To my mother,
    Santosh

my wife,
    Neeta

and my children,
    Agam, Neha, and Param

Data Structures, Algorithms, and Applications in C++

Sartaj Sahni

University of Florida

Boston   Burr Ridge, IL   Dubuque, IA   Madison, WI   New York   San Francisco   St. Louis
Bangkok   Bogota   Caracas   Lisbon   London   Madrid Mexico City   Milan   New Delhi   Seoul
Singapore   Sydney   Taipei   Toronto

WCB/McGraw-Hill

*A Division of the **McGraw-Hill** Companies*

DATA STRUCTURES, ALGORITHMS, AND APPLICATIONS IN C++

This book is printed on acid-free paper.

3 4 5 6 7 8 9 10 DOC/DOC 0 9 8 7 6 5 4 3 2 1 0

ISBN 0-07-109219-6

Vice president and editorial director: *Kevin T. Kane*
Publisher: *Tom Casson*
Executive editor: *Elizabeth A. Jones*
Developmental editor: *Bradley Kosirog*
Marketing manager: *John T. Wannemacher*
Senior project manager: *Beth Cigler*
Senior production supervisor: *Madelyn S. Underwood*
Designer: *Michael Warrell*
Printer: *R. R. Donnelley & Sons Company*

Library of Congress Cataloging-in-Publication Data
Sahni, Sartaj
    Data Structures, algorithms, and applications in C++ / Sartaj Sahni.
       p.   cm.
    Includes index.
    ISBN 0-07-109219-6
    1. C++ (Computer program language) I. Title.
QA76.73.C153S24 1998   97-31865
005. 13'3-dc21

http://www.mhhe.com

PREFACE

The study of data structures and algorithms is fundamental to computer science and engineering. A mastery of these areas is essential for us to develop computer programs that utilize computer resources in an effective manner. Consequently, all computer science and engineering curriculums include one or more courses devoted to these subjects. Typically, the first programming course introduces students to basic data structures (such as stacks and queues) and basic algorithms (such as those for sorting and matrix algebra). The second programming course covers more data structures and algorithms. The next one or two courses are usually dedicated to the study of data structures and algorithms.

The explosion of courses in the undergraduate computer science and engineering curriculums has forced many universities and colleges to consolidate material into fewer courses. At the University of Florida, for example, we offer a single one-semester undergraduate data structures and algorithms course. Students coming into this course have had a one semester course in C++ programming and another in discrete mathematics/structures.

Data Structures, Algorithms, and Applications in C++ has been developed for use in programs that cover this material in a unified course as well as in programs that spread out the study of data structures and algorithms over two or more courses. The book is divided into three parts. Part I, which consists of Chapters 1 and 2, is intended as a review of C++ programming concepts and of algorithm analysis and measurement methods. Students who are familiar with programming in C should be able to read Chapter 1 and bridge the gap between

C and C++. Although Chapter 1 is not a primer on C++, it covers most of the C++ constructs with which students might have become rusty. These concepts include modes of parameter passing, template functions, recursion, dynamic memory allocation, classes, and throwing and catching exceptions. More advanced C++ concepts such as inheritence, virtual functions, and abstract classes are described in the chapters where they are first used. Chapter 2 is a review of methods to analyze the performance of a program—operation counts, step counts, asymptotic notation (big oh, omega, theta, and little oh); it also reviews methods to measure performance experimentally. The applications considered in Chapter 2 explore fundamental problems typically studied in a beginning programming course—simple sort methods such as bubble, selection, insertion, and rank (or count) sort; simple search methods such as sequential and binary search; polynomial evaluation using Horner's rule; and matrix operations such as matrix addition, transpose, and multiply. Even though the primary purpose of Chapter 2 is to study performance analysis and measurement methods, this chapter also ensures that all students are familiar with a set of fundamental algorithms.

Chapters 3 through 12 form the second part of the book. These chapters provide an in-depth study of data structures. Chapter 3 forms the backbone of this study by examining various methods of representing data—formula-based, linked, simulated pointer, and indirect addressing. This chapter develops C++ classes to represent the linear list data structure, using each representation method. At the end of the chapter, we compare the different representation schemes with respect to their effectiveness in representing linear lists. The remaining chapters on data structures use the representation methods of Chapter 3 to arrive at representations for other data structures such as arrays and matrices (Chapter 4), stacks (Chapter 5), queues (Chapter 6), dictionaries (Chapters 7 and 11), binary trees (Chapter 8), priority queues (Chapter 9), tournament trees (Chapter 10), and graphs (Chapter 12).

The third part of this book, which comprises Chapters 13 through 17, is a study of common algorithm-design methods. The methods we study are greedy (Chapter 13), divide and conquer (Chapter 14), dynamic programming (Chapter 15), backtracking (Chapter 16), and branch and bound (Chapter 17). Two lower-bound proofs (one for the minmax problem and the other for sorting) are provided in Section 14.4; approximation algorithms for machine scheduling (Section 9.5.2), bin packing (Section 10.5), and the 0/1 knapsack problem (Section 13.3.2) are also covered. NP-hard problems are introduced, informally, in Section 9.5.2.

A unique feature of this book is the emphasis on applications. Several real-world applications illustrate the use of each data structure and algorithm-design method developed in this book. Typically, the last section of each chapter is dedicated to applications of the data structure or design method studied earlier in the chapter. In many cases additional applications are also introduced early in the chapter. We have drawn applications from various areas—sorting (bubble, selection, insertion, rank, heap, merge, quick, bin, radix, and topological sort); matrix algebra (matrix addition, transpose, and multiplication); electronic design automation (finding the nets in a circuit, wire routing, component stack folding, switch-box routing, placement of signal boosters, crossing distribution, and backplane board ordering); compression and coding (LZW compression, Huffman coding, and variable bit-length codes); computational geometry (convex hull and closest pair of points); simulation (machine-shop simulation); image processing (component labeling); recreational mathematics (Towers of Hanoi, tiling a defective chessboard, and rat in a maze); scheduling (LPT schedules); optimization (bin packing, container loading, 0/1 knapsack, and matrix multiplication chains); statistics (histogramming, finding the minimum and maximum, and finding the kth smallest); and graph algorithms (spanning trees, components, shortest paths, max clique, bipartite graph covers, and traveling salesperson). Our treatment of these applications does not require prior knowledge of the application areas. The material covered in this book is self-contained and gives students a flavor for what these application areas entail.

By closely tying the applications to the more basic treatment of data structures and algorithm-design methods, we hope to give the student a greater appreciation of the subject. Further enrichment can be obtained by working through the almost 600 exercises in the book and from the associated Web site.

WEB SITE

The URL for the Web site for this book is www.cise.ufl.edu/~sahni/dsac. From this Web site you can obtain all the programs in the book together with sample data and generated output. The sample data is not intended to serve as a good test set for a given program; rather it is just something you can use to run the program and compare the output produced with the given output.

All programs in this book have been compiled and run using Borland's C++ compiler version 5.01 as well as GNU's C++ compiler version 2.7.2.1. The files have been zipped together and placed on the Web site as two separate zip files—one for Borland C++ and the other for GNU C++. The mapping between program numbers in the text and file names is available from the `readme` file, which is included in the zip file.

The Web site also includes solutions to many of the exercises that appear in each chapter, sample tests and solutions to these tests, additional applications, and enhanced discussions of some of the material covered in the text.

ICONS

We have used several icons throughout the book to highlight various features. The icon for a section that provides a bird's-eye view of the chapter contents is

The icon for the explanation of a C++ language construct is

The icon for the treatment of an application is

The icon for a topic on which more material can be found at the Web site is

Some of the exercises have been labeled with the symbol ✯. This denotes an exercise whose solution requires development beyond what is done in the chapter. As a result, these exercises are somewhat harder than those without the symbol.

HOW TO USE THIS BOOK

There are several ways in which this book may be used to teach the subject of data structures and/or algorithms. Instructors should make a decision based on the background of their students, the amount of emphasis they want to put on applications, and the number of semesters or quarters devoted to the subject. We give a few of the possible course outlines below. We recommend that the assignments require students to write and debug several programs beginning with a collection of short programs and working up to larger programs as the course progresses. Students should read the text at a pace commensurate with classroom coverage of topics.

TWO-QUARTER SCHEDULE—QUARTER 1

One week of review. Data structures and algorithms sequence.

Week	Topic	Reading
1	Review of C++ and program performance.	Chapters 1 and 2. Assignment 1 given out.
2	Formula-based and linked representations.	Sections 3.1–3.4. Assignment 1 due.
3	Linked, indirect addressing, and simulated pointer.	Sections 3.4–3.7. Assignment 2 given out.
4	Bin sort and equivalence classes.	Section 3.8. Assignment 2 due.
5	Arrays and matrices.	Chapter 4. Examination.
6	Stacks and queues.	Chapters 5 and 6. Assignment 3 given out.
7	Skip lists and hashing.	Chapter 7. Assignment 3 due.
8	Binary and other trees.	Sections 8.1–8.9. Assignment 4 given out.
9	Union/find application. Heaps and heap sort.	Sections 8.10.2, 9.1–9.3, and 9.5.1. Assignment 4 due.
10	Leftist trees, Huffman codes, and tournament trees.	Sections 9.4 and 9.5 and Chapter 10.

TWO-QUARTER SCHEDULE—QUARTER 2
Data structures and algorithms sequence.

Week	Topic	Reading
1	Search trees. Do either AVL or red-black trees. Histogramming.	Chapter 11. Assignment 1 given out.
2	Graphs	Sections 12.1–12.7. Assignment 1 due.
3	Graphs.	Sections 12.8–12.11. Assignment 2 given out.
4	The greedy method.	Sections 13.1–13.3.5. Assignment 2 due.
5	The greedy method and the divide-and-conquer method.	Sections 13.3.6 and 14.1. Assignment 3 given out.
6	Divide-and-conquer applications.	Section 14.2. Examination.
7	Solving recurrences, lower bounds, and dynamic programming.	Sections 14.3, 14.4, and 15.1. Assignment 3 due.
8	Dynamic programming applications.	Sections 15.2.1 and 15.2.2. Assignment 4 given out.
9	Dynamic programming applications.	Sections 15.2.3–15.2.5. Assignment 4 due.
10	Backtracking and branch-and-bound methods.	Chapters 16 and 17.

SEMESTER SCHEDULE
Two weeks of review. Data structures course.

Week	Topic	Reading
1	Review of C++.	Chapter 1. Assignment 1 given out.
2	Review of program performance.	Chapter 2.
3	Formula-based and linked representations.	Sections 3.1–3.4. Assignment 1 due.
4	Linked, indirect addressing, and simulated pointer.	Sections 3.4–3.7. Assignment 2 given out.
5	Bin sort and equivalence classes.	Section 3.8.
6	Arrays and matrices.	Chapter 4. Assignment 2 due. First examination.
7	Stacks. Do one or two applications.	Chapter 5. Assignment 3 given out.
8	Queues. Do two applications.	Chapter 6.
9	Skip lists and hashing.	Chapter 7. Assignment 3 due.
10	Binary and other trees.	Sections 8.1–8.9. Assignment 4 given out.
11	Union/find application.	Section 8.10.2. Second examination.
12	Priority queues, heap sort, and Huffman codes.	Chapter 9. Assignment 4 due.
13	Tournament trees and bin packing.	Chapter 10. Assignment 5 given out.
14	Search trees. Do either AVL or red-black trees. Histogramming.	Chapter 11.
15	Graphs	Sections 12.1–12.7. Assignment 5 due.
16	Graphs. Merge sort and quick sort.	Sections 12.8–12.11, 14.2.2, and 14.2.3.

SEMESTER SCHEDULE
One week of review. Data structures and algorithms course.

Week	Topic	Reading
1	Review of program performance.	Chapters 1 and 2.
2	Formula-based and linked representations.	Sections 3.1–3.4. Assignment 1 given out.
3	Linked, indirect addressing, and simulated pointer.	Sections 3.4–3.8.
4	Arrays and matrices.	Chapter 4. Assignment 1 due.
5	Stacks and queues. Do one or two applications.	Chapters 5 and 6. Assignment 2 given out.
6	Skip lists and hashing.	Chapter 7. First examination. Assignment 2 due.
7	Binary and other trees.	Sections 8.1–8.9. Assignment 3 given out.
8	Union/find application. Heaps and heap sort.	Sections 8.10.2, 9.1–9.3, and 9.5.1.
9	Leftist trees, Huffman codes, and tournament trees.	Sections 9.4 and 9.5 and Chapter 10. Assignment 3 due.
10	Search trees. Do either AVL or red-black trees. Histogramming.	Chapter 11. Assignment 4 given out.
11	Graphs	Sections 12.1–12.7.
12	Graphs and the greedy method.	Sections 12.8–12.11 and 13.1–13.2. Assignment 4 due.
13	Container loading, 0/1 knapsack, shortest paths, and spanning trees.	Section 13.3. Assignment 5 given out.
14	Divide-and-conquer method.	Chapter 14.
15	Dynamic programming.	Chapter 15. Assignment 5 due.
16	Backtracking and branch-and-bound methods.	Chapters 16 and 17.

ACKNOWLEDGMENTS

This book would not have been possible without the assistance, comments, and suggestions of many individuals. I am deeply indebted to the following reviewers for their valuable comments, which have resulted in a better manuscript:

Jacobo Carrasquel	Carnegie Mellon University
Yu Lo Cyrus Chang	University of New Hampshire
Teofilo F. Gonzalez	University of California at Santa Barbara
Laxmikant V. Kale	University of Illinois
Donald H. Kraft	Louisiana State University
Sang W. Lee	University of Michigan
Jorge Lobo	University of Illinois at Chicago
Brian Malloy	Clemson University
Thomas Miller	University of Idaho
Richard Rasala	Northeastern University
Craig E. Wills	Worchester Polytechnic Institute
Neal E. Young	Dartmouth College

Special thanks go to the students in my data structures and algorithms class who provided valuable feedback and helped debug the manuscript. Additionally, I am grateful to the following individuals at the University of Florida for their contributions: Justin Bullard, Edward Y. C. Cheng, Rajesh Dasari, Thomas Davies, Vinayak Goel, Haejae Jung, Jawalant Patel, Sanguthevar Rajasekeran, Gauri Sukhatankar, Gayathri Venkataraman, and Joe Wilson.

The WCB/McGraw-Hill book team has been a pleasure to work with. Everyone contributed immensely to the quality of the final manuscript. The members of this team are Tom Casson, Beth Cigler, Betsy Jones, Brad Kosirog, Madelyn Underwood, John Wannemacher, and Michael Warrell.

Finally, I am indebted to the copy editor, June Waldman, for having done an excellent job.

Sartaj Sahni
Gainesville
October 1997

BRIEF CONTENTS

CONTENTS

PART II DATA STRUCTURES

PART III   ALGORITHM-DESIGN METHODS

PROGRAMMING IN C++

BIRD'S-EYE VIEW

Well folks, we are about to begin a journey through the world of data structures, algorithms, and computer programs that solve many real-life problems. The program development process will require us to (1) represent data in an effective way and (2) develop a suitable step-by-step procedure (or algorithm), which can be implemented as a computer program. Effective data representation requires expertise in the field of data structures, while the development of a suitable step-by-step procedure requires expertise in the field of algorithm design methods.

Before you embark on the study of data structures and algorithm design methods, you need to be a proficient C++ programmer and an adept analyst of computer programs. These essential skills are typically gained from introductory C++ and discrete structures courses. The first two chapters of this book are intended as a review of these skills and much of the material covered in these chapters should already be familar to you.

In this first chapter we review some features of the C++ language. This chapter is not intended as a C++ primer and we do not cover basic constructs such as assignment statements, `if` statements, and looping statements (e.g., `for` and `while`). This chapter covers some C++ language features with which you may have become a bit rusty:

- The different modes of parameter passing in C++ (by value, by reference, and by const reference).
- The different modes in which a function may return a value (by value, by reference, and by const reference).
- Template functions.
- Recursive functions.
- Constant functions.
- The C++ space allocation and deallocation functions `new` and `delete`.
- The C++ exception handling constructs `try`, `catch`, and `throw`.
- Classes and template classes.
- Public, protected, and private class members.
- Friends of a class.
- Operator overloading.

Additional C++ features that may not have been covered in a first C++ course are introduced in later chapters as needed. Chapter 1 also includes codes for the following applications:

- Dynamic allocation and deallocation of one- and two-dimensional arrays.
- Finding the roots of a quadratic function.
- Generating all permutations of n items.
- Finding the maximum of n elements.

Chapter 1 concludes with tips on how to test and debug a program.

1.1 INTRODUCTION

Some of the questions we should ask when examining a computer program are

- Is it correct?
- How easy is it to read the program and understand the code?
- Is the program well documented?
- How easy is it to make changes to the program?
- How much memory is needed to run the program?
- For how long will the program run?
- How general is the code? Will it solve problems over a large range of inputs without modification?
- Can the code be compiled and run on a variety of computers, or are modifications needed to run it on different computers?

The relative importance of some of these questions depends on the application environment. For example, if we are writing a program that is to be run once and discarded, then correctness, memory and time requirements, and the ability to compile and run the code on a single computer are the dominating considerations. Regardless of the application, the most important attribute of a program is correctness. An incorrect program, no matter how fast, how general, or how well documented is of little use (until it is corrected). Although we do not explicitly dwell on techniques to establish program correctness, we provide informal proofs of correctness and implicitly develop programming habits conducive to the production of correct codes. The goal is to teach techniques that will enable you to develop correct, elegant, and efficient solutions.

Before we can begin the study of these techniques, we must review some essential aspects of the C++ language, techniques to test and debug programs, and techniques to analyze and measure the performance of a program. This chapter focuses on the first two items. Chapter 2 reviews performance analysis and measurement techniques.

1.2 FUNCTIONS AND PARAMETERS

1.2.1 Value Parameters

Consider the function Abc (Program 1.1). This function computes the expression a+b+b*c+(a+b-c)/(a+b)+4 for the case when a, b, and c are integers. The result is also an integer.

```
int Abc(int a, int b, int c)
{
    return a+b+b*c+(a+b-c)/(a+b)+4;
}
```

Program 1.1 Compute an integer expression

In Program 1.1 a, b, and c are the **formal parameters** of the function Abc. Each is of type integer. If the function is invoked by the statement

```
z = Abc(2,x,y)
```

then 2, x, and y are the **actual parameters** that correspond to a, b, and c, respectively. When the invocation Abc(2,x,y) is executed, a is assigned the value 2, b is assigned the value of x, and c is assigned the value of y. In case x and/or y are not of type int, then a type conversion between their type and int is performed prior to the assignment of values to b and c. For example, if x is of type float and has the value 3.8, then b is assigned the value 3. In Program 1.1 the formal parameters a, b, and c are **value** parameters.

At run time the value of the actual parameter that corresponds to a value formal parameter is copied into the formal parameter before the function is executed. This copying is done using the **copy constructor** for the data type of the formal parameter. If the actual and value formal parameters are of different data types, a type conversion is performed from the type of the actual parameter to that of the value formal parameter provided such a type conversion is defined.

When a function terminates, **destructors** for the data types of the formal parameters destroy the value formal parameters. *When a function terminates, formal parameter values are not copied back into the actual parameters.* Consequently, function invocation does not change the actual parameters that correspond to value formal parameters.

1.2.2 Template Functions

Suppose we wish to write another function to compute the same expression as computed by Program 1.1. However, this time a, b, and c are of type float, and the result is also of this type. Program 1.2 gives the code. Programs 1.1 and 1.2 differ only in the data type of the formal parameters and of the value returned.

```
float Abc(float a, float b, float c)
{
    return a+b+b*c+(a+b-c)/(a+b)+4;
}
```

Program 1.2 Compute a floating-point expression

Rather than write a new version of the code for every possible data type of the formal parameters, we can write a generic code in which the data type is a variable whose value is to be determined by the compiler. This generic code is written using the `template` statement as shown in Program 1.3.

```
template<class T>
T Abc(T a, T b, T c)
{
    return a+b+b*c+(a+b-c)/(a+b)+4;
}
```

Program 1.3 Compute an expression using a template function

From this generic code the compiler can construct Program 1.1 by substituting `int` for `T` and Program 1.2 by substituting `float` for `T`. In fact, the compiler can construct a double-precision version or a long-integer version (or both) of the code by substituting `double` or `long` for `T`. Writing `Abc` as a template function eliminates the need to know the data type of the formal parameters when we write the code.

1.2.3   Reference Parameters

The use of value parameters in Program 1.3 increases the run-time cost. For example, consider the operations involved when a function is invoked and when it terminates. When `a`, `b`, and `c` are value parameters, the copy constructor for type `T` copies the values of the corresponding actual parameters into the formal parameters `a`, `b`, and `c` upon entry into the function. At the time of exiting the function, the destructor for type `T` is invoked, and the formal parameters `a`, `b`, and `c` are destroyed.

Suppose that `T` is the user-defined data type `Matrix` whose copy constructor copies all entries of the matrix and whose destructor destroys the matrix entries one by one (assume that the operators `+`, `*`, and `/` have been defined for the data type `Matrix`). If `Abc` is invoked with each actual parameter being a matrix with 1000 elements, then copying the three actual parameters into a, b, and c would require 3000 operations. When Abc terminates, the Matrix destructor is invoked to destroy a, b, and c at a cost of an additional 3000 operations.

In the code of Program 1.4, a, b, and c are **reference parameters**. If Abc is invoked by the statement Abc(x,y,z) where x, y, and z are of the same data type, then these actual parameters are bound to the names a, b, and c, respectively. Therefore, during execution of the function Abc, the names x, y, and z, respectively, are used in place of the names a, b, and c. Unlike the case of value parameters, this program does not copy actual parameter values at the time of invocation and does not invoke the type T destructor upon exit.

```
template<class T>
T Abc(T& a, T& b, T& c)
{
    return a+b+b*c+(a+b-c)/(a+b)+4;
}
```

Program 1.4 Compute an expression using reference parameters

Consider the case when the actual parameters that correspond to a, b, and c are matrices x, y, and z with 1000 elements each. Since the values of x, y, and z are now not copied into the formal parameters, we save the 3000 operations needed to do the copying when value parameters are used.

1.2.4 Const Reference Parameters

C++ provides yet another mode of parameter passing, **const reference**. This mode designates reference parameters that are not changed by the function. For example, in Program 1.4 the values of a, b, and c do not change, so we may rewrite the code as shown in Program 1.5.

Using the const qualifier to designate reference paremeters that the function does not change has an important software-engineering value. The function header tells the user that the function will not change the actual parameters.

For simple data types such as int, float, and char, we will use value formal parameters when the function does not change the values of the actual parameters. For the case of all other data types including template types, we will use const reference parameters when the function does not change the values of the actual parameters.

```
template<class T>
T Abc(const T& a, const T& b, const T& c)
{
    return a+b+b*c+(a+b-c)/(a+b)+4;
}
```

Program 1.5 Compute an expression using const reference parameters

Using the syntax of Program 1.6, we can obtain a more general version of Program 1.5. In the new version each formal parameter may be of a different type, and the result is of the same type as the first parameter (for example).

```
template<class Ta, class Tb, class Tc>
Ta Abc(const Ta& a, const Tb& b, const Tc& c)
{
    return a+b+b*c+(a+b-c)/(a+b)+4;
}
```

Program 1.6 A more general version of Program 1.5

1.2.5 Return Values

A function may make a value return, a reference return, or a const reference return. The preceding examples make value returns. In such a return, the object that is being returned is copied into the invoking (or return) environment. This copying is necessary in all versions of the function Abc, as the result of the expression computed by this function is saved in a local temporary variable. When the function terminates, the space allocated to this temporary variable (as well as to all other temporary variables and value formal parameters) is freed and its value no longer available. To avoid losing this value, we copy it from the temporary variable into the return environment before releasing the space allocated to local variables and value formal parameters.

We specify a reference return by adding the symbol & as a suffix to the return type. The function header

```
T& X(int i, T& z)
```

defines a function X that makes a reference return of type T. It could, for example, return z using the following statement:

```
return z;
```

Such a return would not involve copying the value of z into the return environment. When function X terminates, the space allocated to the value formal parameter i and all local variables is released. Because z is simply a reference to an actual parameter, it is not affected.

A const reference return is specified by adding the keyword const to the function header as in

```
const T& X(int i, T& z)
```

A const reference return is similar to a reference return except that the item returned is designated a constant object.

1.2.6   Recursive Functions

A **recursive function** is a function that invokes itself. In **direct recursion** the code for function F contains a statement that invokes F, whereas in **indirect recursion** function F invokes a function G, which invokes a function H, and so on until function F is again invoked. Before delving into recursive C++ functions, we examine two related concepts from mathematics—recursive definitions of mathematical functions and proofs by induction.

In mathematics, we often define a function in terms of itself. For example, the factorial function $f(n) = n!$, for n an integer, is defined as follows:

$$f(n) = \begin{cases} 1 & n \le 1 \\ nf(n-1) & n > 1 \end{cases} \qquad (1.1)$$

This definition states that $f(n)$ equals 1 whenever n is less than or equal to 1; for example, $f(-3) = f(0) = f(1) = 1$. However, when n is more than 1, $f(n)$ is defined recursively, as the definition of f now contains an occurrence of f on the right side. This use of f on the right side does not result in a circular definition, as the parameter of f on the right side is smaller than that on the left side. For example, from Equation 1.1 we obtain $f(2) = 2f(1)$. From Equation 1.1 we also obtain $f(1) = 1$, and substituting for $f(1)$ in $f(2) = 2f(1)$, we obtain $f(2) = 2$. Similarly, from Equation 1.1 we obtain $f(3) = 3f(2)$. We have already seen that Equation 1.1 yields $f(2) = 2$. So $f(3) = 3*2 = 6$.

For a recursive definition of $f(n)$ (we assume direct recursion) to be a complete specification of f, it must meet the following requirements:

- The definition must include a **base** component in which $f(n)$ is defined directly (i.e., nonrecursively) for one or more values of n. For simplicity, we assume that the base covers the case $n \le k$ for some constant k. (It is possible to have recursive definitions in which the base covers the case $n \ge k$ instead, but we encounter these definitions less frequently.)

- In the **recursive component** all occurrences of f on the right side should have a parameter smaller than n so that repeated application of the recursive component transforms all occurrences of f on the right side to occurrences of f in the base.

In Equation 1.1 the base is $f(n) = 1$ for $n \le 1$; in the recursive component $f(n) = nf(n-1)$, the parameter of f is $n-1$, which is smaller than n. Repeated application of the recursive component transforms $f(n-1)$ to $f(n-2)$, $f(n-3)$, $\cdots$, and finally to $f(1)$ which is included in the base. For example, repeated application of the recursive component gives the following:

$$f(5) \ = \ 5f(4) \ = \ 20f(3) \ = \ 60f(2) \ = \ 120f(1)$$

Notice that each application of the recursive component gets us closer to the base. Finally, an application of the base gives $f(5) = 120$. From the example, we see that $f(n) = n(n-1)(n-2)\cdots1$ for $n \ge 1$.

As another example of a recursive definition, consider the Fibonacci numbers that are defined recursively as below:

$$F_0 = 0, \quad F_1 = 1, \quad F_n = F_{n-1} + F_{n-2} \quad \text{for } n > 1 \tag{1.2}$$

In this definition, $F_0 = 0$ and $F_1 = 1$ make up the base component, and $F_n = F_{n-1} + F_{n-2}$ is the recursive component. The function parameters on the right side are smaller than n. For Equation 1.2 to be a complete recursive specification of F, repeated application of the recursive component beginning with any value of $n > 1$ should transform all occurrences of F on the right side to occurrences in the base. Since repeated subtraction of 1 or 2 from an integer $n > 1$ reduces it to either 0 or 1, right-side occurrences of F are always transformed to a base occurrence. For example, $F_4 = F_3 + F_2 = F_2 + F_1 + F_1 + F_0 = 3F_1 + 2F_0 = 3$.

Now we turn our attention to the second concept related to recursive computer functions—proofs by induction. In a proof by induction, we establish the validity of a claim such as

$$\sum_{i=1}^{n} i = n(n+1)/2, \, n \ge 0 \tag{1.3}$$

by showing that the claim is true for one or more base values of n (e.g., $n = 0$ or $n = 0$ and 1); we assume the claim is true for values of n from 0 through m where m is an arbitrary integer greater than or equal to the largest n covered in the base; and finally using this assumption, we show the claim is true for the next value of n (i.e., $m + 1$). This methodology leads to a proof that has three components—**induction base**, **induction hypothesis**, and **induction step**.

Suppose we are to prove Equation 1.3 by induction on n. In the induction base we establish correctness for $n = 0$. At this time the left side is $\sum_{i=1}^{0} i = 0$, and the right side is also 0. So Equation 1.3 is valid when $n = 0$. In the induction hypothesis we assume the equation is valid for $n \leq m$ where m is an arbitrary integer ≥ 0. (For the ensuing induction step proof, it is sufficient to assume that Equation 1.3 is valid only for $n = m$.) In the induction step we show that the equation is valid for $n = m + 1$. For this value of n, the left side is $\sum\limits_{i=1}^{m+1} i$, which equals $m + 1 + \sum\limits_{i=1}^{m} i$. From the induction hypothesis we get $\sum\limits_{i=1}^{m} i = m(m+1)/2$. So when $n = m + 1$, the left side becomes $m + 1 + m(m+1)/2$, $= (m+1)(m+2)/2$, which equals the right side.

At first glance, a proof by induction appears to be a circular proof—we establish a result assuming it is correct. However, a proof by induction is not a circular proof for the same reasons that a recursive definition is not circular. A correct proof by induction has an induction base similar to the base component of a recursive definition, and the induction step proves correctness using correctness for smaller values of n. Repeated application of the induction step reduces the proof to one that is solely in terms of the base.

C++ allows us to write recursive functions. A proper recursive function must include a base component. The recursive component of the function should use smaller values of the function parameters so that repeated invocation of the function results in parameters equal to those included in the base component.

Example 1.1 [*Factorial*] Program 1.7 gives a C++ recursive function that uses Equation 1.1 to compute `n!`. The base component covers the cases when $n \leq 1$. Consider the invocation `Factorial(2)`. To compute `2*Factorial(1)` in the `else` statement, the computation of `Factorial(2)` is suspended and `Factorial` invoked with `n = 1`. When the computation of `Factorial(2)` is suspended, the program state (i.e., values of local variables and value formal parameters, bindings of reference formal parameters, location in code, etc.) is saved in a recursion stack. This state is restored when the computation of `Factorial(1)` completes. The invocation `Factorial(1)` returns the value 1. The computation of `Factorial(2)` resumes, and the expression $2 * 1$ is computed.

```
int Factorial(int n)
{// Compute n!.
    if (n <= 1) return 1;
    else return n * Factorial(n - 1);
}
```

Program 1.7 Recursive function to compute `n!`

When computing `Factorial(3)`, the computation is suspended when the `else` statement is reached so that `Factorial(2)` may be computed. We have already seen how the invocation `Factorial(2)` works to produce the result 2. When the computation of `Factorial(2)` completes, the computation of `Factorial(3)` resumes and the expression $3 * 2$ is computed.

Because of the similarity between the code of Program 1.7 and Equation 1.1, the correctness of the code follows from the correctness of the equation. ∎

Example 1.2 The template function `Sum` (Program 1.8) computes the sum of the elements `a[0]` through `a[n-1]` (abbreviated `a[0:n-1]`). This code results from a recursive formulation of the problem—when `n` is zero, the sum is zero; when `n` is greater than zero, the sum of `n` elements is the sum of the first `n-1` elements plus the last element. ∎

```
template<class T>
T Sum(T a[], int n)
{// Return sum of numbers a[0:n - 1].
   T tsum = 0;
   for (int i = 0; i < n; i++)
     tsum += a[i];
   return tsum;
}
```

Program 1.8 Add `a[0:n-1]`

```
template<class T>
T Rsum(T a[], int n)
{// Return sum of numbers a[0:n - 1].
   if (n > 0)
      return Rsum(a, n-1) + a[n-1];
   return 0;
}
```

Program 1.9 Recursive code to add `a[0:n-1]`

Example 1.3 [*Permutations*] Often we wish to examine all permutations of *n* distinct elements to determine the best one. For example, the permutations of the elements *a*, *b*, and *c* are *abc*, *acb*, *bac*, *bca*, *cba*, and *cab*. The number of permutations of *n* elements is *n*!.

Although developing a nonrecursive C++ function to output all permutations of n elements is quite difficult, we can develop a recursive one with modest effort. Let $E = \{e_1, \cdots, e_n\}$ denote the set of n elements whose permutations are to be generated; let E_i be the set obtained by removing element i from E; let $perm(X)$ denote the permutations of the elements in set X; and let $e_i.perm(X)$ denote the permutation list obtained by prefixing each permutation in $perm(X)$ with e_i. For example, if $E = \{a,b,c\}$, then $E_1 = \{b,c\}$, $perm(E_1) = (bc,cb)$, and $e_1.perm(E_1) = (abc,acb)$.

For the recursion base, we use $n = 1$. Since only one permutation is possible when we have only one element, $perm(E) = (e)$ where e is the lone element in E. When $n > 1$, $perm(E)$ is the list $e_1.perm(E_1)$ followed by $e_2.perm(E_2)$ followed by $e_3.perm(E_3) \cdots$ followed by $e_n.perm(E_n)$. This recursive definition of $perm(E)$ defines $perm(E)$ in terms of n $perm(X)$s, each of which involves an X with $n-1$ elements. Both the base component and recursive component requirements of a complete recursive definition are satisfied.

When $n = 3$ and $E = (a,b,c)$, the preceding definition of $perm(E)$ yields $perm(E) = a.perm(\{b,c\})$, $b.perm(\{a,c\})$, $c.perm(\{b,a\})$. From the recursive definition $perm(\{b,c\})$ is $b.perm(\{c\})$, $c.perm(\{b\})$. So $a.perm(\{b,c\})$ is $ab.perm(\{c\})$, $ac.perm(\{b\}) = ab.c,ac.b = (abc,acb)$. Proceeding in a similar way, we obtain $b.perm(\{a,c\})$ is $ba.perm(\{c\})$, $bc.perm(\{a\}) = ba.c,bc.a = (bac,bca)$ and $c.perm(\{b,a\})$ is $cb.perm(\{a\})$, $ca.perm(\{b\}) = cb.a,ca.b = (cba,cab)$. So $perm(E) = (abc,acb,bac,bca,cba,cab)$.

Notice that $a.perm(\{b,c\})$ is actually the two permutations abc and acb. a is the prefix of these permutations, and $perm(\{b,c\})$ gives their suffixes. Similarly, $ac.perm(\{b\})$ denotes permutations whose prefix is ac and whose suffixes are the permutations $perm(\{b\})$.

Program 1.10 transforms the preceding recursive definition of $perm(E)$ into a C++ function. This code outputs all permutations whose prefix is `list[0:k-1]` and whose suffixes are the permutations of `list[k:m]`. The invocation `Perm(list,0,n-1)` outputs all n! permutations of `list[0:n-1]`. With this invocation k is zero and m is n-1. So the prefix of the generated permutations is null, and their suffixes are the permutations of `list[0:n-1]`. When k equals m, there is only one suffix `list[m]`, and now `list[0:m]` defines a permutation that is to be output. When k < m, each element in `list[k:m]` is swapped with the element in position `list[k]`, and the permutations of the elements in `list[k+1:m]` are computed and used as suffixes to `list[0:k]`. Swap is an inline function that exchanges or swaps the values of its two parameters. It is defined in Program 1.11. The correctness of Perm may be established by induction. ∎

```
template<class T>
void Perm(T list[], int k, int m)
{// Generate all permutations of list[k:m].
   int i;
   if (k == m) {// output a permutation
             for (i = 0; i <= m; i++)
                cout << list[i];
             cout << endl;
             }
    else   // list[k:m] has more than one permutation
           // generate these recursively
           for (i = k; i <= m; i++) {
               Swap(list[k], list[i]);
               Perm(list, k+1, m);
               Swap(list[k], list[i]);
               }
}
```

Program 1.10 Recursive function for permutations

```
template<class T>
inline void Swap(T& a, T& b)
{// Swap a and b.
   T temp = a; a = b; b = temp;
}
```

Program 1.11 Swap two values

EXERCISES

1. Write a template function Input to input a nonnegative value and verify
    that the value input is, in fact, ≥ 0. If it is not, tell the user to input a new
    value because the input is invalid. Give the user three attempts before your
    function quits unsuccessfully. If successful, you should return the input via
    a reference parameter. Your function should return false if it is unsuc-
    cessful and true otherwise. Test your function.

2. Write a template function to determine whether the elements in the array a
    are in sorted order (i.e., a[i] ≤ a[i+1], 0 ≤ i < n-1). Your function
    should return false if a is not sorted and true if it is. Test your code.

3. Write a nonrecursive function to compute $n!$. Test the correctness of your function.

4. (a) Write a recursive function to compute the Fibonacci number F_n. Test its correctness.

    (b) Show that your code for part (a) computes the same F_i more than once when it is invoked to compute F_n for any $n > 2$.

    (c) Write a nonrecursive function to compute the Fibonacci number F_n. Your code should compute each Fibonacci number just once. Test the correctness of your code.

5. Write a recursive function to output all subsets of n elements. For example, the subsets of the three-element set $\{a,b,c\}$ are $\{\}$ (empty set), $\{a\}$, $\{b\}$, $\{c\}$, $\{a,b\}$, $\{a,c\}$, $\{b,c\}$, and $\{a,b,c\}$.

6. Write a recursive function to determine whether element x is one of the elements in the array $a[0:n-1]$.

1.3   DYNAMIC MEMORY ALLOCATION

1.3.1   The Operator `new`

Run-time or dynamic allocation of memory may be done using the C++ operator `new`. This operator returns a pointer to the allocated memory. For example, to dynamically allocate memory for an integer, we must declare a variable (e.g., `y`) to be a pointer to an integer using this statement:

```
int *y;
```

When the program needs to actually use the integer, memory may be allocated to it using this syntax:

```
y = new int;
```

The operator `new` allocates enough memory to hold an integer, and a pointer to this memory is returned and saved in `y`. The variable `y` references the pointer to the integer, and `*y` references the integer. To store an integer value, for example 10, in the newly allocated memory, we can use the following syntax:

```
*y = 10;
```

We can combine the three steps—declare `y`, allocate memory, and assign a value to `*y`—into a smaller number of steps as shown in the following examples:

```
int *y = new int;
*y = 10;
```

or

```
int *y = new int (10);
```

or

```
int *y;
y = new int (10);
```

1.3.2 One-Dimensional Arrays

This text includes many examples of functions that work with one- and two-dimensional arrays. The dimensions of these arrays may not be known at compile time and may, in fact, change from one invocation of the function to the next. Consequently, memory for these arrays needs to be allocated dynamically.

To create a one-dimensional floating-point array x at run time, we must declare x as a pointer to a float and then allocate enough memory for the array. For example, a floating-point array of size n may be created as follows:

```
float *x = new float [n];
```

The operator new allocates memory for n floating-point numbers and returns a pointer to the first of these. The array elements may be addressed using the syntax x[0], x[1], ···, x[n-1].

1.3.3 Exception Handling

What happens when the statement

```
float *x = new float [n];
```

is executed and the computer doesn't have enough memory for n floating-point numbers? In this case new cannot possibly allocate the desired amount of memory, and an **exception** occurs. In Borland C++ the exception xalloc (defined in except.h) is **thrown** by new when it is unable to allocate sufficient memory. We may detect the failure of new by **catching** the exception with the try - catch construct:

```
float *x;
try {x = new float [n];}
catch (xalloc) {// enter only when new fails
     cerr << "Out of Memory" << endl;
     exit(1);}
```

When an exception is thrown, the program resumes operation in the most recent `catch` block set up for that specific exception. In the preceding example, the `catch(xalloc)` block is entered only if the `xalloc` exception is thrown while we are executing the `try` block. The statement `exit(1)` (this function is defined in `stdlib.h`) terminates the program with the termination code 1.

A common way to handle error conditions in C++ programs is to throw an exception whenever such a condition is detected. When an exception is thrown, an exception type (such as `xalloc` above) is associated with it. We enclose program code that may cause an exception to occur in a `try` block which must be followed by one or more `catch` blocks. Each `catch` block is designed to handle exceptions of a particular type; for example, the `catch(xalloc)` block catches exceptions of type `xalloc` only. The syntax `catch(...)` defines a `catch` block that can catch all exceptions. When an exception is thrown, we check the most recent `try-catch` code encountered in the program execution. If one of its `catch` blocks is designed to handle an exception of the type thrown, program execution continues from this catch block. Otherwise, we check the next `try-catch` block and so on until we find one with a matching `catch` block. If we do not find a matching `catch` block, the program terminates with the message `Abnormal program termination`. If no exception is thrown within a `try` block, program execution continues after the last `catch` block associated with this `try` block.

1.3.4   The Operator `delete`

Dynamically allocated memory should be freed when it is no longer needed. The freed memory can then be reused to create new dynamically allocated structures. We can use the C++ operator `delete` to free space allocated using the operator `new`. The statements

```
delete y;
delete [] x;
```

free the memory allocated to `*y` and the one-dimensional array `x`.

1.3.5 Two-Dimensional Arrays

Although C++ provides several mechanisms for declaring two-dimensional arrays, most of these mechanisms require that both dimensions be known at compile time. Further, when these mechanisms are used, it is difficult to write functions that allow a formal parameter which is a two-dimensional array whose second dimension is unknown. This is so because when a formal parameter is a two-dimensional array, we must specify the value of the second dimension. For example, `a[][10]` is a valid formal parameter for a function; `a[][]` is not.

An effective way to overcome these limitations is to use dynamic memory allocation for all two-dimensional arrays. Throughout this text we use dynamically allocated two-dimensional arrays.

When both dimensions of the array are known at compile time, the array may be created using a syntax similar to that used for one-dimensional arrays. For example, a seven by five array of type `char` may be declared using the syntax:

```
char c[7][5];
```

When at least one of the dimensions is unknown at compile time, the array must be created at run time using the `new` operator. A two-dimensional character array for which the number of columns—for example, 5—is known at compile time may be allocated using the following syntax:

```
char (*c)[5];
try {c = new char [n][5];}
catch (xalloc) {// enter only when new fails
     cerr << "Out of Memory" << endl;
     exit(1);}
```

The number of rows `n` may be determined at run time either via computation or user input. When the number of columns is not known at compile time, the array cannot be allocated by a simple invocation of `new` (even if the number of rows is known). To construct the two-dimensional array, we view it as composed of several rows. Each row is a one-dimensional array and may be created using `new` as discussed earlier. Pointers to each row may be saved in another one-dimensional array. Figure 1.1 shows the structure that needs to be established for the case of a three by five array `x`.

`x[0]`, `x[1]`, and `x[2]` point to the first element of rows 0, 1, and 2, respectively. So if `x` is to be a character array, then `x[0:2]` are pointers to characters and `x` is itself a pointer to a pointer to a character. `x` may be declared using the follwoing syntax:

```
char **x;
```

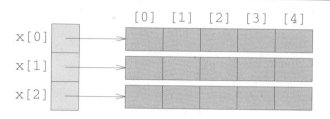

Figure 1.1 Memory structure for a three by five array

To create the memory structure of Figure 1.1, we can use the code of Program
1.12, which creates a two-dimensional array of type T. The array has rows
rows and cols columns. The code first gets memory for the pointers x[0]
through x[rows-1]. Next it gets memory for each row of the array. This
code invokes new rows + 1 times. If one of these invocations of new
throws an exception, program control is transferred to the catch block and the
value false is returned. If none of the invocations of new throws an exception, the array construction is successful and Make2DArray returns the value
true. The elements of the created array x may be indexed using the standard
x[i][j] notation, $0 \le i <$ rows, $0 \le j <$ cols.

```
template <class T>
bool Make2DArray(T ** &x, int rows, int cols)
{// Create a two-dimensional array.

   try {
      // create pointers for the rows
      x = new T * [rows];

      // get memory for each row
      for (int i = 0; i < rows; i++)
         x[i] = new int [cols];
      return true;
      }
   catch (xalloc) {return false;}
}
```

Program 1.12 Allocate memory for a two-dimensional array

In Program 1.12 the exception (if any) thrown by new is reported to the invoking function as the Boolean value false. The failure of Make2DArray may also be reported to the invoking function by simply doing nothing. If we use the code of Program 1.13, the invoking function can catch any exception thrown by new.

```
template <class T>
void Make2DArray(T ** &x, int rows, int cols)
{// Create a two-dimensional array.
 // Do not catch exceptions.

   // create pointers for the rows
   x = new T * [rows];

   // get memory for each row
   for (int i = 0; i < rows; i++)
      x[i] = new int [cols];
}
```

Program 1.13 Make a two-dimensional array but do not catch exceptions

When Make2DArray is defined as in Program 1.13, we can use the code

```
try {Make2DArray(x,r,c);}
catch (xalloc) {cerr << "Could not create x" << endl;
               exit(1);}
```

to determine a shortage of memory. Not catching the exception within Make2DArray not only simplifies the code for this function but also allows the exception to be caught at a point where the user is better able to report a meaningful error or attempt error recovery.

We can free the memory allocated to a two-dimensional array by Program 1.12 by first freeing the memory allocated in the for loop to each row and then freeing the memory allocated for the row pointers, as shown in Program 1.14. Notice that this code sets x to zero, which prevents the user from accessing the memory that was freed.

EXERCISES

7. Suppose that a one-dimensional array a[0:size-1] stores a collection of elements. If we have n elements, these are stored in positions 0

```
template <class T>
void Delete2DArray(T ** &x, int rows)
{// Delete the two-dimensional array x.

   // delete the memory for each row
   for (int i = 0; i < rows; i++)
      delete [] x[i];

   // delete the row pointers
   delete [] x;
   x = 0;
}
```

Program 1.14 Free the memory allocated by `Make2DArray`

through `n-1` of `a`. When `n` exceeds `size`, the array isn't large enough to hold the elements and we need to allocate a larger array. Similarly, if the number of elements in the array becomes much smaller than `size`, we might wish to reduce the size of the array thereby freeing memory for other purposes. Write a template function `ChangeSize1D` to change the size of array `a` to the size `ToSize`. Your function should allocate space for a new one-dimensional array of size `ToSize`; copy the `n` elements of the old `a` into the new `a`; and free the space allocated to the old `a`. Test your code.

8. Write a function `ChangeSize2D` that changes the size of a two-dimensional array (see Exercise 7). Test your code.

1.4　CLASSES

1.4.1　The Class `Currency`

The C++ language supports data types such `int`, `float`, and `char`. Many of the applications we develop in this text require additional data types that are not supported by the language. The most flexible way to define your own data types in C++ is to use the `class` construct. Suppose you wish to deal with objects of type `Currency`. Instances of type `Currency` have a sign component (plus or minus), a dollar component, and a cents component. Two examples are $2.35 (sign is plus, 2 dollars, and 35 cents) and −$6.05 (sign is minus, 6 dollars, and 5 cents). Some of the functions or operations we wish to perform on objects of this type follow:

- Set their value.
- Determine the components (i.e., sign, dollar amount, and number of cents).
- Add two objects of type currency.
- Increment the value.
- Output.

Suppose we choose to represent objects of type currency using an unsigned long variable `dollars`, an unsigned integer `cents`, and a variable `sgn` of type `sign` where the data type `sign` is defined as

```
enum sign {plus, minus};
```

We may declare a C++ class `Currency` using the syntax of Program 1.15. The first line simply says that we are declaring a class whose name is `Currency`. The class declaration is then enclosed in braces ({}). The class declaration has been divided into two sections `public` and `private`. The `public` section declares functions (or methods) that operate on objects (or instances) of type `Currency`. These functions are *visible* to the users of the class and are the only means by which users can interact with objects of type `Currency`. The `private` section declares functions and data members (simple variables, arrays, and so on that may hold data values) that are not visible to users of the class. By having a `public` section and a `private` section, we can show the user see only what he or she needs to see while we hide the remaining information (generally having to do with implementation details). *Although C++ syntax permits you to declare data members in the* `public` *section, good software-engineering practice discourages this procedure.*

The first function in the `public` section has the same name as the class name. Functions with this property are called **constructor** functions. Constructor functions specify how to create an object of a given type and are not permitted to return a value. In our case the constructor has three parameters whose default values are `plus`, 0, and 0. The implementation of the constructor function is provided later in this section. Constructor functions are invoked automatically when an object of type `Currency` is being created. Two ways to create objects of type `Currency` are

```
Currency f, g(plus, 3, 45), h(minus, 10);
Currency *m = new Currency (plus, 8, 12);
```

The first line declares three variables (`f`, `g`, and `h`) of type `Currency`. `f` is to be initialized using the default values `plus`, 0, and 0, whereas `g` is to be initialized to $3.45 and `h` to −$10.00. Notice that the initialization values correspond to the constructor parameters from left to right. If the number of initialization values is less than the number of constructor parameters, the

```
class Currency {
   public:
       // constructor
       Currency(sign s = plus, unsigned long d = 0,
                             unsigned int c = 0);
       // destructor
       ~Currency() {}
       bool Set(sign s, unsigned long d,
                       unsigned int c);
       bool Set(float a);
       sign Sign() const {return sgn;}
       unsigned long Dollars() const {return dollars;}
       unsigned int Cents() const {return cents;}
       Currency Add(const Currency& x) const;
       Currency& Increment(const Currency& x);
       void Output() const;
   private:
       sign sgn;
       unsigned long dollars;
       unsigned int cents;
};
```

Program 1.15 Declaration of the class `Currency`

remaining parameters are assigned their default values. Line 2 declares `m` as a pointer to an object of type `Currency`. We invoke the `new` function to create an object of type `Currency` and store a pointer to this object in `m`. The created object is to be initialized to $8.12.

The next function, `~Currency`, has a name that is the class name preceded by a tilde (`~`). This function is called the **destructor**. It is automatically invoked whenever an object of type `Currency` goes out of scope. The object is destroyed using this function. In our case the destructor is defined as the null function (`{}`). For other classes, the class constructor might create dynamic arrays (for example). The destructor will need to free this space when the object goes out of scope. Destructor functions are not permitted to return a value.

The next two functions allow the user to set the value of a currency object. The first requires the user to provide three parameters, while the second permits setting the value by providing a single floating-point number. Both return the value `true` if they succeed and `false` if they fail. The implementations are provided later in this section. Notice first that both functions have the same name. The compiler and user are able to tell the functions apart because they have different sets of parameters. C++ allows the reuse of function names as long as their parameter lists are different! Notice also that we have not specified the name of the object whose sign, dollars, and cents values are to be set. This is because the syntax to invoke a class member function is

```
g.Set(minus,33,0);
h.Set(20.52);
```

where g and h are variables of type Currency. In the first case g is the object that invokes Set, while in the second the object h invokes Set. When we write the code for the Set functions, we will have a means to access the object that invoked them. Therefore we do not need to include the name of the invoking object in the parameter list.

The functions Sign, Dollars, and Cents return the appropriate data member of the invoking object. The key word const states that these functions do not change the invoking object. We refer to functions of this type as **constant functions**.

The function Add sums the currency amounts of the invoking object and x and then returns the resultant amount. Since this function does not change the invoking object, Add is a constant function. Increment adds the currency amount x to the invoking object. This function changes the invoking object and is not a constant function. The last public member function is Output, which displays the invoking object. The function Output, which does not change the invoking object, is a constant function.

Although both Add and Increment return objects of type Currency, Add does a value return, while Increment does a reference return. As mentioned in Section 1.2.5, value and reference returns work like value and reference parameters. In the case of a value return, the object being returned is copied into the return environment. A reference return avoids this copying, and the return environment makes direct use of the return object. Reference returns are faster than value returns, as no copying is done. The code for Add shows that that it returns a local object, which is destroyed when the function terminates. Therefore the return statement must copy this object. In the case of Increment, a global object is returned and there is no need to copy it.

A **copy constructor** performs the copying for value returns as well as for value parameters. Program 1.15 does not specify a copy constructor, so C++ uses the default copy constructor, which copies the data members only. The use of the default copy constructor is adequate for the class Currency. We will also see classes where the use of the default copy constructor is not sufficient.

In the private section, we declared the three data members needed to represent an object of type Currency. Each object of type Currency has its own copy of these three data members.

The functions whose implementation is not given inside the class declaration must be defined outside of it by using the scope resolution operator `::` to specify that the function we are defining is a member of the class `Currency`. So the syntax `Currency::Currency` denotes the constructor of the class `Currency`, while `Currency::Output` denotes the output function of this class. Program 1.16 gives the `Currency` constructor.

```
Currency::Currency(sign s, unsigned long d,
                              unsigned int c)
{// Create a Currency object.
   if (c > 99)
      {// too many cents
       cerr << "Cents should be < 100" << endl;
       exit(1);}

   sgn = s; dollars = d; cents = c;
}
```

Program 1.16 Constructor for `Currency`

The constructor validates the parameters before initializing the `sgn`, `dollars`, and `cents` data members of the invoking object. If the parameter values are erroneous, the constructor outputs an error message and the program aborts by calling the function `exit`. In our case only the value of `c` needs to be validated.

Program 1.17 gives the codes for the two `Set` functions. The first function validates the input and sets the `private` data members of the invoking object only if the parameter values pass the validation test. The second function does not perform validation and uses only the first two digits after the decimal point. Numbers of the form $d_1.d_2d_3$ may not have an exact computer representation. For example, the computer representation of the number 5.29 is slightly smaller than 5.29. This representation creates an error when extracting the cents component using the following statement:

```
cents = (a - dollars) * 100
```

`(a - dollars) * 100` is slightly smaller than 29, and when the program converts the right side to an integer, it assigns `cents` the value 28 rather than 29. Adding 0.001 to `a` solves our problem so long as the computer representation of $d_1.d_2d_3$ is not less by more than 0.001 or more by ≥ 0.009. For example, if the computer representation of 5.29 is equivalent to 5.28999, then adding 0.001 yields 5.29099 and the computed cents amount is 29.

```
bool Currency::Set(sign s, unsigned long d,
                             unsigned int c)
{// Reset value.
   if (c > 99) return false;
   sgn = s; dollars = d; cents = c;
   return true;
}

bool Currency::Set(float a)
{// Reset value.
   if (a < 0) {sgn = minus; a = -a;}
   else sgn = plus;
   dollars = a; // extract integer part
   // get two decimal digits
   cents = (a + 0.005 - dollars) * 100;
   return true;
}
```

Program 1.17 Setting the `private` data members

Program 1.18 gives the code for the `Add` function. This function begins by converting into integers the two currency values to be added. The amount $2.32 becomes the integer 232, and −$4.75 becomes the integer −475. Notice the difference in syntax used to reference the data members of the invoking object and those of the parameter `x`. `x.dollars` specifies the `dollars` data member of `x`, while the use of `dollars` with no object name before it refers to the `dollars` member of the invoking object. When function `Add` terminates, the local variables `a1`, `a2`, `a3`, and `ans` are destroyed by the destructor for `long` and the space allocated to these variables freed. Since the currency object `ans` is to be returned as the value of the invocation, it must be copied into the invoking environment. So `Add` must do a value return.

Program 1.19 gives the `Increment` and `Output` codes. In C++, the reserved word `this` points to the invoking object; `*this` is the invoking object itself. Consider the invocation `g.Increment(h)`. The first line of function `Increment` invokes the `public` member function `Add`, which adds `x` (i.e., `h`) to the invoking object `g`. The result is returned and assigned to the object `*this`, which is `g`. So the value of `g` is incremented by `h`. The function returns `*this`, which is the invoking object. Since this object is not local to function `Increment`, it will not be automatically destroyed upon termination of the function. Hence we may do a reference return and save the copying that would take place during a value return.

```
Currency Currency::Add(const Currency& x) const
{// Add x and *this.
   long a1, a2, a3;
   Currency ans;
   // convert invoking object to signed integers
   a1 = dollars * 100 + cents;
   if (sgn == minus) a1 = -a1;

   // convert x to signed integer
   a2 = x.dollars * 100 + x.cents;
   if (x.sgn == minus) a2 = -a2;

   a3 = a1 + a2;

   // convert to currency representation
   if (a3 < 0) {ans.sgn = minus; a3 = -a3;}
   else ans.sgn = plus;
   ans.dollars = a3 / 100;
   ans.cents = a3 - ans.dollars * 100;

   return ans;
}
```

Program 1.18 Adding two currency values

By making the data members of the class Currency private, we deny access to these members to the user. So the user cannot change their values using statements such as

```
h.cents = 20;
h.dollars = 100;
h.sgn = plus;
```

We can assure the integrity of the data members by writing the member functions to leave behind valid values if they begin with valid data member values. Our codes for the constructor and Set functions validate the data before using it. The remaining functions have the property they leave behind valid data if they start with valid data. As a result, the codes for functions such as Add and Output do not need to verify that the number of cents is, in fact, between 0 and 99. If the data members are declared as public members, their integrity cannot be assured. The user might (erroneously) set cents equal to 305, which would cause functions such as Output to malfunction. As a result, all functions would need to validate the data before proceeding with their tasks. This

```
Currency& Currency::Increment(const Currency& x)
{// Increment by x.
   *this = Add(x);
   return *this;
}

void Currency::Output() const
{// Output currency value.
   if (sgn == minus) cout << '-';
   cout << '$' << dollars << '.';
   if (cents < 10) cout << "0";
   cout << cents;
}
```

Program 1.19 Increment and Output

validation would slow down the codes and also make them less elegant.

Program 1.20 gives a sample application of the class Currency. This code assumes that the class declaration and all implementation codes are in the file curr1.h. We would normally keep the class declaration and the function implementations in separate files. However, such a separation causes difficulties with template functions and template classes that we use heavily in subsequent sections and chapters.

Line 1 of the function main declares four variables, g, h, i, and j of type Currency. The class constructor initializes all but h to $0.00 by the class constructor. h has the initial value $3.50. In the next two lines, g and i are, respectively, set to −$2.25 and −$6.45. Then the call to function Add adds h and g and returns the resulting object whose value is $1.25. The returned object is assigned to j, using the default assignment procedure that copies the data members of the object on the right side into the corresponding data members of the object on the left side. This copying results in j having the value $1.25. This value of j is output by the next line of code.

The next two lines increment i by h and output the new value of i, −$2.95. The following line first adds i and g together and returns a temporary object with value −$5.20. Next h is added to this temporary object and a new temporary object with value −$1.70 returned. The new temporary object in turn is copied into j. The next line outputs the value of j (i.e., −$1.70). Notice that a sequence of '.'s is handled from left to right.

The next line first increments i by g using Increment, which returns a reference to i. Add returns the sum of the incremented i and h, and = assigns this sum to j. The ouput of j causes −$1.70 to be displayed, while that of i causes −$5.20 to be displayed.

```
#include <iostream.h>
#include "curr1.h"

void main(void)
{
    Currency g, h(plus, 3, 50), i, j;
    g.Set(minus, 2, 25);
    i.Set(-6.45);
    j = h.Add(g);
    j.Output(); cout << endl;
    i.Increment(h);
    i.Output(); cout << endl;
    j = i.Add(g).Add(h);
    j.Output(); cout << endl;
    j = i.Increment(g).Add(h);
    j.Output(); cout << endl;
    i.Output(); cout << endl;
}
```

Program 1.20 Application of the class `Currency`

1.4.2 Using a Different Representation

Suppose that many application codes have been developed using the class `Currency` of Program 1.15. Now we desire to change the representation of a currency object to one that results in faster codes for the more frequently performed operations of `Add` and `Increment` and hence speed the application codes. Since the user interacts with the class `Currency` only through the interface provided in the `public` section, changes made to the `private` section do not affect the correctness of the application codes. Hence we can change the `private` section without making any changes in the applications!

The new representation of a currency object has just one private data member, which is of type `long`. The number 132 represents $1.32, while −20 represents −$0.20. Programs 1.21, 1.22, and 1.23 give the new declaration of `Currency` and the implementation of the various member functions.

Notice that if the new code is placed in the file `curr1.h`, we can run the application code of Program 1.20 with no change at all! *An important benefit of hiding the implementation details from the user is that we can replace old representations with new more efficient ones without changing the application codes.*

```
class Currency {
   public:
      // constructor
      Currency(sign s = plus, unsigned long d = 0,
                              unsigned int c = 0);
      // destructor
      ~Currency() {}
      bool Set(sign s, unsigned long d,
                       unsigned int c);
      bool Set(float a);
      sign Sign() const
         {if (amount < 0) return minus;
          else return plus;}
      unsigned long Dollars() const
         {if (amount < 0) return (-amount) / 100;
          else return amount / 100;}
      unsigned int Cents() const
         {if (amount < 0)
              return -amount - Dollars() * 100;
          else return amount - Dollars() * 100;}
      Currency Add(const Currency& x) const;
      Currency& Increment(const Currency& x)
         {amount += x.amount; return *this;}
      void Output() const;
   private:
      long amount;
};
```

Program 1.21 New declaration of the class `Currency`

1.4.3 Operator Overloading

The class `Currency` includes several member functions that resemble some of the standard operators of C++. For example, `Add` does what `+` does, and `Increment` does what `+=` does. Using these standard C++ operators is more natural than defining new ones such as `Add` and `Increment`. We can use `+` and `+=` by a process called **operator overloading** that permits us to extend the applicability of existing C++ operators so that they work with new data types or classes.

Program 1.24 gives the class declaration that substitutes the standard operators `+` and `+=` for `Add` and `Increment`. The `Output` function now takes the name of an output stream as a parameter. These changes require us to

```
Currency::Currency(sign s, unsigned long d,
                              unsigned int c)
{// Create a Currency object.
   if (c > 99)
      {// too many cents
       cerr << "Cents should be < 100" << endl;
       exit(1);;}

   amount = d * 100 + c;
   if (s == minus) amount = -amount;
}

bool Currency::Set(sign s, unsigned long d,
                            unsigned int c)
{// Reset value.
   if (c > 99) return false;

   amount = d * 100 + c;
   if (s == minus) amount = -amount;
   return true;
}

bool Currency::Set(float a)
{// Reset value.
   sign sgn;
   if (a < 0) {sgn = minus; a = -a;}
   else sgn = plus;
   amount = (a + 0.001) * 100;
   if (sgn == minus) amount = -amount;
   return true;
}
```

Program 1.22 New constructor and set codes

change the codes for Add and Output (Program 1.23) only. Program 1.25 gives the changed codes. This program also includes code to overload the C++ stream insertion operator <<.

Notice that we overload the stream insertion operator without declaring a corresponding member function in the class Currency, and overload + and += by defining these operators as members of the class. We can also overload the stream extraction operator >> without defining this operator as a class member. Further, notice the use of the function Output to assist in the

```
Currency Currency::Add(const Currency& x) const
{// Add x and *this.
   Currency y;
   y.amount = amount + x.amount;
   return y;
}

void Currency::Output() const
{// Output currency value.
    long a = amount;
    if (a < 0) {cout << '-';
                a = -a;}
    long d = a / 100; // dollars
    cout << '$' << d << '.';
    int c = a - d * 100; // cents
    if (c < 10) cout << "0";
    cout << c;
}
```

Program 1.23 New code for Add and Output

overloading of <<. Since the private members of Currency objects are not accessible from functions that are not class members (the overloaded << is not a class member, while the overloaded + is), the code that overloads << may not reference the private members of the object x that it is to insert into the output stream. In particular, the code

```
// overload <<
ostream& operator<<(ostream& out, const Currency& x)
   {out << x.amount; return out;}
```

is erroneous, as the member amount is not accessible.

Program 1.26 is a version of Program 1.20 that assumes that operators have been overloaded and that the codes of Programs 1.24 and 1.25 are in the file curr3.h

```
class Currency {
   public:
      // constructor
      Currency(sign s = plus, unsigned long d = 0,
                               unsigned int c = 0);
      // destructor
      ~Currency() {}
      bool Set(sign s, unsigned long d,
                       unsigned int c);
      bool Set(float a);
      sign Sign() const
        {if (amount < 0) return minus;
         else return plus;}
      unsigned long Dollars() const
        {if (amount < 0) return (-amount) / 100;
         else return amount / 100;}
      unsigned int Cents() const
        {if (amount < 0)
            return -amount - Dollars() * 100;
         else return amount - Dollars() * 100;}
      Currency operator+(const Currency& x) const;
      Currency& operator+=(const Currency& x)
        {amount += x.amount; return *this;}
      void Output(ostream& out) const;
   private:
      long amount;
};
```

Program 1.24 Class declaration using operator overloading

1.4.4 Throwing Exceptions

Class members such as the constructor and Set may fail to perform their appointed tasks. In the first case we handled the error condition by exiting the program, and in the latter by returning a failure signal (false) to the invoking environment. We may, instead, handle these errors by throwing an exception, which may then be caught at a level of the code best suited to handle the error. To throw an exception, we must first define an exception class such as BadIn- itializers (Program 1.27).

   We can change the declarations of Set in Program 1.21 to have return type void. We can also change the codes for the constructor and the first Set function to that of Program 1.28. The remaining codes are unchanged.

```
Currency Currency::operator+(const Currency& x) const
{// Add x and *this.
   Currency y;
   y.amount = amount + x.amount;
   return y;
}

void Currency::Output(ostream& out) const
{// Insert currency value into stream out.
   long a = amount;
   if (a < 0) {out << '-';
              a = -a;}
   long d = a / 100; // dollars
   out << '$' << d << '.';
   int c = a - d * 100; // cents
   if (c < 10) out << "0";
   out << c;
}

// overload <<
ostream& operator<<(ostream& out, const Currency& x)
   {x.Output(out); return out;}
```

Program 1.25 Codes for +, Output, and <<

1.4.5 Friends and Protected Class Members

As pointed out earlier, private members of a class are visible only to class member functions. In some applications, we must grant access to these private members to other classes and functions. This access may be granted by declaring these other classes or functions as friends.

In our Currency class example (Program 1.24), we defined a member function Output to facilitate the overloading of the operator <<. Defining this member function was necessary, as the function

```
ostream& operator<<(ostream& out, const Currency& x)
```

cannot access the private member amount. We may avoid defining the additional function Output by declaring ostream& operator<< a friend of the class Currency. Thus we grant this function access to all members (private and public) of Currency. To make friends, we introduce friend statements into the declaration of the class Currency. For consistency, we shall always place friend statements just after the class

```
#include <iostream.h>
#include "curr3.h"

void main(void)
{
    Currency g, h(plus, 3, 50), i, j;
    g.Set(minus, 2, 25);
    i.Set(-6.45);
    j = h + g;
    cout << j << endl;
    i += h;
    cout << i << endl;
    j = i + g + h;
    cout << j << endl;
    j = (i+=g) + h;
    cout << j << endl;
    cout << i << endl;
}
```

Program 1.26 Using overloaded operators

```
// bad initializers
class BadInitializers {
    public:
        BadInitializers() {}
};
```

Program 1.27 Exception class `BadInitializers`

header statement as in

```
class Currency {
    friend ostream& operator<<(ostream&,
                                const Currency&);
    public:
```

With this friend declaration in place, we may overload the $<<$ operator using the code of Program 1.29. When the `private` members of `Currency` are changed, we will need to examine its friends and make appropriate changes.

Later we shall see how a class A may be derived from another class B. Class A is called the **derived class**, and B is the **base class**. The derived class

```
Currency::Currency(sign s, unsigned long d,
                              unsigned int c)
{// Create a Currency object.
   if (c > 99) throw BadInitializers();

   amount = d * 100 + c;
   if (s == minus) amount = -amount;
}

void Currency::Set(sign s, unsigned long d,
                            unsigned int c)
{// Reset value.
   if (c > 99) throw BadInitializers();

   amount = d * 100 + c;
   if (s == minus) amount = -amount;
}
```

Program 1.28 Throwing an exception

```
// overload <<
ostream& operator<<(ostream& out, const Currency& x)
{// Insert currency value into stream out.
   long a = x.amount;
   if (a < 0) {out << '-';
               a = -a;}
   long d = a / 100; // dollars
   out << '$' << d << '.';
   int c = a - d * 100; // cents
   if (c < 10) out << "0";
   out << c;
   return out;
}
```

Program 1.29 Overloading the friend <<

will need access to some or all of the data members of the base class. To facilitate granting this access, C++ allows for a third category of members called protected. Protected members behave like private members except that derived classes can access protected members.

Class members that are to be accessible by user applications should be declared `public` members. Data members should never be in this category. The remaining members should be divided between the categories `protected` and `private`. Good software-engineering principles dictate that data members remain private. By adding protected member functions to access and change the value of data members, derived classes obtain indirect access to the data members of the base class. At the same time, we can change the implementation of the base class without having to change its derived classes.

1.4.6   Addition of `#ifndef`, `#define`, and `#endif` Statements

The entire contents of the file `curr1.h` (or `curr3.h`) that contains the declaration and implementation of the class `Currency` should be preceded by the statements

```
#ifndef Currency_
#define Currency_
```

and followed by the statement

```
#endif
```

These statements ensure that the code for `Currency` gets included and compiled only once per program. *You should add corresponding statements to the program listings provided for the remaining class definitions in this book.*

EXERCISES

9. (a)   What are the maximum and minimum currency values permissible when the representation of Program 1.15 is used? Assume that an object of type `long` is represented as 4 bytes and one of type `int` is represented as 2 bytes. So an `unsigned long` has the range 0 through $2^{32} - 1$ and an `unsigned int` has range 0 through 65,535.

   (b)   What are the maximum and minimum currency values permissible when the representation of Program 1.15 is used and the data types of `dollars` and `cents` are changed to `int`?

   (c)   If function `Add` (Program 1.18) is used to add two currency amounts, what are their largest possible values so that no error occurs when converting from type `currency` to type `long int` as is done to set `a1` and `a2`?

10. Extend the class `Currency` of Program 1.15 by adding the following `public` member functions:

    (a) `Input()` inputs a currency value from the standard input stream and assign it to the invoking object.

    (b) `Subtract(x)` subtracts the value of the currency object `x` from that of the invoking object and returns the result.

    (c) `Percent(x)` returns a currency object whose value is `x` percent of the value of the invoking object. `x` is a floating-point number.

    (d) `Multiply(x)` returns the currency object that results from multiplying the invoking object and the floating-point number `x`.

    (e) `Divide(x)` returns the currency object that results from dividing the invoking object by the floating-point number `x`.

    Implement all member functions and test their correctness using suitable test data.

11. Do Exercise 10 using the implementation of Program 1.21.

12. (a) Do Exercise 10 using the implementation of Program 1.24. Overload the operators `>>`, `-`, `%`, `*`, and `/`. When overloading `>>`, declare it as a friend function and do not define a `public` input function to facilitate the input.

    (b) Replace the two `Set` functions by overloading the assignment operator `=`. An overload of the type `operator=(int x)` that assigns an integer to an object of type `Currency` should replace the first `Set` function. `x` represents the sign, dollar amount, and cents rolled into a single integer. An overload of the type `operator=(float x)` should replace the second `Set` function.

1.5 TESTING AND DEBUGGING

1.5.1 What Is Testing?

As indicated in Section 1.1, correctness is the most important attribute of a program. Because providing a mathematically rigorous proof of correctness for even a small program is quite difficult, we resort to a process called **program testing** in which we execute the program on the target computer using input data, called **test data**, and compare the program's behavior with the expected behavior. If these two behaviors are different, we have a problem with the program. Unfortunately, however, even if the two behaviors are the same, we cannot conclude that the program is correct, as the two behaviors may not be the same on other input data. By using many sets of input data and verifying that the observed and expected behaviors are the same, we can increase our confidence in the correctness of the program. By using all possible input data we can verify that the program is correct. However, for most practical programs, the number of possible input data is too large to perform such exhaustive testing. The subset of the input data space that is actually used for testing is called the **test set**.

Example 1.4 [*Quadratic Roots*] A **quadratic function** (or simply a **quadratic**) in x is a function that has the form

$$ax^2 + bx + c$$

where the values of a, b, and c are known and $a \neq 0$. $3x^2 - 2x + 4$, $-9x^2 - 7x$, $3.5x^2 + 4$, and $5.8x^2 + 3.2x + 5$ are examples of quadratic functions. $5x + 3$ is not a quadratic function.

The **roots** of a quadratic function are the values of x at which the function value is zero. For example, the roots of $f(x) = x^2 - 5x + 6$ are 2 and 3, as $f(2) = f(3) = 0$. Every quadratic has exactly two roots, and these roots are given by the formula:

$$\frac{-b \pm \sqrt{b^2 - 4ac}}{2a}$$

For the function $f(x) = x^2 - 5x + 6$, $a = 1$, $b = -5$, and $c = 6$. Substituting these into the above formula, we get

$$\frac{5 \pm \sqrt{25 - 4*1*6}}{2} = \frac{5 \pm 1}{2}$$

So the roots of $f(x)$ are $x = 3$ and $x = 1$.

When $d = b^2 - 4ac = 0$, the two roots are the same; when $d > 0$, the two roots are different and real numbers; and when $d < 0$, the two roots are different and complex numbers. In this last case each root has a *real* part and an *imaginary* part. The real part is $real = -b/2a$, and the imaginary part is $imag = \sqrt{-d}$. The complex roots are $real + imag * i$ and $real - imag * i$ where $i = \sqrt{-1}$.

The function OutputRoots (Program 1.30) computes and outputs the roots of a quadratic. We shall not attempt a formal correctness proof for this function. Rather, we wish to establish correctness by testing. The number of possible inputs is the number of different triples (a,b,c) with $a \neq 0$. Even if a, b, and c are restricted to integers, the number of possible input triples is too large for us to test the program on all inputs. With 16 bits per integer, there are 2^{16} different values for b and c and $2^{16} - 1$ for a (recall that a cannot be zero). The number of different triples is $2^{32}(2^{16} - 1)$. If our target computer can test at the rate of 1,000,000 triples per second, it would take almost nine years to complete! A faster computer that is executing at the rate of 1,000,000,000 triples per

```
template<class T>
void OutputRoots(T a, T b, T c)
{// Compute and output the roots of the quadratic.

   T d = b*b-4*a*c;
   if (d > 0) {// two real roots
              float sqrtd = sqrt(d);
              cout << "There are two real roots "
                   << (-b+sqrtd)/(2*a) << " and "
                   << (-b-sqrtd)/(2*a)
                   << endl;}
   else if (d == 0)
           // both roots are the same
           cout << "There is only one distinct root "
                << -b/(2*a)
                << endl;
      else //  complex conjugate roots
           cout << "The roots are complex"
                << endl
                << "The real part is "
                << -b/(2*a) << endl
                << "The imaginary part is "
                << sqrt(-d)/(2*a) << endl;
   }
```

Program 1.30 Compute and output the roots of a quadratic

second would take almost three days. So a practical test set can contain only a small subset of the entire space of input data.

If we run the program using the data set $(a,b,c) = (1,-5,6)$, the roots 2 and 3 are output. The program behavior agrees with the expected behavior, and we conclude the program is correct for this input. However, verifying agreement between observed and expected behavior on a proper subset of the possible inputs does not prove that the program works correctly on all inputs. ∎

Since the number of different inputs that can be provided to a program is generally very large, testing is often limited to a very small subset of the possible inputs. Testing with this subset cannot conclusively establish the correctness of the program. As a result, *the objective of testing is not to establish correctness, but to expose the presence of errors*. The test set must be chosen so as to expose any errors that may be present in the program. Different test sets can expose different errors in a program.

Example 1.5 The test data $(a,b,c) = (1,-5,6)$ causes `OutputRoots` to execute the code for the case when there are two real roots. If the roots 2 and 3 are output, we can have some confidence that the statements executed during this test are correct. Notice that an erroneous code could still give the correct results. For example, if we omitted the `a` from the expression for `d` and mistakenly typed

```
T d = b*b-4*c;
```

the value of `d` is the same as our test data because `a = 1`. Since the test data $(1,-5,6)$ did not execute all statements of the code, we have less confidence in the correctness of the statements that are not executed.

  The test set $\{(1,-5,6), (1,3,2), (2,5,2)\}$ can expose errors only in the first seven lines of `OutputRoots`, as each triple in this test set executes only these seven lines of code. However, the test set $\{(1,-5,6), (1,-8,16), (1,2,5)\}$ causes all statements of `OutputRoots` to execute and so has a better chance of exposing the errors in the code. ■

1.5.2   Designing Test Data

When developing test data, we should keep in mind that the objective of testing is to expose the presence of errors. If data designed to expose errors fails to expose any errors, then we may have confidence in the correctness of the program. To tell whether or not a program malfunctions on a given test data, we must be able to verify the correctness of the program behavior on the test data.

Example 1.6 For our quadratic roots example, the behavior on any test data may be verified in one of two ways. First, we might know the roots of the test quadratic. For example, the roots of the quadratic with $(a,b,c) = (1,-5,6)$ are 2 and 3. We can verify the correctness of Program 1.30 on the test data $(1,-5,6)$ by comparing the output roots with the correct roots 2 and 3. Another possiblity is to substitute the roots produced by the program into the quadratic function and verify that the function value is zero. So if our program outputs 2 and 3 as the roots, we compute $f(2) = 2^2 - 5*2 + 6 = 0$ and $f(3) = 3^2 - 5*3 + 6 = 0$. We can implement these verfication methods as computer programs. In the first the test program inputs the triple (a,b,c) as well as the expected roots and then checks the computed roots against the expected ones. For the second method we write code to evaluate the quadratic at the computed roots and verify that the result is zero. ■

We can evaluate any candidate test data using the following criteria:

- What is this data's potential to expose errors?
- Can we verify the correctness of the program behavior on this data?

Techniques for test data development fall into two categories: black box methods and white box methods. In a **black box method**, we consider the program's function, not the actual code, when we develop test data. In a **white box method**, we examine the code in an attempt to develop test data whose execution results in a good coverage of the program's statements and execution paths.

Black Box Methods

The most popular black box methods are I/O partitioning and cause-effect graphing. This section elaborates on the I/O partitioning method only. In this method we partition the input and/or output data space into classes. The data in different classes cause the program to exhibit qualitatively different behaviors while data in the same class cause qualitatively similar behaviors. The quadratic roots example has three different qualitiative behaviors: the roots are complex; the roots are real and distinct; and the roots are real and the same. We can use these three behaviors to partition the input space into three classes. Data in the first class cause the first kind of behavior; data in the second cause the second kind of behavior; and data in the third cause the third kind of behavior. A test set should include at least one input from each class.

White Box Methods

White box methods create test data based on an examination of the code to be generated. The weakest condition we can place on a test set is that it results in each program statement being executed at least once. This condition is called **statement coverage**. For our quadratic roots example, the test set $\{(1,-5,6),$ $(1,-8,16), (1,2,5)\}$ causes all statements in Program 1.30 to execute. So this test set provides statement coverage. The test set $\{(1,-5,6), (1,3,2), (2,5,2)\}$ does not provide statement coverage.

In **decision coverage** we require the test set to cause each conditional in the program to take on both true and false values. The code of Program 1.30 has two conditionals: $d > 0$ and $d == 0$. In decision coverage, we require at least one set of test data for which $d > 0$ is true and at least one for which it is false. We also require that there be at least one set of test data for which $d == 0$ is true and at least one for which it is false.

Example 1.7 [*Maximum Element*] Program 1.31 returns the position of the largest element in the array `a[0:n-1]`. It finds this position by scanning the array from positions 0 to `n-1` using variable `pos` to keep track of the position of the largest element seen so far. The data set `a[0:4]` = [2,4,6,8,9] provides statement coverage, but not decision coverage, as the condition `a[pos]<a[i]` never becomes false. The data set [4,2,6,8,9] provides both decision and statement coverage. ∎

```
template<class T>
int Max(T a[], int n)
{// Locate the largest element in a[0:n-1].
   int pos = 0;
   for (int i = 1; i < n; i++)
      if (a[pos] < a[i])
         pos = i;
   return pos;
}
```

Program 1.31 Finding the largest element

We can strengthen the decision coverage criterion to require each clause of each conditional to take on both true and false values. This strengthened criterion is called **clause coverage**. A **clause** is formally defined to be a Boolean expression that contains no Boolean operator (i.e., &&, ||, !). The expressions $x > y$, $x + y < y * z$, and c (where c is of type Boolean) are examples of clauses. Consider the statement

```
if ((C1 && C2)|| (C3 && C4)) S1;
else S2;
```

where `C1`, `C2`, `C3`, and `C4` are clauses and `S1` and `S2` are statements. Under the decision coverage criterion, we need to use one test set that causes `((C1 && C2)|| (C3 && C4))` to be true and another that results in this conditional being false. Clause coverage requires us to use a test set that causes each of the four clauses `C1` through `C4` to evaluate to true at least once and to false at least once.

We can further strengthen clause coverage to require testing for all combinations of clause values. In the case of the conditional `((C1 && C2)|| (C3 && C4))`, this strengthening requires the use of 16 sets of test data: one for each truth combination of the four conditions. However, several of these combinations may not be possible.

If we sequence the statements of a program in their order of execution by a certain set of test data, we get an execution path. Different test data may yield different execution paths. Program 1.30 has only three execution paths—lines 1 through 7; lines 1, 2, 8 through 12; and lines 1, 2, 8, 13 through 19. The number of execution paths of Program 1.31 grows as n increases. When n = 1, there is just one path—lines 1, 2, 5; when n = 2, there are two paths—1, 2, 3, 2, 5 and 1, 2, 3, 4, 2, 5; when n = 3, there are four paths—1, 2, 3, 2, 3, 2, 5; 1, 2, 3, 4, 2, 3, 2, 5; 1, 2, 3, 2, 3, 4, 2, 5; and 1, 2, 3, 4, 2, 3, 4, 5. For a general n, the number of execution paths is 2^{n-1}. **Execution path** coverage requires the use of a test set that causes all execution paths to be executed. For the quadratic roots code, statement coverage, decision coverage, clause coverage, and execution path coverage are equivalent requirements. But for Program 1.31 statement coverage, decision coverage, and execution path coverage are different, while decision and clause coverage are equivalent.

Of the white box coverage criteria we have discussed, execution path coverage is generally the most demanding. A test set that results in total execution path coverage also results in statement and decision coverage. It may, however, not result in clause coverage. Total execution path coverage often requires an infinite number of test data or at least a prohibitively large number of test data. Hence total path coverage is often impossible in practice.

Many exercises in this book ask you to test the correctness of your codes. The test data you use should at least provide statement coverage. Additionally, you should test for special cases that could cause your program to malfunction. For example, a program designed to sort $n \geq 0$ elements should be tested with $n = 0$ and 1 in addition to other values of n. If such a program uses an array a[0:99], it should also be tested with $n = 100$. $n = 0$, 1, and 100 represent the boundary conditions empty, singleton, and full.

1.5.3 Debugging

Testing exposes the presence of errors in a program. Once a test run produces a result different from the one expected, we know that something is wrong with the program. The process of determining and correcting the cause of the discrepency between the desired and observed behaviors is called **debugging**. Although a thorough study of debugging methods is beyond the scope of this book, we do provide some suggestions for debugging.

- Try to determine the cause of an error by logical reasoning. If this method fails, then you may wish to perform a program trace to determine when the program started performing incorrectly. This approach becomes infeasible when the program executes many instructions with that test data and the program trace becomes too long to examine manually. In this case you must try to isolate the part of the code that is suspect and obtain a trace of this part.

- Do not attempt to correct errors by creating exceptions. The number of exceptions will soon be very large. Errors should be corrected by first determining their cause and then redesigning your solution as necessary.

- When correcting an error, be certain that your correction does not result in errors where there were none before. Run your corrected program on the test data on which it originally worked correctly to ensure that it still works correctly on this data.

- When testing and debugging a multifunction program, begin with a single function that is independent of the others. This function would typically be an input or output function. Then introduce additional functions one at a time, testing and debugging the larger program for correctness. This strategy is called **incremental testing and debugging**. When this strategy is used, the cause of a detected error can reasonably be expected to lie in the most recently introduced function.

EXERCISES

13. Show that test sets that provide statement coverage for Program 1.30 also provide decision and execution path coverage.

14. Develop a test set for Program 1.31 that provides execution path coverage when $n = 4$.

15. How many execution paths are in Program 1.8?

16. How many execution paths are in Program 1.9?

1.6   REFERENCES AND SELECTED READINGS

A good introduction to programming in C++ can be found in the texts *C++ Program Design: An Introduction to Programming and Object-Oriented Design* by J. Cohoon and J. Davidson, Richard D. Irwin, Inc., Chicago, IL, 1997 and *C++ How to Program* by H. Deitel and P. Deitel, Prentice Hall, Englewood Cliffs, NJ, 1994.

The Art of Software Testing by G. Myers, John Wiley, New York, NY, 1979 and *Software Testing Techniques* by Boris Beizer, Second Edition, Van Nostrand Reinhold, New York, NY, 1990 have more thorough treatments of software testing and debugging techniques.

CHAPTER 2

PROGRAM PERFORMANCE

BIRD'S-EYE VIEW

The following concepts related to program performance analysis and measurement are reviewed in this chapter:

- Determining the memory and time requirements of a program.

- Measuring the time requirements of a program using the operation count and step count approaches.

- Using asymptotic notations such as big oh, omega, theta, and little oh.

- Measuring the actual run time of a program using a clocking function.

In addition to these concepts, this chapter presents many application codes that will prove useful in later chapters. These applications include

- Searching an array of elements for one with a specified characteristic. The methods considered in this chapter are sequential search and binary search.

- Sorting an array of elements. Codes for the rank (or count) sort, selection sort, bubble sort, and insertion sort methods are developed.

45

- Evaluating a polynomial using Horner's rule.
- Performing matrix operations such as add, transpose, and multiply.

2.1 INTRODUCTION

By the **performance of a program**, we mean the amount of computer memory and time needed to run a program. We use two approaches to determine the performance of a program. One is analytical, and the other experimental. In **performance analysis** we use analytical methods, while in **performance measurement** we conduct experiments.

The **space complexity** of a program is the amount of memory it needs to run to completion. We are interested in the space complexity of a program for the following reasons:

- If the program is to be run on a multiuser computer system, then we may need to specify the amount of memory to be allocated to the program.

- For any computer system, we would like to know in advance whether or not sufficient memory is available to run the program.

- A problem might have several possible solutions with different space requirements. For instance, one C++ compiler for your computer might need only 1MB of memory, while another might need 4MB. The 1MB compiler is the only choice if your computer has less than 4MB of memory. Even users whose computers have the extra memory will prefer the smaller compiler if its capabilities are comparable to those of the bigger compiler. The smaller compiler leaves the user with more memory for other tasks.

- We can use the space complexity to estimate the size of the largest problem that a program can solve. For example, we may have a circuit simulation program that requires $280K + 10(c + w)$ bytes of memory to simulate circuits with c components and w wires. If the total amount of memory available is 640K bytes, then we can simulate circuits with $c + w \le 36K$.

The **time complexity** of a program is the amount of computer time it needs to run to completion. We are interested in the time complexity of a program for the following reasons:

- Some computer systems require the user to provide an upper limit on the amount of time the program will run. Once this upper limit is reached, the program is aborted. An easy way out is to simply specify a time limit of a few thousand years. However, this solution could result in serious fiscal problems if the program runs into an infinite loop caused by some discrepency in the data and you actually get billed for the computer time used. We would like to provide a time limit that is just slightly above the expected run time.

- The program we are developing might need to provide a satisfactory real-time response. For example, all interactive programs must provide such a response. A text editor that takes a minute to move the cursor one page down or one page up will not be acceptable to many users. A spreadsheet program that takes several minutes to reevaluate the cells in a sheet will be satisfactory only to very patient users. A database management system that allows its users adequate time to drink two cups of coffee while it is sorting a relation will not find too much acceptance. Programs designed for interactive use must provide satisfactory real-time response. From the time complexity of the program or program module, we can decide whether or not the response time will be acceptable. If not, we need to either redesign the algorithm in use or give the user a faster computer.

- If we have alternative ways to solve a problem, then the decision on which to use will be based primarily on the expected performance difference among these solutions. We will use some weighted measure of the space and time complexities of the alternative solutions.

EXERCISES

1. Give two more reasons why analysts are interested in the space complexity of a program.

2. Give two more reasons why analysts are interested in the time complexity of a program.

2.2   SPACE COMPLEXITY

2.2.1   Components of Space Complexity

The space needed by a program has the following components:

- *Instruction space*
  Instruction space is the space needed to store the compiled version of the program instructions.

- *Data space*
  Data space is the space needed to store all constant and variable values. Data space has two components:

  1. Space needed by constants (for example, the numbers 0, 1, and 4 in Programs 1.1 to 1.9 and simple variables (such as a, b, and c in Programs 1.1 to 1.6).

  2. Space needed by component variables such as the array a in Programs 1.8 and 1.9. This category includes space needed by structures and dynamically allocated memory.

- *Environment stack space*
  The environment stack is used to save information needed to resume execution of partially completed functions. For example, if function `fun1` invokes function `fun2`, then we must at least save a pointer to the instruction of `fun1` to be executed when `fun2` terminates.

Instruction Space

The amount of instruction space that is needed depends on factors such as

- The compiler used to compile the program into machine code.
- The compiler options in effect at the time of compilation.
- The target computer.

The compiler is a very important factor in determining how much space the resulting code needs. Figure 2.1 shows three possible codes for the evaluation of `a+b+b*c+(a+b-c)/(a+b)+4`. They all perform exactly the same arithmetic operations (i.e., every operator has the same operands), but each needs a different amount of space. The compiler in use determines exactly which code will be generated.

Even with the same compiler, the size of the generated program code can vary. For example, a compiler might provide the user with optimization options. These could include code-size optimization as well as execution-time optimization. In Figure 2.1, for instance, the compiler might generate the code of Figure 2.1(b) in nonoptimization mode. In optimization mode, the compiler might use the knowledge that `a+b+b*c = b*c+(a+b)` and generate the shorter and more time-efficient code of Figure 2.1(c). The use of the optimization mode will generally increase the time needed to compile the program.

The example of Figure 2.1 brings to light an additional contribution to the space requirements of a program. Space is needed for temporary variables such as `t1, t2, ⋯, t6`.

Another option that can have a significant effect on program space is the overlay option in which space is assigned only to the program module that is currently executing. When a new module is invoked, it is read in from a disk or other device, and the code for the new module overwrites the code of the old module. So program space corresponding to the size of the largest module (rather than the sum of the module sizes) is needed.

The configuration of the target computer can also affect code size. If the computer has floating-point hardware, then floating-point operations will translate into one machine instruction per operation. If this hardware is not installed, then code to simulate floating-point computations will be generated.

```
        LOAD   a          LOAD   a          LOAD   a
        ADD    b          ADD    b          ADD    b
        STORE  t1         STORE  t1         STORE  t1
        LOAD   b          SUB    c          SUB    c
        MULT   c          DIV    t1         DIV    t1
        STORE  t2         STORE  t2         STORE  t2
        LOAD   t1         LOAD   b          LOAD   b
        ADD    t2         MUL    c          MUL    c
        STORE  t3         STORE  t3         ADD    t2
        LOAD   a          LOAD   t1         ADD    t1
        ADD    b          ADD    t3         ADD    4
        SUB    c          ADD    t2
        STORE  t4         ADD    4
        LOAD   a
        ADD    b
        STORE  t5
        LOAD   t4
        DIV    t5
        STORE  t6
        LOAD   t3
        ADD    t6
        ADD    4

          (a)               (b)               (c)
```

Figure 2.1 Three equivalent codes

Data Space

For simple variables and constants, the space requirements are a function of the computer and compiler used as well as the size of the numbers involved. The reason is that we will normally be concerned with the number of bytes of memory required. Since the number of bits per byte varies from computer to computer, the number of bytes needed per variable also varies. Also, it takes more bits to store the number 2^{100} than it does to store 2^3.

Figure 2.2 shows the space taken by simple variables in Borland C++. We can obtain the space requirement for a structured variable by adding up the space requirements of all its components. Similarly, we can obtain the space requirement of an array variable by multiplying the array size and the space needs of a single array element.

Type	Space (bytes)	Range
char	1	-128-127
unsigned char	1	0-255
short	2	$-32,768$-32,767
int	2	$-32,768$-32,767
unsigned int	2	0-65,535
long	4	-2^{31}-$2^{31}-1$
unsigned long	4	0-$2^{32}-1$
float	4	± 3.4 E± 38
double	8	± 1.7 E± 308
long double	10	3.4 E-4932-1.1 E$+4932$
pointer	2	(near, _cs, _ds, _es, _ss pointers)
pointer	4	(far, huge pointers)

Note that type int is 4 bytes in a 32-bit Borland C++ program

Figure 2.2 Space allocated to simple variables in Borland C++ (Reproduced from *Borland C++ Programmer's Guide*, Borland International, Inc., Scotts Valley, CA, 1996.)

Consider the following array declarations:

```
double a[100];
int maze[rows][cols];
```

The array a has space for 100 elements of type double, each taking 8 bytes. The total space allocated to the array is therefore 800 bytes. The array maze has space for rows*cols elements of type int. The total space taken by this array is 2*rows*cols bytes.

Environment Stack

Beginning performance analysts often ignore the space needed by the environment stack because they don't understand how functions (and in particular recursive ones) are invoked and what happens on termination. Each time a function is invoked the following data are saved on the environment stack:

- The return address.

- The values of all local variables and value formal parameters in the function being invoked (necessary for recursive functions only).

- The binding of all reference and const reference parameters.

Each time the recursive function Rsum (Program 1.9) is invoked, whether from outside or from line 4, the current binding of a, the value of n, and the program location to return to on completion are saved in the environment stack.

It is worth noting that some compilers save the values of the local variables and value formal parameters as well as the bindings of reference and const reference parameters for both recursive and nonrecursive functions, while others do so for recursive functions alone. So the compiler in use will affect the amount of space needed by the environment stack.

Summary

The space needed by a program depends on several factors. Some of these factors are not known at the time the program is conceived or written (e.g., the computer or the compiler that will be used). Until these factors have been determined, we cannot make an accurate analysis of the space requirements of a program.

We can, however, determine the contribution of those components that depend on characteristics of the problem instance to be solved. These characteristics typically include factors that determine the size of the problem instance (e.g., the number of inputs and outputs or magnitude of the numbers involved) being solved. For example, if we have a program that sorts n elements, we can determine space requirements as a function of n. For a program that adds two $n \times n$ matrices, we may use n as the instance characteristic, and for one that adds two $m \times n$ matrices, we may use m and n as the instance characteristics.

The size of the instruction space is relatively insensitive to the particular problem instance being solved. The contribution of the constants and simple variables to the data space is also independent of the characteristics of the problem instance to be solved except when the magnitude of the numbers involved becomes too large for the chosen data type. At this time we will need to either change the data type or rewrite the program using multiprecision arithmetic and then analyze the new program.

The space needed by some of the component variables and some of the dynamically allocated memory may also be independent of the problem size. The environment stack space is generally independent of the instance characteristics unless recursive functions are in use. When recursive functions are in use, the instance characteristics will generally (but not always) affect the amount of space needed for the environment stack.

The amount of stack space needed by recursive functions is called the **recursion stack space**. For each recursive function, this space depends on the space needed by the local variables and the formal parameters. In addition, this space depends on the maximum depth of recursion (i.e., the maximum number of nested recursive calls). For Program 1.9 recursive calls get nested until n equals zero. At this time, the nesting resembles Figure 2.3. The maximum depth of recursion for this program is therefore n+1.

```
Rsum(a,n)
    Rsum(a,n-1)
        Rsum(a,n-2)
              .
              .
              .

            Rsum(a,1)
                Rsum(a,0)
```

Figure 2.3 Nesting of recursive calls for Program 1.9.

We can divide the total space needed by a program into two parts:

- A fixed part that is independent of the instance characteristics. This part typically includes the instruction space (i.e., space for the code); space for simple variables and fixed-size component variables; space for constants, and so on.

- A variable part that consists of the space needed by component variables whose size depends on the particular problem instance being solved; dynamically allocated space (to the extent that this space depends on the instance characteristics); and the recursion stack space (in so far as this space depends on the instance characteristics).

The space requirement $S(P)$ of any program P may therefore be written as

$$S(P) = c + S_P(\text{instance characteristics})$$

where c is a constant that denotes the fixed part of the space requirements and S_P denotes the variable component. An accurate analysis should also include the space needed by temporary variables generated during compilation (refer to Figure 2.1). This space is compiler dependent and, except in the case of recursive functions, independent of the instance characteristics. We will ignore the space needs of these compiler-generated variables.

When analyzing the space complexity of a program, we will concentrate solely on estimating S_P (instance characteristics). For any given problem we need to first determine which instance characteristics to use to measure the space requirements. The choice of instance characteristics is very problem specific, and we will resort to examples to illustrate the various possibilities. Generally speaking, our choices are limited to quantities related to the number and magnitude of the inputs to and outputs from the program. At times we also use more complex measures of the interrelationships among the data items.

2.2.2   Examples

Example 2.1 Consider Program 1.4. Before we can determine S_P, we must select the instance characteristics to be used for the analysis. Two possibilities are (1) the data type T and (2) the magnitude of a, b, and c. Suppose we use T as the instance characteristic. Since a, b, and c are reference parameters, no space is actually allocated for their values in the function. However, we may need space to store pointers to the actual parameters. If each such pointer requires 2 bytes, then we need 6 bytes of pointer space. The total space needed by the function is a constant, and S_{Abc}(instance characteristics) = 0. Had the parameters of function Abc been value parameters, then sizeof(T) space is assigned for each. In this case the space needed by a, b, and c is 3 * sizeof(T). The remaining space needed is independent of T. As a result, S_{Abc}(instance characteristics) = 3 * sizeof(T). If we use the magnitude of a, b, and c as the instance characteristic, then S_{Abc}(instance characteristics) = 0 when either reference or value parameters are used. For the case of value parameters, note that the space allocated to each of a, b, and c is sizeof(T) regardless of the actual values being stored in the variables. For example, if T is double, then each variable is allocated 8 bytes. ∎

Example 2.2 [*Sequential Search*] Program 2.1 examines the elements of the array a[0:n-1] from left to right to see if one of these elements equals x. If an element equal to x is found, the function returns the position of the first occurrence of x. If the array has no element equal to x, the function returns −1.

```
template<class T>
int SequentialSearch(T a[], const T& x, int n)
{// Search the unordered list a[0:n-1] for x.
 // Return position if found; return -1 otherwise.
   int i;
   for (i = 0; i < n && a[i] != x; i++);
   if (i == n) return -1;
   return i;
}
```

Program 2.1 Sequential search

We wish to obtain the space complexity of this function in terms of the instance characteristic n. Let us assume that T is int. We need 2 bytes for each of the pointers to the array a and the actual parameter corresponding to x; 2 bytes for the formal value parameter n; 2 bytes for the local variable i; and 2 bytes for each of the integer constants 0 and −1. The total data space needed is 12 bytes. Since this space is independent of n, $S_{SequentialSearch}(n) = 0$.

Note that the array a must be large enough to hold the n elements being searched. The space needed by this array is, however, allocated in the function where the actual parameter corresponding to a is declared. As a result, we do not add the space requirements of this array into the space requirements of function SequentialSearch. ∎

Example 2.3 For function Sum (Program 1.8), suppose we are interested in measuring space requirements as a function of the number of elements to be summed. Space is required for a, n, i, and tsum. The amount of space needed does not depend on the value of n, so $S_{Sum}(n) = 0$. ∎

Example 2.4 Consider the function Rsum (Program 1.9). As in the case of Sum, assume that the instances are characterized by n. The recursion stack space includes space for the formal parameters a and n and the return address. In the case of a, a pointer is saved, while in the case of n, a value of type int is saved on the recursion stack. If we assume that the pointer is a *near pointer*, it requires 2 bytes of space. If we assume that the return address also takes 2 bytes, then using the knowledge that an int requires 2 bytes, we determine that each call to Rsum requires 6 bytes. Since the depth of recursion is n+1, the recursion stack space needed is 6(n+1) bytes. So $S_{Rsum}(n) = 6(n+1)$.

Program 1.8 has a smaller space requirement than does Program 1.9. ∎

Example 2.5 [*Factorial*] The space complexity of Program 1.7, which computes the factorial function, is analyzed as a function of n rather than as a function of the number of inputs (one) or outputs (one). The recursion depth is max{n, 1}. The recursion stack saves a return address (2 bytes) and the value of n (2 bytes) each time Factorial is invoked. No additional space that is dependent on n is used, so $S_{Factorial}(n) = 4 * \max\{n, 1\}$. ∎

Example 2.6 [*Permutations*] Program 1.10 outputs all permutations of a list of elements. With the initial invocation Perm(list, 0, n−1), the depth of recursion is n. Since each recursive call requires 10 bytes of recursion stack space (2 for each of return address, list, k, m, and i), the recursion stack space needed is 10n bytes, so $S_{Perm}(n) = 10n$. ∎

EXERCISES

3. Compile a sample C++ program using two C++ compilers. Is the code length the same or different?

4. List additional factors that may influence the space complexity of a program.

5. Using the data provided in Figure 2.2, determine the number of bytes needed by the following arrays:

   (a) `int matrix[10][100]`

   (b) `double x[100][5][20]`

   (c) `long double y[3]`

   (d) `float z[10][10][10][5]`

   (e) `short a[2][3][4]`

   (f) `long double b[3][3][3][3]`

6. Program 2.2 gives a recursive function that searches the elements `a[0:n-1]` for the element `x`. If `x` is found, the function returns the position of `x` in `a`. Otherwise, the function returns −1. Obtain $S_P(n)$.

```
template<class T>
int SequentialSearch(T a[], const T& x, int n)
{// Search the unordered list a[0:n-1] for x.
 // Return position if found; return -1 otherwise.
   if (n < 1) return -1;
   if (a[n-1] == x) return n - 1;
   return SequentialSearch(a, x, n-1);
}
```

Program 2.2 Recursive sequential search function

7. Write a nonrecursive function to compute $n!$ (see Example 1.1). Compare the space requirments of your nonrecursive function and those of the recursive version (Program 1.7).

2.3   TIME COMPLEXITY

2.3.1   Components of Time Complexity

The time complexity of a program depends on all the factors that the space complexity depends on. A program will run faster on a computer capable of executing 10^9 instructions per second than on one that can execute only 10^6 instructions per second. The code of Figure 2.1(c) will require less execution time than the code of Figure 2.1(a). Some compilers will take less time than others to generate the corresponding computer code. Smaller problem instances will generally take less time than larger instances.

The time $T(P)$ taken by a program P is the sum of the compile time and the run (or execution) time. The compile time does not depend on the instance characteristics. Also, we can assume that a compiled program will be run several times without recompilation. Consequently, we will concern ourselves with just the run time of a program. This run time is denoted by t_P (instance characteristics).

Because many of the factors t_P depends on are not known when a program is conceived, it is reasonable to only estimate t_P. If we knew the characteristics of the compiler to be used, we could determine the number of additions, subtractions, multiplications, divisions, compares, loads, stores, and so on that the code for P would make. Then we could obtain a formula for t_P. Letting n denote the instance characteristics, we might have an expression for $t_P(n)$ of the form

$$t_P(n) = c_a ADD(n) + c_s SUB(n) + c_m MUL(n) + c_d DIV(n) + \cdots$$

where c_a, c_s, c_m, and c_d respectively denote the time needed for an addition, subtraction, multiplication, and division, and ADD, SUB, MUL, and DIV are functions whose value is the number of additions, subtractions, multiplications, and divisions that will be performed when the code for P is used on an instance with characteristic n.

The fact that the time needed for an arithmetic operation depends on the type (`int`, `float`, `double`, etc.) of the numbers in the operation makes obtaining such an exact formula more cumbersome. So we must separate the operation counts by data type.

Two more manageable approaches to estimating run time are (1) identify one or more key operations and determine the number of times these are performed and (2) determine the total number of steps executed by the program.

2.3.2   Operation Counts

One way to estimate the time complexity of a program or function is to select one or more operations, such as add, multiply, and compare, and to determine how many of each is done. The success of this method depends on our ability to identify the operations that contribute most to the time complexity. Several examples of this method follow.

Example 2.7 [*Max Element*] Program 1.31 returns the position of the largest element in the array $a[0:n-1]$. We can estimate its time complexity by the number of comparisons made between elements of the array a. Each iteration of the for loop makes one such comparison, so the total number of element comparisons is $n-1$. The function Max does other comparisons (each iteration of the for loop is preceded by a comparison between i and n) that are not included in the estimate. Other operations such as initializing pos and incrementing the for loop index i are also not included in the estimate. If we included these other operations into our count, the count would increase by a constant factor. ∎

Example 2.8 [*Polynomial Evaluation*] Consider the polynomial $P(x) = \sum\limits_{i=0}^{n} c_i x^n$. If $c_n \neq 0$, P is a polynomial of degree n. Program 2.3 gives one way to compute $P(x)$ for a given value of x. Suppose we estimate its time complexity by the number of additions and multiplications performed inside the for loop. We shall use the degree n as the instance characteristic. The for loop is entered a total of n times, and each time one addition and two multiplications are done. (This operation count excludes the add performed each time the loop variable i is incremented.) The number of additions is n, and the number of multiplications is 2n.

```
template<class T>
T PolyEval(T coeff[], int n, const T& x)
{// Evaluate the degree n polynomial with
 // coefficients coeff[0:n] at the point x.
   T y = 1, value = coeff[0];
   for (int i = 1; i <= n; i++) {
      // add in next term
      y *= x;
      value += y * coeff[i];
      }
   return value;
}
```

Program 2.3 A function to evaluate a polynomial

Horner's rule to evaluate a polynomial uses the parsing

$$P(x) = (\cdots (c_n * x + c_{n-1}) * x + c_{n-2}) * x + c_{n-3}) * x \cdots) * x + c_0$$

The corresponding C++ function is given in Program 2.4. Using the same measure as used for Program 2.3, we estimate its complexity as n additions and n multiplications. Since `PolyEval` performs the same number of additions but twice as many multiplications as does `Horner`, we expect function `Horner` to be faster. ∎

```
template<class T>
T Horner(T coeff[], int n, const T& x)
{// Evaluate the degree n polynomial with
 // coefficients coeff[0:n] at the point x.
   T value = coeff[n];
   for (int i = 1; i <= n; i++)
      value = value * x + coeff[n - i];
   return value;
}
```

Program 2.4 Horner's rule for polynomial evaluation

Example 2.9 [*Ranking*] The **rank** of an element in a sequence is the number of smaller elements in the sequence plus the number of equal elements that appear to its left. For example if the sequence is given as the array a = [4, 3, 9, 3, 7], then the ranks are r = [2, 0, 4, 1, 3]. Function Rank (Program 2.5) computes the ranks of the elements of array a[0:n-1]. We can estimate the complexity of Rank by counting the number of comparisons between elements of a. These comparisons are done in the if statement. For each value of i, the number of element comparisons is i. So the total number of element comparisons is $1 + 2 + 3 + \cdots + n{-}1 = (n{-}1)n/2$ (see Equation 2.3).

```
template<class T>
void Rank(T a[], int n, int r[])
{// Rank the n elements a[0:n-1].
   for (int i = 0; i < n; i++)
      r[i] = 0; //initialize
   // compare all element pairs
   for (int i = 1; i < n; i++)
      for (int j = 0; j < i; j++)
         if (a[j] <= a[i]) r[i]++;
         else r[j]++;
}
```

Program 2.5 Computing ranks

Note that our complexity estimate excludes the overhead associated with the `for` loops, the cost of initializing the array `r`, and the cost of incrementing `r` each time two elements of `a` are compared. ∎

Example 2.10 [*Rank Sort*] Once the elements have been ranked using Program 2.5, they may be rearranged in nondecreasing order so that `a[0]` ≤ `a[1]` ≤ ··· ≤ `a[n-1]` by moving elements to positions corresponding to their ranks. If we have space for an additional array `u`, we can use the function `Rearrange` given in Program 2.6.

```
template<class T>
void Rearrange(T a[], int n, int r[])
{// Rearrange the elements of a into sorted order
 // using an additional array u.
   T *u = new T [n+1];
   // move to correct place in u
   for (int i = 0; i < n; i++)
      u[r[i]] = a[i];
   // move back to a
   for (int i = 0; i < n; i++)
      a[i] = u[i];
   delete [] u;
}
```

Program 2.6 Rearranging elements using an additional array

The number of element moves performed during the execution of function `Rearrange` is `2n`. (Exercise 11 examines how to reduce the number of moves to `n`.) The complete sort requires `(n-1)n/2` comparisons and `2n` element moves. This method of sorting is known as **rank** or **count** sort. An alternative function to rearrange the elements is considered later (Program 2.11). This function does not use an additional array such as `u`. ∎

Example 2.11 [*Selection Sort*] Example 2.10 examined one way to rearrange the elements in an array `a[0:n-1]` so that `a[0]` ≤ `a[1]` ≤ ··· ≤ `a[n-1]`. An alternative strategy is to determine the largest element and move it to `a[n-1]`, then determine the largest of the remaining `n-1` elements and move it to `a[n-2]`, and so on. Program 2.7 gives the resulting C++ function, `SelectionSort`. Program 1.31 gave the function `Max`. We can estimate the complexity of `SelectionSort` by counting the number of element comparisons made. From Example 2.7 we know that each invocation `Max(a,size)` results in `size-1` comparisons being made. So the total number of

comparisons is $1 + 2 + 3 + \cdots + n-1 = (n-1)n/2$. The number of element moves is $3(n-1)$. Selection sort uses the same number of comparisons as rank sort (Example 2.10, but requires 50 percent more element moves. We consider another version of selection sort later in this section. ■

```
template<class T>
void SelectionSort(T a[], int n)
{// Sort the n elements a[0:n-1].
   for (int size = n; size > 1; size--) {
      int j = Max(a, size);
      Swap(a[j], a[size - 1]);
      }
}
```

Program 2.7 Selection sort

Example 2.12 [*Bubble Sort*] Bubble sort is another simple way to sort elements. This sort employs a ''bubbling strategy'' to get the largest element to the right. In a bubbling pass, pairs of adjacent elements are compared. The elements are swapped in case the one on the left is greater than the one on the right. Suppose we have four integers in the order [5, 3, 7, 1]. The 5 and the 3 are compared and swapped to get the sequence [3, 5, 7, 1]. Next the 5 and 7 are compared, and no swap takes place. Then 7 and 1 are compared and swapped to get the sequence [3, 5, 1, 7]. At the end of one bubbling pass, we are assured that the largest element is in the right-most position. The function Bubble (Program 2.8) performs a bubbling pass. The number of comparisons between pairs of elements of a is n-1.

```
template<class T>
void Bubble(T a[], int n)
{// Bubble largest element in a[0:n-1] to right.
   for (int i = 0; i < n - 1; i++)
      if (a[i] > a[i+1]) Swap(a[i], a[i + 1]);
}
```

Program 2.8 A bubbling pass

Since function Bubble causes the largest element to move to the right-most position, it can be used in place of function Max in SelectionSort (Program 2.7) to obtain a new sorting function (Program 2.9). The number of element comparisons is $(n-1)n/2$, as it is for SelectionSort. ■

```
template<class T>
void BubbleSort(T a[], int n)
{// Sort a[0:n - 1] using bubble sort.
   for (int i = n; i > 1; i--)
      Bubble(a, i);
}
```

Program 2.9 Bubble sort

Best, Worst, and Average Operation Counts

In the examples so far, the operation counts were nice functions of fairly simple instance characteristics like the number of inputs and/or outputs. Some of our examples would have been more complicated if we had chosen to count some other operations. For example, the number of swaps performed by Bubble (Program 2.8) depends not only on the instance characteristic n but also on the particular values of the as. The number of swaps varies from a low of zero to a high of $n - 1$. Since the operation count isn't always uniquely determined by the chosen instance characteristics, we ask for the best, worst, and average counts. These are defined below.

Let P be a program. Suppose we wish to determine an operration count $o_P(n_1, n_2, \cdots, n_k)$ as a function of the characteristics $n_1, n_2, \cdots, n_k$. For any instance I, let $operation_P(I)$ be the operation count for instance I. Let $S(n_1, n_2, \cdots, n_k)$ be the set $\{I \mid I \text{ has the characteristics } n_1, n_2, \cdots, n_k\}$. The *best* operation count of P is

$$o_P^{BC}(n_1, n_2, \cdots, n_k) = \min\{operation_P(I) \mid I \in S(n_1, n_2, \cdots, n_k)\}$$

The *worst* operation count of P is

$$o_P^{WC}(n_1, n_2, \cdots, n_k) = \max\{operation_P(I) \mid I \in S(n_1, n_2, \cdots, n_k)\}$$

The *average* or *expected* operation count of P is

$$o_P^{AVG}(n_1, n_2, \cdots, n_k) = \frac{1}{\mid S(n_1, n_2, \cdots, n_k) \mid} \sum_{I \in S(n_1, \cdots, n_k)} operation_P(I)$$

The formulation for o_P^{AVG} assumes that all $I \in S$ are equally likely instances. Otherwise, the equation needs to be modified to

$$o_P^{AVG}(n_1, n_2, \cdots, n_k) = \sum_{I \in S(n_1, \cdots, n_k)} p(I) operation_P(I)$$

where $p(I)$ is the normalized frequency (or probability) (frequency/ $\mid S(n_1, n_2, \cdots, n_k) \mid$) with which instance I will be solved.

The average operation count is often quite difficult to determine. As a result, in several of the following examples, we limit our analysis to determining the best and worst counts.

Example 2.13 [*Sequential Search*] We are interested in determining the number of comparisons between x and the elements of a during an execution of the sequential search code of Program 2.1. A natural instance characteristic to use is n. Unfortunately, the number of comparisons isn't uniquely determined by n. For example, if n = 100 and x = a[0], then only one comparison is made. However, if x isn't equal to any of the as, then 100 comparisons are made.

A search is **successful** when x is one of the as. All other searches are **unsuccessful**. Whenever we have an unsuccessful search, the number of comparisons is n. For successful searches the best comparison count is one and the worst is n. For the average count, assume that all array elements are distinct and that each is searched for with equal frequency. The average count for a successful search is

$$\frac{1}{n}\sum_{i=1}^{n} i = (n+1)/2.$$

(When equations involving program variables are displayed separate from text or in tables, we shall use the math font rather than the code font.) ∎

Example 2.14 [*Insertion into a Sorted Array*] Program 2.10 inserts an element into an ordered array a[0:n-1]. The elements of a are in nondecreasing order before and after the insertion. For example, if we insert 4 into the array a[0:5] = [1,2,6,8,9,11], the result is a[0:6] = [1,2,4,6,8,9,11]. The insertion is done by beginning at the right end and successively moving array elements one position right until we find the location for the new element. In our example we moved 11, 9, 8, and 6 and inserted 4 into the now-vacant spot a[2].

```
template<class T>
void Insert(T a[], int& n, const T& x)
{// Insert x into the sorted array a[0:n-1].
 // Assume a is of size > n.
   int i;
   for (i = n-1; i >= 0 && x < a[i]; i--)
      a[i+1] = a[i];
   a[i+1] = x;
   n++; // one element added to a
}
```

Program 2.10 Inserting into a sorted array

We wish to determine the number of comparisons made between x and the elements of a. The natural instance characteristic to use is the number n of elements initially in a. The best or minimum number of comparisons is one, which happens when the new element x is to be inserted at the right end. The maximum number of comparisons is n, which happens when x is to be inserted at the left end. For the average assume that x has an equal chance of being inserted into any of the possible n+1 positions. If x is eventually inserted into position i+1 of a, i ≥ 0, then the number of comparisons is n−i. If x is inserted into a[0], the number of comparisons is n. So the average count is

$$\frac{1}{n+1}\left(\sum_{i=0}^{n-1}(n-i) + n\right) = \frac{1}{n+1}\left(\sum_{j=1}^{n} j + n\right)$$
$$= \frac{1}{n+1}(n(n+1)/2 + n)$$
$$= n/2 + n/(n+1) \quad \blacksquare$$

Example 2.15 [*Rank Sort Revisited*] Suppose the elements of an array have been ranked using function Rank (Program 2.5, Example 2.9). We can perform an in-place rearrangement of elements into sorted order by examining the array positions one at a time beginning with position 0. If we are currently examining position i and r[i] = i, then we may advance to the next position. If r[i] ≠ i, then we swap the elements in positions i and r[i]. This swap moves the element previously in position i into its correct sorted position. The swap operation is repeated at position i until the element that belongs in position i in the sorted order is swapped into position i. Then we advance i to the next position. Program 2.11 gives the in-place rearrangement function Rearrange.

```
template<class T>
void Rearrange(T a[], int n, int r[])
{// In-place rearrangement into sorted order.
   for (int i = 0; i < n; i++)
      // get proper element to a[i]
      while (r[i] != i) {
         int t = r[i];
         Swap(a[i], a[t]);
         Swap(r[i], r[t]);
         }
}
```

Program 2.11 In-place rearrangement of elements

The number of swaps performed varies from a low of zero (when the elements are initially in sorted order) to a high of 2(n-1). Notice that each swap involving the as moves at least one element into its sorted position (i.e., element a[i]). So after n-1 swaps, all n elements must be in sorted order. Exercise 12 establishes that this many element swaps may be needed on certain inputs. Hence the number of swaps is zero in the best case and 2(n-1) in the worst case (includes rank swaps). When this rearrangement function is used in place of the one in Program 2.6, the worst-case execution time increases because we need more element moves (each swap requires three moves). However, the space requirements are reduced. ∎

 Example 2.16 [*Selection Sort Revisited*] A shortcoming of the selection sort code of Program 2.7 is that it continues to work even after the elements have been sorted. For example, the for loop iterates n-1 times, even though the array may be sorted after the second iteration. To eliminate the unnecessary iterations, during the scan for the largest element, we can check to see if the array is already sorted. Program 2.12 gives the resulting selection sort function. Here we have incorporated the loop to find the largest element directly into function SelectionSort, rather than write it as a separate function.

```
template<class T>
void SelectionSort(T a[], int n)
{// Early-terminating version of selection sort.
   bool sorted = false;
   for (int size = n; !sorted && (size > 1); size--) {
      int pos = 0;
      sorted = true;
      // find largest
      for (int i = 1; i < size; i++)
         if (a[pos] <= a[i]) pos = i;
         else sorted = false; // out of order
      Swap(a[pos], a[size - 1]);
      }
}
```

Program 2.12 Early-terminating version of selection sort

The best case for the early-terminating version of selection sort arises when the array a is sorted to begin with. Now the outer for loop iterates just once, and the number of comparisons between elements of a is n-1. In the worst case the outer for loop is iterated until size = 1 and the number of comparisons is (n-1)n/2. The best- and worst-case number of swaps remains the same as for Program 2.7. Notice that in the worst case we expect the early-terminating version to be slightly slower because of the additional work to maintain the variable done. ∎

Example 2.17 [*Bubble Sort Revisited*] As in the case of selection sort, we can devise an early-terminating version of bubble sort. If a bubbling pass results in no swaps, then the array is in sorted order and no further bubbling passes are necessary. Program 2.13 gives the early-terminating version of bubble sort. The worst-case number of comparisons is unchanged from the original version (Program 2.9). The best-case number of comparisons is n-1. ∎

```cpp
template<class T>
bool Bubble(T a[], int n)
{// Bubble largest element in a[0:n-1] to right.
   bool swapped = false; // no swaps so far
   for (int i = 0; i < n - 1; i++)
      if (a[i] > a[i+1]) {
         Swap(a[i], a[i + 1]);
         swapped = true; // swap was done
         }
   return swapped;
}


template<class T>
void BubbleSort(T a[], int n)
{// Early-terminating version of bubble sort.
   for (int i = n; i > 1 && Bubble(a, i); i--);
}
```

Program 2.13 Early-terminating bubble sort

Example 2.18 [*Insertion Sort*] Program 2.10 can be used as the basis of a function to sort n elements. Since an array with one element is a sorted array, we start with an array that contains just the first of the n elements to be sorted. By inserting the second element into this one element array, we get a sorted array of size 2. The insertion of the third element yields a sorted array of size 3. Continuing in this way, we obtain a sorted array of size n. Function Insertion-Sort (Program 2.14) implements this strategy. We have rewritten function Insert for this application, as the original version (Program 2.10) performs some unnecessary operations. Actually, we could have embedded the code of Insert directly into the sort function to get the insertion sort version of Program 2.15. Equivalently, we could make Insert an inline function. Note that replacing the body of the for loop of InsertionSort (Program 2.14)

with the code `Insert(a,i,a[i])` doesn't work, as the formal parameter x
of `Insert` is a reference parameter.

```
template<class T>
void Insert(T a[], int n, const T& x)
{// Insert x into the sorted array a[0:n-1].
   int i;
   for (i = n-1; i >= 0 && x < a[i]; i--)
      a[i+1] = a[i];
   a[i+1] = x;
}

template<class T>
void InsertionSort(T a[], int n)
{//  Sort a[0:n-1].
for (int i = 1; i < n; i++) {
   T t = a[i];
   Insert(a, i, t);
   }
}
```

Program 2.14 Insertion sort

```
template<class T>
void InsertionSort(T a[], int n)
{
   for (int i = 1; i < n; i++) {
      // insert a[i] into a[0:i-1]
      T t = a[i];
      int j;
      for (j = i-1; j >= 0 && t < a[j]; j--)
         a[j+1] = a[j];
      a[j+1] = t;
      }
}
```

Program 2.15 Another version of insertion sort

Both versions perform the same number of comparisons. In the best case
the number of comparisons is `n-1` in the worst case it is `(n-1)n/2`. ∎

2.3.3   Step Counts

As noted in some of the examples on operation counts, the operation-count method of estimating time complexity omits accounting for the time spent on all but the chosen operations. In the **step-count** method, we attempt to account for the time spent in all parts of the program/function. As was the case for operation counts, the step count is a function of the instance characteristics. Although any specific instance may have several characteristics (e.g., the number of inputs, the number of outputs, the magnitudes of the inputs and outputs), the number of steps is computed as a function of some subset of these. Usually we choose the characteristics that are of interest to us. For example, we might wish to know how the computing (or run) time (i.e., time complexity) increases as the number of inputs increases. In this case the number of steps will be computed as a function of the number of inputs alone. For a different program we might want to determine how the computing time increases as the magnitude of one of the inputs increases. In this case the number of steps will be computed as a function of the magnitude of this input alone. Thus before the step count of a program can be determined, we need to know exactly which characteristics of the problem instance are to be used. These characteristics define not only the variables in the expression for the step count but also how much computing can be counted as a single step.

After the relevant instance characteristics have been selected, we can define a step. A **step** is any computation unit that is independent of the selected characteristics. Thus 10 additions can be one step; 100 multiplications can also be one step; but n additions, where n is an instance characteristic, cannot. Nor can $m/2$ additions or $p+q$ subtractions, where m, p, and q are instance characteristics, be counted as one step.

Definition A **program step** is loosely defined to be a syntactically or semantically meaningful segment of a program for which the execution time is independent of the instance characteristics. ∎

The amount of computing represented by one program step may be different from that represented by another. For example, the entire statement

```
return a+b+b*c+(a+b-c)/(a+b)+4;
```

can be regarded as a single step if its execution time is independent of the instance characteristics we are using. We may also count a statement such as

```
x = y;
```

as a single step.

We can determine the number of steps that a program or function takes to complete its task by creating a global variable `count` with initial value zero. Next we introduce into the program statements to increment `count` by the appropriate amount. Therefore each time a statement in the original program or function is executed, `count` is incremented by the step count of that statement. The value of `count` when the program or function terminates is the number of steps taken.

Example 2.19 When statements to increment `count` are introduced into Program 1.8, the result is Program 2.16. The change in the value of `count` by the time this program terminates is the number of steps executed by Program 1.8.

```
template<class T>
T Sum(T a[], int n)
{// Return sum of numbers a[0:n - 1].
   T tsum = 0;
   count++; // for tsum = 0
   for (int i = 0; i < n; i++) {
      count++; // for the for statement
      tsum += a[i];
      count++; // for assignment
   }
   count++; // for last execution of for statement
   count++; // for return
   return tsum;
}
```

Program 2.16 Counting steps in Program 1.8

Program 2.17, which is a simplified version of Program 2.16, determines only the change in the value of `count`. We see that for every initial value of `count`, both Programs 2.16 and 2.17 compute the same final value for `count`. In the `for` loop of Program 2.17, the value of `count` increases by a total of 2n. If `count` is zero to start with, then it will be 2n+3 on termination. Therefore each invocation of `Sum` (Program 1.8) executes a total of 2n+3 steps. ∎

Example 2.20 When we introduce statements to increment `count` into Program 1.9, we obtain Program 2.18.

Let $t_{Rsum}(n)$ be the increase in the value of `count` when Program 2.18 terminates. We see that $t_{Rsum}(0) = 2$. When n > 0, count increases by two plus whatever increase results from the invocation of `Rsum` from within the then clause. From the definition of t_{Rsum}, it follows that this additional increase

```
template<class T>
T Sum(T a[], int n)
{// Return sum of numbers a[0:n - 1].
   for (int i = 0; i < n; i++)
      count += 2;
   count += 3;
   return 0;
}
```

Program 2.17 Simplified version of Program 2.16

```
template<class T>
T Rsum(T a[], int n)
{// Return sum of numbers a[0:n - 1].
   count++; // for if conditional
   if (n > 0) {count++; // for return and RSum invoc.
             return Rsum(a, n-1) + a[n-1];}
   count++; // for return
   return 0;
}
```

Program 2.18 Counting steps in Program 1.9

is t_{Rsum} (n-1). So if the value of count is zero initially, its value at the time of termination is $2 + t_{Rsum}$ (n-1), n>0.

When analyzing a recursive program for its step count, we often obtain a recursive formula for the step count (such as t_{Rsum} (n) $= 2 + t_{Rsum}$ (n-1), n > 0 and $t_{Rsum}(0) = 2$). This recursive formula is referred to as a **recurrence equation** (or simply as a **recurrence**). We can solve this recurrence by repeatedly substituting for t_{Rsum} as shown:

$$
\begin{aligned}
t_{Rsum}(n) &= 2 + t_{Rsum}(n-1) \\
&= 2 + 2 + t_{Rsum}(n-2) \\
&= 4 + t_{Rsum}(n-2) \\
&\quad . \\
&\quad . \\
&\quad . \\
&= 2n + t_{Rsum}(0) \\
&= 2(n+1), n \geq 0
\end{aligned}
$$

So the step count for function Rsum (Program 1.9) is 2 (n+1). ∎

Comparing the step counts of Programs 1.8 and 1.9, we see that the count for Program 1.9 is less than that for Program 1.8. However, we cannot conclude that Program 1.8 is slower than Program 1.9, because a step doesn't correspond to a definite time unit. A step of Rsum may take more time than a step of Sum, so Rsum might well be (and we expect it to be) slower than Sum.

The step count is useful in that it tells us how the run time for a program changes with changes in the instance characteristics. From the step count for Sum, we see that if n is doubled, the run time will also double (approximately); if n increases by a factor of 10, we expect the run time to increase by a factor of 10; and so on. So we expect the run time to grow *linearly* in n. We say that Sum is a linear program (the time complexity is linear in the instance characteristic n).

Example 2.21 [*Matrix Addition*] Consider Program 2.19, which adds two matrices that are stored as the two-dimensional arrays a[0:rows-1][0:cols-1] and b[0:rows-1][0:cols-1].

```
template<class T>
void Add(T **a, T **b, T **c, int rows, int cols)
{// Add matrices a and b to obtain matrix c.
   for (int i = 0;  i < rows;  i++)
      for (int j = 0;   j < cols; j++)
         c[i][j]  = a[i][j]  + b[i][j];
}
```

Program 2.19 Matrix addition

Introducing the count incrementing statements leads to Program 2.20. Program 2.21, which is a simplified version of Program 2.20, computes the same value for count. Examining Program 2.21, we see that if count is zero to begin with, it will be 2rows*cols+2rows+1 when Program 2.21 terminates.

From this analysis we see that if rows > cols, then it is better to interchange the two for statements in Program 2.19. If this is done, the step count will become 2rows*cols+2cols+1. Note that in this example the instance characteristics are given by rows and cols. ■

Rather than introduce statements to increment count, we can build a table in which we list the total number of steps that each statement contributes to count. We can arrive at this figure by first determining the number of steps per execution of the statement and the total number of times (i.e., frequency) each statement is executed. Combining these two quantities gives us the total contribution of each statement. We can then add the contributions of all statements to obtain the step count for the entire program.

```
template<class T>
void Add(T **a, T **b, T **c, int rows, int cols)
{// Add matrices a and b to obtain matrix c.
   for (int i = 0; i < rows; i++) {
      count++; // preceding for loop
      for (int j = 0;  j < cols; j++) {
         count++; // preceding for loop
         c[i][j] = a[i][j] + b[i][j];
         count++; // assignment
         }
      count++; // last time of j for loop
      }
   count++; // last time of i for loop
}
```

Program 2.20 Counting steps in Program 2.19

```
template<class T>
void Add(T **a, T **b, T ** c, int rows, int cols)
{// Add matrices a and b to obtain matrix c.
   for (int i = 0; i < rows; i++) {
      for (int j = 0;  j < cols; j++) {
         c[i][j] = a[i][j] + b[i][j];
         count += 2;
         }
      count += 2;
      }
   count++;
}
```

Program 2.21 Simplified version of Program 2.20

An important difference between the step count of a statement and its steps per execution (s/e) is that the step count does not necessarily reflect the complexity of the statement. For example, the statement

```
x = Sum(a,m);
```

has a step count of one, while the total change in count resulting from the execution of this statement is actually one plus the change resulting from the invocation of Sum (i.e., $2m+3$). The steps per execution of the above statement is

$1+2m+3 = 2m+4$. *The s/e of a statement is the amount by which* `count` changes as a result of the execution of that statement.

Figure 2.4 lists the number of steps per execution and the frequency of each of the statements in function `Sum` (Program 1.8). The total number of steps required by the program is $2n+3$. Note that the frequency of the `for` statement is $n+1$ and not n because `i` has to be incremented to `n` before the `for` loop can terminate.

Statement	s/e	Frequency	Total steps
T Sum(T a[], int n)	0	0	0
{	0	0	0
T tsum = 0;	1	1	1
for (int i = 0; i < n; i++)	1	$n+1$	$n+1$
tsum += a[i];	1	n	n
return tsum;	1	1	1
}	0	0	0
Total			$2n+3$

Figure 2.4 Step table for Program 1.8

Figure 2.5 uses the s/e or table method to obtain the step count for `Rsum` (Program 1.9), and Figure 2.6 does the same for `Add` (Program 2.19).

Statement	s/e	Frequency	Total steps
T Rsum(T a[], int n)	0	0	0
{	0	0	0
if (n > 0)	1	$n+1$	$n+1$
return Rsum(a,n−1) + a[n−1];	1	n	n
return 0;	1	1	1
}	0	0	0
Total			$2n+2$

Figure 2.5 Step table for Program 1.9

Program 2.22 transposes a `rows × rows` matrix `a[0:rows-1][0:rows-1]`. Recall that `b` is the transpose of `a` iff (if and only if) `b[i][j] = a[j][i]` for all `i` and `j`.

Statement	s/e	Frequency	Total steps
void Add(T **a · · ·)	0	0	0
{	0	0	0
for (int i=0; i<rows; i++)	1	$rows + 1$	$rows + 1$
for (int j = 0; j < cols; j++)	1	$rows \cdot (cols + 1)$	$rows \cdot cols + rows$
c[i][j] = a[i][j] + b[i][j];	1	$rows \cdot cols$	$rows \cdot cols$
}	0	0	0
Total			$2rows \cdot cols + 2rows + 1$

Figure 2.6 Step table for Program 2.19

```
template<class T>
void Transpose(T **a, int rows)
{// In-place transpose of matrix a[0:rows-1][0:rows-1].
   for (int i = 0; i < rows; i++)
      for (int j = i+1;  j < rows; j++)
         Swap(a[i][j], a[j][i]);
}
```

Program 2.22 Matrix transpose

Figure 2.7 gives the step-count table. Let us derive the frequency of the second `for` statement. For each value of `i`, this statement is executed `rows-i` times. So its frequency is

$$\sum_{i=0}^{rows-1} (rows - i) = \sum_{1}^{rows} i = rows\,(rows + 1)/2$$

The frequency for the `Swap` statement is

$$\sum_{i=0}^{rows-1} (rows - i - 1) = \sum_{i=0}^{rows-1} i = rows\,(rows - 1)/2$$

In some cases the number of steps per execution of a statement varies from one execution to the next, for example, for the assignment statement of function `Inef` (Program 2.23). Function `Inef` is a very inefficient way to compute the prefix sums

$$\sum_{i=0}^{j} a[i] \text{ for } j = 0, 1, \cdots, n - 1$$

Statement	s/e	Frequency	Total steps
void Transpose(T **a, int rows)	0	0	0
{	0	0	0
for (int i = 0; i < rows; i++)	1	$rows + 1$	$rows + 1$
for (int j = i+1; j < rows; j++)	1	$rows(rows + 1)/2$	$rows(rows + 1)/2$
Swap(a[i][j], a[j][i]);	1	$rows(rows - 1)/2$	$rows(rows - 1)/2$
}	0	0	0
Total			$rows^2 + rows + 1$

Figure 2.7 Step table for Program 2.22

```
template <class T>
void Inef(T a[], T b[], int n)
{// Compute prefix sums.
   for (int j = 0; j < n; j++)
      b[j] = Sum(a, j + 1);
}
```

Program 2.23 Inefficient prefix sums

The step count for `Sum(a,n)` has already been determined to be `2n+3`. The number of steps per execution of the assignment statement of function `Inef` is `2j+6`. We have added one to the step count of function `Sum` to account for the cost of invoking the function and of assigning the function value to `b[j]`. The frequency of the assignment statement of function `Inef` is `n`. But the total number of steps resulting from this statement is not `(2j+6)n`. Instead, it is

$$\sum_{j=0}^{n-1} (2j+6) = n(n+5)$$

Figure 2.8 gives the complete analysis for this function.

The notions of best, worst, and average operation counts are easily extended to the case of step counts. The following examples illustrate these notions.

Statement	s/e	Frequency	Total steps
void Inef(T a[], T b[], int n)	0	0	0
{	0	0	0
for (int j = 0; j < n; j++)	1	$n + 1$	$n + 1$
b[j] = Sum(a, j + 1);	$2j + 6$	n	$n(n + 5)$
}	0	0	0
Total			$n^2 + 6n + 1$

Figure 2.8 Step table for Program 2.23

Example 2.22 [*Sequential Search*] Figures 2.9 and 2.10 show the best- and worst-case step-count analyses for function `SequentialSearch` (Program 2.1).

Statement	s/e	Frequency	Total steps
int SequentialSearch(T a[], T& x, int n)	0	0	0
{	0	0	0
int i;	1	1	1
for (int i = 0; i < n && a[i] != x; i++)	1	1	1
if (i == n) return -1;	1	1	1
return i;	1	1	1
}	0	0	0
Total			4

Figure 2.9 Best-case step count for Program 2.1

For the average step-count analysis for a successful search, we assume that the n values in a are distinct and that in a successful search, x has an equal probability of being any one of these values. Under these assumptions, the average step count for a successful search is the sum of the step counts for the n possible successful searches divided by n. To obtain this average, we first obtain the step count for the case x = a[j] where j is in the range [0, n−1] (see Figure 2.11).

Now we obtain the average step count for successful searches:

$$t^{AVG}_{SequentialSearch}(n) = \frac{1}{n}\sum_{j=0}^{n-1}(j + 4) = (n + 7)/2$$

Statement	s/e	Frequency	Total steps
int SequentialSearch(T a[], T& x, int n)	0	0	0
{	0	0	0
int i;	1	1	1
for (i = 0; i < n && a[i] != x; i++)	1	$n+1$	$n+1$
if (i == n) return -1;	1	1	1
return i;	1	0	0
}	0	0	0
Total			$n+3$

Figure 2.10 Worst-case step count for Program 2.1

Statement	s/e	Frequency	Total steps
int SequentialSearch(T a[], T& x, int n)	0	0	0
{	0	0	0
int i;	1	1	1
for (i = 0; i < n && a[i] != x; i++)	1	$j+1$	$j+1$
if (i == n) return -1;	1	1	1
return i;	1	1	1
}	0	0	0
Total			$j+4$

Figure 2.11 Step count for Program 2.1 when `x = a[j]`

This value is a little more than half the step count for an unsuccessful search.

Now suppose that successful searches occur only 80 percent of the time and that each `a[i]` still has the same probability of being searched for. The average step count for `SequentialSearch` is

.8 * (average count for successful searches) + .2 * (count for an unsuccessful search)
= $.8(n+7)/2 + .2(n+3)$
= $.6n + 3.4$ ∎

Example 2.23 [*Insertion into a Sorted Array*] The best- and worst-case step counts for function `Insert` are obtained in Figures 2.12 and 2.13, respectively.

Statement	s/e	Frequency	Total steps
void Insert(T a[], int& n, const T& x)	0	0	0
{	0	0	0
for (int i = n-1; i >= 0 && x < a[i]; i--)	1	1	1
a[i+1] = a[i];	0	0	0
a[i+1] = x;	1	1	1
n++; // one element added to a	1	1	1
}	0	0	0
Total			3

Figure 2.12 Best-case step count for Program 2.10

Statement	s/e	Frequency	Total steps
void Insert(T a[], int& n, const T& x)	0	0	0
{	0	0	0
for (int i = n-1; i >= 0 && x < a[i]; i--)	1	$n + 1$	$n + 1$
a[i+1] = a[i];	1	n	n
a[i+1] = x;	1	1	1
n++; // one element added to a	1	1	1
}	0	0	0
Total			$2n + 3$

Figure 2.13 Worst-case step count for Program 2.10

For the average step count, assume that `x` has an equal chance of being inserted into any of the possible `n+1` positions. If `x` is eventually inserted into position j, $j \geq 0$, then the step count is `2n-2j+3`. So the average count is

$$\frac{1}{n+1}(\sum_{j=0}^{n}(2n - 2j + 3)) = \frac{1}{n+1}[2\sum_{k=0}^{n}k + 3(n + 1)] = n + 3 \quad \blacksquare$$

EXERCISES

8. List additional factors that may influence the time complexity of a program.

9. How many additions are done in the `for` loop of function `Sum` (Program 1.8)?

10. How many multiplications are performed by the function `Factorial` (Program 1.7)?

11. Modify Program 2.6, replacing the code following the first `for` loop by code to free the space occupied by `a` and updating `a` to `u`. You will also need to change the parameter `T a[]` to `T* &a`. For the new code to work, the actual parameter corresponding to `a` must be a dynamically allocated array. Test your new code.

12. Create an input array `a` that causes function `Rearrange` (Program 2.11) to do `n-1` element swaps and `n-1` rank swaps.

13. How many additions are performed between pairs of matrix elements by function `Add` (Program 2.19)?

14. How many `Swap` operations are performed by function `Transpose` (Program 2.22)?

15. Determine the number of multiplications done by function `Mult` (Program 2.24), which multiplies two $n \times n$ matrices.

```
template<class T>
void Mult(T **a, T **b, T **c, int n)
{// Multiply the n x n matrices a and b to get c.
   for (int i = 0; i < n; i++)
      for (int j = 0; j < n; j++) {
         T sum = 0;
         for (int k = 0; k < n; k++)
            sum += a[i][k] * b[k][j];
         c[i][j] = sum;
         }
}
```

Program 2.24 Multiply two $n \times n$ matrices

16. Determine the number of multiplications done by function `Mult` (Program 2.25), which multiplies an $m \times n$ matrix and an $n \times p$ matrix.

```
template<class T>
void Mult(T **a, T **b, T **c, int m, int n, int p)
{// Multiply the m x n matrix a and the n x p matrix b
 // to get c.
   for (int i = 0; i < m; i++)
      for (int j = 0; j < p; j++) {
         T sum = 0;
         for (int k = 0; k < n; k++)
            sum += a[i][k] * b[k][j];
         c[i][j] = sum;
         }
}
```

Program 2.25 Multiply an $m \times n$ and an $n \times p$ matrix

17.   Determine the number of Swap operations performed by function Perm
      (Program 1.10).

18.   Function MinMax (Program 2.26) determines the locations of the
      minimum and maximum elements in an array a[0:n-1]. Let n be the
      instance characteristic. What is the number of comparisons between ele-
      ments of a? Program 2.27 gives an alternative function to determine the
      locations of the minimum and maximum elements. What is the best-case
      and worst-case number of comparisons between elements of a? What can
      you say about the expected relative performance of the two functions?

```
template<class T>
bool MinMax(T a[], int n, int& Min, int& Max)
{// Locate min and max elements in a[0:n-1].
 // Return false if less than one element.
   if (n < 1) return false;
   Min = Max = 0; // initial guess
   for (int i = 1; i < n; i++) {
      if (a[Min] > a[i]) Min = i;
      if (a[Max] < a[i]) Max = i;
      }
   return true;
}
```

Program 2.26 Finding the minimum and maximum

```
template<class T>
bool MinMax(T a[], int n, int& Min, int& Max)
{// Locate min and max elements in a[0:n-1].
 // Return false if less than one element.
   if (n < 1) return false;
   Min = Max = 0; // initial guess
   for (int i = 1; i < n; i++)
      if (a[Min] > a[i]) Min = i;
      else if (a[Max] < a[i]) Max = i;
   return true;
}
```

Program 2.27 Another function to find the minimum and maximum

19. How many comparisons between the as and x are made by the recursive function `SequentialSearch` (Program 2.2)?

20. Program 2.28 gives an alternative iterative sequential search function. What is the worst-case number of comparisons between x and the elements of a? Compare this number with the corresponding number for Program 2.1. Which function should run faster? Why?

```
template<class T>
int SequentialSearch(T a[], const T& x, int n)
{// Search the unordered list a[0:n-1] for x.
 // Return position if found; return -1 otherwise.
   a[n] = x; // assume extra position available
   int i;
   for (i = 0; a[i] != x; i++);
   if (i == n) return -1;
   return i;
}
```

Program 2.28 Another sequential search function

21. (a) Introduce statements to increment count at all appropriate points in Program 2.29.

    (b) Simplify the resulting program by eliminating statements. The simplified program should compute the same value for count as computed by the program of (a).

```
void D(int x[], int n)
{
   for (int i = 0; i < n; i += 2)
      x[i] += 2;
   int i = 1;
   while (i <= n/2) {
      x[i] += x[i+1];
      i++;
      }
}
```

Program 2.29 Function for Exercise 21

  (c) What is the exact value of `count` when the program terminates? You may assume that the initial value of `count` is zero.

  (d) Obtain the step count for Program 2.29 using the frequency method. Clearly show the step-count table.

22. Do Exercise 21 for each of the following functions:

  (a) `Max` (Program 1.31).

  (b) `MinMax` (Program 2.26).

  (c) `MinMax` (Program 2.27). Obtain the worst-case step count.

  (d) `Factorial` (Program 1.7).

  (e) `PolyEval` (Program 2.3).

  (f) `Horner` (Program 2.4).

  (g) `Rank` (Program 2.5).

  (h) `Perm` (Program 1.10).

  (i) `SequentialSearch` (Program 2.28). Obtain the worst-case step count.

  (j) `SelectionSort` (Program 2.7). Obtain the best- and worst-case step counts.

  (k) `SelectionSort` (Program 2.12). Obtain the best- and worst-case step counts.

  (l) `InsertionSort` (Program 2.14). Obtain the worst-case step count.

  (m) `InsertionSort` (Program 2.15). Obtain the worst-case step count.

    (n)   `BubbleSort` (Program 2.9). Obtain the worst-case step count.

    (o)   `BubbleSort` (Program 2.13). Obtain the worst-case step count.

    (p)   `Mult` (Program 2.24).

23.   Do Exercise 21 parts (a), (b), and (c) for the following functions:

    (a)   `Transpose` (Program 2.22).

    (b)   `Inef` (Program 2.23).

24.   Obtain the average step counts for the following functions:

    (a)   `SequentialSearch` (Program 2.2).

    (b)   `SequentialSearch` (Program 2.28).

    (c)   `Insert` (Program 2.10).

25.   (a)   Do Exercise 21 for Program 2.25.

    (b)   Under what conditions will it be profitable to interchange the two outermost `for` loops?

26.   Compare the worst-case number of element moves made by functions `SelectionSort` (Program 2.12), `InsertionSort` (Program 2.15), `BubbleSort` (Program 2.13), and rank sort using Program 2.11. What can you say about the expected relative performance of these sort methods when sorting very large records?

27.   Must a program exhibit its worst-case time behavior and worst-case space behavior at the same time (i.e., for the same input)? Prove your answer.

2.4   ASYMPTOTIC NOTATION (O, Ω, Θ, o)

Two important reasons to determine operation and step counts are (1) to compare the time complexities of two programs that compute the same function and (2) to predict the growth in run time as the instance characteristics change. Neither of these counts yield a very accurate measure of time complexity. When using operation counts, we focus on certain "key" operations and ignore all others. Step counts attempt to overcome this deficiency by accounting for all operations. However, the notion of a step is itself inexact. Both the instructions `x = y` and `x = y+z+(x/y)` count as one step. Because of the inexactness of what a step stands for, the exact step count isn't very useful for comparative purposes. An exception to this observation is when the difference in the step counts of two programs is very large as in $3n + 3$ versus $100n + 10$. We might feel quite safe in predicting that the program with step count $3n + 3$ will run in less time than the one with step count $100n + 10$. But in this case it isn't necessary to know that the exact step count is $100n + 10$. Something like "it's about $80n$ or $85n$ or $75n$" is adequate to arrive at the same conclusion.

If we have two programs with a complexity of $c_1n^2 + c_2n$ and c_3n, respectively, then we know that the program with complexity c_3n will be faster than the one with complexity $c_1n^2 + c_2n$ for sufficiently large values of n. For small values of n, either program could be faster (depending on c_1, c_2, and c_3). If $c_1 = 1, c_2 = 2$, and $c_3 = 100$, then $c_1n^2 + c_2n \leq c_3n$ for $n \leq 98$ and $c_1n^2 + c_2n > c_3n$ for $n > 98$. If $c_1 = 1, c_2 = 2$, and $c_3 = 1000$, then $c_1n^2 + c_2n \leq c_3n$ for $n \leq 998$. Therefore, for most situations it is adequate to be able to make a statement such as $c_1n^2 \leq t_P^{WC}(n) \leq c_2n^2$ or $t_Q^{WC}(n,m) = c_1n + c_2m$, where c_1 and c_2 are nonnegative constants.

No matter what the values of c_1, c_2, and c_3, there will be an n beyond which the program with complexity c_3n will be faster than the program with complexity $c_1n^2 + c_2n$. This value of n is the **breakeven point**. If the breakeven point is zero, then the program with complexity c_3n is always faster (or at least as fast) than the program with complexity $c_1n^2 + c_2n$. The exact breakeven point cannot be determined analytically. The programs have to be run on a computer to determine the breakeven point, so there is little advantage in determining the exact values of c_1, c_2, and c_3.

With the previous discussion as motivation, we introduce notation that will enable us to make meaningful (though inexact) statements about the time and space complexities of a program. This notation is called **asymptotic notation**, and it describes the behavior of the time or space complexity for large instance characteristics. In the following discussion the function $f(n)$ denotes the time or space complexity of a program measured as a function of the instance characteristic n. Since the time and space requirements of a program are nonnegative quantities, we assume that the function f has a nonnegative value for all values of n. Further, since n denotes an instance characteristic, we assume that $n \geq 0$. The asymptotic notation we are about to study will permit us to provide upper and/or lower bounds on the value of f for suitably large values of n.

2.4.1 Big Oh Notation (O)

The big oh notation provides an upper bound for the function f.

Definition [*Big oh*] $f(n) = O(g(n))$ (read as "f of n is big oh of g of n") iff positive constants c and n_0 exist such that $f(n) \leq cg(n)$ for all $n, n \geq n_0$. ∎

The definition states that the function f is at most c times the function g except possibly when n is smaller than n_0. Here c is some positive constant. Thus g is an upper bound (except for a constant factor c) on the value of f for all suitably large n (i.e., $n \geq n_0$). When providing an upper-bound function g for f, we will normally use only simple functional forms. These typically contain a single term in n with a multiplicative constant of one. Figure 2.14 gives some of the more commonly used g functions and their names. We do not associate a logarithmic base with the functions in Figure 2.14 that include $\log n$ because for any constants a and b greater than one, $\log_a n = \log_b n / \log_b a$. So $\log_a n$ and $\log_b n$ are related by the multiplicative factor $1/\log_b a$, which is a constant.

Function	Name
1	constant
$\log n$	logarithmic
n	linear
$n \log n$	$n \log n$
n^2	quadratic
n^3	cubic
2^n	exponential
$n!$	factorial

Figure 2.14 Common asymptotic functions

Example 2.24 [*Linear Function*] Consider $f(n) = 3n + 2$. When n is at least 2, $3n + 2 \leq 3n + n \leq 4n$. So $f(n) = O(n)$. Thus $f(n)$ is bounded from above by a linear function. We can arrive at the same conclusion in other ways. For example, $3n + 2 \leq 10n$ for $n > 0$. Therefore we can also satisfy the definition of big oh by selecting $c = 10$ and n_0 equal to any integer greater than zero. Alternatively, $3n + 2 \leq 3n + 2n = 5n$ for $n \geq 1$, so we can satisfy the definition of big oh by setting $c = 5$ and $n_0 = 1$. The values of c and n_0 used to satisfy the definition of big oh are not important because we will be saying only that $f(n)$ is big oh of $g(n)$ and in this statement neither c nor n_0 play a role.

For $f(n) = 3n + 3$, we note that for $n \geq 3$, $3n + 3 \leq 3n + n \leq 4n$. So $f(n) = O(n)$. Similarly, $f(n) = 100n + 6 \leq 100n + n = 101n$ for $n \geq n_0 = 6$. Therefore, $100n + 6 = O(n)$. As expected, $3n + 2$, $3n + 3$, and $100n + 6$ are all big oh of n; that is, they are bounded from above by a linear function (for suitably large n). ∎

Example 2.25 [*Quadratic Function*] Suppose that $f(n) = 10n^2 + 4n + 2$. We see that for $n \geq 2$, $f(n) \leq 10n^2 + 5n$. Now we note that for $n \geq 5$, $5n \leq n^2$. Hence for $n \geq n_0 = 5$, $f(n) \leq 10n^2 + n^2 = 11n^2$. Therefore, $f(n) = O(n^2)$.

As another example of a quadratic complexity, consider $f(n) = 1000n^2 + 100n - 6$. We easily see that $f(n) \leq 1000n^2 + 100n$ for all n. Furthermore, $100n \leq n^2$ for $n \geq 100$. Hence $f(n) < 1001n^2$ for $n \geq n_0 = 100$. So $f(n) = O(n^2)$. ∎

Example 2.26 [*Exponential Function*] As an example of exponential complexity, consider $f(n) = 6 * 2^n + n^2$. Observe that for $n \geq 4$, $n^2 \leq 2^n$. So $f(n) \leq 6 * 2^n + 2^n = 7 * 2^n$ for $n \geq 4$. Therefore, $6 * 2^n + n^2 = O(2^n)$. ∎

Example 2.27 [*Constant Function*] When $f(n)$ is a constant, as in $f(n) = 9$ or $f(n) = 2033$, we write $f(n) = O(1)$. The correctness of this is easily established. For example, $f(n) = 9 \leq 9 * 1$; setting $c = 9$ and $n_0 = 0$ satisfies the definition of big oh. Similarly, $f(n) = 2033 \leq 2033 * 1$, and the definition of big oh is satisfied by setting $c = 2033$ and $n_0 = 0$. ∎

Example 2.28 [*Loose Bounds*] $3n + 3 = O(n^2)$ as $3n + 3 \leq 3n^2$ for $n \geq 2$. Although n^2 is an upper bound for $3n + 3$, it is not a tight upper bound; we can find a smaller function (in this case linear) that also satisfies the big oh relation.
$10n^2 + 4n + 2 = O(n^4)$ as $10n^2 + 4n + 2 \leq 10n^4$ for $n \geq 2$. Once again, n^4 does not provide a tight upper bound for $100n^2 + 4n + 2$.
Similarly, $6n\,2^n + 20 = O(n^2 2^n)$, but it is not a tight upper bound because we can find a smaller function, namely, $n2^n$, for which the definition of big oh is satisfied. That is, $6n\,2^n + 20 = O(n\,2^n)$. ∎

Note that the strategy in each of the preceding derivations is to replace the low-order terms by higher-order ones until only a single term remains.

Example 2.29 [*Incorrect Bounds*] $3n + 2 \neq O(1)$, as there is no $c > 0$ and n_0 such that $3n + 2 < c$ for all $n, n \geq n_0$. We can use contradiction to prove this condition formally. Suppose that such a c and n_0 exist. Then $n < (c - 2)/3$ for all n, $n \geq n_0$. This is not true for $n > \max\{n_0, (c-2)/3\}$.
To prove $10n^2 + 4n + 2 \neq O(n)$, suppose it is false. That is, $10n^2 + 4n + 2 = O(n)$. There exists a positive c and an n_0 such that $10n^2 + 4n + 2 \leq cn$ for all $n \geq n_0$. Dividing both sides of the relation by n, we get $10n + 4 + 2/n \leq c$ for $n \geq n_0$. This relation cannot be true because the left side increases as n increases, whereas the right side does not change. In particular, we get a contradiction for $n \geq \max\{n_0, (c - 4)/10\}$.
$f(n) = 3n^2 2^n + 4n2^n + 8n^2 \neq O(2^n)$. To prove this inequality, suppose that $f(n) = O(2^n)$. Then a $c > 0$ and an n_0 exist such that $f(n) \leq c*2^n$ for $n \geq n_0$. Dividing both sides by 2^n, we get $3n^2 + 4n + 8n^2/2^n \leq c$ for $n \geq n_0$. Once again, the left side of the relation is an increasing function of n while the right side is constant. So the relation cannot hold for "large" n. ∎

As illustrated in Example 2.28, the statement $f(n) = O(g(n))$ states only that $cg(n)$ is an upper bound on the value of $f(n)$ for all $n, n \geq n_0$. It doesn't say anything about how good or tight this bound is. Notice that $n = O(n^2)$, $n = O(n^{2.5})$, $n = O(n^3)$, and $n = O(2^n)$. For the statement $f(n) = O(g(n))$ to be informative, $g(n)$ should be as small a function of n as possible for which $f(n) = O(g(n))$. So although we often say $3n + 3 = O(n)$, we almost never say $3n + 3 = O(n^2)$, even though the latter statement is correct.
Notice that $f(n) = O(g(n))$ is not the same as $O(g(n)) = f(n)$. In fact, saying that $O(g(n)) = f(n)$ is meaningless. The use of the symbol = is unfortunate, as this symbol commonly denotes the equals relation. We can avoid some of the

confusion that results from the use of this symbol (which is standard terminology) by reading the symbol = as "is" and not as "equals."

Theorem 2.1 obtains a very useful result concerning the order of $f(n)$ (i.e., the $g(n)$ in $f(n) = O(g(n))$) when $f(n)$ is a polynomial in n.

Theorem 2.1 If $f(n) = a_m n^m + \cdots + a_1 n + a_0$ and $a_m > 0$, then $f(n) = O(n^m)$.

Proof $f(n) \le \displaystyle\sum_{i=0}^{m} |a_i| n^i$

$$\le n^m \sum_{0}^{m} |a_i| n^{i-m}$$

$$\le n^m \sum_{0}^{m} |a_i| \text{ for } n \ge 1$$

So $f(n) = O(n^m)$. ∎

Example 2.30 Let us apply Theorem 2.1 to the functions of Examples 2.24, 2.25, and 2.27. For the three linear functions of Example 2.24, $m = 1$, and so these functions are $O(n)$. For the functions of Example 2.25, $m = 2$, and so all are $O(n^2)$. For the constants of Example 2.27, $m = 0$, so both constants are $O(1)$. ∎

We can extend the strategy used in Example 2.29 to show that an upper bound is incorrect to the case when an upper bound is correct, as shown in the following theorem. *It is usually easier to show $f(n) = O(g(n))$ using this theorem than by using the definition of big oh.*

Theorem 2.2 [*Big oh ratio theorem*] Let $f(n)$ and $g(n)$ be such that $\lim_{n \to \infty} f(n)/g(n)$ exists. $f(n) = O(g(n))$ iff $\lim_{n \to \infty} f(n)/g(n) \le c$ for some finite constant c.

Proof If $f(n) = O(g(n))$, then positive c and an n_0 exist such that $f(n)/g(n) \le c$ for all $n \ge n_0$. Hence $\lim_{n \to \infty} f(n)/g(n) \le c$. Next suppose that $\lim_{n \to \infty} f(n)/g(n) \le c$. It follows that an n_0 exists such that $f(n) \le \max\{1, c\} * g(n)$ for all $n \ge n_0$. ∎

Example 2.31 $3n + 2 = O(n)$ as $\lim_{n \to \infty} (3n + 2)/n = 3$. $10n^2 + 4n + 2 = O(n^2)$ as $\lim_{n \to \infty} (10n^2 + 4n + 2)/n^2 = 10$. $6 * 2^n + n^2 = O(2^n)$ as $\lim_{n \to \infty} (6 * 2^n + n^2)/2^n = 6$. $2n^2 - 3 = O(n^4)$ as $\lim_{n \to \infty} (2n^2 - 3)/n^4 = 0$. $3n^2 + 5 \ne O(n)$ as $\lim_{n \to \infty} (3n^2 + 5)/n = \infty$. ∎

2.4.2 Omega Notation (Ω)

The omega notation, which is the lower bound analog of the big oh notation, permits us to bound the value of f from below.

Definition [*Omega*] $f(n) = \Omega(g(n))$ (read as "f of n is omega of g of n") iff positive constants c and n_0 exist such that $f(n) \geq cg(n)$ for all n, $n \geq n_0$. ∎

When we write $f(n) = \Omega(g(n))$, we are saying that f is at least c times the function g except possibly when n is smaller than n_0. Here c is some positive constant. Thus g is a lower bound (except for a constant factor c) on the value of f for all suitably large n (i.e., $n \geq n_0$). As in the case of the big oh notation, we normally use only simple functional forms for g.

Example 2.32 $f(n) = 3n + 2 > 3n$ for all n. So $f(n) = \Omega(n)$. Also, $f(n) = 3n + 3 > 3n$, and so $f(n) = \Omega(n)$. Since $f(n) = 100n + 6 > 100n$, $100n + 6 = \Omega(n)$. So $3n + 2$, $3n + 3$, and $100n + 6$ are all bounded from below by a linear function.

$f(n) = 10n^2 + 4n + 2 > 10n^2$ for $n \geq 0$. So $f(n) = \Omega(n^2)$. Similarly, $1000n^2 + 100n - 6 = \Omega(n^2)$. Furthermore, since $6 * 2^n + n^2 > 6 * 2^n$, $6 * 2^n + n^2 = \Omega(2^n)$.

Observe also that $3n + 3 = \Omega(1)$; $10n^2 + 4n + 2 = \Omega(n)$; $10n^2 + 4n + 2 = \Omega(1)$; $6 * 2^n + n^2 = \Omega(n^{100})$; $6 * 2^n + n^2 = \Omega(n^{50.2})$; $6 * 2^n + n^2 = \Omega(n^2)$; $6 * 2^n + n^2 = \Omega(n)$; and $6 * 2^n + n^2 = \Omega(1)$.

To see that $3n + 2 \neq \Omega(n^2)$, suppose that $3n + 2 = \Omega(n^2)$. Then positive c and n_0 exist such that $3n + 2 \geq cn^2$ for all $n \geq n_0$. So $cn^2/(3n + 2) \leq 1$ for all $n \geq n_0$. This relation cannot be true because its left side increases to infinity as n becomes large. ∎

As in the case of the big oh notation, there are several functions $g(n)$ for which $f(n) = \Omega(g(n))$. $g(n)$ is only a lower bound on $f(n)$. For the statement $f(n) = \Omega(g(n))$ to be informative, $g(n)$ should be as large a function of n as possible for which the statement $f(n) = \Omega(g(n))$ is true. So although we say that $3n + 3 = \Omega(n)$ and that $6 * 2^n + n^2 = \Omega(2^n)$, we almost never say that $3n + 3 = \Omega(1)$ or that $6 * 2^n + n^2 = \Omega(1)$, even though both these statements are correct.

Theorem 2.3 is the analog of Theorem 2.1 for the omega notation.

Theorem 2.3 If $f(n) = a_m n^m + \cdots + a_1 n + a_0$ and $a_m > 0$, then $f(n) = \Omega(n^m)$.

Proof See Exercise 31. ∎

Example 2.33 From Theorem 2.3, it follows that $3n + 2 = \Omega(n)$, $10n^2 + 4n + 2 = \Omega(n^2)$, and $100n^4 + 3500n^2 + 82n + 8 = \Omega(n^4)$. ∎

Theorem 2.4 is the analog of Theorem 2.2 and it is usually easier to show $f(n) = \Omega(g(n))$ using this theorem than by using the definition of omega.

Theorem 2.4 [*Omega ratio theorem*] Let $f(n)$ and $g(n)$ be such that $\lim_{n\to\infty} g(n)/f(n)$ exists. $f(n) = \Omega(g(n))$ iff $\lim_{n\to\infty} g(n)/f(n) \leq c$ for some finite constant c. ■

Proof See Exercise 32. ■

Example 2.34 $3n + 2 = \Omega(n)$ as $\lim_{n\to\infty} n/(3n+2) = 1/3$. $10n^2 + 4n + 2 = \Omega(n^2)$ as $\lim_{n\to\infty} n^2/(10n^2 + 4n + 2) = 0.1$. $6 * 2^n + n^2 = \Omega(2^n)$ as $\lim_{n\to\infty} 2^n/(6 * 2^n + n^2) = 1/6$. $6n^2 + 2 = \Omega(n)$ as $\lim_{n\to\infty} n/(6n^2 + 2) = 0$. $3n^2 + 5 \neq \Omega(n^3)$ as $\lim_{n\to\infty} n^3/(3n^2 + 5) = \infty$. ■

2.4.3   Theta Notation (Θ)

The theta notation is used when the function f can be bounded both from above and below by the same function g.

Definition [*Theta*] $f(n) = \Theta(g(n))$ (read as "f of n is theta of g of n") iff positive constants c_1 and c_2 and an n_0 exist such that $c_1 g(n) \leq f(n) \leq c_2 g(n)$ for all n, $n \geq n_0$. ■

When we write $f(n) = \Theta(g(n))$, we are saying that f lies between c_1 times the function g and c_2 times the function g except possibly when n is smaller than n_0. Here c_1 and c_2 are positive constants. Thus g is both a lower and upper bound (except for a constant factor c) on the value of f for all suitably large n (i.e., $n \geq n_0$). Another way to view the theta notation is that it says $f(n)$ is both $\Omega(g(n))$ and O($g(n)$). As in the case of the big oh and omega notations, we normally use only simple functional forms for g.

Example 2.35 From Examples 2.24, 2.25, 2.26, and 2.32, it follows that $3n + 2 = \Theta(n)$; $3n + 3 = \Theta(n)$; $100n + 6 = \Theta(n)$; $10n^2 + 4n + 2 = \Theta(n^2)$; $1000n^2 + 100n - 6 = \Theta(n^2)$; and $6 * 2^n + n^2 = \Theta(2^n)$.

$10 * \log_2 n + 4 = \Theta(\log_2 n)$ as $\log_2 n < 10\log_2 n + 4 \leq 11\log_2 n$ for $n \geq 16$. As remarked earlier $\log_a n$ is $\log_b n$ times a constant, and we write $\Theta(\log_a n)$ simply as $\Theta(\log n)$.

In Example 2.29 we showed that $3n + 2 \neq$ O(1). So $3n + 2 \neq \Theta(1)$. Similarly, we may show that $3n + 3 \neq \Theta(1)$ and $100n + 6 \neq \Theta(1)$. Since $3n + 3 \neq \Omega(n^2)$, $3n + 3 \neq \Theta(n^2)$. Since $10n^2 + 4n + 2 \neq$ O(n), $10n^2 + 4n + 2 \neq \Theta(n)$. Also, since $10n^2 + 4n + 2 \neq$ O(1), it is not $\Theta(1)$.

Since $6 * 2^n + n^2$ is not $O(n^2)$, it is not $\Theta(n^2)$. Similarly, $6 * 2^n + n^2 \neq \Theta(n^{100})$; and $6 * 2^n + n^2 \neq \Theta(1)$. ■

As mentioned earlier it is common practice to use only g functions with a multiplicative factor of one. We almost never say that $3n + 3 = O(3n)$ or $10 = O(100)$ or $10n^2 + 4n + 2 = \Omega(4 * n^2)$ or $6 * 2^n + n^2 = \Omega(6 * 2^n)$ or $6 * 2^n + n^2 = \Theta(4 * 2^n)$, even though each of these statements is true.

Theorem 2.5 If $f(n) = a_m n^m + \cdots + a_1 n + a_0$ and $a_m > 0$, then $f(n) = \Theta(n^m)$.

Proof See Exercise 31. ■

Example 2.36 From Theorem 2.5, it follows that $3n + 2 = \Theta(n)$, $10n^2 + 4n + 2 = \Theta(n^2)$, and $100n^4 + 3500n^2 + 82n + 8 = \Theta(n^4)$. ■

Theorem 2.6 is the analog of Theorems 2.2 and 2.4.

Theorem 2.6 [***Theta ratio theorem***] Let $f(n)$ and $g(n)$ be such that $\lim_{n \to \infty} f(n)/g(n)$ and $\lim_{n \to \infty} g(n)/f(n)$ exist. $f(n) = \Theta(g(n))$ iff $\lim_{n \to \infty} f(n)/g(n) \leq c$ and $\lim_{n \to \infty} g(n)/f(n) \leq c$ for some finite constant c.

Proof See Exercise 32. ■

Example 2.37 $3n + 2 = \Theta(n)$ as $\lim_{n \to \infty} (3n + 2)/n = 3$ and $\lim_{n \to \infty} n/(3n + 2) = 1/3 < 3$; $10n^2 + 4n + 2 = \Theta(n^2)$ as $\lim_{n \to \infty} (10n^2 + 4n + 2)/n^2 = 10$; and $\lim_{n \to \infty} n^2/(10n^2 + 4n + 2) = 0.1 < 10$. $6 * 2^n + n^2 = \Omega(2^n)$ as $\lim_{n \to \infty} (6 * 2^n + n^2)/2^n = 6$ and $\lim_{n \to \infty} 2^n/(6 * 2^n + n^2) = 1/6 < 6$. $6n^2 + 2 \neq \Theta(n)$ as $\lim_{n \to \infty} (6n^2 + 2)/n = \infty$. ■

2.4.4   Little Oh (o)

Definition [***Little oh***] $f(n) = o(g(n))$ (read as "f of n is little oh of g of n") iff $f(n) = O(g(n))$ and $f(n) \neq \Omega(g(n))$. ■

Example 2.38 [***Little oh***] $3n + 2 = o(n^2)$ as $3n + 2 = O(n^2)$ and $3n + 2 \neq \Omega(n^2)$. However, $3n + 2 \neq o(n)$. Similarly, $10n^2 + 4n + 2 = o(n^3)$, but is not $o(n^2)$. ■

2.4.5   Properties

The following theorem is useful in computations involving asymptotic notation.

Theorem 2.7 These statements are true for every real number x, $x > 0$ and for every real ε, $\varepsilon > 0$:

1. An n_0 exists such that $(\log n)^x < (\log n)^{x+\varepsilon}$ for every n, $n \geq n_0$.
2. An n_0 exists such that $(\log n)^x < n$ for every n, $n \geq n_0$.
3. An n_0 exists such that $n^x < n^{x+\varepsilon}$ for every n, $n \geq n_0$.
4. For every real y, an n_0 exists such that $n^x(\log n)^y < n^{x+\varepsilon}$ for every n, $n \geq n_0$.
5. An n_0 exists such that $n^x < 2^n$ for every n, $n \geq n_0$.

Proof Follows from the definition of the individual functions. ∎

Example   2.39   From   Theorem   2.7,   we   obtain   the   following: $n^3 + n^2 \log n = \Theta(n^3)$; $2^n / n^2 = \Omega(n^k)$ for   every   natural   number k; $n^4 + n^{2.5}\log^{20} n = \Theta(n^4)$; $2^n n^4 \log^3 n + 2^n n^4 / \log n = \Theta(2^n n^4 \log^3 n)$. ∎

Figure 2.15 lists some of the more useful identities involving the big oh, omega, and theta notations. In this table all symbols other than n are positive constants. Figure 2.16 lists some useful inference rules for sums and products.

Figures 2.15 and 2.16 prepare you to use asymptotic notation to describe the time complexity (or step count) of a program.

2.4.6   Complexity Analysis Examples

Let us reexamine some of the time complexity analyses of Section 2.3.3. For procedure Sum (Program 1.8), we had determined that $t_{Sum}(n) = 2n+3$. So $t_{Sum}(n) = \Theta(n)$. $t_{Rsum}(n) = n(m+1)+2 = \Theta(mn)$; $t_{Add}(m,n) = 2mn+2n+1 = \Theta(mn)$; $t_{Transpose}(n) = (n-1)(4n+2)/2 = \Theta(n^2)$.

We have already determined that $t_{SequentialSearch}^{WC}(n) = n+3 = \Theta(n)$. Since $n+3$ is the worst-case complexity, it is an upper bound on the value of $t_{SequentialSearch}(n)$. Hence $t_{SequentialSearch}(n) = O(n)$. This last equality states that positive constants c and n_0 exist such that the computing time of Sequen- tialSearch is bounded by cn for all inputs of size n, $n \geq n_0$. Note that $t_{SequentialSearch}(n)$ is really a multivalued function, as its value is different for different instances of size n. Also, $t_{SequentialSearch}(n) = \Omega(1)$ because the best situation is when x = a[0]. For this case $t_{SequentialSearch}(n) = 4$. $t_{SequentialSearch}^{AVG}(n) = \alpha(n+7)/2+(1-\alpha)(n+3) = \Theta(n)$. ($\alpha$ is the probability that x is one of the as.)

	$f(n)$	Asymptotic
E1	c	$\oplus(1)$
E2	$\displaystyle\sum_{i=0}^{k} c_i n^i$	$\oplus(n^k)$
E3	$\displaystyle\sum_{i=1}^{n} i$	$\oplus(n^2)$
E4	$\displaystyle\sum_{i=1}^{n} i^2$	$\oplus(n^3)$
E5	$\displaystyle\sum_{i=1}^{n} i^k, k>0$	$\oplus(n^{k+1})$
E6	$\displaystyle\sum_{i=0}^{n} r^i, r>1$	$\oplus(r^n)$
E7	$n!$	$\oplus((n/e)^n)$
E8	$\displaystyle\sum_{i=1}^{n} 1/i$	$\oplus(\log n)$

$\oplus$ can be any one of O, Ω, and Θ

Figure 2.15 Asymptotic identities

I1 $\{f(n) = \oplus(g(n))\} \rightarrow \displaystyle\sum_{n=a}^{b} f(n) = \oplus(\sum_{n=a}^{b} g(n))$

I2 $\{f_i(n) = \oplus(g_i(n)), 1 \le i \le k\} \rightarrow \displaystyle\sum_{1}^{k} f_i(n) = \oplus(\max_{1 \le i \le k}\{g_i(n)\})$

I3 $\{f_i(n) = \oplus(g_i(n)), 1 \le i \le k\} \rightarrow \displaystyle\prod_{1}^{k} f_i(n) = \oplus(\prod_{1}^{k} g_i(n))$

I4 $\{f_1(n) = O(g_1(n)), f_2(n) = \Theta(g_2(n))\} \rightarrow f_1(n)+f_2(n) = O(g_1(n)+g_2(n))$

I5 $\{f_1(n) = \Theta(g_1(n)), f_2(n) = \Omega(g_2(n))\} \rightarrow f_1(n)+f_2(n) = \Omega(g_1(n)+g_2(n))$

I6 $\{f_1(n) = O(g(n)), f_2(n) = \Theta(g(n))\} \rightarrow f_1(n)+f_2(n) = \Theta(g(n))$

Figure 2.16 Inference rules for $\oplus \in \{O,\Omega,\Theta\}$

Although the preceding paragraph uses the O, Ω, and Θ notations correctly, it relies on an exact step-count analysis. Actually, we can determine the asymptotic complexity (i.e., the complexity in terms of O, Ω, and Θ) quite easily without determining the exact step count. The procedure is to first determine the asymptotic complexity of each statement (or group of statements) in the program and then add up these complexities. Figures 2.17 to 2.22 determine the asumptotic complexity of several functions without performing an exact step-count analysis.

Statement	s/e	Frequency	Total steps
T Sum(T a[], int n)	0	0	$\Theta(0)$
{	0	0	$\Theta(0)$
T tsum = 0;	1	1	$\Theta(1)$
for (int i = 0; i < n; i++)	1	$n + 1$	$\Theta(n)$
tsum += a[i];	1	n	$\Theta(n)$
return tsum;	1	1	$\Theta(1)$
}	0	0	$\Theta(0)$

$$t_{Sum}(n) = \Theta(\max\{g_i(n)\}) = \Theta(n)$$

Figure 2.17 Asymptotic complexity of Sum (Program 1.8)

Statement	s/e	Frequency	Total steps
T Rsum(T a[], int n)	0	0	$\Theta(0)$
{	0	0	$\Theta(0)$
if (n)	1	$n + 1$	$\Theta(n)$
return Rsum(a,n−1) + a[n−1];	1	n	$\Theta(n)$
return 0;	1	1	$\Theta(1)$
}	0	0	$\Theta(0)$

$$t_{Rsum}(n) = \Theta(n)$$

Figure 2.18 Asymptotic complexity of Rsum (Program 1.9)

At times it is useful to interpret $O(g(n))$, $\Omega(g(n))$, and $\Theta(g(n))$ as being the following sets:

$$O(g(n)) = \{f(n) \,|\, f(n) = O(g(n))\}$$
$$\Omega(g(n)) = \{f(n) \,|\, f(n) = \Omega(g(n))\}$$
$$\Theta(g(n)) = \{f(n) \,|\, f(n) = \Theta(g(n))\}$$

Statement	s/e	Frequency	Total steps
void Add(T **a $\cdots$)	0	0	$\Theta(0)$
{	0	0	$\Theta(0)$
for (int i = 0; i<rows; i++)	1	$\Theta(rows)$	$\Theta(rows)$
for (int j = 0; j < cols; j++)	1	$\Theta(rows \cdot cols)$	$\Theta(rows \cdot cols)$
c[i][j] = a[i][j] + b[i][j];	1	$\Theta(rows \cdot cols)$	$\Theta(rows \cdot cols)$
}	0	0	$\Theta(0)$

$$t_{Add}(rows, cols) = \Theta(rows \cdot cols)$$

Figure 2.19 Asymptotic complexity of Add (Program 2.19)

Statement	s/e	Frequency	Total steps
void Transpose(T **a, int rows)	0	0	$\Theta(0)$
{	0	0	$\Theta(0)$
for (int i = 0; i < rows; i++)	1	$\Theta(rows)$	$\Theta(rows)$
for (int j = i+1; j < rows; j++)	1	$\Theta(rows^2)$	$\Theta(rows^2)$
Swap(a[i][j], a[j][i]);	1	$\Theta(rows^2)$	$\Theta(rows^2)$
}	0	0	$\Theta(0)$

$$t_{Transpose}(rows) = \Theta(rows^2)$$

Figure 2.20 Asymptotic complexity of Transpose (Program 2.22)

Statement	s/e	Frequency	Total steps
void Inef(T a[], T b[], int n)	0	0	$\Theta(0)$
{	0	0	$\Theta(0)$
for (int j = 0; j < n; j++)	1	$\Theta(n)$	$\Theta(n)$
b[j] = Sum(a, j + 1);	$2j + 6$	n	$\Theta(n^2)$
}	0	0	$\Theta(0)$

$$t_{Inef}(n) = \Theta(n^2)$$

Figure 2.21 Asymptotic complexity of Inef (Program 2.23)

Statement	s/e	Frequency	Total steps
int SequentialSearch(T a[], T& x, int n)	0	0	$\Theta(0)$
{	0	0	$\Theta(0)$
int i;	1	1	$\Theta(1)$
for (i = 0; i < n && a[i] != x; i++)	1	$\Omega(1), O(n)$	$\Omega(1), O(n)$
if (i == n) return -1;	1	1	$\Theta(1)$
return i;	1	$\Omega(0), O(1)$	
}	0	0	$\Theta(0)$

$$t_{SequentialSearch}(n) = \Omega(1)$$
$$t_{SequentialSearch}(n) = O(n)$$

Figure 2.22 Asymptotic complexity of `SequentialSearch` (Program 2.1)

Under this interpretation statements such as $O(g_1(n)) = O(g_2(n))$ and $\Theta(g_1(n)) = \Theta(g_2(n))$ are meaningful. When using this interpretation, it is also convenient to read $f(n) = O(g(n))$ as "f of n is in (or is a member of) big oh of g of n" and so on.

While the analyses of Figures 2.17 through 2.22 are actually carried out in terms of step counts, it is correct to interpret $t_P(n) = \Theta(g(n))$, $t_P(n) = O(g(n))$, or $t_P(n) = \Omega(g(n))$ as a statement about the computing time of program P because each step takes only $\Theta(1)$ time to execute.

After you have had some experience using the table method, you will be in a position to arrive at the asymptotic complexity of a program by taking a more global approach. We elaborate on this method in the following examples.

Example 2.40 [*Permutations*] Consider the permutation generation code of Program 1.10. Assume that `m = n-1`. When `k = m`, the time taken is $\Theta(n)$. When `k < m`, the `else` clause is entered. At this time the `for` loop is entered `m-k+1` times. Each iteration of this loop takes $\Theta(t_{Perm}(\texttt{k+1,m}))$ time. So $t_{Perm}(\texttt{k,m}) = \Theta((\texttt{m-k+1})\, t_{Perm}(\texttt{k+1,m}))$ when `k<m`. Using the substitution method, we obtain $t_{Perm}(\texttt{0,m}) = \Theta((\texttt{m+1}) * (\texttt{m+1})!) = \Theta(\texttt{n*n!})$, `n >= 1`. ∎

Example 2.41 [*Binary Search*] Program 2.30 is a function to search a sorted array `a[0:n-1]` for the element `x`. The variables `left` and `right` record the two ends of the array to be searched. Initially we are to search between positions 0 and `n-1`. So `left` and `right` are initialized to these values. We maintain the invariant throughout:

x is one of `a[0:n-1]` *iff* x *is one of* `a[left:right]`

```
template<class T>
int BinarySearch(T a[], const T& x, int n)
{// Search a[0] <= a[1] <= ... <= a[n-1] for x.
 // Return position if found; return -1 otherwise.
   int left = 0; int right = n - 1;
   while (left <= right) {
      int middle = (left + right)/2;
      if (x == a[middle]) return middle;
      if (x > a[middle]) left = middle + 1;
      else right = middle - 1;
      }
   return -1; // x not found
}
```

Program 2.30 Binary search

The search begins by comparing x with the number in the middle of the array. If x equals this number, the search terminates. If x is smaller than this number, then we need only search the left half and so right is updated to middle-1. If x is bigger than the middle element, only the right half needs to be searched and left is updated to middle+1.

Each iteration of the while loop—except the last one—results in a decrease in the size of the segment of a that has to be searched (i.e., the portion between left and right) by a factor of about two. So this loop iterates $\Theta(\log n)$ times in the worst case. As each iteration takes $\Theta(1)$ time, the overall worst-case complexity is $\Theta(\log n)$. ∎

Example 2.42 [*Insertion Sort*] Program 2.15 uses the insertion sort method to sort n elements. For each value of i, the innermost for loop has a worst-case complexity $\Theta(i)$. As a result, the worst-case time complexity of Program 2.15 is *at most* $\Theta(1 + 2 + 3 + \cdots + n-1) = \Theta(n^2)$. The best-case time complexity of Program 2.15 is $\Theta(n)$. Its asymptotic complexity is also given by $\Omega(n)$ and $O(n^2)$. ∎

The little oh notation is often used in step-count analyses. A step count of $3n + o(n)$ would mean that the step count is $3n$ plus terms that are asymptotically smaller than n. When performing such an analysis, one can ignore portions of the program that are known to contribute less than $\Theta(n)$ steps.

The definitions of O, Ω, Θ, and o can be extended to include functions of more than one variable. For example, $f(n,m) = O(g(n,m))$ iff positive constants c, n_0, and m_0 exist such that $f(n,m) \leq cg(n,m)$ for all $n \geq n_0$ and all $m \geq m_0$.

EXERCISES

28. Show that the following equalities are correct, using the definitions of O, Ω, Θ, and o only. Do not use Theorems 2.1 through 2.6, or Figures 2.15 and 2.16.
    (a) $5n^2 - 6n = \Theta(n^2)$.
    (b) $n! = O(n^n)$.
    (c) $2n^2 2^n + n\log n = \Theta(n^2 2^n)$.
    (d) $\sum_{i=0}^{n} i^2 = \Theta(n^3)$.
    (e) $\sum_{i=0}^{n} i^3 = \Theta(n^4)$.
    (f) $n^{2^n} + 6*2^n = \Theta(n^{2^n})$.
    (g) $n^3 + 10^6 n^2 = \Theta(n^3)$.
    (h) $6n^3/(\log n + 1) = O(n^3)$.
    (i) $n^{1.001} + n\log n = \Theta(n^{1.001})$.
    (j) $n^{k+\varepsilon} + n^k \log n = \Theta(n^{k+\varepsilon})$ for all k and ε, $k \geq 0$, and $\varepsilon > 0$.

29. Do Exercise 28 using Theorems 2.2, 2.4, and 2.6.

30. Show that the following equalities are incorrect:
    (a) $10n^2 + 9 = O(n)$.
    (b) $n^2 \log n = \Theta(n^2)$.
    (c) $n^2/\log n = \Theta(n^2)$.
    (d) $n^3 2^n + 6n^2 3^n = O(n^3 2^n)$.

31. Prove Theorems 2.3 and 2.5.

32. Prove Theorems 2.4 and 2.6.

33. Prove that $f(n) = o(g(n))$ iff $\lim_{n \to \infty} f(n)/g(n) = 0$.

34. Prove that equivalences E5 to E8 (Figure 2.15) are correct.

35. Prove the correctness of inference rules I1 to I6 (Figure 2.16).

36. Which of the following inferences are true? Why?
    (a) $\{f(n) = O(F(n)), g(n) = O(G(n))\} \to f(n)/g(n) = O(F(n)/G(n))$.
    (b) $\{f(n) = O(F(n)), g(n) = O(G(n))\} \to f(n)/g(n) = \Omega(F(n)/G(n))$.
    (c) $\{f(n) = O(F(n)), g(n) = O(G(n))\} \to f(n)/g(n) = \Theta(F(n)/G(n))$.
    (d) $\{f(n) = \Omega(F(n)), g(n) = \Omega(G(n))\} \to f(n)/g(n) = \Omega(F(n)/G(n))$.
    (e) $\{f(n) = \Omega(F(n)), g(n) = \Omega(G(n))\} \to f(n)/g(n) = O(F(n)/G(n))$.
    (f) $\{f(n) = \Omega(F(n)), g(n) = \Omega(G(n))\} \to f(n)/g(n) = \Theta(F(n)/G(n))$.

(g) $\{f(n) = \Theta(F(n)), g(n) = \Theta(G(n))\} \rightarrow f(n)/g(n) = \Theta(F(n)/G(n))$.

(h) $\{f(n) = \Theta(F(n)), g(n) = \Theta(G(n))\} \rightarrow f(n)/g(n) = \Omega(F(n)/G(n))$.

(i) $\{f(n) = \Theta(F(n)), g(n) = \Theta(G(n))\} \rightarrow f(n)/g(n) = O(F(n)/G(n))$.

37.   Obtain the asymptotic time complexity of the following functions. Set up a frequency table similar to Figures 2.19 to 2.22.

(a)   `Factorial` (Program 1.7).

(b)   `MinMax` (Program 2.26).

(c)   `MinMax` (Program 2.27).

(d)   `Mult` (Program 2.24).

(e)   `Mult` (Program 2.25).

(f)   `Max` (Program 1.31).

(g)   `PolyEval` (Program 2.3).

(h)   `Horner` (Program 2.4).

(i)   `Rank` (Program 2.5).

(j)   `Perm` (Program 1.10).

(k)   `SelectionSort` (Program 2.7).

(l)   `SelectionSort` (Program 2.12).

(m)   `InsertionSort` (Program 2.14).

(n)   `InsertionSort` (Program 2.15).

(o)   `BubbleSort` (Program 2.9).

(p)   `BubbleSort` (Program 2.13).

2.5   PRACTICAL COMPLEXITIES

We have seen that the time complexity of a program is generally some function of the instance characteristics. This function is very useful in determining how the time requirements vary as the instance characteristics change. We can also use the complexity function to compare two programs P and Q that perform the same task. Assume that program P has complexity $\Theta(n)$ and that program Q has complexity $\Theta(n^2)$. We can assert that program P is faster than program Q for "sufficiently large" n. To see the validity of this assertion, observe that the actual computing time of P is bounded from above by cn for some constant c and for all n, $n \geq n_1$, while that of Q is bounded from below by dn^2 for some constant d and all n, $n \geq n_2$. Since $cn \leq dn^2$ for $n \geq c/d$, program P is faster than program Q whenever $n \geq \max\{n_1, n_2, c/d\}$.

One should always be cautiously aware of the presence of the phrase *sufficiently large* in the assertion of the preceding discussion. When deciding which of the two programs to use, we must know whether the n we are dealing with is, in fact, sufficiently large. If program P actually runs in $10^6 n$ milliseconds while program Q runs in n^2 milliseconds and if we always have $n \le 10^6$, then program Q is the one to use.

To get a feel for how the various functions grow with n, you should study Figures 2.23 and 2.24 very closely. These figures show that 2^n grows very rapidly with n. In fact, if a program needs 2^n steps for execution, then when $n = 40$, the number of steps needed is approximately $1.1 * 10^{12}$. On a computer performing 1,000,000,000 steps per second, this program would require about 18.3 minutes. If $n = 50$, the same program would run for about 13 days on this computer. When $n = 60$, about 310.56 years will be required to execute the program, and when $n = 100$, about $4 * 10^{13}$ years will be needed. We can conclude that the utility of programs with exponential complexity is limited to small n (typically $n \le 40$).

$\log n$	n	$n \log n$	n^2	n^3	2^n
0	1	0	1	1	2
1	2	2	4	8	4
2	4	8	16	64	16
3	8	24	64	512	256
4	16	64	256	4096	65,536
5	32	160	1024	32,768	4,294,967,296

Figure 2.23 Value of various functions

Programs that have a complexity that is a high-degree polynomial are also of limited utility. For example, if a program needs n^{10} steps, then our 1,000,000,000 steps per second computer needs 10 seconds when $n = 10$, 3171 years when $n = 100$, and $3.17 * 10^{13}$ years when $n = 1000$. If the program's complexity had been n^3 steps instead, then the computer would need one second when $n = 1000$, 110.67 minutes when $n = 10,000$, and 11.57 days when $n = 100,000$.

Figure 2.25 gives the time that a 1,000,000,000 instructions per second computer needs to execute a program of complexity $f(n)$ instructions. One should note that currently only the fastest computers can execute about 1,000,000,000 instructions per second. From a practical standpoint, it is evident that for reasonably large n (say $n > 100$) only programs of small complexity (such as n, $n\log n$, n^2, and n^3) are feasible. Further, this is the case even if we could build a computer capable of executing 10^{12} instructions per second. In

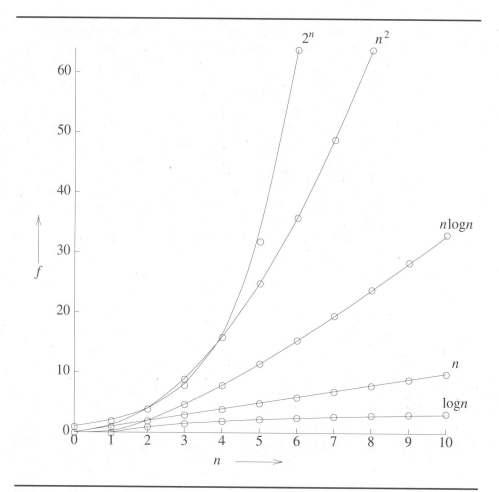

Figure 2.24 Plot of various functions

this case the computing times of Figure 2.25 would decrease by a factor of 1000. Now when $n = 100$, it would take 3.17 years to execute n^{10} instructions and $4 * 10^{10}$ years to execute 2^n instructions.

			$f(n)$				
n	n	$n\log_2 n$	n^2	n^3	n^4	n^{10}	2^n
10	.01µs	.03µs	.1µs	1µs	10µs	10s	1µs
20	.02µs	.09µs	.4µs	8µs	160µs	2.84h	1ms
30	.03µs	.15µs	.9µs	27µs	810µs	6.83d	1s
40	.04µs	.21µs	1.6µs	64µs	2.56ms	121d	18m
50	.05µs	.28µs	2.5µs	125µs	6.25ms	3.1y	13d
100	.10µs	.66µs	10µs	1ms	100ms	3171y	$4*10^{13}$y
10^3	1µs	9.96µs	1ms	1s	16.67m	$3.17*10^{13}$y	$32*10^{283}$y
10^4	10µs	130µs	100ms	16.67m	115.7d	$3.17*10^{23}$y	
10^5	100µs	1.66ms	10s	11.57d	3171y	$3.17*10^{33}$y	
10^6	1ms	19.92ms	16.67m	31.71y	$3.17*10^7$y	$3.17*10^{43}$y	

µs = microsecond = 10^{-6} seconds; ms = milliseconds = 10^{-3} seconds;
s = seconds; m = minutes; h = hours; d = days; y = years

Figure 2.25 Run times on a 1,000,000,000 instruction per second computer

EXERCISES

38. Let A and B be two programs that perform the same task. Let $t_A(n)$ and $t_B(n)$, respectively, denote their run times. For each of the following pairs, find the range of n values for which program A is faster than program B.

    (a) $t_A(n) = 1000n$, $t_B(n) = 10n^2$.

    (b) $t_A(n) = 2n^2$, $t_B(n) = n^3$.

    (c) $t_A(n) = 2^n$, $t_B(n) = 100n$.

    (d) $t_A(n) = 1000n\log_2 n$, $t_B(n) = n^2$.

39. Redo Figure 2.25 assuming a computer capable of doing 1 trillion instructions per second.

40. Suppose that using a certain program and computer, it is possible to solve problems of size up to $n = N$ in a ''reasonable amount of time.'' Create a table that shows the largest value of n for which solutions can be found in reasonable time using the same program and a computer that is x times as fast. Do this exercise for $x = 10$, 100, 1000, and 1,000,000 and $t_A(n) = n$, n^2, n^3, n^5, and 2^n.

2.6 PERFORMANCE MEASUREMENT

Performance measurement is concerned with obtaining the actual space and time requirements of a program. As noted in earlier sections, these quantities are very dependent on the particular compiler and options used as well as on the specific computer on which the program is run. Unless otherwise stated, all performance values in this book were obtained using 486/DX50 PC, the Borland C++ compiler version 5.01 for Windows 95, and the default compiler options.

We ignore the space and time needed for compilation because each program (after it has been fully debugged) will be compiled once and then executed several times. However, the space and time needed for compilation are important during program testing when more time may be spent on this task than in actually running the compiled code.

We do not explicitly consider measuring the run-time space requirements of a program for the following reasons:

- The size of the instruction and data space are provided by the compiler following compilation, so no measurement techniques are needed to obtain these figures.

- We can get a fairly accurate estimate of the recursion stack space and the space needed by dynamically allocated variables using the analytical methods of the earlier sections.

To obtain the execution (or run) time of a program, we need a clocking mechanism. Most C++ implementations provide an appropriate function. For example, Borland C++ has the function `clock()` in its `time.h` unit. This function returns the number of clock ticks since the program started. We can determine the elapsed time in seconds by dividing the elapsed ticks by `CLK_TCK`. On our PC, `CLK_TCK` = 18.2.

Suppose we wish to measure the worst-case time requirements of function `InsertionSort` (Program 2.15). First we need to

1. Decide on the values of n for which the times are to be obtained.

2. Determine, for each of the above values of n, the data that exhibits the worst-case behavior.

2.6.1 Choosing Instance Size

We decide on which values of n to use according to two factors: the amount of timing we want to perform and what we expect to do with the times. Suppose we want to predict how long it will take, in the worst case, to sort an array of n numbers using *InsertionSort*. From Example 2.42 we know that the worst-case complexity of `InsertionSort` is $\Theta(n^2)$; that is, it is quadratic in n. In theory, if we know the times for any three values of n, we can determine the quadratic function that describes the worst-case run time of `InsertionSort` and we can obtain the time for all other values of n from this quadratic function. In practice, we need the times for more than three values of n for the following two reasons:

1. Asymptotic analysis tells us the behavior only for sufficiently large values of n. For smaller values of n, the run time may not follow the asymptotic curve. To determine the point beyond which the asymptotic curve is followed, we need to examine the times for several values of n.

2. Even in the region where the asymptotic behavior is exhibited, the times may not lie exactly on the predicted curve (quadratic in the case of `InsertionSort`) because of the effects of low-order terms that are discarded in the asymptotic analysis. For instance, a program with asymptotic complexity $\Theta(n^2)$ can have an actual complexity that is $c_1 n^2 + c_2 n \log n + c_3 n + c_4$—or any other function of n in which the highest order term is $c_1 n^2$ for some constant $c_1, c_1 > 0$.

We expect the asymptotic behavior of Program 2.15 to begin for some n that is smaller than 100. So for n > 100 we shall obtain the run time for just a few values. A reasonable choice is n = 200, 300, 400, $\cdots$, 1000. There is nothing magical about this choice of values. We can just as well use n = 500, 1000, 1500, $\cdots$, 10,000 or n = 512, 1024, 2048, $\cdots$, 2^{15}. The latter choices will cost us more in terms of computer time and probably will not provide any better information about the run time of our function.

For n in the range [0, 100], we will carry out a more refined measurement, as we aren't quite sure where the asymptotic behavior begins. Of course, if our measurements show that the quadratic behavior doesn't begin in this range, we shall have to perform a more detailed measurement in the range [100, 200] and so on until we detect the onset of this behavior. Times in the range [0, 100] will be obtained in steps of 10 beginning at n = 0.

2.6.2 Developing the Test Data

For many programs, we can generate manually or by computer the data that exhibits the best- and worst-case time complexity. The average complexity, however, is usually quite difficult to demonstrate. For `InsertionSort`, the worst-case data for any n is a decreasing sequence such as n, n-1, n-2, $\cdots$, 1. The best-case data is a sorted sequence such as 0, 1, 2, $\cdots$, n-1. It is difficult to envison the data that would cause `InsertionSort` to exhibit its average behavior.

When we are unable to develop the data that exhibits the complexity we want to measure, we can pick the least (maximum, average) measured time from some randomly generated data as an estimate of the best (worst, average) behavior.

2.6.3   Setting Up the Experiment

Having selected the instance sizes and developed the test data, we are ready to write a program that will measure the desired run times. For our insertion sort example, this program takes the form given in Program 2.31. The measured times are given in Figure 2.26.

```
#include <iostream.h>
#include <time.h>
#include "insort.h"

void main(void)
{
   int a[1000], step = 10;
   clock_t start, finish;
   for (int n = 0; n <= 1000; n += step) {
      // get time for size n
      for (int i = 0; i < n; i++)
         a[i] = n - i; // initialize
      start = clock( );
      InsertionSort(a, n);
      finish = clock( );
      cout << n << ' '
           << (finish - start) / CLK_TCK << endl;
      if (n == 100) step = 100;
      }
}
```

Program 2.31 Program to obtain worst-case run times for insertion sort

Figure 2.26 suggests that no time is needed to sort arrays with 100 or fewer numbers and that there is no difference in the times to sort 500 through 600 numbers. This conclusion, of course, isn't true. Anomalies are also noted for other values of n. The problem is that the time needed is too small for clock() to measure. Furthermore, all measurements are accurate to within one clock tick. Since CLK_TCK = 18.2 on our computer, the actual times may deviate from the measured times by up to one tick or 1/18.2 ~ 0.055 seconds. The reported time for n = 1000 is six ticks. So the actual time could be anywhere between five and seven ticks. If we wish our measurements to be accurate to within 10 percent, finish-start should be at least 10 clock ticks or 0.55 seconds, which isn't the case for any of the times in Figure 2.26.

n	Time	n	Time
0	0	100	0
10	0	200	0.054945
20	0	300	0
30	0	400	0.054945
40	0	500	0.10989
50	0	600	0.109890
60	0	700	0.164835
70	0	800	0.164835
80	0	900	0.274725
90	0	1000	0.32967

Times are in seconds

Figure 2.26 Times using Program 2.31

To improve the accuracy of our measurements, we need to repeat the sort several times for each value of n. Since the sort changes the array a, we need to initialize this array before each sort. Program 2.32 gives the new timing program. Notice that now the measured time is the time to sort plus the time to initialize a and the overhead associated with the while loop. Figure 2.27 gives the measured times.

We can determine the overhead associated with the while loop and the initialization of the array a by running Program 2.32 without the statement InsertionSort(a,n). Figure 2.28 gives the output from this run for selected values of n. Subtracting the overhead time from the time per sort (Figure 2.27), gives us the worst-case time for InsertionSort. Nevertheless, inaccuracy remains because the while conditional is actually tested counter+1 times, whereas the body of the while is executed counter times. However, since the number of repetitions is large for small n and the overhead is negligible for large n, we can overlook this inaccuracy. Notice how for larger n the times of Figure 2.27 almost quadruple each time n is doubled. We expect this pattern, as the worst-case complexity is $\Theta(n^2)$.

```
#include <iostream.h>
#include <time.h>
#include "insort.h"

void main(void)
{
    int a[1000], n, i, step = 10;
    long counter;
    float seconds;
    clock_t start, finish;
    for (n = 0; n <= 1000; n += step) {
        // get time for size n
        start = clock( ); counter = 0;
        while (clock( ) - start < 10) {
            counter++;
            for (i = 0; i < n; i++)
                a[i] = n - i; // initialize
            InsertionSort(a, n);
            }
        finish = clock( );
        seconds = (finish - start) / CLK_TCK;
        cout << n << ' ' << counter << ' ' << seconds
             << ' ' << seconds / counter << endl;
        if (n == 100) step = 100;
        }
}
```

Program 2.32 Program to obtain times with an accuracy of 10 percent

EXERCISES

41. Why does the timing program of Program 2.33 not measure run times to an accuracy of 10 percent.

42. Use Program 2.32 to obtain the worst-case run times for the two versions of insertion sort given in Programs 2.14 and 2.15. Use the same values of n as used in Program 2.32. Evaluate the relative merits of using the Insert function versus incorporating the code for an insert directly into the sort function.

43. Use Program 2.32 to obtain the worst-case run times for the versions of bubble sort given in Programs 2.9 and 2.13. Use the same values of n as used in Program 2.32. However, you will need to verify that the worst-case

n	Repetitions	Total time	Time per sort
0	34228	0.549451	0.000016
10	10365	0.549451	0.000053
20	3525	0.549451	0.000156
30	1701	0.549451	0.000323
40	992	0.549451	0.000554
50	647	0.549451	0.000849
60	454	0.549451	0.001210
70	337	0.549451	0.001630
80	259	0.549451	0.002121
90	206	0.549451	0.002667
100	167	0.549451	0.003290
200	43	0.549451	0.012778
300	19	0.549451	0.028918
400	11	0.549451	0.049950
500	7	0.549451	0.078493
600	5	0.604396	0.120879
700	4	0.604396	0.151099
800	3	0.659341	0.219780
900	3	0.769231	0.256410
1000	2	0.604396	0.302198

Times are in seconds

Figure 2.27 Output from Program 2.32

n	Repetitions	Total time	Overhead
0	36141	0.549451	0.000015
10	32321	0.549451	0.000017
50	19186	0.549451	0.000029
100	12999	0.549451	0.000042
500	3557	0.549451	0.000154
1000	1864	0.549451	0.000295

Times are in seconds

Figure 2.28 Overhead in measurements of Figure 2.27

```
#include <iostream.h>
#include <time.h>
#include "insort.h"

void main(void)
{
   int a[1000], n, i, step = 10;
   long counter;
   float seconds;
   clock_t start, elapsed;
   for (n = 0; n <= 1000; n += step) {
      // get time for size n
      elapsed = 0; counter = 0;
      while (elapsed < 10) {
         counter++;
         for (i = 0; i < n; i++)
            a[i] = n - i; // initialize
         start = clock( );
         InsertionSort(a, n);
         elapsed += clock( ) - start;
         }
      seconds = elapsed / CLK_TCK;
      cout << n << ' ' << counter << ' ' << seconds
           << ' ' << seconds / counter << endl;
      if (n == 100) step = 100;
      }
}
```

Program 2.33 Inaccurate way to time `InsertionSort`

data used by Program 2.32 is, in fact, worst-case data for the two bubble sort functions. Present your results as a table with three columns: n, Program 2.9, Program 2.13. What can you say about the worst-case performance of the two bubble sorts?

44. (a) Devise worst-case data for the two versions of selection sort given in Programs 2.7 and 2.12.

(b) Use a suitably modified version of Program 2.32 to determine the worst-case times for the two selection sort functions. Use the same values of n as used in Program 2.32.

(c)   Present your results as a single table with three columns: n, Program 2.7, Program 2.12.

(d)   What can you say about the worst-case performance of the two selection sorts?

45.   This exercise compares the worst-case run times of insertion sort (Program 2.34) and the early-terminating versions of selection sort (Program 2.12) and bubble sort (Program 2.13). To level the playing field, rewrite Program 2.13 as a single function.

(a)   Devise data that show the worst-case behavior of each function.

(b)   Using the data of (a) and the timing program of Program 2.32, obtain worst-case run times.

(c)   Provide these times both as a single table with columns labeled n, selection sort, bubble sort, and insertion sort and as a single graph showing three curves (one for each method). The x-axis of the graph is labeled by n values, and the y-axis by time values.

(d)   What conclusions can you draw about the relative worst-case performance of the three sort functions?

(e)   Measure the overheads for each value of n and report these in a table as in Figure 2.28. Subtract this overhead from the times obtained in (b) and present a new table of times and a new graph.

(f)   Are there any changes to your conclusions about relative performance as a result of subtracting the overhead?

(g)   Using the data you have obtained, estimate the worst-case time to sort 2000, 4000, and 10,000 numbers using each sort function.

46.   Modify Program 2.32 so that it obtains an estimate of the average run time of InsertionSort (Program 2.15). Do the following:

(a)   Sort a random permutation of the numbers 0, 1, $\cdots$, n−1 on each iteration of the while loop, This permutation is generated using a random permutation generator. In case you don't have such a function available, try to write one using a random number generator, or simply generate a random sequence of n numbers.

(b)   Set the while loop so that at least 20 random permutations are sorted and so that at least 10 clock ticks have elapsed.

(c)   Estimate the average sort time by dividing the elapsed time by the number of permutations sorted.
Present the estimated average times as a table.

47.   Use the strategy of Exercise 46 to estimate the average run times of the bubble sort functions given in Programs 2.9 and 2.13. Use the same values of n as in Program 2.32. Present your results as a table.

48.   Use the strategy of Exercise 46 to estimate the average run times of the selection sort functions given in Programs 2.7 and 2.12. Use the same values of n as in Program 2.32. Present your results as a table.

49.   Use the strategy of Exercise 46 to estimate and compare the average run times of the functions of Programs 2.12, 2.13, and 2.15. Use the same values of n as in Program 2.32. Present your results as a table and as a graph.

50.   Devise experiments to determine the average time taken by sequential search (Program 2.1) and binary search (Program 2.30) to perform a successful search. Assume that each element of the array being searched is looked for with equal probability. Present your results as a table and as a graph.

51.   Devise experiments to determine the worst-case time taken by sequential search (Program 2.1) and binary search (Program 2.30) to perform a successful search. Present your results as a table and as a graph.

52.   Determine the run time of function `Add` (Program 2.19) for n = 10, 20, 30, $\cdots$, 100. Present your measured times as a table and as a graph.

53.   Determine the run time of function `Transpose` (Program 2.22) for n = 10, 20, 30, $\cdots$, 100. Present your measured times as a table and as a graph.

54.   Determine the run time of function `Mult` (Program 2.24) for n = 10, 20, 30, $\cdots$, 100. Present your measured times as a table and as a graph.

2.7   REFERENCES AND SELECTED READINGS

The following books provide asymptotic analyses for several programs: *Fundamentals of Computer Algorithms/C++* by E. Horowitz, S. Sahni, and S. Rajasekaran, W. H. Freeman and Co., New York, NY, 1997; *Fundamentals of Data Structures in C++* by E. Horowitz, S. Sahni, and D. Mehta, W. H. Freeman and Co., New York, NY, 1995; *Introduction to Algorithms* by T. Cormen, C. Leiserson, and R. Rivest, McGraw-Hill, New York, NY, 1992; *Compared to What: An Introduction to the Analysis of Algorithms* by G. Rawlins, W. H. Freeman and Co., New York, NY, 1992; and *Algorithms from P to NP. Volume I: Design and Efficiency* by B. Moret and H. Shapiro, Benjamin-Cummings, Menlo Park, CA, 1991.

CHAPTER 3

DATA REPRESENTATION

BIRD'S-EYE VIEW

We are now ready to begin the study of data structures, which continues through Chapter 12 of this book. Although Chapter 3 focuses on the data structure *linear list*, its primary purpose is to introduce the different ways in which data may be represented or stored in a computer's memory. The common data representation methods are formula based, linked (or pointer based), indirect addressing, and simulated pointer.

Formula-based representation uses a mathematical formula to determine where (i.e., the memory address) to store each element of a list. In the simplest cases the formula stores successive elements of a list in successive memory locations, and we obtain what is commonly known as the sequential representation of a list.

In a linked representation the elements of a list may be stored in any arbitrary set of memory locations. Each element has an explicit pointer (or link) that tells us the location (i.e., the address) of the next element in the list. Similarly, in indirect addressing the list elements may be stored in any arbitrary set of locations. This time, however, we maintain a table such that the *i*th table entry tells

111

us where the ith list element is. So the table stores the addresses of the list elements.

In a formula-based representation, the element addresses are determined using a mathematical formula; in a linked representation, the element addresses are distributed across the list elements; and in indirect addressing, the addresses are collected into a table.

A simulated-pointer representation is very similar to a linked representation. However, integers replace the C++ pointers; both integers and pointers play the same role.

This chapter covers all four ways to represent a linear list. We highlight the merits and demerits of each by examining the complexity of common list operations such as insert and delete. We shall also see how to use arrays to simulate the C++ pointer facility.

The data structure concepts introduced in this chapter are

- Abstract data types.

- Formula-based, linked, indirect addressing, and simulated-pointer representations.

- Chains, circular lists, and doubly linked lists.

The applications section concentrates on the use of linked lists because all the programs developed in Chapters 1 and 2 use formula-based respresentations, and our intention now is to get some experience using linked representations. Bin sort, radix sort, and the equivalence class application use chains, while the convex hull application uses a doubly linked list. Bin sort and radix sort can sort n elements in $\Theta(n)$ time provided the key values are in an "appropriate range." Although the sort methods developed in Chapter 2 take $O(n^2)$ time, they do not require the keys to lie in an appropriate range. Bin sort and radix sort are considerably faster than the sort methods of Chapter 2 when the key values lie in an appropriate range. The bin sort application also shows you how to use a function name as a parameter to a C++ function.

3.1 INTRODUCTION

A **data object** is a set of *instances* or *values*. Some examples are

1. *Boolean* = {*false*, *true*}
2. *Digit* = {0, 1, 2, 3, 4, 5, 6, 7, 8, 9}
3. *Letter* = {A, B, C, $\cdots$, Z, a, b, $\cdots$, z}
4. *NaturalNumber* = {0, 1, 2, $\cdots$}
5. *Integer* = {0, ±1, ±2, ±3, $\cdots$}
6. *String* = {a, b, $\cdots$, aa, ab, ac, $\cdots$}

Boolean, *Digit*, *Letter*, *NaturalNumber*, *Integer*, and *String* are data objects. *true* and *false* are the instances of *Boolean* while 0, 1, $\cdots$, and 9 are the instances of *Digit*. We may regard the individual instances of a data object as being either **primitive** (or **atomic**) or as being composed of instances of another (possibly the same) data object. In the latter case we use the term **element** to refer to the individual components of an instance of an object.

For example, each instance of the data object *NaturalNumber* can be regarded as atomic. In this case we are not concerned with a further decomposition of the instances of this data object. Another view is to regard each instance of a *NaturalNumber* as being composed of several instances of the data object *Digit*. In this view the number 675 comprises the digits 6, 7, and 5 (in that order).

The data object *String* is the set of all possible string instances. Each instance of a string is composed of characters. Some example instances are *good*, *a trip to Hawaii*, *going down hill*, and *abcabcdabcde*. The first string has the four elements *g*, *o*, *o*, and *d* (in that order). Each element is an instance of the data object *Letter*.

The instances of a data object as well as the elements that constitute individual instances are generally related in some way. For example, the natural number 0 is the smallest natural number; 1 is the next; and 2 is the next. In the natural number 675, 6 is the most significant digit, 7 is the next, and 5 is the least significant digit. In the string *good*, *g* is the first letter, *o* the second and third, and *d* the last.

In addition to interrelationships, a set of functions is generally associated with any data object. These functions may transform one instance of an object into another instance of that object, into an instance of another data object, or into both. The function could simply create a new instance without transforming the instances from which the new one is created. For example, the function *add* defined on the natural numbers, creates a new natural number that is the sum of the two numbers to be added. The two numbers that get added are unaltered.

A **data structure** is a data object together with the relationships that exist among the instances and among the individual elements that compose an instance. These relationships are provided by specifying the functions of interest.

When we study data structures, we are concerned with the representation of data objects (actually of the instances) as well as the implementation of the functions of interest for the data objects. The representation of each data object should facilitate an efficient[1] implementation of the functions.

The most frequently used data objects together with their frequently used functions are already implemented in C++ as a standard data type. The objects *Integer* (int), *Real* (float), and *Boolean* (bool) fall into this category. All other data objects can be represented using the standard data types, enumeration, and the grouping ability provided by the class, array, and pointer features of C++. For example, we can represent instances of *String* by using a character array s declared as

```
char s[MaxSize];
```

Our study of data structures has two parts. This chapter is organized by methods to represent data: formula based, linked, indirect addressing, simulated pointer. We use the data object *linear list* to illustrate these methods. In succeeding chapters we study the representation of other popular data objects such as matrices, stacks, queues, dictionaries, priority queues, and graphs.

3.2 LINEAR LISTS

A **linear list** is a data object whose instances are of the form $(e_1, e_2, \cdots, e_n)$ where n is a finite natural number. The e_i terms are the elements of the list, and n is its length. The elements may be viewed as atomic as their individual structure is not relevant to the structure of the list. When $n = 0$, the list is *empty*. When $n > 0$, e_1 is the first element and e_n the last. We say that e_1 comes before (or precedes) e_2, e_2 comes before e_3, and so on. Other than this precedence relation, no other structure exists in a linear list. We shall use s to denote the number of bytes needed by each element e_i. Therefore, s is the size of an element.

Some examples of linear lists are (1) an alphabetized (i.e., ordered by name) list of students in a class; (2) a list of exam scores in nondecreasing order; (3) an alphabetized list of members of Congress; and (4) a list of gold-medal winners in the Olympics men's basketball event ordered by year. With these examples in mind, we see the need to perform the following operations on a linear list:

---

1. The term *efficient* is used here in a very liberal sense. It includes performance efficiency as well as measures of the complexity of development and maintenance of associated software.

- Create a linear list.

- Determine whether the list is empty.

- Determine the length of the list.

- Find the kth element.

- Search for a given element.

- Delete the kth element.

- Insert a new element just after the kth.

A linear list may be specified as an **abstract data type** (ADT) in which we provide a specification of the instances as well as of the operations that are to be performed (see ADT 3.1). Notice the similarity between this abstract data type specification and a C++ class definition. The abstract data type specification is independent of any representation we have in mind. All representations of the abstract data type must satisfy the specification, and the specification becomes a way to validate the representation. In addition, all representations that satisfy the specification may be used interchangeably in applications of the data type.

AbstractDataType *LinearList* {
   instances
      ordered finite collections of zero or more elements
   operations
      Create (): create an empty linear list
      Destroy (): erase the list
      IsEmpty (): return `true` if the list is empty, `false` otherwise
      Length (): return the list size (i.e., number of elements in the list)
      Find (k,x): return the kth element of the list in x
                  return `false` if there is no kth element
      Search (x): return the position of x in the list
                  return 0 if x is not in the list
      Delete (k,x): delete the kth element and return it in x
                  function returns the modified linear list
      Insert (k,x): insert x just after the kth element
                  function returns the modified linear list
      Output (*out*): put the list into the output stream *out*;
}

ADT 3.1 Abstract data type specification of a linear list

Rather than use the informal English approach to specify an abstract data type as in ADT 3.1, we may use a C++ abstract class. This approach uses derived classes, abstract classes, and virtual functions; topics on which we elaborate in Chapters 5 and 12. For now, we shall limit ourselves to using informal English to specify abstract data types. If you are already familiar with derived and abstract classes, you may want to peek at Section 12.9.4 and see how the abstract data type *LinearList* is specified as a C++ abstract class.

3.3 FORMULA-BASED REPRESENTATION

3.3.1 Representation

A **formula-based** representation uses an array to represent the instances of an object. Each position of the array is called a **cell** or **node** and is large enough to hold one of the elements that make up an instance of the data object. In some cases we use a separate array for each instance, while in other cases one array can represent several instances. Individual elements of an instance are located in the array using a mathematical formula.

Suppose we decide to use one array for each list to be represented. We need to map the elements of a list to positions in the array used to represent it. Where does the first element reside? Where does the second reside? In a formula-based representation, a mathematical formula determines the location of each element. A simple mapping formula is

$$location\,(i) = i - 1 \tag{3.1}$$

Equation 3.1 states that the ith element of the list (if it exists) is in position $i - 1$ of the array. Figure 3.1(a) shows a five-element list represented in the array `element` using the mapping of Equation 3.1. (An even simpler formula is *location* $(i) = i$, which does not use position zero of the array. We examine the use of this formula in Exercises 8 through 13.)

To completely specify the list, we need to know its current length or size. We use the variable `length` for this purpose. `length` is zero when the list is empty. Program 3.1 gives the resulting C++ class definition. Since the data type of the list elements may vary from application to application, we have defined a template class in which the user specifies the element data type `T`. The data members `length`, `MaxSize`, and `element` are private members, while the remaining members are public. `Insert` and `Delete` have been defined to return a reference to a linear list. As we shall see, the actual implementations modify the list `*this` and then return a reference to the modified list. Consequently, it is possible to concatenate several list operations as in `X.Insert(0,a).Delete(3,b)`.

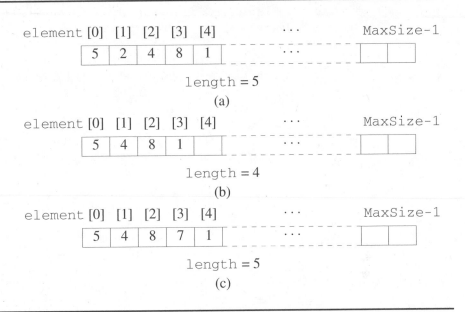

Figure 3.1 Linear lists

3.3.2 The Exception Class NoMem

Many of the codes we write in this book throw an exception if enough memory isn't available. At times the exception will be thrown by new, and at other times we will need to throw the exception ourselves. We desire to throw the same exception in all cases; therefore, we define the exception class NoMem as shown in Program 3.2. The function my_new_handler simply throws an exception of type NoMem. The last line of Program 3.2 invokes the C++ function set_new_handler that causes the operator new to invoke my_new_handler whenever it is unable to allocate the requested memory. Consequently, new causes the exception NoMem to be thrown instead of the exception xalloc. The call to set_new_handler returns a pointer to the function previously called by new whenever it failed. We save the returned pointer in the variable Old_Handler_. To restore the original behavior of new, we can make the following invocation:

```
set_new_handler(Old_Handler_);
```

Notice that Program 3.2 uses a function name as an actual parameter. In addition, Program 3.2 changes the exception that new throws to NoMem regardless of the type of exception new previously threw. Therefore, we can use Program

```
template<class T>
class LinearList {
   public:
      LinearList(int MaxListSize = 10); // constructor
      ~LinearList() {delete [] element;} // destructor
      bool IsEmpty() const {return length == 0;}
      int Length() const {return length;}
      bool Find(int k, T& x) const;
         // return the k'th element of list in x
      int Search(const T& x) const;
         // return position of x
      LinearList<T>& Delete(int k, T& x);
         // delete k'th element and return in x
      LinearList<T>& Insert(int k, const T& x);
         // insert x just after k'th element
      void Output(ostream& out) const;
   private:
      int length;
      int MaxSize;
      T *element; // dynamic 1D array
};
```

Program 3.1 Formula-based class `LinearList`

3.2 even with C++ implementations in which new throws an exception of a type other than `xalloc`.

3.3.3   Operations

The operations *Create* and *Destroy* are implemented as the class constructor and destructor, respectively. The constructor (Program 3.3) creates a list whose maximum default length is 10. When our computer does not have adequate memory to create an array of the desired length, the operator new throws an exception of type `NoMem`. Our constructor code does not catch this exception. If a thrown exception is not caught anywhere in the program, the program makes an abnormal termination. In most of our codes, we expect the application code to catch thrown exceptions.

   The following statement creates a linear list y of integers having maximum length 100:

```
LinearList<int> y(100);
```

```
// insufficient memory
class NoMem {
   public:
      NoMem() {}
};

// change new to throw NoMem instead of xalloc
void my_new_handler()
{
   throw NoMem();
}
new_handler Old_Handler_ =
               set_new_handler(my_new_handler);
```

Program 3.2 Cause `new` to throw `NoMem` exceptions instead of `xalloc` exceptions

The destructor function (Program 3.1) invokes `delete` so as to free the space allocated to the array `element` by the constructor. Program 3.1 includes the code for `IsEmpty` and `Length`, while Program 3.3 gives the code for `Find` and `Search`. The complexity of `IsEmpty`, `Length`, and `Find` is $\Theta(1)$, while that of `Search` is O(length).

To delete the kth element from a list, we need to first ascertain that the list contains a kth element and then delete this element. If the list does not have a kth element, an exception occurs. The ADT *LinearList* (ADT 3.1) doesn't tell us what to do at this time. Our code will throw an exception of type `OutOfBounds`. We throw exceptions of this type whenever one of the parameters to the function being implemented falls outside of the expected range.

When there is a kth element, we can perform the deletion by moving elements k+1, k+2, $\cdots$, length down one position and reducing the value of length by one. For example, to delete the second element (2) from the list of Figure 3.1(a), we have to move the elements 4, 8, and 1 to positions 2, 3, and 4, respectively, of the list. These list positions correspond to positions 1, 2, and 3 of the array `element`. Figure 3.1(b) shows the list following the deletion. The value of length following the deletion is four.

Function `Delete` (Program 3.4) implements the delete operation when linear lists are represented using formula (3.1). When there is no kth element, an exception is thrown and the time taken by `Delete` is $\Theta(1)$. When the list has a kth element, length-k elements are moved taking $\Theta((\text{length-k}) s)$ time where s is the size of each element. In addition, the deleted element is moved to x. Hence the overall complexity is O((length-k) s).

```
template<class T>
LinearList<T>::LinearList(int MaxListSize)
{// Constructor for formula-based linear list.
   MaxSize = MaxListSize;
   element = new T[MaxSize];
   length = 0;
}

template<class T>
bool LinearList<T>::Find(int k, T& x) const
{// Set x to the k'th element in the list.
 // Return false if no k'th; true otherwise.
   if (k < 1 || k > length) return false; // no k'th
   x = element[k - 1];
   return true;
}

template<class T>
int LinearList<T>::Search(const T& x) const
{// Locate x.  Return position of x if found.
 // Return 0 if x not in list.
   for (int i = 0; i < length; i++)
      if (element[i] == x) return ++i;
   return 0;
}
```

Program 3.3 Elementary list operations

To insert a new element after the kth element in the list, we need to first move elements k+1 through length one position up and then insert the new element in position k+1. For example, inserting 7 after the third element of the list of Figure 3.1(b) results in the list of Figure 3.1(c). Program 3.5 gives the complete C++ code to insert an element. As you can see, two kinds of exceptions can occur during an insertion. The first is when the insertion point is not well specified and happens when the list has fewer than k−1 elements prior to the insertion as well as when k < 0. In this case we throw an OutOfBounds exception. The second exception occurs when the list is full. The array has no space left to accomodate the new element, so a NoMem exception is thrown. The complexity of Insert is O((length−k)·*s*).

Program 3.6 gives the code for Output. Its complexity is Θ(length). This code simply inserts the list elements into the output stream out. To actually display the list we can overload the operator << as is done in Program 3.6.

```
template<class T>
LinearList<T>& LinearList<T>::Delete(int k, T& x)
{// Set x to the k'th element and delete it.
 // Throw OutOfBounds exception if no k'th element.
   if (Find(k, x)) {// move elements k+1, ..., down
      for (int i = k; i < length; i++)
         element[i-1] = element[i];
      length--;
      return *this;
      }
   else throw OutOfBounds();
}
```

Program 3.4 Deletion from a linear list

```
template<class T>
LinearList<T>& LinearList<T>::Insert(int k, const T& x)
{// Insert x after the k'th element.
 // Throw OutOfBounds exception if no k'th element.
 // Throw NoMem exception if list is already full.
   if (k < 0 || k > length) throw OutOfBounds();
   if (length == MaxSize) throw NoMem();
   // move one up
   for (int i = length-1; i >= k; i--)
      element[i+1] = element[i];
   element[k] = x;
   length++;
   return *this;
}
```

Program 3.5 Insertion into a linear list

Program 3.7, which is a sample C++ program that uses the class Linear-List, assumes that the codes of Programs 3.1 through 3.6 are stored in the file llist.h and that the exception class definitions are in the file xcept.h. The example creates an integer list L of capacity 5; outputs its length (0); inserts 2 after the 0th element; inserts 6 after the first element (now the list is 2, 6); finds and outputs the first element (2); outputs the current list length (2); and deletes and outputs the first element. Figure 3.2 gives the output generated by Program 3.7.

```
template<class T>
void LinearList<T>::Output(ostream& out) const
{// Put the list into the stream out.
   for (int i = 0; i < length; i++)
      out << element[i] << "   ";
}

// overload <<
template <class T>
ostream& operator<<(ostream& out,
                    const LinearList<T>& x)
   {x.Output(out); return out;}
```

Program 3.6 Inserting a list into the output stream

3.3.4   Evaluation

Before accepting the formula-based representation of a linear list, let us reflect on its merits. Certainly, the operations to be performed on a linear list can be implemented as very simple C++ functions. The C++ functions to search, delete, and insert have a worst complexity that is linear in the size of the individual list. We might regard this complexity as quite satisfactory. (In Chapters 7 and 11 we shall see representations that allow us to perform these operations even faster.)

A negative aspect of the representation is its inefficient use of space. Consider the following situation. We are to maintain three lists. We know that the three lists together will never have more than 5000 elements in them at any time. However, it is quite possible for a list to have 5000 elements at one time and for another list to have 5000 elements at another time. Using the class `Linear-List`, each of the three lists will need to be of capacity 5000. So space for a total of 15,000 elements is required even though we will never have more than 5000 elements at any time.

To allow for this situation, we must represent all our lists in a single array `list` and use two additional arrays `first` and `last` to index into this one. Figure 3.3 shows three lists represented in the single array `list`. We adopt the convention that the lists are numbered 1 through m if there are m lists and that `first[i]` is actually one less than the actual position of the first element in list i. This convention on `first[i]` makes it easier to use the representation. `last[i]` is the actual position of the last element in list i. Notice that with this convention, `last[i] > first[i]` whenever the ith list is not empty. We shall have `first[i] = last[i]` whenever list i is empty. So in the example of Figure 3.3, list 2 is empty. The lists are represented in the array in the order 1, 2, 3, $\cdots$, m from left to right.

```
#include <iostream.h>
#include "llist.h"
#include "xcept.h"

void main(void)
{
    try {
        LinearList<int> L(5);
        cout << "Length = " << L.Length() << endl;
        cout << "IsEmpty = " << L.IsEmpty() << endl;
        L.Insert(0,2).Insert(1,6);
        cout << "List is " << L << endl;
        cout << "IsEmpty = " << L.IsEmpty() << endl;
        int z;
        L.Find(1,z);
        cout << "First element is " << z << endl;
        cout << "Length = " << L.Length() << endl;
        L.Delete(1,z);
        cout << "Deleted element is " << z << endl;
        cout << "List is " << L << endl;
        }
    catch (...) {
        cerr << "An exception has occurred" << endl;
        }
}
```

Program 3.7 Example using the class `LinearList`

```
Length = 0
IsEmpty = 1
List is 2   6
IsEmpty = 0
First element is 2
Length = 2
Deleted element is 2
List is 6
```

Figure 3.2 Output generated by Program 3.7

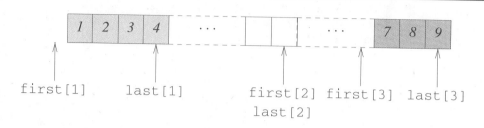

Figure 3.3 All lists in a single array

To avoid having to handle the first and last lists differently from others, we define two boundary lists 0 and `m+1` with `first[0] = last[0] =−1` and `first[m+1] = last[m+1] = MaxSize-1`.

To insert an element following the `kth` element of list `i`, we need to first create space for the new element. If `last[i] = first[i+1]`, then there is no space between lists `i` and `i+1` and we cannot move elements `k+1` through the last one up one position. At this time we can check whether it is possible to move elements 1 through `k-1` of the `ith` list one position down by checking the relation `last[i-1] < first[i]`. If this relation does not hold, then we need to either shift some of the lists 1 through `i-1` down or some of the lists `i+1` through `m` up and create space for list `i` to grow. This shifting is possible when the total number of elements in all the lists is fewer than `MaxSize`.

Figure 3.4 is a pseudo C++ version of the function to insert an element into list `i` and may be refined into compilable C++ code.

Although representing several lists in a single array uses space more efficiently than using a separate array for each list, insertions take more time in the worst case. In fact, a single insertion could require us to move as many as `MaxSize-1` elements.

EXERCISES

1. A shortcoming of the class `LinearList` is the need to predict the maximum possible size of the list. One way around this shortcoming is to set `MaxSize = 1` at the time the list is created. Then during an insert operation, if we already have `MaxSize` elements in the list, `MaxSize` is doubled, a new array of this size is allocated, elements are copied from the old array into the new one, and the old array is deleted. Similarly, during a delete operation, if the list size drops to one-fourth of the current value of `MaxSize`, a smaller array of size `MaxSize/2` is allocated, the elements

```
int insert(int i, int k, int y)
{// Insert y after the kth element in list i.
 // first and last are global.
 int j, m;
 m = last[i] - first[i]; //number of elements in list i
 if (k < 0 || k > m) return 0;
 // Is there space on the right?
```
Find the least j, $j \geq i$ such that last[j] < first[j+1];
If such a j exists, then move lists $i+1$ through j and elements $k+1$ through the last one of list i up one position and insert y into list i;
This move should update appropriate last and first values;

```
 // Is there space on the left?
```
If no j was found above, then find the largest j, $j < i$ such that last[j] < first[j+1];
If such a j is found, then move lists j through $i-1$ and elements 1 through $k-1$ of list i one position left and insert y;
This move should update appropriate last and first values;

```
 // Success?
 return ((no j was found above) ? 0 : 1);
}
```

Figure 3.4 Pseudocode to insert an element in the many lists per array representation

are copied from the old array into the new one, and the old array is deleted.

(a) Obtain a new implementation of the class LinearList that uses this idea. The constructor should have no parameters and should set MaxSize to one, allocate an array of size one, and set length to zero.

(b) Consider any sequence of n linear list operations beginning with an empty list. Suppose that the total step count is $f(n)$ using the old implementation. Show that with the new implementation, the step count is at most $cf(n)$ for some constant c.

2. Assume the representation of a linear list defined by Equation 3.1.

(a) Extend the definition of the class LinearList (Program 3.1) to include a function Reverse to reverse the order of the elements in the list. The reversal is to be done in-place (i.e., within the array element). Note that before the reversal, the kth element (if it exists) of the list is in element[k-1]; following the reversal it is in element[length-k].

(b) The complexity of your function should be linear in the list length. Show that this is the case.

(c) Test the correctness of your code using your own test data.

(d) Now write another in-place function to reverse an object of type LinearList. This function is not a member of the class and should use the member functions of LinearList to produce the reversed list.

(e) What is the time complexity of your new function?

(f) Compare the run-time performance of the two reversal functions using linear lists of size 1000, 5000, and 10,000.

3. Extend the class LinearList by adding the member function Half(). The invocation X.Half() eliminates every other element of X. So if X.length is initially 7 and X.element[] = [2, 13, 4, 5, 17, 8, 29], then following the execution of X.Half(), X.length is 4 and X.element[] = [2, 4, 17, 29]. If X.length is initially 4 and X.element[] = [2, 13, 4, 5], then following the execution of X.Half(), X.length is 2 and X.element[] = [2, 4]. If X is initially empty, then it is empty following the execution of X.Half().

(a) Write code for the member function Half(). You should not use any of the other member functions of LinearList. The complexity of your code should be $\Theta(length)$.

(b) Show that the complexity of your code is, in fact, $\Theta(length)$.

(c) Test the correctness of your code using suitable test data.

4. The default copy constructor for LinearList copies only the values of length, MaxSize, and element. As a result, when the linear list L is the actual parameter corresponding to the value parameter X of a function F and F is invoked, the values of L.length, L.MaxSize, and L.element are copied into the corresponding members of X. On exiting the function F, the LinearList destructor is invoked for X and the array X.element (which is the same as the array L.element) is deleted. One way to avoid the deletion of L.element is to define a copy constructor

```
LinearList<T>::LinearList(const LinearList<T>& L)
```

that copies the values of length and MaxSize and then creates a new array element into which L.element[0:MaxSize-1] is copied. Write such a copy constructor. What is its complexity?

5. In several applications we need to move back and forth on a list. Extend the definition of the class LinearList by adding the private member current that records the current location in the list. The list of public

members is extended to include

(a) Reset—Set current to one.

(b) Current(x)—Return the current element in x.

(c) End—Return true iff at the last element of the list.

(d) Front—Return true iff at the first element of the list.

(e) Next—Move current to the next element in the list; throw an exception if the operation fails.

(f) Previous—Move current to the preceding element in the list; throw an exception if the operation fails.

Write C++ code for the extended class. Test the correctness of your code using suitable test data.

6. Let A and B be two objects of type LinearList.

(a) Write a member function Alternate(A,B) to create a new linear list that contains elements alternately from A and B beginning with the first element of A. If you run out of elements in one of the lists, then append the remaining elements of the other list to the list being created. The complexity of your code should be linear in the lengths of the two input lists.

(b) Show that your code has linear complexity.

(c) Test the correctness of your code using suitable test data.

7. Let A and B be objects of type LinearList. Assume that the elements of A and B are in sorted order (i.e., nondecreasing from left to right).

(a) Write a member function Merge(A,B) to create a new sorted linear list that contains all the elements in A and B.

(b) What is the complexity of your function?

(c) Test the correctness of your code using suitable test data.

8. (a) Write the function LinearList::Split(A,B) to create two linear lists A and B. A contains all elements in odd positions of *this (note that the odd elements of a list are in even positions of element), and B contains the remaining elements.

(b) What is the complexity of your function?

(c) Test the correctness of your code using suitable test data.

9. Suppose that a linear list is represented using the formula

$$location(i) = i \qquad (3.2)$$

    (a)   Are any changes needed to the class definition of Program 3.1? If so, write the new definition.

    (b)   What is the length of the longest list that can be represented?

    (c)   Modify the implementation of all functions of Program 3.1 to conform to this formula.

    (d)   Test the correctness of your code using suitable test data.

    (e)   What is the complexity of each function?

10. Do Exercise 2 using Equation 3.2 instead of 3.1.

11. Do Exercise 6 using Equation 3.2 instead of 3.1.

12. Do Exercise 7 using Equation 3.2 instead of 3.1.

13. Do Exercise 8 using Equation 3.2 instead of 3.1.

14. Suppose that we are to represent a linear list using the formula

$$location\,(i) = (location\,(1) + i - 1)\,\%\,MaxSize \qquad (3.3)$$

where *MaxSize* is the size of the array in which the elements are stored. Rather than storing the list size explicitly, we keep variables `first` and `last` that give the locations of the first and last elements of the list.

    (a)   Develop a class similar to `LinearList` for this representation.

    (b)   What should the initial values of `first` and `last` be?

    (c)   Write codes for all member functions of your class. (You can make the `Delete` and `Insert` codes more efficient by properly choosing to move either elements to the left or right of the delted/inserted element.)

    (d)   What is the time complexity of each of your functions?

    (e)   Test the correctness of your code using suitable test data.

15. Do Exercise 2 using Equation 3.3 instead of 3.1.

16. Do Exercise 6 using Equation 3.3 instead of 3.1.

17. Do Exercise 7 using Equation 3.3 instead of 3.1.

18. Do Exercise 8 using Equation 3.3 instead of 3.1.

19. Refine Figure 3.4 into a C++ function and test its correctness.

20. Write a C++ function to insert an element after the *k*th element in list *i*. Assume that a single array represents *n* lists. If you have to move lists to accomodate the new element, your procedure should first determine the amount of available space. You should move the lists so that each has about the same amount of space available for future growth. Test the correctness of your code by compiling and executing it.

21. Write a C++ function to delete the *k*th element from list *i*. Assume that a single array represents *n* lists. Test the correctness of your code by compiling and executing it.

3.4 LINKED REPRESENTATION

3.4.1 The Classes `ChainNode` and `Chain`

In a linked representation each element of an instance of a data object is represented in a cell or node. The nodes, however, need not be components of an array, and no formula is used to locate individual elements. Instead, each node keeps explicit information about the location of other relevant nodes. This explicit information about the location of another node is called a **link** or **pointer**.

Let $L = (e_1, e_2, ..., e_n)$ be a linear list. In one possible linked representation for this list, each element e_i is represented in a separate node. Each node has exactly one link field that is used to locate the next element in the linear list. So the node for e_i links to that for e_{i+1}, $1 \leq i < n$. The node for e_n has no node to link to and so its link field is to `NULL` (or zero). The pointer variable `first` locates the first node in the representation. Figure 3.5 shows the linked representation of the list $L = (e_1, e_2, ..., e_n)$.

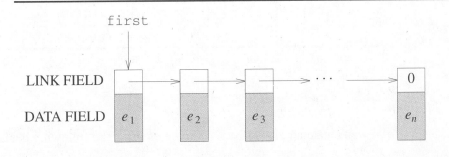

Figure 3.5 Linked representation of a linear list

Since each node in the linked representation of Figure 3.5 has exactly one link, the structure of this figure is called a **singly linked list**. Also, since the first node links to the second, the second to the third, $\cdots$, and the last has a `NULL` (i.e., zero) link, the structure is also called a **chain**. To represent a linear list as a chain, we use the class definitions `ChainNode` and `Chain` of Program 3.8. Since `Chain<T>` is a friend of `ChainNode<T>`, `Chain<T>` has access to all members (in particular, private members) of `ChainNode<T>`. The specification of the public members `Length`, `Find`, `Delete`, and `Insert` is identical to that of Program 3.1.

```
template <class T>
class ChainNode {
    friend Chain<T>;
    private:
       T data;
       ChainNode<T> *link;
};

template<class T>
class Chain {
    public:
       Chain() {first = 0;}
       ~Chain();
       bool IsEmpty() const {return first == 0;}
       int Length() const;
       bool Find(int k, T& x) const;
       int Search(const T& x) const;
       Chain<T>& Delete(int k, T& x);
       Chain<T>& Insert(int k, const T& x);
       void Output(ostream& out) const;
    private:
       ChainNode<T> *first;  // pointer to first node
};
```

Program 3.8 Class definition for a chain

3.4.2 Operations

We can create an empty list L of integers using the following declaration:

```
Chain<int> L;
```

Notice that the linked representation of a linear list does not specify the maximum size of the list.

Program 3.9 gives the code for the destructor function. Its complexity is $\Theta(n)$ where n is the length of the chain. The codes of Programs 3.10 and 3.11 implement the operations Length and Find, respectively. The complexity of Length is $\Theta(n)$ and that of Find is $O(k)$. Function Search (Program 3.12) assumes that the operation != is defined for elements of type T. Its complexity is $O(n)$. The complexity of Output (Program 3.13) is $\Theta(n)$, and it requires that the operation << be defined on the data type T.

```
template<class T>
Chain<T>::~Chain()
{// Chain destructor. Delete all nodes in chain.
   ChainNode<T> *next;   // next node
   while (first) {
      next = first->link;
      delete first;
      first = next;
      }
}
```

Program 3.9 Delete all nodes in a chain

```
template<class T>
int Chain<T>::Length() const
{// Return the number of elements in the chain.
   ChainNode<T> *current = first;
   int len = 0;
   while (current) {
     len++;
     current = current->link;
     }
   return len;
}
```

Program 3.10 Determine the length of a chain

To delete the fourth element from the chain of Figure 3.6, we do the following:

- Locate the third and fourth nodes.
- Link the third node to the fifth.
- Free the fourth node so that it becomes available for reuse.

Program 3.14 gives the code for the delete operation. There are three cases to consider. The first is when k is less than one or when the chain is empty; the delete fails because there is no kth element to delete. The second case is when the first element is to be deleted and the chain is not empty. The final case is when an element other than the first is to be deleted from a nonempty chain.

```
template<class T>
bool Chain<T>::Find(int k, T& x) const
{// Set x to the k'th element in the chain.
 // Return false if no k'th; return true otherwise.
   if (k < 1) return false;
   ChainNode<T> *current = first;
   int index = 1;   // index of current
   while (index < k && current) {
      current = current->link;
      index++;
      }
   if (current) {x = current->data;
                 return true;}
   return false; // no k'th element
}
```

Program 3.11 Find the kth element of a chain

```
template<class T>
int Chain<T>::Search(const T& x) const
{// Locate x.  Return position of x if found.
 // Return 0 if x not in the chain.
   ChainNode<T> *current = first;
   int index = 1;   // index of current
   while (current && current->data != x) {
      current = current->link;
      index++;
      }
   if (current) return index;
   return 0;
}
```

Program 3.12 Search a chain

The code of Program 3.14 begins by handling the first case, which throws the exception OutOfBounds. For the remaining two cases, a pointer variable p is defined and initialized to point to the first node in the chain. If k is one, p is pointing to the kth node of the chain; the statement first = first->link removes this node from the chain. If k is more than one, a pointer variable q locates node k-1 of the chain. This is done using a for loop. When we exit this for loop, q points to node k-1 provided the chain has this many

```
template<class T>
void Chain<T>::Output(ostream& out) const
{// Insert the chain elements into the stream out.
   ChainNode<T> *current;
   for (current = first; current;
                          current = current->link)
      out << current->data << "   ";
}

// overload <<
template <class T>
ostream& operator<<(ostream& out, const Chain<T>& x)
   {x.Output(out); return out;}
```

Program 3.13 Output a chain

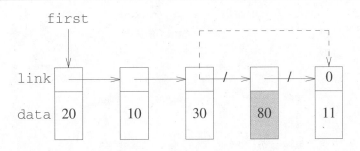

Figure 3.6 Deleting the fourth node

nodes. If the chain has fewer than k-1 nodes, q is zero. The conditional of the following if first checks to see whether q is zero. If it isn't zero, the conditional checks to see whether the chain has a kth node by inspecting the value of q->link. If both tests succeed, p is updated to point to the kth node. This kth node is removed from the chain by setting the pointer in the preceding node (i.e., node q) to point to the node just after node p.

When we exit the if - else construct, p points to the kth node and this node has been removed from the chain. We need to save the data field of p in the parameter x and free the space allocated to the node p.

To check the correctness of Program 3.14, try it on an initially empty list as well as on lists that contain at least one node. In addition, try out values of k, such as $k \le 0$, $k = n$, $k \ge n$, and $0 < k < n$, where n is the list length.

```
template<class T>
Chain<T>& Chain<T>::Delete(int k, T& x)
{// Set x to the k'th element and delete it.
 // Throw OutOfBounds exception if no k'th element.
   if (k < 1 || !first)
      throw OutOfBounds(); // no k'th

   // p will eventually point to k'th node
   ChainNode<T> *p = first;

   // move p to k'th & remove from chain
   if (k == 1) // p already at k'th
      first = first->link; // remove
   else { // use q to get to k-1'st
      ChainNode<T> *q = first;
      for (int index = 1; index < k - 1 && q;
                          index++)
         q = q->link;
      if (!q || !q->link)
         throw OutOfBounds(); // no k'th
      p = q->link; // k'th
      q->link = p->link;} // remove from chain

   // save k'th element and free node p
   x = p->data;
   delete p;
   return *this;
}
```

Program 3.14 Deletion from a chain

Insertion and deletion work in a similar way. To insert a new element immediately following the kth in a chain, we need to first locate the kth element and then insert a new node just after it. Figure 3.7 shows the link changes needed for the two cases $k = 0$ and $k \neq 0$. Solid pointers exist prior to the insert and broken ones following the insert. Program 3.15 gives the C++ code. Its complexity is O(k). Although the code for the insert operation invokes new, it does not attempt to catch any exception that might get thrown. We leave it to the user of Insert to catch this exception.

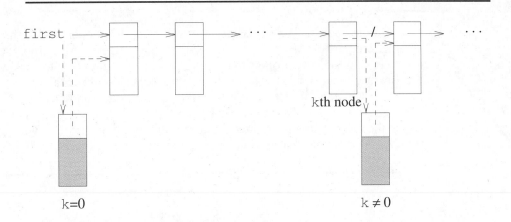

Figure 3.7 Insertion into a chain

```
template<class T>
Chain<T>& Chain<T>::Insert(int k, const T& x)
{// Insert x after the k'th element.
 // Throw OutOfBounds exception if no k'th element.
 // Pass NoMem exception if inadequate space.
   if (k < 0) throw OutOfBounds();
   // p will eventually point to k'th node
   ChainNode<T> *p = first;
   for (int index = 1; index < k && p;
                        index++)  // move p to k'th
      p = p->link;
   if (k > 0 && !p) throw OutOfBounds(); // no k'th

   // insert
   ChainNode<T> *y = new ChainNode<T>;
   y->data = x;
   if (k) {// insert after p
           y->link = p->link;
           p->link = y;}
   else {// insert as first element
           y->link = first;
           first = y;}
   return *this;
}
```

Program 3.15 Insert into a chain

3.4.3 Extensions to the Class `Chain`

In some applications of chains, we wish to perform operations other than those that are part of the abstract data type `LinearList` (ADT 3.1). So it is useful to extend the definition of the class `Chain` (Program 3.8) to include additional functions such as `Erase` (delete the nodes in the chain), `Zero` (set the `first` pointer to zero, but do not delete any node), and `Append` (add an element to the end of a chain). The function `Erase` (Program 3.16) is equivalent to the class destructor. In fact, with this definition of `Erase`, we may define the class destructor as simply a call to `Erase`.

```
template<class T>
void Chain<T>::Erase()
{// Delete all nodes in chain.
   ChainNode<T> *next;
   while (first) {
      next = first->link;
      delete first;
      first = next;}
}
```

Program 3.16 Deleting the nodes in a chain

The function `Zero` may be defined inline as in

```
void Zero() {first = 0;}
```

To append an element in $\Theta(1)$ time, we need to keep track of the last node in the chain by using a new private member `last` that is of type `ChainNode<T>*`. Program 3.17 gives the code for `Append`. For this code to work properly, it is necessary to add the statement

```
if (p == last) last = q;
```

just after the statement

```
p = q->link; // k'th
```

of `Delete` (Program 3.14) and the statement

```
if (!y->link) last = y; // new last element
```

just before the `return *this` statement of `Insert` (Program 3.15).

```
template<class T>
Chain<T>& Chain<T>::Append(const T& x)
{// Add x at right end.
   ChainNode<T> *y;
   y = new ChainNode<T>;
   y->data = x; y->link = 0;
   if (first) {// chain is not empty
               last->link = y;
               last = y;}
   else // chain is empty
        first = last = y;
   return *this;
}
```

Program 3.17 Add an element to the right end

3.4.4   A Chain Iterator Class

Suppose for a moment that `Output()` is not a member function of `Chain` and that `<<` is not overloaded for this class. To output the chain `X`, we would have to execute the code

```
int len = X.Length();
for (int i = 1; i <= len; i++) {
   X.Find(i,x);
   cout << x << ' ';}
```

The complexity of this code is $\Theta(n^2)$, while that of the member function `Output()` is $\Theta(n)$, where n is the chain length. Like the output function, many of the application codes that use chains require us to start at the first element and then examine the remainder from left to right. The use of an *iterator* that records the current position and advances one position right each time it is invoked facilitates this left-to-right examination of the chain elements.

The iterator (Program 3.18) for a chain has two public members `Initialize` and `Next`. `Initialize` returns a pointer to the data contained in the first node of the chain. It also initializes a private variable `location` to point to the first chain node. This variable keeps track of where we are in the chain. The member `Next` advances `location` to the next node in the chain and returns a pointer to its data field. Since the class `ChainIterator` accesses a private member `first` of the class `Chain`, it should be declared a friend of `Chain`.

```
template<class T>
class ChainIterator {
   public:
      T* Initialize(const Chain<T>& c)
            {location = c.first;
             if (location) return &location->data;
             return 0;}
      T* Next()
             {if (!location) return 0;
              location = location->link;
              if (location) return &location->data;
              return 0;}
   private:
      ChainNode<T> *location;
};
```

Program 3.18 Chain iterator class

As before, assume that `Output()` is not a member function of `Chain` and that `<<` is not overloaded. Using a chain iterator, we can output the chain in linear time with Program 3.19.

```
int *x;
ChainIterator<int> c;
x = c.Initialize(X);
while (x) {
   cout << *x << ' ';
   x = c.Next();
   }
cout << endl;
```

Program 3.19 Outputting the integer chain X using a chain iterator

3.4.5 Circular List Representation

Application codes that result from the use of chains can often be simplified and made to run faster by doing one or both of the following: (1) represent the linear list as a **singly linked circular list** (or simply **circular list**), rather than as a chain, and (2) add an additional node, called the **head node**, at the front. A circular list is obtained from a chain by linking the last node back to the first as in

Figure 3.8(a). Figure 3.8(b) shows a nonempty circular list with a head node, and Figure 3.8(c) shows an empty circular list with a head node.

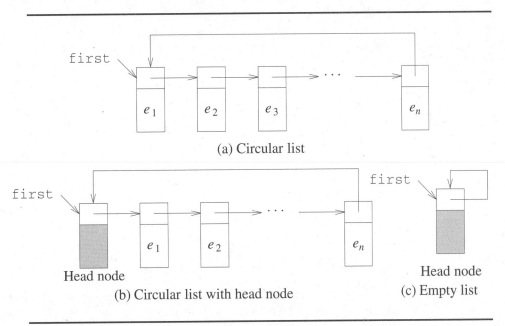

(a) Circular list

(b) Circular list with head node   (c) Empty list

Figure 3.8 Circular linked lists

The use of head nodes is a very common practice when linked lists are used, as their presence generally leads to simpler and faster programs. Program 3.20 gives the search operation for a circular list with a head node. The class `CircularList` is defined analogously to the class `Chain`. Although the complexity remains $O(n)$, the code is slightly simpler than that for a chain search (Program 3.12). Since Program 3.20 makes fewer comparisons on each iteration of the `for` loop, it will run slightly faster than Program 3.12 except possibly when we are looking for an element near the left end of the chain.

3.4.6 Comparison with Formula-Based Representation

Although the formula-based representation of a linear list requires only as much space as is needed to store the elements plus the list length, the chain and circular list representations require additional space for a link field. One link field is needed for every element in the list. The run time of the procedures to insert into and delete from a linear list will generally be smaller when the linked representation is used than when the formula-based representation is used. This expectation is easily justified when each element is many bytes long.

```
template<class T>
int CircularList<T>::Search(const T& x) const
{// Locate x in a circular list with head node.
   ChainNode<T> *current = first->link;
   int index = 1; // index of current
   first->data = x; // put x in head node

   // search for x
   while (current->data != x) {
      current = current->link);
      index++;
      }

   // are we at head?
   return ((current == first) ? 0 : index);
}
```

Program 3.20 Searching a circular linked list with a head node

We can use the linked schemes to represent many lists. Doing so does not decrease the space efficiency nor does it degrade run-time performance. For the formula-based representation to utilize space efficiently, we have to represent all lists in a single array and use two additional arrays to index into this one. Further, the procedures for insertion and deletion are more complex than those for the single list case, and they have a significantly inferior worst-case run time.

Using a formula-based representation, we can access the kth element of a list in $\Theta(1)$ time. In a linked list this operation requires $O(k)$ time.

3.4.7 Doubly Linked List Representation

For most applications of linear lists, the chain and/or circular list representations are adequate. However, in some applications it is convenient to have a pointer from each element to both the next and previous elements. A **doubly linked list** is an ordered sequence of nodes in which each node has two pointers: `left` and `right`. The `left` pointer points to the node (if any) on the left, and the `right` pointer points to the node (if any) on the right. Figure 3.9 shows the doubly linked list representation of the linear list (1, 2, 3, 4).

In C++ we can represent a doubly linked list using the class definition given in Program 3.21. This definition defines functions with respect to the left end. For example, `Find(k,x)` finds the kth element counting from the left. We can also define companion functions that work relative to the right end.

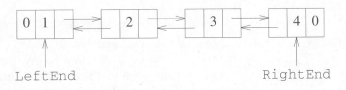

LeftEnd   RightEnd

Figure 3.9 A doubly linked list

```
template <class T>
class DoubleNode {
   friend Double<T>;
   private:
      T data;
      DoubleNode<T> *left, *right;
};

template<class T>
class Double {
   public:
      Double() {LeftEnd = RightEnd = 0;};
      ~Double();
      int Length() const;
      bool Find(int k, T& x) const;
      int Search(const T& x) const;
      Double<T>& Delete(int k, T& x);
      Double<T>& Insert(int k, const T& x);
      void Output(ostream& out) const;
   private:
      DoubleNode<T> *LeftEnd, *RightEnd;
};
```

Program 3.21 Class definition for doubly linked lists

We can enhance doubly linked lists by adding a head node at the left and/or right ends and by making them circular lists. In a nonempty circular doubly linked list, `LeftEnd->left` is a pointer to the right-most node (i.e., it equals `RightEnd`) and `RightEnd->right` is a pointer to the left-most node. So we can dispense with the variable `RightEnd` and simply keep track of the list using the variable `LeftEnd`.

3.4.8 Summary

This section introduced the following important concepts:

- *Chain*. This is a singly linked list of nodes. Let x be a chain. x is empty iff x.first = 0. If x is not empty, then x.first points to the first node in the chain. The first node links to the second; the second to the third; and so on. The link field of the last node is zero.

- *Singly linked circular list*. This differs from a chain only in that the last node links back to the first. When the circular list x is empty, x.first = 0.

- *Head node*. This is an additional node introduced into a linked list. The use of this additional node generally results in simpler programs, as we can often avoid treating the empty list as a special case. When a head node is used, every list (including the empty list) contains at least one node (i.e., the head node).

- *Doubly linked list*. A doubly linked list consists of nodes ordered from left to right. Nodes are linked from left to right using a pointer field (say) right. The right-most node has this field set to zero. Nodes are also linked from right to left using a pointer field (say) left. The leftmost node has this field set to zero.

- *Circular doubly linked list*. This differs from a doubly linked list only in that the left-most node uses its left field to point to the right-most node and the right-most node uses its right field to point to the left-most node.

EXERCISES

22. Write a copy constructor Chain<T>::Chain(const Chain<T>& C) to copy the elements of the chain C into new nodes. What is the complexity of your constructor?

23. Write a function to convert a linear list represented as an array into a chain. Use the Find function for members of LinearList and the Insert function for members of Chain. What is the time complexity of your function? Test the correctness of your code.

24. Write a function to convert a linear list represented as a chain into one represented as an array.

    (a) First use the Find function for members of Chain and the Insert function for members of LinearList. What is the time complexity of your function? Test the correctness of your code.

(b)   Now use a chain iterator. What is the time complexity of the new code? Test it using your own test data.

25.   Extend the class definition `Chain` to include functions to convert a `LinearList` to a `Chain` and vice versa. Specifically, write a function `FromList(L)` to convert a linear list `L` into a chain and another function `ToList(L)` to convert a chain into a linear list `L`. What is the time complexity of each function? Test the correctness of your code.

26.   Compare the run-time performance of the search functions of Programs 3.12 and 3.20. Do this for both worst-case and average run times using linear lists of size 100, 1000, 10,000, and 100,000. Present your times in tabular form and in graph form.

27.   (a)   Extend the definition of the class `Chain` to include a function `Reverse` to reverse the order of the elements in `x`. Do the reversal in-place and do not allocate any new nodes.

      (b)   What is the complexity of your function?

      (c)   Test the correctness of your function by compiling and then executing the code. Use your own test data.

28.   Do Exercise 27 but this time `Reverse` is not a member function of `Chain`. Instead, use the member functions of `Chain` to accomplish the reversal. Your new function will have two parameters `A` and `B`. `A` is the input chain, and `B` is set to be its reverse. Following the reversal, `A` is the empty chain.

29.   Let `A` and `B` be of type `Chain`.

      (a)   Write a function `Alternate` to create a new linear list `C` that contains elements alternately from `A` and `B` beginning with the first element of `A`. If you run out of elements in one of the lists, then append the remaining elements of the other list to `C`. The complexity of your code should be linear in the lengths of the two input lists.

      (b)   Show that your code has linear complexity.

      (c)   Test the correctness of your function by compiling and then executing the code. Use your own test data.

30.   Extend the class `Chain` to include a function `Alternate` that is similar to the function `Alternate` of Exercise 29. Your function should use the same physical nodes used by the chains `A` and `B`. Following a call to `Alternate`, the input chains `A` and `B` are empty.

      (a)   Write the code for `Alternate`. The complexity of your code should be linear in the lengths of initial chains.

      (b)   Show that your code has linear complexity.

(c)   Test the correctness of your code by compiling and then executing the code. Use your own test data.

31.   Let A and B be of type Chain. Assume that the elements of A and B are in sorted order (i.e., nondecreasing from left to right).

(a)   Write a function Merge to create a new sorted linear list C that contains all the elements in A and B.

(b)   What is the complexity of your function?

(c)   Test the correctness of your function by compiling and then executing the code. Use your own test data.

32.   Redo Exercise 31 but this time your function is to be a member of Chain and should use the same nodes as the two input chains use. Following the merge, the input chains are empty.

33.   Let C be of type Chain.

(a)   Write a function Split to create two chains A and B. A contains all elements in odd positions of C, and B contains the remaining elements. Your function should not change list C.

(b)   What is the complexity of your function?

(c)   Test the correctness of your function by compiling and then executing the code. Use your own test data.

34.   Write a function Split that is a member of the class Chain. The function is similar to Split of Exercise 33. However, it destroys the input chain and uses its nodes to construct A and B.

35.   Develop the class Circular. Objects of this type are circular linked lists, as in Figure 3.8, except the lists do not have a head node. Your must implement all the functions defined for the class Chain (Program 3.8). What is the time complexity of each function? Test the correctness of your code.

36.   Do Exercise 35 for the case when each list is to have a head node.

37.   Do Exercise 27 using circular lists instead of chains.

38.   Do Exercise 29 using circular lists instead of chains.

39.   Do Exercise 31 using circular lists instead of chains.

40.   Do Exercise 33 using circular lists instead of chains.

41.   Let x point to an arbitrary node in a circular list z.

(a)   Write a procedure to delete the element in node x. *Hint:* Since we do not know which node precedes x, it is difficult to delete the node x from the list; however, to delete the element in x, it is sufficient to replace the data field of x by the data field of the node y that follows it and then delete the node y.

(b) What is the complexity of your function?

(c) Test the correctness of your function by compiling and then executing the code. Use your own test data.

42. Do Exercise 35 using circular lists with head nodes instead of plain circular lists.

43. Do Exercise 27 using circular lists with head nodes instead of chains.

44. Do Exercise 29 using circular lists with head nodes instead of chains. The extra head node is to be freed.

45. Do Exercise 31 using circular lists with head nodes instead of chains. The extra head node is to be freed.

46. Do Exercise 33 using circular lists with head nodes instead of chains. You will need to allocate one new node, as each new list needs a head node.

47. Do Exercise 35 using doubly linked lists instead of plain circular lists.

48. Do Exercise 27 using doubly linked lists instead of chains.

49. Do Exercise 29 using doubly linked lists instead of chains.

50. Do Exercise 31 using doubly linked lists instead of chains.

51. Do Exercise 33 using doubly linked lists instead of chains.

52. Do Exercise 35 using doubly linked circular lists with a single head node.

53. Do Exercise 27 using doubly linked circular lists with a single head node.

54. Do Exercise 29 using doubly linked circular lists with a single head node. The extra head node is to be freed.

55. Do Exercise 31 using doubly linked circular lists with a single head node. The extra head node is to be freed.

56. Do Exercise 33 using doubly linked circular lists with a single head node. You will need to allocate one new node, as each new list needs a head node.

57. To efficiently support moving back and forth on a doubly linked list, we may extend the definition of the class `Double` (Program 3.21) by adding the private member `current` that records our current location in the list. The list of public functions is extended to include

(a) `ResetLeft`—Set `current` to `LeftEnd`.

(b) `ResetRight`—Set `current` to `RightEnd`.

(c) `Current(x)`—Return the current element in `x`. The function returns `false` if `current > length` and `true` otherwise.

(d) `End`—Return `true` if at the last (i.e., right-most) element of the list; return `false` otherwise.

(e) Front—Return `true` if at the first (i.e., left-most) element of the list; return `false` otherwise.

(f) Next—Move `current` to next element in list. Function returns `false` if there is no next element and `true` otherwise.

(g) Previous—Move `current` to the preceding element in list. Function returns `false` if there is no preceding element and `true` otherwise.

Write C++ code for the extended class. Test the correctness of your code using suitable test data.

58. Write code for the `Chain` member function `InsertionSort`, which uses the insertion sort method of Program 2.15 to reorder the chain elements into nondecreasing order. Do not create new nodes or delete old ones.

(a) What is the worst-case time complexity of your program? How much time does your program need if the elements are already in sorted order?

(b) Test the correctness of your program by compiling and then executing the code. Use your own test data.

59. Do Exercise 58 for the following sort methods (see Chapter 2 for descriptions):

(a) Bubble sort.

(b) Selection sort.

(c) Count or rank sort.

3.5 INDIRECT ADDRESSING

3.5.1 Representation

Indirect addressing is a combination of a formula-based and a linked representation. Using this representation method, we retain many of the advantages of the formula-based method—elements can be accessed by index in $\Theta(1)$ time, a sorted list can be searched in logarithmic time using a binary search, and so forth. At the same time we gain an important advantage of the linked method—elements are not physically moved during operations such as insert and delete. As a result, the time complexity of most operations on an indirectly addressed list is independent of the element size.

In indirect addressing we use a table of pointers to the list elements. A formula (such as Equation 3.1) is used to locate the position of the pointer to the desired element. The elements may themselves be stored in dynamically allocated nodes or in an array of nodes. Figure 3.10 shows a linear list of five elements that is represented using the indirect addressing table `table`. `table[i]` is a pointer to the `i+1`st element in the list, and `length` is the current size of the list.

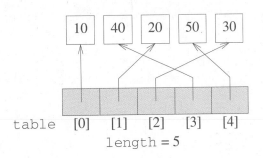

Figure 3.10 Indirect addressing

Although we can use Equation (3.1) to locate the pointer to the `i`th element in the list, this formula does not, by itself, locate the `i`th element. `table` provides one level of *indirection* in the addressing scheme for the elements of the list.

When the indirect addressing scheme of Figure 3.10 is compared with the linked representation of Figure 3.5, we see that both use pointer (or link) fields. In the linked scheme the pointers are in each node. In the indirect addressing scheme, the pointers are in the array `table` much like an index in a book. To locate an item in a book, we first look in the index. The index tells us where the item is.

When the elements are stored in dynamically allocated nodes, the class definition is as in Program 3.22. The private members are `table`, `length`, and `MaxSize`. `table` is an array of pointers to elements of type `T`; `MaxSize` is the size of this array and has a default value of 10; `length` is the current size of the list.

3.5.2 Operations

Program 3.23 gives the codes for the constructor and destructor. To create an empty linear list `x` of integers whose size is not to exceed 20, we use the declaration:

```
IndirectList<int> x(20);
```

```
template<class T>
class IndirectList {
   public:
       IndirectList(int MaxListSize = 10);
       ~IndirectList();
       bool IsEmpty() const {return length == 0;}
       int Length() const {return length;}
       bool Find(int k, T& x) const;
       int Search(const T& x) const;
       IndirectList<T>& Delete(int k, T& x);
       IndirectList<T>& Insert(int k, const T& x);
       void Output(ostream& out) const;
   private:
       T **table; // 1D array of T pointers
       int length, MaxSize;
};
```

Program 3.22 Class definition for an indirectly addressed list

```
template<class T>
IndirectList<T>::IndirectList(int MaxListSize)
{// Constructor.
   MaxSize = MaxListSize;
   table = new T *[MaxSize];
   length = 0;
}


template<class T>
IndirectList<T>::~IndirectList()
{// Delete the list.
   for (int i = 0; i < length; i++)
      delete table[i];
   delete [] table;
}
```

Program 3.23 Constructor and destructor for indirect addressing

The length of list x is given by `length` and `Length` is defined as an inline function in Program 3.22. `IsEmpty` is also defined as an inline function in Program 3.22. The kth element can be found by following the pointer in `table[k-1]` provided $1 \leq k \leq$ `length` and a search for x may be done by examining the list elements pointed to by `table[0]`, `table[1]`, $\cdots$. Program 3.24 gives the codes for `Find`. The complexity of `Length`, `IsEmpty`, and `Find` is $\Theta(1)$. Notice the similarity with the corresponding codes for the class `LinearList`.

```
template<class T>
bool IndirectList<T>::Find(int k, T& x) const
{// Set x to the k'th element in the list.
 // Return false if no k'th; return true otherwise.
   if (k < 1 || k > length) return false; // no k'th
   x = *table[k - 1];
   return true;
}
```

Program 3.24 Find operation for indirect lists

To delete the third element from the list of Figure 3.10, we need to free the space used by the third element, move the pointers in `table[3:4]` to `table[2:3]`, and reduce `length` by one. Program 3.25 is the indirect addressing counterpart of the linear list deletion functions given in Programs 3.4 and 3.14. Notice the similarity between Programs 3.4 and 3.25. The complexity of both Programs 3.14 and 3.25 is independent of the size of a list element. Regardless of whether each list element is 10 bytes long or 1000 bytes long, these functions to delete an item take the same time. Program 3.4 takes more time to delete an element when each element is 1000 bytes than when each is 10 bytes because it moves list elements, and each such move takes $\Theta(s)$ time where s is the size of an element.

```
template<class T>
IndirectList<T>& IndirectList<T>::Delete(int k, T& x)
{// Set x to the k'th element and delete it.
 // Throw OutOfBounds exception if no k'th element.
   if (Find(k, x)) {// move pointers k+1, ..., down
      for (int i = k; i < length; i++)
         table[i-1] = table[i];
      length--;
      return *this;
      }
   else throw OutOfBounds();
}
```

Program 3.25 Deletion from an indirect list

Suppose we wish to insert the element x between the second and third elements of the list of Figure 3.10. We need to create the configuration shown in
Figure 3.11. This configuration may be created by first moving the pointers in
table[2:4] one position to the right and then inserting a pointer to y at
table[2]. Program 3.26 inserts an element just after element k of a linear
list x. The worst-case asymptotic complexity of this program is seen to be the
same as that for Program 3.15 (insertion into a chain). That is, it is O(length).
The complexity of the formula-based insertion function of Program 3.5 is
O($s*$length) where s is the size of an element of type T.

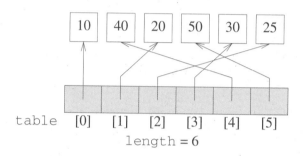

Figure 3.11 Insertion into an indirectly addressed list

```
template<class T>
IndirectList<T>& IndirectList<T>
                  ::Insert(int k, const T& x)
{// Insert x after the k'th element.
 // Throw OutOfBounds exception if no k'th element.
 // Pass NoMem exception if inadequate space.
   if (k < 0 || k > length) throw OutOfBounds();
   if (length == MaxSize) throw NoMem();
   // move one up
   for (int i = length-1; i >= k; i--)
      table[i+1] = table[i];
   table[k] = new T;
   *table[k] = x;
   length++;
   return *this;
}
```

Program 3.26 Insertion into an indirectly addressed list

EXERCISES

60. Provide an implementation of the `IndirectList` member function `Output`. Then use this member function to overload the operator `<<`. Test your codes.

61. Provide an implementation of the `IndirectList` member function `Search`. Test its correctness. What is the time complexity of your function?

62. Develop an iterator class for indirect lists. Model it after the class `ChainIterator` (Program 3.18). Test its correctness by using it to output a linear list from left to right.

63. (a) Write a binary search (see Program 2.30) function to search an indirectly addressed linear list. Assume that `*table[i]` ≤ `*table[i+1]` for all `i` ≤ `length-2`. The complexity of your function should be O(log (`length`)). Show that this is the case.

    (b) Test the correctness of your function by compiling and executing the code. Use your own test data.

    (c) How fast can a sorted chain be searched? Write a search function for chains that has this complexity.

64. Let `x` be an object of type `IndirectList`.

    (a) Write a function to sort `x` into nondecreasing order; after the sort `*table[i]` ≤ `*table[i+1]` for all `i` ≤ `length-2`. Base your function on the insertion sort method (see Program 2.15). The complexity of your function should be O(`length`^{2}) and independent of the size of each element. Show that this is the case.

    (b) Test the correctness of your function by compiling and executing the code. Use your own test data.

65. Do Exercise 64 for each of the following sort methods (see Chapter 2 for a description of each):

    (a) Bubble sort.

    (b) Selection sort.

    (c) Count sort.

66. You are given a type `T` array `element[0:length-1]` and an integer array `table[0:length-1]`. `table[]` is a permutation of [0, 1, $\cdots$, length-1] such that

    element[table[i]] ≤ element[table[i+1]]

    for 0 ≤ i ≤ length-2.

    (a)   Write a function to reorder `element[]` so that `element[i]` $\leq$ `element[i+1]` for all `i`. Your function must have time complexity O(s * `length`) where s is the size of each element. Its space complexity should be O(s). Show that this is the case.

    (b)   Test the correctness of your function.

3.6 SIMULATING POINTERS

In most applications, we can implement the desired linked and indirect addressing representations using dynamic allocation and C++ pointers. At times, however, it is more convenient and efficient to use an array of nodes and simulate C++ pointers by integers that are indexes into this array.

Suppose we use an array `node`, each element of which has the two fields `data` and `link`. The nodes are `node[0]`, `node[1]`, $\cdots$, `node[NumberOfNodes-1]`. We shall refer to `node[i]` as node `i`. Now if a chain `c` consists of nodes 10, 5, and 24 (in that order), we shall have `c = 10` (pointer to first node on the chain `c` is of type `int`); `node[10].link = 5` (pointer to second node on chain); `node[5].link = 24` (pointer to next node); and `node[24].link = -1` (indicating that node 24 is the last node on the chain). When drawing the chain, the links are drawn as arrows in the same way as when C++ pointers are used (Figure 3.12).

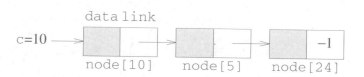

Figure 3.12 Chain using simulated pointers

To complete the simulation of pointers, we need to design procedures to allocate and deallocate a node. Nodes that are presently not in use will be kept in a **storage pool**. Initially, this pool contains all the nodes `node[0:NumberOfNodes-1]`. `Allocate` takes nodes out of this pool, one at a time. `Deallocate` puts nodes into this pool one at a time. Hence `Allocate` and `Deallocate`, respectively, perform deletes and inserts on the storage pool and are equivalent to the `delete` and `new` functions of C++. These functions can be performed efficiently if the storage pool is set up as a chain of nodes (as in Figure 3.13). This chain is called the **available space list**. It contains all nodes that are currently free. `first` is a variable of type `int` that points to the first node on this chain. Additions to and deletions from this chain are made at the front.

Figure 3.13 Available space list

To implement a simulated pointer system, we define the classes `SimNode` and `SimSpace` as in Program 3.27.

```
template <class T>
class SimNode {
   friend SimSpace<T>;
   private:
      T data;
      int link;
};

template <class T>
class SimSpace {
   public:
      SimSpace(int MaxSpaceSize = 100);
      ~SimSpace() {delete [] node;}
      int Allocate(); // allocate a node
      void Deallocate(int& i); // deallocate node i
   private:
      int NumberOfNodes, first;
      SimNode<T> *node; // array of nodes
};
```

Program 3.27 Class definition for simulated pointers

3.6.1   `SimSpace` Operations

Since all nodes are initially free, the available space list contains `NumberOf-Nodes` nodes at the time it is created. Program 3.28 initializes the available space list. Programs 3.29 and 3.30 perform the `Allocate` and `Deallo-cate` operations.

```
template<class T>
SimSpace<T>::SimSpace(int MaxSpaceSize)
{// Constructor.
   NumberOfNodes = MaxSpaceSize;
   node = new SimNode<T> [NumberOfNodes];
   // initialize available space list
   // create a chain of nodes
   for (int i = 0; i < NumberOfNodes-1; i++)
      node[i].link = i+1;
   // last node of chain
   node[NumberOfNodes-1].link = -1;
   // first node of chain
   first = 0;
}
```

Program 3.28 Initialize available space list

```
template<class T>
int SimSpace<T>::Allocate()
{// Allocate a free node.
   if (first == -1) throw NoMem();
   int i = first;            // allocate first node
   first = node[i].link;     // first points to next
                             // free node
   return i;
}
```

Program 3.29 Allocate a node using simulated pointers

```
template<class T>
void SimSpace<T>::Deallocate(int& i)
{// Free node i.
   // make i first node on avail list
   node[i].link = first;
   first = i;
   i = -1;
}
```

Program 3.30 Deallocate a node with simulated pointers

We readily see that the three functions have time complexity Θ(NumberOfNodes), $\Theta(1)$, and $\Theta(1)$, respectively. We can reduce the run time of the constructor (Program 3.28) by maintaining two available space lists. One contains all free nodes that haven't been used yet. The second contains all free nodes that have been used at least once. Whenever a node is deallocated, it is put onto the second list. When a new node is needed, we provide it from the second list in case this list is not empty. Otherwise, we attempt to provide it from the first list. Let first1 and first2, respectively, point to the front of the first and second space lists. Because of the way nodes are allocated, the nodes on the first list are node[i], first1 ≤ i < NumberOfNodes. The code to deallocate a node differs from Program 3.30 only in that all occurences of the variable first are replaced by first2. The new constructor and allocation codes are given in Programs 3.31 and 3.32. For these codes to work, we make the integer variables first1 and first2 private members of SimSpace.

```
template<class T>
SimSpace<T>::SimSpace(int MaxSpaceSize)
{// Dual available list constructor.
   NumberOfNodes = MaxSpaceSize;
   node = new SimNode<T> [NumberOfNodes];
   // initialize available space lists
   first1 = 0;
   first2 = -1;
}
```

Program 3.31 Initialization of dual available space list

```
template<class T>
int SimSpace<T>::Allocate()
{// Allocate a free node.
   if (first2 == -1) {// 2nd list empty
      if (first1 == NumberOfNodes) throw NoMem();
      return first1++;}
   // allocate first node of chain
   int i = first2;
   first2 = node[i].link;
   return i;
}
```

Program 3.32 Dual available space list version of Allocate

We expect the dual available space list of Programs 3.31 and 3.32 to provide better performance than the single space list version in most applications. We make the following observations:

- Program 3.32 takes the same time as does Program 3.29 except when the node is to be provided from the first list. This exception occurs at most NumberOfNodes times. The extra time spent on these cases is balanced by the savings during initialization. In fact, we will frequently need fewer than NumberOfNodes nodes (especially during debugging runs and in software designed to handle problems with widely varying instance characteristics), and the dual scheme will be faster.

- The reduction in the initialization time is very desirable in an interactive environment. The startup time for the program is significantly reduced.

- When the single list scheme is in use, chains can be built without explicitly setting the link fields in any but the last node because the appropriate link values are already present in the nodes (see Figure 3.13). This advantage can also be incorporated into the dual available space list scheme by writing a function Get(n) that provides a chain with n nodes on it. This function will explicitly set links only when nodes are taken from the first list.

- Chains can be disposed more efficiently using either of these schemes than when C++ pointers are used. For instance, if we know the front f and end e of a chain, all nodes on it are freed by the following statements:

  ```
  node[e].link = first; first = f;
  ```

- If c is a circular list, then all nodes on it are disposed in $\Theta(1)$ time using Program 3.33. Figure 3.14 shows the link changes that take place.

```
template<class T>
void SimSpace<T>::DeallocateCircular(int& c)
{// Deallocate the circular list c.
   if (c != -1) {
      int next = node[c].link;
      node[c].link = first;
      first = next;
      c = -1;
      }
}
```

Program 3.33 Deallocate a circular list

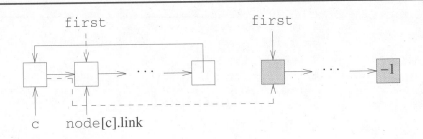

Figure 3.14 Deallocating a circular list

3.6.2 Chains Using Simulated Pointers

We may define a class for chains using the simulated space S (see Program 3.34). S is declared as a static member so that all simulated chains of the same type T share the same simulated space. Programs 3.35 to 3.38 give the code for the public methods other than Search and Output. The code assumes that SimChain has been declared a friend of both SimNode and SimSpace. Notice the similarity between these codes and the codes for the corresponding members of Chain. Program 3.39 gives a sample program that uses a simulated chain. In this program simul.h and schain.h are files that contain the codes for SimSpace and SimChain, respectively.

```
template<class T>
class SimChain {
    public:
        SimChain() {first = -1;}
        ~SimChain() {Destroy();}
        void Destroy(); // make list null
        int Length() const;
        bool Find(int k, T& x) const;
        int Search(const T& x) const;
        SimChain<T>& Delete(int k, T& x);
        SimChain<T>& Insert(int k, const T& x);
        void Output(ostream& out) const;
    private:
        int first;  // index of first node
        static SimSpace<T> S;
};
```

Program 3.34 Class definition for simulated chains

```
template<class T>
void SimChain<T>::Destroy()
{// Deallocate chain nodes.
   int next;
   while (first != -1) {
      next = S.node[first].link;
      S.Deallocate(first);
      first = next;}
}
template<class T>
int SimChain<T>::Length() const
{// Return the number of elements in the chain.
   int current = first,  // chain node cursor
       len = 0;          // element counter
   while (current != -1) {
      current = S.node[current].link;
      len++;}
   return len;
}
```

Program 3.35 Destructor and length using simulated pointers

```
template<class T>
bool SimChain<T>::Find(int k, T& x) const
{// Set x to the k'th element of the chain.
 // Return false if no k'th; return true otherwise.
   if (k < 1) return false;
   int current = first,  // cursor for chain nodes
       index = 1;        // index of current node
   // move current to k'th node
   while (index < k && current != -1) {
      current = S.node[current].link;
      index++;}
   // verify that we got to the k'th node
   if (current != -1) {x = S.node[current].data;
                       return true;}
   return false; // no k'th element
}
```

Program 3.36 Find using simulated pointers

```
template<class T>
SimChain<T>& SimChain<T>::Delete(int k, T& x)
{// Set x to the k'th element and delete it.
 // Throw OutOfBounds exception if no k'th element.

   if (k < 1 || first == -1)
      throw OutOfBounds(); // no k'th

   // p will eventually point to k'th node
   int p = first;

   // move p to k'th & remove from chain
   if (k == 1) // p already at k'th
      first = S.node[first].link; // remove from chain
   else { // use q to get to k-1'st
      int q = first;
      for (int index = 1; index < k - 1 && q != -1;
                          index++)
         q = S.node[q].link;

      // verify presence of k'th element
      if (q == -1 || S.node[q].link == -1)
         throw OutOfBounds(); // no k'th

      // make p point to k'th element
      p = S.node[q].link;

      // remove k'th element from chain
      S.node[q].link = S.node[p].link;
      }

   // save k'th element and free node p
   x = S.node[p].data;
   S.Deallocate(p);
   return *this;
}
```

Program 3.37 Delete using simulated pointers

```
template<class T>
SimChain<T>& SimChain<T>::Insert(int k, const T& x)
{// Insert x after the k'th element.
 // Throw OutOfBounds exception if no k'th element.
 // Pass NoMem exception if inadequate space.

   if (k < 0) throw OutOfBounds();

   // define a cursor p that will
   // eventually point to k'th node
   int p = first;

   // move p to k'th node
   for (int index = 1; index < k && p != -1;
                       index++)
      p = S.node[p].link;

   // verify presence of k'th element
   if (k > 0 && p == -1)
      throw OutOfBounds();

   // prepare a new node for insertion
   int y = S.Allocate();
   S.node[y].data = x;

   // insert the new node into the chain
   // first check if the new node is to be the
   // first one in the chain
   if (k) {// insert after p
           S.node[y].link = S.node[p].link;
           S.node[p].link = y;}
   else {// insert as first element
         S.node[y].link = first;
         first = y;}

   return *this;
}
```

Program 3.38 Insert using simulated pointers

```
#include <iostream.h>
#include "schain.h"

SimSpace<int> SimChain<int>::S;

void main(void)
{
    int x;
    SimChain<int> c;
    cout << "Chain length is " << c.Length() << endl;
    c.Insert(0,2).Insert(1,6);
    cout << "Chain length is " << c.Length() << endl;
    c.Find(1,x);
    cout <<"First element is " << x << endl;
    c.Delete(1,x);
    cout << "Deleted " << x << endl;
    cout << "New length is " << c.Length() << endl;
    cout << "Position of 2 is " << c.Search(2) << endl;
    cout << "Position of 6 is " << c.Search(6) << endl;
    c.Insert(0,9).Insert(1,8).Insert(2,7);
    cout << "Current chain is " << c << endl;
    cout << "Its length is " << c.Length() << endl;
}
```

Program 3.39 Using a simulated chain

EXERCISES

67. Develop an iterator class `SimIterator` for the class `SimChain`. See Program 3.18 for the definition of an iterator class defined for `Chains` (Program 3.8). `SimIterator` should contain the same functions as does `ChainIterator`. Write and test your code.

68. (a) Modify the class `SimSpace` so that `Allocate` returns a pointer to `node[i]` rather than the index `i`. Similarly, `Deallocate` takes as input a pointer to the node that is to be deallocated.

    (b) Rewrite the code for `SimChain` using the `SimSpace` codes of (a). Notice the similarity between your new code and that for the class `Chain`.

69. (a) Modify the definition of the class `SimNode` so that it contains a static member `S` of type `SimSpace<T>`. All nodes of the type `SimSpace<T>` can now share the same simulated space. Overload

the functions `new` and `delete` so as to get/return `SimNodes` from/to the simulated space `S`.

(b)   Suppose that `SimSpace` is implemented as in Exercise 68 and that `SimNode` is as in (a). Change the code for the class `Chain` (Program 3.8) so that it works properly using `SimNodes` in place of `ChainNodes`. Test your code and perform run-time measurements to determine which version of `Chain` is faster.

70.   Assume that a chain is represented using simulated pointers. The nodes are of type `SimNode`.

(a)   Write a procedure that uses the insertion sort method to sort the chain into nondecreasing order of the field `data`.

(b)   What is the time complexity of your code? In case it isn't $O(n^2)$, where n is the chain length, rewrite the code to have this complexity.

(c)   Test the correctness of your code.

71.   Do Exercise 70 using selection sort.

72.   Do Exercise 70 using bubble sort.

73.   Do Exercise 70 using rank sort.

74.   Calls to the functions `new` and `delete` are usually quite expensive and we can often improve the run time of our code by replacing the use of `delete` by a call to our own deallocating function which saves the deleted node on a chain of free nodes. Calls to `new` are replaced by calls to our own node allocator which invokes `new` only when the free node chain is empty. Modify the class `Chain` (Program 3.8) to operate in this way. Write functions to allocate and deallocate a node as described, and to initialize the chain of free nodes. Compare the run times of the two versions of the class `Chain`. Comment on the merits/demerits of the new implementation.

75.   Consider the operation XOR (exclusive OR, also written as $\oplus$) defined as below (for i and j binary):

$$i \oplus j = \begin{cases} 0 & \text{if } i \text{ and } j \text{ are identical} \\ 1 & \text{otherwise} \end{cases}$$

The XOR of two binary strings i and j is obtained by take the XOR of corresponding bits of i and j. For example, if $i = 10110$ and $j = 01100$, then $i \text{ XOR } j = i \oplus j = 11010$. Note that

$$a \oplus (a \oplus b) = (a \oplus a) \oplus b = b$$

and

$$(a \oplus b) \oplus b = a \oplus (b \oplus b) = a$$

This observation gives us a space-saving device for storing the right and left links of a doubly linked list. We assume that the available nodes are in an array `node` and that the node indexes are 1, 2, $\cdots$. So `node[0]` is not used. A `NULL` link can now be represented as a zero rather than as -1. Each node has two fields: `data` and `link`. If `l` is to the left of node `x` and `r` is to its right, then `link(x) = l` $\oplus$ `r`. For the left-most node `l = 0`, and for the right-most node `r = 0`. Let `(l, r)` be a doubly linked list represented in this way; `l` points to the left-most node and `r` points to the right-most node in the list.

(a) Write a function to traverse the doubly linked list `(l, r)` from left to right, listing out the contents of the `data` field of each node.

(b) Write a function to traverse the list from right to left, listing out the contents of the `data` field of each node.

(c) Test the correctness of your codes.

3.7 A COMPARISON

The table of Figure 3.15 compares the asymptotic complexity of performing various functions on a linear list, using each of the four representation methods discussed in this chapter. In this table s and n, respectively, denote `sizeof(T)` and the list length. Since the asymptotic complexity of the operations is the same when C++ pointers and simulated pointers are used, the table contains a single row for both.

Representation	Function		
	Find kth	Delete kth	Insert after kth
Formula (3.1)	$\Theta(1)$	$O((n-k)s)$	$O((n-k)s)$
Linked List (C++ & Simulated)	$O(k)$	$O(k)$	$O(k+s)$
Indirect	$\Theta(1)$	$O(n-k)$	$O(n-k)$

Figure 3.15 Comparison of four representation methods

Indirect addressing uses about the same space as does a chain. Both use more space than a formula-based representation. The time complexity of the functions that perform the linear list operations of insert and delete are independent of the size of list elements when either a chain or indirect addressing is used. However, this complexity is linearly dependent on the element size when a formula-based representation is in use. So if the size s of a list element is large, we expect the chain and indirect addressing representations to be superior for applications that perform many inserts and deletes.

We can determine the length of a list and access the kth element of a list in $\Theta(1)$ time using the formula-based and indirect-addressing representations. These operations take, respectively, $\Theta(\texttt{length})$ and $O(k)$ time when a chain is used. So the chain representation is inferior in applications where these two operations dominate.

From this discussion, we note that indirect addressing is the superior representation in applications in which the element size is large and in which we determine the list length, access the kth element, and insert and delete elements frequently. Note also that if the list is ordered by value, then we can peform a search in $O(\log n)$ time when we use a formula-based or indirect-addressing scheme. When we use a linked representation, this search takes $O(n)$ time.

3.8   APPLICATIONS

3.8.1   Bin Sort

Suppose that a chain maintains a list of students in a class. Each node has fields for the student's name, social security number, score on each assignment and test, and for the weighted aggregate score of all assignments and tests. Assume that all scores are integers in the range 0 through 100. We are to sort the nodes in order of the aggregate score. This sort takes $O(n^2)$ time (n is the number of students in the class) if we use one of the sort methods of Chapter 2. A faster way to accomplish the sort is to use **bin sort**. In a bin sort the nodes are placed into bins, each bin containing nodes with the same score. Then we combine the bins to create a sorted chain.

Figure 3.16(a) shows a sample chain with 10 nodes. This figure shows only the name and score fields of each node. The first field is the name, and the second is the score. For simplicity, we assume that each name is a single character and that the scores are in the range 0 through 5. We will need six bins, one for each of the possible score values 0 through 5. Figure 3.16(b) shows the 10 nodes distributed into bins by score. We can obtain this distribution by moving down the chain and examining the nodes one at a time. When a node is examined, it is placed into the bin that corresponds to its score. So the first node is placed into bin 2, the second into bin 4, and so forth. Now if we collect the nodes from the bins, beginning with those in bin 0, we will have a sorted list as shown in Figure 3.16(c).

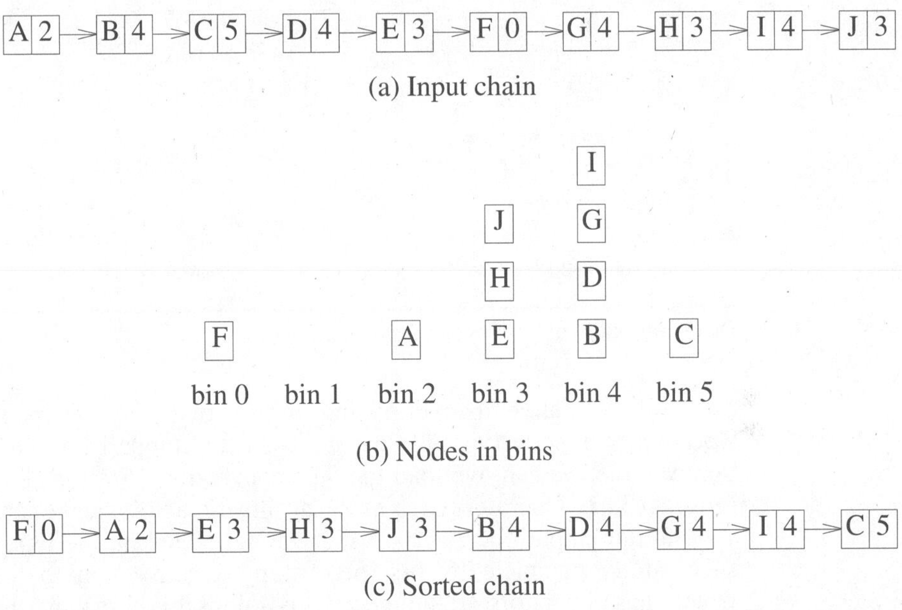

A|2 → B|4 → C|5 → D|4 → E|3 → F|0 → G|4 → H|3 → I|4 → J|3

(a) Input chain

```
                                    I
                        J           G
                        H           D
        F           A   E   B       C
      bin 0   bin 1  bin 2  bin 3  bin 4  bin 5
```

(b) Nodes in bins

F|0 → A|2 → E|3 → H|3 → J|3 → B|4 → D|4 → G|4 → I|4 → C|5

(c) Sorted chain

Figure 3.16 Bin sort example

To implement the bins, we note that each bin is a linear list of nodes. The number of nodes in a bin may vary from zero to as many as n. A simple way to represent the bins is as chains. Before we begin the node distribution step, all bins are empty.

For bin sort we need to be able to (1) move down the input chain deleting nodes from this chain and adding them to the chain for the appropriate bin and (2) collect and concatenate chains from the bins into a single sorted chain. If the input chain is of type Chain (Program 3.8), we can do (1) by successively deleting the first element from the chain and inserting it as the first element in the appropriate bin chain; we can do (2) by deleting the elements from the bins (beginning with the last bin) and inserting into the first position of an initially empty chain.

The data fields of the chain nodes will be of type Node (Program 3.40). The operators != and << have been overloaded, as these operators are used by the class Chain.

```
class Node {
   friend ostream& operator<<(ostream&, const Node &);
   public:
      int operator !=(Node x) const
         {return (score != x.score);}
   private:
      int score;
      char *name;
};

ostream& operator<<(ostream& out, const Node& x)
   {out << x.score << ' '; return out;}
```

Program 3.40 Possible node class for bin sort

An alternative to overloading is to provide a conversion from the type Node to a numeric type that can be used for comparison and output purposes. For example, we can overload the type conversion operator int() as shown in Program 3.41. Operators such as the arithmetic and logical operators +, /, <=, != and the output operator << that are undefined on the type Node can now successfully complete by first performing a conversion to the type int for which these operators are defined. This solution is somewhat more general than our earlier one in which we explicitly overloaded the operators != and <<, as now the code works even when we extend the class Chain to include functions that perform other operations on T->data.

```
class Node {
   public:
      // overload type conversion operator
      operator int() const {return score;}
   private:
      int score;
      char *name;
};
```

Program 3.41 An alternative way to handle operator overloading

We can combine both overloading approaches so that type conversion to int occurs only when the operator will fail without the type conversion. So we may, for example, use the definition of Program 3.42. Type conversion to int will now take place only for operators other than != and <<.

```
class Node {
    friend ostream& operator<<(ostream&, const Node &);
    public:
        int operator !=(Node x) const
        {return (score != x.score
                || name[0] != x.name[0]);}
        operator int() const {return score;}
    private:
        int score;
        char *name;
};

ostream& operator<<(ostream& out, const Node& x)
{
    out << x.score << ' ' << x.name[0] << ' ';
    return out;
}
```

Program 3.42 Another way to handle operator overloading

Program 3.43 gives the code for the bin sort function. It assumes that BinSort is a friend of Node. The sort function allows the exception NoMem to pass through in case there isn't enough space to create the bins. Each of the inserts and deletes performed in the two for loops takes $\Theta(1)$ time. Therefore, the complexity of the first for loop is $\Theta(n)$ where n is the length of the input chain, the complexity of the second for loop is $\Theta(n + \text{range})$, and the overall complexity of BinSort (when it is successful) is $\Theta(n + \text{range})$.

Bin Sort as a Member of the Class Chain
Efficiency concious readers have probably noticed that we can avoid much of the work done by function BinSort by developing BinSort as a member function of Chain. This approach enables us to use the same physical nodes when an element is a chain member and when it is in a bin and also eliminates all calls to new and delete (other than the ones associated with bin). Further, by keeping track of the front and end of each bin chain, we could concatenate the bin chains in the "collection phase," as shown in Program 3.44.

The chain for each bin begins with the node at the bottom of the bin and goes to the node at the top of the bin. Each chain has two pointers, bottom and top, to it. bottom[b] points to the node at the bottom of bin b while top[b] points to the node at the top of this bin. The initial configuration of empty bins is represented by setting bottom[b] = 0 for all bins (first for loop of Program 3.44). As nodes are examined, they are added to the top of the

```
void BinSort(Chain<Node>& X, int range)
{// Sort by score.
   int len = X.Length();
   Node x;
   Chain<Node> *bin;
   bin = new Chain<Node> [range + 1];

   // distribute to bins
   for (int i = 1; i <= len; i++) {
      X.Delete(1,x);
      bin[x.score].Insert(0,x);
      }

   // collect from bins
   for (int j = range; j >= 0; j--)
      while (!bin[j].IsEmpty()) {
         bin[j].Delete(1,x);
         X.Insert(0,x);
         }

   delete [] bin;
}
```

Program 3.43 Bin sort using class definitions

required bin (second `for` loop of Program 3.44). The code of the second `for` loop assumes that type conversion from `Node` to `int` has been defined so as to return the `score` field. The third `for` loop examines the bins beginning with bin 0 and concatenates the chains in the nonempty bins to form the sorted chain.

For the time complexity of `BinSort`, we see that the first and third `for` loops take $\Theta(\text{range})$ time and the second takes $\Theta(n)$ time. So the overall complexity is $\Theta(n+\text{range})$.

Notice that `BinSort` (Program 3.44) does not change the relative order of nodes that have the same score. For example, suppose that E, G, and H all have the score 3 and that E comes before G, which comes before H in the input chain. In the sorted chain, too, E comes before G, which comes before H. In some applications of sorting, the sort method must not change the relative order of elements that have the same value. A sort method that preserves the relative order of elements with the same value is called a **stable sort**.

```
template<class T>
void Chain<T>::BinSort(int range)
{// Sort by score.
   int b;  // bin index
   ChainNode<T> **bottom, **top;
   // initialize the bins
   bottom = new ChainNode<T>* [range + 1];
   top = new ChainNode<T>* [range + 1];
   for (b = 0; b <= range; b++)
      bottom[b] = 0;

   // distribute to bins
   for (; first; first = first->link) {// add to bin
      b = first->data;
      if (bottom[b]) {// bin not empty
         top[b]->link = first;
         top[b] = first;}
      else // bin empty
         bottom[b] = top[b] = first;
      }

   // collect from bins into sorted chain
   ChainNode<T> *y = 0;
   for (b = 0; b <= range; b++)
      if (bottom[b]) {// bin not empty
         if (y) // not first nonempty bin
            y->link = bottom[b];
         else // first nonempty bin
            first = bottom[b];
         y = top[b];}
   if (y) y->link = 0;

   delete [] bottom;
   delete [] top;
}
```

Program 3.44 Bin sort as a class member of Chain

A Generalization

Suppose each element of Node has the fields exam1, exam2, and exam3 plus additional fields. In one part of our program, we may wish to sort on the field exam1; at a later time we may wish to sort on exam3; and at an even later stage, by `exam1+exam2+exam3`. We can use the code of Program 3.44 to perform these three sorts if we define the data types `Node1`, `Node2`, and `Node3`. In `Node1`, the function `int()` is defined to return the value of the field `exam1`, in `Node2` it returns `exam2`, and in `Node3` it returns `exam1+exam2+exam3`. Before invoking `BinSort`, the data to be sorted will need to be copied into a chain of type `Node1` or `Node2` or `Node3`, depending on the kind of sort we want.

We can avoid the overhead of copying the elements from a chain of one type to another by defining `BinSort` so that it has an additional parameter `value`, which is a function that returns the value to be used for the sort. The syntax is

```
void Chain<T>::BinSort(int range, int(*value)(T& x))
```

The above statement declares the function `Chain<T>::BinSort` as one that has two parameters and returns nothing. The first parameter, `range`, is of type `int`. The second parameter, `value`, is the name of a function that has a single parameter `x` of type `T&` and returns an `int`.

When `BinSort` is defined as above, the statement

```
j = first->data;
```

of Program 3.44 needs to be changed to

```
j = value(first->data);
```

We can now sort using code such as that of Program 3.45.

3.8.2 Radix Sort

The bin sort method of Section 3.8.1 may be extended to sort, in $\Theta(n)$ time, n integers in the range 0 through $n^c - 1$ where c is a constant. Notice that if we use function `BinSort` with `range` $= n^c$, the sort complexity will be $\Theta(n + \text{range}) = \Theta(n^c)$. Instead of using `BinSort` directly on the numbers to be sorted, we shall decompose these numbers using some radix r. For example, the number 928 decomposes into the digits 9, 2, and 8 using the radix 10 (i.e., $928 = 9*10^2 + 2*10^1 + 8*10^0$). The most siginificant digit is 9 and the least is 8. 3725 has the radix 10 decomposition 3, 7, 2, and 5, while using the radix 60 its decomposition is 1, 2, and 5 (i.e., $(3725)_{10} = (125)_{60}$). In a **radix sort**, we decompose the numbers into digits using some radix r and then sort by digits.

```
inline int F1(Node& x) {return x.exam1;}
inline int F2(Node& x) {return x.exam2;}
inline int F3(Node& x)
    {return x.exam1 + x.exam2 + x.exam3;}

void main(void)
{
   Node x;
   Chain<Node> L;
   randomize();
   for (int i = 1; i <= 20; i++) {
       x.exam1 = i/2;
       x.exam2 = 20 - i;
       x.exam3 = random(100);
       x.name = i;
       L.Insert(0,x);}
   L.BinSort(10, F1);
   cout << "Sort on exam 1" << endl;
   cout << L << endl;
   L.BinSort(20, F2);
   cout << "Sort on exam 2" << endl;
   cout << L << endl;
   L.BinSort(130, F3);
   cout << "Sort on sum of exams" << endl;
   cout << L << endl;
}
```

Program 3.45 Sorting on different fields

Example 3.1 Suppose that we are sorting 10 integers in the range 0 through 999.
If we use `BinSort` with `range = 1000`, then the bin initialization takes 1000
steps, the node distribution takes 10 steps, and collecting from the bins takes
1000 steps. The total step count is 2010. Another approach is:

1. Use `BinSort` to sort the 10 numbers by their least significant digit.
    Since each digit ranges from 0 through 9, we have `range = 10`. Figure
    3.17(a) shows a sample 10-number chain, and Figure 3.17(b) shows the
    chain sorted by least significant digit.

2. Use bin sort to sort the chain from (1) by the second most significant digit.
    Again, `range = 10`. Since bin sort is a stable sort, nodes that have the
    same second digit remain sorted by the least significant digit. As a result,
    the chain is now sorted by the last two digits. Figure 3.17(c) shows our
    chain following this sort.

3. Use bin sort to sort the chain from (2) by the third most significant digit. (If a number has only two digits, then its third most significant digit is zero.) Since the sort on the most significant digit is a stable one, nodes with the same most significant digit remain sorted on the remaining two digits. As a result, the chain is sorted on the first three digits. Figure 3.17(d) shows the chain following this sort.

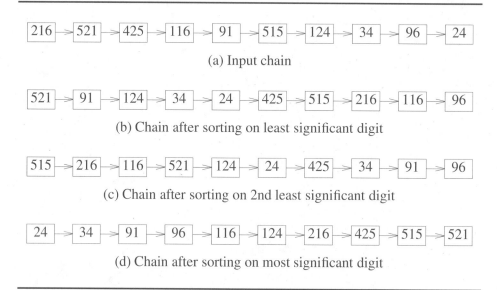

(a) Input chain

(b) Chain after sorting on least significant digit

(c) Chain after sorting on 2nd least significant digit

(d) Chain after sorting on most significant digit

Figure 3.17 Radix sort with $r = 10$ and $d = 3$

The preceding sorting scheme describes a radix 10 sort. The numbers to be sorted are decomposed into their decimal (or base 10) digits, and the numbers are sorted on these digits. Since each number has at most three digits, three sort passes are made. Each sort pass is done using a bin sort with `range = 10`. In each of these three bin sorts, we spend 10 steps in initializing the bins, 10 in distributing the records, and 10 in bin collection. The total number of steps is 90, which is less than when the 10 numbers are sorted using a single bin-sort with `range = 1000`. The single bin-sort scheme is really a radix sort with $r = 1000$.
∎

Example 3.2 Suppose that 1000 integers in the range 0 through $10^6 - 1$ are to be sorted. Using a radix of $r = 10^6$ corresponds to using `BinSort` directly on the numbers and takes 10^6 steps to initialize the bins, 1000 steps to distribute the numbers into bins, and another 10^6 to collect from the bins. The total number of steps is therefore 2,001,000. With $r = 1000$, the sort proceeds as follows:

1. Sort using the three least significant decimal digits of each number and use range = 1000.

2. Sort the result of (1) using the next three decimal digits of each number.

Each of the preceding sorts takes 3000 steps, so the sort is accomplished in a total of 6000 steps. When $r = 100$ is used, three bin sorts on pairs of decimal digits are performed. Each of these sorts takes 1200 steps, and the total steps needed for the sort become 3600. If we use $r = 10$, six bin sorts will be done, one on each decimal digit. The total number of steps will be $6(10 + 1000 + 10) = 6120$. For our example, we expect radix sort with $r = 100$ to be most efficient. ■

To implement the radix sorts of Examples 3.1 and 3.2, we need to decompose a number given a certain radix. This decomposing can be done using the division and mod operators. If we are performing a radix 10 decomposition, then the radix 10 digits may be computed (from least significant to most significant) using the following expressions:

$$x\%10; \ (x\%100)/10; \ (x\%1000)/100; \ \cdots$$

When $r = 100$, these expressions become

$$x\%100; \ (x\%10000)/100; \ (x\%1000000)/10000; \ \cdots$$

For a general radix r, the expressions are

$$x\%r; \ (x\%r^2)/r; \ (x\%r^3)/r^2; \ \cdots$$

When we use the radix $r = n$ to decompose n integers in the range 0 through $n^c - 1$, the number of digits is c. So the n numbers can be sorted using c bin sort passes with range = n. The time needed for the sort is $\Theta(cn) = \Theta(n)$ as c is a constant.

3.8.3 Equivalence Classes

Definitions and Motivation

Suppose we have a set $U = \{1, 2, \cdots, n\}$ of n elements and a set $R = \{(i_1, j_1), (i_2, j_2), \cdots, (i_r, j_r)\}$ of r relations. The relation R is an **equivalence relation** iff the following conditions are true:

• $(a,a) \in R$ for all a (the relation is reflexive).

• $(a,b) \in R$ iff $(b,a) \in R$ (the relation is symmetric).

• $(a,b) \in R$ and $(b,c) \in R$ imply that $(a,c) \in R$. In other words, the relation is transitive.

Often when we specify an equivalence relation R, we shall omit some of the pairs in R. The omitted pairs may be obtained by applying the reflexive, symmetric, and transitive properties of an equivalence relation.

Example 3.3 Suppose $n = 14$ and $R = \{(1,11), (7,11), (2,12), (12,8), (11,12), (3,13), (4,13), (13,14), (14,9), (5,14), (6,10)\}$. We have omitted all pairs of the form (a,a) because these pairs are implied by the reflexive property. Similarly, we have omitted all symmetric pairs. Since $(1,11) \in R$, the symmetric property requires $(11,1) \in R$. Other omitted pairs are obtained by applying the transitive property. For example, $(7,11)$ and $(11,12)$ imply $(7,12)$. ■

Two elements a and b are equivalent if $(a,b) \in R$. An **equivalence class** is defined to be a maximal set of equivalent elements. Maximal means that no element outside the class is equivalent to an element in the class.

Example 3.4 Consider the equivalence relation of Example 3.3. Since elements 1 and 11, and 11 and 12 are equivalent, elements 1, 11, and 12 are equivalent. They are therefore in the same class. These three elements do not, however, form an equivalence class, as they are equivalent to other elements (e.g., 7). So $\{1, 11, 12\}$ is not a maximal set of equivalent elements. The set $\{1, 2, 7, 8, 11, 12\}$ is an equivalence class. The relation R defines two other equivalence classes: $\{3, 4, 5, 9, 13, 14\}$ and $\{6, 10\}$. ■

In the **offline equivalence class** problem, we are given n and R and are to determine the equivalence classes. Notice that each element will be in exactly one equivalence class. In the **online equivalence class** problem, we begin with n elements, each in a separate equivalence class. We are to process a sequence of the operations: (1) `Combine(a,b)` ... combine the equivalence classes that contain elements `a` and `b` into a single class and (2) `Find(e)` ... determine the class that currently contains element `e`. The purpose of the find operation is to determine whether two elements are in the same class. Hence the find operation is to be implemented to return the same answer for elements in the same class and different answers for elements in different classes.

We can write the combine operation in terms of two `Finds` and a `Union` that actually takes two different classes and makes one. So `Combine(a,b)` is equivalent to

```
i = Find(a); j = Find(b);
if (i != j) Union(i,j);
```

Notice that with the find and union operations, we can add new relations to R. For instance, to add the relation (a,b), we determine whether a and b are already in the same class. If they are, then the new relation is redundant. If they aren't, then we perform a `Union` on the two classes that contain a and b.

In this section we are concerned primarily with the online version which is also often referred to as the **union-find** problem. Although the solutions developed in this section are rather simple, they are not the most efficient. Faster solutions are developed in Section 8.10.2. A fast solution for the offline equivalence problem is developed in Section 5.5.5.

Example 3.5 [*Scheduling with Deadlines*] A certain factory has a single machine that is to perform n tasks. Task i has an integer release time r_i and an integer deadline d_i. The completion of each task requires one unit of time on this machine. A **feasible schedule** is an assignment of tasks to time slots on the machine such that task i is assigned to a time slot between its release time and deadline and no slot has more than one task assigned to it.

Consider the following four tasks:

Task	1	2	3	4
Release time	0	0	1	2
Deadline	4	4	2	3

Tasks 1 and 2 are released at time 0, task 3 is released at time 1, and task 4 is released at time 2. The following task-to-slot assignment is a feasible schedule: do task 1 from 0 to 1; task 3 from 1 to 2; task 4 from 2 to 3; and task 2 from 3 to 4. An intuitively appealing method to construct the schedule is

1. Sort the tasks into nonincreasing order of release time.

2. Consider the tasks in this nonincreasing order. For each task determine the free slot nearest to, but not after, its deadline. If this free slot is before the task's release time, fail. Otherwise, assign the task to this slot.

Exercise 83 asks you to prove that the strategy just described fails to find a feasible schedule only when such a schedule does not exist.

The online equivalence class problem can be used to implement step (2). For this step, let d denote the latest deadline of any task. The usable time slots are of the form "from $i - 1$ to i" where $1 \leq i \leq d$. We shall refer to these usable slots as slots 1 through d. For any slot a, define *near*(a) as the largest i such that $i \leq a$ and slot i is free. If no such i exists, define *near*$(a) =$ *near*$(0) = 0$. Two slots a and b are in the same equivalence class iff *near*$(a) =$ *near*(b).

Prior to the scheduling of any task, *near*$(a) = a$ for all slots and each slot is in a separate equivalence class. When slot a is assigned a task in step (2), *near* changes for all slots b with *near*$(b) = a$. For these slots the new value of *near* is *near*$(a-1)$. Hence when slot a is assigned a task, we need to perform a Union on the equivalence classes that currently contain slots a and $a - 1$. If with each equivalence class E we retain, in $N[E]$, the value of *near* of its members, then *near*(a) is given by $N[\text{Find}(a)]$. (Assume that the class name is taken to be whatever the Find operation returns.) ∎

Example 3.6 [*From Wires to Nets*] An electronic circuit consists of components, pins, and wires. Figure 3.18 shows a circuit with the three components A, B, and C. Each wire connects a pair of pins. Two pins a and b are **electrically equivalent** iff they are either connected by a wire or there is a sequence $a_1, a_2,$ ... a_k of pins such that a, a_1; a_1, a_2; a_2, a_3; $\cdots$; a_{k-1}, a_k; and a_k, b are all connected by wires. A **net** is a maximal set of electrically equivalent pins. *Maximal* means that no pin outside the net is electrically equivalent to a pin in the net.

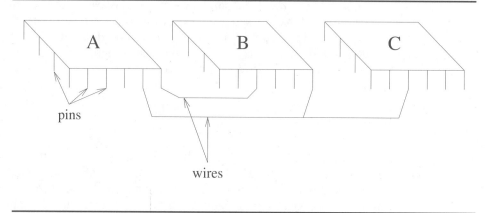

Figure 3.18 A 3-chip circuit on a printed circuit board

Consider the circuit shown in Figure 3.19. In this figure only the pins and wires have been shown. The fourteen pins are numbered 1 through 14. Each wire may be described by the two pins that it connects. For instance, the wire connecting pins 1 and 11 is described by the pair (1,11), which is equivalent to the pair (11,1). The set of wires is {(1,11), (7,11), (2,12), (12,8), (11,12), (3,13), (4,13), (13,14), (14,9), (5,14), (6,10)}. The nets are {1, 2, 7, 8, 11, 12}, {3, 4, 5, 9, 13, 14} and {6, 10}.

In the **offline net finding problem**, we are given the pins and wires and are to determine the nets. This problem is modeled by the offline equivalence problem with each pin being a member of U and each wire a member of R.

In the **online** version we begin with a collection of pins and no wires and are to perform a sequence of operations of the form (1) add a wire to connect pins a and b and (2) find the net that contains pin a. The purpose of the find operation is to determine whether two pins are in the same net or in different nets. This version of the net problem may be modeled by the online equivalence class problem. Initially, there are no wires, and we have $R = \varnothing$. The net find operation corresponds to the equivalence class Find operation and adding a wire (a, b) corresponds to Combine(a,b). ∎

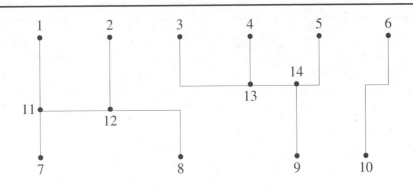

Figure 3.19 Circuit with pins and wires shown

First Solution

A simple solution to the online equivalence class problem is to use an array `E` and let `E[e]` be the class that currently contains element `e`. The functions to initialize, union, and find take the form given in Program 3.46. `n` is the number of elements. `n` and `E` are both assumed to be global variables. To unite two different classes, we arbitrarily pick one of these classes and change the `E` values of all elements in this class to correspond to the `E` values of the elements of the other class. The `Initialize` and `Union` functions have complexity $\Theta(n)$ (we assume that `new` does not throw an exception when invoked by `Initialize`), and the complexity of `Find` is $\Theta(1)$. From Examples 3.5 and 3.6, we see that in any application of these functions, we will perform one initialization, u unions, and f finds. The time needed for all of these operations is $\Theta(n+u*n+f) = \Theta(u*n+f)$.

Second Solution

The time complexity of the union operation can be reduced by keeping a chain for each equivalence class because now we can find all elements with `E[k]` equal to `j` by going down the chain for class `j`, rather than by examining all `E` values. In fact, if each equivalence knows its size, we can choose to change the `E` values of the smaller class and perform the the union operation even faster. By using simulated pointers, we get quick access to the node that represents element `e`. We adopt the following conventions:

- `EquivNode` is a class with private data members `E`, `size`, and `link`. Each of these data members is of type `int`.

- The functions `Initialize`, `Union`, and `Find` are friends of `EquivNode`.

```
void Initialize(int n)
{// Initialize n classes with one element each.
   E = new int [n + 1];
   for (int e = 1; e <= n; e++)
      E[e] = e;
}

void Union(int i, int j)
{// Union the classes i and j.
   for (int k = 1; k <= n; k++)
      if (E[k] == j) E[k] = i;
}

int Find(int e)
{// Find the class that contains element i.
   return E[e];
}
```

Program 3.46 Online equivalence class functions using arrays

- Nodes node[1:n] is used to represent the n elements together with the equivalence class chains.

- node[e].E is both the value to be returned by Find(e) and a pointer to the first node in the chain for class node[e].E.

- node[e].size is defined only if e is the first node on a chain. In this case it gives the number of nodes on the chain that begins at node[e].

- node[e].link gives the next node on the chain that contains node e. Since the nodes in use are numbered 1 through n, a NULL pointer can be simulated by zero rather than by -1.

Program 3.47 gives the new code for Initialize and Union. The code for Find is the same as in Program 3.46.

Since an equivalence class is of size $O(n)$, the complexity of the union operation is $O(n)$ when chains are used. The complexity of the initialization and find operations remain $\Theta(n)$ and $\Theta(1)$, respectively. To determine the complexity of performing one initialization and a sequence of u unions and f finds, we shall use the following lemma.

```
void Initialize(int n)
{// Initialize n classes with one element each.
   node = new EquivNode [n + 1];

   for (int e = 1; e <= n; e++) {
      node[e].E = e;
      node[e].link = 0;
      node[e].size = 1;
      }
}

void Union(int i, int j)
{// Union the classes i and j.

   // make i smaller class
   if (node[i].size > node[j].size)
      Swap(i,j);

   //  change E values of smaller class
   int k;
   for (k = i; node[k].link; k = node[k].link)
      node[k].E = j;
   node[k].E = j; // last node in chain

   // insert chain i after first node in chain j
   // and update new chain size
   node[j].size += node[i].size;
   node[k].link = node[j].link;
   node[j].link = i;
}

int Find(int e)
{// Find the class that contains element i.
   return node[e].E;
}
```

Program 3.47 Online equivalence class functions using chains

Lemma 3.1 If we start with n classes that have one element each and perform u unions, then

(a)   No class has more than $u + 1$ elements.

(b)   At least $n - 2u$ singleton classes remain.

(c) $u < n$.

Proof See Exercise 81. ∎

The complexity of the initialize and f finds is $\Theta(n+f)$. For the u unions, we note that the cost of each union is Θ(size of smaller class). Let `i` denote the smaller class in the union operation. During the union, each element of `i` is moved from class `i` to class `j`. The number of elements moved is therefore `size[i]`, which equals the size of the smaller class and also equals the work done during the union. Therefore, the complexity of the u unions is given by the total number of element moves. Following a move, each element of class `i` is in a class whose size is at least twice that of `i` (as `size[i]` $\leq$ `size[j]` prior to the move and the class size is `size[i]` + `size[j]` after the move). Therefore, since at the end no class has more than $u+1$ elements (Lemma 3.1(a)), no element can be moved more than $\log_2(u+1)$ times during the u unions. Furthermore, from Lemma 3.1(b), at most $2u$ elements can move. So the total number of element moves cannot exceed $2u\log_2(u+1)$. As a result, the time needed to perform the u unions is $O(u\log u)$. The complexity of the initialization and the sequence of u unions and f finds is therefore $O(n+u\log u+f)$.

3.8.4   Convex Hull

A **polygon** is a closed planar figure with three or more straight edges. The polygon of Figure 3.20(a) has six edges and that of Figure 3.20(b) has eight. A polgon **contains** all points that are either on its edges or inside the region it encloses. A polygon is **convex** iff all line segments that join two points on or in the polygon include no point that is outside the polygon. The polygon of Figure 3.20(a) is convex, while that of Figure 3.20(b) is not. Figure 3.20(b) shows two line segments (broken lines) whose endpoints are on or in the polygon. Both of these segments contain points that are outside the polygon.

The **convex hull** of a set S of points in the plane is the smallest convex polygon that contains all these points. The corners of this polygon are the **extreme points** of S. Figure 3.21 shows 13 points in the plane. The convex hull is the polygon defined by the solid lines. The extreme points have been identified by circles. When all points of S lie on a straight line (i.e., they are colinear), we have a degenerate case for which the convex hull is defined to be the smallest straight line that includes all the points.

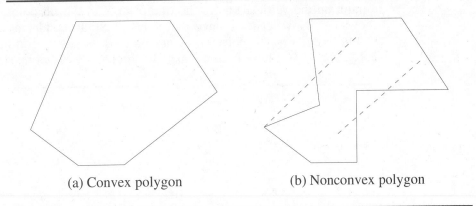

(a) Convex polygon   (b) Nonconvex polygon

Figure 3.20 Convex and nonconvex polygons

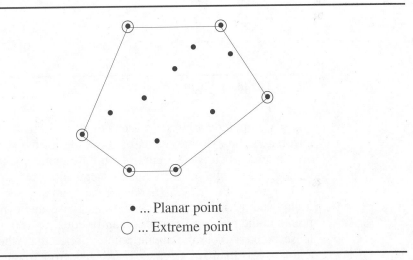

• ... Planar point
○ ... Extreme point

Figure 3.21 Convex hull of planar points

   The problem of finding the convex hull of a set of points in the plane is a fundamental problem in computational geometry. The solutions to several other problems in computational geometry (e.g., find the smallest rectangle that encloses a set of points in the plane) require the computation of the convex hull. In addition, the convex hull finds application in image processing and statistics.
   Suppose we pick a point X in the interior of the convex hull of S and draw a vertical line downwards from X (Figure 3.22(a)). Exercise 85 describes how we can select the point X. Let a_i be the (polar) angle made by this line and the

line from X to the ith point of S. a_i is measured by going counterclockwise from a point on the vertical line to the line from X to the ith point. Figure 3.22(a) shows a_2. Now let us arrange the points of S into nondecreasing order of a_i. Points with the same polar angle are ordered by distance from X. In Figure 3.22(a), the points have been numbered 1 through 13 in the stated order.

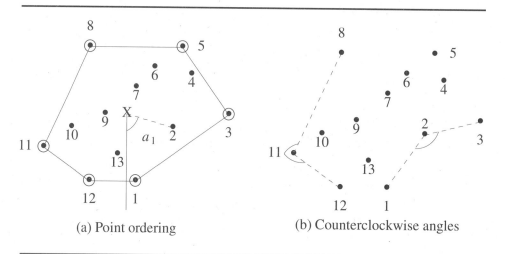

(a) Point ordering   (b) Counterclockwise angles

Figure 3.22 Identifying extreme points

A counterclockwise sweep of the vertical line downwards from X encounters the extreme points of S in order of the polar angle a_i. If u, v, and w are three consecutive extreme points in counterclockwise order, then the counterclockwise angle made by the line segments from u to v and w to v is more than 180 degrees. (Figure 3.22(b) shows the counterclockwise angle made by points 8, 11, and 12.) When the counterclockwise angle made by three consecutive points in the polar order is less than or equal to 180 degrees, then the second of these points is not an extreme point. Notice that when the angle made by u, v, and w is less than 180 degrees, if we walk from u to v to w, we make a right turn at v. When we walk counterclockwise around a convex polygon, all our turns are left turns. The observations made so far result in the algorithm of Figure 3.23, which finds the extreme points and convex hull of S.

Step 1 of the algorithm handles the degenerate cases when the number of points in S is zero or one, as well as when all points of S are colinear. This step can be done in $\Theta(n)$ time where n is the number of points in S. For the colinearity test, we select any two points and compute the equation of the line through them. Next we examine the remaining $n-2$ points and determine whether they lie on this line. During this process, we can also determine the endpoints of the shortest line that includes all points in case they are colinear.

Step 1: [Handle degenerate cases]
If S has fewer than three points, return S.
If all points lie on a straight line, compute the endpoints of the smallest line that includes all points of S and return these two points.

Step 2: [Sort by polar angle]
Find a point X that is inside the convex hull of S.
Sort S by polar angle and within polar angle by distance from X.
Create a doubly linked circular list of points using the above order. Let `right` link to the next point in the order and `left` link to the previous point.

Step 3: [Eliminate nonextreme points]
Let `p` be the point that has the smallest y-coordinate (break a tie, if any, by selecting the one with largest x-coordinate).

```
for (x = p, rx = point to the right of x; x != rx; ) {
    rrx = point to the right of rx;
    if (angle formed by x, rx, and rrx is ≤ 180 degrees) {
        delete rx from the list;
        rx = x; x = point on left of rx;}
    else {x = rx; rx = rrx;}
}
```

Figure 3.23 Pseudocode to find the convex hull of S

In step 2 the points are ordered by polar angle and collected into a doubly linked list, because in step 3 we shall be eliminating points that are not extreme points and also moving backwards on the list. Both operations are straightforward in a doubly linked list. Exercise 85 asks you to explore the use of a singly linked list. Because of the sort, this step takes $O(n^2)$ time if we use any of the sorts from Chapter 2. In Chapters 9 and 14, we shall see that we can sort in $O(n \log n)$ time. As a result, the complexity of step 2 is counted as $O(n \log n)$.

In step 3 we repeatedly examine sets of three consecutive points in counterclockwise order and check whether the angle they make is less than or equal to 180 degrees. If it is, then the middle point `rx` is not an extreme point and is eliminated. If the angle exceeds 180 degrees, `rx` may or may not be an extreme point and we advance `x` to the next vertex `rx`. When the `for` loop is exited, every point `x` on the doubly linked circular list satisfies the property that the angle made by `x`, `rx`, and `rrx` exceeds 180 degrees. Hence all of these points are extreme points. By going around the list using the `right` fields, we traverse the boundary of the convex hull in counterclockwise order. We begin at the point with lowest y, as this point must be in the convex hull.

For the complexity of step 3, we note that following each angle check in the `for` loop either (1) a vertex `rx` is eliminated and `x` is moved back one node on the list or (2) `x` is moved forward on the list. Since the number of eliminated vertices is O(n), `x` can be moved back at most a total of O(n) nodes. Hence we can be in case (2) only O(n) times, so the `for` loop is iterated O(n) times. Since an angle check takes $\Theta(1)$ time, the complexity of step 3 is O(n). As a result, we can find the convex hull of n points in O($n\log n$) time.

EXERCISES

76. Is Program 3.43 a stable sort program?

77. Compare the run times of the bin sort functions given in Programs 3.43 and 3.48. Use n = 10,000, 50,000, and 100,000. What can you say about the overhead introduced by using the class `Chain`?

78. You are given a chain with n nodes of type `ChainNode<Node>`. The chain is to be sorted on the field `score`.

    (a) Write a function to accomplish the sort using the radix sort method. The chain, radix r, and number of digits d in the radix r decomposition are inputs to your function. The complexity of your function should be $\Theta(d(r+n))$. Show that this is the case.

    (b) Test the correctness of your function by compiling and executing it with your own test data.

    (c) Compare the performance of your function with one that performs a linked insertion sort. Do so for n = 100, 1000, and 10,000; r = 10; and $d = 3$.

79. (a) Write a function to sort n integers in the range 0 through $n^c - 1$ using the radix sort method and $r = n$. The complexity of your function should be $\Theta(cn)$. Show that this is the case. Assume the input is a chain.

    (b) Test the correctness of your function.

    (c) Measure the run time of your function for n = 10, 100, 1000, and 10,000 and c = 2. Present your results in tabular form and in graph form.

80. You are given a pile of n card decks. Each card has three fields: deck number, suit, and face value. Since each deck has at most 52 cards (some cards may be missing from a deck), the pile has at most $52n$ cards. You may assume there is at least one card from each deck. So the number of cards in the pile is at least n.

(a) Explain how to sort this pile by deck number, within deck number by suit, and within suit by face value. You should make three bin sort passes over the pile to accomplish the sort.

(b) Write a program to input n and a card pile and to output the sorted pile. You should represent the card pile as a linked chain. Each node of the chain has the fields: `deck`, `suit`, `face`, and `link`. The complexity of your program should be $\Theta(n)$. Show that this is the case.

(c) Test the correctness of your program.

81. Prove Lemma 3.1.

82. Write a C++ program for the online net finding problem of Example 3.6. Model the problem as the online equivalence class problem and use the chain method. Test the correctness of your program.

83. Prove that the strategy outlined in Example 3.5 fails to find a feasible schedule only when such a schedule does not exist.

84. Write a C++ program for the scheduling problem of Example 3.5. Model the problem as the online equivalence class problem and use the chain method. Test the correctness of your program.

85. [*Convex Hull*]

(a) Let u, v, and w be three points in the plane. Assume that they are not colinear. Write a function to find a point inside the triangle formed by these three points.

(b) Let S be a set of points in the plane. Write a function to determine whether all the points are colinear. In case they are, your function should compute the endpoints of the shortest line that includes all the points. In case the points are not colinear, then you should find three noncolinear points from the given point set. You can use these three points together with your function for part (a) to determine a point inside the convex hull of S. The complexity of your function should be $\Theta(n)$. Show that this is the case.

(c) Use the codes of (a) and (b) to refine Figure 3.23 into a C++ program that inputs S and outputs the convex hull of S. During input, the points may be collected into a doubly linked list that is later sorted by polar angle. For the sort step you may use one of the sort methods of Chapter 2, or if you have access to an $O(n\log n)$ sort, you may use it.

(d) Write additional convex hull programs that replace the use of a doubly linked list with (i) a chain and (ii) a formula-based linear list.

(e) Test the correctness of your convex hull programs.

86. Let c be a linked chain. Suppose that as we move to the right, we reverse the direction of the chain pointers; therefore, when we are at node p, the chain is split into two chains. One is a chain that begins at p and goes to the last node of c. The other begins at the node l that precedes p in chain c and goes back to the first node c. Initially, p = c and l = 0.

    (a) Draw a chain with six nodes and show the configuration when p is at the third node and l is at the second.

    (b) Write a function to advance l and p by one node.

    (c) Write a function to move l and p back by one node.

    (d) Test your codes using suitable data.

87. Do Exercise 85 using a singly linked list. Use the ideas of Exercise 86 to ensure that the for loop of step 3 of Figure 3.23 has complexity $\Theta(n)$.

88. Use the ideas of Exercise 86 to extend the class definition Chain of Program 3.8 so that it is possible to efficiently move back and forth on a chain. For this, add the private members l and p as in Exercise 86 and add the following public methods:

    (a) Reset—Set p to first and l to 0.

    (b) Current(x) —Return the element pointed to by p in x; throw an exception if the operation fails.

    (c) End—Return true if p is at the last element of the list; return false otherwise.

    (d) Front—Return true if p is at the first element of the list; return false otherwise.

    (e) Next—Move p and l one position right; throw an exception if the operation fails.

    (f) Previous—Move p and l one position back; throw an exception if the operation fails.

    Write C++ code for the extended class definition. To implement the Insert, Delete, and Find functions efficiently, it will be useful to have another private member current that gives you the index of the element p points to (i.e., is it the first, second, etc., element of the list). Test the correctness of your code using suitable test data.

★ 89. Obtain a representation for integers that is suitable for performing arithmetic on arbitrarily large integers. The arithmetic is to be performed with no loss of accuracy. Write C++ functions to input and output large integers and to perform the arithmetic operations: add, subtract, multiply, and divide. The function for division will return two integers: the quotient and the remainder. Also, write a function to dispose of an integer. This function should free the space currently used by the integer being disposed.

★ 90. [*Polynomials*] A **univariate polynomial** of degree d has the form

$$c_d x^d + c_{d-1} x^{d-1} + c_{d-2} x^{d-2} \cdots + c_0$$

where $c_d \neq 0$. The c_is are the coefficients, and the e_is are the exponents. By definition the exponents are nonnegative integers. Each $c_i x^i$ is a term of the polynomial. We wish to develop a template class to support arithmetic involving polynomials. For this, we shall represent each polynomial as a linear list, $(c_0, c_1, c_2, \cdots, c_d)$, of coefficients.

Develop a C++ template class `Polynomial<T>` where `T` gives the type of the coefficients. The class `Polynomial` should have a private member `degree`, which is the degree of the polynomial. It may have other private members also. Your polynomial class should support the following operations:

(a) `Polynomial()`—Create the zero polynomial. The degree of this polynomial is zero and it has no terms. `Polynomial()` is the class constructor.

(b) `Degree()`—Return the degree of the polynomial.

(c) `Input()`—Read in a polynomial. You may assume the input consists of the polynomial degree and a list of coefficients in ascending order of exponents.

(d) `Output()`—Output the polynomial. The output format should be the same as the input format.

(e) `Add(b)`—Add to polynomial `b` and return the result polynomial.

(f) `Subtract(b)`—Subtract the polynomial `b` and return the result.

(g) `Multiply(b)`—Multiply with polynomial `b` and return the result.

(h) `Divide(b)`—Divide by polynomial `b` and return the quotient.

(i) `Value(x)`—Return the value of the polynomial at point `x`.

You should overload the operators `<<`, `>>`, `+`, `-`, `*`, `/`, and `()` for (c) through (i). For (i), the syntax `P(x)` where `P` is of type `Polynomial` should return the value of the polynomial at `x`. Test your package.

★ 91. [*Polynomials*] Design a linked class to represent and manipulate univariate polynomials (see Exercise 90). Use circular linked lists with head nodes. The `data` field of each node includes a coefficient and exponent field. In addition to the head node, the circular list representation of a polynomial has one node for each term that has a nonzero coefficient. Terms with zero coefficient are not represented. The terms are in decreasing order of exponent and the head node has its exponent field equal to -1. Figure 3.24 gives some examples.

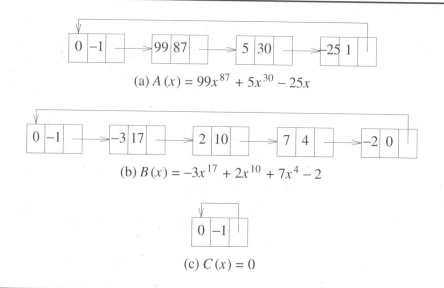

(a) $A(x) = 99x^{87} + 5x^{30} - 25x$

(b) $B(x) = -3x^{17} + 2x^{10} + 7x^4 - 2$

(c) $C(x) = 0$

Figure 3.24 Sample polynomials

The external (i.e., for input or output) representation of a univariate polynomial will be assumed to be a sequence of numbers of the form $n, e_1, c_1, e_2, c_2, e_3, c_3, \ldots, e_n, c_n$, where the e_i represent the exponents and the c_i the coefficients; n gives the number of terms in the polynomial. The exponents are in decreasing order; that is, $e_1 > e_2 > \ldots > e_n$.

Your class should support all the functions of Exercise 90. Test the correctness of your code using suitable polynomials.

3.9   REFERENCES AND SELECTED READINGS

Additional material on data structures in C++ may be found in the texts *Fundamentals of Data Structures in C++* by E. Horowitz, S. Sahni, and D. Mehta, W. H. Freeman, New York, NY, 1994; *Data Abstraction and Problem Solving with C++* by F. Carrano, Benjamin/Cummings Publishing Company, Redwood City, CA, 1995; *Data Structures and Algorithms in C++* by A. Drozdek, PWS Publishing Company, Boston, 1996; *Algorithms, Data Structures, and Problem Solving with C++* by M. Weiss, Addison-Wesley, Menlo Park, CA, 1996; and *Classic Data Structures in C++* by T. Budd, Addison-Wesley, Reading, MA, 1994.

CHAPTER 4

ARRAYS AND MATRICES

BIRD'S-EYE VIEW

In practice, data is often available in tabular form. Although arrays are the most natural way to represent tabular data, we can often reduce both the space and time requirements of our programs by using a customized representation. This reduction is possible, for example, when a large fraction of the table entries are zero.

This chapter begins by examining the row-major and column-major representations of a multidimensional array. These representations map a multidimensional array into a one-dimensional array.

Although C++ supports multidimensional arrays, it does not validate array subscripts. Nor does it provide for the input and output of arrays or the performing of simple arithmetic operations such as assignment and addition. To overcome these deficiencies of the supported array data structure, we develop the classes `Array1D` and `Array2D` for one- and two-dimensional arrays.

The data object matrix is often represented as a two-dimensional array. However, matrices are normally indexed beginning at one rather than zero and we use the notation $A(i,j)$ rather than $A[i][j]$ to reference element (i,j) of a matrix. Therefore, we develop another class `Matrix` that conforms more closely to the data object matrix.

We also consider the representation of matrices with special structure. These matrices include diagonal, tridiagonal, triangular, and symmetric matrices. Using customized formula-based (or sequential) representations, we can reduce the space requirements of these matrices considerably when compared to the space used by the natural two-dimensional array representation. The customized representations also result in significant savings in run time for operations such as matrix addition and subtraction.

The final section of this chapter develops sequential and linked representations for sparse matrices (i.e., ones with a large number of zeroes) in which the positions of the zeroes do not necessarily define a regular pattern.

4.1   ARRAYS

4.1.1   The Abstract Data Type

Each instance of the data object *array* is a set of pairs of the form (index, value). No two pairs in this set have the same index. The functions performed on the array follow.

- *Create*—Creates an initially empty array (i.e., one that has no pairs).

- *Store*—Adds a pair of the form (index, value) to the set, and if a pair with the same index already exists, deletes the old pair.

- *Retrieve*—Retrieves the value of the pair that has a given index.

These three functions together with the data object array define the abstract data type *Array* (ADT 4.1).

AbstractDataType *Array* {
  instances
    set of (index, value) pairs, no two pairs have the same index
  operations
    Create (): create an empty array
    Store (*index*,*value*): add this pair to set deleting existing pair (if any)
                with the same index
    Retrieve (*index*): return the pair with this index value
}

ADT 4.1 Abstract data type specification of an array

Example 4.1 The high temperature (in degrees Farenheit) for each day of last week may be represented by the following array:

high = {(sunday, 82), (monday, 79), (tuesday, 85), (wednesday, 92),
                (thursday, 88), (friday, 89), (saturday, 91)}

Each pair of the array is composed of an index (day of week) and a value (the high temperature for that day). The name of the array is *high*. We can change the high temperature recorded for monday to 83 by performing the following operation:

Store (monday,83)

We can determine the high temperature for friday by performing this operation:

Retrieve (friday)

An alternative array to represent the daily high temperature is

$$high = \{(0, 82), (1, 79), (2, 85), (3, 92), (4, 88), (5, 89), (6, 91)\}$$

In this array the index is a number rather than the name of the day. The numbers $(0, 1, 2, \cdots)$ replace the names of the days of the week (sunday, monday, tuesday, $\cdots$).

4.1.2 Indexing a C++ Array

Although arrays are a standard data structure in C++, the index (also called **subscript**) of an array in C++ must be of the form

$$[i_1][i_2][i_3] \cdots [i_k]$$

where each i_j is a nonnegative integer. If k is one, the array is a one-dimensional array, and if k is two, it is a two-dimensional array. i_1 is the first coordinate of the index, i_2 the second, and i_k the kth. A k-dimensional array `score`, whose values are of type integer, may be *created* in C++ using the statement

$$\texttt{int score}[u_1][u_2][u_3] \cdots [u_k]$$

where the u_is are positive constants or positive expressions derived from constants. With such a declaration, indexes with i_j in the range $0 \le i_j < u_j, 1 \le j \le k$ are permitted. So the array can hold a maximum of $n = u_1 u_2 u_3 \cdots u_k$ values. Since each value in the array `score` is an integer, `sizeof(int)` bytes are needed for each. The memory `size(score)` needed for the entire array is therefore $n * \texttt{sizeof(int)}$ bytes. The C++ compiler reserves this much memory for the array. This memory begins at byte *start* (say) and extends up to and including byte *start* + `size(score)` − 1.

4.1.3 Row- and Column-Major Mappings

To implement the `Store` and `Retrieve` functions associated with arrays, we need a mapping of index values to bytes in the range [*start*, *start* + $n *$ `sizeof(score)` − 1]. Actually, the mapping transforms each array index $[i_1][i_2][i_3] \cdots [i_k]$ to a number $map(i_1, i_2, \cdots, i_k)$ in the range $[0, n − 1]$ such that the value of the pair with index $[i_1][i_2][i_3] \cdots [i_k]$ is stored in `sizeof(int)` bytes beginning with the following byte:

$$start + map(i_1, i_2, \cdots, i_k) * \texttt{sizeof(int)}.$$

When the number of dimensions is one (i.e., $k = 1$), the function

$$map(i_1) = i_1$$

is used. When the number of dimensions is two, the indexes may be arranged into a table with indexes that have the same first coordinate forming a row of the table and those with the same second coordinate forming a column (see Figure 4.1).

[0][0]	[0][1]	[0][2]	[0][3]	[0][4]	[0][5]
[1][0]	[1][1]	[1][2]	[1][3]	[1][4]	[1][5]
[2][0]	[2][1]	[2][2]	[2][3]	[2][4]	[2][5]

Figure 4.1 Tabular arrangement of indexes for `int score[3][6]`

The mapping is obtained by numbering the indexes by row beginning with those in the first (i.e., top) row. Within each row numbers are assigned from left to right. The result is shown in Figure 4.2(a). This way of mapping the positions in a two-dimensional array into a number in the range 0 through $n - 1$ is called **row major**. The numbers are assigned in row-major order. C++ uses this scheme. Figure 4.2(b) shows an alternative scheme, called **column major**. In column-major order, the numbers are assigned by column beginning with the left-most column. Within a column, the numbers are assigned from top to bottom.

0	1	2	3	4	5
6	7	8	9	10	11
12	13	14	15	16	17

0	3	6	9	12	15
1	4	7	10	13	16
2	5	8	11	14	17

(a) Row-major mapping   (b) Column-major mapping

Figure 4.2 Mapping a two-dimensional array

When row-major order is used, the mapping function is

$$map(i_1, i_2) = i_1 u_2 + i_2$$

where u_2 is the number of columns in the array. To verify the correctness of the above mapping function, note that by the time the index $[i_1][i_2]$ is numbered in the row-major scheme, i_1u_2 elements from the rows 0, $\cdots$, i_1-1 as well as i_2 elements from row i_1 have been numbered.

Let us try out the row-major mapping function on the sample 3×6 array of Figure 4.2(a). Since the number of columns, u_2, is six, the formula becomes

$$map(i_1,i_2) = 6i_1 + i_2$$

So $map(1,3) = 6 + 3 = 9$, and $map(2,5) = 6*2 + 5 = 17$. Both agree with the numbers given in Figure 4.2(a).

The row-major scheme may be extended to obtain mapping functions for arrays with more than two dimensions. Notice that in row-major order, we list first all indexes with first coordinate equal to zero, then those with this coordinate equal to one, and so on. Indexes with the same first coordinate are listed in increasing order of the second coordinate; that is, the indexes are listed in lexicographic order. For a three-dimensional array, we list first all indexes with first coordinate equal to zero; then those with this coordinate equal to one; and so on. Indexes with the same first coordinate are listed in order of the second coordinate, and indexes that agree on the first two coordinates are listed in order of the third. For example, the indexes of `score[3][2][4]` in row-major order are

[0][0][0], [0][0][1], [0][0][2], [0][0][3], [0][1][0], [0][1][1], [0][1][2], [0][1][3],
[1][0][0], [1][0][1], [1][0][2], [1][0][3], [1][1][0], [1][1][1], [1][1][2], [1][1][3],
[2][0][0], [2][0][1], [2][0][2], [2][0][3], [2][1][0], [2][1][1], [2][1][2], [2][1][3]

The mapping function for a three-dimensional array is

$$map(i_1,i_2,i_3) = i_1u_2u_3 + i_2u_3 + i_3$$

To see that this mapping function is correct, observe that the elements with first coordinate i_1 are preceded by all elements with first coordinate less than i_1. There are u_2u_3 elements that have the same first coordinate. So there are $i_1u_2u_3$ elements with first coordinate less than i_1. The number of elements with first coordinate equal to i_1 and second coordinate less than i_2 is i_2u_3, and the number with first coordinate equal to i_1, second equal to i_2, and third less than i_3 is i_3.

4.1.4 The Class `Array1D`

Although C++ supports one-dimensional arrays, this support is rather primitive. For instance, we are permitted to use array indexes that fall outside the declared range. Consider the array `a` declared as

```
int a[9]
```

Accessing array elements `a[-3]`, `a[9]`, and `a[90]`, for example, is permitted, even though −3, 9, and 90 are invalid indexes. Permitting the use of invalid array indexes often causes a program to behave in an unpredictable manner and makes debugging difficult. Other shortcomings are that the array cannot be output using the statement

```
cout << a << endl;
```

and we cannot perform operations such as add and subtract (using the operators + and -) on one-dimensional arrays. To overcome these deficiencies, we define the class Array1D (Program 4.1). Each instance X of this class is a one-dimensional array. The elements of X are stored in the array X.element with the ith element being in X.element[i], $0 \le i < size$.

```
template<class T>
class Array1D {
   public:
      Array1D(int size = 0);
      Array1D(const Array1D<T>& v); // copy constructor
      ~Array1D() {delete [] element;}
      T& operator[](int i) const;
      int Size() {return size;}
      Array1D<T>& operator=(const Array1D<T>& v);
      Array1D<T> operator+() const; // unary +
      Array1D<T> operator+(const Array1D<T>& v) const;
      Array1D<T> operator-() const; // unary minus
      Array1D<T> operator-(const Array1D<T>& v) const;
      Array1D<T> operator*(const Array1D<T>& v) const;
      Array1D<T>& operator+=(const T& x);
   private:
      int size;
      T *element; // 1D array
};
```

Program 4.1 A one-dimensional array class

The public members of this class include a constructor, a copy constructor, a destructor, the array indexing operator [], a function Size that returns the array size, and the arithmetic operators +, -, *, and +=. Additional operators may be added. Program 4.2 gives the constructor and copy constructor. The constructor deviates slightly from ANSI C++ and permits arrays with zero elements. If we do not wish this deviation, the code may be appropriately modified.

Program 4.3 overloads the array index operator []. The code returns a reference to the ith element and so enables both the store and retrieve functions to be performed in a natural way. The statement

```
X[1] = 2 * Y[3];
```

```
template<class T>
Array1D<T>::Array1D(int sz)
{// Constructor for one-dimensional arrays.
   if (sz < 0) throw BadInitializers();
   size = sz;
   element = new T[sz];
}

template<class T>
Array1D<T>::Array1D(const Array1D<T>& v)
{// Copy constructor for one-dimensional arrays.
   size = v.size;
   element = new T[size];   // get space
   for (int i = 0; i < size; i++) // copy elements
      element[i] = v.element[i];
}
```

Program 4.2 Constructors for a one-dimensional array

where X and Y are of type Array1D works as you would expect. The code
Y[3] invokes the [] operator on object Y. The operator returns a reference to
element 3, which is then multiplied by two. The code X[1] also invokes the
[] operator, and a reference to X[1] is returned. The result of 2 * Y[3] is
then stored in this referenced position.

```
template<class T>
T& Array1D<T>::operator[](int i) const
{// Return reference to element i.
   if (i < 0 || i >= size) throw OutOfBounds();
   return element[i];
}
```

Program 4.3 Overloading the array indexing operator

Program 4.4 gives the code for the assignment operator. This code avoids
doing assignments of the type X = X (self-assignments) by verifying that the
objects on the left and right side are different. To do the assignment, we first free
the space assigned to the destination array *this. Next enough space is allocated to accomodate the source array v. Although the call to new may fail, we
do not catch the thrown exception; we leave it to be caught by a part of the
overall code better equipped to handle the exception. If no exception is thrown

by new, the elements are copied one by one from the source array to the destination.

```
template<class T>
Array1D<T>& Array1D<T>::operator=(const Array1D<T>& v)
{// Overload assignment operator.
   if (this != &v) {// not self-assignment
      size = v.size;
      delete [] element; // free old space
      element = new T[size]; // get right amount
      for (int i = 0; i < size; i++) // copy elements
         element[i] = v.element[i];
      }
   return *this;
}
```

Program 4.4 Overloading the assignment operator

Program 4.5 gives the codes for the binary minus, unary minus, and increment operators. The codes for the remaining operators are similar.

Complexity
The complexity of the constructor and destructor is $\Theta(1)$ when T is an internal C++ data type (e.g., int, float, and char) and O(size) when T is a user-defined class. This difference in complexities is due to the fact that when T is a user-defined class, the constructor (destructor) for T is invoked once for each element of the array element when this array is created (deleted) by new (delete). The complexity of the subscript operator ([]) is $\Theta(1)$, while that of the remaining operators is O(size). (Note that the complexity is not $\Theta(size)$, as all the operators for which we have provided code may throw an exception and terminate early.)

4.1.5 The Class Array2D

We may define a class Array2D for two-dimensional arrays as in Program 4.6. This implementation uses a representation similar to that of Figure 1.1. A two-dimensional array is viewed as a collection of one-dimensional arrays. Although Figure 1.1 uses a one-dimensional array to point to the row arrays, in Program 4.6 we use a one-dimensional array row to directly store the row arrays. The array row is set up as a standard C++ one-dimensional array, rather than as an instance of Array1D because we have complete control over how its elements are accessed (row is a private member). Therefore, we can ensure that valid

```
template<class T>
Array1D<T> Array1D<T>::
           operator-(const Array1D<T>& v) const
{// Return w = (*this) - v.
   if (size != v.size) throw SizeMismatch();

   // create result array w
   Array1D<T> w(size);
   for (int i = 0; i < size; i++)
      w.element[i] = element[i] - v.element[i];

   return w;
}

template<class T>
Array1D<T> Array1D<T>::operator-() const
{// Return w = -(*this).
   // create result array w
   Array1D<T> w(size);
   for (int i = 0; i < size; i++)
      w.element[i] = -element[i];

   return w;
}

template<class T>
Array1D<T>& Array1D<T>::operator+=(const T& x)
{// Add x to each element of (*this).
   for (int i = 0; i < size; i++)
      element[i] += x;
   return *this;
   }
```

Program 4.5 Overloading binary minus, unary minus, and increment

indexes are used. We have no need for the added functionality provided by Array1D. row[i] is the one-dimensional array of type Array1D that denotes row i of the two-dimensional array. Note that, unlike Figure 1.1, row[i] is not a pointer to a one-dimensional array. An alternative representation using row-major mapping is considered in Section 4.2.2.

```
template<class T>
class Array2D {
   public:
      Array2D(int r = 0, int c = 0);
      Array2D(const Array2D<T>& m); // copy constructor
      ~Array2D() {delete [] row;}
      int Rows() const {return rows;}
      int Columns() const {return cols;}
      Array1D<T>& operator[](int i) const;
      Array2D<T>& operator=(const Array2D<T>& m);
      Array2D<T> operator+() const; // unary +
      Array2D<T> operator+(const Array2D<T>& m) const;
      Array2D<T> operator-() const; // unary minus
      Array2D<T> operator-(const Array2D<T>& m) const;
      Array2D<T> operator*(const Array2D<T>& m) const;
      Array2D<T>& operator+=(const T& x);
   private:
      int rows, cols;  // number of rows and columns
      Array1D<T> *row; // array of 1D arrays
};
```

Program 4.6 A class for two-dimensional arrays

Program 4.7 gives the code for the constructor function. The default is an array with zero rows and columns. Arrays with zero rows and a nonzero number of columns, and vice-versa, are not permitted. The statement

```
row = new Array1D<T> [r];
```

makes row a one-dimensional array with r positions. Each position is of type Array1D<T>. When the array row is created, the Array1D constructor is called for each position. So row[i] is a default size (i.e., zero) one-dimensional array, $0 \le i < r$. Since only default constructors may be invoked when creating an array, the creation of the array row is followed by a for loop in which each element of row is changed to the right size. ReSize is a new member function of Array1D, which changes the size of a one-dimensional array to sz by executing the following code:

```
delete [] element;
size = sz;
element = new T [size];
```

```
template<class T>
Array2D<T>::Array2D(int r, int c)
{// Constructor for two-dimensional arrays.

   // validate r and c
   if (r < 0 || c < 0) throw BadInitializers();
   if ((!r || !c) && (r || c))
      throw BadInitializers();

   rows = r;
   cols = c;

   // allocate r 1D arrays of default size
   row = new Array1D<T> [r];

   // make them right size
   for (int i = 0; i < r; i++)
      row[i].ReSize(c);
}
```

Program 4.7 Constructor for a two-dimensional array

Notice that the destructor does not explicitly free the space allocated to the rows of the two-dimensional array. However, when `delete [] row` is executed, the operator `delete` invokes the `Array1D` destructor for each element of the array `row` and the `Array1D` destructor frees the space allocated to the rows.

The copy constructor (Program 4.8) first creates an array `row` that has the correct number of positions and then uses the assignment operator for one-dimensional arrays to copy each row of the two-dimensional array. Unlike the constructor of Program 4.7, the copy constructor does not validate the values of `m.rows` and `m.cols`, as these values were validated when `m` was created. The code for the assignment operator is similar to that of the copy constructor. However, like the assignment operator code of Program 4.4, the assignment code for `Array2D` checks for self-assignment.

`X[i][j]` where `X` is of type `Array2D<T>` is parsed as `(X.operator[i]).operator[j]`. So `Array2D<T>::operator[]` is invoked first with actual parameter `i`. If this operator returns the object `Y`, then `typeof(Y)::operator[]` is invoked with actual parameter `j`. So if `typeof(Y)` is different from `Array2D<T>`, then

`Array2D<T>::operator[]`

```
template<class T>
Array2D<T>::Array2D(const Array2D<T>& m)
{// Copy constructor for two-dimensional arrays.
    rows = m.rows;
    cols = m.cols;

    // allocate array of 1D arrays
    row = new Array1D<T> [rows];

    // copy each row
    for (int i = 0; i < rows; i++)
        row[i] = m.row[i];
}
```

Program 4.8 Copy constructor for two-dimensional arrays

is invoked only with the first index of the two-dimensional array. With this understanding we arrive at the code of Program 4.9, which simply returns a reference to the one-dimensional array corresponding to the first index. When executing the code X[i][j], X[i] invokes Array2D<T>::operator[], which returns a reference to X.row[i] (or the ith row of X). Since this reference is of type Array1D<T>, Array1D<T>::operator[] is invoked next and returns a reference to the correct array element.

```
template<class T>
Array1D<T>& Array2D<T>::operator[](int i) const
{// First index of 2D array.
    if (i < 0 || i >= rows) throw OutOfBounds();
    return row[i];
}
```

Program 4.9 Overloading [] for a two-dimensional array

The code for the binary minus operator given in Program 4.10 simply invokes Array1D<T>::operator- for each row of the two-dimensional array. The codes for addition, unary minus, increment, and output are similar.

The multiplication operator may be implemented to correspond to a matrix multiply (see Program 2.25). The code is very similar to that of Program 2.25 and is given in Program 4.11.

```
template<class T>
Array2D<T> Array2D<T>::
          operator-(const Array2D<T>& m) const
{// Return w = (*this) - m.
   if (rows != m.rows || cols != m.cols)
      throw SizeMismatch();

   // create result array w
   Array2D<T> w(rows,cols);
   for (int i = 0; i < rows; i++)
      w.row[i] = row[i] - m.row[i];

   return w;
}
```

Program 4.10 Subtraction

```
template<class T>
Array2D<T> Array2D<T>::
          operator*(const Array2D<T>& m) const
{// A matrix product. Return w = (*this) * m.
   if (cols != m.rows) throw SizeMismatch();

   // create result array w
   Array2D<T> w(rows, m.cols);
   for (int i = 0; i < rows; i++)
      for (int j = 0; j < m.cols; j++) {
         T sum = (*this)[i][0] * m[0][j];
         for (int k = 1; k < cols; k++)
            sum += (*this)[i][k] * m[k][j];
         w[i][j] = sum;
      }

   return w;
}
```

Program 4.11 Matrix multiplication

Complexity

The complexity of the constructor and destructor is O(rows) when T is an internal data type and is O(rows*cols) when T is a user-defined data type. The copy constructor and operator- have complexity O(rows*cols), while the complexity of the subscript operator [] is Θ(1). The multiplication operator has complexity O(rows*cols*m.cols).

EXERCISES

1. Extend the class Array1D (Program 4.1) by overloading the operators << (input an array), + (unary plus), *= (multiply each element by the type T element on the right side), /=, and -=. Test your codes.

2. Develop a class Array1D<T1,T2> for one-dimensional arrays. T1 is the data type of the array index, and T2 that of the array elements. T1 may be any enumerated type. For example, if T1 is bool, then the permissible indexes are true and false. Your class should include all the public members in Array1D (Program 4.1).

3. Do Exercise 1 for the class Array2D. Also include an operator to multiply corresponding pairs of elements of two arrays of the same size.

4. Write the template functions Make3DArray and Delete3DArray corresponding to the make and delete functions for two-dimensional arrays (Programs 1.13 and 1.14). If an integer array *s* is to be created, the user would have the declaration

   ```
   int ***x
   ```

   and access elements using the syntax x[i][j][k]. Test the correctness of your codes.

5. Develop a class Array3D<T> for three-dimensional arrays, analogous to Array2D<T>.

6. List the indexes of score[2][3][2][2] in row-major order.

7. Obtain the row-major mapping function for a four-dimensional array.

8. Obtain the row-major mapping function for a five-dimensional array.

9. Obtain the row-major mapping function for a *k*-dimensional array.

10. List the indexes of score[2][3][4] in column-major order. Note that now, all indexes with third coordinate equal to 0 are listed first, then those with this coordinate equal to 1, and so on. Indexes with the same third coordinate are listed in order of the second and those with the same last two coordinates in order of the first.

11. Obtain the column-major mapping function for a three-dimensional array (see preceding exercise).

12. List the indexes of `score[2][3][2][2]` in column-major order.

13. Obtain the column-major mapping function for a four-dimensional array.

14. Obtain the column-major mapping function for a k-dimensional array.

15. We wish to map the elements of a two-dimensional array beginning with the bottom-most row and within a row from left to right.

   (a) List the indexes of `score[3][5]` in this order.

   (b) Obtain the mapping function for $score[u_1][u_2]$.

16. We wish to map the elements of a two-dimensional array beginning with the right-most column and within a column from top to bottom.

   (a) List the indexes of `score[3][5]` in this order.

   (b) Obtain the mapping function for $score[u_1][u_2]$.

4.2 MATRICES

4.2.1 Definitions and Operations

An $m \times n$ **matrix** is a table with m rows and n columns (Figure 4.3). m and n are the **dimensions** of the matrix.

	col 1	col 2	col 3	col 4
row 1	7	2	0	9
row 2	0	1	0	5
row 3	6	4	2	0
row 4	8	2	7	3
row 5	1	4	9	6

Figure 4.3 A 5×4 matrix

Matrices are often used to organize data. For instance, in an effort to document the assets of the world, we might first produce a list of asset types of interest. This list could include mineral deposits (silver, gold, etc.); animals (lions, elephants, etc.); people (physicians, engineers, etc.); and so on. For each asset we can determine the amount present in the country. We can organize the data into a table with one column for each country and one row for each asset type (i.e., a row for silver, another for lions, etc.). The result is an asset matrix with a number of columns n equal to the number of countries and a number of rows m equal to the number of asset types. We use the notation $M(i,j)$ to refer to the element in row i and column j of matrix M, $1 \leq i \leq m$, $1 \leq j \leq n$. If in our asset matrix example, row i represents cats and column j represents USA, then $asset(i,j)$ would be the number of cats in the USA.

The operations most commonly performed on matrices are transpose, addition or sum, and multiplication or product. The transpose of an $m \times n$ matrix M is an $n \times m$ matrix M^T with the property

$$M^T(i,j) = M(j,i), \ 1 \leq i \leq n, \ 1 \leq j \leq m$$

The sum of two matrices is defined only when the two matrices have the same dimensions (i.e., the same number of rows and the same number of columns). The sum of two $m \times n$ matrices A and B is a third $m \times n$ matrix C such that

$$C(i,j) = A(i,j) + B(i,j), \ 1 \leq i \leq n, \ 1 \leq j \leq m$$

The product, $A * B$, of an $m \times n$ matrix A and a $q \times p$ matrix B is defined only when the number of columns in A equals the number of rows in B, i.e., $n = q$. When $n = q$, the product is an $m \times p$ matrix C with the property

$$C(i,j) = \sum_{k=1}^{n} A(i,k) * B(k,j), \ 1 \leq i \leq m, \ 1 \leq j \leq p$$

Example 4.2 Consider the asset matrix described above. Suppose that the data is being accumulated by two agencies and neither duplicates the work of the other. The result is two $m \times n$ matrices $asset\,1$ and $asset\,2$. To get the desired asset matrix, we add the two matrices $asset\,1$ and $asset\,2$.

Next, suppose we have another matrix $value$ that is an $m \times s$ matrix. $value(i,j)$ is the value of one unit of asset i under scenario j. Let $CV(i,j)$ be the value of country i under scenario j. CV is an $n \times s$ matrix that satisfies the equation

$$CV = asset^T * value$$

∎

C++ functions to compute the transpose of a matrix and to add and multiply two matrices represented as two-dimensional arrays were considered in Chapter 2 (Programs 2.19, 2.22, 2.24, and 2.25).

4.2.2 The Class `Matrix`

An m × n matrix M all of whose elements are integer may be represented as a two-dimensional integer array

```
int x[m][n];              or              Array2D<int> x[m][n];
```

with $M(i,j)$ being stored as `x[i-1][j-1]`. This representation requires the user to write applications using array indexes that differ from matrix indexes by one and also to use `[][]` rather than `()` to index matrix elements. These changes reduce the readability of the application codes and also increase the likelihood of errors. We can overcome these problems by defining a class `Matrix`, in which we use `()` to index matrix elements and which permits the user to use indexes that begin at one.

The class `Matrix` (Program 4.12) uses a one-dimensional array `element` to store the `rows * cols` elements of a `rows × cols` matrix.

```
template<class T>
class Matrix {
   public:
      Matrix(int r = 0, int c = 0);
      Matrix(const Matrix<T>& m); // copy constructor
      ~Matrix() {delete [] element;}
      int Rows() const {return rows;}
      int Columns() const {return cols;}
      T& operator()(int i, int j) const;
      Matrix<T>& operator=(const Matrix<T>& m);
      Matrix<T> operator+() const; // unary +
      Matrix<T> operator+(const Matrix<T>& m) const;
      Matrix<T> operator-() const; // unary minus
      Matrix<T> operator-(const Matrix<T>& m) const;
      Matrix<T> operator*(const Matrix<T>& m) const;
      Matrix<T>& operator+=(const T& x);
   private:
      int rows, cols; // matrix dimensions
      T *element;      // element array
};
```

Program 4.12 The class `Matrix`

Program 4.13 gives the code for the constructor. The code for the copy constructor and assignment operator are similar and may be modeled after the corresponding codes for `Array1D`.

```
template<class T>
Matrix<T>::Matrix(int r, int c)
{// Matrix constructor.
   // validate r and c
   if (r < 0 || c < 0) throw BadInitializers();
   if ((!r || !c) && (r || c))
    throw BadInitializers();

   // create the matrix
   rows = r; cols = c;
   element = new T [r * c];
}
```

Program 4.13 Matrix constructor

To overload the matrix indexing operator (), we use the C++ function operator (), which, unlike the array indexing operator [], can take any number of parameters. For a matrix we need two integer parameters. The code of Program 4.14 returns a reference to the (i,j)th element of the matrix.

```
template<class T>
T& Matrix<T>::operator()(int i, int j) const
{// Return a reference to element (i,j).
   if (i < 1 || i > rows || j < 1
           || j > cols) throw OutOfBounds();
   return element[(i - 1) * cols + j - 1];
}
```

Program 4.14 Indexing a matrix

Program 4.15 gives the code for the subtraction operator. This code is closer to the code for one-dimensional array subtraction (Program 4.5) than for two-dimensional array subtraction (Program 4.10). The codes for addition, unary minus, increment, and output are similar.

Although we can fashion the matrix multiplication code after the code for two-dimensional arrays (Program 4.11), it is more efficient to write customized code. The loop structure of the matrix multiplication code (Program 4.16) is similar to that of our other matrix multiplication codes (Programs 2.25 and 4.11). There are three nested for loops. The innermost loop computes the (i,j)th element of the result by multiplying the ith row of *this and the jth column of m. When we enter the innermost loop, element[ct] is the first

```
template<class T>
Matrix<T> Matrix<T>::
          operator-(const Matrix<T>& m) const
{// Return (*this) - m.
   if (rows != m.rows || cols != m.cols)
      throw SizeMismatch();

   // create result matrix w
   Matrix<T> w(rows, cols);
   for (int i = 0; i < rows * cols; i++)
      w.element[i] = element[i] - m.element[i];

   return w;
}
```

Program 4.15 Matrix subtraction

element of row i and m.element[cm] the first of column j. To go to the
next element of row i, ct is to be incremented by one, as in row-major order
the elements of a row occupy consecutive positions. To go the next element of
column j, cm is to be incremented by m.cols, as consecutive elements of a
column are m.cols positions apart in row-major order. When the innermost
loop completes, ct is positioned at the end of row i and cm is at the end of
column j. For the next iteration of the for j loop, ct needs to be at the
start of row i and cm at the start of the next column of m. The resetting that
occurs after the innermost loop completes positions ct. When the for j
loop completes, ct should be set to the position of the first element of the next
row and cm to that of the first element of the first column.

Complexity
The complexity of the matrix constructor is O(1) when T is an internal data type
and O(row*cols) when T is a user-defined class. The asymptotic complexity
of all remaining matrix operators is the same as that for their counterparts in the
class Array2D.

EXERCISES

17. Extend the class Matrix (Program 4.12) by overloading the operators
    << (input a matrix), + (unary plus), *= (multiply each element by the
    type T element on the right side, /=, and -=. Test your codes.

```
template<class T>
Matrix<T> Matrix<T>::
          operator*(const Matrix<T>& m) const
{// Matrix multiply.  Return w = (*this) * m.
   if (cols != m.rows) throw SizeMismatch();

   Matrix<T> w(rows, m.cols);   // result matrix

   // define cursors for *this, m, and w
   // and initialize to location of (1,1)
   int ct = 0, cm = 0, cw = 0;

   // compute w(i,j) for all i and j
   for (int i = 1; i <= rows; i++) {

      // compute row i of result
      for (int j = 1; j <= m.cols; j++) {

         // compute first term of w(i,j)
         T sum =  element[ct] * m.element[cm];

         // add in remaining terms
         for (int k = 2; k <= cols; k++) {
            ct++;   // next term in row i of *this
            cm += m.cols;   // next in column j of m
            sum += element[ct] * m.element[cm];
            }
         w.element[cw++] = sum;   // save w(i,j)

         // reset to start of row and next column
         ct -= cols - 1;
         cm = j;
         }

      // reset to start of next row and first column
      ct += cols;
      cm = 0;
      }

   return w;
}
```

Program 4.16 Matrix multiplication

18. Extend the class `Matrix` by adding a public member `Transpose` that returns the transposed matrix.

19. Compare the performance of the two classes `Array2D` and `Matrix` by measuring the time needed to subtract as well as to multiply. What can you say about the merits of using the row-major mapping over that used in the class `Array2D`?

4.3 SPECIAL MATRICES

4.3.1 Definitions and Applications

A **square** matrix has the same number of rows and columns. Some special forms of square matrices that arise frequently are:

- **Diagonal.** M is diagonal iff $M(i,j) = 0$ for $i \neq j$; see Figure 4.4(a).

- **Tridiagonal.** M is tridiagonal iff $M(i,j) = 0$ for $|i-j| > 1$; see Figure 4.4(b).

- **Lower triangular.** M is lower triangular iff $M(i,j) = 0$ for $i < j$; see Figure 4.4(c).

- **Upper triangular.** M is upper triangular iff $M(i,j) = 0$ for $i > j$; see Figure 4.4(d).

- **Symmetric.** Matrix M is symmetric iff $M(i,j) = M(j,i)$ for all i and j; see Figure 4.4(e).

```
2 0 0 0          2 1 0 0          2 0 0 0
0 1 0 0          3 1 3 0          5 1 0 0
0 0 4 0          0 5 2 7          0 3 1 0
0 0 0 6          0 0 9 0          4 2 7 0

(a) Diagonal     (b) Tridiagonal  (c) Lower triangular


        2 1 3 0          2 4 6 0
        0 1 3 8          4 1 9 5
        0 0 1 6          6 9 4 7
        0 0 0 0          0 5 7 0

      (d) Upper triangular    (e) Symmetric
```

Figure 4.4 4×4 matrices

Example 4.3 Consider the six cities Gainesville, Jacksonville, Miami, Orlando, Tallahassee, and Tampa, which are all in Florida. We may number these cities 1 through 6 in the listed order. The distance between pairs of these cities may be represented using a 6×6 matrix *distance*. The ith row and column of this matrix represent the ith city and *distance* (i,j) is the distance between city i and city j. Figure 4.5 shows the distance matrix. Since *distance* (i,j) = *distance* (j,i) for all i and j, the distance matrix is symmetric. ■

	GN	JX	MI	OD	TL	TM
GN	0	73	333	114	148	129
JX	73	0	348	140	163	194
MI	333	348	0	229	468	250
OD	114	140	229	0	251	84
TL	148	163	468	251	0	273
TM	129	194	250	84	273	0

GN = Gainesville	OD = Orlando
JX = Jacksonville	TL = Tallahassee
MI = Miami	TM = Tampa

Distance in miles

Figure 4.5 A distance matrix (Source: Rand McNally Road Atlas)

Example 4.4 Suppose we have a stack of n cartons with carton 1 at the bottom and carton n at the top. Each carton has width w and depth d. The height of the ith carton is h_i. The volume occupied by the stack is $w * d * \sum_{i=1}^{n} h_i$. In the **stack folding** problem, we are permitted to create substacks of cartons by selecting a fold point i and creating two adjacent stacks. One has cartons 1 through i and the other cartons $i + 1$ through n. By repeating this folding process, we may obtain several stacks of cartons. If we create s stacks, the width of the arrangement is $s * w$, its depth is d, and the height h needed is the the height of the tallest stack. The volume of the space needed for the stacks is $s * w * d * h$. Since h is the height of a stack of boxes i through j for some i and j, $i \leq j$, the possible values for h are given by the $n \times n$ matrix H where $H(i,j)$ is 0 for $i > j$ and is

$\sum\limits_{k=i}^{j} h_k$ for $i \le j$. Since each carton may be assumed to have a height > 0, an $H(i,j)$ value of zero indicates an infeasible stack height. Figure 4.6(a) shows a five-carton stack. The numbers inside each rectangle gives the carton height. Figure 4.6(b) shows a folding of the five-carton stack into three stacks. The height of the largest stack is seven. The matrix H is an upper-triangular matrix, as shown in Figure 4.6(c). ■

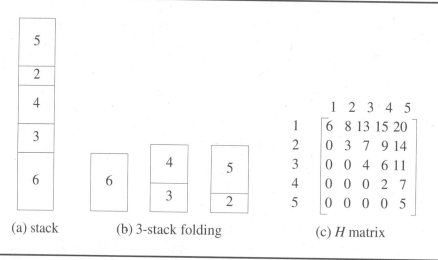

(a) stack   (b) 3-stack folding   (c) H matrix

Figure 4.6 Stack folding

4.3.2 Diagonal Matrices

One way to represent an $n \times n$ diagonal matrix D with values of type T is to use a two-dimensional array created as

```
T d[n][n]
```

and use array element $d[i-1][j-1]$ to represent matrix element $D(i,j)$. This representation requires $n^2 * sizeof(T)$ bytes of memory. However, since a diagonal matrix contains at most n nonzero entries, we may use a one-dimensional array created as

```
T d[n]
```

and use array element $d[i-1]$ to represent $D(i,i)$. The elements of the matrix D that are not represented in the array are all known to be zero. This representation leads to the C++ class `DiagonalMatrix` (Program 4.17).

```
template<class T>
class DiagonalMatrix {
   public:
      DiagonalMatrix(int size = 10)
         {n = size; d = new T [n];}
      ~DiagonalMatrix() {delete [] d;}
      DiagonalMatrix<T>&
         Store(const T& x, int i, int j);
      T Retrieve(int i, int j) const;
   private:
      int n; // matrix dimension
      T *d;  // 1D array for diagonal elements
};

template<class T>
DiagonalMatrix<T>& DiagonalMatrix<T>::
            Store(const T& x, int i, int j)
{// Store x as D(i,j).
   if (i < 1 || j < 1 ||
       i > n || j > n) throw OutOfBounds();
   if (i != j && x != 0) throw MustBeZero();
   if (i == j) d[i-1] = x;
   return *this;
}

template <class T>
T DiagonalMatrix<T>::Retrieve(int i, int j) const
{// Retrieve D(i,j).
   if (i < 1 || j < 1 ||
       i > n || j > n) throw OutOfBounds();
   if (i == j) return d[i-1];
   else return 0;
}
```

Program 4.17 The class `DiagonalMatrix`

We have provided different functions for the store and retrieve functions, rather than provide an overloaded version of the operator ( ), as simply returning a reference to $D(i,j)$ will not do. When we are storing a value, we need to ensure that no attempt is made to place a nonzero value in a nondiagonal position. When we are retrieving, no such check is needed, so we must distinguish between these two cases. As a result, we use different mechanisms for storing and retrieving. The complexity of Store and Retrieve (Program 4.17) is $\Theta(1)$.

4.3.3   Tridiagonal Matrix

In an $n \times n$ tridiagonal matrix T, the nonzero elements lie on one of the three diagonals:

1.   Main diagonal—for this, $i = j$.
2.   Diagonal below main diagonal—for this, $i = j + 1$.
3.   Diagonal above main diagonal—for this, $i = j - 1$.

The number of elements on these three diagonals is $3n - 2$. We can use a one-dimensional array t with $3n - 2$ positions to represent T. Only the elements on the three diagonals are explicitly stored. Consider the 4×4 tridiagonal matrix of Figure 4.4(b). There are 10 elements on the main diagonal and the diagonals just above and below the main diagonal. If these elements are mapped into t by rows, then t[0:9] = [2, 1, 3, 1, 3, 5, 2, 7, 9, 0]; if the mapping is by columns, t = [2, 3, 1, 1, 5, 3, 2, 9, 7, 0]; and if the mapping is by diagonals beginning with the lowest, then t = [3, 5, 9, 2, 1, 2, 0, 1, 3, 7]. As we can see, there are several reasonable choices for the mapping of T into t. Each requires a different code for the Store and Retrieve functions. Program 4.18 defines the C++ class TridiagonalMatrix in which the mapping is done by diagonals.

```
template<class T>
class TridiagonalMatrix {
   public:
      TridiagonalMatrix(int size = 10)
         {n = size; t = new T [3*n-2];}
      ~TridiagonalMatrix() {delete [] t;}
      TridiagonalMatrix<T>& Store
               (const T& x, int i, int j);
      T Retrieve(int i, int j) const;
   private:
      int n; // matrix dimension
      T *t;  // 1D array for tridiagonal
};
```

Program 4.18 The class TridiagonalMatrix (continues)

```
template<class T>
TridiagonalMatrix<T>& TridiagonalMatrix<T>::
                Store(const T& x, int i, int j)
{// Store x as T(i,j).
   if (i < 1 || j < 1 || i > n || j > n)
       throw OutOfBounds();

   switch (i - j) {
      case 1: // lower diagonal
         t[i - 2] = x; break;
      case 0: // main diagonal
         t[n + i - 2] = x; break;
      case -1: // upper diagonal
         t[2 * n + i - 2] = x; break;
      default: if (x != 0) throw MustBeZero();
         }
   return *this;
}

template <class T>
T TridiagonalMatrix<T>::Retrieve(int i, int j) const
{// Retrieve T(i,j).
   if (i < 1 || j < 1 || i > n || j > n)
       throw OutOfBounds();

   switch (i - j) {
      case 1: // lower diagonal
              return t[i - 2];
      case 0: // main diagonal
              return t[n + i - 2];
      case -1: // upper diagonal
              return t[2 * n + i - 2];
      default: return 0;
         }
}
```

Program 4.18 The class `TridiagonalMatrix` (concluded)

4.3.4   Triangular Matrices

In a triangular matrix the nonzero elements lie in the region marked ''nonzero'' in Figure 4.7. In a lower-triangular matrix, the nonzero region has one element in row 1, two in row 2, $\cdots$, and n in row n; and in an upper-triangular matrix, the nonzero region has n elements in row 1, $n - 1$ in row 2, $\cdots$, and one in row n. In both cases, the total number of elements in the nonzero region is

$$\sum_{i=1}^{n} i = n(n+1)/2$$

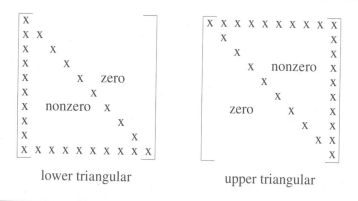

lower triangular   upper triangular

Figure 4.7 Lower- and upper-triangular matrices

Both kinds of triangular matrices may be represented using a one-dimensional array of size $n(n + 1)/2$. Consider a lower-triangular matrix L mapped into a one-dimensional array l. Two possible ways to do the mapping are by rows and by columns. If the mapping is done by rows, then the 4×4 lower-triangular matrix of Figure 4.4(c) has the mapping $l[0:9] = (2, 5, 1, 0, 3, 1, 4, 2, 7, 0)$. The column mapping results in $l = (2, 5, 0, 4, 1, 3, 2, 1, 7, 0)$.

Consider element $L(i,j)$ of a lower-triangular matrix. If $i < j$, the element is in the zero region. If $i \geq j$, the element is in the nonzero region. In a row mapping, the element $L(i,j)$, $i \geq j$, is preceded by $\sum_{k=1}^{i-1} k$ nonzero region elements that are in rows 1 through $i - 1$ and $j - 1$ such elements from row i. The total number of nonzero region elements that precede it in a row mapping is $i(i - 1)/2 + j - 1$. This expression also gives the position of $L(i,j)$ in l. Using this formula, we arrive at the store and retrieve functions given in Program 4.19. Both have time complexity $\Theta(1)$.

```
template<class T>
class LowerMatrix {
   public:
      LowerMatrix(int size = 10)
         {n = size; t = new T [n*(n+1)/2];}
      ~LowerMatrix() {delete [] t;}
      LowerMatrix<T>& Store(const T& x, int i, int j);
      T Retrieve(int i, int j) const;
   private:
      int n; // matrix dimension
      T *t;  // 1D array for lower triangle
};

template<class T>
LowerMatrix<T>& LowerMatrix<T>::
         Store(const T& x, int i, int j)
{// Store x as L(i,j).
   if (i < 1 || j < 1 || i > n || j > n)
      throw OutOfBounds();

   // (i,j) in lower triangle iff i >= j
   if (i >= j) t[i*(i-1)/2+j-1] = x;
   else if (x != 0) throw MustBeZero();

   return *this;
}

template <class T>
T LowerMatrix<T>::Retrieve(int i, int j) const
{// Retrieve L(i,j).
   if (i < 1 || j < 1 || i > n || j > n)
      throw OutOfBounds();

   // (i,j) in lower triangle iff i >= j
   if (i >= j) return t[i*(i-1)/2+j-1];
   else return 0;
}
```

Program 4.19 The class `LowerMatrix`

4.3.5   Symmetric Matrices

An $n \times n$ symmetric matrix can be represented using a one-dimensional array of size $n(n + 1)/2$ by storing either the lower or upper triangle of the matrix using one of the schemes for a triangular matrix. The elements that are not explicitly stored may be computed from those that are.

EXERCISES

20. (a) Extend the class `DiagonalMatrix` (Program 4.17) by adding public members to input, output, add, subtract, multiply, and transpose diagonal matrices represented as one-dimensional arrays. Note that in each case the result is a diagonal matrix represented as a one-dimensional array. Overload the operators `<<`, `>>`, `+`, `-`, and `*`.

    (b) Test the correctness of your codes.

    (c) What is the time complexity of each of your functions?

21. (a) Extend the class `TridiagonalMatrix` (Program 4.18) by adding public members to input, output, add, subtract, and transpose tridiagonal matrices. Overload C++ operators where appropriate.

    (b) Test the correctness of your codes.

    (c) What is the time complexity of each function?

22. (a) Develop a C++ class `TriByCols` that maps a tridiagonal $n \times n$ matrix into a one-dimensional array of size $3n - 2$ by columns. Include public members for the input, output, store, retrieve, add, subtract, and transpose operations.

    (b) Test the correctness of your codes.

    (c) What is the time complexity of each function?

23. Do Exercise 22 for the class `TriByRows` in which the $n \times n$ tridiagonal matrix is mapped into a one-dimensional array of size $3n - 2$ by rows.

24. Is the product of two tridiagonal matrices neccessarily tridiagonal?

25. Develop a C++ class `UpperMatrix` analogous to Program 4.19 for the case of an upper-triangular matrix.

26. Extend the class `LowerMatrix` by including a public member to add two lower-triangular matrices. What is the time complexity of your code?

27. Write a function that starts with a lower-triangular matrix which is a member of the class `LowerMatrix`, and produces its transpose, which is a member of the class `UpperMatrix`. What is the time complexity of your code?

28. In an $n \times n$ **C-matrix**, all terms other than those in row 1, row n, and column 1 (see Figure 4.8)) are zero. A C-matrix has at most $3n-2$ nonzero terms. A C-matrix may be compactly stored in a one-dimensional array by first storing row 1, then row n, and then the remaining column 1 elements.

x denotes a possible nonzero
all other terms are zero

Figure 4.8 A C-matrix

(a) Give a sample 4×4 C-matrix and its compact representation.

(b) Develop a class `CMatrix` that represents an $n \times n$ C-matrix in a one-dimensional array `t` as above. You should include the `Store` and `Retrieve` public members.

(c) Test the correctness of your code using suitable test data.

29. Write a function to multiply two lower-triangular matrices that are members of the class `LowerMatrix` (Program 4.19). The result matrix is in a two-dimensional array. What is the time complexity of your function?

30. Write a function to multiply a lower-triangular and an upper-triangular matrix mapped into one-dimensional arrays by rows. The result matrix is in a two-dimensional array. What is the time complexity of your function?

31. Suppose that symmetric matrices are stored by mapping the lower-triangular region into one-dimensional arrays by rows. Develop a C++ class `LowSymmetric` that includes public members for the store and retrieve functions. The complexity of your functions should be $\Theta(1)$.

32. Let A and B be two $n \times n$ lower-triangular matrices. The total number of elements in the lower triangles of the two matrices is $n(n+1)$. Devise a scheme to represent both triangles in an array `d[n+1][n]`. [*Hint:* If you join the lower triangle of A and the upper-triangle of B^T, you get an $(n+1) \times n$ matrix.] Write the store and retrieve functions for both A and B. The complexity of each should be $\Theta(1)$.

★ 33.   A **square band matrix** $D_{n,a}$ is an $n \times n$ matrix in which all the nonzero terms lie in a band centered around the main diagonal. The band includes the main diagonal and $a - 1$ diagonals below and above the main diagonal (Figure 4.9).

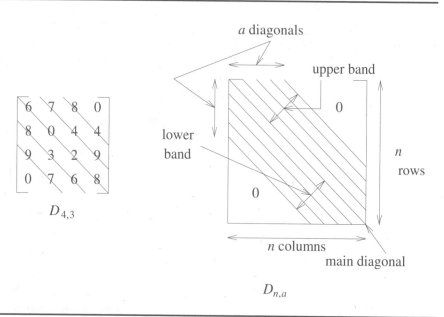

Figure 4.9 Square band matrix

(a)   How many elements are there in the band $D_{n,a}$?

(b)   What is the relationship between i and j for elements $d_{i,j}$ in the band $D_{n,a}$?

(c)   Assume that the band of $D_{n,a}$ is mapped into a one-dimensional array b by diagonals, starting with the lowest diagonal. For example, the band matrix $D_{4,3}$ of Figure 4.9 would have the following representation:

b[0]	b[1]	b[2]	b[3]	b[4]	b[5]	b[6]	b[7]	b[8]	b[9]	b[10]	b[11]	b[12]	b[13]
9	7	8	3	6	6	0	2	8	7	4	9	8	4
d_{20}	d_{31}	d_{10}	d_{21}	d_{32}	d_{00}	d_{11}	d_{22}	d_{33}	d_{01}	d_{12}	d_{23}	d_{02}	d_{13}

Obtain a formula for the location of an element $d_{i,j}$ in the lower band of $D_{n,a}$ (location(d_{10}) = 2 in the example above).

(d) Develop a C++ class `SquareBand` that uses the mapping of (c). Your class must include public members for the store and retrieve functions. What is the time complexity of each?

34. An $n \times n$ matrix `T` is a **Toeplitz matrix** iff $T(i,j) = T(i-1, j-1)$ for all i and j, $i > 1$ and $j > 1$.

(a) Show that a Toeplitz matrix has at most $2n - 1$ distinct elements.

(b) Obtain a mapping of a Toeplitz matrix into a one-dimensional array of size $2n - 1$.

(c) Use the mapping of (b) to obtain a C++ class `Toeplitz` in which a Toeplitz matrix is mapped into a one-dimensional array of size $2n - 1$. Include public members for the store and retrieve functions. The complexity of each should be $\Theta(1)$.

(d) Write a public member to multiply two Toeplitz matrices stored as in (b). The result is stored in a two-dimensional array. What is the time complexity of your code?

35. An $n \times n$ square matrix M is an **antidiagonal** matrix iff all entries $M(i,j)$ with $i + j \neq n + 1$ equal zero.

(a) Give a sample of a 4×4 antidiagonal matrix.

(b) Show that the antidiagonal matrix M has at most n nonzero entries.

(c) Devise a way to represent an antidiagonal matrix in a one-dimensional array of size n.

(d) Use the representation of (c) to arrive at the code for a C++ class `AntiDiagonal` that includes public members for the store and retrieve functions.

(e) What is the time complexity of your store and retrieve codes?

4.4 SPARSE MATRICES

4.4.1 Motivation

An $m \times n$ matrix is said to be **sparse** if "many" of its elements are zero. A matrix that is not sparse is **dense**. The boundary between a dense and a sparse matrix is not precisely defined. Diagonal and tridiagonal $n \times n$ matrices are sparse. Each has O(n) nonzero terms and O(n^2) zero terms. Is an $n \times n$ triangular matrix sparse? It has at least $n(n-1)/2$ zero terms and at most $n(n+1)/2$ nonzero terms. For the representation schemes we shall be looking at in this section to be competitive over the standard two-dimensional array representation, the number of nonzero terms will need to be less that $n^2/3$ and in some cases less that $n^2/5$. In this context we will classify triangular matrices as dense.

Sparse matrices such as diagonal and tridiagonal matrices have sufficient structure in their nonzero regions that we can devise a simple representation scheme whose space requirements equal the size of the nonzero region. In this section we are concerned with sparse matrices with an irregular or unstructured nonzero region.

Example 4.5 A supermarket is conducting a study of the mix of items purchased by its customers. For this study data is gathered for the purchases made by 1000 customers. This data is organized into a matrix, *purchases*, with *purchases* (i,j) being the quantity of item i purchased by customer j. Suppose that the super-market has an inventory of 10,000 different items. The *purchases* matrix is therefore a 10,000 $\times$ 1000 matrix. If the average customer buys 20 different items, only about 20,000 of the 10,000,000 matrix entries are nonzero. However, the distribution of the nonzero entries does not fall into any well-defined struc-ture.

The supermarket has a 10,000 $\times$ 1 matrix, *price*. *price* (i) is the selling price of one unit of item i. The matrix *spent* = *purchases* ^{T} * *price* is a 1000 $\times$ 1 matrix that gives the amount spent by each of the customers. If a two-dimensional array is used to represent the matrix *purchases*, an unnecessarily large amount of memory is used and the time required to compute *spent* is also unnecessarily large. ■

4.4.2 Array Representation

The nonzero entries of an irregular sparse matrix may be mapped into a one-dimensional array in row-major order. For example, the nonzero entries of the 4 $\times$ 8 matrix of Figure 4.10(a) in row-major order are 2, 1, 6, 7, 3, 9, 8, 4, 5.

| 0 0 0 2 0 0 1 0 |
| 0 6 0 0 7 0 0 3 |
| 0 0 0 9 0 8 0 0 |
| 0 4 5 0 0 0 0 0 |

a[]	0	1	2	3	4	5	6	7	8
row	1	1	2	2	2	3	3	4	4
col	4	7	2	5	8	4	6	2	3
value	2	1	6	7	3	9	8	4	5

(a) A 4 $\times$ 8 matrix | (b) Its representation

Figure 4.10 A sparse matrix and its array representation

To reconstruct the matrix structure, we need to record the row and column each nonzero entry comes from. So each element of the array into which the sparse matrix is mapped needs to have three fields: `row` (the row of the matrix entry), `col` (the column of the matrix entry), and `value` (the value of the matrix entry). For this purpose, we define the template class `Term` as shown:

```
template <class T>
class Term {
   private:
       int row, col;
       T value;
};
```

If `a` is an array of type `Term`, the nonzero entries of the matrix of Figure 4.10(a) may be stored in `a` in row-major order as shown in Figure 4.10(b). In addition to storing the array `a`, we need to store the number of rows, columns, and nonzero terms. So the number of bytes of memory used to store the nine nonzero elements of Figure 4.10(a) is `21*sizeof(int)+9*sizeof(T)`. If we had represented our matrix using a 4×8 array, the space used would have been `32*sizeof(T)`. Suppose that `T` is `int` and that `sizeof(T)` is 2 bytes. The representation of Figure 4.10(b) uses 60 bytes, while a 4×8 array takes 64 bytes. The space saving achieved by the one-dimensional array representation isn't much in this case. However, for the matrix *purchase* (see our supermarket example, Example 4.5), the one-dimensional array representation takes `60000*sizeof(int)` bytes, while the two-dimensional array representation needs `10000000*sizeof(int)` bytes. If an integer takes 2 bytes, the space saving is 19,880,000 bytes!

The array representation of a sparse matrix does not lead to efficient implementations of the store and retrieve functions. The store operation takes O(number of nonzero entries) time as we may need to move this many terms to make room for the new term. The retrieve function takes O(log [number of nonzero entries]) time if a binary search is used. Each of these operations takes $\Theta(1)$ time using the standard two-dimensional array representation. However, matrix operations such as transpose, add, and multiply can be performed efficiently.

The Class `SparseMatrix`

We may define a class `SparseMatrix` (Program 4.20) that uses the row-major mapping of a sparse matrix into a one-dimensional array. This class is a friend of `Term`. The private members `rows`, `cols`, and `terms` denote the number of rows, columns, and nonzero terms in the sparse matrix. `MaxTerms` is the capacity of the array `a` used to hold the nonzero terms. In defining the public members, we have chosen not to overload the `+` operator for add because `+` creates a temporary result that then needs to be copied into the return environment. Since the copy constructor for `SparseMatrix` will need to copy every term, this copying is expensive and may be avoided using a function such as `Add` that tells you where to put the result.

```
template<class T>
class SparseMatrix
{
   friend ostream& operator<<
         (ostream&, const SparseMatrix<T>&);
   friend istream& operator>>
         (istream&, SparseMatrix<T>&);
   public:
      SparseMatrix(int maxTerms = 10);
      ~SparseMatrix() {delete [] a;}
      void Transpose(SparseMatrix<T> &b) const;
      void Add(const SparseMatrix<T> &b,
            SparseMatrix<T> &c) const;
   private:
      void Append(const Term<T>& t);
      int rows, cols;  // matrix dimensions
      int terms;   // current number of nonzero terms
      Term<T> *a;    // term array
      int MaxTerms; // size of array a;
};
```

Program 4.20 The class `SparseMatrix`

Program 4.21 gives the class constructor and Program 4.22 gives the input (<<) and output (>>) codes. These latter two codes require that `operator<<` and `operator>>` be friends of the class `Term`. `operator<<` outputs the nonzero terms in row-major order, while `operator<<` inputs the sparse matrix terms in row-major order and sets up the internal representation. Both `operator<<` and `operator>>` take $\Theta(\text{terms})$ time. Exercises 37 and 38 consider refinements of the codes of Program 4.22.

```
template<class T>
SparseMatrix<T>::SparseMatrix(int maxTerms)
{// Sparse matrix constructor.
   if (maxTerms < 1) throw BadInitializers();
   MaxTerms = maxTerms;
   a = new Term<T> [MaxTerms];
   terms = rows = cols = 0;
}
```

Program 4.21 `SparseMatrix` constructor

```
// overload <<
template <class T>
ostream& operator<<(ostream& out,
                    const SparseMatrix<T>& x)
{// Put *this in output stream.

   // put matrix characteristics
   out << "rows = " << x.rows << " columns = "
       << x.cols  << endl;
   out << "nonzero terms = " << x.terms << endl;

   // put terms, one per line
   for (int i = 0; i < x.terms; i++)
      out << "a(" << x.a[i].row << ',' << x.a[i].col
          << ") = " << x.a[i].value << endl;

   return out;
}

// overload >>
template<class T>
istream& operator>>(istream& in, SparseMatrix<T>& x)
{// Input a sparse matrix.

   // input matrix characteristics
   cout << "Enter number of rows, columns, and terms"
        << endl;
   in >> x.rows >> x.cols >> x.terms;
   if (x.terms > x.MaxTerms) throw NoMem();

   // input terms
   for (int i = 0; i < x.terms; i++) {
      cout << "Enter row, column, and value of term "
           << (i + 1) << endl;
      in >> x.a[i].row >> x.a[i].col >> x.a[i].value;
      }

   return in;
}
```

Program 4.22 SparseMatrix input and output codes

`operator>>` throws an exception if the number of terms to be input exceeds the size of the array `*this.a`. An alternative to throwing an exception is to delete the array `a` and allocate a larger one using the `new` operator (Exercise 38).

Matrix Transpose

Program 4.23 gives the code for the `Transpose` function. The transposed matrix is returned in `b`. We first verify that there is enough space in `b` to store the nonzero terms of the transposed matrix. If not, we need to either get a larger array `b.a` or throw an exception. Our code throws an exception. If there is enough space in `b` to accommodate the transpose, two arrays `ColSize` and `RowNext` are created. `ColSize[i]` is the number of nonzero terms of the input matrix that are in column `i`. `RowNext[i]` denotes the location in `b` for the next nonzero term that is in row `i` of the transpose. `ColSize` is computed in the first two `for` loops by simply examining each term of the input matrix. `RowNext` is now computed as in the third `for` loop. Initially, `RowNext[i]` is the number of terms in rows 0 through `i-1` of the transpose and is equal to the number of terms in columns 0 through `i-1` of the input matrix. Finally, in the last `for` loop, the nonzero terms are copied from the input matrix to their correct positions in `b`.

Although Program 4.23 is more complex than its counterpart for matrices stored as two-dimensional arrays (see Program 2.22), for matrices with many zero entries, it is faster. It is not too difficult to see that computing the transpose of the *purchase* matrix of Example 4.5 using the one-dimensional array representation and function `Transpose` is much faster than using a two-dimensional array repsentation and the transpose function of Program 2.22. The time complexity of `Transpose` is O(`cols+terms`).

Adding Two Matrices

Our code to add two matrices uses the function `Append` (Program 4.24) that appends a nonzero term to the end of the array of nonzero terms of a sparse matrix. Its complexity is $\Theta(1)$.

The code of Program 4.25 adds the matrices `*this` and `b` and returns the result in `c`. The result matrix `c` is produced by scanning the terms of the two input matrices from left to right. This scan is done using two cursors (variables that move through a list): `ct` (cursor for matrix `*this`) and `cb` (cursor for matrix `b`). On each iteration of the `while` loop, we need to determine whether the position in `c` of the term `(*this).a[ct]` is before, at the same place as, or after that of `b.a[cb]`. We can make this determination by computing the row-major index of these two terms. It is actually simpler to compute the row-major index plus the number of columns in the matrix, as we do in function `Add`. The index for the term of `*this` is given by `indt` and that for the term of `b` by `indb`.

```
template<class T>
void SparseMatrix<T>::
     Transpose(SparseMatrix<T> &b) const
{// Return transpose of *this in b.

   // make sure b has enough space
   if (terms > b.MaxTerms) throw NoMem();

   // set transpose characteristics
   b.cols = rows;
   b.rows = cols;
   b.terms = terms;

   // initialize to compute transpose
   int *ColSize, *RowNext;
   ColSize = new int[cols + 1];
   RowNext = new int[rows + 1];

   // find number of entries in each column of *this
   for (int i = 1; i <= cols; i++) // initialize
      ColSize[i] = 0;
   for (int i = 0; i < terms; i++)
      ColSize[a[i].col]++;

   // find the starting point of each row of b
   RowNext[1] = 0;
   for (int i = 2; i <= cols; i++)
      RowNext[i] = RowNext[i - 1] + ColSize[i - 1];

   // perform the transpose copying from *this to b
   for (int i = 0; i < terms; i++) {
      int j = RowNext[a[i].col]++; // position in b
      b.a[j].row = a[i].col;
      b.a[j].col = a[i].row;
      b.a[j].value = a[i].value;
      }
}
```

Program 4.23 Transposing a sparse matrix

```
template<class T>
void SparseMatrix<T>::Append(const Term<T>& t)
{// Append a nonzero term t to *this.
   if (terms >= MaxTerms) throw NoMem();
   a[terms] = t;
   terms++;
}
```

Program 4.24 Appending a nonzero term

```
template<class T>
void SparseMatrix<T>::Add(const SparseMatrix<T> &b,
                              SparseMatrix<T> &c) const
{// Compute c = (*this) + b.

   // verify compatibility
   if (rows != b.rows || cols != b.cols)
     throw SizeMismatch(); // incompatible matrices

   // set characteristics of result c
   c.rows = rows;
   c.cols = cols;
   c.terms = 0; // initial value

   // define cursors to move through *this and b
   int ct = 0, cb = 0;

   // move through *this and b adding like terms
   while (ct < terms && cb < b.terms) {

      // Row-major index plus cols of each term
      int indt = a[ct].row * cols + a[ct].col;
      int indb = b.a[cb].row * cols + b.a[cb].col;

      if (indt < indb) {// b term comes later
      c.Append(a[ct]);
          ct++;} // next term of *this
```

Program 4.25 Adding two sparse matrices (continues)

```
      else {if (indt == indb) {// both in same position

            // append to c only if sum not zero
            if (a[ct].value + b.a[cb].value) {
               Term<T> t;
               t.row = a[ct].row;
               t.col = a[ct].col;
               t.value = a[ct].value + b.a[cb].value;
               c.Append(t);}

            ct++; cb++;}  // next terms of *this and b
         else {c.Append(b.a[cb]);
               cb++;} // next term of b
      }
   }

   // copy over remaining terms
   for (; ct < terms; ct++)
      c.Append(a[ct]);
   for (; cb < b.terms; cb++)
      c.Append(b.a[cb]);
}
```

Program 4.25 Adding two sparse matrices (concluded)

The `while` loop of function `Add` is iterated at most `terms+b.terms` times, as on each iteration `ct`, `cb`, or both are incremented. The first `for` loop is iterated at most `terms` times, while the second is iterated O(`b.terms`) times. Also, each iteration of each loop takes constant time. So the complexity of `Add` is O(`terms+b.terms`). If the two matrices were represented as two-dimensional arrays, it would take O(`rows*cols`) time to add them. When `terms+b.terms` is much less than `rows*cols`, the sparse matrix representation results in a much faster implementation.

4.4.3   Linked Representation

A shortcoming of the one-dimensional array representation of a sparse matrix is that we need to know the number of nonzero terms in each of the sparse matrices we plan to use when the array is created. Although this number is known for arrays being input, the number of nonzero terms in the matrix that results from the addition, subtraction, and multiplication of two matrices cannot be accurately computed without actually performing the operation. Without this information, we can estimate the number of nonzero terms in each matrix and declare each array to have this estimated size. We adopted this strategy when we wrote the codes for the class `SparseMatrix`. Although our codes for this class throw an exception when the number of terms in the result matrix exceeds the estimated number, the codes could be rewritten so as to allocate a new larger array, copy the terms over from the old array, and delete the old array. This extra work slows the algorithms and leaves us with the question of how much larger the new array should be. If it isn't large enough, we will have to repeat the allocate and copy process, and if it is too large, we waste space. An alternative is to use a pointer-based representation. This alternative incurs a space overhead to store pointers and other information not stored in the array representation. However, it requires no storage reallocation and copying of partial results.

The Representation

One possibility for a linked representation is to link together the nonzero entries in each row to form a chain, as is shown by the unshaded nodes of Figure 4.11. Each unshaded node represents a nonzero term of the sparse matrix and has three fields—col (the column number for the term), value (the value of the term), and link (pointer to next unshaded node). These row chains are created only for rows that have at least one nonzero term. The nodes on a row chain are linked in ascending order of their col value.

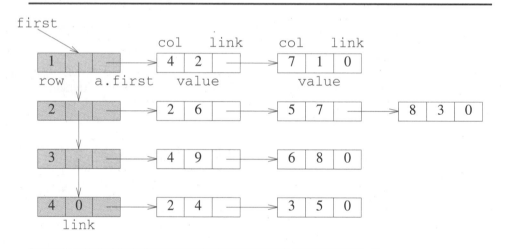

Figure 4.11 Linked representation of matrix of Figure 4.10(a)

The row chains (i.e., unshaded chains) are collected together by using another chain as shown by the shaded nodes of Figure 4.11. Each shaded node has three fields—row (row number for corresponding row chain), link (pointer to next shaded node), and a (the chain of unshaded nodes, a.first points to the first unshaded node). The shaded nodes are linked together in ascending order of their row value. Each shaded node may be viewed as the head node of a row chain and the shaded chain may be viewed as a head node chain. An empty head node chain represents a matrix with no nonzero terms.

Chain Node Types

The chains defined by the unshaded nodes of Figure 4.11 may be represented as members of the class Chain<CNode<T> > where CNode is as in Program 4.26. The chain defined by the shaded nodes is a member of the class Chain<Headnode<T> > where HeadNode<T> is as in Program 4.26.

The Class LinkedMatrix

The class LinkedMatrix may now be defined as in Program 4.27. The implementations of the public member functions as well as the overloading of the operators >> and << require that LinkedMatrix, operator>>, and operator<< be friends of the classes CNode and HeadNode.

Overloading >>

Program 4.28 inputs the nonzero terms in row-major order and creates the linked representation of Figure 4.11. It begins by inputting the dimensions of the matrix as well as the number of nonzero terms. Next, the terms are input and assembled into row chains. We use variable H as the head node of the row chain that is currently being assembled. If the new term does not belong to the current row, the current row chain is appended to the head node chain x.a of the input matrix x (unless this chain is for the fictional row 0). Following this, H is set to start a new row chain and the new term appended to this new row chain. If the new term belongs to the current row chain, it is simply appended to this chain . (i.e., to the chain H.a). Note that the functions Append and Zero are members of the extended chain class defined in Section 3.4.3. Append adds a node at the end of a chain while Zero sets first to zero but does not delete the nodes on the chain. The complexity of operator>> is O(terms).

```
template<class T>
class CNode {
   public:
      int operator !=(const CNode<T>& y)
         {return (value != y.value);}
      void Output(ostream& out) const
         {out << "column " << col
              << " value " << value;}
   private:
      int col;
      T value;
};

template<class T>
ostream& operator<<(ostream& out, const CNode<T>& x)
   {x.Output(out); out << endl; return out;}

template<class T>
class HeadNode {
   public:
      int operator !=(const HeadNode<T>& y)
         {return (row != y.row);}
      void Output(ostream& out) const
         {out << "row " << row;}
   private:
      int row;
      Chain<CNode<T> > a; // row chain
};

template<class T>
ostream& operator<<(ostream& out,
                    const HeadNode<T>& x)
   {x.Output(out); out << endl; return out;}
```

Program 4.26 Chain nodes used in sparse matrix representation

```
template<class T>
class LinkedMatrix
{
   public:
      LinkedMatrix(){}
      ~LinkedMatrix(){}
      void Transpose(LinkedMatrix<T> &b) const;
      void Add(const LinkedMatrix<T> &b,
               LinkedMatrix<T> &c) const;
   private:
      int rows, cols;            // matrix dimensions
      Chain<HeadNode<T> > a;   // head node chain
};
```

Program 4.27 Class definition for a linked sparse matrix

```
template<class T>
istream& operator>>(istream& in, LinkedMatrix<T>& x)
{// Input matrix x from the stream in.
   x.a.Erase(); // delete all nodes from x

   // get matrix characteristics
   int terms;   // number of terms to be input
   cout << "Enter number of rows, columns, and terms"
        << endl;
   in >> x.rows >> x.cols >> terms;

   // create fictional row zero
   HeadNode<T> H;   // head node for current row
   H.row = 0;       // current row number

   // get terms of matrix x
   for (int i = 1; i <= terms; i++) {
      // get next term
      cout << "Enter row, column, and value of term "
           << i << endl;
      int row, col;
      T value;
      in >> row >> col >> value;
```

Program 4.28 Input a sparse matrix (continues)

```
      // check if new term is part of current row
   if (row > H.row) {// start a new row
      // append head node H of current row to
      // head node chain x.a only if row not zero
      if (H.row) x.a.Append(H);

      // prepare H for new row
      H.row = row;
      H.a.Zero();}  // save from chain destructor

   // add new term to row chain
   CNode<T> *c = new CNode<T>;
   c->col = col;
   c->value = value;
   H.a.Append(*c);
   }
// take care of last row of matrix
if (H.row) x.a.Append(H);
H.a.Zero(); // save from chain destructor

return in;
}
```

Program 4.28 Input a sparse matrix (concluded)

Overloading <<
To output a linked sparse matrix, we use a chain iterator (see Section 3.4.4) to move down the head node chain one node at a time. At each node of this head node chain, the row chain is output. Program 4.29 gives the code. Its complexity is linear in the number of nonzero terms.

The Function Transpose
For the transpose operation, we use bins to collect the terms of the input matrix *this that belong in the same row of the result. bin[i] is a chain for the terms of row i (column i) of the result matrix b. In the while loop of Program 4.30, we examine the terms of *this in row-major order by going down the head node chain of the input matrix and making a left to right traversal of each row chain. We move along the head node and row chains using a chain iterator p for the head node chain and another iterator q for the row chain. Each term encountered in this ordered traversal of the matrix *this is appended to the bin chain for its row in the result. The bin chains are collected together in the for loop to create the head node chain of the result.

```
template<class T>
ostream& operator<<(ostream& out,
                    const LinkedMatrix<T>& x)
{// Put matrix x into the output stream out.
   ChainIterator<HeadNode<T> > p;// head node iterator

   // output matrix dimensions
   out << "rows = " << x.rows << " columns = "
      << x.cols << endl;

   // set h to point to first head node
   HeadNode<T> *h = p.Initialize(x.a);
   if (!h) {out << "No nonzero terms" << endl;
               return out;}

   // output one row at a time
   while (h) {
      out << "row " << h->row << endl;
      out << h->a << endl;  // output row chain
      h = p.Next();          // next head node
      }

   return out;
}
```

Program 4.29 Output a sparse matrix

```
template<class T>
void LinkedMatrix<T>::
    Transpose(LinkedMatrix<T> &b) const
{// Return transpose of *this as matrix b.
   b.a.Erase(); // delete all nodes from b

   // create bins to collect rows of b
   Chain<CNode<T> > *bin;
   bin = new Chain<CNode<T> > [cols + 1];

   // head node iterator
   ChainIterator<HeadNode<T> > p;
```

Program 4.30 Transpose a sparse matrix (continues)

```
// set h to point to first head node of *this
HeadNode<T> *h = p.Initialize(a);

// copy terms of *this into bins
while (h) { // examine all rows
   int r = h->row; // row number for row chain

   // row chain iterator
   ChainIterator<CNode<T> > q;
   // set z to point to first node in row chain
   CNode<T> *z = q.Initialize(h->a);

   CNode<T> x;   // temporary node
   // terms from row r of *this go to column r of b
   x.col = r;

   // examine all terms in row r of *this
   while (z) {// go down row r
      x.value = z->value;
      // append term to bin for row z->col of b
      bin[z->col].Append(x);
      z = q.Next();   // next term in row
            }

   h = p.Next(); // go to next row
         }

// set dimensions of b and empty it
b.rows = cols;
b.cols = rows;

// assemble head node chain of b
HeadNode<T> H;
// scan bins
for (int i = 1; i <= cols; i++)
   if (!bin[i].IsEmpty()) {// row i of transpose
      H.row = i;
      H.a = bin[i];
      b.a.Append(H);
      bin[i].Zero();} // save from destructor
```

Program 4.30 Transpose a sparse matrix (continues)

```
    H.a.Zero(); // save from destructor

    delete [] bin;
}
```

Program 4.30 Transpose a sparse matrix (concluded)

The time spent in the `while` loop is linear in the number of nonzero terms, while that spent in the `for` loop is linear in the number of columns in the input matrix. The overall time is therefore linear in the sum of these two quantities.

Exercise 45 asks you to implement the `Add` function as well as other basic functions.

EXERCISES

36. Write the store and retrieve functions for a sparse matrix stored in row-major order in a one-dimensional array. What is the time complexity of your functions?

37. Refine the code for `operator>>` (Program 4.22) so that it verifies that the terms are in fact input in row-major order, that the row and column indexes of each term are valid, and that each term is nonzero.

38. Modify the code for `operator>>` (Program 4.22) so that it tries to get a larger array for the terms in case `x.MaxSize` is smaller than `x.terms`.

39. Write a copy constructor for the class `SparseMatrix`.

40. Modify the code for `Append` (Program 4.24) so that it tries to get a larger array `a` in case the current `a` does not have adequate space.

41. Extend the class `SparseMatrix` (Program 4.20) by adding public members to multiply and subtract matrices.

42. Suppose that a sparse matrix is mapped into a one-dimensional array in column-major order of the nonzero entries.

    (a) Obtain the representation of the sparse matrix of Figure 4.10(a).

    (b) Write the store and retrieve functions for sparse matrices stored in this way.

    (c) What is the time complexity of your functions?

★43. Write a function to multiply two sparse matrices represented using a one-dimensional array. Assume both are mapped in row-major order. The result matrix is similarly represented.

⋆ 44. Write a function to multiply two sparse matrices represented using a one-dimensional array. Assume both are mapped in column-major order. The result matrix is similarly represented.

⋆ 45. Extend the class `LinkedMatrix` by adding public members for the following operations:

   (a) Store a term given the row index, column index, and value of the term.

   (b) Retrieve the term with a given row and column of the matrix.

   (c) Add two sparse matrices.

   (d) Subtract two sparse matrices.

   (e) Multiply two sparse matrices.

   Also, refine the code for `operator>>` as desribed in Exercise 37. Test your code.

⋆ 46. An alternative linked representation for sparse matrices uses nodes that have the fields `down`, `right`, `row`, `col`, and `value`. Each nonzero entry of the sparse matrix is represented by a node. The zero entries are not explicitly stored. The nodes are linked together to form two circular lists. The first list, the row list, is made up by linking nodes by rows and within rows by columns using the `right` field. The second list, the column list, is made up by linking nodes via the `down` field. In this list, nodes are linked by columns and within columns by rows. These two lists share a common head node. In addition, a node is added to contain the dimensions of the matrix.

   (a) Write down any 5×8 matrix that has exactly nine nonzero terms such that there is at least one nonzero term in each row and each column. For this sparse matrix, draw the linked representation.

   (b) Suppose that an $m \times n$ matrix with t nonzero terms is represented as above. How small must t be so that the above linked scheme uses less space than an $m \times n$ array uses?

   (c) Design a suitable external (i.e., one that can be used for input and output) representation for a sparse matrix. Your representation should not require explicit input of the zero terms.

   (d) Do Exercise 37 using the representation of (b).

   (e) For each of the public members of the class, obtain its asymptotic time complexity. How do these complexities compare with the corresponding complexities using two-dimensional arrays?

CHAPTER 5

STACKS

BIRD'S-EYE VIEW

Stacks and queues are, perhaps, the most frequently used data structures. Both are restricted versions of the linear or ordered list data structure covered in Chapter 3. We shall study stacks in this chapter and queues in the next. The stack data structure is obtained from a linear list by restricting the insertions and deletions to take place from the same end. As a result, a stack is a last-in-first-out (LIFO) structure.

Since a stack is a special kind of linear list, it is natural to derive stack classes from corresponding linear list classes. Therefore, we may derive a formula-based stack class from the class `LinearList` (Program 3.1) and a linked-stack class from the class `Chain` (Program 3.8). While these derivations simplify the programming task, they result in code that incurs a significant run-time penalty. Since a stack is a very basic data structure that many applications employ, we also develop formula-based and linked-stack classes from scratch (i.e., not derived from any other class). These latter classes provide improved run-time performance over their derived counterparts.

Six application codes that make use of stacks are also developed. The first is a simple program to match left and right parentheses in an expression. The second is the classical towers of Hanoi problem in which we move disks one at a time from a source tower to a destination tower using one intermediary tower; each tower operates as a stack. The third application uses stacks to represent shunting tracks in a railroad yard. The objective is to rearrange the cars in a train into the desired order. The fourth application is from the computer-aided design of circuits field. In this application, we use a stack to determine whether a switch box can be feasibly routed. The fifth application revisits the offline equivalence class problem introduced in Section 3.8.3. A stack enables us to determine the equivalence classes in linear time. The final application considered in this chapter is the classical rat in a maze problem in which we are to find a path from the entrance of a maze to its exit. You are urged to go through this application very carefully, as its treatment in this chapter illustrates many software-engineering principles.

The new C++ language features used in this chapter are derived classes and inheritance.

5.1 THE ABSTRACT DATA TYPE

Definition A **stack** is a linear list in which insertions (also called additions) and deletions take place at the same end. This end is called the **top**. The other end of the list is called the **bottom**. ∎

Figure 5.1(a) shows a stack with four elements Suppose we wish to add the element E to the stack of Figure 5.1(a). This element will have to be placed on top of the element D, giving us the configuration of Figure 5.1(b). If we are to delete an element from the stack of Figure 5.1(b), it will be the element E. Following the deletion, the configuration of Figure 5.1(a) results. If we perform three successive deletions on the stack of Figure 5.1(b), the stack of Figure 5.1(c) results.

```
                          E←top
D←top                     D
C                         C
B                         B                      B←top
A←bottom                  A←bottom               A←bottom

   (a)                       (b)                     (c)
```

Figure 5.1 Stack configurations

From the preceding discussion, we see that a stack is a LIFO (last-in-first-out) list. Lists of this type appear frequently in computing. The ADT stack is specified in ADT 5.1.

5.2 DERIVED CLASSES AND INHERITANCE

We often have to deal with a new data object that is a specialized or restricted version of a more general data object. For example, in this chapter we are considering the data object stack that is a restricted version of the more general data object linear list. Every instance of the data object stack is also an instance of the data object linear list. Moreover, all the stack operations can be performed as linear list operations. For example, if we designate the left end of the list as the stack bottom and the right as the stack top, then the stack add operation is equivalent to inserting at the right end of a linear list and the stack delete operation is equivalent to deleting from this same end.

AbstractDataType *Stack* {
   instances
      linear list of elements; one end is called the *bottom*; the other is the *top*;
   operations
     Create (): Create an empty stack;
     IsEmpty (): Return `true` if stack is empty, return `false` otherwise;
     IsFull (): Return `true` if stack is full, return `false` otherwise;
     Top (): Return top element of stack;
     Add (x): Add element x to the stack;
     Delete (x): Delete top element from stack and put it in x;
}

ADT 5.1 The abstract data type stack

As a result of these observations, we expect that the implementation of C++ classes for the data object stack will be simplified if we can explicitly declare a stack to be a special type of linear list and also define the stack operations in terms of linear list operations.

A class `B` that is a specialized or restricted version of another class `A` may be derived from `A`. We call `A` the base class and `B` the derived class. A class `B` that derives from class `A` **inherits** all of the members—public, protected, and private—of the base class `A`, and all data members and functions of `A` are associated with every object of type `B`. Class `B` may inherit these members of class `A` in one of three basic ways (or modes): public, protected, and private. A public inheritance, for example, may be specified using the class header syntax

```
class B : public A
```

A class may derive from more than one class. The class header syntax when `B` derives from both `A` and `C` and inherits publically from `A` but privately from `C` is

```
class B : public A, private C
```

In all modes of inheritance, the private members of the base class `A` remain private to `A` and are not accessible from members of `B`. The different inheritance modes affect the accessiblity of protected and public members of the base class only.

When `B` inherits publically from `A`, the protected members of `A` become protected members of `B` and the public members of `A` become public members of `B`. So when writing the code for the explicitly declared members of `B`, we have access to the public and protected members of `A` but not to the private members of `A`. If `X` is of type `B`, then the user may perform function `F` on `X` by writing `X.F()` only when `F` is a public member of either `B` or `A`.

When the inheritance mode is protected, both the public and protected members of A become protected members of B. If X and F are as stated, the user may do X.F() only for functions F that are public members of B.

If the derivation mode is private, then the public and protected members of A become private in B.

All derivation modes may be prefixed by the word virtual. We shall see the significance of this prefixing in Chapter 12.

5.3 FORMULA-BASED REPRESENTATION

Since a stack is a linear list with the restriction that additions and deletions take place at the same end, we may use the linear list representation of Section 3.3. The top element of the stack is stored in element[length-1], and the bottom element in element[0]. The class Stack defined in Program 5.1 is a derived class of LinearList (Program 3.1). Since the inheritance mode is private, the protected and public members of LinearList are accessible by members of Stack, but not by stack instances. The public and protected members of LinearList become private to Stack. However, the private members of LinearList are not accessible to members of Stack.

```
template<class T>
class Stack : private LinearList <T> {
// LIFO objects.
   public:
      Stack(int MaxStackSize = 10)
        : LinearList<T> (MaxStackSize) {}
      bool IsEmpty() const
          {return LinearList<T>::IsEmpty();}
      bool IsFull() const
         {return (Length() == GetMaxSize());}
      T Top() const
         {if (IsEmpty()) throw OutOfBounds();
          T x; Find(Length(), x); return x;}
      Stack<T>& Add(const T& x)
         {Insert(Length(), x); return *this;}
      Stack<T>& Delete(T& x)
         {LinearList<T>::Delete(Length(), x);
          return *this;}
};
```

Program 5.1 Formula-based class Stack

The constructor for `Stack` simply invokes the linear list constructor passing to it the desired stack size `MaxStackSize`. We have defined no destructor for our class. When objects of type `Stack` are to be destroyed, the destructor for `LinearList` will be invoked automatically. The `IsEmpty` function is simply a call to the corresponding function for a linear list. We use the scope resolution operator `::` to distinguish between functions and members that have the same name in the base and derived class.

The fact that private members of `LinearList` are not accessible to members of `Stack` poses a problem when implementing the function `IsFull`. To implement this function, we need to know the value of `LinearList<T>::MaxSize`. We could overcome this problem by making `MaxSize` a protected member of `LinearList`. However, if we later change the implementation of `LinearList` and no longer have this data member, we would also need to change our `Stack` implementation. This fact is not known to `LinearList`, as its code does not record all the classes derived from it. A better solution is to add a protected member `GetMaxSize()`, defined as below, to the class `LinearList`.

```
protected:
    int GetMaxSize() const {return MaxSize;}
```

This function is accessible to members of `Stack`. Should the implementation of `LinearList` change, we would need to change the implementation of `GetMaxSize`, but not that of any of the derived classes. An alternative is to define an `IsFull` function for `LinearList`.

In the definition of `Stack<T>::IsFull` (Program 5.1), we do not need to use the syntax `LinearList<T>::Length()`, as there is no `Length()` function for stacks.

The function `Top` first verifies whether the stack is empty. If so, there is no top element and an `OutOfBounds` exception is thrown. When the stack is not empty, it invokes the linear list `Find` function to determine the element at the right end.

The function `Add` adds the element `x` to the top of the stack by inserting `x` at the right end of the linear list. `Delete` removes the top element of the stack and puts it in `x`. This operation is accomplished by performing a deletion from the right end of a linear list. Both add and delete functions return the modified stack. Neither `Add` nor `Delete` catch the exception that might be thrown by `Insert` or `LinearList<T>::Delete`. They leave it to the function that invoked them to catch the thrown exception.

Suppose that `X` is an object of type `Stack`. Users of `X` may perform `X.F` where `F` is any one of the public members of `Stack`. However, users may not perform `X.F` for `LinearList` functions (such as `Length`) as none of these functions are public members of `Stack` (because the inheritance mode is private).

Efficiency of `Stack`

The complexity of the stack constructor and destructor is $\Theta(1)$ when `T` is an internal data type and O(`MaxStackSize`) when `T` is a user-defined class. The complexity of each of the remaining stack operations is $\Theta(1)$. Notice that deriving `Stack` from `LinearList` reduces the effort we need to code the class `Stack`. Also, we have significantly improved our chances of obtaining a correct implementation as the methods for `LinearList` have already been tested and are known to be correct. Unfortunately, this simplification has come at the cost of increased run time. For example, to add an element to a stack, we first determine its `Length()` and then invoke `Insert`, which checks whether the insert is in range. Following this check, a `for` loop overhead is paid to perform zero element moves. We can eliminate these overheads by developing `Stack` as a base class rather than as a derived class.

Another potential difficulty is that the derived class `Stack` is subject to all the limitations of the class `LinearList`. For instance, the operations `<<` and `==` need to be defined on members of the data type `T` as the former is used in the overloading of `<<` for linear lists and the latter in `LinearList::Search`.

A Customized Definition of `Stack`

Program 5.2 defines the class `Stack` as a base class. The representation used is the same as for a linear list. The stack elements are stored in an array `stack` with `top` pointing to the top (or last) element. The stack capacity is `MaxTop+1`.

```
template<class T>
class Stack {
// LIFO objects.
   public:
      Stack(int MaxStackSize = 10);
      ~Stack() {delete [] stack;}
      bool IsEmpty() const {return top == -1;}
      bool IsFull() const {return top == MaxTop;}
      T Top() const;
      Stack<T>& Add(const T& x);
      Stack<T>& Delete(T& x);
   private:
      int top;     // current top of stack
      int MaxTop;  // max value for top
      T *stack;    // element array
};
```

Program 5.2 Customized version of `Stack` (continues)

```
template<class T>
Stack<T>::Stack(int MaxStackSize)
{// Stack constructor.
   MaxTop = MaxStackSize - 1;
   stack = new T[MaxStackSize];
   top = -1;
}

template<class T>
T Stack<T>::Top() const
{// Return top element.
   if (IsEmpty()) throw OutOfBounds(); // top fails
   else return stack[top];
}

template<class T>
Stack<T>& Stack<T>::Add(const T& x)
{// Add x to stack.
   if (IsFull()) throw NoMem(); // add fails
   stack[++top] = x;
   return *this;
}

template<class T>
Stack<T>& Stack<T>::Delete(T& x)
{// Delete top element and put in x.
   if (IsEmpty()) throw OutOfBounds(); // delete fails
   x = stack[top--];
   return *this;
}
```

Program 5.2 Customized version of `Stack` (concluded)

In a run-time test that involved a `for` with 100,000 stack add and delete operations, the code of Program 5.1 took 50 percent more time than did the code of Program 5.2.

EXERCISES

1. Extend the stack ADT by adding functions to:

   (a) Determine the size (i.e., number of elements) of the stack.

   (b) Input a stack.

   (c) Output a stack.

   Now extend the class definition of a formula-based stack to include these functions. Write and test the codes.

2. Extend the stack ADT by adding functions to

   (a) Split a stack in two. The first contains the bottom half elements, and the second the remaining elements.

   (b) Combine two stacks by placing all elements of the second stack on top of those in the first. The relative order of elements from the second stack is unchanged. Following the combine, the second stack is empty.

   Now extend the class definition of a formula-based stack to include code for these functions. Write and test the codes.

3. A shortcoming of the formula-based representation of a stack is the need to specify the value of `MaxStackSize` when the stack is created. One way around this shortcoming is to set `MaxTop = 0` when the stack is created. If, during an `Add` operation, we do not have space to accomodate the new element, `MaxTop` is changed to `2*MaxTop+1`, a new array of size `MaxTop+1` is allocated, elements are copied from the old array into the new one, and the old array is deleted. Similarly, during a delete operation, if the list size drops to one-fourth of the array capacity, a smaller array of half the size is allocated, the elements are copied from the old array into the new one, and the old array is deleted.

   (a) Obtain a new implementation of the customized class `Stack` that uses this idea. The constructor should have no parameters and should set `MaxTop` to 0, allocate an array of size 1, and set `top` to −1.

   (b) Consider any sequence of n add and delete operations beginning with an empty stack. Suppose that the total step count is $f(n)$ using the old implementation. Show that with the new implementation, it is at most $cf(n)$ for some constant c.

5.4   LINKED REPRESENTATION

While the array representation of a stack considered in the previous section is both elegant and efficient, it is wasteful of space when multiple stacks are to coexist. The reasons are the same as those cited in Section 3.3.4 for the inefficiency of the separate arrays for separate lists representation. An exception is when only two stacks are to coexist. We can maintain space and time efficiency by pegging the bottom of one stack at position 0 and the bottom of the other at position `MaxSize-1`. The two stacks grow toward the middle of the array (see Figure 5.2). When more than two stacks are to be represented, the multiple lists in a single array representation may be adapted to the case of multiple stacks. While this adaptation results in a space-efficient implementation, the worst-case add time becomes O(`ArraySize`) rather than $\Theta(1)$. The delete time remains $\Theta(1)$.

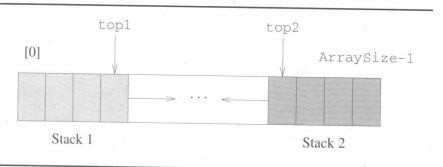

Figure 5.2 Two stacks in an array

Multiple stacks can be represented efficiently using a chain for each stack. This representation incurs a space penalty of one pointer field for each stack element. However, each stack operation can be performed in $\Theta(1)$ time.

When using a chain to represent a stack, we must decide which end of the chain corresponds to the stack top. If we associate the right end of the chain with the stack top, then stack additions and deletions are implemented using the chain operations `Insert(n,x)` and `Delete(n,x)` where n is the number of nodes in the chain. Each of these chain operations takes $\Theta(n)$ time. On the other hand, if we associate the left end of the chain with the stack top, then chain operations to use are `Insert(0,x)` and `Delete(1,x)`. Each of these operations takes $\Theta(1)$ time. This analysis shows that we should use the left end of the chain to represent the stack top.

Program 5.3 defines a linked stack that derives from the class `Chain`. The left end of the chain is the stack top, and the right end is the stack bottom.

```
template<class T>
class LinkedStack : private Chain<T> {
   public:
      bool IsEmpty() const
         {return Chain<T>::IsEmpty();}
      bool IsFull() const;
      T Top() const
         {if (IsEmpty()) throw OutOfBounds();
          T x; Find(1, x); return x;}
      LinkedStack<T>& Add(const T& x)
         {Insert(0, x); return *this;}
      LinkedStack<T>& Delete(T& x)
         {Chain<T>::Delete(1, x); return *this;}
};

template<class T>
bool LinkedStack<T>::IsFull() const
{// Is stack full?
   try {ChainNode<T> *p = new ChainNode<T>;
        delete p; return false;}
   catch (NoMem) {return true;}
}
```

Program 5.3 Linked stack derived from `Chain`

The implementation of `IsFull` is inelegant because the only way to know whether or not we can add an element to a stack is to see whether enough space exists to create a node of type `Node`. This check is done by invoking new and then deleting the created node as we do not intend to use it.

As in the case of the class `Stack` (Program 5.1), we can improve the run-time performance by customizing the code. Program 5.4 gives the customized code.

The code of Program 5.3 took 25 percent more time to execute a `for` loop of 100,000 add and delete operations than did the customized code of Program 5.4.

```
template <class T>
class Node {
   friend LinkedStack<T>;
   private:
      T data;
      Node<T> *link;
};

template<class T>
class LinkedStack {
   public:
      LinkedStack() {top = 0;}
      ~LinkedStack();
      bool IsEmpty() const {return top == 0;}
      bool IsFull() const;
      T Top() const;
      LinkedStack<T>& Add(const T& x);
      LinkedStack<T>& Delete(T& x);
   private:
      Node<T> *top; // pointer to top node
};

template<class T>
LinkedStack<T>::~LinkedStack()
{// Stack destructor..
   Node<T> *next;
   while (top) {
      next = top->link;
      delete top;
      top = next;
      }
}

template<class T>
bool LinkedStack<T>::IsFull() const
{// Is the stack full?
   try {Node<T> *p = new Node<T>;
        delete p;
        return false;}
   catch (NoMem) {return true;}
}
```

Program 5.4 Customized linked stack (continues)

```
template<class T>
T LinkedStack<T>::Top() const
{// Return top element.
   if (IsEmpty()) throw OutOfBounds();
   return top->data;
}

template<class T>
LinkedStack<T>& LinkedStack<T>::Add(const T& x)
{// Add x to stack.
   Node<T> *p = new Node<T>;
   p->data = x;
   p->link = top;
   top = p;
   return *this;
}

template<class T>
LinkedStack<T>& LinkedStack<T>::Delete(T& x)
{// Delete top element and put in x.
   if (IsEmpty()) throw OutOfBounds();
   x = top->data;
   Node<T> *p = top;
   top = top->link;
   delete p;
   return *this;
}
```

Program 5.4 Customized linked stack (concluded)

EXERCISES

4. (a) Write a program to measure the run time of an alternating sequence of 100,000 stack add and delete operations. Measure the times needed by Programs 5.1, 5.2, 5.3, 5.4, and the implementation of Exercise 3.

   (b) An alternating sequence of add and delete operations represents the best case for the code of Exercise 3. Develop worst-case data for this implementation and obtain the worst-case time for 100,000 stack operations.

5. Extend the class `LinkedStack` to include the following stack operations:

    (a) Determine the size (i.e., number of elements) of the stack.

    (b) Input a stack.

    (c) Output a stack.

6. Extend the class `LinkedStack` to include the following operations:

    (a) Split a stack in two. The first stack contains the bottom half elements, and the second contains the remaining elements.

    (b) Combine two stacks by placing all elements of the second stack on top of those in the first. The relative ordering of elements from the second stack is unchanged. Following the combine, the second stack is empty.

5.5   APPLICATIONS

5.5.1   Parenthesis Matching

In this problem we are to match the left and right parentheses in a character string. For example, the string (a * (b + c) + d) has left parentheses at positions 1 and 4 and right parentheses at positions 8 and 11. The left parenthesis at position 1 matches the right at position 11, while the left parenthesis at position 4 matches the right parenthesis at position 8. In the string (a + b))(, the right parenthesis at position 6 has no matching left parenthesis, and the left parenthesis at position 7 has no matching right parenthesis. Our objective is to write a C++ program that inputs a string and outputs the pairs of matched parentheses as well as those parentheses for which there is no match. Notice that the parenthesis matching problem is equivalent to the problem of matching braces ({ and }) in a C++ program.

We observe that if we scan the input string from left to right, then each right parenthesis is matched to the most recently seen unmatched left parenthesis. This observation motivates us to save the position of left parentheses on a stack as they are encountered in a left-to-right scan. When a right parenthesis is encountered, it is matched to the left parenthesis (if any) at the top of the stack. The matched left parenthesis is deleted from the stack. Program 5.5 gives the complete C++ program. Figure 5.3 gives a sample input/output dialogue. The time complexity of Program 5.5 is $\Theta(n)$ where n is the length of the input string.

```
#include <iostream.h>
#include <string.h>
#include <stdio.h>
#include "stack.h"

const int MaxLength = 100; // max expression length

void PrintMatchedPairs(char *expr)
{// Parenthesis matching.
   Stack<int> s(MaxLength);
   int j, length = strlen(expr);

   // scan expression expr for ( and )
   for (int i = 1; i <= length; i++) {
      if (expr[i - 1] == '(') s.Add(i);
      else if (expr[i - 1] == ')')
         try {s.Delete(j);   // unstack match
              cout << j << ' ' << i << endl;}
          catch (OutOfBounds)
              {cout << "No match for right parenthesis"
                    << " at " << i << endl;}

      }

   // remaining ( in stack are unmatched
   while (!s.IsEmpty()) {
      s.Delete(j);
      cout << "No match for left parenthesis at "
           << j << endl;}
}

void main(void)
{
   char expr[MaxLength];
   cout << "Type an expression of length at most "
        << MaxLength << endl;
   cin.getline(expr, MaxLength);
   cout <<"The pairs of matching parentheses in"
        << endl;
   puts(expr);
   cout <<"are" << endl;
   PrintMatchedPairs(expr);
}
```

Program 5.5 Program to output matched parentheses

Type an expression of length at most 100
(d+(a+b)*c*(d+e)-f))(()
The pairs of matching parentheses in the expression
(d+(a+b)*c*(d+e)-f))(()
are
4 8
12 16
1 19
No match for right parenthesis at 20
22 23
No match for left parenthesis at 21

Figure 5.3 Sample run of parenthesis-matching program

5.5.2   Towers of Hanoi

The **Towers of Hanoi** problem is fashioned after the ancient Tower of Brahma ritual. According to legend, when the world was created there was a diamond tower (tower 1) with sixty-four golden disks (Figure 5.4). The disks were of decreasing size and were stacked on the tower in decreasing order of size from bottom to top. Next to this tower are two other diamond towers (towers 2 and 3). Since the time of creation, Brahman priests have been attempting to move the disks from tower 1 to tower 2, using tower 3 for intermediate storage. As the disks are very heavy, they can be moved only one at a time. In addition, at no time can a disk be on top of a smaller disk. According to legend, the world will come to an end when the priests have completed their task.

In the Towers of Hanoi problem, we are given n disks and three towers. The disks are initially stacked on tower 1 in decreasing order of size from bottom to top. We are to move the disks to tower 2, one disk at a time, such that no disk is ever on top of a smaller one. You may wish to attempt a solution to this problem for $n = 2$, 3, and 4 before reading further.

A very elegant solution results from the use of recursion. To get the largest disk to the bottom of tower 2, we move the remaining $n-1$ disks to tower 3 and then move the largest to tower 2. Now we are left with the task of moving the $n-1$ disks from tower 3 to tower 2. To perform this task, we can use towers 1 and 2. We can safely ignore the fact that tower 2 has a disk on it because this disk is larger than the disks being moved from tower 3. Therefore, we can place any disk on top of it. Program 5.6 gives recursive C++ code for this solution. The initial invocation is `TowersOfHanoi(n,1,2,3)`. The correctness of Program 5.6 is easily established.

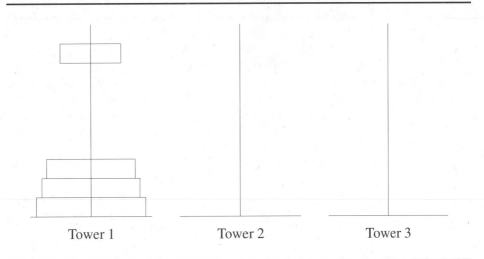

Tower 1   Tower 2   Tower 3

Figure 5.4 Towers of Hanoi

```
void TowersOfHanoi(int n, int x, int y, int z)
{// Move the top n disks from tower x to tower y.
 // Use tower z for intermediate storage.
   if (n > 0) {
      TowersOfHanoi(n-1, x, z, y);
      cout << "Move top disk from tower " << x
           << " to top of tower " << y << endl;
      TowersOfHanoi(n-1, z, y, x);}
}
```

Program 5.6 Recursive function for Towers of Hanoi

The time taken by Program 5.6 is proportional to the number of lines of output generated, and the number of lines output is equal to the number of disk moves performed. Examining Program 5.6, we obtain the following recurrence for the number of moves, *moves* (*n*):

$$moves\,(n) = \begin{cases} 0 & n = 0 \\ 2moves\,(n-1) + 1 & n > 0 \end{cases}$$

This recurrence may be solved using the substitution method of Chapter 2 (see Example 2.20). The result is *moves* (*n*) = $2^n - 1$. We can show that $2^n - 1$ is, in fact, the least number of moves in which the disks can be moved. Since $n = 60$ in the Tower of Brahma, it will take the Brahman priests quite a few years to finish their task. From the solution to the above recurrence, we conclude that the time complexity of function `TowersOfHanoi` is $\Theta(2^n)$.

The output from Program 5.6 gives us the disk-move sequence needed to move the disks from tower 1 to tower 2. Suppose we wish to show the state (i.e., the disks together with their order bottom to top) of the three towers following each move. To show this state, we must store the state of the towers in memory and change the state of each as disks are moved. Following each move, we can output the tower states to an output device such as the computer screen, printer, or video maker.

Since disks are removed from each tower in a LIFO manner, each tower may be represented as a stack. The three towers together contain exactly n disks at any time. Using linked stacks, we can get by with space for n elements. If formula-based stacks are used, towers 1 and 2 must have a capacity of n disks each, while tower 3 must have a capacity of $n-1$. Therefore, we need space for a total of $3n-1$ disks. As our earlier analysis has shown, the complexity of the Towers of Hanoi problem is exponential in n. So using a reasonable amount of computer time, the problem can be solved only for small values of n (say $n \leq 30$). For these small values of n, the difference in space required by the formula-based and linked representations is sufficiently small that either may be used.

The code of Program 5.7 uses formula-based stacks. `TowersOfHanoi(n)` is just a preprocessor for the recursive function `Hanoi::TowersOfHanoi`, which is modeled after the function of Program 5.6. The preprocessor creates the three stacks `S[1:3]` that will store the states of the three towers. The disks are numbered 1 (smallest) through n (largest). As a result, each stack is of type `int`. In case there isn't enough memory to create the three stacks, the stack constructor throws an exception of type `NoMem` and the preprocessor function is exited. When enough space is available, it invokes `Hanoi::TowersOfHanoi`. The function `ShowState` that is invoked by `Hanoi::TowersOfHanoi` is not specified, as the code for this function depends on the nature of the output device (computer screen, printer, video maker).

5.5.3 Rearranging Railroad Cars

A freight train has n railroad cars. Each is to be left at a different station. Assume that the n stations are numbered 1 through n and that the freight train visits these stations in the order n through 1. The railroad cars are labeled by their destination. To facilitate removal of the railroad cars from the train, we must reorder the cars so that they are in the order 1 through n from front to back. When the cars are in this order, the last car is detached at each station. We rearrange the cars at a shunting yard that has an *input track*, an *output track*, and k

```
class Hanoi {
   friend void TowersOfHanoi(int);
   public:
      void TowersOfHanoi(int n, int x, int y, int z);
   private:
      Stack<int> *S[4]; // array of pointers to stacks
};

void Hanoi::TowersOfHanoi(int n, int x, int y, int z)
{// Move the top n disks from tower x to tower y.
 // Use tower z for intermediate storage.
   int d;  // disk number
   if (n > 0) {
      TowersOfHanoi(n-1, x, z, y);
      S[x]->Delete(d);  // remove a disk from x
      S[y]->Add(d);     // put this disk on tower y
      ShowState();
      TowersOfHanoi(n-1, z, y, x);}
}

void TowersOfHanoi(int n)
{// Preprocessor for Hanoi::towersOfHanoi.
   Hanoi X;
   // create three stacks of size n each
   X.S[1] = new Stack<int> (n);
   X.S[2] = new Stack<int> (n);
   X.S[3] = new Stack<int> (n);

   for (int d = n; d > 0; d--) // initialize
      X.S[1]->Add(d); // add disk d to tower 1

   // move n disks from tower 1 to 3 using 2 as
   // intermediate tower
   X.TowersOfHanoi(n, 1, 2, 3);
}
```

Program 5.7 Towers of Hanoi using stacks

holding tracks between the input and output tracks. Figure 5.5(a) shows a shunting yard with $k = 3$ holding tracks $H1$, $H2$, and $H3$. The n cars of the freight train begin in the input track and are to end up in the output track in the order 1 through n from right to left. In Figure 5.5(a), $n = 9$; the cars are initially in the order 5, 8, 1, 7, 4, 2, 9, 6, 3 from back to front. Figure 5.5(b) shows the cars rearranged in the desired order.

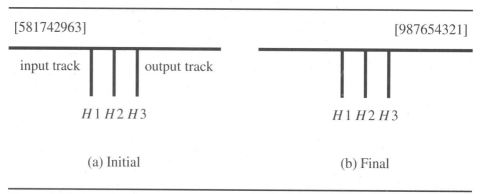

[581742963]   [987654321]

input track   output track

H1 H2 H3   H1 H2 H3

(a) Initial   (b) Final

Figure 5.5 A three-track example

To rearrange the cars, we examine the cars on the input track from front to back. If the car being examined is the next one in the output arrangement, we move it directly to the output track. If not, we move it to a holding track and leave it there until it is time to place it in the output. The holding tracks operate in a LIFO manner as cars enter and leave these tracks from the top. When rearranging cars, only the following moves are permitted:

- A car may be moved from the front (i.e., right end) of the input track to the top of one of the holding tracks or to the left end of the output track.

- A car may be moved from the top of a holding track to the left end of the output track.

Consider the input arrangement of Figure 5.5(a). Car 3 is at the front and cannot be output yet as it is to be preceded by cars 1 and 2. So car 3 is detached and moved to the holding track $H1$. The next car, car 6, is also to be moved to a holding track. If it is moved to $H1$, the rearrangement cannot be completed because car 3 will be below car 6. However, car 3 is to be output before car 6 and so must leave $H1$ before car 6 does. So car 6 is put into $H2$. The next car, car 9, is put into $H3$ because putting it into either $H1$ or $H2$ will make it impossible to complete the rearrangement. *Notice that whenever the car labels in a holding track are not in increasing order from top to bottom, the rearrangement cannot be completed.* The current state of the holding tracks is shown in Figure 5.6(a).

Car 2 is considered next. It can be moved into any of the holding tracks while satisfying the requirement that car labels in any holding track be in increasing order, but moving it to $H1$ is preferred. If it is moved to $H3$, then we have no place to move cars 7 and 8. If we move it to $H2$, then the next car, car 4,

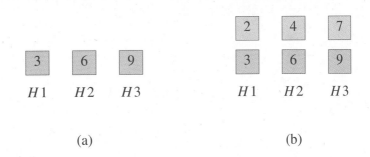

Figure 5.6 Track states

will have to be moved to $H3$ and we will have no place for cars 5, 7, and 8. *The least restrictions on future car placement arise when the new car u is moved to the holding track that has at its top a car with smallest label v such that v > u.* We shall use this **assignment rule** to select the holding track.

When car 4 is considered, the cars at the top of the three holding tracks are 2, 6, and 9. Using our assignment rule, car 4 is moved to $H2$. Car 7 is then moved to $H3$. Figure 5.6(b) shows the current state of the holding tracks. The next car, car 1, is moved to the output track. It is now time to move car 2 from $H1$ to the output track. Next, car 3 is moved from $H1$ and then car 4 moved from $H2$. No other cars can be moved to the output at this time.

The next input car, car 8, is moved to $H1$. Then car 5 is moved from the input track to the output track. Following this move, car 6 is moved from $H2$. Then car 7 is moved from $H3$, car 8 from $H1$, and car 9 from $H3$.

While three holding tracks are sufficient to rearrange the cars from the initial ordering of Figure 5.5(a), other initial arrangements may need more tracks. For example, the initial arrangement 1, n, $n-1$, $\cdots$, 2 requires $n-1$ holding tracks.

To implement the preceding rearrangement scheme, we use k linked stacks to represent the k holding tracks. We use linked stacks rather than formula-based stacks because linked stacks need space for only $n-1$ elements. Function `Railroad` (Program 5.8) determines a sequence of moves that results in rearranging n cars with initial ordering `p[1:n]` using at most k holding tracks. If such a sequence does not exist, `Railroad` returns `false`. Otherwise, it returns `true`. If the function fails to complete for lack of sufficient memory, a `NoMem` exception is thrown.

Function `Railroad` begins by creating an array `H` of linked stacks. `H[i]` represents holding track `i, 1 ≤ i ≤ k`. `NowOut` is the label of the car that is to go to the output track next; `minH` is the smallest label in any of the holding tracks, and `minS` is the holding track (or stack) that contains the car

```
bool Railroad(int p[], int n, int k)
{// k track rearrangement of car order p[1:n].
 // Return true if successful, false if impossible.
 // Throw NoMem exception if inadequate space.

    // create stacks for holding tracks
    LinkedStack<int> *H;
    H = new LinkedStack<int> [k + 1];

    int NowOut = 1;   // next car to output
    int minH = n+1;   // smallest car in a track
    int minS;         // track with car minH

    // rearrange cars
    for (int i = 1; i <= n; i++)
       if (p[i] == NowOut) {// send straight out
          cout << "Move car " << p[i] <<
                  " from input to output" << endl;
          NowOut++;

          // output from holding tracks
          while (minH == NowOut) {
             Output(minH, minS, H, k, n);
             NowOut++;
             }
          }
       else {// put car p[i] in a holding track
          if (!Hold(p[i], minH, minS, H, k, n))
          return false;}

    return true;
}
```

Program 5.8 Railroad car rearrangement program

with label minH. The for loop maintains the invariant: *at the start of this loop, the car with label* NowOut *is not in a holding track*.

In iteration i of the for loop, car p[i] is moved from the input track. This car is to move to the output track only if p[i] equals NowOut. If car p[i] is moved to the output track, NowOut increases by one, and it may be possible to move one or more of the cars in the holding tracks out. These cars are moved to the output by the while loop. If car p[i] cannot be moved to the output, then no car can be so moved. Consequently, `p[i]` is added to a holding track using the stated track assignment rule.

Programs 5.9 and 5.10, respectively, give the functions `Output` and `Hold` utilized by `Railroad`. `Output` outputs instructions to move a car from a holding track to the output track. It also updates `minH` and `minS`. The function `Hold` puts car *c* into a holding track using the track assignment rule. It also outputs instructions to move the car to the chosen holding track and updates `minH` and `minS` if necessary.

```
void Output(int& minH, int& minS,
        LinkedStack<int> H[], int k, int n)
{// Move from hold to output and update minH and minS.
   int c;   // car index

   // delete smallest car minH from stack minS
   H[minS].Delete(c);
   cout << "Move car " << minH << " from holding track "
        << minS << " to output" << endl;

   // find new minH and minS
   // by checking top of all stacks
   minH = n + 2;
   for (int i = 1; i <= k; i++)
      if (!H[i].IsEmpty() &&
               (c = H[i].Top()) < minH) {
         minH = c;
         minS = i;}
}
```

Program 5.9 `Output` function used in Program 5.8

For the time complexity of Program 5.8, we first observe that both `Output` and `Hold` have complexity $\Theta(k)$. Since at most `n-1` cars can be output from the `while` loop of `Railroad` and at most `n-1` put into holding tracks from the `else` clause, the total time spent in functions `Output` and `Hold` is $O(kn)$. The remainder of the `for` loop of `Railroad` takes $\Theta(n)$ time. So the overall complexity of Program 5.8 is $O(kn)$. This complexity can be reduced to $O(n \log k)$ by using a balanced binary search tree (such as an AVL tree) to store the labels of the cars at the top of the holding tracks (see Chapter 11). When a balanced binary search tree is used in this way, functions `Output` and `Hold` can be rewritten to have complexity $O(\log k)$. The use of a balanced binary search tree for this application is recommended only when `k` is large.

```
bool Hold(int c, int& minH, int &minS,
        LinkedStack<int> H[], int k, int n)
{// Add car c to a holding track.
 // Return false if no feasible holding track.
 // Throw NoMem exception if no stack space.
 // Return true otherwise.

    // find best holding track for car c
    // initialize
    int BestTrack = 0,     // best track so far
        BestTop = n + 1,   // top car in BestTrack
        x;                 // a car index

    // scan tracks
    for (int i = 1; i <= k; i++)
       if (!H[i].IsEmpty()) {// track i not empty
          x = H[i].Top();
          if (c < x && x < BestTop) {
             // track i has smaller car at top
             BestTop = x;
             BestTrack = i;}
          }
       else // track i empty
          if (!BestTrack) BestTrack = i;

    if (!BestTrack) return false; // no feasible track

    // add c to best track
    H[BestTrack].Add(c);
    cout << "Move car " << c << " from input "
         << "to holding track " << BestTrack << endl;

    // update minH and minS if needed
    if (c < minH) {minH = c;
                   minS = BestTrack;}

    return true;
}
```

Program 5.10 Hold function used by Program 5.8

5.5.4 Switch Box Routing

In the switch box routing problem, we are given a rectangular routing region with pins at the periphery. Pairs of pins are to be connected together by laying a metal path between the two pins. This path is confined to the routing region and is called a wire. If two wires intersect, an electrical short occurs. So wire intersections are forbidden. Each pair of pins that is to be connected is called a **net**. We are to determine whether the given nets can be routed with no intersections. Figure 5.7(a) shows a sample switch box instance with eight pins and four nets. The nets are (1, 4), (2, 3), (5, 6), and (7, 8). The wire routing of Figure 5.7(b) has a pair of intersecting wires (those for nets (1, 4) and (2, 3)) while the routing of Figure 5.7(c) has no intersections. Since the four nets can be routed with no intersections, the given switch box is a **routable switch box**. (In practice, we also require a minimum separation between adjacent wires. We ignore this additional requirement here.) Our problem is to input a switch box routing instance and determine whether it is routable.

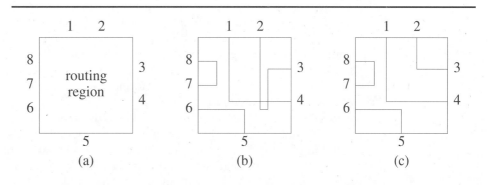

Figure 5.7 Sample switch box

While the wires in both Figures 5.7 (b) and (c) are composed of straight line segments parallel to the x- and y-axes, it is permissible to have segments that are not parallel to these axes as well as segments that are not straight lines.

To solve the switch box routing problem, we note that when a net is connected, the wire partitions the routing region into two regions. The pins that fall on the boundary of a partition do not depend on the wire path, but only on the pins of the net that was routed. For instance, when net (1, 4) is routed, we get two regions. One contains the pins 2 and 3, and the other contains the pins 5 through 8. If there is now a net with one pin in one region and the other in a different region, this new net cannot be routed and the routing instance is unroutable. If there is no net with this property, then since the wires cannot cross between regions, we can attempt to determine whether each region is independently routable. To make this determination, we pick a net in one of the regions; this net partitions its region into two regions and none of the remaining nets should have a pin in one partition and another in the other partition.

We can implement this strategy by traversing around the periphery of the switch box in either clockwise or counterclockwise order, beginning at any pin. If we traverse the pins of Figure 5.7(a) in clockwise order, beginning at pin 1, the pins are examined in the order, 1, 2, $\cdots$, 8. The pins that lie between pin 1 and its net partner, pin 4, define one region of the first partition, and those that lie between pins 4 and 1 define the other. We shall place pin 1 on a stack and continue processing pins until pin 4 is encountered. This procedure allows us to process one of the regions before going on to the other. The next pin, pin 2, together with its net partner, pin 3, partition the current region into two regions. As before, pin 2 is placed on the stack, and we proceed to pin 3. Since pin 3's partner, pin 2, is at the top of the stack, we have completed a region and pin 2 is deleted from the stack. Next we encounter pin 4 whose partner is now at the top of the stack. The processing of a region is now complete, and pin 1 is deleted from the stack. Proceeding in this way, we are able to complete the processing of all created regions and the stack is empty after pin 8 is examined.

What happens on a nonroutable instance? Suppose the nets for Figure 5.7(a) are (1,5), (2, 3), (4, 7), and (6,8). Pins 1 and 2 are put on the stack initially. When pin 3 is examined, pin 2 is deleted from the stack. Next pin 4 is added to the stack, as pin 4 and the pin at the stack top do not define a region boundary. When pin 5 is examined, it is also added to the stack. Even though pins 1 and 5 have both been seen, we are unable to complete the processing of the first region defined by this net, as pin 4's routing has to cross the boundary. As a result, when we complete the examination of all pins, the stack will not be empty.

Program 5.11 gives a C++ program that implements this strategy. It requires that the nets be numbered and that each pin have a net number. So for the example in Figure 5.7(c), the input array `net` is [1, 2, 2, 1, 3, 3, 4, 4]. The complexity of the program is $\Theta(n)$ where n is the number of pins.

5.5.5 Offline Equivalence Problem

The offline equivalence problem was defined in Section 3.8.3. The inputs to this problem are the number of elements n, the number of relation pairs r, and the r relation pairs. We are to partition the n elements into equivalence classes. Program 5.12 gives a two-part program to do this partitioning. In the first part, n, r, and the r pairs are input and a chain is constructed for each of the n elements. A chain `chain[i]` for element i contains all elements j such that `(i,j)` or `(j,i)` is an input relation pair. The second part outputs the equivalence classes. For the second part we maintain an array `out` such that `out[i]` = `true` iff element i has been output as a member of some

```
bool CheckBox(int net[], int n)
{// Determine whether the switch box is routable.
   Stack<int> *s = new Stack<int> (n);

   // scan nets clockwise
   for (int i = 0; i < n; i++) {
      // examine net[i]
      if (!s->IsEmpty()) {// check with top net
         if (net[i] == net[s->Top()]) {
            // net[i] routable, delete from stack
            int x;
            s->Delete(x);}
         else s->Add(i);}
      else s->Add(i);
      }

   // any unrouted nets left?
   if (s->IsEmpty()) {// no nets remain
      delete s;
      cout << "Switch box is routable" << endl;
      return true;}

   delete s;
   cout << "Switch box is not routable" << endl;
   return false;
}
```

Program 5.11 Switch box routing

equivalence class. A stack stack assists in locating all elements of an equivalence class. This stack holds all elements that have been output as part of the current class and that may lead us to additional elements of the class.

To find the first member of the next equivalence class, we scan the array out for an element not yet output. If there is no such element, then there is no next class. If such an element is found, it begins the next class. We put this element on the stack. Then we continually examine elements from this stack to see whether they have been defined equivalent to an element not yet output. For this examination, we delete an element m from the stack and examine all elements on chain[m]. When the stack is empty, no member m of the current equivalence class has an input pair (m,p) such that p has not been output (since p must be on chain[m] and hence output when m was deleted from the stack). Consequently, the elements output in each iteration of the **do** loop define an equivalence class.

```
void main(void)
{// Offline equivalenece classes.
   int n, r;

   // input n and r
   cout << "Enter number of elements" << endl;
   cin >> n;
   if (n < 2) {cerr << "Too few elements" << endl;
              exit(1);}
   cout << "Enter number of relations" << endl;
   cin >> r;
   if (r < 1) {cerr << "Too few relations" << endl;
              exit(1);}

   // create an array of n chains
   Chain<int> *chain;
   try {chain = new Chain<int> [n+1];}
   catch (NoMem) {cerr << "Out of memory" << endl;
                 exit(1);}

   // input the r relations and put on chains
   for (int i = 1; i <= r; i++) {
      cout << "Enter next relation/pair" << endl;
      int a, b;
      cin >> a >> b;
      chain[a].Insert(0,b);
      chain[b].Insert(0,a);
      }
```

Program 5.12 Offline equivalence class program (continues)

   To analyze the complexity of the equivalence class program, we note that since each chain insert occurs at the front of the chain, each takes $\Theta(1)$ time. Hence part 1 of the program (input and initialize chains) takes $\Theta(n+r)$ time. For part 2 we note that since each of the n elements is output exactly once, each is added to the stack once and deleted from the stack once. So the total time spent on stack adds and deletes is $\Theta(n)$. Finally, when an element is deleted from the stack, all elements on its chain are deleted from the chain. Each delete is from the chain front and so takes $\Theta(1)$ time. The total number of elements on all n chains following input is $2r$. All $2r$ are deleted during part 2. Hence the time spent deleting chain elements is $\Theta(r)$. The overall complexity of Program 5.12 is therefore $\Theta(n+r)$.

```
// initialize to output classes
LinkedStack<int> stack;
bool *out;
try {out = new bool [n+1];}
catch (NoMem) {cerr << "Out of memory" << endl;
               exit(1);}
for (int i = 1; i <= n; i++)
   out[i] = false;

// output classes
for (int i = 1; i <= n; i++)
  if (!out[i]) {// start of a new class
      cout << "Next class is: " << i << ' ';
      out[i] = true;
      stack.Add(i);
      // get rest of class from stack
      while (!stack.IsEmpty()) {
          int *q, j;
          stack.Delete(j);

          // elements on chain[j] are in
          // same class, use iterator c
          // to get them
          ChainIterator<int> c;
          q = c.Initialize(chain[j]);
          while (q) {// q is in same class
              if (!out[*q]) {
                  cout << *q << ' ';
                  out[*q] = true;
                  stack.Add(*q);}
              q = c.Next();
              }
          }
      cout << endl;
      }

   cout << endl << "End of class list" << endl;
}
```

Program 5.12 Offline equivalence class program (concluded)

Notice that Program 5.12 does not delete the space allocated to the arrays `chain` and `out`. There is no need to delete this space because when the program terminates all space allocated to the program gets freed. If Program 5.12 is to be made into a function, then we should add statements to delete these two arrays so that the space they use is freed and becomes available to the rest of the program.

5.5.6 Rat in a Maze

Specification

A **maze** (Figure 5.8) is a rectangular area with an entrance and an exit. The interior of the maze contains walls or obstacles that one cannot walk through. In our mazes these obstacles are placed along rows and columns that are parallel to the rectangular boundary of the maze. The entrance is at the upper-left corner, and the exit is at the lower-right corner.

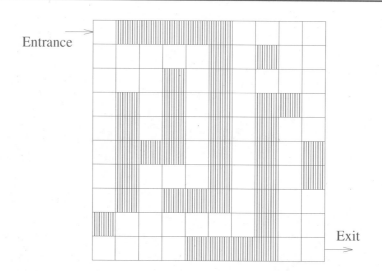

Figure 5.8 A maze

Suppose that the maze is to be modeled as an $n \times m$ matrix with position (1,1) of the matrix representing the entrance and position (n, m) representing the exit. n and m are, respectively, the number of rows and columns in the maze. Each maze position is described by its row and column intersection. The matrix has a one in position (i, j) iff there is an obstacle at the corresponding maze position. Otherwise, there is a zero at this matrix position. Figure 5.9 shows the matrix representation of the maze of Figure 5.8. The **rat in a maze** problem is to find a path from the entrance to the exit of a maze. A **path** is a sequence of positions, none of which is blocked, and such that each (other than the first) is the north, south, east, or west neighbor of the preceding position (Figure 5.10).

```
0 1 1 1 1 1 0 0 0 0
0 0 0 0 0 1 0 1 0 0
0 0 0 1 0 1 0 0 0 0
0 1 0 1 0 1 0 1 1 0
0 1 0 1 0 1 0 1 0 0
0 1 1 1 0 1 0 1 0 1
0 1 0 0 0 1 0 1 0 1
0 1 0 1 1 1 0 1 0 0
1 0 0 0 0 0 0 1 0 0
0 0 0 0 1 1 1 1 0 0
```

Figure 5.9 Matrix representation of maze of Figure 5.8

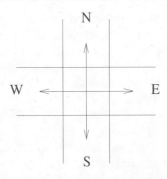

Figure 5.10 The four options for a move from any position in the maze

You are to write a program to solve the rat in a maze problem. You may assume that the mazes for which your program is to work are square (i.e., $m = n$) and are sufficiently small that the entire maze can be represented in the memory of the target computer. Your program will be a stand-alone product that will be used directly by persons wishing to find a path in a maze of their choice.

Design

We shall use the top-down modular methodology to design the program. It is not too difficult to see the three aspects to the problem: input the maze, find a path, and output the path. We will use one program module for each task. A fourth module that displays a welcome message and identifies the program and its author is also desirable. While this module is not directly related to the problem at hand, the use of such a module enhances the user-friendliness of the program.

The module that finds the path does not interact directly with the user and will therefore contain no help facility and will not be menu driven. The remaining three modules interact with the user, and we need to expend some effort designing their user interface. The user interface should make the user want to use your program rather than competing programs.

Let us begin with the welcome module. We wish to display a message such as

Welcome To
RAT IN A MAZE
© Joe Bloe, 1998

While displaying this message might seem like a trivial task, we can use various design elements to obtain a pleasing effect. For example, the message can be muticolored to take advantage of the user's color display. The three lines of the welcome display need to be positioned on the screen, and we can change the character size from one line to the next (or even from character to character). The welcome message can be introduced on the display with a reasonable time lapse between the introduction of one character and the next. Alternatively, the time lapse can be very small. In addition, we might consider the use of sound effects. We also need to determine the duration for which the message is to be displayed. It should be displayed long enough so that the user can read it, but not so long as to leave the user yawning. As you can see, the design of the welcome message (and the whole user interface in general) requires strong artistic skills.

The input module needs to inform the user that the input is expected as a matrix of ones and zeros. We need to decide whether this matrix is to be provided by rows or by columns. Since it is more natural to ask for this matrix by rows, let us decide to ask for it this way. The user must first provide us with the number of rows (which is also the number of columns). We can ask for this information by displaying the message shown in Figure 5.11.

Next, we may ask for the rows one by one:

Please Enter Row 1
Press <Enter> when done

> Please enter the number of rows in the maze.
>
> I work on square mazes only.
>
> Enter -1 to terminate the program.
>
> Press <Enter> when done.

Figure 5.11 Screen to get maze size

As each row is entered, we can display the row on the screen and ask the user to verify the entries. An edit facility to correct errors will be quite helpful. Such an edit facility is certainly preferable (from the user's standpoint) to reentering the entire row. The input module can also verify that the entrance and exit of the maze are not blocked. If they are, then no path exists. In all likelihood the user made an error in input. The following discussion assumes that the input module performs this verification and that the entrance and exit are not blocked.

Some other issues in the design of the user interface for the input module are use of color and sound; size of characters in request messages; positioning of request messages on the display screen; whether the screen should scroll up as we go from one row to the next, or whether we should erase the previous row from the display and show the next row at the same place.

Once again, we see that what initially appeared to be a simple task (read in a matrix) is actually quite complex if we want to do it in a user-friendly way.

The output module design involves essentially the same considerations as the design of the input module.

Program Plan

The design phase has already pointed out the need for four program modules. We also need a root (or main) module that invokes these four modules in the following sequence: welcome module, input module, find path module, and output module.

Our program will have the modular structure of Figure 5.12. Each program module can be coded independently. The root module will be coded as the function `main`; the welcome, input, find path, and output path modules will each be a single function.

At this point we see that our program is going to have the form given in Figure 5.13.

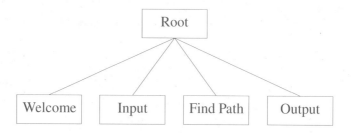

Figure 5.12 Modular structure of rat in a maze program

```
// function modules
// module Welcome
// module InputMaze
// module FindPath
// module OutputPath

void main(void)
{
  Welcome();
  InputMaze();
  if (FindPath()) OutputPath;
  else cout << "No path" << endl;
}
```

Figure 5.13 Form of rat in a maze program

Program Development

Substantial data structure and algorithm issues arise in the development of the path-finding module only. Consequently, we shall develop just this module here. Exercise 16 asks you to develop the remaining modules. Without thinking too much about the coding of the path-finding module, we can arrive at the C++ pseudocode given in Figure 5.14. This code is readily seen to be correct. Unfortunately, we cannot present it to a computer in this form, and we need to refine the pseudocode into pure C++ code.

Before attempting a refinement of Figure 5.14 that will get us closer to C++ code, let us figure out how we are to search the maze for a path. We begin with the entrance as our present position. If the present position is the exit, then we

```
bool FindPath()
{
    Search the maze for a path to the exit;
    if (a path is found) return true;
    else return false;
}
```

Figure 5.14 First version of FindPath

have found a path and we are done. If we are not at the exit, then we block the present position (i.e., place an obstacle there) so as to prevent the search from returning here. Next we see whether there is an adjacent maze position that is not blocked. If so, we move to this new adjacent position and attempt to find a path from there to the exit. If we are unsuccessful, we attempt to move to some other unblocked adjacent maze position and try to find a path from there. To facilitate this move, we save the current position on a stack before advancing to a new adjacent position. If all adjacent unblocked positions have been tried and no path is found, there is no path from entrance to exit in the maze.

Let us use the above strategy on the maze of Figure 5.8. We begin with the position (1,1) on the stack and move to its only unblocked neighbor (2,1). The position (1,1) is blocked to prevent the search path from moving through this position later. From (2,1) we can move to (3,1) or (2,2). Suppose we decide to move to (3,1). Prior to the move, we block (2,1) and add it to the stack. From (3,1) we may move to either (4,1) or (3,2). If we move to (4,1), (4,1) gets blocked and added to the stack. From (4,1) we move to (5,1), (6,1), (7,1), and (8,1). The path cannot be extended from (8,1). Our stack now contains the path from (1,1) to (8,1). To try another path, we back up to (7,1) by deleting this position from the stack. As there are no ublocked positions adjacent to (7,1), we back up to (6,1) by deleting this position from the stack. In this way we back up to position (3,1) from which we are again able to move forward (i.e., move to (3,2)). Notice that the stack always contains the path from the entrance to the current position. If we reach the exit, the entrance-to-exit path will be on the stack.

To refine Figure 5.14, we need representations for the maze, which is a matrix of zeros and ones, each maze position, and the stack. Let us consider the maze first. The maze is naturally represented as a two-dimensional array maze of type int. (Since each array position can take on only one of the values 0 and 1, we could pack 16 maze positions into a single variable of type int, assuming each such variable is 2 bytes long. This packing reduces the space needed for the maze by a factor of 16. However, the run time increases because of the increased difficulty of accessing a maze position.) Position (i,j) of the maze matrix corresponds to position [i][j] of the array maze.

From interior (i.e., nonboundary) positions of the maze, four moves are possible: right, down, left, and up. From positions on the boundary of the maze, either two or three moves are possible. To avoid having to handle positions on the boundaries of the maze differently from interior positions, we shall surround the maze with a wall of obstacles. For an $m \times m$ maze, this wall will occupy rows 0 and $m+1$ and columns 0 and $m+1$ of the array `maze` (see Figure 5.15).

```
1 1 1 1 1 1 1 1 1 1 1 1
1 0 1 1 1 1 1 0 0 0 0 1
1 0 0 0 0 0 1 0 1 0 0 1
1 0 0 0 1 0 1 0 0 0 0 1
1 0 1 0 1 0 1 0 1 1 0 1
1 0 1 0 1 0 1 0 1 0 0 1
1 0 1 1 1 0 1 0 1 0 1 1
1 0 1 0 0 0 1 0 1 0 1 1
1 0 1 0 1 1 1 0 1 0 0 1
1 1 0 0 0 0 0 0 1 0 0 1
1 0 0 0 0 1 1 1 1 0 0 1
1 1 1 1 1 1 1 1 1 1 1 1
```

Figure 5.15 Maze of Figure 5.8 with wall of ones around it

All positions in the maze are now within the boundary of the surrounding wall, and we can move to four possible positions from each position (some of these four positions may have obstacles). By surrounding the maze with our own boundary, we have eliminated the need for our program to handle boundary conditions, which significantly simplifies the code. This simplification is achieved at the cost of a slightly increased space requirement for the array `maze`.

Each maze position is described by its row and column index, which are, respectively, called the row and column coordinates of the position. We may define a class `Position` with private integer members `row` and `col`. We can use objects of type `Position` to keep track of maze positions. The stack that maintains the path from the entrance to the current position may be represented as a formula-based stack:

```
Stack<Position> path(MaxPathLength);
```

Here `MaxPathLength` is the maximum number of positions on a path from the entrance to any position in the maze. An $m \times m$ maze with no blockages can have paths with as many as m^2 positions (see Figure 5.16(a)). Since no path repeats a position and the maze has only m^2 positions, no path can have more than m^2 positions. Further, as the last position on a path is not stored on the stack, it suffices to define `MaxPathLength = ` $m^2 - 1$. Notice that in a maze with no blockages there is always a path with at most 2m positions between any two points (see, for example, Figure 5.16(b)). However, we have no assurance at this time that our path finder will find the shortest path.

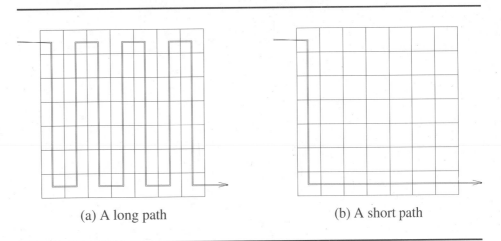

        (a) A long path   (b) A short path

Figure 5.16 Paths in a maze with no blockages

    We can now refine Figure 5.14 and obtain Figure 5.17, which is closer to being a C++ program. Now we need to tackle the problem of determining a neighbor of position `here` that can be moved to. The task of trying out alternative moves is simplified if we select from the options available at any position in some systematic way. For example, we may first attempt to move right, then down, then left, and finally up. Once an option has been selected, we need to know the coordinates of the position to move to. These coordinates are easily computed by maintaining a table of offsets as in Figure 5.18. The moves right, down, left, and up have, respectively, been numbered 0, 1, 2, and 3. In the table of Figure 5.18, `offset[i].row` and `offset[i].col`, respectively, give the amounts to be added to the `row` and `col` coordinates of the present position to move to the adjacent position in the direction `i`. For example, if we are presently at the position (3, 4), then the position on the right has row coordinate `3+offset[0].row = 3` and column coordinate `4+offset[0].col = 5`.

    Incorporating these refinements into the code of Figure 5.17 results in the C++ code of Program 5.13. The code of Program 5.13 assumes that `maze`, `m` (maze size), and `path` have been defined as global variables as below

```
int **maze, m;
Stack<Position> *path;   // pointer to stack
```

and that `FindPath` is a friend of `Position`. The variables `maze` and `m` are initialized by function `InputMaze`.

```
bool FindPath()
{// Find a path from (1,1) to the exit (m,m).
   Initialize wall of obstacles around maze;

   // initialize variable to keep track of
   // our current position in the maze
   Position here;
   here.row = 1;
   here.col = 1;

   maze[1][1] = 1;   // prevent return to entrance

   // search for a path to the exit
   while (not at exit) do {
      find a neighbor to move to;
      if (there is such a neighbor) {
        add position here to path stack;
        // move to and block neighbor
        here = neighbor;
        maze[here.row][here.col] = 1;}
      else {
        // cannot move forward, backup
        if (path empty) return false;
        back up to position here which is at top of path stack;}
      }
   return true;
}
```

Figure 5.17 Refined version of Figure 5.14

move	direction	offset[move].row	offset[move].col
0	right	0	1
1	down	1	0
2	left	0	−1
3	up	−1	0

Figure 5.18 Table of offsets

```
bool FindPath()
{// Find a path from (1,1) to the exit (m,m).
 // Return true if successful, false if impossible.
 // Throw NoMem exception if inadequate space.

    path = new Stack<Position>(m * m - 1);

    // initialize offsets
    Position offset[4];
    offset[0].row = 0; offset[0].col = 1; // right
    offset[1].row = 1; offset[1].col = 0; // down
    offset[2].row = 0; offset[2].col = -1; // left
    offset[3].row = -1; offset[3].col = 0; // up

    // initialize wall of obstacles around maze
    for (int i = 0; i <= m+1; i++) {
        maze[0][i] = maze[m+1][i] = 1; // bottom and top
        maze[i][0] = maze[i][m+1] = 1; // left and right
        }

    Position here;
    here.row = 1;
    here.col = 1;
    maze[1][1] = 1; // prevent return to entrance
    int option = 0; // next move
    int LastOption = 3;

    // search for a path
    while (here.row != m || here.col != m) {// not exit
        // find a neighbor to move to
        int r, c;
        while (option <= LastOption) {
            r = here.row + offset[option].row;
            c = here.col + offset[option].col;
            if (maze[r][c] == 0) break;
            option++; // next option
            }
```

Program 5.13 Code to find a path in a maze (continues)

```
        // was a neighbor found?
    if (option <= LastOption) {// move to maze[r][c]
        path->Add(here);
        here.row = r; here.col = c;
        // set to 1 to prevent revisit
        maze[r][c] = 1;
        option = 0;
        }
    else {// no neighbor to move to, back up
        if (path->IsEmpty()) return false;
        Position next;
        path->Delete(next);
        if (next.row == here.row)
            option = 2 + next.col - here.col;
        else option = 3 + next.row - here.row;
        here = next;
        }
    }

    return true;   // at exit
}
```

Program 5.13 Code to find a path in a maze (concluded)

FindPath begins by creating a large enough stack *path. It then initializes the array of offsets and builds a wall of obstacles around the maze. In the while loop, we attempt to advance the path forward from the current position here by trying the move options in the following order: right, down, left, and up. If we are able to move forward, the present location is stored on the stack path and a forward move is made. If a forward move isn't possible, we try to back up to a previous position. If there is no position to back up to (i.e., the stack is empty), there is no path to the exit. Otherwise, we can back up. Once we back up to the top position on the stack (next), we need to move forward by trying the next move option. This option can be computed from the positions next and here. Notice that here is a neighbor of next. In fact, at some previous time in the program, we moved from next to here, and this move was the last move made from next. The next move option to try is correctly computed by the code

```
if (next.row == here.row)
    option = 2 + next.col - here.col;
else option = 3 + next.row - here.row;
```

For the time complexity analysis, we see that in the worst case we may move to each unblocked position of the input maze. Each such position may get added to the stack at most four times. (Each time we move forward from a position, it is added to the stack; only four forward moves are possible from any position.) Hence each position may be deleted from the stack at most four times. Further, at each position $\Theta(1)$ time is spent examining its neighbors. So the time complexity is O(*unblocked*) where *unblocked* is the number of unblocked positions in the input maze. This complexity is O(m^2).

EXERCISES

7. Establish the correctness of Program 5.6 by induction on the number of disks.

8. Assume that the Towers of Hanoi disks are labeled 1 through n with the smallest disk being disk 1. Modify Program 5.6 so that it also outputs the label of the disk that is being moved. This modification requires a simple change to the `cout` statement. Do not make any other changes.

9. Write code for the `ShowState` function of Program 5.7 assuming that the output device is a computer screen. You will need to introduce a time delay so that the display does not change too rapidly. Show each disk in a different color.

10. When the output device is a computer screen, can we show the state of the three towers following each move without explicitly storing these states in memory? Explain.

11. Suppose that k formula-based stacks are used for the k holding tracks of the railroad car rearrangement problem. How large must each stack be?

★ 12. (a) Does Program 5.8 succeed in rearranging the cars whenever it is possible to do this rearrangement using k tracks?

   (b) The total number of car moves required is n + (number of cars moved to a holding track). Suppose that the initial car arrangement can be rearranged using k tracks and Program 5.8. Does Program 5.8 perform the rearrangement using the minimum number of moves? Prove your answer.

13. Develop a program for the railroad car switching problem under the assumption that holding track i can hold at most s_i cars, $1 \leq i \leq k$.

14. In the switch box routing application, we noted that processing can stop when two pins of the same net get on to the stack. Suppose that the input to the switch box routing problem is a collection of nets, each net being a pair of pins. Write a C++ program to input the nets and determine whether the switch box is routable. Make this determination using a new

CheckBox function that terminates if the addition of a pin to the stack results in two pins of the same net being on the stack. The time complexity of your program should be $\Theta(n)$ where n is the number of pins. How large a stack do you need?

15. The offline equivalence problem used the classes Chain and Link-edStack. When generating the equivalence classes, nodes are deleted by the function Chain::Delete and created by the function LinkedStack::Add. We can avoid this deletion and creation of nodes at the expense of writing our own code to add and delete from a linked chain and stack. In this case nodes on chain[j] with data field x such that out[x] is zero are added to the stack. That is, every node on the stack was at one time on a chain. Following input of the relations and the creation of the array out, no more calls are made to function new. Also, since the program terminates following output of all classes, nodes cannot be reused. Hence we may omit calls to the function delete.

(a) Write an offline equivalence class program that does not use the classes Chain and LinkedStack. Rather, it uses customized code to add and delete from chains and stacks. Furthermore, no calls to delete are ever made and no calls to new are made after the creation of the array out. The complexity of your program should be linear in the number of elements and relations. Show that your code has this complexity.

(b) Compare the run-time performance of this code with Program 5.12 using suitable test data.

16. Complete the rat in a maze code. Write a pleasing C++ program by doing the following:

(a) Write a nice Welcome function.

(b) Write a robust InputMaze function. For example, there may not be enough memory to create the array maze. Check for this condition and output an error message. Also provide user prompts for input.

(c) Write the OutputPath function so as to output the path from the maze to the exit (not from the exit to the entrance).
Test your codes using sample mazes.

17. Redo the rat in a maze code so as to display the maze in Figure 5.8 using different colors to indicate initially blocked positions, positions blocked by the algorithm, unblocked positions, and the path from the entrance to the current location. Your FindPath function will need to modify the display with each move. To enable the user to follow your attempt at finding the path, you will need to slow down your code so that it makes approximately one move per second. Do so by inserting a wait loop into

the code. In the loop you will wait for one second (say) to elapse. Test your code using sample mazes.

18. Modify `FindPath` so that it works for mazes in which you are allowed to move to the north, northeast, east, southeast, south, southwest, west, and northwest neighbors of a position. Test the correctness of the modified code using suitable mazes.

19. Develop a better bound than m^2-1 for the maximum size of the stack `path`.

20. Since the stack `path` is defined dynamically, its size can be set to be the number of unblocked positions in the input maze minus one. Modify the codes of Programs 5.13 and 5.14 to set the stack size in this way.

21. Modify the codes of Programs 5.13 and 5.14 to use a linked stack for `path`. What are the pros and cons of using a linked stack versus a formula-based stack for this application?

22. In the code of Program 5.13, we know that the stack is large enough to accept all requests to add elements. Therefore, the test for stack full in the stack add routine of the class `Stack` is superfluous. The use of a member of `Stack` also makes it difficult to output the path in the order *entrance* to *exit*. Rewrite the codes of Programs 5.13 and 5.14 to use a customized stack; that is, use a dynamically defined one-dimensional array `path` and a variable `top`. The final path can be output by looking at positions 1 through `top` of this array. Test your code using sample mazes.

23. The strategy used to find a path in a maze is really a recursive one. From the present position we find a neighbor to move to and then determine whether there is a path from this neighbor to the exit. If so, we are done. If not, we find another neighbor to move to. Rewrite function `FindPath` (Program 5.13) using recursion. Test the correctness of your code using suitable mazes.

5.6 REFERENCES AND SELECTED READINGS

The switch box routing algorithm is from Hsu and Pinter. It is described in the papers ''General River Routing Algorithm'' by C. Hsu, *ACM/IEEE Design Automation Conference*, pages 578–583, 1983, and ''River-routing: Methodology and Analysis'' by R. Pinter, *Third Caltech Conference on VLSI*, March 1983.

CHAPTER 6
QUEUES

BIRD'S-EYE VIEW

A queue, like a stack, is a special kind of linear list. In a queue insertions and deletions take place from different ends of the linear list. Consequently, a queue is a first-in-first-out (FIFO) list. Although queue classes may be easily derived from the linear list classes `LinearList` (Program 3.1) and `Chain` (Program 3.8), we do not do so in this chapter. For run-time efficiency reasons, the formula-based and linked classes for a queue are developed as base classes.

In the applications section, we develop four sample codes that use a queue. The first is for the railroad-switching problem considered initially in Section 5.5.3. In this chapter the problem has been modified so that the shunting tracks at the railroad yard are FIFO rather than LIFO. The second application is the classical Lee's algorithm to find the shortest path for a wire that is to connect two given points. This application may also be viewed as a variant of the rat in a maze problem of Section 5.5.6. In this variant we must find the shortest path between the maze entrance and exit. Notice that the code developed in Section 5.5.6 does not guarantee to find a shortest path. It simply guarantees to find a path (of unspecifed length) whenever the maze has at least one entrance-to-exit

283

path. The third application, from the computer-vision field, labels the pixels of a binary image so that two pixels have the same label iff they are part of the same image component. The final application is a machine shop simulation. The machine shop has several machines, each capable of performing a different task. Each job in the shop requires one or more tasks to be performed. We provide a program to simulate the flow of jobs through the machine shop. Our program determines the total time each job spends waiting to be processed as well as the total wait at each machine. We can use this information to improve the machine shop.

Each application in this chapter uses the queue data structure to obtain an efficient solution. Several additional queue applications appear in later chapters.

6.1 THE ABSTRACT DATA TYPE

Definition A **queue** is a linear list in which additions and deletions take place at different ends. The end at which new elements are added is called the **rear**, and that from which old elements are deleted is called the **front**. ∎

A queue with three elements is shown in Figure 6.1(a). The first element we delete from the queue of Figure 6.1(a), is A. Following the deletion, the configuration of Figure 6.1(b) results. To add the element D to the queue of Figure 6.1(b) we must place it after element C. The new configuration is shown in Figure 6.1(c).

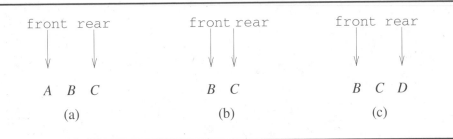

Figure 6.1 Sample queues

So a queue is a first-in-first-out (FIFO) list, while a stack is a last-in-first-out (LIFO) list. The ADT queue is specified in ADT 6.1.

AbstractDataType *Queue* {
   instances
      ordered list of elements; one end is called the `front`; the other is the `rear`;
   operations:
      Create (): Create an empty queue;
      IsEmpty (): Return `true` if queue is empty, return `false` otherwise;
      IsFull (): Return `true` if queue is full, return `false` otherwise;
      First (): Return first element of queue;
      Last (): Return last element of queue;
      Add (x): Add element x to the queue;
      Delete (x): Delete front element from queue and put it in x;
}

ADT 6.1 The abstract data type queue

6.2 FORMULA-BASED REPRESENTATION

Suppose a queue is represented using the Equation 6.1.

$$location\,(i) = i - 1 \tag{6.1}$$

This equation worked well for the formula-based representation of a stack. If the queue is represented in the array `queue[MaxSize]` using Equation 6.1, then the first element is in `queue[0]`, the second is in `queue[1]`, and so on. `front` always equals zero, `rear` is the location of the last element, and the queue size is `rear+1`. An empty queue has `rear = −1`. Using Equation 6.1, the queues of Figure 6.1 are represented as in Figure 6.2.

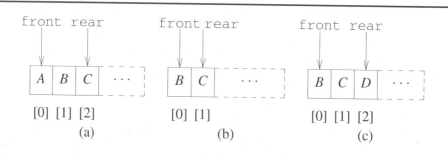

Figure 6.2 Queues of Figure 6.1 using Equation 6.1

To add an element to a queue, we need to increase `rear` by 1 and place the new element at `queue[rear]`, which means that an addition requires O(1) time. To delete an element, we must slide the elements in positions 1 through `rear` one position down the array. Sliding the elements takes $\Theta(n)$ time where n is the number of elements in the queue following the deletion. Therefore, while Equation 6.1 results in $\Theta(1)$ time algorithms for both stack addition and deletion, it results in a $\Theta(n)$ time algorithm for queue deletion.

We can delete in $\Theta(1)$ time if we use the Equation 6.2.

$$location\,(i) = location\,(1) + i - 1 \tag{6.2}$$

Equation 6.2 does not require us to shift the queue one position left each time an element is deleted from the queue. Instead, we simply increase *location*(1) by 1. Figure 6.3 shows the representation of the queues of Figure 6.1 that results when Equation 6.2 is used. Notice that `front` = *location*(1), `rear` = *location*(*last element*), and an empty queue has `rear < front`.

As Figure 6.3(b) shows, each deletion causes `front` to move right by 1. Hence there will be times when `rear = MaxSize-1` and `front > 0`. At these times the queue is not full, and there is space for additional elements at the left end of the array. To continue adding to the queue, we can shift all elements

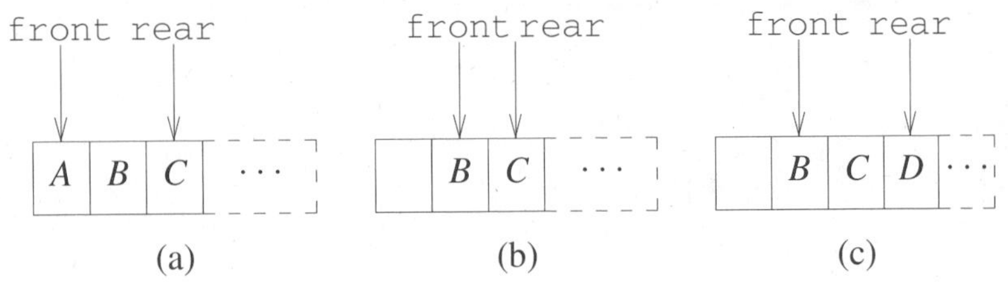

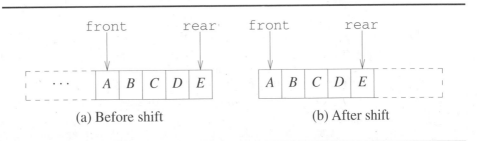

Figure 6.3 Queues of Figure 6.1 using Equation 6.2

to the left end of the queue (as in Figure 6.4) and create space at the right end. This shifting increases the worst-case add time from $\Theta(1)$, when Equation 6.1 is used, to $\Theta(n)$ (n is the number of elements in the queue) when Equation 6.2 is used. So the trade-off for improved efficiency of a delete is loss of efficiency for an addition.

Figure 6.4 Shifting a queue

The worst-case add and delete times become $\Theta(1)$ when the equation

$$location\,(i) = (location\,(1) + i - 1)\,\%\,MaxSize \qquad (6.3)$$

is used. Now the array in which the queue is represented is regarded as circular (Figure 6.5). Notice that we have changed the convention for the variable front. It now points one position counterclockwise from the location of the first element in the queue. The convention for rear is unchanged. Adding an element to the queue of Figure 6.5(a) results in the queue of Figure 6.5(b). Deleting an element from the queue of Figure 6.5(b) results in the queue of Figure 6.5(c).

A queue is empty iff front = rear. The initial condition front = rear = 0 defines an initially empty queue. We need to determine the condition for a full queue. If we add elements to the queue of Figure 6.5(b), until it gets full, we obtain the configuration of Figure 6.6. This configuration has front =

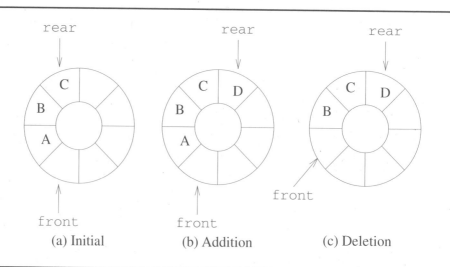

Figure 6.5 Circular queues

rear, which is the same condition as when the queue is empty! Therefore, we cannot distinguish between an empty and a full queue. To avoid this difficulty, we shall not permit a queue to get full. Before adding an element to a queue, we verify whether this addition will cause it to get full. If so, a queue-full error is given. Hence the maximum number of elements that can be in the queue is actually MaxSize-1.

The abstract data type Queue may be implemented as a C++ class as in Program 6.1. In our implementation of a formula-based stack (Program 5.1), we were able to reuse the definition of the class LinearList (Program 3.1) to simplify the code. However, we are unable to reuse LinearList for the implementation of the class Queue; the implementation of Queue is based on Equation 6.3, whereas that of LinearList is based on Equation 6.1. Programs 6.2 and 6.3 give the codes for the member functions of Queue. Notice how the queue constructor allows for the fact that a circular queue can accomodate one fewer element than the array size. As a result, the statement

```
Queue<int> Q(12);
```

creates a queue Q that can hold up to 12 integers.

The queue functions are similar to their stack counterparts and we shall not explain them further. The complexity of the queue constructor and destructor is $\Theta(1)$ when T is an internal data type and O(MaxStackSize) when T is a user-defined class. The complexity of each of the remaining queue oprations is $\Theta(1)$.

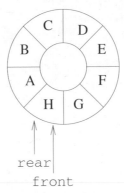

rear|
front

Figure 6.6 A circular queue with MaxSize elements

```
template<class T>
class Queue {
// FIFO objects
   public:
      Queue(int MaxQueueSize = 10);
      ~Queue() {delete [] queue;}
      bool IsEmpty() const {return front == rear;}
      bool IsFull() const {return (
         ((rear + 1) % MaxSize == front) ? 1 : 0);}
      T First() const; // return front element
      T Last() const; // return last element
      Queue<T>& Add(const T& x);
      Queue<T>& Delete(T& x);
   private:
      int front;   // one counterclockwise from first
      int rear;    // last element
      int MaxSize; // size of array queue
      T *queue;    // element array
};
```

Program 6.1 Formula-based class Queue

```
template<class T>
Queue<T>::Queue(int MaxQueueSize)
{// Create an empty queue whose capacity
 // is MaxQueueSize.
   MaxSize = MaxQueueSize + 1;
   queue = new T[MaxSize];
   front = rear = 0;
}

template<class T>
T Queue<T>::First() const
{// Return first element of queue.  Throw
 // OutOfBounds exception if the queue is empty.
   if (IsEmpty()) throw OutOfBounds();
   return queue[(front + 1) % MaxSize];
}

template<class T>
T Queue<T>::Last() const
{// Return last element of queue.  Throw
 // OutOfBounds exception if the queue is empty.
   if (IsEmpty()) throw OutOfBounds();
   return queue[rear];
}
```

Program 6.2 Queue functions using formula-based representation

EXERCISES

1. Extend the queue ADT by adding functions to
   (a) Determine the size (i.e., number of elements) of the queue.
   (b) Input a queue.
   (c) Output a queue.
   Now extend the class definition of a formula-based queue to include code for these functions. Write and test your code.

2. Extend the queue ADT by adding functions to
   (a) Split a queue into two queues. The first of the resulting two queues contains the first, third, fifth, ··· elements of the original queue; the second contains the remaining elements.

```
template<class T>
Queue<T>& Queue<T>::Add(const T& x)
{// Add x to the rear of the queue.   Throw
 // NoMem exception if the queue is full.
   if (IsFull()) throw NoMem();
   rear = (rear + 1) % MaxSize;
   queue[rear] = x;
   return *this;
}


template<class T>
Queue<T>& Queue<T>::Delete(T& x)
{// Delete first element and put it in x.   Throw
 // OutOfBounds exception if the queue is empty.
   if (IsEmpty()) throw OutOfBounds();
   front = (front + 1) % MaxSize;
   x = queue[front];
   return *this;
}
```

Program 6.3 Queue functions using formula-based representation

(b) Combine two queues by selecting elements alternately from the two queues beginning with queue 1. When a queue exhausts, append the remaining elements from the other queue to the combined queue. The relative order of elements from each queue is unchanged.
Now extend the class definition of a formula-based queue to include code for these functions. Write and test your code.

3. Develop a C++ class for queues using Equation 6.2. Write and test all codes.

4. Modify the representation used in the class Queue (Program 6.1) so that a queue can hold as many elements as the size of the array queue. For this modification, introduce another private member LastOp that keeps track of the last operation performed on the queue. Notice that if the last operation performed was Add, the queue cannot be empty. Also, if the last operation was Delete, the queue cannot be full. So LastOp can be used to distinguish between an empty and full queue when front = rear. Test the correctness of your modifed code.

5. A **deque** (pronounced *deck*) is an ordered list to/from which we can make additions and deletions at/from either end. Therefore, we can call it a double-ended queue.

(a) Define the ADT *Deque*. Include the operations: *Create*, *IsEmpty*, *IsFull*, *Left*, *Right*, *AddLeft*, *AddRight*, *DeleteLeft*, and *DeleteRight*.

(b) Use Equation 6.3 to represent a deque. Develop a C++ class `Deque` that corresponds to the ADT *Deque* and write code for all class members.

(c) Test your code using suitable test data.

6.3 LINKED REPRESENTATION

A queue, like a stack, can be represented as a chain. We need two variables `front` and `rear` to keep track of the two ends of a queue. There are two possibilities for binding these two variables to the two ends of a chain. The nodes can be linked from front to rear (Figure 6.7(a)) or from rear to front (Figure 6.7(b)). The direction of linkage is determined by the relative difficulty of performing additions and deletions. Figures 6.8 and 6.9, respectively, illustrate the mechanics of an add and a delete. We can see that both linkage directions are well suited for additions. but the front-to-rear linkage is more efficient for deletions. Hence we shall link the nodes in a queue from front to rear.

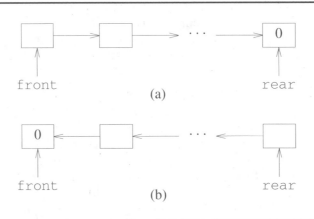

Figure 6.7 Linked queues

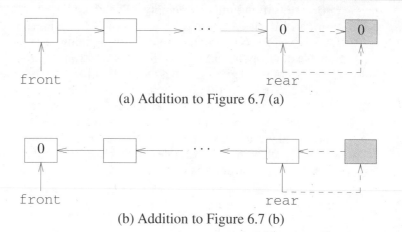

(a) Addition to Figure 6.7 (a)

(b) Addition to Figure 6.7 (b)

Figure 6.8 Addition to a linked queue

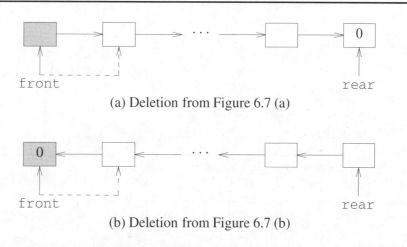

(a) Deletion from Figure 6.7 (a)

(b) Deletion from Figure 6.7 (b)

Figure 6.9 Deletion from a linked queue

We can use the initial values front = rear = 0 and the boundary value front = 0 iff the queue is empty. The class LinkedQueue may be defined as a derived class of Chain (Program 3.8), using the extensions of Section 3.4.3. Exercise 6 considers this way of defining LinkedQueue. In this section, we develop the class LinkedQueue from scratch.

Program 6.4 gives the class definition for a linked queue, and Programs 6.5 and 6.6 give the function implementations. The class Node is the same as used for a customized linked stack (Program 5.4). However, LinkedQueue needs to be declared a friend of Node. You should run through the LinkedQueue codes by hand using an empty queue, a queue with one element, and a queue with many elements as examples. The complexity of all linked queue functions other than the destructor is $\Theta(1)$.

```
template<class T>
class LinkedQueue {
// FIFO objects
   public:
      LinkedQueue() {front = rear = 0;} // constructor
      ~LinkedQueue(); // destructor
      bool IsEmpty() const
           {return ((front) ? false : true);}
      bool IsFull() const;
      T First() const; // return first element
      T Last() const; // return last element
      LinkedQueue<T>& Add(const T& x);
      LinkedQueue<T>& Delete(T& x);
   private:
      Node<T> *front;  // pointer to first node
      Node<T> *rear;   // pointer to last node
};
```

Program 6.4 Class definition for a linked queue

```
template<class T>
LinkedQueue<T>::~LinkedQueue()
{// Queue destructor.  Delete all nodes.
   Node<T> *next;
   while (front) {
      next = front->link;
      delete front;
      front = next;
      }
}

template<class T>
bool LinkedQueue<T>::IsFull() const
{// Is the queue full?
   Node<T> *p;
   try {p = new Node<T>;
        delete p;
        return false;}
   catch (NoMem) {return true;}
}

template<class T>
T LinkedQueue<T>::First() const
{// Return first element of queue.  Throw
 // OutOfBounds exception if the queue is empty.
   if (IsEmpty()) throw OutOfBounds();
   return front->data;
}

template<class T>
T LinkedQueue<T>::Last() const
{// Return last element of queue.  Throw
 // OutOfBounds exception if the queue is empty.
   if (IsEmpty()) throw OutOfBounds();
   return rear->data;
}
```

Program 6.5 Linked queue function implementations

```
template<class T>
LinkedQueue<T>& LinkedQueue<T>::Add(const T& x)
{// Add x to rear of queue.  Do not catch
 // possible NoMem exception thrown by new.

   // create node for new element
   Node<T> *p = new Node<T>;
   p->data = x;
   p->link = 0;

   // add new node to rear of queue
   if (front) rear->link = p;   // queue not empty
   else front = p;              // queue empty
   rear = p;

   return *this;
}

template<class T>
LinkedQueue<T>& LinkedQueue<T>::Delete(T& x)
{// Delete first element and put it in x.  Throw
 // OutOfBounds exception if the queue is empty.

   if (IsEmpty()) throw OutOfBounds();

   // save element in first node
   x = front->data;

   // delete first node
   Node<T> *p = front;
   front = front->link;
   delete p;

   return *this;
}
```

Program 6.6 Linked queue function implementations

EXERCISES

6. Develop `LinkedQueue` as a derived class of `Chain` (Program 3.8). Use the extended version of `Chain` that includes the function `Append` (see Section 3.4.3). Customize the chain operations as needed.

7. Do Exercise 1 using a linked queue.

8. Do Exercise 2 using a linked queue. However, this time, perform the operations in place without the use of new nodes. The input queue(s) is (are) empty following each operation.

9. Do Exercise 5 using a chain. What is the complexity of each operation?

10. Do Exercise 5 using a doubly linked list to represent a deque. What is the complexity of each operation?

6.4 APPLICATIONS

6.4.1 Railroad Car Rearrangement

We shall reconsider the railroad car rearrangement problem of Section 5.5.3. This time the holding tracks lie between the input and output track as in Figure 6.10. These tracks operate in a FIFO manner and so may be regarded as queues. As in the case of Section 5.5.3, moving a car from a holding track to the input track or from the output track to a holding track is forbidden. All car motion is in the direction indicated by the arrowheads of Figure 6.10.

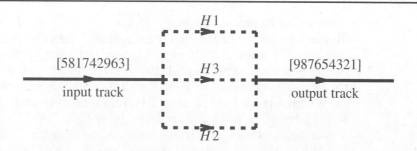

Figure 6.10 A three-track example

We reserve track Hk for moving cars directly from the input track to the output track. So the number of tracks available to hold cars that are not ready to be output becomes $k - 1$.

Consider rearranging nine cars that have the initial ordering 5, 8, 1, 7, 4, 2, 9, 6, 3. Assume that $k = 3$. Car 3 cannot be moved directly to the output track, as cars 1 and 2 must come before it. So it is moved to $H1$. Car 6 can be placed behind car 3 in $H1$, as car 6 is to be output after car 3. Car 9 can now be placed after car 6 in $H1$. Car 2 cannot be placed after car 9, as car 2 is to be output before car 9. So it is placed at the front of $H2$. Car 4 can now be placed after car 2 in $H2$, and car 7 can be placed after it. Car 1 can be moved to the output using $H3$. Next car 2 is moved from $H2$ to the output. Then car 3 is moved from $H1$ to the output, and car 4 is moved from $H2$ to the output. Car 5 is to be output next. It is still in the input track. So car 8 is moved from the input track to $H2$. Then car 5 is moved to the output track. Now cars 6, 7, 8, and 9 are moved from their holding tracks to the output track.

When a car is to be moved to a holding track, we can use the following track selection to decide which holding track to move it to. *Move car c to a holding track that contains only cars with a smaller label; if there are several such tracks, select one with largest label at its left end; otherwise, select an empty track (if one remains).*

First Implementation

We can implement the car rearrangement algorithm by using linked queues for the $k-1$ holding tracks that can hold cars. We can model the code after Programs 5.8, 5.9, and 5.10. Program 6.7 gives the new code for the `Output` and `Hold` functions. The function `Railroad` of Program 5.8 needs to be modified. The changes are (1) decrease `k` by 1, (2) change the type of `H` to `LinkedQueue<int> *`, (3) change `MinS` to `MinQ`, and (4) delete the last parameter (`n`) from the invocation of `Hold`. The time needed to perform the rearrangement is O(nk). We can use AVL trees (see Chapter 11) to reduce this time to O(nlogk).

Alternative Implementation

To animate the progress of the rearrangement algorithm, it is useful to keep the queues of Program 6.7. If our objective is to simply output the sequence of moves necessary to accomplish the rearrangement, then we need to know only the last member of each holding track (or queue) together with which track each car is currently in. Let `last[i]` be zero if holding track `i` is empty, and let it be the label of the last car in the track, otherwise. Let `track[i]` be zero if car `i` is in the input track, and let it be the holding track car `i` is (was) in, otherwise. Initially `last[i]` = 0, $1 \le$ `i` $<$ `k`, and `track[i]` = 0, $1 \le$ `i` $\le$ `n`. Program 6.8 produces the same output as does Program 6.7 but uses no queues. Both programs have the same asymptotic complexity.

```
void Output(int& minH, int& minQ,
       LinkedQueue<int> H[], int k, int n)
{// Move from hold to output and update minH and minQ.

   int c;  // car index

   // delete smallest car minH from queue minQ
   H[minQ].Delete(c);
   cout << "Move car " << minH << " from holding track "
        << minQ << " to output" << endl;

   // find new minH and minQ
   // by checking front of all queues
   minH = n + 2;
   for (int i = 1; i <= k; i++)
      if (!H[i].IsEmpty() &&
              (c = H[i].First()) < minH) {
         minH = c;
         minQ = i; }
}
```

Program 6.7 Rearranging cars using queues (continues)

6.4.2 Wire Routing

As noted in Section 5.5.6, our solution to the rat in a maze problem does not guarantee to find a shortest path from maze entrance to exit. By using a queue, we can find such a path. The problem of finding a shortest path in a maze arises in other situations also. For example, a common approach to the wire-routing problem for electrical circuits is to impose a grid over the wire-routing region. The grid divides the routing region into an $n \times m$ array of squares much like a maze (Figure 6.11(a)). A wire runs from the midpoint of one square a to the midpoint of another b. In doing so, the wire may make right-angle turns (Figure 6.11(b)). Grid squares that already have a wire through them are blocked. To minimize signal delay, we wish to route the wire using a shortest path between a and b.

The following discussion assumes that you are familiar with the rat in a maze development of Section 5.5.6. If not, you should review this development before proceeding. To find the shortest path between grid positions a and b, we begin at position a and label its reachable neighbors 1 (i.e., they are distance 1 from a). Next the reachable neighbors of squares labeled 1 are labeled 2. This labeling process is continued until we either reach b or have no more reachable

```
bool Hold(int c, int& minH, int &minQ,
      LinkedQueue<int> H[], int k)
{// Add car c to a holding track.
 // Return false if no feasible holding track.
 // Throw NoMem exception if no queue space.
 // Return true otherwise.

   // find best holding track for car c
   // initialize
   int BestTrack = 0,   // best track so far
       BestLast = 0,    // last car in BestTrack
       x;               // a car index

   // scan holding tracks
   for (int i = 1; i <= k; i++)
      if (!H[i].IsEmpty()) {// track i not empty
         x = H[i].Last();
         if (c > x && x > BestLast) {
            // track i has bigger car at end
          BestLast = x;
            BestTrack = i;}
         }
      else // track i empty
         if (!BestTrack) BestTrack = i;

   if (!BestTrack) return false; // no track available

   // add c to best track
   H[BestTrack].Add(c);
   cout << "Move car " << c << " from input "
      << "to holding track " << BestTrack << endl;

   // update minH and minQ if needed
   if (c < minH) {minH = c;
                  minQ = BestTrack;}

   return true;
}
```

Program 6.7 Rearranging cars using queues (concluded)

```
void Output(int NowOut, int Track, int& Last)
{// Move car NowOut from hold to output, update Last.
   cout << "Move car " << NowOut
        << " from holding track "
        << Track << " to output" << endl;
   if (NowOut == Last) Last = 0;
}

bool Hold(int c, int last[], int track[], int k)
{// Add car c to a holding track.
 // Return false if no feasible holding track.
 // Return true otherwise.

   // find best holding track for car c
   // initialize
   int BestTrack = 0,  // best track so far
       BestLast = 0;   // last car in BestTrack

   // scan holding tracks
   for (int i = 1; i <= k; i++) // find best track
      if (last[i]) {// track i not empty
          if (c > last[i] && last[i] > BestLast) {
              // track i has bigger car at end
            BestLast = last[i];
              BestTrack = i;}
          }
      else // track i empty
          if (!BestTrack) BestTrack = i;

   if (!BestTrack) return false; // no track available

   // add c to best track
   track[c] = BestTrack;
   last[BestTrack] = c;
   cout << "Move car " << c << " from input "
        << "to holding track " << BestTrack << endl;

   return true;
}
```

Program 6.8 Rearranging cars without the use of a queue (continues)

```
bool Railroad(int p[], int n, int k)
{// k track rearrangement of car order p[1:n].
 // Return true if successful, false if impossible.
 // Throw NoMem exception if inadequate space.

    // initialize arrays last and track
    int *last = new int [k + 1];
    int *track = new int [n + 1];
    for (int i = 1; i <= k; i++)
       last[i] = 0;   // track i is empty
    for (int i = 1; i <= n; i++)
       track[i] = 0;   // car i is on no track
    k--; // keep track k open for direct moves

    // initialize index of next car
    // that goes to output
    int NowOut = 1;

    // output cars in order
    for (int i = 1; i <= n; i++)
       if (p[i] == NowOut) {// send straight to output
          cout << "Move car " << p[i] <<
                    " from input to output" << endl;
          NowOut++;

          // output from holding tracks
          while (NowOut <= n && track[NowOut]) {
             Output(NowOut, track[NowOut], last[NowOut]);
             NowOut++;
             }
          }
       else {// put car p[i] in a holding track
          if (!Hold(p[i], last, track, k))
          return false;}

    return true;
}
```

Program 6.8 Rearranging cars without the use of a queue (concluded)

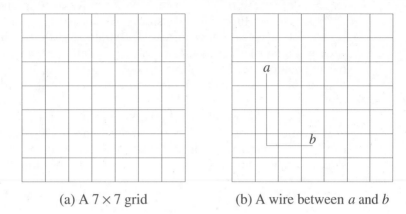

(a) A 7×7 grid   (b) A wire between a and b

Figure 6.11 Wire-routing example

neighbors. Figure 6.12(a) shows this process for the case $a = (3,2)$ and $b = (4,6)$. The shaded squares are blocked squares.

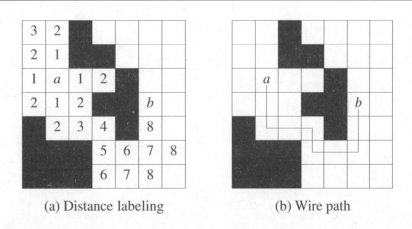

(a) Distance labeling   (b) Wire path

Figure 6.12 Wire routing

Once we have reached b, we can label it with its distance (9 in the case of Figure 6.12(a)). To construct a shortest path between a and b, we begin at b and move to any one its neighbors labeled one less than b's label. Such a neighbor must exist as each grid's label is one more than that of at least one of its neighbors. In the case of Figure 6.12(a), we move from b to (5,6). From here we move to one of its neighbors whose label is one less, and so on until we reach a. In the example of Figure 6.12(a), from (5,6) we move to (6,6) and then to (6,5), (6,4), (5,4), and so on. Figure 6.12(b) shows the constructed path.

Now let us see how to take the strategy outlined above and obtain C++ code to find a shortest path in a grid. We shall use many ideas from the rat in a maze solution of Section 5.5.6. An $m \times m$ grid is represented as a two-dimensional array with a 0 representing an open position and a 1 a blocked position; the grid is surrounded by a ''wall'' of 1s; the array `offsets` helps us move from a position to its neighbors; and a linked queue keeps track of labeled grid positions whose neighbors have yet to be labeled. A formula-based queue can be used instead, but in this case we need to estimate the maximum queue size, just as we had to estimate the stack size in the rat in a maze code.

```
bool FindPath(Position start, Position finish,
              int& PathLen, Position * &path)
{// Find a path from start to finish.
 // Return true if successful, false if impossible.
 // Throw NoMem exception if inadequate space.

   if ((start.row == finish.row) &&
       (start.col == finish.col))
          {PathLen = 0; return true;} // start = finish

   // initialize wall of blocks around grid
   for (int i = 0; i <= m+1; i++) {
      grid[0][i] = grid[m+1][i] = 1; // bottom & top
      grid[i][0] = grid[i][m+1] = 1; // left & right
      }
   // initialize offsets
   Position offset[4];
   offset[0].row = 0; offset[0].col = 1; // right
   offset[1].row = 1; offset[1].col = 0; // down
   offset[2].row = 0; offset[2].col = -1; // left
   offset[3].row = -1; offset[3].col = 0; // up

   int NumOfNbrs = 4; // neighbors of a grid position
   Position here, nbr;
   here.row = start.row;
   here.col = start.col;
   grid[start.row][start.col] = 2; // block
```

Program 6.9 Find a wire route (continues)

```
// label reachable grid positions
LinkedQueue<Position> Q;
do {// label neighbors of here
   for (int i = 0; i < NumOfNbrs; i++) {
      nbr.row = here.row + offset[i].row;
      nbr.col = here.col + offset[i].col;
      if (grid[nbr.row][nbr.col] == 0) {
         // unlabeled nbr, label it
         grid[nbr.row][nbr.col]
            = grid[here.row][here.col] + 1;
         if ((nbr.row == finish.row) &&
            (nbr.col == finish.col)) break; // done
      Q.Add(nbr);} // end of if
      } // end of for

   // have we reached finish?
   if ((nbr.row == finish.row) &&
      (nbr.col == finish.col)) break; // done

   // finish not reached, can we move to a nbr?
   if (Q.IsEmpty()) return false; // no path
   Q.Delete(here); // get next position
} while(true);

// construct path
PathLen = grid[finish.row][finish.col] - 2;
path = new Position [PathLen];

// trace backwards from finish
here = finish;
for (int j = PathLen-1; j >= 0; j--) {
   path[j] = here;
   // find predecessor position
   for (int i = 0; i < NumOfNbrs; i++) {
      nbr.row = here.row + offset[i].row;
      nbr.col = here.col + offset[i].col;
      if (grid[nbr.row][nbr.col] == j+2) break;
      }
   here = nbr;  // move to predecessor
   }
return true;
}
```

Program 6.9 Find a wire route (concluded)

In the code of Program 6.9, we assume that the start (*a*) and finish (*b*) positions are unblocked. The code begins with a check to see whether the start and finish positions are the same. In this case the path length is 0, and the code terminates. Otherwise, we set up a wall of blocked positions around the grid; initialize the offset array, and label the start position with a distance of 2. (All distance labels have been increased by two as the grid uses the numbers 0 and 1 to denote open and blocked positions, respectively. To get the corresponding distances as shown in Figure 6.12(a), we need to subtract two from the labeled distance.) Using the queue Q and beginning at position start, we move to reachable grid positions that are distance 1 from the start and then to those that are distance 2, and so on until we either reach the finish position or are unable to move to a new, unblocked position. In the latter case there is no path to the finish position. In the former case the finish position is labeled by its distance value.

If we reach the finish position, the path is reconstructed using the distance labels. The positions on the path (except for start) are stored in the array path.

Since no grid position can get on the queue more than once, it takes $O(m^2)$ time (for an $m \times m$ grid) to complete the distance-labeling phase. The time needed for the path-construction phase is $\Theta(PathLen)$ where *PathLen* is the length of the shortest path.

6.4.3 Image-Component Labeling

A digitized image is an $m \times m$ matrix of pixels. In a binary image each pixel is either 0 or 1. A 0 pixel represents image background, while a 1 represents a point on an image component. We shall refer to pixels whose value is 1 as component pixels. Two pixels are adjacent if one is to the left, above, right, or below the other. Two component pixels that are adjacent are pixels of the same image component. The objective of component labeling is to label the component pixels so that two pixels get the same label iff they are pixels of the same image component.

Consider Figure 6.13(a) that shows a 7×7 image. The blank squares represent background pixels, and the 1s represent component pixels. Pixels (1,3) and (2,3) are pixels of the same component because they are adjacent. Since component pixels (2,3) and (2,4) are adjacent, they are also of the same component. Hence the three pixels (1,3), (2,3), and (2,4) are from the same component. Since there are no other image pixels adjacent to these three pixels, these three define an image component. The image of Figure 6.13(a) has four components. The first component is defined by the pixel set {(1,3), (2,3), (2,4)}; the second is {(3,5), (4,4), (4,5), (5,5)}; the third is {(5,2), (6,1), (6,2), (6,3), (7,1), (7,2), (7,3)}; and the fourth is {(5,7), (6,7), (7,6), (7,7)}. In Figure 6.13(b) the component pixels have been given labels so that two of them have the same label iff they are part of the same component.

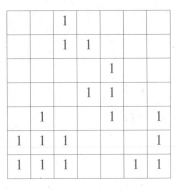

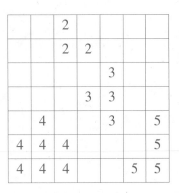

(a) A 7×7 image

(b) Labeled components

Figure 6.13 Image-component labeling

Our program to label component pixels uses much of the development used for the wire-routing problem. To move around the image with ease, we surround the image with a wall of blank (i.e., 0) pixels. We use the offset array to determine the pixels adjacent to a given pixel. The components are determined by scanning the pixels by rows and within rows by columns. When an unlabeled component pixel is encountered, it is given a component identifier/label. (We use the numbers $2, 3, 4, \cdots$ as component identifiers.) This pixel forms the seed of a new component. We determine the remaining pixels in the component by identifying and labeling all component pixels that are adjacent to the seed. Call the pixels that are adjacent to the seed the distance 1 pixels. Then unlabeled component pixels that are adjacent to the distance 1 pixels are identified and labeled. These newly labeled pixels are the distance 2 pixels. Then unlabeled component pixels adjacent to the distance 2 pixels are identified and labeled. This process continues until no new unlabeled adjacent component pixels are found.

The labeling process just described is very similar to the process used to label squares in a wiring grid by their distance from the start square. This similarity results in a component-labeling code (Program 6.10) that is similar to Program 6.9.

Program 6.10 begins by setting up a wall of background (0) pixels around the image and initializing the array of neighbor/adjacent pixel offsets. The next two for loops scan the image for a seed for the next component. The seed is an unmarked component pixel. For such a pixel, pixel[r][c] is 1. The

```
void Label()
{// Label image components.
   // initialize wall of 0 pixels
   for (int i = 0; i <= m+1; i++) {
      pixel[0][i] = pixel[m+1][i] = 0; // bottom & top
      pixel[i][0] = pixel[i][m+1] = 0; // left & right
      }
   // initialize offsets
   Position offset[4];
   offset[0].row = 0; offset[0].col = 1; // right
   offset[1].row = 1; offset[1].col = 0; // down
   offset[2].row = 0; offset[2].col = -1; // left
   offset[3].row = -1; offset[3].col = 0; // up

   int NumOfNbrs = 4; // neighbors of a pixel position
   LinkedQueue<Position> Q;
   int id = 1;  // component id
   Position here, nbr;

   // scan all pixels labeling components
   for (int r = 1; r <= m; r++)   // row r of image
      for (int c = 1; c <= m; c++)    // column c
         if (pixel[r][c] == 1) {// new component}
            pixel[r][c] = ++id; // get next id
            here.row = r; here.col = c;

            do {// find rest of component
               for (int i = 0; i < NumOfNbrs; i++) {
                  // check all neighbors of here
                  nbr.row = here.row + offset[i].row;
                  nbr.col = here.col + offset[i].col;
                  if (pixel[nbr.row][nbr.col] == 1) {
                     pixel[nbr.row][nbr.col] = id;
                     Q.Add(nbr);}} // end of if and for

               // any unexplored pixels in component?
               if (Q.IsEmpty()) break;
               Q.Delete(here); // a component pixel
            } while(true);

         } // end of if, for c, and for r
}
```

Program 6.10 Component labeling

seed is assigned a component label by changing `pixel[r][c]` from 1 to a component identifier/label (`id`). Then with the help of a linked queue (a formula-based queue, linked stack, or formula-based stack can be used instead), the remaining pixels in this component are identified. By the time function `Label` terminates, all component pixels have been assigned a label.

It takes $\Theta(m)$ time to initialize the wall of background pixels and $\Theta(1)$ time to initialize `offsets`. Although the condition `pixel[r][c] == 1` is checked m^2 times, it is true only as many times as the number of components in the image. For each component Θ(number of pixels in component) time is spent identifying and labeling its pixels (other than the component seed). Since no pixel is in two or more components, the total time spent identifying and labeling nonseed component pixels is Θ(number of component pixels in image) = Θ(number of pixels with value 1 in input image) = $O(m^2)$. The overall time complexity of function `Label` is $\Theta(m^2)$.

6.4.4 Machine Shop Simulation

Problem Description

A machine shop (or factory or plant) comprises m machines or work stations. The machine shop works on jobs, and each job comprises several tasks. Each machine can process one task of one job at any time, and different machines perform different tasks. Once a machine begins to process a task, it continues processing that task until the task completes.

Example 6.1 A sheet metal plant might have one machine (or station) for each of the following tasks: design; cut the sheet metal to size; drill holes; cut holes; trim edges; shape the metal; and seal seams. Each of these machines/stations can work on one task at a time.

Each job includes several tasks. For example, to fabricate the heating and air-conditioning ducts for a new house, we would need to spend some time in the design phase, and then some time cutting the sheet metal stock to the right size pieces. We need to drill or cut the holes (depending on their size), shape the cut pieces into ducts, seal the seams, and trim any rough edges. ∎

For each task of a job, there is a task time (i.e., how long does it take) and a machine on which it is to be performed. The tasks of a job are to be performed in a specified order. So a job goes first to the machine for its first task. When this first task is complete, the job goes to the machine for its second task, and so on until its last task completes. When a job arrives at a machine, it may have to wait because the machine might be busy. In fact, several jobs might already waiting for that machine.

Each machine in our machine shop can be in one of three states: active, idle, and change over. In the active state the machine is working on a task of some job; in the idle state it is doing nothing; and in the change-over state the machine has completed a task and work needed to prepare it for a new task is in progress. In the change-over state, the machine operator might, for example, clean the machine, put away tools used for the last task, and take a break. The time each machine must spend in its change-over state varies from machine to machine.

When a machine becomes available for a new job, it will need to pick one of the waiting jobs to work on. In our machine shop each machine serves its waiting jobs in a FIFO manner, and so the waiting jobs at each machine form a (FIFO) queue. In other machine shops the next job may be selected by priority. Each job has a priority associated with it. When a machine becomes free, the waiting job with highest priority is selected.

The time at which a job's last task completes is called its **finish time**. The **length** of a job is the sum of its task times. If a job of length l arrives at the machine shop at time 0 and completes at time f, then it must have spent exactly $f-l$ amount of time waiting in machine queues. To keep customers happy, it is desirable to minimize the time a job spends waiting in machine queues. Machine shop performance can be improved if we know how much time jobs spend waiting and which machines are contributing most to this wait.

When simulating a machine shop, we follow the jobs from machine to machine without physically performing the tasks. We simulate time by using a simulated clock that is advanced each time a task completes or a new job enters the machine shop. As tasks complete, new tasks are scheduled. Each time a task completes or a new job enters the shop, we say that an **event** has occurred. In addition, a **start event** initiates the simulation. The following example illustrates how the simulation works when no new jobs enter the machine shop during the simulation.

Example 6.2 Consider a machine shop that has $m = 3$ machines and $n = 6$ jobs. We assume that all six are available at time 0 and that no new jobs become available during the simulation. The simulation will continue until all jobs have completed.

The three machines, $M1$, $M2$, and $M3$, have a change-over time of 2, 0, and 1, respectively. So when a task completes, machine 1 must wait two time units before starting another, machine 2 can start the next task immediately, and machine 3 must wait one time unit. Figure 6.14(a) gives the characteristics of the six jobs. Job 1, for example, has three tasks. Each task is specified as a pair of the form (machine, time). The first task of job 1 is to be done on $M1$ and takes two time units, the second is to be done on $M2$ and takes four time units, the third is to be done on $M1$ and takes one time unit. The job lengths (i.e., the sum of their task times) are 7, 6, 8, and 4, respectively.

Job#	#Tasks	Tasks
1	3	(1,2) (2,4) (1,1)
2	2	(3,4) (1,2)
3	2	(1,4) (2,4)
4	2	(3,1) (2,3)

(a) Job characteristics

Time	Machine Queues			Active Jobs			Finish Times		
	$M1$	$M2$	$M3$	$M1$	$M2$	$M3$	$M1$	$M2$	$M3$
Init	1,3	–	2,4	I	I	I	L	L	L
0	3	–	4	1	I	2	2	L	4
2	3	–	4	C	1	2	4	6	4
4	2	–	4	3	1	C	8	6	5
5	2	–	–	3	1	4	8	6	6
6	2,1	4	–	3	C	C	8	9	7
7	2,1	4	–	3	C	I	8	9	L
8	2,1	4,3	–	C	C	I	10	9	L
9	2,1	3	–	C	4	I	10	12	L
10	1	3	–	2	4	I	12	12	L
12	1	3	–	C	C	I	14	15	L
14	–	3	–	1	C	I	15	15	L
15	–	–	–	C	3	I	17	16	L
16	–	–	–	C	C	I	19	19	L

(b) Simulation

Figure 6.14 Machine shop simulation example

Figure 6.14(b) shows the machine shop simulation. Initially, the four jobs are placed into queues corresponding to their first tasks. The first task for jobs 1 and 3 are to be done on $M1$, so these jobs are placed on the queue for $M1$. The first tasks for jobs 2 and 4 are to be done on $M3$. Consequently, these jobs begin on the queue for $M3$. The queue for $M2$ is empty. At the start all three machines are idle. We use the symbol I to indicate that the machines have no active job at this time. Since no machine is active, the time at which they will finish their current active task is undefined and denoted by the symbol L (large time).

The simulation begins at time 0. That is, the first event, the start event, occurs at time 0. At this time the first job in each machine queue is scheduled on the corresponding machine. Job 1's first task is scheduled on $M1$, and job 2's first task on $M3$. The queue for $M1$ now contains job 3 only, while that for $M3$ contains job 4 only. The queue for $M2$ remains empty. Job 1 becomes the active job on $M1$, and job 2 the active job on $M3$. $M2$ remains idle. The finish time for $M1$ becomes 2 (current time of 0 plus task time of 2) while the finish time for $M3$ becomes 4.

The next event occurs at time 2. This time is determined by finding the minimum of the machine finish times. At time 2 $M1$ completes its active task. This task is a job 1 task. Job 1 is moved to machine $M2$ for its next task. Since $M2$ is idle, the processing of job 1's second task begins immediately. This task will complete at time 6 (current time of 2, plus task time of 4). $M1$ goes into its change-over state and will remain in this state for two time units. Its active job is set to C (change over), and its finish time to 4.

At time 4 both $M1$ and $M3$ complete their active tasks. As $M1$ completes a change-over task, it begins a new job. From its queue, the first job, job 3, is selected. The task length is 4. So the task will complete at time 8. This time becomes the finish time for $M1$. $M3$'s active job, job 2, needs to be serviced next on $M1$. $M1$ is busy, so the job is added to $M1$'s job queue. $M3$ moves into its change-over state and completes this change-over task at time 5.

You should now be able to follow the remaining sequence of events. Jobs 2 and 4 finish at time 12, job 1 finishes at time 15, and job 3 finishes at time 19. Since the length of job 2 is 6 and its finish time 12, job 2 must have spent a total of $12-6 = 6$ time units waiting in machine queues. Similarly, job 4 must have spent $12-4 = 8$ time units waiting in queues. The wait time for jobs 1 and 3 is 8 and 11, respectively. The total wait time is 33.

We may determine the distribution of these 33 units of wait time across the three machines. For example, job 4 joined the queue for $M3$ at time 0 and did not become active until time 5. So this job waited at $M3$ for five time units. No other job experienced a wait at $M3$. The total wait time at $M3$ was, therefore, five time units. Going through Figure 6.14(b), we can compute the wait times for $M1$ and $M2$. The numbers are 18 and 10, respectively. As expected, the sum of the job wait times (33) equals the sum of the machine wait times. ∎

High-Level Simulator Design

In designing our simulator, we shall assume that all jobs are available initially (i.e., no jobs enter the shop during the simulation). Further, we assume that the simulation is to be run until all jobs complete.

Since the simulator is a fairly complex program, we break it into modules. The tasks to be performed by the simulator are input the data and put the jobs into the queues for their first tasks; perform the start event (i.e., do the initial loading of jobs onto the machines); run through all the events (i.e., perform the actual simulation); and output the machine wait times. We shall have one C++ function for each task. Each function may throw exceptions such as `NoMem` and `BadInput` (invalid input data). As a result, our main function takes the form of Program 6.11. The `catch` block could be replaced by several `catch` blocks, one for each kind of exception that may be thrown, and a different message output from each. Exercise 19 asks you to make this refinement.

```
void main(void)
{// Machine shop simulation.
   try {
       InputData();      // get machine and job data
       StartShop();      // initial machine loading
       Simulate();       // run all jobs through shop
       OutputStats();}   // output machine wait times
   catch (...) {
       cout << "An exception has occurred" << endl;}
   }
```

Program 6.11 Main function for machine shop simulation

The Class Task

Before we can develop the code for the four functions invoked by Program 6.11, we must develop representations for the data objects that are needed. These objects include tasks, jobs, machines, and an event list. Each task has two components: machine (the machine on which it is to be performed) and time (the time needed to complete the task). Program 6.12 gives the class definition. Since machines are assumed to be numbered 1 through m, machine is of type int (type unsigned may be used instead). We shall assume that all times are integral. The data type of time is declared as long to permit very long simulations. The class Task has two friends: the class Job and the function MoveToNextMachine. Task and Job have been declared friends because they need access to the private members of Task. We may avoid granting this access by defining public member functions of Task to set and retrieve the values of the machine and time components.

The Class Job

Each job has a list of associated tasks that are performed in list order. Consequently, the task list may be represented as a queue TaskQ. To determine the total wait time experienced by a job, we need to know its length and finish time. The finish time is determined by the event clock, while the length is the sum of task times. To determine a job's length, we associate a private data member Length with it.

Program 6.12 gives the class Job. TaskQ has been defined as a linked queue of tasks. Since the number of tasks associated with a job is known at the time of input, we could have defined TaskQ to be a pointer to a dynamically constructed formula-based queue just large enough to hold the desired number of

```
class Task {
    friend class Job;
    friend bool MoveToNextMachine(Job*);
    private:
        long time;
        int  machine;
};


class Job {
    friend bool MoveToNextMachine(Job*);
    friend Job* ChangeState(int);
    friend void Simulate();
    friend class Machine;
    public:
        Job(long id) {ID = id;
                Length = ArriveTime = 0;}
        void AddTask(int p, long t) {
                Task x;
                x.machine = p;
                x.time = t;
                TaskQ.Add(x);}
        long DeleteTask() {// delete next task
                Task x;
                TaskQ.Delete(x);
                Length += x.time;
                return x.time;}
    private:
        LinkedQueue<Task> TaskQ;
        long Length;    // sum of scheduled task times
        long ArriveTime;// arrival time at current queue
        long ID;        // job identifier
};
```

Program 6.12 The classes Task and Job

tasks. This definition would work quite well for our limited simulator, as we
assume no jobs enter the shop after the simulation begins. In a more general
simulator, jobs are permitted to enter the shop during simulation. When linked
queues are used, task queue nodes may be freed as soon as a task completes.
These freed nodes may be reused to construct the task queue for new jobs. When
formula-based queues are used, the task queue space may be freed only when the

entire job has completed. Consequently, the simulation may fail for lack of sufficient space, even though very few unfinished tasks remain in the shop.

The private member `ArriveTime` records the time at which a job enters its current machine queue and determines the time the job waits in this queue. The job identifier is stored in `ID` and is used only when outputting the total wait time encountered by this job.

The public member `AddTask` adds a task to the job's task queue. The task is to be performed on machine `p` and takes `t` time. This function is used only during data input. The public member `DeleteTask` is used when a job is moved from a mchine queue to active status. At this time, its first task is deleted from the task queue (the task queue maintains a list of tasks yet to be scheduled on machines), the job length is incremented by the task time, and the task time returned. `Length` becomes equal to the job length when we schedule the last task for the job.

The Class `Machine`

Each machine has a change-over time, an active job, and a queue of waiting jobs. Since a job is a rather large object (it has a task queue and other data members), it is more efficient to define the queue of waiting jobs as a queue of pointers to jobs. Therefore, each machine queue operation deals with pointers (which are small objects) rather than with jobs.

Since each job can be in at most one machine queue at any time, the total space needed for all queues is bounded by the number of jobs. However, the distribution of jobs over the machine queues changes as the simulation proceeds. It is possible to have a few very long queues at one time. These queues might become very short later, and some other queues become long. If we use formula-based queues, we must declare the queue size for each machine at its maximum possible value. (Alternatively, we must dynamically adjust the size of the array that holds the queue.) As a result, we need space for $m*(n+1)$ job pointers (m is the number of machines and n the number of jobs). When we use linked queues, we need space for n job pointers and link fields, so we use linked queues.

Program 6.13 gives the class `Machine`. The private members `JobQ`, `ChangeTime`, `TotalWait`, `NumTasks`, and `Active`, respectively, denote the queue of pointers to waiting jobs, the change-over time for the machine, the total time jobs have spent waiting at this machine, the number of tasks processed by the machine, and a pointer to the currently active job. The active job pointer is zero whenever the machine is idle or in its change-over state.

The public member `IsEmpty` returns `true` iff the job queue is empty; the public member `AddJob` adds a job to the queue of waiting jobs; `SetChange` sets the value of `ChangeTime` (change-over time) during input; and `Stats` returns the total wait time experienced at this machine as well as the number of tasks processed.

```
class Machine {
   friend Job* ChangeState(int);
   public:
      Machine() {TotalWait = NumTasks = 0;
                 Active = 0;}
      bool IsEmpty() {return JobQ.IsEmpty();}
      void AddJob(Job* x) {JobQ.Add(x);}
      void SetChange(long w) {ChangeTime = w;}
      void Stats(long& tw, long& nt)
            {tw = TotalWait;
             nt = NumTasks;}
   private:
      LinkedQueue<Job*> JobQ; // queue of waiting jobs
      long ChangeTime;   // machine changeover time
      long TotalWait;    // total delay at this machine
      long  NumTasks;    // number of tasks processed
      Job *Active;       // pointer to current job
};
```

Program 6.13 The class `Machine`

We store the finish times of all machines in an event list. To go from one event to the next, we need to determine the minimum of the machine finish times. Our simulator also needs an operation that sets the finish time of a particular machine. This operation has to be done each time a new job is scheduled on a machine. When a machine becomes idle, its finish time is set to some large number.

The Class `EventList`

Program 6.14 gives the class `EventList` that implements the event list as a one-dimensional array `FinishTime`, with `FinishTime[p]` being the finish time of machine `p`. When the machine shop is initialized, all machines are idle and their finish time is set to `BigT`. For correct operation, the simulation should complete before time `BigT`. The number of machines in the shop is recorded in `NumMachines`.

The function `NextEvent` returns, in `p`, the machine that completes its active task next, and in `t`, the time at which this task completes. For an `m` machine shop, it takes $\Theta(m)$ time to find the minimum of the finish times, so the complexity of `NextEvent` is $\Theta(m)$. The function to set the finish time of a machine, `SetFinishTime`, runs in $\Theta(1)$ time. In Chapter 9 we will see two data structures—heaps and leftist trees—that may also represent an event list. When we use either of these data structures, the complexity of both

```
class EventList {
   public:
      EventList(int m, long BigT);
      ~EventList(){delete [] FinishTime;}
     void NextEvent(int& p, long& t);
      long NextEvent(int p) {return FinishTime[p];}
      void SetFinishTime(int p, long t)
             {FinishTime[p] = t;}
   private:
      long *FinishTime; // finish time array
      int NumMachines;  // number of machines in shop
};

EventList::EventList(int m, long BigT)
{// Initialize finish times for m machines.
   if (m < 1) throw BadInitializers();
   FinishTime = new long [m+1];
   NumMachines = m;
   // all machines idle, initialize with
   // large finish time
   for (int i = 1; i <= m; i++)
      FinishTime[i] = BigT;
}

void EventList::NextEvent(int& p, long& t)
{// Return machine and time for next event.
   // find first machine to finish, this is
   // machine with smallest finish time
   p = 1;
   t = FinishTime[1];
   for (int i = 2; i <= NumMachines; i++)
      if (FinishTime[i] < t) {// i finishes earlier
         p = i;
         t = FinishTime[i];}
}
```

Program 6.14 The class `EventList`

`NextEvent` and `SetFinishTime` becomes $O(\log m)$. If the total number of tasks across all jobs is T, then our simulator will invoke `NextEvent` and `SetFinishTime` $\Theta(T)$ times each. Using the event list implementation of Program 6.14, these invocations take $\Theta(Tm)$ time; using one of the data structures of

Chapter 9, the invocations take O(Tlogm) time. Even though the data structures of Chapter 9 are more complex, they result in a faster simulation when m is suitably large.

Global Variables

Our code for the four functions of Program 6.11 uses the global variables defined in Program 6.15. The significance of most of these variables is self-evident. Now is the simulated clock and records the current time. Each time an event occurs, it is updated to the event time. LargeTime is a time that exceeds the finish time of the last job and denotes the finish time of an idle machine.

```
// globals
long Now = 0;                // current time
int m;                       // number of machines
long n;                      // number of jobs
long LargeTime = 10000;      // finish before this time
EventList *EL;               // pointer to event list
Machine *M;                  // array of machines
```

Program 6.15 Global variables used by the simulator

The Function InputData

The code for the function InputData (Program 6.16) begins by inputting the number of machines and jobs in the shop. Next, we create the initial event list *EL, with finish times equal to LargeTime for each machine, and the array M of machines. Then, we input the change-over times for the machines. Next, we input the jobs one by one. For each job we first input the number of tasks it has, and then we input the tasks as pairs of the form (machine, time). The machine for the first task of the job is recorded in the variable p. When all tasks of a job have been input, the job (actually a pointer to the job) is added to the queue for its first task's machine.

The Functions StartShop and ChangeState

To start the simulation, we need to move the first job from each machine's job queue to the machine and commence processing. Since each machine is initialized in its idle state, we perform the initial loading in the same way as we change a machine from its idle state, which may happen during simulation, to an active state. Function ChangeState(i) performs this change over for machine i. The function to start the shop, Program 6.17, needs merely invoke ChangeState for each machine.

```
void InputData()
{// Input machine shop data.
   cout << "Enter number of machines and jobs" << endl;
   cin >> m >> n;
   if (m < 1 || n < 1) throw BadInput();

   // create event and machine queues
   EL = new EventList(m,LargeTime);
   M = new Machine [m+1];

   // input the machine wait times
   cout << "Enter change-over times for machines"
        << endl;
   for (int j = 1; j <= m; j++) {
      long ct;  // change-over time
      cin >> ct;
      if (ct < 0) throw BadInput();
      M[j].SetChange(ct);
      }
   // input the n jobs
   Job *J;
   for (int i = 1; i <= n; i++) {
      cout << "Enter number of tasks for job " << i
           << endl;
      int tasks;  // number of tasks
      int first;  // machine for first task of job
      cin >> tasks;
      if (tasks < 1) throw BadInput();
      J = new Job(i);
      cout << "Enter the tasks (machine, time)"
           << " in process order" << endl;
      for (int j = 1; j <= tasks; j++) {// get tasks
         int p;      // machine number
         long tt;   // task time
         cin >> p >> tt;
         if (p < 1 || p > m || tt < 1) throw BadInput();
         if (j == 1) first = p; // job's first machine
         J->AddTask(p,tt);   // add task to task queue
         }
      M[first].AddJob(J);   // add job to machine for
      }                     // first task
}
```

Program 6.16 Code to input shop data

```
void StartShop()
{// Load first jobs onto each machine.
   for (int p = 1; p <= m; p++)
      ChangeState(p);
}
```

Program 6.17 Initial loading of machines

Program 6.18 gives the code for ChangeState. If machine p is idle or in its change-over state, ChangeState returns 0. Otherwise, it returns a pointer to the job that it has been working on. Additionally, ChangeState(p) changes the state of machine p. If machine p was previously idle or in its change-over state, then it begins to process the next job on its queue. If its queue is empty, the machine's new state is "idle". If machine p was previously processing a job, machine p moves into its change-over state.

If M[p].Active is 0, then machine p is either in its idle or change-over state; the job pointer, LastJob, to return is 0. If the job queue is empty, the machine moves into its idle state and its finish time is set to LargeTime. If its job queue is not empty, the first job is deleted and becomes machine p's active job. The time this job has spent waiting in machine p's queue is added to the total wait time for this machine, and the number of tasks processed by the machine incremented by 1. Next the task that this machine is going to work on is deleted from the job's task list, and the finish time of the machine is set to the time at which the new task will complete.

If M[p].Active is nonzero, the machine has been working on a job whose task has just completed. A pointer to this job is to be returned, so the pointer is saved in LastJob. The machine should now move into its change-over state and remain in that state for ChangeTime time units.

The Functions Simulate **and** MoveToNextMachine
The function Simulate, Program 6.19, cycles through all shop events until the last job completes. n is the number of incomplete jobs, so the while loop of Program 6.19 terminates when no incomplete jobs remain. In each iteration of the while loop, the time for the next event is determined and the clock time Now updated to this event time. A change-job operation is performed on the machine p on which the event occurred. If this machine has just finished a task of a job (J is not zero), job *J moves to the machine on which its next task is to be performed. The function MoveToNextMachine performs this move. If there is no next task for job *J, the job has completed, function MoveToNextMachine returns false, and n is decremented by 1.

```
Job* ChangeState(int p)
{// Task on machine p has finished, schedule next one.
 // Return last job.
   Job* LastJob;
   if (!M[p].Active) {// in idle or change-over state
      LastJob = 0;
      // wait over, ready for new job
      if (M[p].JobQ.IsEmpty()) // no waiting job
          EL->SetFinishTime(p,LargeTime);
      else {// take job off Q and work on it
         M[p].JobQ.Delete(M[p].Active);
         M[p].TotalWait +=
               Now - M[p].Active->ArriveTime;
         M[p].NumTasks++;
         long t = M[p].Active->DeleteTask();
         EL->SetFinishTime(p, Now + t);}
      }
   else {// task has just finished on M[p]
         // schedule change-over time
         LastJob = M[p].Active;
         M[p].Active = 0;
         EL->SetFinishTime(p, Now + M[p].ChangeTime);}
   return LastJob;
}
```

Program 6.18 Code to change the active job at a machine

Function `MoveToNextMachine` (Program 6.20) first checks to see whether any unprocessed tasks remain for the job, `*J`. If not, the job has completed and its finish time and wait time are output. The function returns `false` to indicate there was no next machine for this job.

When the job `*J` to be moved has a next task, the machine `p` for this task is determined and the job added to this machine's queue of waiting jobs. In case machine `p` is idle, `ChangeState` is invoked to change its state.

The Function `OutputStats`
Since the time at which a job finishes as well as the time a job spends waiting in machine queues is output by `MoveToNextMachine`, `OutputStats` needs to output only the time at which the machine shop completes all jobs (this time is also the time at which the last job completed and has been output by `MoveToNextMachine`) and the statistics (total wait time and number of tasks processed) for each machine. Program 6.21 gives the code.

```
void Simulate()
{// Process all n jobs to completion.
   int p;
   long t;
   while (n) {// at least one job left
      EL->NextEvent(p,t); // next machine to finish
      Now = t; // present time
      // change job on machine p
      Job *J = ChangeState(p);
      // move job J to its next machine
      // decrement n if J has finished
      if (J && !MoveToNextMachine(J)) n--;
      }
}
```

Program 6.19 Run all jobs through their machines

```
bool MoveToNextMachine(Job *J)
{// Move J to machine for next task.
 // Return false if no next machine for this job.
  if (J->TaskQ.IsEmpty()) {// no next task
     cout << "Job " << J->ID << " has completed at "
          << Now << " Total wait was "
          << (Now-J->Length) << endl;
     return false;}
  else {// job has a next task
        // get machine for next task
        int p = J->TaskQ.First().machine;
        // put on p's wait queue
        M[p].AddJob(J);
        J->ArriveTime = Now;
        // if p idle, schedule immediately
        if (EL->NextEvent(p) == LargeTime) {
           // machine is idle
           ChangeState(p);}
        return true;}
}
```

Program 6.20 Move a job to the machine for its next task

```
void OutputStats()
{// Output wait times at machine.
   cout << "Finish time = " << Now << endl;
   long TotalWait, NumTasks;
   for (int p = 1; p <= m; p++) {
      M[p].Stats(TotalWait, NumTasks);
      cout << "Machine " << p << " completed "
           << NumTasks << " tasks" << endl;
      cout << "The total wait time was " << TotalWait;
      cout << endl << endl;
      }
}
```

Program 6.21 Output the wait times at each machine

EXERCISES

11. Does Program 6.7 successfully rearrange all input car permutations that can be rearranged using *k* holding tracks? Prove your answer.

12. Rewrite Program 6.7 under the assumption that at most s_i cars can be in holding track *i* at any time. Reserve the track with smallest s_i for direct input to output moves.

13. Obtain a complete C++ program for wire routing. Your program should include a Welcome function that displays the program name and functionality; a function to input the wire grid size, blocked and unblocked grid positions, and wire endpoints; the function FindPath (Program 6.9); and a function to output the input grid with wire path shown. Test the correctness of your program using sample wire grids.

14. Obtain a complete C++ program for image component labeling. Your program should include a Welcome function that displays the program name and functionality; a function to input the image size and binary image, the function Label (Program 6.10); and a function to output the image using a different color for pixels that are in different components. Test the correctness of your program using sample images.

15. Rewrite function Label (Program 6.10) using a formula-based queue. What are the advantages/disadvantages of using a formula-based queue rather than a linked queue?

16. Rewrite function `Label` using a stack. What are the relative merits/demerits of using a stack rather than a queue for this function?

17. Can we replace the stack in Program 5.5 with a queue? Why?

18. Can we replace the stack in Program 5.12 with a queue? Why?

19. Refine Program 6.11 by having several `catch` blocks that output different error messages. You should have one `catch` block for each of the exception types that might get thrown during execution.

★ 20. Write an enhanced machine shop simulator that allows you to specify a minimum wait time between successive tasks of the same job. Your simulator must move a job into a wait state following the completion of each of its tasks (including the last one). Therefore, a job is placed on its next queue immediately upon completion of a task. Upon arriving in this queue, the job enters its wait state. When a machine is ready to start a new task, it must bypass jobs at the front of the queue that are still in a wait state. The bypassed jobs could, for example, be moved to the end of the queue.

★ 21. Write an enhanced machine shop simulator that allows jobs to enter the shop during simulation. The simulation stops at a prespecified time. Jobs that have not been completed by this time are left in an incomplete state.

6.5 REFERENCES AND SELECTED READINGS

The wire-routing algorithm of Section 6.4.2 is known as Lee's router. The book *Algorithms for VLSI Physical Design Automation*, 2nd edition, by N. Sherwani, Kluwer Academic Publishers, Boston, 1995, contains a detailed discussion of this and other routing algorithms.

CHAPTER 7

SKIP LISTS AND HASHING

BIRD'S-EYE VIEW

Although a sorted array of *n* elements can be searched in O(log*n*) time using the binary search method, the search operation on a sorted chain takes O(*n*) time. We can improve the search performance of a sorted chain by placing additional pointers in some or all of the chain nodes. These additional pointers permit us to skip over several nodes of the chain during a search. Thus it is no longer necessary to examine all chain nodes from left to right during a search.

Chains augmented with additional forward pointers are called skip lists. By improving the search performance of a sorted chain, skip lists also improve performance for the insert and delete operations. Skip lists employ a randomization technique to determine which chain nodes are to be augmented by additional forward pointers and how many additional pointers are to be placed in the node. Using this randomization technique, skip lists deliver an expected search, insert, and delete performance of O(log*n*). However, the worst-case performance is Θ(*n*). By comparison, the expected time to insert and/or delete into/from a sorted array or chain is O(*n*), and the worst-case time is Θ(*n*).

Hashing is another randomization scheme that may be used to search, insert, and delete records. It provides improved expected performance, $\Theta(1)$, over skip lists but has the same worst-case performance, $\Theta(n)$. Despite this performance, skip lists have an advantage over hashing in applications where we need to frequently output all elements in sorted order and/or search by element rank (i.e., find the 10th-smallest element). These latter two operations can be performed more efficiently when skip lists are in use.

One application of hashing is developed in this chapter. This application is text compression and decompression. The program we develop is based on the popular Liv-Zempel-Welch algorithm.

7.1 DICTIONARIES

A **dictionary** is a collection of elements; each element has a field called `key`, and no two elements have the same `key` value. The operations to be performed on a dictionary are

- Insert an element with a specified key value.

- Search the dictionary for an element with a specified key value.

- Delete an element with a specified key value.

The abstract data type *Dictionary* is specified in ADT 7.1. The access mode for elements in a dictionary is called **random access**, as any element in the collection may be retrieved by simply performing a search on its key. By contrast, in the **sequential access** mode elements are retrieved one by one in ascending order of the key field. Sequential access requires operations such as *Begin* (which retrieves the element with smallest key) and *Next* (which retrieves the next element). Some of the dictionary implementations in this chapter are suitable for both random and sequential access modes.

AbstractDataType *Dictionary* {
   instances
      collection of elements with distinct keys
   operations
     Create (): create an empty dictionary
     Search (k,x): return element with key k in x;
               return `false` if the operation fails, `true` if it succeeds
     Insert (x): insert x into the dictionary
     Delete (k,x): delete element with key k and return it in x
}

ADT 7.1 Dictionary abstract data type

A **dictionary with duplicates** is similar to a dictionary as defined **above**. However, it permits elements to have equal keys. In a dictionary with duplicates, we need a rule to remove the ambiguity in the search and delete operations. That is, if we are to search for (or delete) an element with key k, then which of the several elements with this key is to be returned (or deleted)? In the case of both dictionaries and dictionaries with duplicates, some applications require a different form of the delete operation in which all elements inserted since a particular time are to be deleted.

Example 7.1 The class list for the data structures course is a dictionary with as many elements as students registered for the course. When a new student registers, an element/record corresponding to this student is inserted into the dictionary; when a student drops the course, his/her record may be deleted. During the course the instructor may query the dictionary to determine the record corresponding to a particular student and make changes to the record (for example, add/change test or assignment scores). The student name may be used as the element key. ∎

Example 7.2 A compiler uses a dictionary with duplicates, called the **symbol table**, of user-defined identifiers. When an identifier is defined, a record is created for it and inserted into the symbol table. This record includes the identifier as key as well as other information, such as identifier type (`int`, `float`, etc.) and (relative) memory address for its value. Since the same identifier name may be defined more than once (in different program blocks), the symbol table must be able to hold multiple records/elements with the same key. A search should return the most recently inserted element with the given key. Deletions are done only when the end of a program block is reached. All elements inserted since the start of that block are to be deleted. ∎

7.2   LINEAR LIST REPRESENTATION

A dictionary can be maintained as an ordered linear list $(e_1, e_2, \cdots)$ where the e_is are dictionary elements and their keys increase from left to right. To facilitate this representation, we may define two classes `SortedList` and `SortedChain`. The first uses a formula-based representation of a linear list, for example, the class `LinearList` (Program 3.1), while the latter use a linked representation, for example, the class `Chain` (Program 3.8).

Exercise 1 asks you to develop the class `SortedList`. We note that you can search for an element in a `SortedList` using the binary search method. So the *Search* operation takes O(log$n$) time for an n element dictionary. To make an insertion, we need to verify that the dictionary doesn't already contain an element with the same key. This verification is done by performing a search. Following this search, the insertion may be done in O(n) additional time, as O(n) elements must be moved to make room for the new element. Each delete is done by first searching for the element to be deleted and then deleting the found element. Following the search, the deletion takes O(n) time as O(n) elements must be moved to fill up the vacancy left by the deleted element.

Programs 7.1, 7.2, and 7.3 define the class `SortedChain`. E denotes the data type of the chain elements, and K that of the keys on which the chain is sorted. The class `SortedChainNode`, like the class `ChainNode` (Program 3.8), simply has the two private members `data` and `link`. `SortedChain` is a friend of `SortedChainNode`.

```
template<class E, class K>
class SortedChain {
    public:
        SortedChain() {first = 0;}
        ~SortedChain();
        bool IsEmpty() const {return first == 0;}
        int Length() const;
        bool Search(const K& k, E& e) const;
        SortedChain<E,K>& Delete(const K& k, E& e);
        SortedChain<E,K>& Insert(const E& e);
        SortedChain<E,K>& DistinctInsert(const E& e);
    private:
        SortedChainNode<E,K> *first;
};
```

Program 7.1 The class `SortedChain`

The class `SortedChain` provides two kinds of insert operations. The operation `DistinctInsert` ensures that all elements in the chain have distinct keys, and `Insert` allows for multiple entries with the same key. Although the dictionary application requires the `DistinctInsert` operation, other applications of sorted chains may require the `Insert` operation.

The codes for the destructor, `Length`, `Output`, and the overloading of `<<` are the same as for the class `Chain` (Program 3.8) and are not repeated here. The code for `Insert` is obtained from that for `DistintInsrt` by omitting the check for a duplicate (first `if` statement of Program 7.3). As we can see from the code, search, insert, and delete each take O(n) time on an n node chain.

The class `SortedChain` requires that the operators `<<`, `==`, `!=`, and `<` be defined on the data type `E`. User-defined types can use the operator overloading features of C++ to provide this definition. Many applications require these operators to work with a single field (`key`) of `E`. A simple way to accomplish this type of overloading is to overload the type conversion operator so as to convert elements of type `E` to elements of type `K` (`K` is the type of `key`). For example, when `K` is `long`, we can add the statement

```
operator long() const {return key;}
```

to the class definition of `E`.

Both `SortedList` and `SortedChain` may be extended to provide efficient sequential access. In either case `Begin` and `Next` will take $\Theta(1)$ time per element retrieved.

```
template<class E, class K>
bool SortedChain<E,K>::Search(const K& k, E& e) const
{// Put element that matches k in e.
 // Return false if no match.

   SortedChainNode<E,K> *p = first;

   // search for match with k
   for (; p && p->data < k; p = p->link);

   // verify match
   if (p && p->data == k) // yes, found match
      {e = p->data; return true;}
   return false; // no match
}

template<class E, class K>
SortedChain<E,K>& SortedChain<E,K>
                  ::Delete(const K& k, E& e)
{// Delete element that matches k.
 // Put deleted element in e.
 // Throw BadInput exception if no match.

   SortedChainNode<E,K> *p = first,
                        *tp = 0; // trail p

   // search for match with k
   for (; p && p->data < k; tp = p, p = p->link);

   // verify match
   if (p && p->data == k) {// found a match
         e = p->data;   // save data

         // remove p from chain
         if (tp) tp->link = p->link;
         else first = p->link;  // p is first node

         delete p;
         return *this;}
   throw BadInput();// no match
}
```

Program 7.2 Search and delete members of `SortedChain`

```
template<class E, class K>
SortedChain<E,K>& SortedChain<E,K>
                ::DistinctInsert(const E& e)
{// Insert e only if no element with same key
 // currently in list.
 // Throw BadInput exception if duplicate.

   SortedChainNode<E,K> *p = first,
                        *tp = 0; // trail p

   // move tp so that e can be inserted after tp
   for (; p && p->data < e; tp = p, p = p->link);

   // check if duplicate
   if (p && p->data == e) throw BadInput();

   // not duplicate, set up node for e
   SortedChainNode<E,K> *q = new SortedChainNode<E,K>;
   q->data = e;

   // insert node just after tp
   q->link = p;
   if (tp) tp->link = q;
   else first = q;

   return *this;
}
```

Program 7.3 Insertion into a sorted chain

EXERCISES

1. Develop the C++ class `SortedList` that uses a formula-based representation. Provide the same member functions as provided in the class `SortedChain`. Write code for all functions and test the code using suitable test data.

2. Extend the class `SortedChain` by including the sequential access functions `Begin` and `Next`, which, respectively, return a pointer to the first and next element (in ascending order) of a dictionary. Both return zero in case there is no first or next element. The complexity of both functions should be $\Theta(1)$. Test the correctness of your codes.

3. Modify the class `SortedChain` so as to use a chain that has both a head node and a tail node. Use the tail node to keep an element with value larger than that of any other element. The use of a tail element should simplify your code.

7.3   SKIP LIST REPRESENTATION

7.3.1   The Ideal Case

A search in an n-element dictionary that is represented as a sorted chain requires up to n element comparisons. The number of comparisons can be reduced to $n/2 + 1$ if we keep a pointer to the middle element. Now to search for an element, we first compare with the middle one. If we are looking for a smaller element, we need search only the left half of the sorted chain. If we are looking for a larger element, we need compare only the right half of the chain.

Example 7.3 Consider the seven-element sorted chain of Figure 7.1(a). The sorted chain has been augmented by a head and tail node. The number inside a node is its value. A search of this chain may involve up to seven element comparisons. We can reduce this worst-case number of comparisons to four by keeping a pointer to the middle element as in Figure 7.1(b). Now to search for an element, we first compare with the middle element and then, depending on the outcome, compare with either the left or right half of the chain. If we are looking for an element with value 26, then we begin by comparing 26 with the middle value 40. Since 26 < 40, we need not examine the elements to the right of 40. If we are searching for an element with value 75, then we can limit the search to the elements that follow 40. ∎

We can reduce the worst-case number of element comparisons by keeping pointers to the middle elements of each half as in Figure 7.1(c). In this figure we have three chains. The level 0 chain is essentially that of Figure 7.1(a) and includes all seven elements of the dictionary. The level 1 chain includes the second, fourth, and sixth elements, while the level 2 chain includes only the fourth element. To search for an element with value 30, we begin with a comparison against the middle element. This element is found in $\Theta(1)$ time using the level 2 chain. Since 30 < 40, the search continues by examining the middle element of the left half. This element is also found in $\Theta(1)$ time using the level 1 chain. Since 30 > 24, we continue the search by dropping into the level 0 chain and comparing with the next element in this chain.

As another example, consider the search for an element with value 77. The first comparison is with 40. Since 77 > 40, we drop into the level 1 chain and compare with the element (75) in this chain that comes just after 40. Since 77 > 75, we drop into the level 0 chain and compare with the element (80) in this

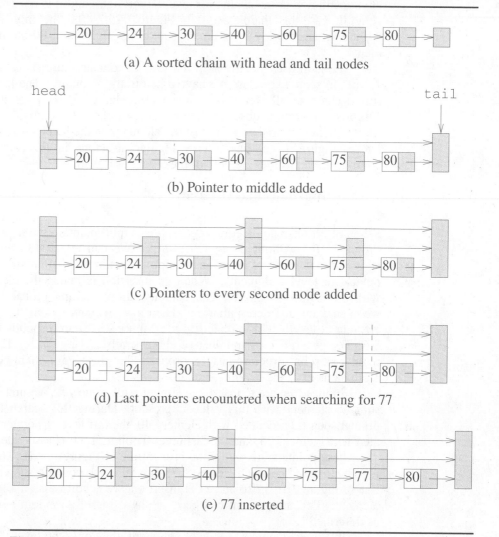

(a) A sorted chain with head and tail nodes

(b) Pointer to middle added

(c) Pointers to every second node added

(d) Last pointers encountered when searching for 77

(e) 77 inserted

Figure 7.1 Fast searching of a sorted chain

chain that comes just after 75. At this time we know that 77 is not in the dictionary. Using the three-chain structure of Figure 7.1(c), we can perform all searches using at most three comparisons. The three-chain structure allows us to perform a binary search in the sorted chain.

For general n, the level 0 chain includes all elements; the level 1 chain includes every second element; the level 2 chain every fourth element; and the level i chain every 2^ith element. We shall say that an element is a **level** i

element iff it is in the chains for levels 0 through i and it is not on the level $i + 1$ chain (in case this chain exists). In Figure 7.1(c), 40 is the only level 2 element; 24 and 75 are the level 1 elements; and 20, 30, 60, and 80 are the level 0 elements.

We shall use the term **skip list** to refer to a structure such as that of Figure 7.1(c). In such a structure we have a heirarchy of chains. The level 0 chain is a sorted chain of all elements. The level 1 chain is also a sorted chain that is comprised of some subset of the elements on the level 0 chain. In general, the level i chain comprises a subset of the elements in the level $i - 1$ chain. The skip list of Figure 7.1(c) has a very regular structure in that the level i chain comprises every other element of the level $i - 1$ chain.

7.3.2   Insertions and Deletions

When insertions and deletions occur, we cannot maintain the regular structure of Figure 7.1(c) without doing O(n) work. We can attempt to approximate this structure in the face of insertions by noting that in the regular structure, $n/2^i$ elements are level i elements. When an insertion is made, the element level is i with probability $1/2^i$. We can actually allow for any probability to be used when making this determination. Therefore, we can assign the newly inserted element at level i with probability p^i. Figure 7.1(c) corresponds to the case $p = 0.5$. For general p, the number of chain levels is $\lfloor \log_{1/p} n \rfloor + 1$. In this case a regular skip list structure has the property that the level i chain comprises every $1/p$th element of the level $i - 1$ chain.

Suppose we are to insert an element with value 77. We first search to make sure no element with this value is present. During this search the last level 2 pointer seen is associated with element 40, the last level 1 pointer seen is associated with element 75, and the last level 0 pointer seen is associated with element 75. These pointers are cut by the broken line of Figure 7.1(d). The new element is to be inserted between elements 75 and 80 at the position shown by the broken line of Figure 7.1(d). To make the insertion, we need to assign a level to the new element. This assignment can be made by using of a random number generator as described later.

If the new element is a level i element, then only the level 0 through level i pointers cut by the broken line are affected. Figure 7.1(e) shows the list structure following the insertion of 77 as a level 1 element.

We have no control over the structure that is left following a deletion. To delete the 77 from the skip list structure of Figure 7.1(e), we first search for 77. The last pointers encountered in the chains are the level 2 pointer in the node with 40, and the level 1 and level 0 pointers in the node with 75. Of these pointers, only the level 0 and level 1 pointers are to be changed as 77 is a level 1 element. When these pointers are changed to point to the element after 77 in their respective chains, we get the structure of Figure 7.1(d).

7.3.3 Assigning Levels

The basis of level assignment is the observation that in a regular skip list structure, a fraction p of the elements on the level $i - 1$ chain are also on the level i chain. Therefore, the probablity that an element that is on the level $i - 1$ chain is also on the level i chain is p. Suppose we have a uniform random number generator that generates numbers in the range 0 through RAND_MAX. Then the probability that the next random number is $\leq$ CutOff $= p *$RAND_MAX is p. Consequently, if the next random number is $\leq$ CutOff, then the new element should be on the level 1 chain. Now we need to decide whether it should also be on the level 2 chain. To make this decision, we simply generate another random number. If the new random number is $\leq$ CutOff, then the element is also on the level 2 chain. We can continue this process until a random number $>$ CutOff is generated.

As a result, we can use the following code to assign a level number to the element that is being inserted:

```
int lev = 0;
while (rand() <= CutOff) lev++;
```

A potential shortcoming of this way of assigning levels is that some elements may be assigned a very large level, resulting in a number of chains far in excess of $\log_{1/p}N$ where N is the maximum number of elements expected in the dictionary. To prevent this possibility, we can set an upper limit to the value of lev. In a regular skip list structure with N elements, the maximum level MaxLevel is

$$\lceil \log_{1/p}N \rceil - 1 \qquad (7.1)$$

We can use this value as the upper limit.

Another shortcoming is that even with the use of an upper limit as above, we may find ourselves in a situation where, for example, we have 3 chains just before the insertion and 10 just after. In this case, the new element was assigned the level 9 even though there were no elements at levels 3 through 8 prior to the insertion. In other words, prior to and following the insertion, there are no level 3, 4, $\cdots$, 8 elements. Since there is no immediate benefit to having these empty levels, we may alter the level assignment of the element to three.

Example 7.4 We are using a skip list to represent a dictionary that will have no more than 1024 elements. We have decided to use $p = 0.5$, so MaxLevel is $\log_2 1024 - 1 = 9$. If our random number generator has RAND_MAX $= 2^{32} - 1$, then CutOff $= 2^{16} - 1$ and there is a 0.5 probability that any randomly generated number will be $\leq$ CutOff.

Suppose we start with an empty dictionary that is represented by a skip list structure that has a head and a tail. The head has 10 pointers, one for each of the 10 chains we might have. Each pointer goes from the head to the tail.

When the first element is inserted, it is assigned a level. The permissible levels are zero through nine (MaxLevel). If the level assigned is nine, then to insert the first element, we will need to change nine chain pointers. On the other hand, as we have no level 0, level 1, $\cdots$, level 8 elements, we may alter the level assignment to zero and change only one chain pointer. ■

An alternative way to assign levels is to divide the range of values the random number generator outputs into segments. The first segment contains $1 - 1/p$ of the range, the second $1/p - 1/p^2$ of the range, and so on. If the random number generated falls in the ith segment, the element to be inserted is a level $i - 1$ element.

7.3.4 The Class SkipNode

The head node of a skip list structure needs sufficient pointer fields for the maximum number of level chains that might be constructed. The tail node needs no pointer field. Each node that contains an element needs a data field for the element and a number of pointer fields that is one more than its level number. The needs of all kinds of nodes can be met using the class definition of Program 7.4. The pointer fields are represented by the array link with link[i] being the pointer for the level i chain. The constructor allocates space for the array of pointers. When invoked, the value of size should be lev+1 for a level lev element.

```
template<class E, class K>
class SkipNode {
   friend SkipList<E,K>;
   private:
      SkipNode(int size)
         {link = new SkipNode<E,K> *[size];}
      ~SkipNode() {delete [] link;}
      E data;
      SkipNode<E,K> **link;   // 1D array of pointers
};
```

Program 7.4 The class SkipNode

7.3.5 The Class SkipList

The class SkipList is defined in Program 7.5. MaxE is the maximum number of elements the dictionary is to hold. Although our codes permit more elements than MaxE, the expected performance is better if the number of elements does not exceed MaxE as the number of chains is limited by substituting MaxE for N in Equation 7.1. p is the probablity that an element in the level $i - 1$ chain is also in the level i chain, and Large is a value larger than that of an element to be kept in the dictionary. The value Large is used in the tail node. The values in the level 0 chain (excluding the head node, which has no value) are in ascending order from left to right.

```
template<class E, class K>
class SkipList {
    public:
        SkipList(K Large, int MaxE = 10000,
                          float p = 0.5);
        ~SkipList();
        bool Search(const K& k, E& e) const;
        SkipList<E,K>& Insert(const E& e);
        SkipList<E,K>& Delete(const K& k, E& e);
    private:
        int Level();
        SkipNode<E,K> *SaveSearch(const K& k);
        int MaxLevel;   // max permissible chain level
        int Levels;     // max current nonempty chain
        int CutOff;     // used to decide level number
        K TailKey;      // a large key
        SkipNode<E,K> *head;  // head node pointer
        SkipNode<E,K> *tail;  // tail node pointer
        SkipNode<E,K> **last; // array of pointers
};
```

Program 7.5 The class SkipList

Program 7.6 gives the constructor and destructor functions. The constructor initializes CutOff, Levels (the current maximum level of any element), MaxLevel, TailKey (all elements must have smaller value than this), and the random number generator that is used to assign levels to new elements. It also allocates space for the head and tail nodes and an array last that is used to keep track of the last node encountered in each chain during the search phase that precedes an insert and delete. The skip list is also initialized to the empty configuration in which we have `MaxLevel+1` pointers from the head node to the tail node. The complexity of the constructor is $\Theta(\texttt{MaxLevel})$.

```
template<class E, class K>
SkipList<E,K>::SkipList(K Large, int MaxE, float p)
{// Constructor.
   CutOff = p * RAND_MAX;
   MaxLevel = ceil(log(MaxE) / log(1/p)) - 1;
   TailKey = Large;
   randomize(); // initialize random generator
   Levels = 0;  // initial number of levels

   // create head & tail nodes and last array
   head = new SkipNode<E,K> (MaxLevel+1);
   tail = new SkipNode<E,K> (0);
   last = new SkipNode<E,K> *[MaxLevel+1];
   tail->data = Large;

   // head points to tail at all levels as empty
   for (int i = 0; i <= MaxLevel; i++)
      head->link[i] = tail;
}

template<class E, class K>
SkipList<E,K>::~SkipList()
{// Delete all nodes and array last.
   SkipNode<E,K> *next;

   // delete all nodes by deleting level 0
   while (head != tail) {
      next = head->link[0];
      delete head;
      head = next;
      }
   delete tail;

   delete [] last;
}
```

Program 7.6 Constructor and destructor

The destructor frees all space currently in use by the chains. Its complexity is Θ(length of the level 0 chain). The functions to search, insert, and delete require that E be overloaded so that comparisons between members of E, as well between a member of E and one of K, be well-defined. An assignment from a K to an E and the reverse are also required. When each element has the integer field data and the long field key, and the element value is given by key, the overloading of Program 7.7 may be used.

```
class element {
    friend void main(void);
    public:
        operator long() const {return key;}
        element& operator =(long y)
        {key = y; return *this;}
    private:
        int data;
        long key;
};
```

Program 7.7 Operator overloading for skip lists

There are two search functions (Program 7.8) for the skip list class. Search is a public member used when we wish to locate an element with a certain value k. The element, if found, is returned in e. The function returns false if no element with value k is found and true otherwise. Search begins with the highest level chain—the level Levels chain—that contains an element and works its way down to the level 0 chain. At each level we advance as close to the element being searched as possible without advancing to the right of the element. Although we can terminate the search at level i if we reach an element whose value equals k, the additional comparison needed to test for equality isn't justified as the majority of the elements are expected to be only in the level 0 chain. When we exit from the for loop, we are positioned just to the left of the element we seek. Comparing with the next element on the level 0 chain permits us to determine whether or not the element we seek is in the structure.

The second search function, SaveSearch, is a private member that is invoked during an insert and delete operation. SaveSearch not only does the work of Search but also saves, in the array last, the last node encountered at each level.

Program 7.9 gives the code to assign a level to an element that is to be inserted along with the code to insert an element. Insert throws a BadInput exception in case the value of the element to be inserted is not smaller than TailKey, as well as when the structure already contains an element with the

```
template<class E, class K>
bool SkipList<E,K>::Search(const K& k, E& e) const
{// Search for element that matches k.
 // Put matching element in e.
 // Return false if no match.
   if (k >= TailKey) return false;

   // position p just before possible node with k
   SkipNode<E,K> *p = head;
   for (int i = Levels; i >= 0; i--) // go down levels
      while (p->link[i]->data < k)    // follow level i
         p = p->link[i];              // pointers

   // check if next node has key k
   e = p->link[0]->data;
   return (e == k);
}

template<class E, class K>
SkipNode<E,K> * SkipList<E,K>::SaveSearch(const K& k)
{// Search for k and save last position
 // visited at each level.
   // position p just before possible node with k
   SkipNode<E,K> *p = head;
   for (int i = Levels; i >= 0; i--) {
      while (p->link[i]->data < k)
         p = p->link[i];
      last[i] = p;   // last level i node seen
      }
   return (p->link[0]);
}
```

Program 7.8 Skip list search functions

same value. The call to new throws a NoMem exception in case there isn't
enough space to make the insertion. Insert returns the skip list if the element
e is successfully inserted.

Program 7.10 gives the code to delete an element with value k and return
it in e, a BadInput exception is thrown if there is no element with value k.
The while loop updates Levels so that there is at least one level Levels
element unless the skip list is empty. In the latter case Levels is set to zero.

```
template<class E, class K>
int SkipList<E,K>::Level()
{// Generate a random level number <= MaxLevel.
   int lev = 0;
   while (rand() <= CutOff)
      lev++;
   return (lev <= MaxLevel) ? lev : MaxLevel;
}

template<class E, class K>
SkipList<E,K>& SkipList<E,K>::Insert(const E& e)
{// Insert e if not duplicate.
   K k = e; // extract key
   if (k >= TailKey) throw BadInput(); // too large

   // see if duplicate
   SkipNode<E,K> *p = SaveSearch(k);
   if (p->data == e) throw BadInput(); // duplicate

   // not duplicate, determine level for new node
   int lev = Level(); // level of new node
   // fix lev to be <= Levels + 1
   if (lev > Levels) {lev = ++Levels;
                      last[lev] = head;}

   // get and insert new node just after p
   SkipNode<E,K> *y = new SkipNode<E,K> (lev+1);
   y->data = e;
   for (int i = 0; i <= lev; i++) {
      // insert into level i chain
      y->link[i] = last[i]->link[i];
      last[i]->link[i] = y;
      }

   return *this;
}
```

Program 7.9 Skip list insertion

```
template<class E, class K>
SkipList<E,K>& SkipList<E,K>::Delete(const K& k, E& e)
{// Delete element that matches k. Put deleted
 // element in e.  Throw BadInput if no match.
   if (k >= TailKey) throw BadInput(); // too large

   // see if matching element present
   SkipNode<E,K> *p = SaveSearch(k);
   if (p->data != k) throw BadInput(); // not present

   // delete node from skip list
   for (int i = 0; i <= Levels &&
                      last[i]->link[i] == p; i++)
      last[i]->link[i] = p->link[i];

   // update Levels
   while (Levels > 0 && head->link[Levels] == tail)
      Levels--;

   e = p->data;
   delete p;
   return *this;
}
```

Program 7.10 Deletion from a skip list

7.3.6 Complexity

The complexity of a search, insert, and delete operation is $O(n+\texttt{MaxLevel})$ where n is the number of elements in the structure. In the worst case there may be only one level $\texttt{MaxLevel}$ element, and the remaining elements may all be level 0 elements. Now $\Theta(\texttt{MaxLevel})$ time is spent on the level i chains for $i > 0$ and $O(n)$ time on the level 0 chain. Despite this poor worst-case performance, skip lists are a valuable representation method as the expected complexity of each of the operations (search, insert, delete) is $O(\log n)$. The proof of this claim is beyond the scope of this book.

As for the space complexity, we note that in the worst case each element might be a level $\texttt{MaxLevel}$ element requiring $\texttt{MaxLevel}+1$ pointers. Therefore, in addition to the space needed to store the n elements (i.e., $n*\texttt{sizeof(element)}$), we need $O(n*\texttt{MaxLevel})$ space for the chain pointers. On the average, however, only $n*p$ of the elements are expected to be on the level 1 chain, $n*p^2$ on the level 2 chain, and $n*p^i$ on the level i chain.

So the expected number of pointer fields (excluding those in the head and tail nodes) is $n\sum_i p^i = n/(1-p)$. So while the worst-case space requirements are large, the expected requirements are not. When $p = 0.5$, the expected space requirements (in addition to that for the n elements) is that for approximately $2n$ pointers!

EXERCISES

4. Since the level 0 chain of a skip list is sorted, a skip list can support sequential access in $\Theta(1)$ time per element retrieved. Extend the class `SkipList` by including the sequential access functions `Begin` and `Next`, which, respectively, return a pointer to the first and next element (in ascending order) of a dictionary. Both return zero in case there is no first or next element. The complexity of both functions should be $\Theta(1)$. Test the correctness of your codes.

5. Write a level allocation program that divides the range of random number values into segments as described in the text and then determines the level on the basis of which segment a random number falls into.

6. Modify the class `SkipList` to allow for the presence of elements that have the same value. Each chain is now in nondecreasing order of value from left to right. Test your code using suitable data.

7. Extend the class `SkipList` by including functions to delete the element with least value, delete the element with largest value, and output the elements in ascending order of value. What is the expected complexity of each operation?

7.4 HASH TABLE REPRESENTATION

7.4.1 Ideal Hashing

Another possibility for the representation of a dictionary is to use **hashing**. This method uses a **hash function** to map keys into positions in a table called the **hash table**. In the ideal situation, if element e has the key k and f is the hash function, then e is stored in position $f(k)$ of the table. To search for an element with key k, we compute $f(k)$ and see if there is an element at position $f(k)$ of the table. If so, we have found the element. If not, the dictionary contains no element with this key. In the former case the element may be deleted (if desired) by making position $f(k)$ of the table empty. In the latter case the element may be inserted by placing it in position $f(k)$.

Example 7.5 Consider the student records dictionary of Example 7.1. Suppose that instead of using student names as the key, we use student ID numbers, which are six-digit integers. For our class, assume we will have at most 100 students and their ID numbers will be in the range 951000 and 952000. The function $f(k) = k - 951000$ maps student IDs into table positions 0 through 1000. We may use an array `ht[1001]` of type `E` as the hash table. This table is initialized so that `ht[i].key` is zero for $0 \le$ `i` $<= 1000$. To search for an element with key k, we compute $f(k) = k - 951000$. The element is at `ht[`$f(k)$`]` provided the key field of the element at this position is not zero. If the key field of the element at this position is zero, the dictionary contains no element with key k. In this latter case the element may be inserted at this position. In the former case the element may be deleted by setting `ht[`$f(k)$`].key` to 0. ∎

In the ideal situation just described, it takes $\Theta(b)$ time to initialize an empty dictionary (b is the number of positions in the hash table) and $\Theta(1)$ time to perform a search, insert, or delete operation. Although the ideal hashing solution just described may be used in many applications of a dictionary, there are many other applications where the range in key values is so large that it isn't possible to have a table this large. For instance, suppose that in the class list example (Example 7.1), each student's name is truncated to be at most 12 characters long, uppercase letters are replaced by corresponding lowercase letters, and special characters such as hyphens are deleted. Suppose now that this truncated name is used as the key. A key that is less than 12 characters long may be made 12 characters long by adding blanks to its front. Each key may be converted into a numeric key by mapping a blank to the number 0, the letter 'a' to the number 1, the letter b to the number 2, $\cdots$, and the letter z to the number 26. This conversion maps the names into integers in the range 1 ('a') through $27^{12} - 1$ ('zzzzzzzzzzzz'). This range is too large for us to create the array `ht` as used in the ideal situation.

7.4.2   Hashing with Linear Open Addressing

The Method
When the key range is too large to use the ideal method described above, we use a hash table whose size is smaller than the range and a hash function that maps several different keys into the same position of the hash table. Although several different hash functions with this property are in use, hashing by division is most common. In hashing by division, the hash function has the form

$$f(k) = k \% D \tag{7.2}$$

where k is the key, D is the size (i.e., number of positions) of the hash table, and $\%$ is the modulo operator. The positions in the hash table are indexed 0 through $D - 1$. Each position is called a **bucket**. In case the key values are not of an integral type (e.g., `int`, `long`, `char`, `unsigned char`), they will need to be converted to non-negative integers before $f(k)$ can be computed. For example, a long string can be converted to an unsigned integer by selecting two of its characters, or to an unsigned long integer by selecting four of its characters. $f(k)$ is the **home bucket** for the element with key value k. Under favorable circumstances the home bucket is the location of the element with key value k.

Figure 7.2(a) shows a hash table `ht` with 11 buckets numbered 0 through 10. This table contains three elements. The divisor D to use is 11. The 80 is in position 3 as 80 % 11 = 3; the 40 is in position 40 % 11 = 7; and the 65 is in position 65 % 11 = 10. Each element is in its home bucket. The remaining buckets in the hash table are empty.

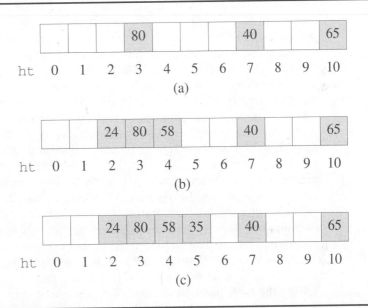

Figure 7.2 Hash tables

Now suppose we wish to enter the value 58 into the table. The home bucket is $f(58) = 58 \% 11 = 3$. This bucket is already occupied by a different value. We say that a **collision** has occurred. In general, a bucket may contain space for more than one element, so a collision may not create any difficulties. An **overflow** occurs if there isn't room in the home bucket for the new element. Since each bucket of our table has space for only one element, collisions and overflows occur at the same time. Where shall we insert 58? The easiest thing to do is search the table for the next available bucket and place 58 into it. This method of handling overflows is called **linear open addressing**.

The 58 gets inserted into position 4. Suppose that the next value to be inserted is 24. 24 % 11 is 2. This bucket is empty, and so the 24 is placed there. Our hash table now has the form shown in Figure 7.2(b). Let us attempt to insert the value 35 into this table. Its home bucket (2) is full. Using linear open addressing, this value is placed in the next available bucket and the table of Figure 7.2(c) results. As a final example, consider inserting 98 into the table. Its home bucket (10) is full. The next available bucket is 0, and the insertion is made into this bucket. So the search for the next available bucket is made by regarding the table as circular!

Having seen how insertions are made into a linear-open-addressed hash table, we can devise a method to search such a table. The search begins at the home bucket $f(k)$ of the key k we are searching for and continues by examining successive buckets in the table (regarding the table as circular) until one of the following happens: (1) a bucket containing an element with key k is reached, in which case we have found the element we were searching for; (2) an empty bucket is reached; and (3) we return to the home bucket. In the latter two cases, the table contains no element with key k.

The deletion of an element must leave behind a table on which the search method just described works correctly. If we are to delete the element with key 58 from the table of Figure 7.2(c), we cannot simply make position 4 of the table empty. Doing so will result in the search method failing to find the element with key 35. A deletion may require us to move several elements. The search for elements to move begins just after the bucket vacated by the deleted element and proceeds to successive buckets until we either reach an empty bucket or we return to the bucket from which the deletion took place. An alternative to this rather cumbersome deletion strategy is to introduce the field `NeverUsed` in each bucket. When the table is initialized, this field is set to `true` for all buckets. When an element is placed into a bucket, its `NeverUsed` field is set to `false`. Now condition (2) for search termination is replaced by (3') a bucket with `NeverUsed` field equal to true is reached. We accomplish a deletion by setting the table position to empty. A new element may be inserted into the first empty bucket encountered during a search that begins at the element's home bucket. Notice that in this alternative scheme, `NeverUsed` is never reset to `true`. After a while, all (or almost all) buckets have this field equal to `false`, and unsuccessful searches examine all buckets. To improve performance, we must reorganize the table when many empty buckets have their `NeverUsed` field equal to `false`. This reorganization could, for example, involve reinserting all remaining elements into an empty hash table.

C++ Implementation

Program 7.11 gives the class definition for a hash table that uses linear open addressing. This definition assumes that each element to be stored in the hash table is of type `E` and has a field `key` of type `K`. The field `key` is used to compute the home bucket. So the type `K` must be one for which the modulo operator % is defined. The hash table is implemented using two arrays: ht and empty. empty[i] is true iff ht[i] does not have an element in it. Program 7.12 gives the implementation of the constructor.

```
template<class E, class K>
class HashTable {
   public:
      HashTable(int divisor = 11);
      ~HashTable() {delete [] ht;
                    delete [] empty;}
      bool Search(const K& k, E& e) const;
      HashTable<E,K>& Insert(const E& e);
   private:
      int hSearch(const K& k) const;
      int D; // hash function divisor
      E *ht; // hash table array
      bool *empty; // 1D array
};
```

Program 7.11 C++ class definition for hash tables

```
template<class E, class K>
HashTable<E,K>::HashTable(int divisor)
{// Constructor.
   D = divisor;

   // allocate hash table arrays
   ht = new E [D];
   empty = new bool [D];

   // set all buckets to empty
   for (int i = 0; i < D; i++)
      empty[i] = true;
}
```

Program 7.12 Constructor for HashTable

Program 7.13 gives the search functions. The public function Search returns false if no element with the search key k is found and true otherwise. Also, when an element is found, the element is returned in the parameter e. The public search function makes use of a private search function hSearch that returns a bucket b in the table that satisfies exactly one of the following: (1) empty[b] is false and ht[b] has the key k; (2) no element in the table has the key k, empty[b] is true, and the element with key k may be inserted into bucket b if desired; and (3) no element in the table has the key k, empty[b] is false, ht[b] has a key other than k, and the table is full.

```cpp
template<class E, class K>
int HashTable<E,K>::hSearch(const K& k) const
{// Search an open addressed table.
 // Return location of k if present.
 // Otherwise return insert point if there is space.
   int i = k % D; // home bucket
   int j = i;      // start at home bucket
   do {
      if (empty[j] || ht[j] == k) return j;
      j = (j + 1) % D;  // next bucket
      } while (j != i); // returned to home?

   return j;  // table full
}

template<class E, class K>
bool HashTable<E,K>::Search(const K& k, E& e) const
{// Put element that matches k in e.
 // Return false if no match.
   int b = hSearch(k);
   if (empty[b] || ht[b] != k) return false;
   e = ht[b];
   return true;
}
```

Program 7.13 Search functions

Program 7.14 gives the implementation of function Insert. This code begins by invoking the private function hSearch. From the specification of hSearch, if the returned bucket i is empty, then there is no element in the table with key k and element e may be inserted into this bucket. If the returned bucket is not empty, then it either contains an element with key k or the table is full. In the former case function Insert throws a BadInput exception; in the latter, it throws a NoMem exception. Exercise 14 asks you to write code for function Delete.

```
template<class E, class K>
HashTable<E,K>& HashTable<E,K>::Insert(const E& e)
{// Hash table insert.
   K k = e; // extract key
   int b = hSearch(k);

   // check if insert is to be done
   if (empty[b]) {empty[b] = false;
                  ht[b] = e;
                  return *this;}

   // no insert, check if duplicate or full
   if (ht[b] == k) throw BadInput(); // duplicate
   throw NoMem(); // table full
}
```

Program 7.14 Insertion into a hash table

When `E` is a user-defined class or data type, it is necessary to overload several operators such as `%`, `!=`, and `==`. See Program 7.7 for a sample overloading.

Performance Analysis

We shall analyze the time complexity only. Let b be the number of buckets in the hash table. When division with divisor D is used as the hash function, $b = D$. The time needed to initialize the table is $\Theta(b)$. The worst-case insert and search time is $\Theta(n)$ when n elements are present in the table. The worst case happens, for instance, when all n key values have the same home bucket. Comparing the worst-case complexity of hashing to that of the linear list method to maintain a dictionary, we see that both have the same worst-case complexity.

For average performance, however, hashing is considerably superior. Let U_n and S_n, respectively, denote the average number of buckets examined during an unsuccessful and a successful search. This average is defined over all possible sequences of n key values being inserted into the table. For linear open addressing, it can be shown that

$$U_n \sim \frac{1}{2}\left[1 + \frac{1}{(1-\alpha)^2}\right]$$

$$S_n \sim \frac{1}{2}\left[1 + \frac{1}{1-\alpha}\right]$$

where $\alpha = n/b$ is the **loading factor**.

So if $\alpha = 0.5$, an unsuccessful search will examine 2.5 buckets on the average and an average successful search will examine 1.5 buckets. When $\alpha = 0.9$, these figures are 50.5 and 5.5. These figures, of course, assume that n is at least 51. When it is possible to work with small loading factors (say about 0.5), the average performance of hashing with linear open addressing is significantly superior to that of the linear list method.

Determining D

In practice, the choice of the divisor D has a significant effect on the performance of hashing. Best results are obtained when D (and therefore the number of buckets b) is either a prime number or has *no prime factors less than* 20.

To determine D, we first determine what constitutes acceptable performance for unsuccessful and successful searches. Using the formulas for U_n and S_n, we can determine the largest α that can be used. From the value of n (or an estimate) and the computed value of α, we obtain the smallest permissible value for b. Next the smallest integer that is at least as large as this value of b and that either is a prime or has no factors smaller than 20 is found. This integer is the value of D and b to use.

Example 7.6 We are to design a hash table for up to 1000 elements. Successful searches should require no more than 4 bucket examinations on the average and unsuccessful searches should examine no more than 50.5 buckets on the average. From the formula for U_n, we obtain $\alpha \leq 0.9$, and from that for S_n, we obtain $4 \geq 0.5 + 1/(2(1-\alpha))$ or $\alpha \leq 6/7$. Therefore, we require $\alpha \leq \min\{0.9, 6/7\} = 6/7$. Hence b should be at least $\lceil 7n/6 \rceil = 1167$. $b = D = 37*37 = 1369$ is a suitable (though not least) choice. ∎

Another way to compute D is to begin with a knowledge of the largest possible value for b as determined by the maximum amount of space available for the hash table. Now we find the largest D no larger than this largest value that is either a prime or has no factors smaller than 20. For instance, if we can allot at most 530 buckets to the table, then $23*23 = 529$ is the right choice for D and b.

7.4.3   Hashing with Chains

The Method

Chains provide a good solution to the overflow problem that arises when hashing is used. Rather than place an element into a bucket other than its home bucket, we maintain chains of elements that have the same home bucket. Figure 7.3 shows a hash table in which overflows are handled by **chaining**. As in our earlier example, the hash function divisor is 11. In this hash table organization, each bucket has space for just a pointer to a node. All elements are kept on chains.

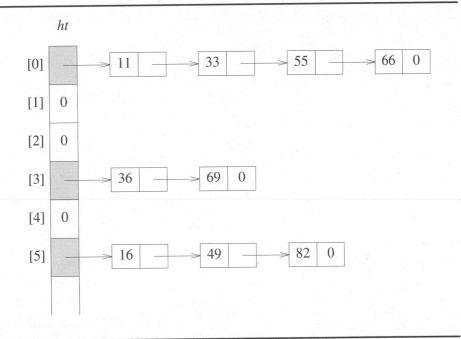

Figure 7.3 A chained hash table

　　To search for an element with key k, we first compute the home bucket, $k \% D$ for the key and then search the chain that begins at this bucket. To insert an element, we need to first verify that the table does not already have an element with the same key. This search can, of course, be limited to the chain for the home bucket of the new element. As each insert is preceded by a search, it is less expensive to maintain the chains in ascending order of the key values (as in Figure 7.3) than in an unordered way. Finally, to delete an element with key k, we access the home bucket chain, search this chain for an element with the given key, and then delete the element.

C++ Implementation of Chained Hash Tables

A chained hash table may now be implemented as an array of sorted chains as in Program 7.15. Since this class utilizes members of the class `SortedChain`, we must define the operators `cout`, `==`, `!=`, and `<` on the data type `E`. A sample overloading of these operators is given in Program 7.7.

```
template<class E, class K>
class ChainHashTable {
   public:
      ChainHashTable(int divisor = 11)
         {D = divisor;
          ht = new SortedChain<E,K> [D];}
      ~ChainHashTable() {delete [] ht;}
      bool Search(const K& k, E& e) const
          {return ht[k % D].Search(k, e);}
      ChainHashTable<E,K>& Insert(const E& e)
          {ht[e % D].DistinctInsert(e);
           return *this;}
      ChainHashTable<E,K>& Delete(const K& k, E& e)
          {ht[k % D].Delete(k, e);
           return *this;}
   private:
      int D;                    // divisor
      SortedChain<E,K> *ht;   // array of chains
};
```

Program 7.15 Chained hash table

An Improved Implementation

We can get slightly improved performance by adding a tail node to the end of each chain as in Figure 7.4. The tail node has a key that is at least as large as that of any element to be inserted into the table. In Figure 7.4 this large key is denoted by the symbol ∞. In practice, when the keys are integer, we can use the constant INT_MAX defined in the file limits.h. With the use of a tail node, we may change all occurrences of i && i->data in the definition of SortedChain to i->data. Also, notice that although Figure 7.4 has been drawn so as to use a separate tail for each chain, in practice, we may use the same tail node for all chains.

Comparison with Linear Open Addressing

We shall explicitly compare linear open addressing with chaining for the case where the chains do not have a tail node. Let s be the space (in bytes) required by an element. Assume that each pointer and each variable of type int takes 2 bytes of space. Further, assume that the hash table has b buckets and n elements. We first note that when linear open addressing is used, $n \leq b$. When chaining is used, n may exceed b.

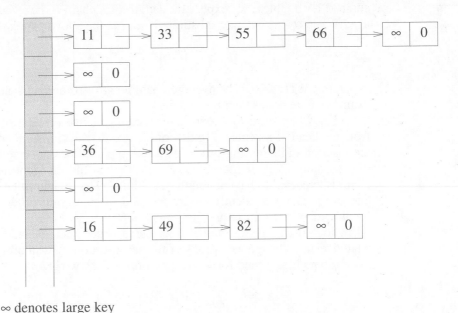

∞ denotes large key

Figure 7.4 Hash table with tail nodes

The space needed when linear open addressing is used is $b(s+2)$ bytes where s is the number of bytes needed by an element. When chaining is used, $2b+2n+ns$ bytes of space are needed. So whenever $n < bs/(s+2)$, chaining takes less space than does linear open addressing. Note that the space comparison changes somewhat if we program linear-open-addressed tables in a space-efficient manner. For example, we could pack the array `empty` into $b/8$ bytes (our current implementation uses $2b$ bytes for this array). Alternatively, when the keys are known to not use the entire integer range, we could use an unused integer (say -1 or `INT_MAX`) in the key field of an empty bucket.

As far as the worst-case time complexities are concerned, a search can require the examination of all n elements in both cases. The average performance of a search when chaining is used can be derived in the following way. An unsuccessful search of an ordered chain with i nodes on it will examine either 1, 2, 3, $\cdots$, or i nodes, for $i \geq 0$. If each of these possibilities happens with equal probability, then the average number of nodes that get examined in an unsuccessful search is

$$\frac{1}{i}\sum_{j=1}^{i} j = \frac{i(i+1)}{2i} = \frac{i+1}{2}$$

when $i \geq 1$. When $i = 0$, the average number of nodes examined is 0. For chained hash tables, we expect the length of a chain to be $n/b = \alpha$ on the average. When $\alpha \geq 1$, we may substitute α for i in the above expression to get

$$U_n \sim \frac{\alpha+1}{2}, \alpha \geq 1$$

When $\alpha < 1$, $U_n \leq \alpha$ as the average chain length is α and no search requires us to examine more nodes than on a chain.

For S_n we need to know the expected distance of each of the n identifiers from the head of its chain. To determine this distance, assume that the identifiers are inserted in increasing order. This assumption does not affect the positioning of identifiers on their respective chains. When the ith identifier is inserted, its chain is expected to have a length of $(i-1)/b$. The ith identifier gets added to the end of the chain as identifiers are inserted in increasing order. Hence a search for this identifier will require us to examine $1 + (i-1)/b$ nodes. Note also that when identifiers are inserted in increasing order, their distance from the chain head does not change as a result of further insertions. Assuming that each of the n identifiers is searched for with equal probability, we get

$$S_n = \frac{1}{n} \sum_{i=1}^{n} \{1 + (i-1)/b\} = 1 + \frac{n-1}{2b} \sim 1 + \frac{\alpha}{2}$$

Comparing the formulas for chaining with those for linear open addressing, we see that the expected performance of chaining is superior to that of linear open addressing. For instance, when $\alpha = 0.9$, an unsuccessful search in a chained hash table is expected to examine 0.9 elements and a successful search, 1.45 elements. On the other hand, when linear open addressing is used, 50.5 elements are expected to be examined if the search is unsuccessful and 5.5 if is successful!

Comparison with Skip Lists

Both skip lists and hashing utilize a randomization process to improve the expected performance of the dictionary operations. In the case of skip lists, randomization is used to assign a level to an element at the time of insertion. This level assignment is done without examining the value of the element being inserted. In the case of hashing, the hash function assigns a bucket so as to randomly distribute the bucket assignments for the different elements being inserted. The hash function does utilize the element value.

By using randomization, skip lists and hashing, respectively, obtain logarithmic and constant time expected performance. However, the worst-case complexity of the skip list method is $\Theta(n+\texttt{MaxLevel})$, while that of hashing is $\Theta(n)$. When skip lists are used, the expected space required for the pointers is approximately $\texttt{MaxLevel}+n/(1-p)$. The worst-case space requirements are considerably larger, a chained hash table requires $D + n$ space for pointers.

The skip list structure is, however, more versatile than hash tables. For example, we can output the elements in ascending order of value in linear time by simply going down the level 0 chain. When a chained hash table is used, it takes $\Theta(D + n)$ time to collect the n elements and an additional $O(n \log n)$ to sort them before they can be output in ascending order of value. Other operations, such as find or delete the element with largest or smallest value, are also more expensive (in terms of expected complexity) when a hash table is used.

EXERCISES

8. Use ideal hashing to implement a C++ class for dictionaries. Assume that element keys are integers in the range 0 through `MaxKey`, where `MaxKey` is specified by the user at the time the dictionary is created. Test the correctness of your code using suitable data.

9. In some applications of ideal hashing, even though we have enough space to construct a hash table with as many positions as the range of key values, the time, $\Theta(b)$, needed to initialize the hash table is too large to make the method competitive. For example, if the key range is 1,000,000 and we expect to perform only 100 operations, the million units of time spent initializing the table dominate the 100 units spent on the operations themselves.

   For these applications, the ideal hash method may be modified to use two arrays: `ht` and `ele`. `ht` is an integer array with positions 0 through `MaxKey` (`MaxKey` is the largest permissible key), and `ele` is of type `E` and has as many positions as the number of distinct keys among all elements to be inserted (generally much less than `MaxKey`). Neither array is initialized.

   In the absence of deletions, positions in `ele` are used in the order 0, 1, 2, $\cdots$. A counter `LastE` indicates the last used position of `ele`. Initially `LastE = -1`. `ht[j]` contains either garbage or an index into `ele` where the element with home address (or key) `j` may be found.

   Develop this idea into initialize, search, insert, and delete functions for ideal hashing. Each of these functions should have complexity $\Theta(1)$. Your functions should be developed as public members of a class `IdealHashTable`. Test the correctness of your code.

10. Comment on the difficulty of providing sequential access when a linear-open-addressed hash table is used.

11. Program the formula-based linear list representation for a dictionary as well as the linear-open-addressing method. For this exercise you do not need the delete function. Assume that the keys are integers and that D is 961. Insert a randomly generated sequence of $n = 500$ distinct integers

into the table and then search for each m times. Measure the average search times for different ms. What conclusions can you draw from your experiment?

12. Obtain a suitable value for the hash function divisor D when linear open addressing is used. Do this for each of the following situations:

 (a) $n = 50, S_n \leq 3, U_n \leq 20$.

 (b) $n = 500, S_n \leq 5, U_n \leq 60$.

 (c) $n = 10, S_n \leq 2, U_n \leq 10$.

13. For each of the following conditions, obtain a suitable value for the hash function divisor D. For this value of D determine S_n and U_n as a function of n. Assume that linear open addressing is used.

 (a) *MaxElements* ≤ 530.

 (b) *MaxElements* ≤ 130.

 (c) *MaxElements* ≤ 150.

★ 14. Write the code for the function `Delete`, which is a public member of the class `HashTable` (Program 7.11). Do not change any of the other members of this class. What is the worst-case time complexity of your code to delete an element? Use suitable data to test its correctness.

15. Write a class definition for hash tables using linear open addressing and the `NeverUsed` concept to handle a delete operation. Write complete C++ code for all functions. Include a function to reorganize the table when (say) 60 percent of the empty buckets have `NeverUsed` equal to `false`. The reorganization should move elements around as necessary and leave a properly configured hash table in which `NeverUsed` is `true` for every empty bucket. Test the correctness of your code.

16. Comment on the difficulty of providing sequential access when a chained hash table is used.

17. Develop a new class `SortedChainWithTail` in which the sorted chain has a tail node. Use the tail node to simplify your code by placing the element or key being searched for, inserted, or deleted into the tail at the start of the operation. Compare the run-time performance of sorted chains with and without tail nodes.

18. Develop the class `ChainHashTable` from basics. Define your own class `HashNode` with the fields `data` and `link` and do not use any version of the chain class. Test your code.

19. Develop a modified version of the class `ChainHashTable` that is derived from the class `SortedChainWithTail` (see Exercise 17). Compare the run-time performance of the two versions.

20. Develop a class `ChainHashWithTail` in which each hash table chain is a sorted chain with a tail node. The tail node for all chains is the same physical node. Compare the run-time performance of this class with that of `ChainHashTable` (Program 7.15).

21. In an effort to simplify the insert and delete codes for chained hash tables, we might consider adding a head node to each chain. The head node is in addition to a tail node as discussed in the text. All insertions and deletions now take place between the head and tail of a chain. As a result, the case of insertion and deletion at/from the front of a chain is eliminated.

   (a) Is it possible to use the same head node for all chains? Why?

   (b) Is it desirable to set the key field(s) of the head node(s) to a particular value? Why?

   (c) Write the class definition for a chained hash table using both head and tail nodes. Write the code for all functions.

   (d) Test the correctness of your code using suitable test data.

   (e) State the merits and demerits of using head and tail nodes versus using only tail nodes versus using neither head nor tail nodes. Of these options which do you recommend? Why?

7.5 AN APPLICATION—TEXT COMPRESSION

We can often reduce the disk storage needed to store a text file by storing a coded version of the file. For example, a text file that is a string of 1000 xs followed by a string of 2000 ys will take 3002 bytes of space (1 byte for each x and y, and 2 bytes to denote the string end) when stored as an uncoded text file. The same file can be coded, using *run-length coding*, as the string $1000x2000y$, which is 10 characters long and can be stored using 12 bytes of space. The space can be further reduced by storing the run lengths (1000 and 2000) using their binary representation. With 2 bytes per run length, the maximum run length is 2^{16}. Our example string can now be stored using 8 bytes. When the coded file is read back from storage, it needs to be decoded into the original file. File coding is done by a **compressor** and decoding by a **decompressor**.

In this section we shall develop C++ code to compress and decompress text files using a technique developed by Lempel, Ziv, and Welch. Hence we shall refer to the technique as the LZW method. The method is relatively simple and employs both ideal hashing and chained hashing.

7.5.1 LZW Compression

The LZW compression method maps strings of text characters into numeric codes. To begin with, all characters that may occur in the text file are assigned a code. For example, suppose the text file to be compressed is the string:

aaabbbbbbaabaaba

This string is composed of the characters 'a' and 'b'. 'a' is assigned the code 0 and 'b' the code 1. The mapping between character strings and their codes is stored in a dictionary. Each dictionary entry has two fields: `key` and `code`. The character string represented by `code` is stored in the field `key`. The initial dictionary for our example is given by the first two columns of Figure 7.5 (i.e., codes 0 and 1).

code	0	1	2	3	4	5	6	7
key	a	b	aa	aab	bb	bbb	bbba	aaba

Figure 7.5 LZW compression dictionary for aaabbbbbbaabaaba

Beginning with the dictionary initialized as above, the LZW compressor repeatedly finds the longest prefix, p, of the unencoded part of the input file that is in the dictionary and outputs its code. If there is a next character c in the input file, then pc (pc is the prefix string p followed by the character c) is assigned the next code and inserted into the dictionary. This strategy is called the **LZW rule**.

Let us try the LZW method on our example string. The longest prefix of the input that is in the initial dictionary is 'a'. Its code, 0, is output, and the string 'aa' is assigned the code 2 and entered into the dictionary. 'aa' is the longest prefix of the remaining string that is in the dictionary. Its code, 2, is output; the string 'aab' is assigned the code 3 and entered into the dictionary. *Notice that even though 'aab' has the code 3 assigned to it, only the code 2 for 'aa' is output. The suffix 'b' will be part of the next code output. The reason for not outputting 3 is that the code table is not part of the compressed file. Instead, the code table is reconstructed during decompression using the compressed file. This reconstruction is possible only if we adhere strictly to the LZW rule.*

Following the output of the code 2, the code for 'b' is output; 'bb' is assigned the code 4 and entered into the code dictionary. Then the code for 'bb' is output, and 'bbb' is entered into the table with code 5. Next the code 5 is output, and 'bbba' is entered with code 6. Then the code 3 is output for 'aab', and 'aaba' is entered into the dictionary with code 7. Finally, the code 7 is output for the remaining string 'aaba'. Our sample string is encoded as the string 0214537.

7.5.2 Implementation of LZW Compression

Input/Output

The input to the compressor is a text file, and the output is a binary file. To simplify matters, we shall assume that the name of the input file contains no period ('.') (i.e., the file name has no extension). If the input file name is `InputFile`, then the output file name is to be `InputFile.zzz`. We further assume that the user is to have the option of providing the input file name on the command line. So if the compression program is called `Compress`, then the command line

```
Compress text
```

should result in the compressed version of the file `text` being saved as the file `text.zzz`. In case the user does not specify the file name on the command line, then we are to prompt the user for this name.

Function `SetFiles` establishes the iostreams for input and output. It assumes that the `main` function has the prototype

```
void main(int argc, char* argv[])
```

and that `in` and `out` are global variables, respectively, of type `ifstream` and `ostream`. `argc` is set to the number of parameters in the command line, and `argv[i]` points to the `i`th argument. If the command line is

```
Compress text
```

then `argc` is 2, `argv[0]` points to the character string `Compress`, and `argv[1]` points to `text`.

Dictionary Organization

Each element of the dictionary is to have the two fields: `code` and `key`. Although `code` is an integer, `key` is a potentially long character string. However, each `key` of length $l > 1$ has the property that its first $l - 1$ characters (called the key prefix) are the key of some other entry in the dictionary. Since each dictionary entry has a unique code (in addition to having a unique key), we may replace the key prefix by its code. So in the example of Figure 7.5, the key 'aa' may be represented as '0a' and 'aaba' as '3a'. The dictionary now takes the form given in Figure 7.6.

To simplify decoding the compressed file, we shall write each code using a fixed number of bits. In further development we shall assume that each code is 12 bits long. Hence we can assign at most $2^{12} = 4096$ codes. Since each character is 8 bits long, a key can be represented using a long integer (32 bits). The least significant 8 bits are used for the last character in the key, and the next 12 bits for the code of its prefix. The dictionary itself may be represented as a chained hash table. If the prime number $D = 4099$ is used as the hash function

```
void SetFiles(int argc, char* argv[])
{// Create input and output streams.
   char OutputFile[50], InputFile[50];
   // see if file name provided
   if (argc >= 2) strcpy(InputFile,argv[1]);
   else {// name not provided, ask for it
        cout << "Enter name of file to compress"
             << endl;
        cout << "File name should have no extension"
             << endl;
        cin >> InputFile;}

   // name should not have an extension
   if (strchr(InputFile,'.')) {
      cerr << "File name has extension" << endl;
      exit(1);}

   // open files in binary mode
   in.open(InputFile,ios::binary);
   if (in.fail()) {cerr << "Cannot open "
                        << InputFile << endl;
                   exit(1);}
   strcpy(OutputFile,InputFile);
   strcat(OutputFile, ".zzz");
   out.open(OutputFile,ios::binary);
}
```

Program 7.16 Establish I/O streams

code	0	1	2	3	4	5	6	7
key	a	b	0a	2b	1b	4b	5a	3a

Figure 7.6 Modified LZW compression dictionary for aaabbbbbbaabaaba

divisor, the loading density will be less than 1, as we can have at most 4096 entries in the dictionary. The declaration

```
ChainHashTable<element, unsigned long> h(D)
```

suffices to create the table. Our application will not use the `Delete` function associated with members of the class `ChainHashTable`.

Output of Codes

Since each code is 12 bits long and each character is 8 bits, we can output only part of a code as a character. Eight bits of the first code are output, and the remaining four are saved for later output. When the next code is to be output, we have 4 bits from before, resulting in a total of 16 bits. These 16 bits can be output as two characters. Program 7.17 gives the C++ code for the output function. `mask1` is 255, `mask12` is 15, `excess` is 4, and `ByteSize` is 8. `status` is 1 if there are 4 bits of the previous code that remain to be ouput. If so, these 4 bits are in the variable `LeftOver`.

```
void Output(unsigned long pcode)
{// Output 8 bits, save rest in LeftOver.
   unsigned char c,d;
   if (status) {// 4 bits remain
      d = pcode & mask1; // right ByteSize bits
      c = (LeftOver << excess) | (pcode >> ByteSize);
      out.put(c);
      out.put(d);
      status = 0;}
   else {
      LeftOver = pcode & mask2; // right excess bits
      c = pcode >> excess;
      out.put(c);
      status = 1;}
}
```

Program 7.17 Code output

Compression

Program 7.18 gives the code for the LZW compression algorithm. We begin by initializing the dictionary with all 256 (`alpha` = 256) 8-bit characters and their codes. The variable `used` keeps track of the number of codes used so far. With 12 bits per code, at most `codes` = 4096 codes may be assigned. To find the longest prefix that is in the dictionary, we examine prefixes of length 1, 2, 3, $\cdots$, in this order until the first one that is not in the table. At this time a code is output and a new code created (unless we have used all 4096 codes).

```
void Compress()
{// Lempel-Ziv-Welch compressor.
   // define and initialize the code dictionary
   ChainHashTable<element, unsigned long> h(D);
   element e;
   for (int i = 0; i < alpha; i++) {// initialize
      e.key = i;
      e.code = i;
      h.Insert(e);
      }
   int used = alpha;  // number of codes used

   // input and compress
   unsigned char c;
   in.get(c);        // first character of input file
   unsigned long pcode = c; // prefix code
   if (!in.eof()) {// file length is > 1
      do {// process rest of file
           in.get(c);
           if (in.eof()) break;   // finished
           unsigned long k = (pcode << ByteSize) + c;
           // see if code for k is in the dictionary
           if (h.Search(k, e)) pcode = e.code;   // yes
           else {// k not in table
                   Output(pcode);
                   if (used < codes) // create new code
                      {e.code = used++;
                       e.key = (pcode << ByteSize) | c;
                       h.Insert(e);}
                   pcode = c;}
      } while(true);

      // output last code(s)
      Output(pcode);
      if (status) {c = LeftOver << excess;
                   out.put(c);}
      }

   out.close();
   in.close();
}
```

Program 7.18 LZW compressor

Headers and Function `main`
Program 7.19 gives the include files, constant definition, data types, global variables, and the `main` function.

```cpp
#include <fstream.h>
#include <iostream.h>
#include <string.h>
#include <stdlib.h>
#include <math.h>
#include "chash.h"

const D = 4099,        // hash function divisor
      codes = 4096,    // 2^12
      ByteSize = 8,
      excess = 4,      // 12 - ByteSize
      alpha = 256,     // 2^ByteSize
      mask1 = 255,     // alpha - 1
      mask2 = 15;      // 2^excess - 1

class element {
   friend void Compress();
   public:
      operator unsigned long() const {return key;}
      element& operator =(unsigned long y)
         {key = y; return *this;}
   private:
      int code;
      unsigned long key;
};

int LeftOver,    // code bits yet to be output
    status = 0; // 0 means no bits in LeftOver
ifstream in;
ofstream out;

void main(int argc, char* argv[])
{
   SetFiles(argc, argv);
   Compress();
}
```

Program 7.19 Function `main` for compression

7.5.3 LZW Decompression

For decompression we input the codes one at a time and replace them by the texts they denote. The code-to-text mapping can be reconstructed in the following way. The codes assigned for single character texts are entered into the dictionary. As before, the dictionary entries are code-text pairs. This time, however, the dictionary is searched for an entry with a given code (rather than with a given text). The first code in the compressed file corresponds to a single character and so may be replaced by the corresponding character. For all other codes p in the compressed file, we have two cases to consider: (1) the code p is in the dictionary, and (b) it is not. When p is in the dictionary, the text $text(p)$ to which it corresponds is extracted from the dictionary and output. Also, from the working of the compressor, we know that if the code that precedes p in the compressed file is q and $text(q)$ is the corresponding text, then the compressor would have created a new code for the text $text(q)$ followed by the first character, $fc(p)$, of $text(p)$. So we enter the pair (next code, $text(q)fc(p)$) into the directory. Case (2) arises only when the current text segment has the form $text(q)text(q)fc(q)$ and $text(p) = text(q)fc(q)$. The corresponding compressed file segment is qp. During compression, $text(q)fc(q)$ is assigned the code p, and the code p is output for the text $text(q)fc(q)$. During decompression, after q is replaced by $text(q)$, we encounter the code p. However, there is no code-to-text mapping for p is our table. We are able to decode p using the fact that this situation arises only when the decompressed text segment is $text(q)text(q)fc(q)$. When we encounter a code p for which the code-to-text mapping is udefined, the code-to-text mapping for p is $text(q)fc(q)$, where q is the code that precedes p.

Let us try this decompression scheme on our earlier sample string

aaabbbbbbaabaaba

which was compressed into the coded string 0214537. To begin, we initialize the dictionary with the pairs (0, a) and (1, b), and obtain the first two entries in the dictionary of Figure 7.5. The first code in the compressed file is 0. It is replaced by the text 'a'. The next code, 2, is undefined. Since the previous code 0 has $text(0)$ = 'a', $fc(0)$ = 'a' and $text(2) = text(0)fc(0)$ = 'aa'. So the code 2 is replaced by 'aa', and (2, 'aa') is entered into the dictionary. The next code, 1, is replaced by $text(1)$ = 'b', and (3, $text(2)fc(1)$) = (3, 'aab') is entered into the dictionary. The next code, 4, is not in the dictionary. The code preceding it is 1, and so $text(4) = text(1)fc(1)$ = 'bb'. The pair (4, 'bb') is entered into the dictionary, and 'bb' is output to the decompressed file. When the next code, 5, is encountered, (5, 'bbb') is entered into the directory; 'bbb' is output to the decompressed file. The next code is 3. $text(3)$ = 'aab' is output to the decompressed file, and the pair (6, $text(5)fc(3)$) = (6, 'bbba') is entered into the dictionary. Finally, when the code 7 is encountered, (7, $text(3)fc(3)$) = (7, 'aaba') is entered into the dictionary and 'aaba' output.

7.5.4 Implementation of LZW Decompression

Input/Output

The function `SetFiles` (Program 7.20) serves the same function as the corresponding function for compression. It inputs the decompressed file's name and adds the extension `.zzz` to get the name of the compressed file.

```cpp
void SetFiles(int argc, char* argv[])
{// Determine file name.
   char OutputFile[50], InputFile[50];

   // see if file name provided
   if (argc == 2) strcpy(OutputFile,argv[1]);
   else {// name not provided, ask for it
         cout << "Enter name of file to decompress"
              << endl;
         cout << "Omit the extension .zzz" << endl;
         cin >> OutputFile;}

   // name should not have an extension
   if (strchr(OutputFile,'.'))
      {cerr << "File name has extension" << endl;
       exit(1);}

   strcpy(InputFile, OutputFile);
   strcat(InputFile, ".zzz");

   // open files in binary mode
   in.open(InputFile,ios::binary);
   // in.open(InputFile);  for g++
   if (in.fail()) {cerr << "Cannot open "
                        << InputFile  << endl;
                   exit(1);}
   out.open(OutputFile,ios::binary);
   // out.open(OutputFile); for g++
}
```

Program 7.20 Establish I/O streams

Dictionary Organization

Since we shall be querying the dictionary by providing a code and since the number of codes is 4096, we can use an array ht[4096] and store *text*(*p*) in ht[*p*]. Using array ht in this way corresponds to ideal hashing with $f(k) = k$. *text*(*p*) may be compactly stored by using the code for the prefix of *text*(*p*) and the last character (suffix) of *text*(*p*) as in Figure 7.6. For our decompression application it is convenient to store the prefix and suffix separately as an integer and character, respectively. So if *text*(*p*) = *text*(*q*)*c*, then ht[*p*].suffix is the character *c* and ht[*p*].code equals *q*.

When this dictionary organization is used, *text*(*p*) may be constructed from right to left beginning with the last character ht[*p*].suffix, as is shown in Program 7.21. This code obtains suffix values of codes $\geq$ alpha from the table ht, and for codes < alpha it uses the knowledge that the code is just the integer representation of the corresponding character. *text*(*p*) is assembled into the array s[] and then output. Since *text*(*p*) is assembled from right to left, the first character of *text*(*p*) is in s[size].

```
void Output(int code)
{// Output string corresponding to code.
   size = -1;
   while (code >= alpha) {// suffix in dictionary
      s[++size] = ht[code].suffix;
      code = ht[code].prefix;
      }
   s[++size] = code;   // code < alpha

   // decompressed string is s[size] ... s[0]
   for (int i = size; i >= 0; i--)
      out.put(s[i]);
}
```

Program 7.21 Compute *text*(code)

Input of Codes

Since the sequence of 12-bit codes is represented as a sequence of 8-bit bytes in the compressed file, we need to reverse the process employed by function Output (Program 7.17). This reversal is done by function GetCode (Program 7.22). The only new constant here is mask. Its value, 15, enables us to extract the low-order 4 bits of a byte.

```
bool GetCode(int& code)
{// Put next code in compressed file into code.
 // Return false if no more codes.
   unsigned char c, d;
   in.get(c);  // input 8 bits
   if (in.eof()) return false;  // no more codes

   // see if any left over bits from before
   // if yes, concatenate with left over 4 bits
   if (status) code = (LeftOver << ByteSize) | c;
   else {// no left over bits, need four more bits
         // to complete code
         in.get(d);  // another 8 bits
         code = (c << excess) | (d >> excess);
         LeftOver = d & mask;}  // save 4 bits
   status = 1 - status;
   return true;
}
```

Program 7.22 Extracting codes from a compressed file

Decompression
Program 7.23 gives the LZW decompressor. The first code in the compressed
file is decoded outside the while loop, and the remaining codes are decoded
inside this loop. Since the first code is always in the range zero through
alpha, it represents a single character that is obtained by doing a type conversion to the type unsigned char. *At the start of each iteration of the*
while *loop,* s[size] *contains the first character of the last decoded text that
was output.* To establish this condition for the first iteration, we set size to
zero and s[0] to the first and only character corresponding to the first code in
the compressed file.

The while loop repeatedly obtains a code ccode from the compressed
file and decodes it. There are two cases for ccode—(1) ccode is in the dictionary and (2) it is not. ccode is in the dictionary iff ccode < used
where ht[0:used] is the defined part of table ht. In this case the code is
decoded using the function Output, and following the LZW rule, a new code
is created with suffix being the first character of the text just output for ccode.
When ccode is not defined, we are in the special case discussed at the beginning of this section and ccode is *text*(pcode)s[size]. This information is
used to create a table entry for code and to output the decoded text to which it
corresponds.

```
void Decompress()
{// Decompress a compressed file.
   int used = alpha; // codes used so far

   // input and decompress
   int pcode,  // previous code
       ccode;  // current code
   if (GetCode(pcode)){// file is not empty
      s[0] = pcode;   // character for pcode
      out.put(s[0]);  // output string for pcode
      size = 0; // s[size] is first character of
                // last string output

      while(GetCode(ccode)) {// get another code
         if (ccode < used) {// ccode is defined
            Output(ccode);
            if (used < codes) {// create new code
               ht[used].prefix = pcode;
               ht[used++].suffix = s[size];}}
         else {// special case, undefined code
               ht[used].prefix = pcode;
               ht[used++].suffix = s[size];
               Output(ccode);}
         pcode = ccode;}
         }

   out.close();
   in.close();
}
```

Program 7.23 LZW decompressor

Headers and Function `main`
Program 7.24 gives the include files, constants, type definitions, function proto-types, and main function for LZW decompression.

```
#include <fstream.h>
#include <iostream.h>
#include <string.h>
#include <stdlib.h>
#include <math.h>

class element {
    friend void Decompress();
    friend void Output(int);
    private:
        int prefix;
        unsigned char suffix;
};

// constants
const codes = 4096,     // 2^12
      ByteSize = 8,
      excess = 4,        // 12 - ByteSize
      alpha = 256,       // 2^ByteSize
      mask = 15;         // 2^excess - 1

// globals
unsigned char s[codes];// used to reconstruct text
int size,              // size of reconstructed text
    LeftOver,          // left over bits from last code
    status = 0;        // 0 iff no left over bits
element ht[codes];     // dictionary
ifstream in;
ofstream out;

void main(int argc, char* argv[])
{
    SetFiles(argc, argv);
    Decompress();
}
```

Program 7.24 Main function for decompression

EXERCISES

22. Is is possible for the compressed file generated by our LZW compressor to be longer than the original file? If so, by how much?

23. Write an LZW compressor and decompressor for files composed of the characters {a, b, $\cdots$, z, 0, 1, $\cdots$, 9, ':', ',', ';', ':'} and the end-of-line character. Use 8 bits per code. Test the correctness of your program. Is it possible for the compressed file to be longer than the original file?

24. Modify the LZW compress and decompress programs so that the code table is reinitialized after every x kbytes of the text file have been compressed/decompressed. Experiment with the modified compression code using text files that are 100K to 200K bytes long and $x = 10, 20, 30, 40,$ and 50. Which value of x gives the best compression?

7.6   REFERENCES AND SELECTED READINGS

Skip lists were proposed by William Pugh. An analysis of their expected complexity can be found in the paper ''Skip Lists: A Probabilistic Alternative to Balanced Trees'' by W. Pugh, *Communications of the ACM*, 33, 6, 1990, 668–676.

Our description of the Lempel-Ziv compression method is based on the paper ''A Technique for High-Performance Data Compression'' by T. Welch, *IEEE Computer*, June 1994, 8–19. For more on data compression see the survey article ''Data Compression'' by D. Lelewer and D. Hirschberg, *ACM Computing Surveys*, 19, 3, 1987, 261–296.

CHAPTER 8

BINARY AND OTHER TREES

BIRD'S-EYE VIEW

Yes, it's a jungle out there. The jungle is populated with many varieties of trees, plants, and animals. The world of data structures also has a wide variety of trees, too many for us to discuss in this book. In the present chapter we study two basic varieties: general trees (or simply trees) and binary trees. Chapters 9, 10, and 11 consider the more popular of the remaining varieties.

Two applications of trees are developed in the applications section. The first is concerned with the placement of signal boosters in a tree distribution network. The second is a revisit of the online equivalence problem introduced in Section 3.8.3. This problem is also known as the union/find problem. By using trees to represent the sets, we can obtain improved run-time performance over the chain representation developed in Section 3.8.3.

In addition, this chapter covers the following topics:

- Tree and binary tree terminology such as height, depth, level, root, leaf, child, parent, and sibling.

- Formula-based and linked representations of binary trees.
- The four common ways to traverse a binary tree: preorder, inorder, postorder, and level order.

8.1 TREES

So far in this text we have seen data structures for linear and tabular data. These data structures are generally not suitable for the representation of hierarchical data. In hierarchical data we have an ancestor-descendant, superior-subordinate, whole-part, or similar relationship among the data elements.

Example 8.1 [*Joe's Descendants*] Figure 8.1 shows the descendants of Joe arranged in a hierarchical manner, beginning with Joe at the top of the hierarchy. Joe's children (Ann, Mary, and John) are listed next in the hierarchy, and a line or edge joins Joe and his children. Ann has no children, while Mary has two and John has one. Mary's children are listed below her, and John's child is listed below him. There is an edge between each parent and his/her children. From this hierarchical representation, it is easy to identify Ann's siblings, Joe's descendants, Chris's ancestors, and so on. ■

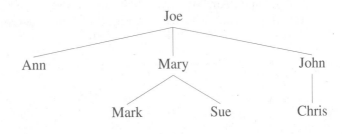

Figure 8.1 Descendants of Joe

Example 8.2 [*Corporate Structure*] As an example of hierarchical data, consider the administrative structure of the corporation of Figure 8.2. The person (in this case the president) highest in the hierarchy appears at the top of the diagram. Those who are next in the hierarchy (i.e., the vice presidents) are shown below the president and so on. The vice presidents are the president's subordinates, and the president is their superior. Each vice president, in turn, has his/her subordinates who may themselves have subordinates. In the diagram we have drawn a line or edge between each person and his/her direct subordinates or superior. ■

Example 8.3 [*Governmental Subdivisions*] Figure 8.3 is a hierarchical drawing of the branches of the federal government. At the top of the hierarchy, we have the entire federal government. At the next level of the hierarchy, we have drawn its major subdivisions (i.e., the different departments). Each department may be

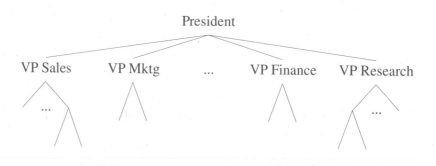

Figure 8.2 Hierarchical administrative structure of a corporation

further subdivided. These subdivisions are drawn at the next level of the hierarchy. For example, the Department of Defense has been subdivided into the Army, Navy, Air Force, and Marines. There is a line between each element and its components. The data of Figure 8.3 is an example of whole-part relationships. ∎

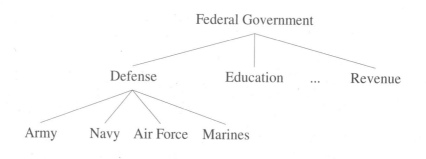

Figure 8.3 Modules of the federal government

Example 8.4 [*Software Engineering*] For another example of hierarchical data, consider the software-engineering technique referred to as modularization. In modularization we decompose a large and complex task into a collection of smaller, less complex tasks. The objective is to divide the software system into many functionally independent parts or **modules** so that each can be developed relatively independently. This decision reduces the overall software development time, as it is much easier to solve several small problems than one large

one. Additionally, different programmers can develop different modules at the same time. If necessary, each module may be further decomposed so as to obtain a hierarchy of modules as shown by the tree of Figure 8.4. This tree represents a possible modular decomposition of a text processor.

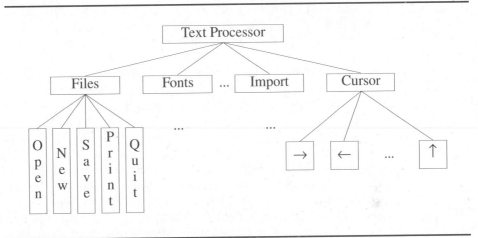

Figure 8.4 Module hierarchy for text processor

At the top level the text processor has been split into several modules. Only four are shown in the figure. The module Files performs functions related to text files such as opening an existing file, opening a new file, saving a file, printing a file, and exiting from the text processor (exiting requires saving files if the user so desires). Each function is represented by a module at the next level of the hierarchy. The module Fonts handles all functions related to the font in use. These functions include changing the font, its size, color, and so on. If modules for these functions were shown in the figure, they would appear below the module Fonts. The Import module handles functions associated with the import of material such as graphics, tables, and text in a format not native to this text processor. The Cursor module handles the movement of the cursor on the screen. Its subordinate modules correspond to various cursor motions. Programmers can carry out the specification, design, and development of each module in a relatively independent manner after the interfaces are fully specified.

When the software system is specified and designed in a modular fashion, it is natural to develop the system itself in this way. The resulting software system will have as many modules as there are nodes in the module hierarchy. Modularization improves the intellectual manageability of a problem. By systematically dividing a large problem into smaller relatively independent problems, we can solve the large problem with much less effort. The independent problems can be assigned to different persons for parallel solution. It is harder to share labor on a single module. Another advantage of developing modular software is that it is much easier to test and verify many small modules independently before testing them as a unit than to do so for one large module. The hierarchical organization clearly shows the relationship among the modules. ∎

Definition A **tree** t is a finite nonempty set of elements. One of these elements is called the **root**, and the remaining elements (if any) are partitioned into trees which are called the **subtrees** of t. ∎

Let us see how this definition relates to our examples of hierarchical data. The element at the highest level of the hierarchy is the root. The elements at the next level are the roots of the subtrees formed by a partitioning of the remaining elements.

Example 8.5 In the descendants-of-Joe example (Example 8.1), the data set is {Joe, Ann, Mary, Mark, Sue, John, Chris}. So $n = 7$. The root of the collection is Joe. The remaining elements are partitioned into the three disjoint sets {Ann}; {Mary, Mark, Sue}; and {John, Chris}. {Ann} is a tree with a single element; its root is Ann. The root of {Mary, Mark, Sue} is Mary, and that of {John, Chris} is John. The remaining elements of {Mary, Mark, Sue} are partitioned into the disjoint sets {Mark} and {Sue}, which are both single-element (sub)trees, and the remaining element of {John, Chris} is also a single-element subtree. ∎

When drawing a tree, each element is represented as a node. The tree root is drawn at the top, and its subtrees are drawn below. There is a line or edge from the tree root to the roots of its subtrees (if any). Each subtree is drawn similarly with its root at the top and its subtrees below. The edges in a tree connect an element node and its **children** nodes. In Figure 8.1, for example, Ann, Mary, and John are the children of Joe, and Joe is their **parent**. Children of the same parent are called **siblings**. Ann, Mary, and John are siblings in the tree of Figure 8.1, but Mark and Chris are not. The extension of this terminology to include the terms **grandchild**, **grandparent**, **ancestor**, **descendent**, and so forth is straightforward. In a tree, elements with no children are called **leaves**. So Ann, Mark, Sue, and Chris are the leaves of the tree of Figure 8.1. The tree root is the only tree element that has no parent.

Example 8.6 In the corporate-structure example (Example 8.2), the company employees are the tree elements. The president is the tree root. The remaining employees are partitioned into disjoint sets, which represent different divisions of the company. Each division has a vice president, who is the root of the subtree that represents the division. The remaining employees of a division are partitioned into disjoint sets representing departments. The department head will be the root of the department subtree. The remaining employees of a department could be partitioned into projects and so on.

The vice presidents are children of the president; department heads are children of their vice president, and so on. The president is the parent of the vice presidents, and each vice president is the parent of the department heads in his/her division.

In Figure 8.3 the root is the element Federal Government. Its subtrees have the roots Defense, Education, $\cdots$, and Revenue which are the children of Federal Government. Federal Government is the parent of its children. Defense has the children Army, Navy, Air Force, and Marines. The children of Defense are siblings and are also leaves. ∎

Another commonly used tree term is **level**. By definition, the tree root is at level 1; its children (if any) are at level 2; their children (if any) are at level 3; and so on. In the tree of Figure 8.3, Federal Government is at level one; Defense, Education, and Revenue are at level 2; and Army, Navy, Air Force, and Marines are at level 3.

The **degree of an element** is the number of children it has. The degree of a leaf is zero. The degree of Files in Figure 8.4 is five. The **degree of a tree** is the maximum of its element degrees.

EXERCISES

1. Obtain a tree representation for the major elements (whole book, chapters, sections, and subsections) of this text.

   (a) What is the total number of elements in your tree?

   (b) Identify the leaf elements.

   (c) Identify the elements on level 3.

   (d) List the degree of each element.

2. Access the World Wide Web home page for your department (Alternatively, access `http://www.cise.ufl.edu`, which is the home page for the computer and information science and engineering department at the University of Florida.) Follow some of the links to lower-level pages and draw the resulting structure. In your drawing the Web pages are represented by nodes, and the links are the edges that join pairs of nodes.

   (a) Is it necessary for the structure to be a tree? Why?

   (b) In case your structure is a tree, identify the root and the leaves.

8.2   BINARY TREES

Definition A **binary tree** t is a finite (possibly empty) collection of elements. When the binary tree is not empty, it has a **root** element and the remaining elements (if any) are partitioned into two binary trees, which are called the left and right subtrees of t. ∎

The essential differences between a binary tree and a tree are

- A binary tree can be empty, whereas a tree cannot.

- Each element in a binary tree has exactly two subtrees (one or both of these subtrees may be empty). Each element in a tree can have any number of subtrees.

- The subtrees of each element in a binary tree are ordered. That is, we distinguish between the left and the right subtrees. The subtrees in a tree are unordered.

Like a tree, a binary tree is drawn with its root at the top. The elements in the left (right) subtree of the root are drawn below and to the left (right) of the root. Between each element and its children is a line or edge.

Figure 8.5 shows some binary trees that represent arithmetic expressions. Each operator (+, −, *, /) may have one or two operands. The left operand (if any) is the left subtree of the operator. The right operand is its right subtree. The leaf elements in an expression tree are either constants or variables. Note that an expression tree contains no parentheses.

One application of expression trees is in the generation of optimal computer code to evaluate an expression. Although we do not study algorithms to generate optimal code from an expression tree, we shall use these trees to illustrate some of the operations that are commonly performed on binary trees.

EXERCISES

3. (a) Identify the leaves of the binary trees of Figure 8.5.

   (b) Identify all level 3 nodes in Figure 8.5(b).

   (c) How many level 4 nodes are in Figure 8.5(c)?

4. Draw the binary expression trees corresponding to each of the following expressions:

   (a) $(a + b)/(c - d * e) + e + g * h / a$

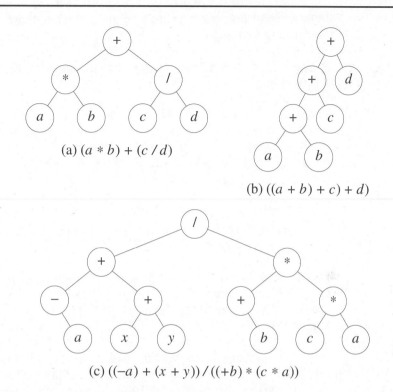

(a) $(a * b) + (c / d)$

(b) $((a + b) + c) + d)$

(c) $((-a) + (x + y)) / ((+b) * (c * a))$

Figure 8.5 Expression trees

(b) $-x - y * z + (a + b + c / d * e)$

(c) $((a + b) > (c - \check{e})) \parallel a < f \&\& (x < y \parallel y > z)$

8.3 PROPERTIES OF BINARY TREES

Property 1 The drawing of every binary tree with n elements, $n > 0$, has exactly $n - 1$ edges.

Proof Every element in a binary tree (except the root) has exactly one parent. There is exactly one edge between each child and its parent. So the number of edges is $n - 1$. ∎

The **height** (or **depth**) of a binary tree is the number of levels in it. The binary tree of Figure 8.5(a) has a height of 3 while those of Figures 8.5(b) and (c) have a height of 4.

Property 2   A binary tree of height h, $h \geq 0$, has at least h and at most $2^h - 1$ elements in it.

Proof   Since there must be at least one element at each level, the number of elements is at least h. As each element can have at most two children, the number of elements at level i is at most 2^{i-1}, $i > 0$. For $h = 0$, the total number of elements is 0, which equals $2^0 - 1$. For $h > 0$, the number of elements cannot exceed

$$\sum_{i=1}^{h} 2^{i-1} = 2^h - 1. \quad \blacksquare$$

Property 3   The height of a binary tree that contains n, $n \geq 0$, elements is at most n and at least $\lceil \log_2(n+1) \rceil$.

Proof   Since there must be at least one element at each level, the height cannot exceed n. From Property 2, we know that a binary tree of height h can have no more than $2^h - 1$ elements. So $n \leq 2^h - 1$. Hence $h \geq \log_2(n + 1)$. Since h is an integer, we get $h \geq \lceil \log_2(n+1) \rceil$. $\quad \blacksquare$

A binary tree of height h that contains exactly $2^h - 1$ elements is called a **full binary tree**. The binary tree of Figure 8.5(a) is a full binary tree of height 3. The binary trees of Figures 8.5(b) and (c) are not full binary trees. Figure 8.6 shows a full binary tree of height 4.

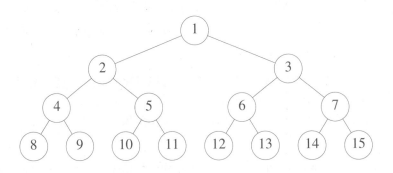

Figure 8.6 Full binary tree of height 4

Suppose we number the elements in a full binary tree of height h using the numbers 1 through $2^h - 1$. We begin at level 1 and go down to level h. Within levels the elements are numbered left to right. The elements of the full binary tree of Figure 8.6 have been numbered in this way. Now suppose we delete the k, $k \geq 0$, elements numbered $2^h - i$, $1 \leq i \leq k$ for any k. The resulting binary tree is called a **complete binary tree**. Figure 8.7 gives some examples. Note that a full binary tree is a special case of a complete binary tree. Also, note that the height of a complete binary tree that contains n elements is $\lceil \log_2(n + 1) \rceil$.

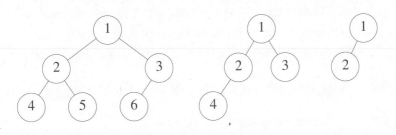

Figure 8.7 Complete binary trees

There is a very nice relationship among the numbers assigned to an element and its children in a complete binary tree, as given by Property 4.

Property 4 Let i, $1 \leq i \leq n$, be the number assigned to an element of a complete binary tree. The following are true:

1. If $i = 1$, then this element is the root of the binary tree. If $i > 1$, then the parent of this element has been assigned the number $\lfloor i/2 \rfloor$.

2. If $2i > n$, then this element has no left child. Otherwise, its left child has been assigned the number $2i$.

3. If $2i + 1 > n$, then this element has no right child. Otherwise, its right child has been assigned the number $2i + 1$.

Proof Can be established by induction on i. ∎

EXERCISES

5. Prove Property 4.

6. In a k-ary tree each node may have up to k children. These children are called, respectively, the first, second, $\cdots$, kth child of the node. A 2-ary tree is a binary tree.

    (a) Obtain the analogue of Property 1 for k-ary trees.

    (b) Obtain the analogue of Property 2 for k-ary trees.

    (c) Obtain the analogue of Property 3 for k-ary trees.

    (d) Obtain the analogue of Property 4 for k-ary trees.

7. What is the maximum number of nodes in a binary tree that has m leaves?

8.4 REPRESENTATION OF BINARY TREES

8.4.1 Formula-Based Representation

The formula-based representation of a binary tree utilizes Property 4. The binary tree to be represented is regarded as a complete binary tree with some missing elements. Figure 8.8 shows two sample binary trees. The first binary tree has three elements (A, B, and C), and the second has five elements (A, B, C, D, and E). Neither is complete. Unshaded circles represent missing elements. All elements (including the missing ones) are numbered as described in the previous section.

In a formula-based representation, the binary tree is represented in an array by storing each element at the array position corresponding to the number assigned to it. Figure 8.8 also shows the formula-based representations for its binary trees. Missing elements are represented by white circles and boxes. As can be seen, this representation scheme is quite wasteful of space when many elements are missing. In fact, a binary tree that has n elements may require an array of size up to $2^n - 1$ for its representation. This maximum size is needed when each element (except the root) of the n-element binary tree is the right child of its parent. Figure 8.9 shows such a binary tree with four elements. Binary trees of this type are called **right-skewed** binary trees.

The formula-based representation is useful only when the number of missing elements is small.

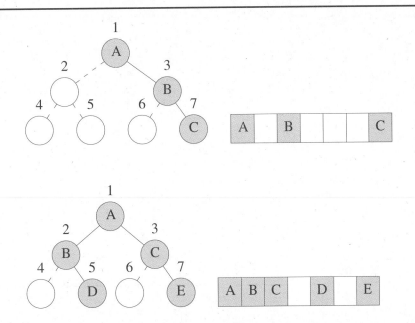

Figure 8.8 Incomplete binary trees

8.4.2 Linked Representation

The most popular way to represent a binary tree is by using links or pointers. Each element is represented by a node that has exactly two link fields. Let us call these link fields `LeftChild` and `RightChild`. In addition to these two link fields, each node has a field named `data`. This node structure may be defined as a C++ template class as in Program 8.1. This definition provides three constructors for a binary tree node. The first takes no parameters and initializes the left and right child fields of the node to zero (i.e., `NULL`); the second takes one parameter and uses this parameter to initialize the data field, the child fields are set to zero; the third takes three parameters and uses these to initialize all three fields of the node.

Each edge in the drawing of a binary tree is represented by a pointer from the parent node to the child node. This pointer is placed in the appropriate link field of the parent node. Since an n-element binary tree has exactly $n-1$ edges, we are left with $2n - (n-1) = n+1$ link fields that have no value. These link fields are set to zero. Figure 8.10 shows the linked representations of the binary trees of Figure 8.8.

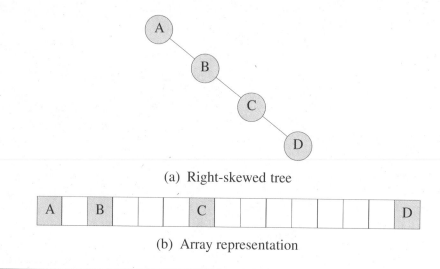

(a) Right-skewed tree

(b) Array representation

Figure 8.9 Right-skewed binary tree

```
template <class T>
class BinaryTreeNode {
   public:
      BinaryTreeNode() {LeftChild = RightChild = 0;}
      BinaryTreeNode(const T& e)
            {data = e;
             LeftChild = RightChild = 0;}
      BinaryTreeNode(const T& e, BinaryTreeNode *l,
                     BinaryTreeNode *r)
            {data = e;
             LeftChild = l;
             RightChild = r;}
   private:
      T data;
      BinaryTreeNode<T> *LeftChild,    // left subtree
                        *RightChild;   // right subtree
};
```

Program 8.1 Node class for linked binary trees

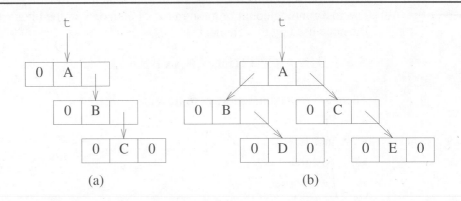

Figure 8.10 Linked representations

A variable (t in Figure 8.10) is used to keep track of the root of the binary tree. We use the name of this variable to refer to the root node as well as to the whole binary tree. So we use the phrases the root t and the binary tree t. We can access all nodes in a binary tree t by starting at the root and following LeftChild and RightChild links. The absence of a parent link from the linked representation of a binary tree generally causes no difficulties, as most of the functions we perform on a binary tree do not require this link. If some application needs this link, we can add another link field to each node.

8.5 COMMON BINARY TREE OPERATIONS

Some of the operations that are commonly performed on binary trees are to

- Determine its height.
- Determine the number of elements in it.
- Make a copy.
- Display the binary tree on a screen or on paper.
- Determine whether two binary trees are identical.
- Delete the tree.
- If it is an expression tree, evaluate the expression.
- If it is an expression tree, obtain the parenthesized form of the expression.

All these operations can be performed by traversing the binary tree in a systematic manner. In a binary tree **traversal**, each element is **visited** exactly once. During this visit all action with respect to this element is taken. This action can include writing the element on a screen or on paper, evaluating the expression represented by the subtree of which this element is the root, adding one to a running count of the number of elements in the binary tree, and deleting the node used by this element,

8.6 BINARY TREE TRAVERSAL

There are four common ways to traverse a binary tree:

- Preorder
- Inorder
- Postorder
- Level order

The first three traversal methods are best described recursively as in Programs 8.2, 8.3, and 8.4. These codes assume that the binary tree being traversed is represented using the linked scheme of the previous section, and BinaryTreeNode is defined as a template structure or class.

```
template <class T>
void PreOrder(BinaryTreeNode<T> *t)
{// Preorder traversal of *t.
   if (t) {
      Visit(t);                      // visit tree root
      PreOrder(t->LeftChild);   // do left subtree
      PreOrder(t->RightChild);  // do right subtree
      }
}
```

Program 8.2 Preorder traversal

```
template <class T>
void InOrder(BinaryTreeNode<T> *t)
{// Inorder traversal of *t.
   if (t) {
      InOrder(t->LeftChild);   // do left subtree
      Visit(t);                     // visit tree root
      InOrder(t->RightChild);  // do right subtree
      }
}
```

Program 8.3 Inorder traversal

```
template <class T>
void PostOrder(BinaryTreeNode<T> *t)
{// Postorder traversal of *t.
   if (t) {
      PostOrder(t->LeftChild);    // do left subtree
      PostOrder(t->RightChild);   // do right subtree
      Visit(t);                   // visit tree root
      }
}
```

Program 8.4 Postorder traversal

In the first three traversal methods, the left subtree of a node is traversed before the right subtree. The difference among the three orders comes from the difference in the time at which a node is visited. In the case of a preorder traversal, each node is visited before its left and right subtrees are traversed. In an inorder traversal, the root of each subtree is visited after its left subtree has been traversed but before the traversal of its right subtree begins. In a postorder traversal, each root is visited after its left and right subtrees have been traversed.

Figure 8.11 shows the output generated by Programs 8.2, 8.3, and 8.4 when Visit(t) is replaced by the statement:

```
cout << t->data;
```

The input binary trees are those of Figure 8.5.

Preorder	$+*ab/cd$	$+++abcd$	$/+-a+xy*+b*ca$
Inorder	$a*b+c/d$	$a+b+c+d$	$-a+x+y/+b*c*a$
Postorder	$ab*cd/+$	$ab+c+d+$	$a-xy++b+ca**/$
	(a)	(b)	(c)

Figure 8.11 Elements of a binary tree listed in pre-, in-, and postorder

When an expression tree is output in in-, pre-, or postorder, we get the infix, prefix, and postfix forms of the expression, respectively. The **infix** form of an expression is the form in which we normally write an expression. In this form each binary operator (i.e., operator with two operands) appears just after the infix form of its left operand and just before the infix form of its right operand. An expression presented as a binary tree is unambiguous in the sense that the association between operators and operands is uniquely determined by the representation. This association is not uniquely determined by the representation when infix form is used. For example, is $x + y * z$ to be interpreted as $(x + y) * z$ or $x + (y * z)$. To resolve this ambiguity, one assigns priorities to operators and employs priority rules. Further, delimiters such as parentheses are used to override these rules if necessary. In a *fully parenthesized* infix representation, each operator and its operands are enclosed in a pair of parentheses. Furthermore, each of the operands of the operator are in fully parenthesized form. Some representations of this type are $((x)+(y))$, $((x)+((y)*(z)))$, and $(((x)+(y))*((y)+(z)))*(w))$. This form of the expression is obtained by modifying inorder traversal as in Program 8.5.

```
template <class T>
void Infix(BinaryTreeNode<T> *t)
{// Output infix form of expression.
   if (t) {cout << '(';
           Infix(t->LeftChild);   // left operand
           cout << t->data;       // operator
           Infix(t->RightChild);  // right operand
           cout << ')';}
}
```

Program 8.5 Output fully parenthesized infix form

In the **postfix form** each operator comes immediately after the postfix form of its operands. The operands themselves appear in left-to-right order. In the **prefix form** each operator comes immediately before the prefix form of its operands. The operands themselves appear in left-to-right order. Like the binary tree representation, the prefix and postfix representations are unambiguous. As a result, neither the prefix nor the postfix representation employs parentheses or operator priorities. The association between operators and operands is easily determined by scanning the expression from right to left or from left to right, and employing a stack of operands. If an operand is encountered during this scan, it is stacked. If an operator is encountered, it is associated with the correct number of operands from the top of the stack. These operands are deleted from the stack and replaced by an operand that represents the result produced by the operator.

In a level-order traversal, elements are visited by level from top to bottom. Within levels, elements are visited from left to right. It is quite difficult to write a recursive function for level-order traversal, as the correct data structure to use here is a queue and not a stack. Program 8.6 traverses a binary tree in level order. It makes use of a linked queue (see the class `LinkedQueue` defined in Section 6.3). The elements of this queue are pointers to binary tree nodes. We could have used a formula-based queue instead.

```
template <class T>
void LevelOrder(BinaryTreeNode<T> *t)
{// Level-order traversal of *t.
   LinkedQueue<BinaryTreeNode<T>*> Q;
   while (t) {
      Visit(t);   // visit t

      // put t's children on queue
      if (t->LeftChild) Q.Add(t->LeftChild);
      if (t->RightChild) Q.Add(t->RightChild);

      // get next node to visit
      try {Q.Delete(t);}
      catch (OutOfBounds) {return;}
      }
}
```

Program 8.6 Level-order traversal

Program 8.6 enters the `while` loop only if the tree is not empty. The root is visted, and its children, if any, are added to the queue. In case a queue add operation fails, a `NoMem` exception is thrown by `Add` and function `LevelOrder` is exited as it does not catch the exception. Following the addition of the children of `t` to the queue, we attempt to delete an element from the queue. If the queue is empty, `Delete` throws an `OutOfBounds` exception, which is caught by the `catch` statement. Since an empty queue signifies the end of the traversal, we execute a `return`. If the queue is not empty, then `Delete` returns the deleted element in `t`. This deleted element points to the next node that is to be visited.

Let n be the number of elements in a binary tree `t`. The space complexity of each of the four traversal programs is O(n), and the time complexity is $\Theta(n)$. To verify this claim, observe that the recursion stack space needed by pre-, in-, and postorder traversal is $\Theta(n)$ when `t` has height n (as is the case for a right-skewed binary tree (Figure 8.9)); the queue space needed by level-order traversal is $\Theta(n)$ when `t` is a full binary tree. For the time complexity, observe that each of the traversal methods spends $\Theta(1)$ time at each node of the tree (assuming the time needed to visit a node is $\Theta(1)$).

EXERCISES

8. Write a procedure to perform a preorder traversal on a binary tree represented using the formula-based scheme. Assume that the elements of the binary tree are stored in the array `a` and that `last` is the position of the last element of the tree. `a[i]` = 0 iff there is no element at position `i`. What is the time complexity of your procedure?

9. Do Exercise 1 for inorder.

10. Do Exercise 1 for postorder.

11. Do Exercise 1 for level order.

12. Write a C++ function to make a copy of a binary tree represented using the formula-based scheme.

13. Write two C++ functions to copy a binary tree `t` that is represented using the template structure `BinaryTreeNode`. The first function should traverse the tree in postorder, and the second in preorder. What is the difference (if any) in the recursion stack space needed by these two functions?

14. Write a function to evaluate an expression tree `t` represented using the template structure `BinaryTreeNode`. Assume that each node has a field `value` that your procedure can use. The value field for nodes representing constants and variables contains the appropriate numeric value.

15. Write a function to erase a binary tree `t` (*Hint:* perform a postorder traversal). Assume that `t` is a linked tree and that the nodes are to be returned to the free-space list using the C++ function `delete`.

16. Write an iterative procedure to traverse a linked binary tree in inorder. Your procedure can use a formula-based stack. Make your procedure as elegant as possible. How much stack space does the traversal need? Give this stack space as a function of the number of nodes n in `t`.

17. Do Exercise 16 for preorder.

18. Do Exercise 16 for postorder.

★ 19. Suppose `t` is a binary tree whose data fields are of type `int`. Each node has a distinct data field. Do the pre- and inorder listings of the data fields uniquely define the binary tree? If so, write a function to construct the binary tree. What is the time complexity of your function?

20. Do Exercise 19 for pre- and postorder.

★ 21. Do Exercise 19 for in- and postorder.

22. Write a C++ function to accept an expression in postfix form and construct its binary tree representation. Assume that each operator may have either one or two operands.

★ 23. Do Exercise 22 beginning with the prefix form.

24. Write a C++ function to transform a postfix expression into its fully parenthesized infix form.

★ 25. Do Exercise 24 beginning with a prefix expression.

★ 26. Begin with an infix expression (not necessarily fully parenthesized) and obtain its postfix form. For this exercise assume that the permissible operators are binary +, -, *, / and the permissible delimiters are (and). Notice that since the order of operands is the same in infix, prefix, and postfix, the translation from infix to prefix or postfix can be done by scanning the infix form from left to right and outputting operands as they are encountered. Operators are held in a stack until the right time to output them, which is determined by assigning priorities to the operators and to (. Use the priorities 1 (for + and -) and 2 (for * and /). Use priority 3 for a (that is outside the stack and 0 for a (that is in the stack.

★ 27. Do Exercise 26 but this time generate the prefix form.

★ 28. Do Exercise 26 but this time generate the binary tree form.

29. Write a function to evaluate an expression that is in its postfix form. Assume a suitable array representation for the expression.

8.7   THE ADT *BinaryTree*

Now that we have some understanding of what a binary tree is, we can specify it as an abstract data type (ADT 8.1). Note that an abstract data type specification is to be independent of any potential implementation. Since the number of operations we may wish to perform on a binary tree is quite large, we list only some of the commonly performed ones. The ADT is extended in Section 8.9.

8.8   THE CLASS `BinaryTree`

Program 8.7 defines a C++ implementation of the ADT binary tree. This implementation defines a C++ class `BinaryTree` that employs a linked representation for binary trees. We have added the function `Visit` as a parameter to the traversal methods so that different operations may be implemented easily.

Program 8.8 gives the code for the public methods `Root`, `MakeTree`, and `BreakTree`, while Programs 8.9 and 8.10 give the codes for the private traversal methods. The codes for `MakeTree` and `BreakTree` require that the three trees involved in the operation be different. If these trees are not different, then the program may produce incorrect results. For example, the

---

AbstractDataType *BinaryTree* {
   instances: collection elements; if not empty, the collection is partitioned into a root, left subtree, and right subtree; each subtree is also a binary tree;

  operations:
     Create(): Create an empty binary tree;
     IsEmpty: Return **true** if empty, return **false** otherwise;
     Root(x): *x* is set to root element;
              return **false** if the operation fails, return **true** otherwise
     MakeTree(root,left,right): create a binary tree with *root* as the root
                  element, *left* (*right*) as the left (right) subtree.
     BreakTree(root,left,right): inverse of create
     PreOrder: preorder traversal of binary tree
     InOrder: inorder traversal of binary tree
     PostOrder: postorder traversal of binary tree
     LevelOrder: level-order traversal of binary tree
}

ADT 8.1 The abstract data type binary tree

invocation `Y.MakeTree(e,X,X)` results in a binary tree whose left and right subtrees share the same nodes. This sharing is correct only when `X` is the empty binary tree. The invocation `X.MakeTree(e,X,Y)` resets `X.root` (`left.root`) to zero just before returning. So regardless of what `X` and `Y` are initially, after `MakeTree`, `X` is the empty binary tree. In Exercise 30 you write a version of `MakeTree` and `BreakTree` that avoids these pitfalls.

    The sample code in Program 8.11 uses this class implementation. This code constructs a four-node binary tree and then performs a preorder traversal to determine the number of nodes in the tree.

8.9 ADT AND CLASS EXTENSIONS

We now extend our ADT definition 8.1 by adding the additional binary tree operations:

1.   *PreOutput():* output the data fields in preorder.

2.   *InOutput():* output the data fields in inorder.

3.   *PostOutput():* output the data fields in postorder.

4.   *LevelOutput():* output the data fields in level order.

```
template<class T>
class BinaryTree {
   public:
      BinaryTree() {root = 0;};
      ~BinaryTree(){};
      bool IsEmpty() const
         {return ((root) ? false : true);}
      bool Root(T& x) const;
      void MakeTree(const T& element,
           BinaryTree<T>& left, BinaryTree<T>& right);
      void BreakTree(T& element, BinaryTree<T>& left,
                       BinaryTree<T>& right);
      void PreOrder(void(*Visit)(BinaryTreeNode<T> *u))
           {PreOrder(Visit, root);}
      void InOrder(void(*Visit)(BinaryTreeNode<T> *u))
           {InOrder(Visit, root);}
      void PostOrder
           (void(*Visit) (BinaryTreeNode<T> *u));
           {PostOrder(Visit, root);}
      void LevelOrder
           (void(*Visit) (BinaryTreeNode<T> *u));
   private:
      BinaryTreeNode<T> *root;   // pointer to root
      void PreOrder(void(*Visit)
        (BinaryTreeNode<T> *u), BinaryTreeNode<T> *t);
      void InOrder(void(*Visit)
        (BinaryTreeNode<T> *u), BinaryTreeNode<T> *t);
      void PostOrder(void(*Visit)
        (BinaryTreeNode<T> *u), BinaryTreeNode<T> *t);
};
```

Program 8.7 Binary tree class

5.   *Delete()*: delete a binary tree, freeing up its nodes.

6.   *Height()*: return the tree height.

7.   *Size()*: return the number of nodes in the tree.

```
template<class T>
bool BinaryTree<T>::Root(T& x) const
{// Set x to root data.
 // Return false if no root.
   if (root) {x = root->data;
              return true;}
   else return false;  // no root
}

template<class T>
void BinaryTree<T>::MakeTree(const T& element,
         BinaryTree<T>& left, BinaryTree<T>& right)
{// Combine left, right, and element to make new tree.
 // left, right, and this must be different trees.
   // create combined tree
   root = new BinaryTreeNode<T>
              (element, left.root, right.root);

   // deny access from trees left and right
   left.root = right.root = 0;
}

template<class T>
void BinaryTree<T>::BreakTree(T& element,
       BinaryTree<T>& left, BinaryTree<T>& right)
{// left, right, and this must be different trees.
   // check if empty
   if (!root) throw BadInput(); // tree empty

   // break the tree
   element = root->data;
   left.root = root->LeftChild;
   right.root = root->RightChild;

   delete root;
   root = 0;
}
```

Program 8.8 Implementation of public members

```
template<class T>
void BinaryTree<T>::PreOrder(
          void(*Visit)(BinaryTreeNode<T> *u),
                         BinaryTreeNode<T> *t)
{// Preorder traversal.
   if (t) {Visit(t);
           PreOrder(Visit, t->LeftChild);
           PreOrder(Visit, t->RightChild);
           }
}

template <class T>
void BinaryTree<T>::InOrder(
          void(*Visit)(BinaryTreeNode<T> *u),
                         BinaryTreeNode<T> *t)
{// Inorder traversal.
   if (t) {InOrder(Visit, t->LeftChild);
           Visit(t);
           InOrder(Visit, t->RightChild);
           }
}

template <class T>
void BinaryTree<T>::PostOrder(
          void(*Visit)(BinaryTreeNode<T> *u),
                         BinaryTreeNode<T> *t)
{// Postorder traversal.
   if (t) {PostOrder(Visit, t->LeftChild);
           PostOrder(Visit, t->RightChild);
           Visit(t);
           }
}
```

Program 8.9 Pre-, in-, and postorder

```
template <class T>
void BinaryTree<T>::LevelOrder(
        void(*Visit)(BinaryTreeNode<T> *u))
{// Level-order traversal.
   LinkedQueue<BinaryTreeNode<T>*> Q;
   BinaryTreeNode<T> *t;
   t = root;
   while (t) {
      Visit(t);
      if (t->LeftChild) Q.Add(t->LeftChild);
      if (t->RightChild) Q.Add(t->RightChild);
      try {Q.Delete(t);}
      catch (OutOfBounds) {return;}
      }
}
```

Program 8.10 Level-order traversal

```
#include <iostream.h>
#include "binary.h"

int count = 0;
BinaryTree<int> a,x,y,z;

template<class T>
void ct(BinaryTreeNode<T> *t) {count++;}

void main(void)
{
   y.MakeTree(1,a,a);
   z.MakeTree(2,a,a);
   x.MakeTree(3,y,z);
   y.MakeTree(4,x,a);
   y.PreOrder(ct);
   cout << count << endl;
}
```

Program 8.11 Application of the class BinaryTree

8.9.1 Output

The four output functions are easily implemented by defining a private static member `Output` for the class. This static member takes the form:

```
static void Output(BinaryTreeNode<T> *t)
          {cout << t->data << ' ';}
```

The four public output functions now take the form:

```
void PreOutput()
     {PreOrder(Output, root); cout << endl;}
void InOutput()
     {InOrder(Output, root); cout << endl;}
void PostOutput()
     {PostOrder(Output, root); cout << endl;}
void LevelOutput()
     {LevelOrder(Output); cout << endl;}
```

When the time complexity of the `Visit` operation is $\Theta(1)$, each traversal method takes $\Theta(n)$ time (assuming the traversal is successful) on a binary tree with n nodes. Hence the time complexity of each output method is $\Theta(n)$.

8.9.2 Delete

To delete a binary tree, we need to delete its nodes. The nodes may be deleted by a postorder traversal in which each node is deleted when it is visited. That is, we first delete the left subtree, then the right subtree, and then the root. The public member function `Delete` takes the form:

```
void Delete() {PostOrder(Free, root); root = 0;}
```

where `Free` is the private member function:

```
static void Free(BinaryTreeNode<T> *t) {delete t;}
```

The time complexity of the `Delete` function is $\Theta(n)$ where n is the number of nodes in the binary tree to be deleted.

8.9.3 Height

We can find the height of a binary tree by performing a postorder traversal. We first determine the height `hl` of the left subtree; then that of the right subtree (`hr`). During the visit step, the height of the tree is determined as

$$\max\{hl, hr\} + 1$$

Unfortunately, we cannot use the postorder traversal code of Program 8.9, as we need a traversal that returns a value (i.e., the height of a subtree). To implement the public member function `Height`, we add the following statement to the public part of Program 8.7:

```
int Height() const {return Height(root);}
```

and the following to the private part:

```
int Height(BinaryTreeNode<T> *t) const;
```

The private member function `Height` is defined in Program 8.12. Its time complexity is $\Theta(n)$ where n is the number of nodes in the binary tree.

```
template <class T>
int BinaryTree<T>::Height(BinaryTreeNode<T> *t) const
{// Return height of tree *t.
   if (!t) return 0;                        // empty tree
   int hl = Height(t->LeftChild);   // height of left
   int hr = Height(t->RightChild); // height of right
   if (hl > hr) return ++hl;
   else return ++hr;
}
```

Program 8.12 Height of a binary tree

8.9.4   Size

We can use any of the four traversal methods to determine the number of nodes in a binary tree. Since each traversal method visits each node exactly once, we need merely add one to a global counter when a node is visited. The sample program of Program 8.11 determines the size using a user-defined function `ct`. We may define an equivalent class member function (called `Size`) by adding the following to the public part of Program 8.7:

```
int Size()
   {_count = 0;
   PreOrder(Add1, root);
   return _count;}
```

`_count` is defined as an integer variable outside the class definition using the statement

```
int _count;
```

and the private member function Add1 is

```
static void Add1(BinaryTreeNode<T> *t) {_count++;}
```

The time complexity of Size is $\Theta(n)$ where n is the number of nodes in the binary tree.

EXERCISES

30. Write a new version of the binary tree member functions MakeTree and BreakTree that checks whether the three trees involved in each operation are distinct. If not, decide what action to take and code your functions appropriately.

31. (a) Extend the ADT *BinaryTree* to include the operation *Compare* (X), which compares a binary tree with the binary tree *X*. It returns true if the two binary trees are identical and false otherwise.

    (b) Now extend the C++ class BinaryTree to include a public compare function. Test your code.

32. (a) Extend the ADT *BinaryTree* to include the operation *Copy* (), which creates a new copy of a binary tree. If the operation fails, throw a suitable exception.

    (b) Now extend the C++ class BinaryTree to include a public copy function. Test your code.

★ 33. Develop a class Expression as a derived class of BinaryTree. The class should permit the following operations:

    (a) Output the fully parenthesized infix form of the expression.

    (b) Output the prefix and postfix forms.

    (c) Convert from prefix to expression tree.

    (d) Convert from postfix to expression tree.

    (e) Convert from infix to expression tree.

    (f) Evaluate an expression tree.

    Test the correctness of your code using suitable data.

8.10   APPLICATIONS

8.10.1   Placement of Signal Boosters

In a distribution network a resource is distributed from its origin to several other sites. For example, petroleum or natural gas can be distributed using a network of pipes from the source of the petroleum/natural gas to the consumption sites. Similarly, electrical power may be distributed using a network of wires from the power plant to the points of consumption. We shall use the term **signal** to refer to the resource (petroleum, natural gas, power, etc.) that is to be distributed. While the signal is being transported through the distribution network, it may experience a loss in or degradation of one or more of its characteristics. For example, there may be a pressure drop along a natural gas pipeline or a voltage drop along an electrical transmission line. In other situations noise may enter the signal as it moves along the network. Between the signal source and point of consumption, we can tolerate only a certain amount, *tolerance*, of signal degradation. To guarantee a degradation that does not exceed this amount, **signal boosters** are placed at strategic places in the network. A signal booster might, for example, increase the signal pressure or voltage so that it equals that at the source or may enhance the signal so that the signal-to-noise ratio is the same as that at the source. In this section we develop an algorithm to determine where to place signal boosters. Our objective is to minimize the number of boosters in use while ensuring that the degradation in signal (relative to that at the source) does not exceed the given tolerance.

To simplify the problem, we assume that the distribution network is a tree with the source as the root. Each node in the tree (other than the root) represents a substation where we can place a booster. Some of these nodes also represent points of consumption. The signal flows from a node to its children. Figure 8.12 shows a distribution network that is a tree. Each edge is labeled by the amount of signal degradation that takes place when a signal flows between the corresponding parent and child. The units of degradation are assumed to be additive. That is, when a signal flows from node p to node v in Figure 8.12, the degradation is 5. The degradation from node q to node x is 3.

Let $d(i)$ denote the degradation between node i and its parent. Therefore, in Figure 8.12, $d(w) = 2$, $d(p) = 0$, and $d(r) = 3$. Since signal boosters can be placed only at nodes of the distribution tree, the presence of a node i with $d(i) >$ *tolerance* implies that no placement of boosters can prevent signal degradation from exceeding *tolerance*. For example, if *tolerance* = 1, then there is no way to place signal boosters so that the degradation between p and r is ≤ 1 in Figure 8.12.

For any node i, let $D(i)$ denote the maximum signal degradation from node i to any leaf in the subtree rooted at i. If i is a leaf node, than $D(i) = 0$. For the example of Figure 8.12, $D(i) = 0$ for $i \in \{ w, x, t, y, z \}$. For the remaining

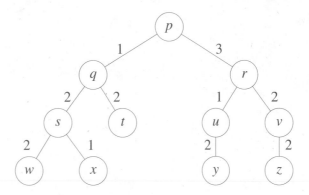

Figure 8.12 Tree distribution network

nodes, $D(i)$ may be computed using the following equality:

$$D(i) = \max_{j \text{ is a child of } i} \{ D(j) + d(j) \}$$

So $D(s) = 2$. To use this equation, we must compute the D value of a node after computing that of its children. Therefore, we must traverse the tree so that we visit a node after we visit its children. We can compute the D value of a node when we visit it. This traversal order is a natural extension of postorder traversal to trees of degree (possibly) more than two.

Suppose that during the computation of D as described above, we encounter a node i with a child j such that $D(j) + d(j) > tolerance$. If we do not place a booster at j, then the signal degradation from i to a leaf will exceed *tolerance* even if a booster is placed at i. For example, in Figure 8.12, when computing $D(q)$, we compute $D(s) + d(s) = 4$. If *tolerance* = 3, then placing a booster at q or at one of its ancestors doesn't reduce signal degradation between q and its descendents. We need to place a booster at s or at one or more of its children. If a booster is placed at s, then $D(q) = 2$.

The pseudocode to place boosters and compute D is

```
D(i) = 0;
for (each child j of i)
    if (D(j) + d(j)) > tolerance) place a booster at j;
    else D(i) = max {D(i), D(j) + d(j)};
```

Applying this computation method to the distribution tree of Figure 8.12 results in the placement of boosters at nodes r, s, and v (see Figure 8.13). The D values for nodes are given inside the node.

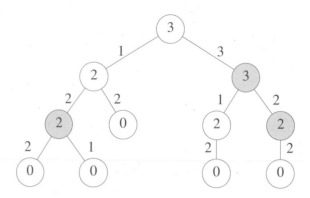

Signal boosters are at shaded nodes
Numbers inside nodes are D values

Figure 8.13 Distribution network with signal boosters

Theorem 8.1 The procedure outlined above uses the minimum number of boosters.

Proof The proof is by induction on the number n of nodes in the distribution tree. If $n = 1$, the theorem is trivially valid. Assume that the theorem is valid for $n \le m$ where m is an arbitrary natural number. Let t be a tree with $n + 1$ nodes. Let X be the set of vertices at which the outlined procedure places boosters and let W be a minimum cardinality placement of boosters that satisfies the tolerance requrements. We need to show that $|X| = |W|$.

If $|X| = 0$, then $|X| = |W|$. If $|X| > 0$, then let z be the first vertex at which a booster is placed by the outlined procedure. Let t_z be the subtree of t rooted at z. Since $D(z) + d(z) > tolerance$, W must contain at least one vertex u that is in t_z. If W contains more than one such u, then W cannot be of minimum cardinality because by placing boosters at $W - \{$ all such $u \} + \{z\}$, we can satisfy the tolerance requirement. Hence W contains exactly one such u. Let W' $= W - \{u\}$. Let t' be the tree that results from the removal of t_z from t except z. We see that W' is a minimum cardinality booster placement for t' that satisfies the tolerance requirement. Also, $X' = $ X $- \{z\}$ satisfies the tolerance requirement for t' and is the booster placement generated by our outlined procedure on the tree t'. Since the number of vertices in t' is less than $m + 1$, $|X'| = |W'|$. Hence $|X| = |X'| + 1 = |W'| + 1 = |W|$. ∎

When no node of the distribution tree has more than two children, it may be represented as a binary tree using the classes `BinaryTree` (Program 8.7) and `Booster` (Program 8.13). The field `boost` is used to differentiate between nodes at which a booster is placed and those where it is not. The data fields of our binary tree will be of type `Booster`. The overloading of the output operator `<<` is necessary as the extensions to Program 8.7 made in Section 8.9 defined a static `Output` function that outputs the data field of a node.

```
class Booster {
   public:
      void Output(ostream& out) const
         {out << boost << ' ' << D << ' ' << d << ' ';}
   private:
      int D,        // degradation to leaf
          d;        // degradation from parent
      bool boost;   // true iff booster here
};

// overload <<
ostream& operator<<(ostream& out, Booster x)
   {x.Output(out); return out;}
```

Program 8.13 The class `Booster`

We can compute the D values for the nodes and the location of a minimum set of boosters by performing a postorder traversal of the binary distribution tree. During the visit step, we execute the code of Program 8.14. The code for `PlaceBoosters` assumes that it is a friend of `Booster` and that `tolerance` is defined as a global variable.

If `X` is a member of the class `BinaryTree<Booster>` whose `d` fields have been set to the degradation values and `boost` fields to 0, then the invocation `X.PostOrder(PlaceBoosters)` will reset the `D` and `boost` fields correctly. The values computed by `PlaceBoosters` can be output using the invocation `X.PostOutput()`. Since the complexity of `PlaceBoosters` is $\Theta(1)$, the invocation `X.PostOrder(PlaceBoosters)` takes $\Theta(n)$ time where n is the number of nodes in the distribution tree.

Binary Tree Representation of a Tree

When the distribution tree `t` contains nodes that have more than two children, we can still represent the tree as a binary tree. This time, for each node `x` of the tree `t`, we link its children into a chain using the `RightChild` fields of the children nodes. The `LeftChild` field of `x` points to the first node in this chain. The `RightChild` field of `x` is used for the chain of `x`'s siblings.

```
void PlaceBoosters(BinaryTreeNode<Booster> *x)
{// Computer degradation at *x.  Place booster
 // here if degradation exceeds tolerance.
   BinaryTreeNode<Booster> *y = x->LeftChild;
   int degradation;
   x->data.D = 0;   // initialize degradation at x
   if (y) {// compute from left child
           degradation = y->data.D + y->data.d;
           if (degradation > tolerance)
              {y->data.boost = true;
                return;}
           else x->data.D = degradation;
           }
   y = x->RightChild;
   if (y) {// compute from right child
           degradation = y->data.D + y->data.d;
           if (degradation > tolerance)
              y->data.boost = true;
           else if (x->data.D < degradation)
                   x->data.D = degradation;
           }
}
```

Program 8.14 Place boosters and determine D for binary distribution trees

Figure 8.14 shows a tree and its binary tree representation. Solid lines represent left child pointers, and right child pointers are shown as dotted lines.

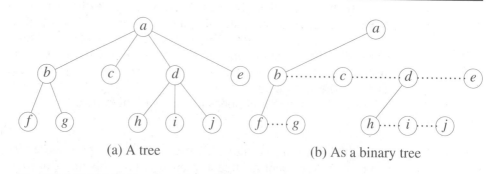

(a) A tree   (b) As a binary tree

Figure 8.14 A tree and its binary tree representation

When the binary tree representation of a tree is used, the invocation `X.PostOrder(PlaceBoosters)` does not have the desired effect. The development of the new function to compute `D` and `boost` is considered in Exercise 37.

8.10.2   Online Equivalence Classes

The online equivalence problem was introduced in Section 3.8.3. Basically, we begin with n elements numbered 1 through n; initially, each is in a class of its own, and we perform a sequence of `Find` and `Combine` operations. The operation `Find(e)` returns a unique characteristic of the class that element `e` is in, and `Combine(a,b)` combines the classes that contain the elements `a` and `b`. In Section 3.8.3 we saw that `Combine(a,b)` is usually implemented using the union operation `Union(i,j)` where `i = Find(a)`, `j = Find(b)`, and `i ≠ j`. The solution provided in Section 3.8.3 used chains and had a complexity $O(n + u\log u + f)$ where u is the number of union operations and f is the number of find operations performed. The online equivalence problem is also known as the **disjoint set union-find** problem. Notice that the equivalence classes may be viewed as disjoint sets of elements.

In this section we explore an alternative solution in which each set (or class) is represented as a tree. Figure 8.15 shows some sets represented as trees. Notice that each node that is not a root points to its parent in the tree; we intend to use the root element as the set identifier. Hence we say that the elements 1, 2, 20, 30, and so on are in the set with root 20; the elements 11, 16, 25, and 28 are in the set with root 16; the element 15 is in the set with root 15; and the elements 26 and 32 are in the set with root 26 (or simply the set 26).

Tree Representation

The solution to the union-find problem is a good example of the use of simulated pointers. A linked representation of the trees is needed. Each node must have a `parent` field. Children fields are, however, not needed. We also have a need to make direct access to nodes. To find the set containing element 10, we need to determine which node represents the element 10 and then follow a sequence of `parent` links to the root. This direct access is best obtained if the nodes are indexed 1 through `n` (the number of elements) and if node e represents element e. Each `parent` field gives the index of the parent node. Hence the `parent` fields are of type `int`. Figure 8.16 represents the trees of Figure 8.15 using this representation. The number inside a node is the value of its parent field. The number outside a node is its index. This index is also the element it represents. The parent field for a root node is set to 0. Since there is no node with index 0, a parent field of 0 is detected as a link to no node (or a null link).

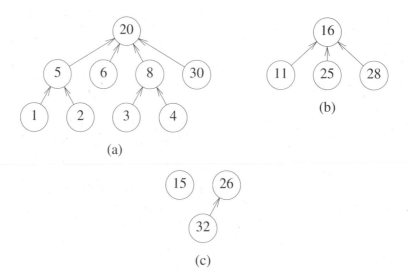

Figure 8.15 Tree representation of disjoint sets

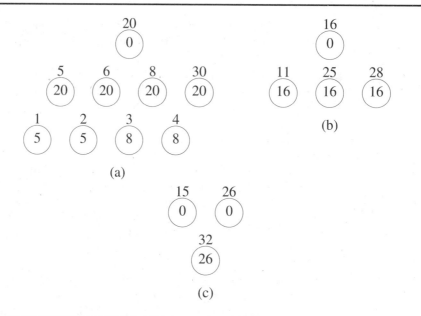

Figure 8.16 Representation of trees of Figure 8.15

Since each node has only one field, the declaration

```
int *parent;
```

suffices.

Operations

Each element starts in a set of its own. To create the initial configuration, we need to allocate space for the array `parent` and to set `parent[1:n]` to 0. This initialization is done by function `Initialize` of Program 8.15. The complexity of `Initialize` is $\Theta(n)$.

```
void Initialize(int n)
{// One element per set/class/tree.
   parent = new int[n+1];
   for (int e = 1; e <= n; e++)
      parent[e] = 0;
}

int Find(int e)
{// Return root of tree containing i.
   while (parent[e])
      e = parent[e];   // move up one level
   return e;
}

void Union(int i, int j)
{// Combine trees with roots i and j.
   parent[j] = i;
}
```

Program 8.15 Simple tree solution to union-find problem

To find the set that contains element `e`, we begin at node `e` and follow `parent` links until we reach the root. For instance, if `e` = 4 and the status of the sets is as in Figure 8.15(a), we begin at 4. The `parent` field gets us to node 8. Its `parent` field gets us to node 20 whose `parent` is 0. Hence 20 is the root and is therefore the set identifier. Function `Find` of Program 8.15 implements this strategy. This function assumes that the test $1 \leq e \leq n$ (i.e., `e` is a valid element) is performed externally. The complexity of `Find` is $O(h)$ where h is the height of the tree that contains element `e`.

The union of the sets with roots `i` and `j`, $i \neq j$, is obtained by making either `i` a subtree of `j` or `j` a subtree of `i`. For instance, if `i` = 16 and `j` =

26 (Figure 8.15), the tree of Figure 8.17(a) results if i is made a subtree of j, while the result is Figure 8.17(b) if j is made a subtree of i. Function Union of Program 8.15 performs a union. It assumes that the check i ≠ j is performed before it is invoked. j is always made a subtree of i. The complexity of Union is $\Theta(1)$.

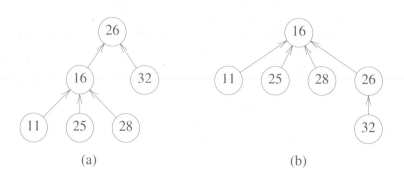

(a) (b)

Figure 8.17 Union

Performance Evaluation

Assume that u unions and f finds are to be performed. Since each union is necessarily preceded by two finds, we may assume that $f > u$. Each union takes $\Theta(1)$ time. The time for each find depends on the height of the trees that get created. In the worst case a tree with m elements can have a height of m. This worst case happens, for example, when the following sequence of unions is performed:

$$Union\,(2,1),\ Union\,(3,2),\ Union\,(4,3),\ Union\,(5,4),\ \cdots$$

Hence each find can take as much as $\Theta(q)$ time where q is the number of unions that have been performed before the find.

Performance Enhancement

We can enhance the performance of the union-find algorithms by using either the **weight** or the **height** rule when performing a union of the trees with roots i and j.

Definition [*Weight rule*] If the number of nodes in tree i is less than the number in tree j, then make j the parent of i; otherwise, make i the parent of j. ■

Definition [*Height rule*] If the height of tree i is less than that of tree j, then make j the parent of i; otherwise, make i the parent of j. ■

If we perform a union on the trees of Figure 8.15 (a) and (b), then the tree with root 16 becomes a subtree of the tree with root 20, regardless of whether the weight or the height rule is used. When we perform a union on the trees of Figure 8.18 (a) and (b), the tree with root 16 becomes a subtree of the tree with root 20 in case the weight rule is used. However, when the height rule is used, the tree with root 20 becomes a subtree of the one with root 16.

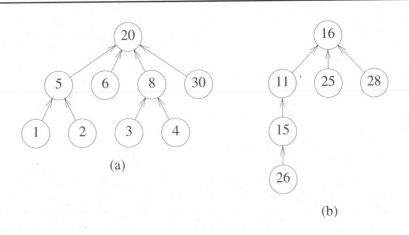

Figure 8.18 Two sample trees

To incorporate the weight rule into the procedure for a union, we add a Boolean field `root` to each node. The `root` field of a node is `true` iff the node is presently a root node. The `parent` field of each root node is used to keep a count of the total number of nodes in the tree. For the trees of Figure 8.15, we have `root[i]` = `true` iff `i` = 20, 16, 15, or 26. Also, `parent[i]` = 9, 4, 1, and 2 for `i` = 20, 16, 15, and 26, respectively. The remaining `parent` fields are unchanged.

The initialization, find, and union procedures now take the form given in Program 8.16. These codes assume that `root` has been declared as follow:

```
bool *root;
```

Exercise 44 asks you to redo these codes using a single array in which each element has the two fields `parent` and `root`.

The time required to perform a union has increased somewhat but is still bounded by a constant; it is $\Theta(1)$. Lemma 8.1 determines the maximum time to perform a find.

```
void Initialize(int n)
{// One element per set/class/tree.
   root = new bool[n+1];
   parent = new int[n+1];
   for (int e = 1; e <= n; e++) {
      parent[e] = 1;
      root[e] = true;}
}

int Find(int e)
{// Return root of tree containing e.
   while (!root[e])
      e = parent[e];   // move up one level
   return e;
}

void Union(int i, int j)
{// Combine trees with roots i and j.
 // Use weighting rule.
   if (parent[i] < parent[j]) {
      // i becomes subtree of j
      parent[j] += parent[i];
      root[i] = false;
      parent[i] = j; }
   else {// j becomes subtree of i
      parent[i] += parent[j];
      root[j] = false;
      parent[j] = i;}
}
```

Program 8.16 Unioning with the weight rule

Lemma 8.1 [*Weight rule lemma*] Assume that we start with singleton sets and perform unions using the weight rule (as in Program 8.16). Let t be a tree with p nodes created in this way. The height of t is at most $\lfloor \log_2 p \rfloor + 1$.

Proof The lemma is clearly true for $p = 1$. Assume it is true for all trees with i nodes, $i \le p - 1$. We shall show that it is also true for $i = p$. Let t be a tree with p nodes created by Program 8.16. Consider the last union operation performed, *union(k,j)*. Let m be the number of nodes in tree j, and let $p - m$ be the number of nodes in k. Without loss of generality we may assume $1 \le m \le p/2$. Then the height of t either is the same as that of k or is one more than that of j. If the former is the case then the height of t is $\leq \lfloor \log_2 (p - m) \rfloor + 1 \leq \lfloor \log_2 p \rfloor + 1$. If the latter is the case then the height of t is $\leq \lfloor \log_2 m \rfloor + 2 \leq \lfloor \log_2 p/2 \rfloor + 2 \leq \lfloor \log_2 p \rfloor + 1$. ■

If we start with singleton sets and perform an intermixed sequence of u unions and f finds, no set will have more than $u + 1$ elements in it. From Lemma 8.1, it follows that when the weight rule is used, the cost of the sequence of union and find operations (excluding the initialization time) is $O(u + f \log u)$. We can show that when the weight rule is replaced by the height rule in Program 8.16, the bound of Lemma 8.1 still governs the height of the resulting trees. Exercises 40, 41, and 42 explore the use of the height rule.

Further improvement in the worst-case performance is possible by modifying the find procedure of Program 8.16 so as to reduce the length of the path from the find element e to the root. This reduction in path length is obtained using a process called **path compression**, which we can do in at least three different ways. In the first way, called **path compaction**, we change the pointers from all nodes on the path from e (the element being searched) to the root so that these nodes point directly to the root. As an example, consider the tree of Figure 8.19. When we perform a Find(10), the nodes 10, 15, and 3 are determined to be on the path from 10 to the root. Their parent fields are changed to 2, and the tree of Figure 8.20 is obtained. (Since node 3 already points to 2, its field doesn't have to be changed; when writing the program, it turns out to be easier to include this node in the set of nodes whose parent field is to be changed.)

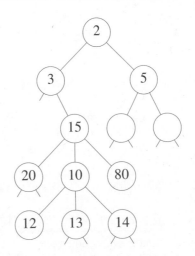

Figure 8.19 Sample tree

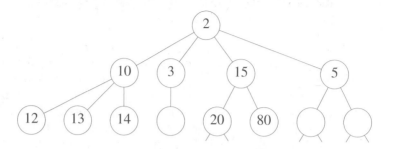

Figure 8.20 Path compaction

Although path compaction increases the time needed for an individual find, it reduces the cost of future finds. For instance, finding the elements in the subtrees of 10 and 15 is quicker in the compacted tree of Figure 8.20. Program 8.17 implements the compaction rule.

```
int Find(int e)
{// Return root of tree containing e.
 // Compact path from e to root.
   int j = e;
   // find root
   while (!root[j])
      j = parent[j];

   // compact
   int f = e;   // start at e
   while (f != j) {// f is not root
      int pf = parent[f];
      parent[f] = j;   // move f to level 2
      f = pf;          // f moves to old parent
      }

   return j;
}
```

Program 8.17 Path compaction

The remaining two path compression methods are **path splitting** and **path halving**. In path splitting we change the parent pointer in each node (except the root and its child) on the path from e to the root to point to the node's original grandparent. In the tree of Figure 8.19, path splitting beginning at node 13 results in the tree of Figure 8.21. Note that when we use path splitting, a single pass from e to the root suffices.

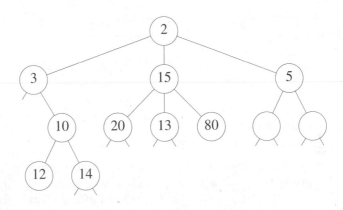

Figure 8.21 Path splitting

In path halving we change the parent pointer of every other node (except the root and its child) on the path from e to the root to point to the node's grandparent. As a result, in path halving, only half as many pointers are changed as in path splitting. As in the case of path splitting, a single pass from e to the root suffices. Figure 8.22 shows the result of path halving beginning at node 13 of Figure 8.19.

With the suggested enhancements to the union and find algorithms, the time needed to process an intermixed sequence of union and finds is almost linear in the number of unions and finds. To state the time complexity more precisely, we first define the Ackermann's function $A(i,j)$ and its inverse $\alpha(p,q)$ as follows:

$$A(1,j) = 2^j, \qquad\qquad \text{for } j \geq 1$$
$$A(i,1) = A(i-1,2) \qquad \text{for } i \geq 2$$
$$A(i,j) = A(i-1, A(i,j-1)) \quad \text{for } i,j \geq 2$$

$$\alpha(p,q) = \min\{z \geq 1 \mid A(z, \lfloor p/q \rfloor) > \log_2 q\}, \; p \geq q \geq 1$$

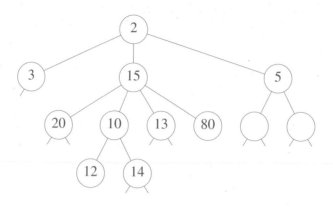

Figure 8.22 Path halving

The function $A(i,j)$ is a very rapidly growing function. Consequently, α grows very slowly as p and q are increased. In fact, since $A(3,1) = 16$, $\alpha(p,q) \leq 3$ for $q < 2^{16} = 65{,}536$ and $p \geq q$. Since $A(4,1)$ is a very, very large number and in our application q will be the number n of set elements and p will be $n + f$ (f is the number of finds), $\alpha(p,q) \leq 4$ for all practical purposes.

Theorem 8.2 [*Tarjan and Van Leeuwen*] Let $T(f,u)$ be the maximum time required to process any intermixed sequence of f finds and u unions. Assume that $u \geq n/2$. Then

$$k_1(n + f\,\alpha(f+n,n)) \leq T(f,u) \leq k_2(n + f\,\alpha(f+n,n))$$

for some positive constants k_1 and k_2. These bounds apply when we start with singleton sets and use either the weight or height rule for unions and any one of the three path compression methods for a find. ∎

The requirement that $u \geq n/2$ in Theorem 8.2 is really not significant becaue when $u < n/2$, some elements are not involved in union operations. These elements remain in singleton sets throughout the sequence of union and find operations, and we can eliminate them from consideration because find operations that involve these elements can be done in O(1) time each. Even though the function $\alpha(f,u)$ is a very slowly growing function, the complexity of *union-find* is not linear in the number of unions and finds. As far as the space requirements are concerned, each element needs one node.

EXERCISES

34. Draw the binary tree representations of the trees of Figures 8.15 (a) and (b), Figures 8.17 (a) and (b), and Figures 8.18 (a) and (b).

35. Draw the binary tree representation of the tree of Figure 8.12. (Note that the binary tree representation of this tree different from that obtained by using the left-child pointer of a node to point to one child and the right-child pointer to point to the other.)

36. A **forest** is a collection of zero or more trees. In the binary tree representation of a tree, the root has no right child. We may use this observation to arrive at a binary tree representation for a forest with m trees. First, we obtain the binary tree representation of each tree in the forest. Next, the ith tree is made the right subtree of the $(i-1)$th, $2 \leq i \leq m$. Draw the binary tree representation of the four-tree forest of Figure 8.15, the two-tree forest of Figure 8.17, and the two-tree forest of Figure 8.18.

37. Let `t` be a member of the class `BinaryTree`. Assume that `t` is the binary tree representation of a distribution tree (see Figure 8.14). Obtain a program to compute the `D` and `boost` values of each node in `t`. Your program should also output these values by invoking `t.PostPrint()`. Test the correctness of your program using suitable distribution trees.

38. Suppose we start with n sets, each containing a distinct element.
    (a) Show that if u unions are peformed, then no set contains more than $u + 1$ elements.
    (b) Show that at most $n - 1$ unions can be performed before the number of sets becomes one.
    (c) Show that if fewer than $\lceil n/2 \rceil$ unions are performed, then at least one set with a single element in it remains.
    (d) Show that if u unions are performed, then at least max $\{n - 2u, 0\}$ singleton sets remain.

39. Give an example of a sequence of unions that start with singleton sets and create trees whose height equals the upper bound given in Lemma 8.1. Assume that each union is performed using the weight rule.

40. Write a version of function `Union` (Program 8.16) that uses the height rule instead of the weight rule.

41. Prove Lemma 8.1 for the case when the height rule is used instead of the weight rule.

42. Give an example of a sequence of unions that start with singleton sets and create trees whose height equals the upper bound given in Lemma 8.1. Assume that each union is performed using the height rule.

43. Compare the average performance of the code of Program 8.15 with that of Program 8.16 (replace the find function of Program 8.16 with that given in Program 8.17). Do this comparison for different values of n. For each value of n, generate a random sequence of pairs $(i\ j)$. Replace each pair by two finds (one for i and the other for j). If the two are in different sets, then a union is to be performed. Repeat the experiment using many different random sequences. Measure the total time taken over these sequences. It is left to you to take this basic description of the experiment and plan a meaningful experiment to compare the average performance of the two sets of programs. Write a report that describes your experiment and your conclusions. Include program listings, a table of average times, and graphs in your report.

44. Rewrite Programs 8.16 and 8.17 using an array of nodes of type `Node`. `Node` may be defined as a class; each instance of this class has the private members `parent` and `root`. If the array is `E[0:n+1]`, then `E[e].parent` is the parent of element `e` and `E[e].root` is `true` iff `e` is a root.

45. Write a function for the find operation that uses path splitting instead of path compaction (as used in Program 8.17).

46. Write a function for the find operation that uses path halving instead of path compaction (as used in Program 8.17).

8.11 REFERENCES AND SELECTED READINGS

The problem of placing boosters is studied in the following papers: ''Deleting Vertices in Dags to Bound Path Lengths'' by D. Paik, S. Reddy, and S. Sahni, *IEEE Transactions on Computers*, 43, 9, 1994, 1091–1096, and ''Heuristics for the Placement of Flip-Flops in Partial Scan Designs and for the Placement of Signal Boosters in Lossy Circuits'' by D. Paik, S. Reddy, and S. Sahni, *Sixth International Conference On VLSI Design*, 1993, 45–50.

A complete analysis of the tree representations for the inline equivalence problem appears in the paper ''Worst Case Analysis of Set Union Algorithms'' by R. Tarjan and J. Leeuwen, *Journal of the ACM*, 31, 2, 1984, 245–281.

CHAPTER 9

PRIORITY QUEUES

BIRD'S-EYE VIEW

Unlike the queues of Chapter 6, which are FIFO structures, the order of deletion from a priority queue is determined by the element priority. Elements are deleted either in increasing or decreasing order of priority rarther than in the order in which they arrived in the queue.

A priority queue is efficiently implemented using the heap data structure, which is a complete binary tree that is most efficiently stored using the formula-based representation described in Section 8.4. Linked data structures suitable for the implementation of a priority queue include height- and weight-balanced leftist trees. This chapter covers both heaps and leftist trees.

In the applications section we use heaps to develop an O($n$log$n$) sorting method called heap sort. The sort methods of Chapter 2 take O(n^2) to sort n elements. Even though the bin sort and radix sort methods of Chapter 3 run in $\Theta(n)$ time, they are limited to elements with keys in an appropriate range. So heap sort is the first general-purpose sort we are seeing that has a complexity better than O(n^2). Chapter 14 discusses other sort methods with this complexity. From the asymptotic-complexity point of view, heap sort is an optimal sorting method, as we can show that every general-purpose sorting method that relies on comparing pairs of elements has a complexity that is $\Omega(n\log n)$ (Section 14.4.2).

The other applications considered in this chapter are machine scheduling and the generation of Huffman codes. The machine-scheduling application allows us to introduce the NP-hard class of problems. This class includes problems for which no polynomial-time algorithms are known. As noted in Chapter 2, for large instances only polynomial-time algorithms are practical. As a result, NP-hard problems are often solved by approximation algorithms or heuristics that complete in a reasonable amount of computer time, but do not guarantee to find the best answer. For the machine-scheduling application, we use the heap data structure to obtain an efficient implementation of a much-studied machine-scheduling approximation algorithm. Although we do not consider any applications of leftist trees in this chapter, the machine-shop simulation problem of Section 6.4.4 is a good application.

9.1   INTRODUCTION

A **priority queue** is a collection of zero or more elements. Each element has a priority or value. The operations performed on a priority queue are (1) find an element, (2) insert a new element, and (3) delete an element. In a **min priority queue** the find operation finds the element with minimum priority, while the delete operation deletes this element. In a **max priority queue**, the find operation finds the element with maximum priority, and the delete operation deletes this element. The elements in a priority queue need not have distinct priorities. The find and delete operations may break ties in any manner.

The abstract data type specification for a max priority queue is given in ADT 9.1. The specification for a min priority queue is the same except that min and delete min operations operations replace the max and delete max operations.

AbstractDataType *MaxPriorityQueue* {
   instances
      finite collection of elements, each has a priority
   operations
      Create( ): create an empty priority queue
      Size( ): return number of elements in the queue
      Max( ): return element with maximum priority
      Insert(x): insert x into the queue
      DeleteMax(x): delete the element with largest priority from the queue;
                    return this element in x;
}

ADT 9.1 Abstract data type specification of a max priority queue

Example 9.1 Suppose that we are selling the services of a machine. Each user pays a fixed amount per use. However, the time needed by each user is different. To maximize the returns from this machine under the assumption that the machine is not to be kept idle unless no user is available, we maintain a min priority queue of all users waiting to use the machine. The priority of a user is the amount of time he/she needs. When a new user requests the machine, his/her request is put into the priority queue. Whenever the machine becomes available, the user with smallest time requirement (i.e., priority) is selected.

If each user needs the same amount of time on the machine but users are willing to pay different amounts for the service, then we can use a priority queue in which the element priorities are the amount of payment. Whenever the machine becomes available, the user paying the most is selected. This selection requires a max priority queue. ∎

Example 9.2 The machine-shop simulation problem was introduced in Section 6.4.4. The operations performed on the event queue are (1) find the machine with minimum finish time and (2) change the finish time of this machine. Suppose we set up a min priority queue in which each element represents a machine, and an element's priority is the finish time of the machine it represents. The find operation of a min priority queue gives us the machine with the smallest finish time. To change a machine's finish time, we may first do a delete min and then an insert with the priority changed to the new finish time. Actually, for event list applications we may extend the ADT min priority queue to include an operation to change the priority of the min element to a new value.

Max priority may also be used in the machine-shop simulation problem. In the simulation programs of Section 6.4.4, each machine served its set of waiting jobs in a first-come-first-served manner. Therefore, we used a FIFO queue at each machine. If the service discipline is changed to "when a machine is ready for a new job, it selects the waiting job with maximum priority," we need a max priority queue at each machine. The operations to be performed at each machine are (1) when a new job arrives at the machine, it is inserted into the max priority queue for that machine, and (2) when a machine is ready to work on a new job, a job with maximum priority is deleted from its queue and made active.

When the service discipline at each machine is changed as above, the simulation problem of Section 6.4.4 requires a min priority queue for the event list and a max priority queue at each machine. In the simulation model of Section 6.4.4, we know the size of the event list in advance. This size equals the number of machines and does not change as the simulation progresses. As a result, a formula-based priority queue is suitable. In a more general simulation, we might allow for the introduction of new machines and the removal of old ones. In this case we might be better off with a linked priority queue; when such a queue is used, we do not need to predict its maximum size at the time the queue is created nor do we need to dynamically change the size of an array.

The priority queues at each machine should, however, be linked queues. The reasoning is the same as for our choice of linked FIFO queues over formula-based ones in Section 6.4.4. The size of individual queues varies widely during simulation, but the sum of the sizes of all queues is at most the number of incomplete jobs. ■

In this chapter we develop efficient representations for priority queues. Since the representations for min and max priority queues are very similar, we explicitly develop only those for max priority queues.

9.2 LINEAR LISTS

The simplest way to represent a max priority queue is as an unordered linear list. Suppose that we have a priority queue with n elements. If Equation (2.1) is used, then insertions are most easily performed at the right end of this list. Hence the insert time is $\Theta(1)$. A deletion requires a search for the element with largest priority followed by its deletion. Since it takes $\Theta(n)$ time to find the largest element in an n-element unordered list, the delete time is $\Theta(n)$. If a chain is used, additions can be performed at the front of the chain in $\Theta(1)$ time. Each deletion takes $\Theta(n)$ time.

An alternative is to use an ordered linear list. The elements are in nondecreasing order when we use Eqation (2.1), and in nonincreasing order when we use an ordered chain. The delete time for each representation is $\Theta(1)$, and the insert time is $O(n)$.

EXERCISES

1. Develop a C++ class for the ADT *MaxPriorityQueue* using an unordered formula-based linear list (i.e., use the class `LinearList` of Program 3.1). The insert time should be $\Theta(1)$, and the delete max time should be $O(n)$ where n is the number of elements in the queue.

2. Do Exercise 1 using an unordered chain (i.e., use the class `Chain` of Program 3.8).

3. Do Exercise 1 using an ordered, formula-based linear list. This time the insert time should be $O(n)$, and the delete max time is $\Theta(1)$.

4. Do Exercise 1 using the class `SortedChain` of Program 7.1.

5. Specify the abstract data type *MinPriorityQueue* and obtain a C++ class definition for this data type using an unordered, formula-based linear list.

9.3 HEAPS

9.3.1 Definitions

Definition A **max tree** (**min tree**) is a tree in which the value in each node is greater (less) than or equal to those in its children (if any). ∎

Some max trees appear in Figure 9.1, and some min trees appear in Figure 9.2. Although these examples are all binary trees, it is not necessary for a max tree to be binary. Nodes of a max or min tree may have more than two children.

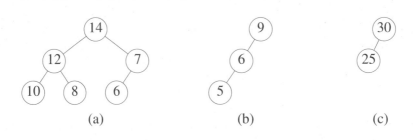

Figure 9.1 Max trees

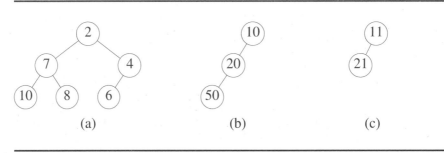

Figure 9.2 Min trees

Definition A **max heap** (**min heap**) is a max (min) tree that is also a complete binary tree. ∎

The max tree of Figure 9.1(b) is not a max heap. The other two max trees are max heaps. The min tree of Figure 9.2(b) is not a min heap. The other two are.

Since a heap is a complete binary tree, a heap can be efficiently represented in a one-dimensional array using the formula-based scheme described in Section 8.4. We can use Property 4 (Section 8.3) to move from a node in the heap to its parent or to one of its children. Our subsequent discussion of heaps will refer to nodes in a heap by their position in the array representation. The position of the root is 1, that of its left child is 2, the root's right child is at 3, and so on. Also, note that since a heap is a complete binary tree, a heap with n elements has height $\lceil \log_2(n+1) \rceil$. Consequently, if we can insert and delete in time O(*height*), then these operations will have complexity O(log$n$).

9.3.2   Insertion into a Max Heap

Figure 9.3(a) shows a max heap with five elements. When an element is added to this heap, the resulting six-element heap must have the structure shown in Figure 9.3(b) because a heap is a complete binary tree. If the element to be inserted has value 1, it may be inserted as the left child of 2. If instead, the value of the new element is 5, the element cannot be inserted as the left child of 2 (as otherwise, we will violate the max tree property). Therefore, the 2 is moved down to its left child (Figure 9.3(c)) and we determine whether placing the 5 at the old position of 2 results in a max heap. Since the parent element (20) is at least as large as the element (5) being inserted, we can insert the new element at the position shown in the figure. Next suppose that the new element has value 21 rather than 5. In this case the 2 moves down to its left child as in Figure 9.3(c). The 21 cannot be inserted into the old position occupied by the 2 as the parent of this position is smaller than 21. Hence the 20 is moved down to its right child, and the 21 inserted in the root of the heap (Figure 9.3(d)).

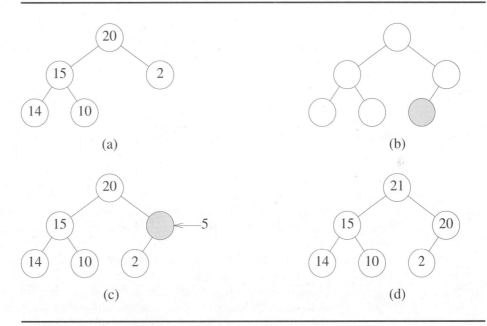

Figure 9.3 Insertion into a max heap

    The insertion strategy just outlined makes a single pass from a leaf towards the root. At each level we do $\Theta(1)$ work, so we should be able to implement the strategy to have complexity $O(height) = O(\log n)$.

9.3.3 Deletion from a Max Heap

When an element is to be deleted from a max heap, it is taken from the root of the heap. For instance, a deletion from the max heap of Figure 9.3(d) results in the removal of the element 21. Since the resulting max heap has only five elements, the binary tree of Figure 9.3(d) needs to be restructured to correspond to a complete binary tree with five elements. To do this restructuring, we remove the element in position 6, that is, the element 2. Now we have the right structure (Figure 9.4(a)), but the root is vacant and the element 2 is not in the heap. If the 2 is inserted into the root, the resulting binary tree is not a max tree. The element at the root should be the largest from among the 2 and the elements in the left and right children of the root. This element is 20. It is moved into the root thereby creating a vacancy in position 3. Since this position has no children, the 2 may be inserted here. The resulting max heap appears in Figure 9.3(a).

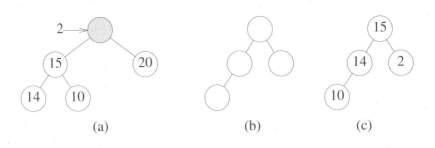

(a)   (b)   (c)

Figure 9.4 Deletion from a max heap

Now suppose we wish to delete 20. Following this deletion, the heap has the binary tree structure shown in Figure 9.4(b). To get this structure, the 10 is removed from position 5. If we put the 10 into the root, the result is not a max heap. The larger of the two children of the root (15 and 2) is moved to the root, and we attempt to insert the 10 into position 2. If the 10 is inserted here, the result is, again, not a max heap. So the 14 is moved up, and the 10 inserted into position 4. The resulting heap is shown in Figure 9.4(c).

The deletion strategy just outlined makes a single pass from the heap root down towards a leaf. At each level $\Theta(1)$ work is done, so we should be able to implement the strategy to have complexity $O(height) = O(\log n)$.

9.3.4 Max Heap Initialization

In several max heap applications, including the event list of the machine shop scheduling problem of Section 6.4.4, we begin with a heap that contains $n > 0$

elements. We can construct this initial nonempty heap by performing n insertions into an initially empty heap. The total time taken by these n inserts is O($n \log n$). We may initialize the heap in $\Theta(n)$ time using a different strategy.

Suppose we begin with an array a of n elements. Assume that $n = 10$ and the keys of the elements in a[1:10] are [20, 12, 35, 15, 10, 80, 30, 17, 2, 1]. This array may be interpreted as representing a complete binary tree as shown in Figure 9.5(a). This complete binary tree is not a max heap.

To convert the complete binary tree of Figure 9.5(a) into a max heap, we begin with the first element that has a child (i.e., 10). This element is at position $i = \lfloor n/2 \rfloor$ of the array. If the subtree that rooted at this position is a max heap, then no work is done here. If this subtree is not a max heap, then we adjust the subtree so that it is a heap. Following this adjustment, we examine the subtree whose root is at $i - 1$, then $i - 2$, and so on until we have examined the root of the entire binary tree, which is at position 1.

Let us try this process on the binary tree of Figure 9.5(a). Initially, $i = 5$. The subtree with root at i is a max heap, as $10 > 1$. Next, we examine the subtree rooted at position 4. This subtree is not a max heap, as $15 < 17$. To convert this subtree into a max heap, the 15 and 17 are interchanged to get the tree of Figure 9.5 (b). The next subtree examined has its root at position 3. To make this subtree into a max heap, we interchange the 80 and 35. Next we examine the subtree with its root at position 2. From the way the restructuring progresses, the subtrees of this element are guaranteed to be max heaps. So restructuring this subtree into a max heap involves determining the larger of its two children, 17. As $12 < 17$, the 17 should be the root of the restructured subtree. Next we compare 12 with the larger of the two children of position 4. As $12 < 15$, the 15 is moved to position 4. The vacant position 8 has no children, and the 12 is inserted here. The resulting binary tree appears in Figure 9.5(c). Finally, we examine position 1. The subtrees with roots at positions 2 and 3 are max heaps at this time. However, $20 < \max\{17, 80\}$. So the 80 should be in the root of the max heap. When the 80 is moved there, it leaves a vacancy at position 3. Since $20 < \max\{35, 30\}$, position 3 is to be occupied by the 35. The 20 can now occupy position 6. Figure 9.5(d) shows the resulting max heap.

9.3.5 The Class MaxHeap

Program 9.1 gives the class definition of a max heap . The private members are n, the number of elements currently in the heap; MaxSize, the maximum number of elements the heap can hold; and heap, the array in which the elements are stored. The default maximum size for a heap is 10 elements.

The implementation of the constructor appears in Program 9.2. The constructor simply allocates an array large enough to hold the desired maximum number of elements. It does not catch the NoMem exception that might be thrown by new. The destructor deletes this array. The size function is

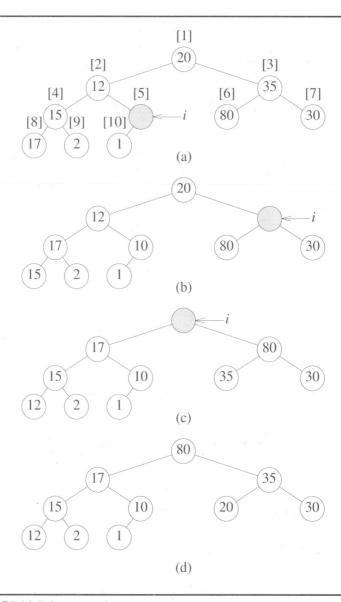

Figure 9.5 Initializing a max heap

particularly simple. It just returns the value of CurrentSize. Another simple function is Max. If the max heap is empty, it throws an OutOfBounds exception. If not, it returns the element in the root of the max tree.

```
template<class T>
class MaxHeap {
   public:
      MaxHeap(int MaxHeapSize = 10);
      ~MaxHeap() {delete [] heap;}
      int Size() const {return CurrentSize;}
      T Max() {if (CurrentSize == 0)
                  throw OutOfBounds();
               return heap[1];}
      MaxHeap<T>& Insert(const T& x);
      MaxHeap<T>& DeleteMax(T& x);
      void Initialize(T a[], int size, int ArraySize);
   private:
      int CurrentSize, MaxSize;
      T *heap;    // element array
};
```

Program 9.1 The class `MaxHeap`

```
template<class T>
MaxHeap<T>::MaxHeap(int MaxHeapSize)
{// Max heap constructor.
   MaxSize = MaxHeapSize;
   heap = new T[MaxSize+1];
   CurrentSize = 0;
}
```

Program 9.2 Constructor for `MaxHeap`

The codes for `Insert` (Program 9.3) and `DeleteMax` (Program 9.4) assume that the the relational operators `<`, `>`, and `>=` have been overloaded to work with operands of type `T`. These codes mirror the discussion of Sections 9.3.2 and 9.3.3.

In the insertion code we start `i` at the newly created leaf position `CurrentSize` of the heap and traverse the path from here to the root. At each positioning of `i`, we check to see whether we are either at the root ($i = 1$) or the insertion of the new element `x` at `i` does not violate the max tree property (`x.key` ≤ `heap[i/2].key`). If either of these conditions holds, we can insert `x` at position `i`. Otherwise, we enter the body of the `while` loop and move the element at `i/2` down to `i` and advance `i` up to its parent (`i/2`). For a max heap with *n* elements (i.e., `CurrentSize` = *n*), the number of

```
template<class T>
MaxHeap<T>& MaxHeap<T>::Insert(const T& x)
{// Insert x into the max heap.
   if (CurrentSize == MaxSize)
      throw NoMem(); // no space

   // find place for x
   // i starts at new leaf and moves up tree
   int i = ++CurrentSize;
   while (i != 1 && x > heap[i/2]) {
      // cannot put x in heap[i]
      heap[i] = heap[i/2]; // move element down
      i /= 2;                 // move to parent
      }

   heap[i] = x;
   return *this;
}
```

Program 9.3 Insertion into a max heap

iterations of the `while` loop is O(*height*) = O(log$n$), and each iteration takes $\Theta(1)$ time. Therefore, the complexity of `Insert` is O(log$n$).

For a `DeleteMax` operation, the maximum element in the heap root (`heap[1]`) is saved in the variable `x`, the element in the last heap position (`heap[CurrentSize]`) is saved in `y`, and the heap size (`CurrentSize`) is reduced by one. In the `while` loop, we begin a search for the proper place to reinsert `y`. This search begins at the root and proceeds down the heap. For an n-element heap, the number of iterations of the `while` loop is O(log$n$), and each iteration takes $\Theta(1)$ time. Therefore, the overall complexity of `DeleteMax` is O(log$n$). Notice that the code works correctly even when the size of the heap following the deletion is zero. In this case the `while` loop is not entered, and a redundant assignment to position 1 of the heap is made.

The function `Initialize` (Program 9.5) initializes the max heap to the elements in the array `a`. This initialization is done in-place by deleting the array to which the private member `heap` is currently pointing and having `heap` point to `a[0]`. `size` is the number of elements in `a`, and `ArraySize` is the maximum number of elements that `a` can hold assuming the first is at `a[1]`. The first four lines of Program 9.5 reset the private members of the max heap so that the array `a` assumes the role of the array `heap`. In the `for` loop we begin at the last node in the binary tree interpretation of the array `heap` (now equivalent to array `a`) that has a child and work our way to the root. At

```
template<class T>
MaxHeap<T>& MaxHeap<T>::DeleteMax(T& x)
{// Set x to max element and delete
 // max element from heap.
   // check if heap is empty
   if (CurrentSize == 0)
      throw OutOfBounds(); // empty

   x = heap[1]; // max element

   // restucture heap
   T y = heap[CurrentSize--]; // last element

   // find place for y starting at root
   int i = 1,  // current node of heap
       ci = 2; // child of i
   while (ci <= CurrentSize) {
      // heap[ci] should be larger child of i
      if (ci < CurrentSize &&
          heap[ci] < heap[ci+1]) ci++;

      // can we put y in heap[ci]?
      if (y >= heap[ci]) break;   // yes

      // no
      heap[i] = heap[ci]; // move child up
      i = ci;                // move down a level
      ci *= 2;
      }
   heap[i] = y;

   return *this;
}
```

Program 9.4 Deletion from a max heap

each positioning of the variable i, the embedded while loop ensures that the subtree rooted at i is a max heap. Notice the similarity between the body of the for loop and the code for DeleteMax (Program 9.4).

The somewhat unusual method used by Initialize to bring an entire array of elements into a class can cause problems when we leave the scope of the max heap but still want access to the elements in the array a. To overcome this

```
template<class T>
void MaxHeap<T>::Initialize(T a[], int size,
                                  int ArraySize)
{// Initialize max heap to array a.
   delete [] heap;
   heap = a;
   CurrentSize = size;
   MaxSize = ArraySize;

   // make into a max heap
   for (int i = CurrentSize/2; i >= 1; i--) {
     T y = heap[i]; // root of subtree

     // find place to put y
     int c = 2*i; // parent of c is target
                  // location for y
     while (c <= CurrentSize) {
        // heap[c] should be larger sibling
        if (c < CurrentSize &&
            heap[c] < heap[c+1]) c++;

        // can we put y in heap[c]?
        if (y >= heap[c]) break;  // yes

        // no
        heap[c/2] = heap[c]; // move child up
        c *= 2;              // move down a level
        }
     heap[c/2] = y;
     }
}
```

Program 9.5 Initialize a nonempty max heap

problem, we add the public member `Deactivate`

```
void Deactivate() {heap = 0;}
```

to the class definition of `MaxHeap`. By deactivating the heap, we avoid the deletion of the array a when the heap destructor is invoked.

Complexity of `Initialize`

If the number of elements is n, each iteration of the `for` loop of `Initialize` (Program 9.5) takes O($\log n$) time and the number of iterations is $n/2$. So the complexity of `Initialize` is O($n\log n$). Recall that the big oh notation provides only an upper bound on the complexity of an algorithm. Consequently, the complexity of `Initialize` could be better. A more careful analysis allows us to conclude that its complexity is actually $\Theta(n)$.

Each iteration of the `while` loop of `Initialize` takes O(h_i) time where h_i is the height of the subtree with root i. The complete binary tree $a[1:n]$ has height $h = \lceil \log_2(n+1) \rceil$. It has at most 2^{j-1} nodes at level j. Hence at most 2^{j-1} of the is have $h_i = h - j + 1$. The time to initialize the max heap is therefore:

$$\text{O}(\sum_{j=1}^{h-1} 2^{j-1}(h-j+1)) = \text{O}(\sum_{k=1}^{h-1} k2^{h-k}) = \text{O}(2^h \sum_{k=1}^{h-1}(k/2^k)) = \text{O}(2^h) = \text{O}(n)$$

Since the `for` loop goes through $n/2$ iterations, the complexity is also $\Omega(n)$. Combining these two bounds, we get $\Theta(n)$ as the complexity of `Initialize`.

EXERCISES

6. Extend the class `MaxHeap` by adding public members `IsEmpty` and `IsFull`. The first returns `true` iff the max heap is empty and the second returns `true` iff it is full.

7. Modify the class definition of a max heap to obtain one for min heaps. Test the correctness of your code.

8. Extend the class `MaxHeap` by adding a public member `ChangeMax(x)` that changes the current maximum element to element `x`. `x` may have a value that is either smaller or larger than that of the current maximum element. Your code should follow a downward path from the root, as is done in the delete max operation. In case the max heap is currently empty, you should throw an `OutOfBounds` exception. The complexity of your code should be O($\log n$) where n is the number of elements in the max heap. Show that this is the case.

9. Since the element `y` that is reinserted into the max heap during a deletion (see Program 9.4) was removed from the bottom of the heap, we expect to reinsert it near the bottom. Write a new version of `DeleteMax` in which the vacancy in the root is first moved down to a leaf, and then the place for `y` is determined making an upward pass from this leaf. Experiment with the new code to see if it works faster than the old one.

10. Rewrite the member functions of `MaxHeap` under the assumptions (a) when a heap is created, the creator provides two elements `MaxElement` and `MinElement`; no element in the heap is larger than `MaxElement` or smaller than `MinElement`, (b) a heap with n elements requires an array `heap[0:2n+1]`, (c) the n elements are stored in `heap[1:n]` as described in this section, (d) `MaxElement` is stored in `heap[0]`, and (e) `MinElement` is stored in `heap[n+1:2n+1]`. These assumption should simplify the codes for `Insert` and `Delete`. Compare the implementation of this section with the one of this exercise experimentally.

9.4 LEFTIST TREES

9.4.1 Height- and Weight-Biased Min and Max Leftist Trees

The heap structure of Section 9.3 is an example of an **implicit data structure**. The complete binary tree representing the heap is stored implicitly (i.e., there are no explicit pointers or other explicit data from which the structure may be deduced) in an array. Since no explicit structural information is stored, the representation is very space efficient; in fact, there is no space overhead. Despite the heap structure being both space and time efficient, it is not suitable for all applications of priority queues. In particular, applications in which we wish to meld (i.e., combine or blend) pairs of priority queues, as well as those in which we have multiple queues of varying size, require a different data structure. Leftist tree structures are suitable for these applications.

Consider a binary tree in which a special node called an **external node** replaces each empty subtree. The remaining nodes are called **internal nodes**. A binary tree with external nodes added is called an **extended binary tree**. Figure 9.6(a) shows a binary tree. Its corresponding extended binary tree is shown in Figure 9.6(b). The external nodes appear as shaded boxes. These nodes have been labeled *a* through *f* for convenience.

Let $s(x)$ be the length of a shortest path from node x to an external node in its subtree. From the definition of $s(x)$, it follows that if x is an external node, its s value is zero. Furthermore, if x is an internal node, its s value is

$$\min\{s(L), s(R)\} + 1$$

where L and R are, respectively, the left and right children of x. The s values for the nodes of the extended binary tree of Figure 9.6(b) appear in Figure 9.6(c).

Definition A binary tree is a *height-biased leftist tree (HBLT)* iff at every internal node, the s value of the left child is greater than or equal to the s value of the right child. ∎

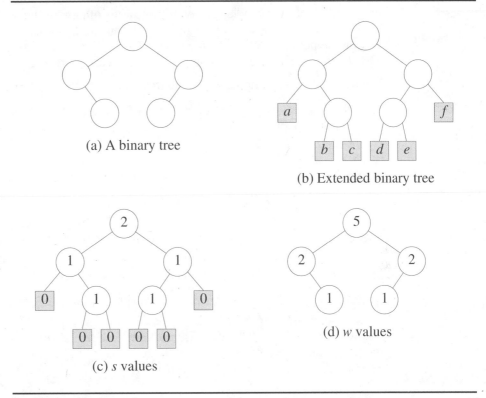

(a) A binary tree

(b) Extended binary tree

(c) s values

(d) w values

Figure 9.6 s and w values

The binary tree of Figure 9.6(a) is not an HBLT. To see this, consider the parent of the external node a. The s value of its left child is zero, while that of its right is one. All other internal nodes satisfy the requirements of the HBLT definition. By swapping the left and right subtrees of the parent of a, the binary tree of Figure 9.6(a) becomes an HBLT.

Theorem 9.1 Let x be any internal node of an HBLT.

(a) The number of nodes in the subtree with root x is at least $2^{s(x)} - 1$.

(b) If the subtree with root x has m nodes, $s(x)$ is at most $\log_2(m + 1)$.

(c) The length of the rightmost path from x to an external node (i.e., the path obtained by beginning at x and making a sequence of right child moves) is $s(x)$.

Proof From the definition of $s(x)$, it follows that there are no external nodes on the $s(x)-1$ levels immediately below node x (as otherwise the s value of x would be less). The subtree with root x has exactly one node on the level at which x is, two on the next level, four on the next, $\cdots$, and $2^{s(x)-1}$ $s(x)-1$ levels below x. The subtree may have additional nodes at levels more than $s(x)-1$ below x. Hence the number of nodes in the subtree x is at least $\sum_{i=0}^{s(x)-1} 2^i = 2^{s(x)} - 1$. (b) follows from (a). (c) follows from the definition of s and the fact that in an HBLT, the s value of the left child of a node is always greater than or equal to that of the right child. ∎

Definition A **max HBLT** is an HBLT that is also a max tree. A **min HBLT** is an HBLT that is also a min tree. ∎

The max trees of Figure 9.1 as well as the min trees of Figure 9.2 are also HBLTs; therefore, the trees of Figure 9.1 are max HBLTs, and those of Figure 9.2 are min HBLTs. A max priority queue may be represented as a max HBLT, and a min priority queue may be represented as a min HBLT.

We arrive at another variety of leftist tree by considering the number of nodes in a subtree rather than the length of a shortest root to external node path. Define the weight, $w(x)$, of node x to be the number of internal nodes in the subtree with root x. Notice that if x is an external node, its weight is zero. If x is an internal node, its weight is one more than the sum of the weights of its children. The weights of the nodes of the binary tree of Figure 9.6(a) appear in Figure 9.6(d)

Definition A binary tree is a **weight-biased leftist tree (WBLT)** iff at every internal node, the w value of the left child is greater than or equal to the w value of the right child. A max (min) WBLT is a max (min) tree that is also a WBLT. ∎

As was the case for HBLTs, the length of the right-most path in a WBLT that has m nodes is at most $\log_2(m+1)$. Using either WBLTs or HBLTs, we can perform the priority queue operations find, insert, and delete in the same asymptotic time as heaps take. Like heaps, WBLTs and HBLTs may be initialized in linear time. Two priority queues represented as WBLTs or HBLTs can be melded into one in logarithmic time. When priority queues are represented as heaps, they cannot be melded in logarithmic time.

The way in which finds, inserts, deletes, melds, and initializations are done in WBLTs and HBLTs is similar. Consequently, we describe these operations for HBLTs only and leave the adaptation of these methods to WBLTs as an exercise (Exercise 12).

9.4.2 Insertion into a Max HBLT

The insertion operation for max HBLTs may be performed using the max HBLT meld operation. Suppose we are to insert an element x into the max HBLT H. If we create a max HBLT with the single element x and then meld this max HBLT and H, the resulting max HBLT will include all elements in H as well as the element x. Hence an insertion may be performed by creating a new max HBLT with just the element that is to be inserted and then melding this max HBLT and the original one.

9.4.3 Deletion from a Max HBLT

The max element is in the root. If the root is deleted, two max HBLTs, the left and right subtrees of the root, remain. By melding these two max HBLTs together, we obtain a max HBLT that contains all elements in the original max HBLT other than the deleted max element. So the delete max operation may be performed by deleting the root and then melding its two subtrees.

9.4.4 Melding Two Max HBLTs

Since the length of the rightmost path of an HBLT with n elements is $O(\log n)$, a meld algorithm that traverses only the rightmost paths of the HBLTs being melded, spending $O(1)$ time at each node on these two paths, will have complexity logarithmic in the total number of elements in the two HBLTs together. With this observation in mind, we develop a meld algorithm that begins at the roots of the two HBLTs and makes right child moves only.

The meld strategy is best described using recursion. Let A and B be the two max HBLTs that are to be melded. If one is empty, then we may use the other as the result. So assume that neither is empty. To perform the meld, we compare the elements in the two roots. The root with the larger element becomes the root of the melded HBLT. Ties may be broken arbitrarily. Suppose that A has the larger root and that its left subtree is L. Let C be the max HBLT that results from melding the right subtree of A and the max HBLT B. The result of melding A and B is the max HBLT that has A as its root and L and C as its subtrees. If the s value of L is smaller than that of C, then C is the left subtree. Otherwise, L is.

Example 9.3 Consider the two max HBLTs of Figure 9.7(a). The s value of a node is shown outside the node, while the element value is shown inside. When drawing two max HBLTs that are to be melded, we shall always draw the one with larger root value on the left. Ties are broken arbitrarily. Because of this convention, the root of the left HBLT always becomes the root of the final HBLT. Also, we shall shade the nodes of the HBLT on the right.

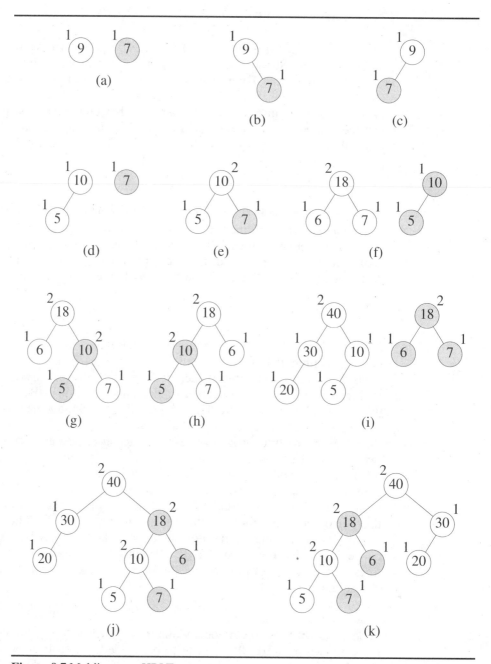

Figure 9.7 Melding max HBLTs

Since the right subtree of 9 is empty, the result of melding this subtree of 9 and the tree with root 7 is just the tree with root 7. We make the tree with root 7 the right subtree of 9 temporarily to get the max tree of Figure 9.7(b). Since the s value of the left subtree of 9 is 0 while that of its right subtree is 1, the left and right subtrees are swapped to get the max HBLT of Figure 9.7(c).

Next consider melding the two max HBLTs of Figure 9.7(d). The root of the left subtree becomes the root of the result. When the right subtree of 10 is melded with the HBLT with root 7, the result is just this latter HBLT. If this HBLT is made the right subtree of 10, we get the max tree of Figure 9.7(e). Comparing the s values of the left and right children of 10, we see that a swap is not neccessary.

Now consider melding the two max HBLTs of Figure 9.7(f). The root of the left subtree is the root of the result. We proceed to meld the right subtree of 18 and the max HBLT with root 10. The two max HBLTs being melded are the same as those melded in Figure 9.7(d). The resultant max HBLT (Figure 9.7(e)) becomes the right subtree of 18, and the max tree of Figure 9.7(g) results. Comparing the s values of the left and right subtrees of 18, we see that these subtrees must be swapped. Swapping results in the max HBLT of Figure 9.7(h).

As a final example, consider melding the two max HBLTs of Figure 9.7(i). The root of the left max HBLT becomes the root of the result. We proceed to meld the right subtree of 40 and the max HBLT with root 18. These max HBLTs were melded in Figure 9.7(f). The resultant max HBLT (Figure 9.7(g)) becomes the right subtree of 40. Since the left subtree of 40 has a smaller s value than the right has, the two subtrees are swapped to get the max HBLT of Figure 9.7(k). Notice that when melding the max HBLTs of Figure 9.7(i), we first move to the right child of 40, then to the right child of 18, and finally to the right child of 10. All moves follow the right-most paths of the initial max HBLTs. ∎

9.4.5 Initialization

It takes O($n \log n$) time to initialize a max HBLT with n elements by inserting these elements into an initially empty max HBLT one at a time. To get a linear time initialization algorithm, we begin by creating n max HBLTs with each containing one of the n elements. These n max HBLTs are placed on a FIFO queue. Then max HBLTs are deleted from this queue in pairs, melded, and added to the end of the queue until only one max HBLT remains.

Example 9.4 We wish to create a max HBLT with the five elements 7, 1, 9, 11, and 2. Five single-element max HBLTs are created and placed in a FIFO queue. The first two, 7 and 1, are deleted from the queue and melded. The result (Figure 9.8(a)) is added to the queue. Next the max HBLTs 9 and 11 are deleted from the queue and melded. The result appears in Figure 9.8(b). This max HBLT is added to the queue. Now the max HBLT 2 and that of Figure 9.8(a) are deleted from the queue and melded. The resulting max HBLT (Figure 9.8(c)) is added to the queue. The next pair to be deleted from the queue consists of the max HBLTs of Figures 9.8 (b) and (c). These HBLTs are melded to get the max HBLT of Figure 9.8(d). This max HBLT is added to the queue. The queue now has just one max HBLT, and we are done with the initialization. ■

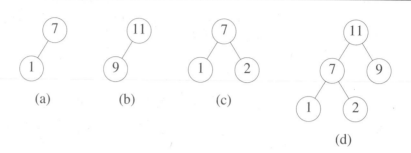

(a)   (b)   (c)

(d)

Figure 9.8 Initializing a max HBLT

9.4.6   The Class MaxHBLT

Each node of a max HBLT needs the fields data, LeftChild, RightChild, and s. HBLTNode (Program 9.6) is the corresponding node class. The constructor for HBLTNode requires that the data field and s value be provided. The left and right child fields are set to zero.

```
template <class T>
class HBLTNode {
   friend MaxHBLT<T>;
   public:
      HBLTNode(const T& e, const int sh)
        {data = e;
         s = sh;
         LeftChild = RightChild = 0;}
   private:
      int s; // s value of node
      T data;
      HBLTNode<T> *LeftChild, *RightChild;
};
```

Program 9.6 Node class for height-biased leftist tees

Max HBLTs may be implemented as the class `MaxHBLT` of Program 9.7. Each object of type `MaxHBLT` has the single private member `root`, which points to the root node of the max HBLT. The constructor initializes `root` to zero, thereby initializing the max HBLT to be empty. The destructor deletes all nodes in the max HBLT by invoking the private member function `Free` that performs a postorder traversal of the max HBLT, deleting nodes in the visit step. The code for `Free` is the same as the code for the private member function `Free` developed in Section 8.9 for binary trees.

```
template<class T>
class MaxHBLT {
   public:
      MaxHBLT() {root = 0;}
      ~MaxHBLT() {Free(root);}
      T Max() {if (!root) throw OutOfBounds();
               return root->data;}
      MaxHBLT<T>& Insert(const T& x);
      MaxHBLT<T>& DeleteMax(T& x);
      MaxHBLT<T>& Meld(MaxHBLT<T>& x) {
               Meld(root,x.root);
               x.root = 0;
               return *this;}
      void Initialize(T a[], int n);
   private:
      void Free(HBLTNode<T> *t);
      void Meld(HBLTNode<T>* &x, HBLTNode<T>* y);
      HBLTNode<T> *root;   // pointer to tree root
};
```

Program 9.7 The class `MaxHBLT`

Since the insert, delete max, and intialize operations use the meld operation, let us examine this operation first. To meld two max HBLTs, the public member function `Meld` invokes a private member function `Meld`, which does the actual melding. This private member function has two parameters `x` and `y`. Both are pointers to the roots of the max HBLTs that are to be melded. A pointer to the resulting max HBLT is returned in `x`. Following the meld of `root` and `x.root`, the public `Meld` function sets the root of `x` to zero (this step prevents the accidental erasure of the old nodes of `x` that have been moved into the melded tree) and returns a reference to the melded tree.

The private meld function given in Program 9.8 begins by handling the special case when at least one of the trees being melded is empty. When neither tree is empty, we make sure that x points to the tree that has the larger element in its root (i.e., the tree with larger root is on the left). If x does not point to this tree, the pointers x and y are swapped. Next the right subtree of x and the max HBLT with root y are melded recursively. Following this meld, x is the root of a max tree whose left and right subtrees may need to be swapped so as to ensure that the entire tree is, in fact, a max HBLT. This swapping is done, if necessary, and the s value of x is computed.

```
template<class T>
void MaxHBLT<T>::Meld(HBLTNode<T>* &x, HBLTNode<T>* y)
{// Meld leftist trees with roots *x and *y.
 // Set x to point to new root.
   if (!y) return; // y is empty
   if (!x) // x is empty
      {x = y;
       return;}

   // neither is empty
   if (x->data < y->data) Swap(x,y);
   // now x->data >= y->data
   Meld(x->RightChild,y);
   if (!x->LeftChild) {// left subtree empty
         // swap subtrees
         x->LeftChild = x->RightChild;
         x->RightChild = 0;
         x->s = 1;}
   else {// see if subtrees to be swapped
         if (x->LeftChild->s < x->RightChild->s)
            Swap(x->LeftChild,x->RightChild);
         x->s = x->RightChild->s + 1;}
}
```

Program 9.8 Melding two leftist trees

To insert an element x into a max HBLT, the code of Program 9.9 creates a max HBLT with the single element x and then uses the private member function `Meld` to meld this tree and the original one. A reference to the resulting max HBLT is returned. The exception, if any, thrown by `new` is not caught by this code.

```
template<class T>
MaxHBLT<T>& MaxHBLT<T>::Insert(const T& x)
{// Insert x into the leftist tree.
 // Create tree with one node.
   HBLTNode<T> *q = new HBLTNode<T> (x,1);
   // meld q and original tree
   Meld(root,q);
   return *this;
}
```

Program 9.9 Inserting into a max HBLT

The code for `DeleteMax` (Program 9.10) throws an `OutOfBounds` in case the max HBLT is empty. When the max HBLT is not empty, pointers to the left and right subtrees of the root are saved in `L` and `R`, respectively; the root is deleted, and the subtrees `L` and `R` melded.

```
template<class T>
MaxHBLT<T>& MaxHBLT<T>::DeleteMax(T& x)
{// Delete max element and put it in x.
   if (!root) throw OutOfBounds();

   // tree not empty
   x = root->data;  // max element
   HBLTNode<T> *L = root->LeftChild;
   HBLTNode<T> *R = root->RightChild;
   delete root;
   root = L;
   Meld(root,R);
   return *this;
}
```

Program 9.10 Deleting the max element from a max HBLT

The max HBLT initialization code is given in Program 9.11. A formula-based FIFO queue is used to hold the intermediate max HBLTs created by the initialization algorithm. In the first `for` loop, n single-element max HBLTs are created and added to an initially empty queue. In the next `for` loop, pairs of max HBLTs are deleted from the queue, melded, and the result added to the queue. When this `for` loop terminates, the queue contains a single max HBLT (provided n > 1), which includes all n elements.

```
template<class T>
void MaxHBLT<T>::Initialize(T a[], int n)
{// Initialize hblt with n elements.
   Queue<HBLTNode<T> *> Q(n);
   Free(root);   // delete old nodes
   // initialize queue of trees
   for (int i = 1; i <= n; i++) {
      // create trees with one node each
      HBLTNode<T> *q = new HBLTNode<T> (a[i],1);
      Q.Add(q);
      }

   // repeatedly meld from queue
   HBLTNode<T> *b, *c;
   for (int i = 1; i <= n - 1; i++) {
      // delete and meld two trees
      Q.Delete(b).Delete(c);
      Meld(b,c);
      // put melded tree on queue
      Q.Add(b);
      }

   if (n) Q.Delete(root);
}
```

Program 9.11 Initializing a max HBLT

Complexity Analysis
The constructor takes $\Theta(1)$ time, while the destructor takes $\Theta(n)$ time where n is the number of elements in the max HBLT being destroyed. The next function, Max, takes $\Theta(1)$ time. The complexity of Insert, DeleteMax, and the public member function Meld is the same as that of the private member function Meld. Since this private member function moves only to right subtrees of the trees with roots *x and *y, that are being melded, the complexity of this private member function is O(x->s + y->s). The s values of *x and *y are at most $\log_2(m + 1)$ and $\log_2(n + 1)$ where m and n are, respectively, the number of elements in the max HBLTs with roots *x and *y. As a result, the complexity of the private member function Meld is O(logmn).

For the complexity analysis of Initialize, assume, for simplicity, that n is a power of 2. The first $n/2$ melds involve max HBLTs with one element each, the next $n/4$ melds involve max HBLTs with two elements each; the next

$n/8$ melds are with trees that have four elements each; and so on. The time needed to meld two trees with 2^i elements each is $O(i+1)$, and so the total time taken by `Initialize` is

$$O(n/2 + 2*(n/4) + 3*(n/8) + \cdots) = O(n\sum\frac{i}{2^i}) = O(n)$$

EXERCISES

11. Write the code for the class `MinHBLT`. This class differs from the class `MaxHBLT` only in that class members are now min HBLTs rather than max HBLTs. The operations `Min` and `DeleteMin` replace the operations `Max` and `DeleteMax`.

12. [*Max WBLTs*]

    (a) Which (if any) of the binary trees of Figure 9.1 are WBLTs?

    (b) Let x be a node in a WBLT. Use induction on $w(x)$ to show that the length of the right-most path from x to an external node is at most $\log_2(w(x) + 1)$.

    (c) Develop the class `WBLTNode` to represent the nodes of a weight-biased leftist tree. Each class member has the fields `w` (weight), `data`, `LeftChild`, and `RightChild`.

    (d) Develop the class `MaxWBLT` as one whose objects are max WBLTs. Your class should include the functions `Max`, `Insert`, `DeleteMax`, `Meld`, and `Initialize`. These functions are equivalent to the corresponding functions for a max HBLT. Your code for each of these functions should have the same asymptotic complexity as the corresponding codes for `MaxHBLT`. Write the code for the private member function `Meld` without using recursion. Note that since the `w` value of a node can be computed on the way down, the bottom-to-top pass made when recursion unfolds as in Program 9.8 is unneccessary when WBLTs are used but necessary when HBLTs are used.

    (e) Compare the merits/demerits of max WBLTs, max HBLTs, and max heaps as a data structure for max priority queues.

13. Replace the use of the `NULL` (or zero) pointer in the representation of a max HBLT by a pointer to a node that has value `MinElement` (see Exercise 10). Modify the max HBLT codes to take advantage of this change. Does the new code run faster than the original code?

9.5 APPLICATIONS

9.5.1 Heap Sort

You might have already noticed that a heap can be used to sort n elements in $O(n\log n)$ time. We begin by initializing a max heap with the n elements to be sorted. Then we extract (i.e., delete) elements from the heap one at a time. The elements appear in nonincreasing order. The initialization takes $\Theta(n)$ time, and each deletion takes $O(\log n)$ time. So the total time is $O(n\log n)$. This time is better than the $O(n^2)$ time taken by the sort methods of Chapter 2.

The sort method that results from the above strategy is called **heap sort**. Its implementation appears in Program 9.12.

```
template <class T>
void HeapSort(T a[], int n)
{// Sort a using the heap sort method.
   // create a max heap of the elements
   MaxHeap<T> H(1);
   H.Initialize(a,n,n);

   // extract one by one from the max heap
   T x;
   for (int i = n-1; i >= 1; i--) {
      H.DeleteMax(x);
      a[i+1] = x;
      }

   // save array a from heap destructor
   H.Deactivate();
}
```

Program 9.12 Heap sort

Figure 9.9 shows the progress of the `for` loop of Program 9.12 for the first few values of `i`. This loop begins with the max heap of Figure 9.5(d).

9.5.2 Machine Scheduling

Consider a machine shop that has m identical machines. We have n jobs that need to be processed. The processing time required by job i is t_i. This time includes the time needed to set up and remove the job on/from a machine. A

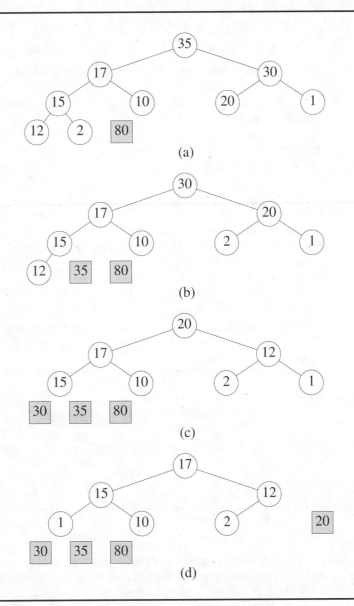

Figure 9.9 Heap sort

schedule is an assignment of jobs to time intervals on machines such that

- No machine processes more than one job at any time.
- No job is processed by more than one machine at any time.
- Each job i is assigned for a total of t_i units of processing.

Each machine is assumed to be available at time 0. The **finish time** or **length** of a schedule is the time at which all jobs have completed. In a nonpremptive schedule, each job i is processed by a single machine from some start time s_i to its completion time $s_i + t_i$. We shall concern ourselves only with nonpreemptive schedules.

Figure 9.10 shows a three-machine schedule for seven jobs with processing requirements (2, 14, 4, 16, 6, 5, 3). The machines are labeled M1, M2, and M3. Each shaded area represents the duration for which a job is scheduled. The number inside the area is the job index. Job 4 is scheduled on machine 1 (M1) from time 0 to time 16. In these 16 units of time, machine 1 completes the processing of job 4. The schedule for machine two is do job 2 from time 0 to time 14 and then do job 7 from time 14 to 17. On machine 3, job 5 is done from 0 to 6, job 6 from 6 to 11, job 3 from 11 to 15, and job 1 from 15 to 17. Notice that each job i is processed on a single machine from a start time s_i to a finish time $s_i + t_i$ and that no machine works on more than one job at any time. The time at which all jobs have completed is 17. So the schedule finish time or length is 17.

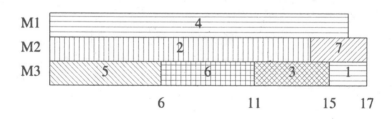

Figure 9.10 A three-machine schedule

Our task is to write a program that constructs a minimum-finish-time m-machine schedule for a given set of n jobs. Constructing such a schedule is very hard. In fact, no one has ever developed a polynomial time algorithm (i.e., an algorithm whose complexity is $O(n^k m^l)$ for any constants k and l) to construct a minimum-finish-time schedule.

The scheduling problem we have just defined is a member of the infamous class of NP-hard (NP stands for **nondeterministic polynomial**) problems. The NP-hard and NP-complete problem classes contain problems for which no one has developed a polynomial-time algorithm. The problems in the class NP-complete are decision problems. That is, for each problem instance, the answer is either yes or no. Our machine-scheduling problem is not a decision problem as the answer, for each instance, is an assignment of jobs to machines such that the finish time is minimum. We may formulate a related machine-scheduling problem in which, in addition to the tasks and machines, we are given a time *TMin* and are asked to determine whether or not there is a schedule with finish time *TMin* or less. For this related problem, the answer to each instance is either yes or no. This related problem is a decision problem that is NP-complete. NP-hard problems may or may not be decision problems.

Thousands of problems of practical interest are NP-hard or NP-complete. If anyone discovers a polynomial-time algorithm for an NP-hard or NP-complete problem, then he/she would have simultaneously discovered a way to solve all NP-complete problems in polynomial time. Although we are unable to prove that NP-complete problems cannot be solved in polynomial time, common wisdom very strongly suggests that this is the case. As a result, optimization problems that are NP-hard are often solved by **approximation algorithms**. Although approximation algorithms do not guarantee to obtain optimal solutions, they guarantee solutions "close" to optimal.

In the case of our scheduling problem, we can generate schedules whose lengths are at most $4/3 - 1/(3m)$ of optimal by employing a simple scheduling strategy called **longest processing time first** (LPT). In LPT, jobs are assigned to machines in descending order of their-processing time requirements t_i. When a job is being assigned to a machine, it is assigned to the machine that becomes idle first. Ties are broken arbitrarily.

For the job set example in Figure 9.10, we may construct an LPT schedule by first sorting the jobs into descending order of processing times. The job order is (4, 2, 5, 6, 3, 7, 1). First, job 4 is assigned to a machine. Since all three machines become available at time 0, job 4 may be assigned to any machine. Suppose we assign it to machine 1. Now machine 1 is unavailable until time 16. Job 2 is next assigned; we can assign it to either machine 2 or 3, as both become available at the same time (i.e., time 0). Assume that we assign job 2 to machine 2. Now machine 2 is unavailable until time 14. Next we assign job 5 to machine 3 from time 0 to time 6. Job 6 is to be assigned next. The first available machine is machine 3. It becomes available at time 6. Following the assignment of job 6 from time 6 to time 11 on this machine, the availability time of machine 3 becomes 11. Job 3 is next considered for scheduling. The first machine to become available is machine 3 at time 11, we assign job 3 to this machine. Continuing in this way, we obtain the schedule of Figure 9.10.

Theorem 9.2 [*Graham*] Let $F * (I)$ be the finish time of an optimal m-machine schedule for a job set I and let $F(I)$ be the finish time of the LPT schedule for this job set. Then

$$\frac{F(I)}{F*(I)} \le \frac{4}{3} - \frac{1}{3m}$$

Proof See the book *Computer Algorithms C++* by E. Horowitz, S. Sahni, and S. Rajasekeran, Computer Science Press, New York, 1996. ∎

In practice, LPT schedules are often much closer to optimal than suggested by the bound of Theorem 9.2. LPT schedules can be constructed in $O(n \log n)$ time using heaps. First, we notice that when $n \leq m$, we need merely assign job i to machine i from time 0 to t_i. When $n > m$, we begin by sorting the jobs into ascending order of processing times using HeapSort (Program 9.12). To construct the LPT schedule, the jobs are assigned in the reverse of this order. To determine which machine a job is to be assigned to, we need to determine which machine becomes available first. To make this determination, we maintain a min heap of the m machines. Each element on this min heap is of type MachineNode (Program 9.13). avail is the time at which the machine becomes available, and ID is the machine identifier. A DeleteMin is used to extract the machine that becomes available first. The machine's availability time is increased, and it is inserted back into the min heap. This min heap is initialized by inserting a node for each machine. Since all machines are initially available at time 0, the avail value for each of these machines is 0. Program 9.14 gives the code. The type T must include at least the fields time and ID. Program 9.13 gives a suitable type JobNode for *a and T. ID gives each job's unique identifier, and time gives the processing requirements of a job.

```
class  JobNode {
    friend void LPT(JobNode *, int, int);
    friend void main(void);
    public:
        operator int () const {return time;}
    private:
        int ID,     // job identifier
            time;   // processing time
};

class  MachineNode {
    friend void LPT(JobNode *, int, int);
    public:
        operator int () const {return avail;}
    private:
        int ID,      // machine identifier
            avail;   // when it becomes free
};
```

Program 9.13 The data types JobNode and MachineNode

```
template <class T>
void LPT(T a[], int n, int m)
{// Construct an m machine LPT schedule.
   if (n <= m) {
      cout << "Schedule one job per machine." << endl;
      return;}

   HeapSort(a,n); // in ascending order
   // initialize m machines and the min heap
   MinHeap<MachineNode> H(m);
   MachineNode x;
   for (int i = 1; i <= m; i++) {
      x.avail = 0;
      x.ID = i;
      H.Insert(x);
      }

   // construct schedule
   for (int i = n; i >= 1; i--) {
      H.DeleteMin(x);  // get first free machine
      cout << "Schedule job " << a[i].ID
           << " on machine " << x.ID << " from "
           << x.avail << " to "
           << (x.avail + a[i].time) << endl;
      x.avail += a[i].time;  // new avail time
      H.Insert(x);
      }
}
```

Program 9.14 LPT schedule construction

Complexity Analysis of LPT
When $n \leq m$, function LPT takes $\Theta(1)$ time. When $n > m$, the heap sort takes $O(n\log n)$ time. The heap initialization takes $\Theta(m)$ time, even though we are doing m inserts, because all elements have the same value; therefore, each insert actually takes only $\Theta(1)$ time. In the second for loop, n DeleteMin and n Insert operations are performed. Each takes $O(\log m)$ time. So the second for loop takes $O(n\log m)$ time. The total time is therefore $O(n\log n + n\log m) = O(n\log n)$ (as $n > m$).

9.5.3   Huffman Codes

In Section 7.5.2 we developed a text compressor based on the LZW method. This method relies on the recurrence of substrings in a text. Another approach to text compression, **Huffman codes**, relies on the relative frequency with which different symbols appear in a piece of text. Suppose our text is a string that comprises the characters a, u, x, and z. If the length of this string is 1000, then storing it as 1000 one-byte characters will take 1000 bytes (or 8000 bits) of space. If we encode the symbols in the string using 2 bits per symbol ($00 = a$, $01 = x$, $10 = u$, $11 = z$), then the 1000 symbols can be represented with 2000 bits of space. We also need space for the code table, which may be stored using the following format:

number of table entries, code 1, symbol 1, code 2, symbol 2, ...

Eight bits are adequate for the number of entries and for each of the symbols. Each code is of size $\lceil \log_2 (\text{number of table entries}) \rceil$ bits. For our example the code table may be saved using $5*8 + 4*2 = 48$ bits. The compression ratio is $8000/2048 = 3.9$.

Using the above encoding, the string aaxuaxz is encoded as 00000110000111. The code for each symbol has the same number of bits (i.e., two). By picking off pairs of bits from the coded string from left to right and using the code table, we can obtain the original string.

In the string *aaxuaxz*, the a occurs three times. The number of occurrences of a symbol is called its **frequency**. The frequencies of a, x, u, and z in the sample string are 3, 2, 1, and 1, respectively. When there is significant variation in the frequencies of different symbols, we can reduce the size of the coded string using variable-length codes. If we use the codes ($0 = a$, $10 = x$, $110 = u$, $111 = z$), the encoded version of *aaxuaxz* is 0010110010111. The length of this encoded version is 13 bits compared to 14 bits using the 2 bits per symbol code! The difference is more dramatic when the spread in frequencies is greater. If the frequencies of the four symbols are (996, 2, 1, 1), then the 2 bits per symbol code results in an encoding that is 2000 bits long, while the variable-length code results in an encoding that is 1006 bits.

But how do we decode the encoded string? When each code is 2 bits long, decoding is easy—just pick off every pair of bits and use the code table to determine what these 2 bits stand for. With variable-length codes, we do not know how many bits to pick off. The string *aaxuaxz* was coded as 0010110010111. When decoding this code from left to right, we need to know whether the code for the first symbol is 0, 00, or 001. Since we have no codes that begin with 00, the first code must be 0. This code is decoded using the code table to get a. The next code is 0, 01, or 010. Again, because no codes begin with 01, the code must be 0. Continuing in this way, we are able to decode the encoded bit string.

What makes this decoding method work? If we examine the four codes in use (0, 10, 110, 111), we observe that no code is a prefix of another. Consequently, when examining the coded bit string from left to right, we can get a match with exactly one code.

We may use extended binary trees (see Section 9.4.1 for a definition) to derive a special class of variable-length codes that satisfy this prefix property. This class of codes is called **Huffman codes**.

The root to external node paths in an extended binary tree may be coded using 0 to represent a move to a left subtree and 1 to represent a move to a right subtree. In Figure 9.6(b) the path from the root to the external node b gets the code 010. The codes for the paths to the nodes (a, b, c, d, e, f) are (00, 010, 011, 100, 101, 11). Notice that since no root to external node path is a prefix of another such path, no path code is a prefix of another path code. Therefore, these codes may be used to encode the symbols $a, b, \cdots, f$ respectively. Let S be a string made up of these symbols, and let $F(x)$ be the frequency of the symbol $x \in \{a, b, c, d, e, f\}$. If S is encoded using these codes, the encoded string has a length

$$2 * F(a) + 3 * F(b) + 3 * F(c) + 3 * F(d) + 3 * F(e) + 2 * F(f)$$

For an extended binary tree with external nodes labeled $1, \cdots, n$, the length of the encoded string is

$$WEP = \sum_{i=1}^{n} L(i) * F(i)$$

where $L(i)$ is the length of the path (i.e., number of edges on the path) from the root to the external node labeled i. *WEP* is called the **weighted external path length** of the binary tree. To minimize the length of the coded string, we must use codes from a binary tree whose external nodes correspond to the symbols in the string being encoded and whose weighted external path length is minimum. A binary tree with minimum weighted external path length for a given set of frequencies (weights) is called a **Huffman tree**.

To encode a string (or piece of text) using Huffman codes, we need to

1. Determine the different symbols in the string and their frequencies.

2. Construct a binary tree with minimum weighted external path length (i.e., a Huffman tree). The external nodes of this tree are labeled by the symbols in the string and the weight of each external node is the frequency of the symbol that is its label.

3. Traverse the root to external node paths and obtain the codes.

4. Replace the symbols in the string by their codes.

To facilitate decoding, we need to save a table that contains the symbol to code mapping or a table that contains the frequency of each symbol. In the latter case the Huffman codes can be reconstructed using the method for (b). We shall elaborate on step (b) only.

A Huffman tree can be constructed by beginning with a collection of binary trees, each having just an external node. Each external node represents a different string symbol and has a **weight** equal to the frequency of this symbol. Then we repeatedly select two binary trees of lowest weight (ties are broken arbitrarily) from the collection and combine them into one by making them subtrees of a new root node. The weight of the newly formed tree is the sum of the weights of the constituent subtrees. The process terminates when only one tree remains.

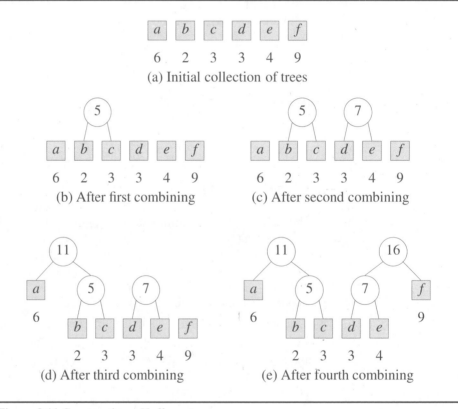

Figure 9.11 Constructing a Huffman tree

Let us try this construction method on a six symbol (a, b, c, d, e, f) example with frequencies $(6, 2, 3, 3, 4, 9)$. The initial binary trees are shown in Figure 9.11(a). The numbers outside the boxes are the tree weights. The tree with the lowest weight is *b*. We have a tie for the tree with the second-lowest weight. Suppose that we select tree *c*. Combining trees *b* and *c* yields the configuration of Figure 9.11(b). The root node is labeled with the tree weight (5). From the five trees of Figure 9.11(b), we select two of lowest weight. Trees *d* and *e* are selected and combined to get a tree of weight 7 (Figure 9.11(c)). From the four trees of Figure 9.11(c), we select two of lowest weight to combine. The trees *a* and the one with weight 5 are selected. Combining these trees results in a tree of weight 11. From the remaining three trees (Figure 9.11(d)), the tree with weight 7 and the tree *f* are selected for combining. When these two trees are combined, the two trees of Figure 9.11(e) remain. These trees are next combined to get the single tree of Figure 9.6(b) whose weight is 27.

Theorem 9.3 The procedure outlined above constructs binary trees with minimum weighted external path length.

Proof Left as an exercise (Exercise 19). ■

The Huffman tree construction procedure can be implemented using a min heap to store the collection of binary trees. Each element of the min heap consists of a binary tree and a value that is the weight of this binary tree. The binary tree itself is a member of the class `BinaryTree` defined in Section 8.8. For an external node the data field is set to the symbol it represents, and for an internal node this field is set to zero. We may assume, for convenience, that the symbols are numbered 1 through n. Function `HuffmanTree` (Program 9.15) assumes that the class `Huffman` has been defined as in Program 9.16.

Function `HuffmanTree` inputs a collection of n frequencies (or weights) in the array a and returns a Huffman tree. It begins by constructing n binary trees, each with just an external node. These trees are saved in the array w, which is later initialized to be a min heap. Each iteration of the second `for` loop extracts two binary trees of minimum weight from the min heap and combines them into a single binary tree, which is then inserted into the min heap.

Complexity of `HuffmanTree`
The time needed to create and delete the array w is $\Theta(1)$ when T is an internal data type and $\Theta(n)$ when T is a user-defined class. The first `for` loop and the heap initialization take $\Theta(n)$ time. In the second `for` loop, a total of `2(n-1)` delete min and `n-1` insert operations are performed, taking O(nlogn) time. The remainder of this function takes $\Theta(1)$ time. So the overall time complexity is O(nlogn).

```
template <class T>
BinaryTree<int> HuffmanTree(T a[], int n)
{// Generate Huffman tree with weights a[1:n].
   // create an array of single node trees
   Huffman<T> *w = new Huffman<T> [n+1];
   BinaryTree<int> z, zero;
   for (int i = 1; i <= n; i++) {
      z.MakeTree(i, zero, zero);
      w[i].weight = a[i];
      w[i].tree = z;
      }

   // make array into a min heap
   MinHeap<Huffman<T> > H(1);
   H.Initialize(w,n,n);

   // repeatedly combine trees from heap
   Huffman<T> x, y;
   for (int i = 1; i < n; i++) {
      H.DeleteMin(x);
      H.DeleteMin(y);
      z.MakeTree(0, x.tree, y.tree);
      x.weight += y.weight; x.tree = z;
      H.Insert(x);
      }

   H.DeleteMin(x); // final tree
   H.Deactivate();
   delete [] w;
   return x.tree;
}
```

Program 9.15 Construct a Huffman tree

```
template<class T>
class  Huffman {
   friend BinaryTree<int> HuffmanTree(T [], int);
   public:
      operator T () const {return weight;}
   private:
      BinaryTree<int> tree;
      T weight;
};
```

Program 9.16 The class `Huffman`

EXERCISES

14. Compare the worst-case run times of heap sort and insertion sort. For heap sort, use some number of random permutations to estimate the worst-case run time. At what value of n does the run time of heap sort become less than that of insertion sort?

15. Use the ideas of Exercises 9 and 10 to arrive at a faster implementation of heap sort than Program 9.12. Experiment with random data and compare the run times of the two implementations.

16. A sort method is said to be **stable** if the relative order of records with equal key is the same after the sort as it was before the sort. Suppose that records 3 and 10 have the same key. In a stable sort, record 3 will precede record 10 following the sort. Is heap sort a stable sort? How about insertion sort?

17. Each iteration of the second `for` loop of Program 9.14 performs one delete min and one insert. The two operations together essentially increase the value of the minimum key by an amount equal to the processing time of the job just scheduled. We can speed Program 9.14 by a constant factor by using an extended min priority queue. The extension includes the functions normally supported by a min priority queue plus the function `IncreaseMinKey(x,e)` that increases the value of the minimum key by x and returns, in `e`, the element that had minimum key originally. This function first increases the key in the root by x and then moves down the heap (as in a delete min operation), moving elements up the heap until it finds an appropriate place for the increased key.

    (a) Develop a new class `ExtendedMinHeap` that provides all the functions provided by the class `MinHeap` plus the function `IncreaseMinKey`. `template <class Te, class Tk> class ExtendedMinHeap` should be derived from the class

MinHeap<Te>; Te is the data type of the elements, and Tk is the data type of the elements. So in the function IncreaseMinKey(x,y), x is of type Tk and e is of type Te. You may assume that the operator += has been overloaded so that the statement e += x increments the key of e by x.

(b) Rewrite Program 9.14 using function IncreaseMinKey.

(c) Determine, experimentally, the improvement in run time of your new code versus that of Program 9.14.

18. n items are to be packed into containers. Item i uses s_i units of space, and each container has a capacity C. The packing is to be done using the **worst-fit** rule in which the items are assigned to containers one at a time. When an item is being assigned, we look for the container with maximum available capacity. If the item fits in this container, the assignment is made; otherwise, this item starts a new container.

(a) Develop a program to input n, the s_is, and C and to output the assignment of items to containers. Use a max heap to keep track of the available space in the containers.

(b) What is the time complexity of your program (as a function of n and the number m of containers used)?

★ 19. Prove Theorem 9.3 by using induction on the number of external nodes. The induction step should establish the existence of a binary tree with minimum weighted external path length that has a subtree with one internal node and two external nodes corresponding to the two lowest frequencies.

20. Write a function to input a Huffman tree as constructed by Huffman-Tree (Program 9.15), and output to a code table. What is the time complexity of your function?

★ 21. Develop a complete compression-decompression package based on Huffman codes. Test its correction using suitable text files.

★ 22. A collection of n integers in the range 0 through 511 is to be stored. Develop a compression-decompression package for this application. Use Huffman codes.

23. A **run** is a sorted sequence of elements. Assume that two runs can be merged into a single run in time $\Theta(r + s)$ where r and s are, respectively, the lengths of the two runs being merged. n runs of different lengths are to be merged into a single run by repeatedly merging pairs of runs until only one run remains. Explain how to use Huffman trees to determine a minimum-cost way to merge the n runs.

9.6 REFERENCES AND SELECTED READINGS

A more detailed study of data structures for priority queues and priority-queue variants can be found in the text *Fundamentals of Data Structures in C++* by E. Horowitz, S. Sahni, and D. Mehta, W. H. Freeman, New York, NY, 1994.

Height-biased leftist trees are described in the monograph *Data Structures and Network Algorithms* by R. Tarjan, SIAM, Philadelphia, PA, 1983, while weight-biased leftist trees are developed in the paper "Weight Biased Leftist Trees and Modified Skip Lists" by S. Cho and S. Sahni, in *Proceedings, Second International Conference, COCOON'96*, Lecture Notes in Computer Science, Springer Verlag, 1090, 1996, 361–370.

You can find out more about NP-hard problems from the books *Computer and Intractability: A Guide to the Theory of NP-Completeness* by M. Garey and D. Johnson, W. H. Freeman, New York, NY, 1979, and *Computer Algorithms/C++* by E. Horowitz, S. Sahni, and S. Rajasekeran, Computer Science Press, New York, NY, 1996.

CHAPTER 10

TOURNAMENT TREES

BIRD'S-EYE VIEW

We have reached the half-way in our journey through the forest of trees. The new tree variety we encounter in this chapter is the tournament tree. Like the heap of Section 9.3, a tournament tree is a complete binary tree that is most efficiently stored using the formula-based binary tree representation of Section 8.4. The basic operation that a tournament tree supports is replacing the maximum (or minimum) element. If we have n elements, this operation takes $\Theta(\log n)$ time. Although this operation can be done with the same asymptotic complexity—in fact, $O(\log n)$—using either a heap or a leftist tree, neither of these structures can implement a predictable tie breaker. The tournament tree becomes the data structure of choice when we need to break ties in a prescribed manner, such as to select the element that was inserted first or to select the element on the left (all elements are assumed to have a left-to-right ordering).

We study two varieties of tournament trees: winner and loser trees. Although winner trees are more intuitive and model real-world tournament trees, loser trees can be implemented more efficiently. The applications section considers another NP-hard problem, bin packing. Tournament trees are used to obtain efficient implementations of two approximation algorithms for the bin-packing problem. You will find it instructive to see whether you can implement these algorithms in the same time bounds using any of the other data structures developed so far in this text.

10.1 INTRODUCTION

Suppose that n players enter a tennis tournament. The tournament is to be played in the *sudden-death* mode in which a player is eliminated upon losing a match. Pairs of players play matches until only one remains undefeated. This surviving player is declared the tournament winner. Figure 10.1(a) shows a possible tennis tournament involving eight players a through h. The tournament is described by a binary tree in which each external node represents a player and each internal node represents a match played between players designated by the children of the node. Each level of internal nodes defines a *round* of matches that can be played in parallel. In the first round players a and b, c and d, e and f, and g and h play. The winner of each match is recorded at the internal node that represents the match. In the case of Figure 10.1(a), the four winners are b, d, e, and h. The remaining four players (i.e., the losers) are eliminated. In the next round of matches, b and d play against each other as do e and h. The winners are b and e who play the final match. The overall winner is e. Figure 10.1(b) shows a possible tournament that involves five players a through e. The winner in this case is c.

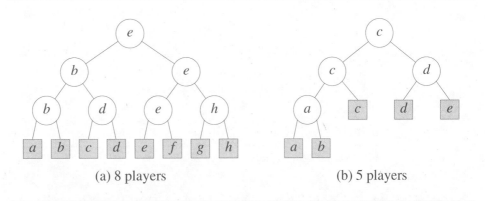

(a) 8 players   (b) 5 players

Figure 10.1 Tournament trees

Although both trees of Figure 10.1 are complete binary trees (actually, tree (a) is also a full binary tree), trees that correspond to real world tournaments do not have to be complete binary trees. However, using complete binary trees minimizes the number of rounds of matches that have to be played. For an n-player tournament, this number is $\lceil \log_2 n \rceil$. The tournament tree depicted in Figure 10.1 is called a **winner tree** because at each internal node, we record the winner of the match played at that node. Section 10.4 considers another variety, called **loser tree**, in which we record the loser at each internal node. Tournament trees are also known as **selection trees**.

Winner trees may be adapted for computer use. In this adaptation, we restrict ourselves to complete binary trees.

Definition A **winner tree** for n players is a complete binary tree with n external and $n-1$ internal nodes. Each internal node records the winner of the match played there. ∎

To determine the winner of a match, we assume that each player has a *value* and that there is a rule to determine the winner based on a comparison of the two players' values. In a **min winner tree**, the player with the smaller value wins, while in a **max winner tree**, the player with the larger value wins. In case of a tie, the player represented by the left child of the node wins. Figure 10.2(a) shows an eight-player min winner tree, while Figure 10.2(b) shows a five-player max winner tree. The number below each external node is the player's value.

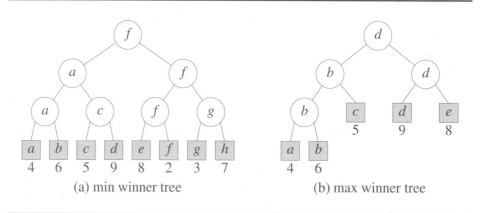

(a) min winner tree   (b) max winner tree

Figure 10.2 Winner trees

One of the nice things about a winner tree is that we can easily modify the tree to accomodate a change in one of the players. For example, if the value of player d changes from 9 to 1, then we need only replay matches on the path from d to the root. The change in this value does not affect the outcome of the remaining matches. In some situations we can avoid replaying some of the matches on the path to the root. For example, if in the min winner tree of Figure 10.2(a), the value of player b changes from 6 to 5, we play at its parent and b loses. There is no need to replay the matches at the grandparent and great grandparent of b, as these matches will have the same outcome as they had before.

Since the number of matches needed to restructure an n-player winner tree following a change in one value ranges from a low of one to a high of $\log_2 n$, the time needed for restructuring is $O(\log n)$. Also, an n player winner tree can be initialized in $\Theta(n)$ time by playing the $n-1$ matches at the internal nodes by beginning with the matches at the lowest level and working up to the root. Alternatively, the tree can be initialized by performing a postorder traversal. During the visit step, a match is played.

Example 10.1 [*Sorting*] We may use a min winner tree to sort n elements in $\Theta(n\log n)$ time. First, the winner tree is initialized with the n elements as the players. The sort key is used to decide the outcome of each match. The overall winner is the element with smallest key. This player's key is now changed to a very large number (say ∞) so that it cannot win against any of the remaining players. We restructure the tree to reflect the change in this player's key. The new overall winner is the element that comes next in sorted order. Its key is changed to ∞, and the tree is restructured. Now the overall winner is the element that is third in sorted order. Continuing in this way, we can sort the n elements. It takes $\Theta(n)$ time to initialize the winner tree. Each key change and restructure operation takes $\Theta(\log n)$ time because when the key of the tournament winner changes, we need to replay all matches on the path to the root. The restructuring needs to be done $n-1$ times, so the overall run time of the sorting method is $\Theta(n\log n)$. ∎

Example 10.2 [**Run Generation**] The sorting methods (insertion sort, heap sort, etc.) we have discussed so far are all **internal sorting methods**. These methods require that the elements to be sorted fit in the memory of our computer. When the element collection does not fit in memory, internal sort methods do not work too well because they require too many accesses to the external storage media (say a disk) on which all or part of the collection resides. In this case sorting is accomplished using an **external sorting method**. A popular approach to external sorting involves (1) generating sorted sequences called **runs** and (2) merging these runs together to create a single run.

Suppose we wish to sort a collection of 16,000 records and we are able to sort up to 1000 records at a time using an internal sort. Then in step 1, we do the following 16 times to create 16 runs:

Input 1000 records.
Sort these records using an internal sort.
Output the sorted sequence (or run).

Following this run-generation step, we initiate the run-merging step, step 2. In this step we repeatedly merge up to k runs creating a single sorted run until a single run remains. In our example of 16 runs, we could perform two levels of four-way merges, as in Figure 10.3. The initial 16 runs are labeled R1 $\cdots$ R16. First, runs R1 $\cdots$ R4 merge to obtain the run $S1$, which is 4000 records long. Then R5 $\cdots$ R8 merge, and so on. At the next level, S1 $\cdots$ S4 merge to create the single run T1, which is the desired output from the external sort.

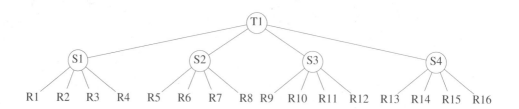

Figure 10.3 Four-way merging of 16 runs

A simple way to merge k runs is to repeatedly remove the element with smallest key from the front of these k runs. This element is moved to the output run being generated. The process is complete when all elements have been moved from the input k runs to the output run. Notice that to determine the next element in the output run we only need to have the key of the front element of each input run in memory. We can merge k runs of arbitrary length as long as we have enough memory to hold k keys. In practice, we will want to input and output many elements at a time so as to reduce the input/output time.

In our 16,000-record example, each run is 1000 records long, and our memory capacity is also 1000 records. To merge the first four runs, we could partition memory into five buffers, each of size 200 records. Four of these buffers are designated input buffers, and the fifth is an output buffer. Two hundred records from each of the first four runs are input into the four input buffers. The output buffer is used to collect the merged records. Records are merged from the input buffers into the output buffer until one of the following conditions occurs:

- *The output buffer becomes full.*
- *An input buffer becomes empty.*

When the first condition occurs, we write the output buffer to disk and resume merging when this write has completed. When the second condition occurs, we read in the next buffer load (if any) for the run that corresponds to the empty input buffer and resume merging when this input has completed. The merge of the four runs is complete when all 4000 records from these runs have been written out as the single run S1. (A more sophisticated run-merging scheme is described in *Fundamentals of Data Structures in C++* by E. Horowitz, S. Sahni, and D. Mehta, Computer Science Press, New York, NY, 1995.)

One of the factors that determines the amount of time spent in the run-merging step is the number of runs generated in step 1. By using a winner tree, we can often reduce the number of runs generated. We begin with a winner tree for p players where each player is an element of the input collection. Each player has a key and run number associated with it. The first p elements are assigned run number one. When a match is played between two players, the element with the smaller run number wins. In case of a tie, the keys are compared, and the element with smaller key wins. If a tie remains, it may be broken arbitrarily. To generate runs, we repeatedly move the overall winner W into the run corresponding to its run-number field and replace the moved element by the next input element N. If the key of N is $\geq$ the key of W, then element N can be output as part of the same run. It is assigned a run number equal to that of W. If the key of N is less than that of W, outputting N after W in the same run violates the sorting constraint on a run. N is assigned a run number that is one more than that of W.

When using this method to generate runs, the average run length is ~ $2p$. When $2p$ is larger than the memory capacity, we expect to get fewer runs than using the simple scheme proposed earlier. In fact, if our input collection is already sorted (or nearly sorted), only one run is generated and we can skip the run-merging step, step 2. ∎

Example 10.3 [*k-Way Merging*] In a k-way merge (see Example 10.2), k runs are merged to generate a single sorted run. The simple scheme, described in Example 10.2, to perform a k-way merge requires $O(k)$ time per element merged to the output run because in each iteration we need to find the smallest of k keys. The total time to generate a run of size n is, therefore, $O(kn)$. We can reduce this time to $\Theta(k + n\log k)$ using a winner tree. First we spend $\Theta(k)$ time to initialize a winner tree for k players. The k players are the first elements of the k runs to be merged. Then the winner is moved to the output run and replaced by the next element from the corresponding input run. If there is no next element in this run, it is replaced by an element with very large key (say ∞). We remove and replace the winner a total of n times at a cost of $\Theta(\log k)$ each time. The total time needed to perform the k-way merge is $\Theta(k + n\log k)$. ∎

EXERCISES

1. (a) Describe how a min heap can be used in place of a min winner tree to generate runs (see Example 10.2). How much time does it take to generate each element of a run?

   (b) What are the merits/demerits of using a min winner tree rather than a heap in this application?

2. (a) Describe how a min heap can be used in place of a min winner tree when performing a k-way merge (see Example 10.3).

   (b) What are the merits/demerits of using a min winner tree rather than a heap in this application?

10.2   THE ADT *WinnerTree*

In specifying the abstract data type *WinnerTree*, we make the assumption that the number of players is static. That is, after the tree is initialized for some number n of players, we do not increase or decrease the number of players. The players themselves are not part of the winner tree. So only the internal nodes of Figure 10.1 make up the winner tree. As a result, the operations that a winner tree needs to support are create an empty winner tree, initialize a winner tree for n players, return the winner, and replay the matches on the path from player i to the root. The specification of these operations is provided in ADT 10.1.

AbstractDataType *WinnerTree* {
  instances
    complete binary trees with each node pointing to the winner of the match played there; the external nodes represent the players
  operations
    Create(): create an empty winner tree
    Initialize(a, n): initialize a winner tree for the n players $a\,[1:n\,]$
    Winner(): return the tournament winner
    RePlay(i): replay matches following a change in player i
}

ADT 10.1 Abstract data type specification of a winner tree

10.3   THE CLASS `WinnerTree`

10.3.1   Representation

We assume that the winner tree is to be represented using the formula-based representation of a complete binary tree. A winner tree of n players requires $n-1$ internal nodes `t[1:n-1]`. The players (or external nodes) are represented as an array `e[1:n]`, so `t[i]` is an index into the array `e` and hence is of type `int`. `t[i]` gives the winner of the match played at node `i` of the winner tree. Figure 10.4 gives the correspondence between the nodes of a winner tree and the arrays `t` and `e` for the case of a five-player tree.

To implement the ADT operations, we must be able to determine the parent `t[p]` of an external node `e[i]`. When the number of external nodes is n, the number of internal nodes is $n-1$. The left-most internal node at the lowest level is numbered 2^s where $s = \lfloor \log_2(n-1) \rfloor$. Therefore, the number of internal nodes at the lowest level is $n-2^s$, and the number *LowExt* of external nodes at the lowest level is twice this number. For example, in the tree of Figure 10.4, $n = 5$

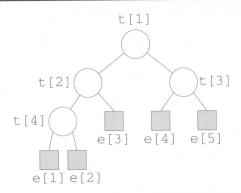

Figure 10.4 Tree-to-array correspondence

and $s = 2$. The left-most internal node at the lowest level is $t[2^s] = t[4]$, and the total number of internal nodes at this level is $n - 4 = 1$. The number of lowest-level external nodes is 2. The left-most external node at the second-lowest level is numbered $LowExt + 1$. Let $offset = 2^{s+1} - 1$. Then we see that for any external node $e[i]$, its parent $t[p]$ is given by

$$p = \begin{cases} (i + offset)/2 & i \le LowExt \\ (i - LowExt + n - 1)/2 & i > LowExt \end{cases} \tag{10.1}$$

10.3.2 Class Specification

The class specification appears in Program 10.1. The private members include `MaxSize` (the largest number of players permissible), `n` (the number of players the winner tree has been initialized for); `t` (internal node array); `e` (external node array); `LowExt`; and `offset`. We have specified `Initialize` and `RePlay` so that the function used to determine the winner of a match is a parameter. `winner(a,b,c)` returns the winner of the match played between `a[b]` and `a[c]`. By suitably defining `winner`, we can construct min winner trees, max winner trees, and so forth.

10.3.3 Constructor, Destructor, and `Winner`

The class constructor in Program 10.2 creates an initially empty winner tree ($n = 0$) that can handle up to `MaxSize` players. The usable internal nodes are `t[1]` through `t[MaxSize-1]`. The class destructor and function `Winner` are defined inline in Program 10.1.

```
template<class T>
class WinnerTree {
   public:
      WinnerTree(int TreeSize = 10);
      ~WinnerTree() {delete [] t;}
      void Initialize(T a[], int size,
          int(*winner)(T a[], int b, int c));
      int Winner()  const {return (n) ? t[1] : 0;}
      void RePlay(int i, int(*winner)
          (T a[], int b, int c));
   private:
      int MaxSize;
      int n;        // current size
      int LowExt;   // lowest-level external nodes
      int offset;   // 2^k - 1
      int *t;       // array for winner tree
      T *e;         // element array
      void Play(int p, int lc, int rc,
          int(*winner)(T a[], int b, int c));
};
```

Program 10.1 Class definition for a winner tree

```
template<class T>
WinnerTree<T>::WinnerTree(int TreeSize)
{// Constructor for winner tree.
   MaxSize = TreeSize;
   t = new int[MaxSize];
   n = 0;
}
```

Program 10.2 Creating a winner tree

10.3.4   Initializing a Winner Tree

The code for the initialization operation appears in Program 10.3.   a is the player array, size is the number of players, and winner computes the winner of a[b] and a[c]. We begin by verifying that the winner tree can handle this many players. If so, n and e are initialized. Next, $s = \lfloor \log_2 (n-1) \rfloor$ is

```
template<class T>
void WinnerTree<T>::Initialize(T a[], int size,
              int(*winner)(T a[], int b, int c))
{// Initialize winner t for array a.
   if (size > MaxSize || size < 2)
      throw BadInput();
   n = size;
   e = a;

   // compute  s = 2^log (n-1)
   int i, s;
   for (s = 1; 2*s <= n-1; s += s);

   LowExt = 2*(n-s);
   offset = 2*s-1;

   // play matches for lowest-level external nodes
   for (i = 2; i <= LowExt; i += 2)
      Play((offset+i)/2, i-1, i, winner);

   // handle remaining external nodes
   if (n % 2) {// special case for odd n, play
               // internal and external node
      Play(n/2, t[n-1], LowExt+1, winner);
      i = LowExt+3;}
   else i = LowExt+2;

   // i is left-most remaining external node
   for (; i <= n; i += 2)
      Play((i-LowExt+n-1)/2, i-1, i, winner);
}
```

Program 10.3 Initializing a winner tree

computed. From `s`, `LowExt` and `offset` are computed. To complete the initialization, we play matches beginning at external node `i` and going up the tree as far as possible. This match playing is done in the order $i = 1, 2, \cdots, n$. For this order we note that a match can be played at an internal node only if we are coming up from its right child. When an internal node is reached from its left child, the winner from its right subtree has yet to be determined and the match cannot be played. In the second `for` loop, match playing is initated by players (external nodes) at the lowest level. The players who are right children are e[2], e[4], ···, e[LowExt]. The match playing is done by the protected method Play (Program 10.4). For such an e[i], the parent is t[(offset+i)/2] (Equation 10.1) and the opponent e[i-1]. To play the matches initiated by the remaining n-LowExt players, we need to determine whether n is odd. If it is, e[LowExt+1] is a right child. Otherwise, it is a left child. If n is odd, the opponent is e[t[n-1]] and the parent is t[(n-1)/2]. The final for loop initiates the match sequence for the remaining external nodes.

```
template<class T>
void WinnerTree<T>::Play(int p, int lc, int rc,
       int (*winner)(T a[], int b, int c))
{// Play matches beginning at t[p].
 // lc and rc are the children of t[p].
   t[p] = winner(e, lc, rc);

   // more matches possible if at right child
   while (p > 1 && p % 2) {// at a right child
      t[p/2] = winner(e, t[p-1], t[p]);
      p /= 2;    // go to parent
      }
}
```

Program 10.4 Playing matches to initialize the tree

Function Play plays matches beginning with the one at internal node t[p]. It then moves up the winner tree playing matches until it moves from a left child to its parent.

To see how Initialize works, consider the five-player example of Figure 10.4. In the second for loop, a match is played between e[1] and e[2], and the winner recorded in t[4]. The match at t[2] is not played at this time, as t[4] is the left child of its parent t[2]. Then since n is odd, the match at t[2] is played between e[t[4]] and e[3]; the winner is recorded in t[2]. In the third for loop, we first play the match at t[3] (this match is between e[4] and e[5]). Then since t[3] is the right child of its parent, the match at t[1] is also played.

To analyze the complexity of Initialize, we see that the computation of s takes $\Theta(\log n)$ time. The second and third for loops take $\Theta(n)$ time exclusive of the time spent in function Play. The total time spent in all invocations of Play equals that needed to play n−1 matches. This time is $\Theta(n)$, so the overall time complexity of Initialize is $\Theta(n)$.

10.3.5   Replaying Matches

When the key corresponding to player i is changed, it is necessary to replay some or all of the matches on the path from external node e[i] to the root t[1]. For simplicity, we shall replay all matches on this path. Actually, in the applications of Examples 10.1, 10.2, and 10.3, only the key of the winner is changed. This change of key necessitates a replay of all matches on the path from the winner's external node to the root. Program 10.5 gives the code.

```
template<class T>
void WinnerTree<T>::RePlay(int i,
          int(*winner)(T a[], int b, int c))
{// Replay matches for element i.
   if (i <= 0 || i > n) throw OutOfBounds();

   int p,    // match node
       lc,   // left child of p
       rc;   // right child of p

   // find first match node and its children
   if (i <= LowExt) {// begin at lowest level
      p = (offset + i)/2;
      lc = 2*p - offset; // left child of p
      rc = lc+1;}
   else {p = (i-LowExt+n-1)/2;
         if (2*p == n-1) {lc = t[2*p];
                          rc = i;}
         else {lc = 2*p - n + 1 + LowExt;
               rc = lc+1;}
        }

   t[p] = winner(e, lc, rc);

   // play remaining matches
   p /= 2;   // move to parent
   for (; p >= 1; p /= 2)
      t[p] = winner(e, t[2*p], t[2*p+1]);
}
```

Program 10.5 Replaying matches when element i changes

For the replay, we use Equation 10.1 to determine the players involved in the first match. The match is played at `t[p]` between `e[lc]` and `e[rc]`, and the winner is recorded in `t[p]`. The remaining matches are played in the `for` loop. The total number of matches played is Θ(height of winner tree) = Θ(logn).

EXERCISES

3. Modify function `RePlay` (Program 10.5) to play only those necessary matches. In particular, we can stop playing when the winner of a match is the same as the previous winner of that match provided this previous winner is not the changed element `i`.

4. Write a sort program that uses a winner tree to repeatedly extract elements in sorted order (see Example 10.1).

10.4   LOSER TREES

Let us examine the `RePlay` operation on a winner tree. In many applications, this operation is performed only after the previous winner has been replaced by a new player (see Examples 10.1, 10.2, and 10.3). In these applications, all matches on the path from the external node that represents the winner up to the root have to be replayed. Consider the min winner tree of Figure 10.2(a). When the winner f is replaced by a player (f') with key 5, the first match is played between e and f'. e is the player who lost the match previously played at this node against f. The winner, f', plays the next match at internal node `t[3]` with g. Notice that g is the player who lost the match previously played at `t[3]` between g and f. The winner at `t[3]` is g. Next, g plays at the root against a. Again, a is the player who lost the match previously played at the root.

We can reduce the work needed to determine the players of each match on the path from the changed winner `e[i]` to the root if we record in each internal node the loser of the match played at that node, rather than the winner. The overall winner may be recorded in `t[0]`. Figure 10.5(a) shows the loser tree for the eight players of Figure 10.2(a). Now when the winner f is changed to have key 5, we move to its parent `t[6]`. The match is to be played between $e[t[6]]$ and `e[6]`. To determine the opponent for f' = `e[6]`, we simply look at `t[6]`. In a winner tree we would need to determine the other child of `t[6]`. After playing the match at `t[6]`, the loser e is recorded here and f' advances to play at `t[3]` with the previous loser of this match. This loser, g, is available from `t[3]`. f' loses, and this fact is recorded in `t[3]`. The winner g plays with the previous loser of the match at `t[1]`. This loser, a, is available from `t[1]`. The new loser tree appears in Figure 10.5(b).

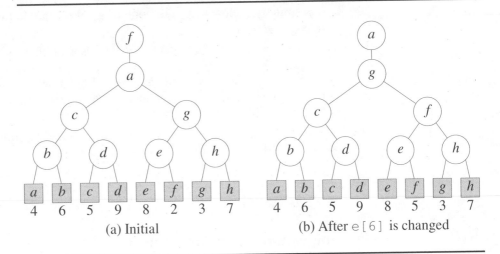

(a) Initial   (b) After e[6] is changed

Figure 10.5 Eight player min loser trees

Although a loser tree simplifies the replaying of matches following a change in the previous winner, it does not result in a similar simplification when a change is made in other players. For example, suppose that the key of player d is changed from 9 to 3. Matches are to be replayed at t[5], t[2], and t[1]. At t[5] d has to play c, but c is not the previous loser of this match. At t[2] d has to play a, but a did not lose the match previously played here. At t[1] d has to play f, not the player who previously lost at t[1]. To replay these matches easily, a winner tree is needed. Therefore, we expect a loser tree to give better performance than a winner tree only when the RePlay(i) function is restricted to the case when e[i] is the previous tournament winner.

EXERCISES

5. (a) Develop a C++ class LoserTree using a representation similar to that used for winner trees (Program 10.1). The tournament winner should be recorded in t[0]. In place of the public function RePlay(i), define the public function RePlay() to replay matches beginning at the winner of the previous tournament.

   (b) A simple way to initialize a loser tree is to first construct a winner tree and then make a level order traversal replacing the entry at each internal node by the loser. The traversal is done from top to bottom. When at t[i], its children tell us who played at t[i], and from this information we can determine who lost. Write `Initialize` using this strategy. Show that your code takes $\Theta(n)$ time to initialize a loser tree with n players.

(c) Write a version of `Initialize` that uses only the strategy used in Program 10.3. Play matches as far as you can, recording losers. When a match cannot be played, record the single player determined for that match. Show that your code takes $\Theta(n)$ time to initialize a loser tree with n players.

6. Write a sort program that uses a loser tree to repeatedly extract elements in sorted order. What is the complexity of your program?

10.5 APPLICATIONS

10.5.1 Bin Packing Using First Fit

In the bin-packing problem, we have bins that have a capacity `c` and `n` objects that need to be packed into these bins. Object `i` requires `s[i]`, $0 < $ `s[i]` $\leq$ `c`, units of capacity. A **feasible** packing is an assignment of objects to bins so that no bin's capacity is exceeded. A feasible packing that uses the fewest number of bins is an **optimal packing**.

Example 10.4 [*Truck Loading*] A freight company needs to pack parcels into trucks. Each parcel has a weight, and each truck has a load limit (assumed to be the same for all trucks). In the truck-loading problem, we are to pack the parcels into trucks using the fewest number of trucks. This problem may be modeled as a bin-packing problem with each truck being a bin and each parcel an object that needs to be packed. ■

Example 10.5 [*Chip Placement*] A collection of electronic chips is to be placed in rows on a circuit board of a given width. The chips have the same height but different widths. The height, and hence area, of the circuit board is minimized by minimizing the number of rows used. The chip-placement problem may also be modeled as a bin-packing problem with each row being a bin and each chip an object that needs to be packed. The board's width is the bin capacity, and the chip's length, the capacity needed by the corresponding object. ■

The bin-packing problem, like the machine-scheduling problem of Section 8.5.2, is an NP-hard problem. As a result, it is often solved using an approximation algorithm. In the case of bin packing, such an algorithm generates solutions that use a number of bins that is close to minimum. Four popular approximation algorithms for this problem are

1.   *First Fit (FF)*
     Objects are considered for packing in the order 1, 2, $\cdots$, n. We assume a large number of bins arranged from left to right. Object `i` is packed into the left-most bin into which it fits.

2.   *Best Fit (BF)*
     Let `cAvail[j]` denote the capacity available in bin `j`. Initially, the available capacity is `c` for all bins. Object `i` is packed into the bin with the least `cAvail` that is at least `s[i]`.

3.   *First Fit Decreasing (FFD)*
     This method is the same as FF except that the objects are first reordered so that `s[i]` $\geq$ `s[i+1]`, $1 \leq$ `i` $<$ `n`.

4.   *Best Fit Decreasing (BFD)*
     This method is the same as BF except that the objects are reordered as for FFD.

You should be able to show that not one of these methods guarantees optimal packings. All four are intuitively appealing and can be expected to perform well in practice.

Let *I* be any instance of the bin-packing problem. Let $b(I)$ be the number of bins used by an optimal packing. The number of bins used by FF and BF never exceeds $\lceil (17/10)b(I) \rceil$, while that used by FFD and BFD does not exceed $(11/9)b(I) + 4$. The proofs of these facts are rather laborious and can be found in the papers "Resource Constrained Scheduling as Generalized Bin-Packing" by M. Garey, R. Graham, D. Johnson, and A. Yao, *Journal of Combinatorial Theory*, Series A, 1976, 257–298, and "Worst-Case Performance Bounds for Simple One-Dimensional Packing Algorithms" by D. Johnson, A. Demers, J. Ullman, M. Garey, and R. Graham, *SIAM Journal on Computing*, 1974, 299–325.

Example 10.6 Four objects with `s[1:4]` = [3, 5, 2, 4] are to be packed in bins of size 7. When FF is used, object 1 goes into bin 1 and object 2 into bin 2. Object 3 fits into the first bin and is placed there. Object 4 does not fit into either of the two bins used so far, and a new bin is used. The solution produced utilizes three bins and has objects 1 and 3 in bin 1, object 2 in bin 2, and object 4 in bin 3.

When BF is used, objects 1 and 2 get into bins 1 and 2, respectively. Object 3 gets into bin 2, as this bin provides a better fit than does bin 1. Object 4 now fits into bin 1. The packing obtained uses only two bins and has objects 1 and 4 in bin 1 and objects 2 and 3 in bin 2.

For FFD and BFD, the objects are packed in the order 2, 4, 1, 3. In both cases a two-bin packing is obtained. Objects 2 and 3 are in bin 1, and objects 1 and 4 are in bin 2. ■

The FF and FFD methods can be implemented so as to run in $\Theta(n\log n)$ time using a winner tree. Since the maximum number of bins ever needed is n, we can begin with n empty bins. Let `avail[j]` be the available space in bin j. Initially, `avail[j] = c` for all n bins. Next, a max winner tree with the `avail[j]`'s as players is initialized. Figure 10.6(a) shows the max winner tree for the case n = 8 and c = 10. The external nodes represent bins 1 through 8 from left to right. The number below an external node is the space available in that bin. Suppose that `s[1] = 8`. To find the left-most bin for this object, we begin at the root `t[1]`. By definition, `avail[t[1]] ≥ s[1]`. This relationship simply means that there is at least one bin into which the object fits. To find the left-most bin, we determine whether there is enough space in one of the bins 1 through 4. One of these bins has enough space iff `avail[t[2]] ≥ s[1]`. In our example this relationship holds, and so we can continue the search for a bin in the subtree with root 2. Now we determine whether there is adequate space in any bin covered by the left subtree of 2 (i.e., the subtree with root 4). If so, we are not interested in bins in the right subtree. In our example we move into the left subtree as `avail[t[4]] ≥ s[1]`. Since the left subtree of 4 is an external node, we know that `s[1]` is to be placed in one of node 4's two children. It goes in the left child provided this child has enough space. When object 1 is placed in bin 1, `avail[1]` reduces to 2 and we must replay matches beginning at `avail[2]`. The new winner tree appears in Figure 10.6(b). Now suppose that `s[2] = 6`. Since `avail[t[2]] ≥ 6`, we know that there is a bin with adequate space in the left subtree. So we move here. Then we move into the left subtree 4 and place object 2 in bin 2. The new configuration appears in Figure 10.6(c). When `s[3] = 5`, the search for a bin leads us into the subtree with root 2. For its left subtree, `avail[t[4]] < s[3]`, so no bin in the subtree with root 4 has enough space. As a result, we move into the right subtree 5 and place the object in bin 3. This placement results in the configuration of Figure 10.6(d). Next, suppose `s[4] = 3`. Our search gets us to the subtree with root 4, as `avail[t4]] ≥ s[3]`, and we add object 3 to bin 2.

With the preceding discussion as motivation, we can develop a program for the first-fit strategy. The main program, which appears in Program 10.6, begins by inputting the number n of objects and the capacity c of each bin. We assume that the bin capacity and object space requirements are all integer. Further, we assume that the program is only for the case n ≥ 2. The cases n = 0 and 1 are trivial. Next, the n objects are entered, and we verify that each has a space requirement ≤ c. Finally, we invoke function `FirstFitPack` (Program 10.7), which does the actual assignment of objects to bins. In case we wish to pack using FFD, we can sort the objects into decreasing order before invoking `FirstFitPack`.

Function `FirstFitPack` begins by initializing a max winner tree for n players. Player i represents the current available capacity of bin i. This capacity is initially c for all bins. The function assumes that when a match is played, the left player is the winner unless the right one is larger. It also assumes that the

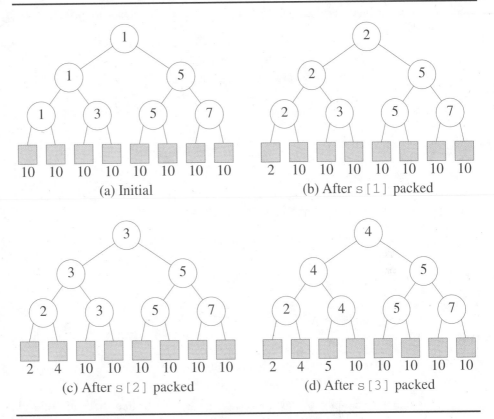

(a) Initial

(b) After s[1] packed

(c) After s[2] packed

(d) After s[3] packed

Figure 10.6 First-fit max winner trees

class definition of `WinnerTree` (Program 10.1) has been extended to add the public method:

```
int Winner(int i) const {return (i < n) ? t[i] : 0;}
```

This public method returns the winner of the match played at internal node `i`. In the second `for` loop, objects are assigned to bins one by one. When object `i` is being assigned, we follow a path beginning at the root and leading to the left-most bin with adequate space to accomodate the object. From our current position, we see whether the left subtree (this subtree has root `p`) has a bin with enough capacity. If not, the right subtree (this subtree has root `p+1`) is guaranteed to have such a bin. A bin in the left subtree is preferred over one in the right. Once we determine which subtree to move to, `p` is updated to the root of its left subtree. The `while` loop is exited when the left subtree of the current

```
void main(void)
{
    int n, c; // number of objects and bin capacity
    cout << "Enter number of objects and bin capacity"
        << endl;
    cin >> n >> c;
    if (n < 2) {cout << "Too few objects" << endl;
                exit(1);}
    int *s = new int[n+1];

    for (int i = 1; i <= n; i++) {
      cout << "Enter space requirement of object "
          << i << endl;
      cin >> s[i];
      if (s[i] > c) {
        cout << "Object too large to fit in a bin"
            << endl;
        exit(1);}
      }
    FirstFitPack(s, n, c);
}
```

Program 10.6 First-fit bin packing

node is an external node (i.e., $p \geq n$). Notice that our code does not explicitly record the current position. However, we can always compute the current position by dividing p by 2 upon exiting the `while` loop. When n is odd, the current position can be an external node. At this time p equals n. In all other cases p is an internal node. When p is at an external node, the bin represented by this node is the winner of the match played at its parent. That is, it is bin `t[p/2]`. When p is at an internal node, we are assured that bin `t[p]` has enough capacity. However, if this bin is not the left child of its parent, it may not be the left-most such bin. So we check with the bin on its left. Once the bin `b` to assign object `i` to has been determined, the available capacity of this bin is reduced by `s[i]` and the winner tree is restructured by replaying the matches on the path from this bin to the root.

Each iteration of the second `for` loop of Program 10.7 takes $\Theta(\log n)$ time. Therefore, this loop takes $\Theta(n \log n)$ time. The remainder of this function takes $\Theta(n)$ time, and the time needed to assign the objects to bins is $\Theta(n \log n)$.

```
void FirstFitPack(int s[], int n, int c)
{// Output first fit packing into bins of size c.
 // n is the number of objects and s[] their size.

   WinnerTree<int> *W = new WinnerTree<int> (n);
   int *avail = new int [n+1]; // bins

   // initialize n bins and winner tree
   for (int i = 1; i <= n; i++)
      avail[i] = c;  // initial available capacity
   W->Initialize(avail, n, winner);

   // put objects in bins
   for (int i = 1; i <= n; i++) {// put s[i] in a bin
      // find first bin with enough capacity
      int p = 2;  // start search at left child of root
      while (p < n) {
         int winp = W->Winner(p);
         if (avail[winp] < s[i])  // first bin is in
            p++ ;                        // right subtree
         p *= 2;    // move to left child
         }

      int b;    // will be set to bin to use
      p /= 2;  // undo last left child move
      if (p < n) {// at a tree node
        b = W->Winner(p);
        // if b is right child, need to check
        // bin b-1.  No harm done by checking
        // bin b-1 even if b is left child.
        if (b > 1 && avail[b-1] >= s[i])
           b--;}
      else  // arises when n is odd
         b = W->Winner(p/2);

      cout << "Pack object " << i << " in bin "
         << b << endl;
      avail[b] -= s[i];   // update avail. capacity
      W->RePlay(b, winner);
      }
}
```

Program 10.7 The function FirstFitPack

Commentary

Function `FirstFitPack` uses intimate details of the implementation of a winner tree. For example, it uses the fact that a winner tree is a complete binary tree represented as an array. As a result, it is able to move down the tree by multplying by two and possibly adding one. Moving down the tree in this way defeats one of the objectives of using a class—information hiding. We wish to insulate the implementation details of the class from the user. When the user and class are so insulated, we can change the implementation while keeping the public aspects of the class unchanged. Such changes do not affect the correctness of the applications. In the interests of information hiding, we may extend the class definition of `WinnerTree` to include public functions to move to the left and right children of an internal node and then use these functions in `FirstFitPack`.

10.5.2 Bin Packing Using Next Fit

Next fit is a bin-packing strategy in which objects are packed into bins one at a time. We begin by packing object 1 in bin 1. For the remaining objects, we determine the next nonempty bin that can accomodate the object by polling the bins in a round-robin fashion, begining at the bin next to the one last used. In such a polling, if bins 1 through b are in use, then these bins are viewed as arranged in a circle. The bin next to (or after) bin i is $i+1$ except when $i = b$; in this case the next bin is bin 1. If the last object placed went into bin j, then the search for a bin for the current object begins at the bin next to bin j. We examine successive bins until we either encounter a bin with enough space or return to bin j. If no bin with sufficient capacity is found, a new bin is started and the object placed into it.

Example 10.7 Six objects with $s[1:6]$ = [3, 5, 3, 4, 2, 1] are to be packed in bins of size 7. When next fit is used, object 1 goes into bin 1. Object 2 doesn't fit into a nonempty bin. So a new bin, bin 2, is started with this object in it. For object 3, we begin by examining the nonempty bin next to the last bin used. The last bin used was bin 2, and the bin next to it is bin 1. Bin 1 has enough space, and object 3 goes in it. For object 4, the search begins at bin 2, as bin 1 was the last one used. This bin doesn't have enough space. The bin next to bin 2 (i.e., bin 1) doesn't have enough space either. So a new bin, bin 3, is started with object 4 in it. The search for a bin for object 5 begins at the bin next to bin 3. This bin is bin 1. From here, the search moves to bin 2 where the object is actually packed. For the last object, we begin by examining bin 3. Since this bin has enough space, the object is placed here. ∎

The next-fit strategy described above is modeled after a dynamic memory allocation strategy that has the same name. In the context of bin packing, there is another next-fit strategy in which objects are packed one at a time. If an object does not fit into the current bin, then the current bin is closed and a new bin is started. We do not consider this variant of the next-fit strategy in this section.

A max winner tree may be used to obtain an efficient implementation of the next-fit strategy. As in the case of first fit, the external nodes represent the bins and matches are played by comparing the available space in the bins. For an n-object problem, we begin with n bins/external nodes. Consider the max winner tree of Figure 10.7, in which six of eight bins are in use. The labeling convention is the same as that used in Figure 10.6. Although the situation shown in Figure 10.7 cannot arise when n = 8, it illustrates how to determine the bin in which to pack the next object. If the last object was placed in bin last and b bins are currently in use, the search for the next bin to use can be broken into two searches as follows:

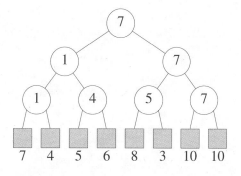

Figure 10.7 A next-fit max winner tree

Step 1: Find the first bin j, j > last into which the object fits. Such a j always exists as the number of bins is n. If this bin is not empty (i.e., j ≤ b), this bin is the bin to use.

Step 2: If step 1 does not find a bin, find the left-most bin into which the object fits. This bin is now the bin to use.

Consider the situation depicted in Figure 10.7 and suppose that the next object to be placed needs seven units of space. If last = 3, then in step 1 we determine that bin 5 has adequate space. Since bin 5 is not an empty bin, the object is placed into it. On the other hand, if last = 5, then in step 1, bin 7 is identified as the bin with enough space. Since bin 7 is empty, we move to step 1 and look for the left-most bin with enough capacity. This left-most bin is bin 1, and the object is placed into it.

To implement step 1, we begin at bin $j = $ last+1. Notice that if last $= $ n, then all n objects must have been packed as the only way to utilize n bins when the number of objects is n is to pack one object in each bin. So $j \le $ n. The pseudocode of Figure 10.8 describes the search process adopted from bin j. Basically, we traverse the path from bin j to the root, examining right subtrees until we find the first one that contains a bin with sufficient available capacity. When we find such a subtree, the bin we seek is the left-most bin in this subtree that has sufficient available capacity.

```
// Find nearest bin to right of
// last into which object i fits.
  j = last + 1;
  if (avail[j] >= s[i]) return j;
  if (avail[j+1] >= s[i]) return j + 1;
  p = parent of avail[j];
  if (p == n - 1) {// special case
    let q be the external node to the right of t[p];
    if (avail[q] >= s[i]) return q;}

// move towards root looking for first right
// subtree that has a bin with enough capacity
// subtree to right of p is p+1

p /= 2; // move to parent
while (avail[t[p+1]] < s[i])
    p /= 2;

return first bin in subtree p+1 into which object i fits;
```

Figure 10.8 Pseudocode for step 1

Consider the winner tree of Figure 10.7. Suppose that last $= 1$ and s[i] $= 7$. We begin with $j = 2$. First, we determine that bin 2 does not have enough capacity. Next, we check bin $j+1 = 3$. It doesn't have enough capacity either. So we move to bin j's parent and set p equal to four. Since $p \ne $ n-1, we reach the while loop and determine that the subtree with root 5 does not have a suitable bin. Next, we move to node 2 and determine that the subtree with root 3 has a suitable bin. The required bin is the left-most bin in this subtree that has seven or more units of space available. This bin, bin 5, can be found following the strategy of Program 10.7. Suppose, instead, that last $= 3$ and s[i] $= 9$. We begin by checking bin 4. Since neither bin 4 nor bin 5 has enough capacity, p is set to 5 and we reach the while loop. The first iteration checks avail[t[6]] and determines that the subtree with root 6 has no suitable bin. p is then moved to node 2, and we determine that the subtree with root 3 has a suitable bin. The left-most suitable bin in this subtree is identified using a process similar to that of Program 10.7. This left-most bin is bin 7. Since this bin is an empty bin, we move to step 2 and determine that bin 7 is, in fact, the bin to use.

Step 1 requires us to follow a path up the tree and then make a downward pass to identify the left-most suitable bin. This step can be done in O(logn) time. Step 2 may be done in Θ(logn) using the strategy of Program 10.7, so the overall complexity of the proposed next-fit implementation is Θ(nlogn).

EXERCISES

7. Function FirstFitPack (Program 10.7) takes Θ(logn) time to assign an object to a bin, even when the number of bins used so far is much less than n. We can reduce this time by beginning the search for a bin at the root of the smallest subtree that includes both bin 1 and bin b where b is the right-most bin currently in use; that is, we begin at the nearest ancestor of external nodes 1 and b. So when b is 3, we begin at internal node 2. In case none of the bins 1 through b has enough space, b is increased by 1. Also, during a replay, matches are played only as far as the nearest common ancestor of 1 and b. Rewrite Program 10.7 using these suggestions and then compare the run times of the two versions using randomly generated instances with n = 1000; 5000; 50,000; and 100,000.

8. (a) Extend the class WinnerTree by adding the public functions LeftChild(i) and RightChild(i) that, respectively, return the left and right children of the internal node i. They should return zero in case the child is an external node.

    (b) Now rewrite FirstFitPack (Program 10.7) so as to conform to the principles of information hiding described in the commentary of Section 10.5.1.

9. Although it is quite difficult to prove that the number of bins used by first fit and best fit never exceeds $\lceil (17/10)b(I) \rceil$, where $b(I)$ is the minimum number of bins needed by instance I, you should be able to prove that the number of bins never exceeds $2b(I)$ with modest effort. Prove this weaker bound.

10. Worst fit is an alternative bin-packing strategy. As in first fit, objects are packed into bins one at a time. When an object is considered, it is packed into a nonempty bin that has maximum available space provided the space is adequate. If the object cannot fit into this bin, a new bin is started for this

object. The worst-fit strategy can be implemented using a max heap. The complexity of the implementation is $O(n\log n)$ where n is the number of objects.

(a) Write a function `WorstFitPack` that differs from `FirstFit-Pack` only in its use of the worst-fit strategy. Use a max heap that is initially empty (no nonempty bins). Examine the bin with maximum available space each time an object is to be packed. If the bin doesn't have enough space, start a new bin and add it to the heap.

(b) Compare the number of bins required using worst fit with that used by first fit. Do this comparison by generating random instances with $n =$ 500, 1000, 2000, and 5000.

11. (a) Write a C++ program for the next fit strategy to pack bins. Use the two-step approach outlined in Section 10.5.2 and base the implementation of step 1 on the pseudocode of Figure 10.8.

(b) Compare the number of bins used by next fit and first fit on randomly generated bin-packing instances.

CHAPTER 11

SEARCH TREES

BIRD'S-EYE VIEW

This last chapter on trees develops tree structures suitable for the representation of a dictionary. The dictionary representations of Chapter 7 provide good expected behavior but poor worst-case behavior. When an n-element dictionary is represented using skip lists, the expected time for a search, insert, or delete is O(log$n$). However, the worst-case time is $\Theta(n)$. When hashing is used, the expected and worst-case times are $\Theta(1)$ and $\Theta(n)$, respectively. Skip lists are readily extended to provide efficient sequential access (i.e., retrieve elements in ascending order) to the dictionary elements. Hash tables, on the other hand, are unable to provide sequential access in an efficient way. When a balanced search tree is used, the expected and worst-case times for search, insert, and delete operations are $\Theta(\log n)$. The operations of search and delete by element rank can also be done in O(log$n$) time, and all dictionary elements can be output in ascending order in linear time. Since dictionary elements can be output in ascending order in linear time (using either balanced or unbalanced search trees), search trees support sequential access in $\Theta(1)$ average time per element retrieved.

In practice, we can expect hashing to outperform balanced search trees when the desired operations are search, insert, and delete (all by key value); therefore, hashing is the preferred method in these applications. When the dictionary operations are done solely by key value, balanced search trees are recommended only in time-critical applications in which we must guarantee that no dictionary operation ever takes more than a specified amount of time. Balanced search trees are also recommended when the search and delete operations are done by rank and for applications in which the dictionary operations are not done by exact key match. An example of the latter would be finding the smallest element with key larger than k.

We begin this chapter by examining binary search trees. These trees provide an asymptotic performance that is comparable to that of skip lists. The expected complexity of a search, insert, or delete operation is O(log$n$), while the worst-case complexity is $\Theta(n)$. Next we consider two of the many known varieties of balanced trees: AVL and red-black trees. When either AVL or red-black trees are used, a search, insert, or delete can be performed in logarithmic time (expected and worst case). The actual run-time performance of both structures is similar, with AVL trees generally being slightly faster. Both balanced tree structures use "rotations" to maintain balance. AVL trees perform at most one rotation following an insert and O(log$n$) rotations following a delete. However, red-black trees perform a single rotation following either an insert or delete. This difference is not important in most applications where a rotation takes $\Theta(1)$ time. It does, however, become important in advanced applications where a rotation cannot be performed in constant time. One such application is the implementation of the balanced priority search trees of McCreight. These priority search trees are used to represent elements with two-dimensional keys. In this case each key is a pair (x,y). A priority search tree is simultaneously a priority queue on y and a search tree on x. When rotations are performed in these trees, each has a cost of O(log$n$). Since red-black trees perform a single rotation following an insert or delete, the overall insert or delete time remains O(log$n$) if we use a red-black tree to represent a priority search tree. When we use an AVL tree, the time for the delete operation becomes O(log$n$).

Although AVL and red-black trees provide good performance when the dictionary being represented is sufficiently small to fit in our computer's memory, they are quite inadequate for larger dictionaries. When the dictionary resides on disk, we need to use search trees with a much higher degree and hence a much smaller height. An example of such a search tree, the B-tree, is also considered in this chapter.

Three applications of search trees are developed in the applications section. The first is the computation of a histogram. The second application is the implementation of the best-fit approximation method for the NP-hard bin-packing problem of Section 10.5.1. The final application is the crossing-distribution problem that arises when we route wires in a routing channel. We can improve the expected performance of the histogram application by using hashing in place of the search tree. In the best-fit application, the searches are not done by an exact match, and so hashing cannot be used. In the crossing-distribution problem, the operations are done by rank, and so hashing cannot be used here either.

11.1   BINARY SEARCH TREES

11.1.1   Definition

The abstract data type *Dictionary* was introduced in Section 7.1, and in Section 7.4, we saw that when a hash table represents a dictionary, the dictionary operations (insert, search, and delete) take $\Theta(1)$ expected time. However, the worst-case time for these operations is linear in the number n of dictionary entries. A hash table no longer provides good expected performance when we extend the ADT *Dictionary* to include operations such as

1.   Output in ascending order of keys.

2.   Find the kth element in ascending order.

3.   Delete the kth element.

To perform operation (1), we need to gather the elements from the table, sort them, and then output them. If a divisor D chained table is used, the elements can be gathered in $\Theta(D + n)$ time, sorted in $O(n\log n)$ time, and output in $\Theta(n)$ time. The total time for operation (1) is therefore $O(D + n\log n)$. If linear open addressing is used for the hash table, the gathering step takes $\Theta(b)$ time where b is the number of buckets. The total time for operation (1) is then $O(b + n\log n)$. Operations (2) and (3) can be done in $O(D + n)$ time when a chained table is used and in $\Theta(b)$ time when linear open addressing is used. To achieve these complexities for operations (2) and (3), we must use a linear-time algorithm to determine the kth element of a collection of n elements (explained in Section 14.5).

The basic dictionary operations (search, insert, delete) can be performed in $O(\log n)$ time when a balanced search tree is used. Operation (1) can then be performed in $\Theta(n)$ time. By using an indexed balanced search tree, we can also perform operations (2) and (3) in $O(\log n)$ time. Section 11.3 examines other applications where a balanced tree results in an efficient solution, while a hash table does not.

Rather than jump straight into the study of balanced trees, we first develop a simpler structure called a binary search tree.

Definition A **binary search tree** is a binary tree that may be empty. A nonempty binary search tree satisfies the following properties:

1.   Every element has a key (or value) and no two elements have the same key; therefore, all keys are distinct.

2.   The keys (if any) in the left subtree of the root are smaller than the key in the root.

3. The keys (if any) in the right subtree of the root are larger than the key in the root.

4. The left and right subtrees of the root are also binary search trees. ∎

There is some redundancy in this definition. Properties 2, 3, and 4 together imply that the keys must be distinct. Therefore, property 1 can be replaced by the following property: The root has a key. The preceding definition is, however, clearer than the nonredundant version.

Some binary trees in which the elements have distinct keys appear in Figure 11.1. The number inside a node is the element key. The tree of Figure 11.1(a) is not a binary search tree despite the fact that it satisfies properties 1, 2, and 3. The right subtree fails to satisfy property 4. This subtree is not a binary search tree as its right subtree has a key value (22) that is smaller than that in the subtrees' root (25). The binary trees of Figures 11.1(b) and (c) are binary search trees.

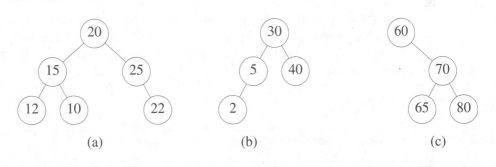

(a)   (b)   (c)

Figure 11.1 Binary trees

We can remove the requirement that all elements in a binary search tree need distinct keys. Now we replace smaller in property 2 by ≤ and larger in property 3 by ≥; the resulting tree is called a **binary search tree with duplicates**.

An **indexed binary search tree** is derived from an ordinary binary search tree by adding the field LeftSize to each tree node. This field gives the number of elements in the node's left subtree plus one. Figure 11.2 shows two indexed binary search trees. The number inside a node is the element key, while that outside is the value of LeftSize. Notice that LeftSize also gives the rank of an element with respect to the elements in its subtree. For example, in the tree of Figure 11.2 (a), the elements (in sorted order) in the subtree with root 20 are 12, 15, 18, 20, 25, and 30. The rank of the root is four (i.e., the element in the root is the fourth element in sorted order). In the subtree with root 25, the elements (in sorted order) are 25 and 30, so the rank of 25 is one and its Left-Size value is 1.

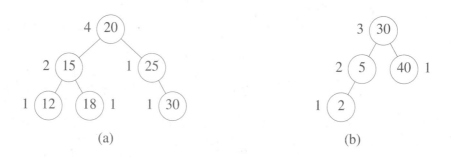

Figure 11.2 Indexed binary search trees

11.1.2 The ADTs *BSTree* and *IndexedBSTree*

ADT 11.1 gives the abstract data type specification for a binary search tree. An indexed binary search tree supports all the binary search tree operations. In addition, it supports search and deletion by rank. Its abstract data type specification is given in ADT 11.2. The abstract data types *DBSTree* (binary search trees with duplicates) and *DIndexedBSTree* may be specified in a similar way.

AbstractDataType *BSTree* {
   instances
      binary trees, each node has an element with a key field; all keys are distinct;
      keys in the left subtree of any node are smaller than the key in the node;
      those in the right subtree are larger.
   operations
      Create(): create an empty binary search tree
      Search(k, e): return in *e* the element with key *k*
                return `false` if the operation fails, return `true` if it succeeds
      Insert(e): insert element *e* into the search tree
      Delete(k, e): delete the element with key *k* and return it in *e*
      Ascend(): Output all elements in ascending order of key
}

ADT 11.1 Abstract data type specification of a binary search tree

---

AbstractDataType *IndexedBSTree* {
  instances
    Same as for `BSTree` except that each node has a `LeftSize` field.
  operations
    Create(): create an empty indexed binary search tree
    Search(k, e): return in *e* the element with key *k*
                  return `false` if the operation fails, return `true` if it succeeds
    IndexSearch(k, e): return in *e* the *k*th element
    Insert(e): insert element *e* into the search tree
    Delete(k, e): delete the element with key *k* and return it in *e*
    IndexDelete(k, e): delete the *k*th element and return it in *e*
    Ascend(): Output all elements in ascending order of key
}

ADT 11.2 Abstract data type specification of an indexed binary search tree

11.1.3 The Class `BSTree`

Since the number of elements in a binary search tree as well as its shape changes as operations are performed, a binary search tree is represented using the linked representation of Section 8.4. We can greatly simplify the task of developing the class `BSTree` if we define this class as a derived class of `BinaryTree` (Program 8.7), as is done in Program 11.1. Since `BSTree` is a derived class of `BinaryTree`, it inherits all members of `BinaryTree`. However, it has access only to the public and protected members. To access the private member `root` of `BinaryTree`, we need to make `BSTree` a friend of `BinaryTree`.

```
template<class E, class K>
class BSTree : public BinaryTree<E> {
   public:
      bool Search(const K& k, E& e) const;
      BSTree<E,K>& Insert(const E& e);
      BSTree<E,K>& Delete(const K& k, E& e);
      void Ascend() {InOutput();}
};
```

Program 11.1 Class definition for binary search trees

The class `IndexedBSTree` may also be defined as a derived class of `BinaryTree` (see Exercise 5). Notice that the elements of a binary tree can be output in ascending order by invoking the inorder output function `InOutput` defined in Section 8.9 for binary trees. This function outputs the elements in the left subtree (i.e., smaller elements), then the root element, and finally those in the right subtree (i.e., larger elements). The time complexity is $\Theta(n)$ for an n-element tree.

11.1.4 Searching

Suppose we wish to search for an element with key k. We begin at the root. If the root is `NULL` (i.e., zero), the search tree contains no elements and the search is unsuccessful. Otherwise, we compare k with the key in the root. If k is less than the key in the root, then no element in the right subtree can have key value k and only the left subtree is to be searched. If k is larger than the key in the root, only the right subtree needs to be searched. If k equals the key in the root, then the search terminates successfully. The subtrees may be searched similarly. Program 11.2 gives the code. The time complexity is $O(h)$ where h is the height of the tree being searched.

```
template<class E, class K>
bool BSTree<E,K>::Search(const K& k, E &e) const
{// Search for element that matches k.
   // pointer p starts at the root and moves through
   // the tree looking for an element with key k
   BinaryTreeNode<E> *p = root;
   while (p) // examine p->data
      if (k < p->data) p = p->LeftChild;
      else if (k > p->data) p = p->RightChild;
           else {// found element
                  e = p->data;
                  return true;}
   return false;
}
```

Program 11.2 Search a binary search tree

We can perform an indexed search in an indexed binary search tree in a similar manner. Suppose we are looking for the third element in the tree of Figure 11.2(a). The `LeftSize` field of the root is 4. So the third element is in the left subtree. The root of the left subtree has `LeftSize = 2`. So the third element is the smallest element in its right subtree. Since the root of this right subtree has `LeftSize` = 1, the desired element is located here. The time complexity of an indexed search is also O(*h*).

11.1.5   Inserting an Element

To insert a new element e into a binary search tree, we must first verify that its key is different from those of existing elements by performing a search for an element with the same key as that of e. If the search is unsuccessful, then the element is inserted at the point the search terminated. For instance, to insert an element with key 80 into the tree of Figure 11.1(b), we first search for 80. This search terminates unsuccessfully, and the last node examined is the one with key 40. The new element is inserted as the right child of this node. The resulting search tree appears in Figure 11.3(a). Figure 11.3(b) shows the result of inserting key 35 into the search tree of Figure 11.3(a). Program 11.3 implements this insert strategy.

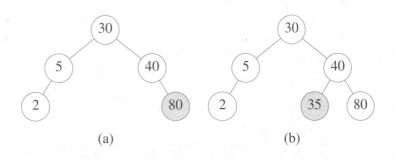

(a)   (b)

Figure 11.3 Inserting into a binary search tree

When inserting into an indexed binary search tree, we use a procedure similar to Program 11.3. This time, though, we also need to update `LeftSize` fields on the path from the root to the newly inserted node. Nevertheless, the insertion can be performed in O(*h*) time where *h* is the height of the search tree.

11.1.6   Deleting an Element

For deletion we consider the three possibilities for the node p that contains the element to be deleted: (1) p is a leaf, (2) p has exactly one nonempty subtree, and (3) p has exactly two nonempty subtrees.

Case (1) is handled by discarding the leaf node. To delete 35 from the tree of Figure 11.3(b), the left-child field of its parent is set to zero and the node discarded. The resulting tree appears in Figure 11.3(a). To delete the 80 from this

```
template<class E, class K>
BSTree<E,K>& BSTree<E,K>::Insert(const E& e)
{// Insert e if not duplicate.
   BinaryTreeNode<E> *p = root,   // search pointer
                     *pp = 0;     // parent of p
   // find place to insert
   while (p) {// examine p->data
      pp = p;
      // move p to a child
      if (e < p->data) p = p->LeftChild;
      else if (e > p->data) p = p->RightChild;
           else throw BadInput(); // duplicate
      }

   // get a node for e and attach to pp
   BinaryTreeNode<E> *r = new BinaryTreeNode<E> (e);
   if (root) {// tree not empty
      if (e < pp->data) pp->LeftChild = r;
      else pp->RightChild = r;}
   else // insertion into empty tree
        root = r;

   return *this;
}
```

Program 11.3 Inserting into a binary search tree

tree, the right-child field of 40 is set to zero, obtaining the tree of Figure 11.1(b), and the node containing 80 is discarded.

Next consider the case when the element to be deleted is in a node p that has only one nonempty subtree. If p has no parent (i.e., it is the root), node p is discarded and the root of its single subtree becomes the new search tree root. If p has a parent pp, then we change the pointer from pp so that it points to p's only child and then delete the node p. For instance, if we wish to delete the element with key 5 from the tree of Figure 11.3(b), we change the left-child field of its parent (i.e., the node containing 30) to point to the node containing the 2.

Finally, to delete an element in a node that has two nonempty subtrees, we replace this element with either the largest element in its left subtree or the smallest element in its right subtree. Suppose we wish to delete the element with key 40 from the tree of Figure 11.4(a). Either the largest element (35) from its left subtree or the smallest (60) from its right subtree can replace this element. If we opt for the smallest element in the right subtree, we move the element with key

60 to the node from which the 40 was deleted, and the leaf from which the 60 is moved is deleted. The resulting tree appears in Figure 11.4(b).

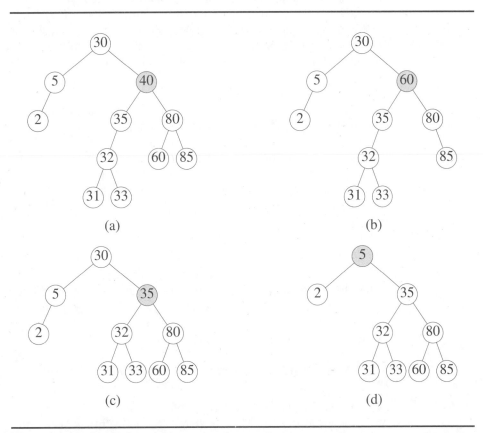

Figure 11.4 Deletion from a binary search tree

Suppose, instead, that when deleting 40 from the search tree of Figure 11.4(a), we had opted for the largest element in the left subtree of 40. This element has key 35 and is in a node of degree 1. We move the element into the node that currently contains 40 and the left-child pointer of this node changes to point to the lone child of the node from which the 35 was moved. The result is shown in Figure 11.4(c).

As another example, consider the deletion of 30 from the tree of Figure 11.4(c). We may replace this element with either the 5 or the 31. If we opt for the 5, then since 5 is currently in a node with degree 1, we change the left-child pointer of the parent node to point to the lone child. The result is the tree of Figure 11.4(d). If we had opted to replace 30 with 31, then since 31 is in a leaf, we need merely delete this leaf.

Notice that the element with smallest key in the right subtree (as well as that with largest key in the right subtree) is guaranteed to be in a node with either zero or one nonempty subtree. Note also that we can find the largest element in the left subtree of a node by moving to the root of that subtree and then following a sequence of right-child pointers until we reach a node whose right-child pointer is 0. Similarly, we can find the smallest element in the right subtree of a node by moving to the root of the right subtree and then following a sequence of left-child pointers until we reach a node whose left-child pointer is 0.

Program 11.4 implements the deletion strategy outlined above. When deleting from a node with two nonempty subtrees, this code always uses the largest element in the left subtree as a replacement. The complexity of this code is O(h). We can perform an indexed deletion from an indexed binary search tree in the same amount of time using an analogous procedure. We first perform an indexed search to locate the element to be deleted. Next we delete the element as outlined here and update `LeftSize` fields on the path from the root to the physically deleted node as necessary.

11.1.7 The Class `DBSTree`

The class for the case when the binary search tree is permitted to contain elements that have the same key is called `DBSTree`. We can implement this class by changing the `while` loop of `BSTree::Insert` (Program 11.3) to that shown in Program 11.5. No other changes are needed.

11.1.8 Height of a Binary Search Tree

Unless care is taken, the height of a binary search tree with n elements can become as large as n. The tree height becomes this large, for instance, when Program 11.3 is used to insert elements with keys [1, 2, 3, $\cdots$, n], in this order, into an initially empty binary search tree. As a result, a search, insert, or delete operation on a binary search tree takes O(n) time. This time is no better than the times for these operations using an unordered chain. However, we can show that when insertions and deletions are made at random using Programs 11.3 and 11.4, the height of the binary search tree is O(log$n$) on the average. As a result, the expected time for each of the search tree operations is O(log$n$).

```
template<class E, class K>
BSTree<E,K>& BSTree<E,K>::Delete(const K& k, E& e)
{// Delete element with key k and put it in e.
   // set p to point to node with key k
   BinaryTreeNode<E> *p = root, // search pointer
                     *pp = 0;   // parent of p
   while (p && p->data != k){// move to a child of p
      pp = p;
      if (k < p->data) p = p->LeftChild;
      else p = p->RightChild;
      }
   if (!p) throw BadInput(); // no element with key k
   e = p->data;  // save element to delete
   // restructure tree
   // handle case when p has two children
   if (p->LeftChild && p->RightChild) {// two children
      // convert to zero or one child case
      // find largest element in left subtree of p
      BinaryTreeNode<E> *s = p->LeftChild,
                        *ps = p;  // parent of s
      while (s->RightChild) {// move to larger element
         ps = s;
         s = s->RightChild;}
      // move largest from s to p
      p->data = s->data;
      p = s;
      pp = ps;}
   // p has at most one child
   // save child pointer in c
   BinaryTreeNode<E> *c;
   if (p->LeftChild) c = p->LeftChild;
   else c = p->RightChild;
   // delete p
   if (p == root) root = c;
   else {// is p left or right child of pp?
         if (p == pp->LeftChild)
            pp->LeftChild = c;
         else pp->RightChild = c;}
   delete p;
   return *this;
}
```

Program 11.4 Deleting from a binary search tree

```
while (p) {
   pp = p;
   if (e <= p->data) p = p->LeftChild;
   else p = p->RightChild;
   }
```

Program 11.5 New `while` loop for Program 11.3 to permit duplicates

EXERCISES

1. How much (expected) time does it take to do the *BSTree* operations of ADT 11.1 using skip lists?

2. Provide a specification for the abstract data type `DBSTree` (binary search tree with duplicates).

3. Provide a specification for the abstract data type *DIndexedBSTree*.

4. Develop the C++ class `DBSTree` as a derived class of `BSTree` (Program 11.1). The complexity of each function should be the same as for `BSTree`. Test the correctness of your implementation.

5. Develop the C++ class `IndexedBSTree` as a derived class of `BSTree`. You may assume that `LeftSize` is a subfield of `data`. Test the correctness of all your functions. Express the time complexity of each function in terms of the number of elements and/or the height of the tree.

6. Develop a class `IndexedBinaryTree` that represents a linear list as a binary tree (not a binary search tree). Your implementation should support all the linear list operations defined in Program 3.1. Other than the operation `Search`, all should run in logarithmic or less expected time. Show that this is the case. You may assume that the expected height of the binary tree constructed is logarithmic in the number of elements.

7. Do Exercise 5 for the class `DIndexedBSTree`. This time, derive from the class `DBSTree` of Exercise 4.

8. Generate a random permutation of the integers 1 through n. Insert the keys 1 through n into an initially empty binary search tree. Perform the insertion in the order specified by the random permutation. Measure the height of the resulting search tree. Repeat this experiment for several random permutations and compute the average of the measured heights. Compare this figure with $2\lceil \log_2(n+1) \rceil$. For n use the values 100; 500; 1000; 10,000; 20,000; and 50,000.

9. Change Program 11.2 so that in the `whle` loop, the first comparison is `k == p->data`. Use the search-tree-generation method described in Exercise 8 to generate random search trees of different size. Measure the time it takes to search for all elements in the tree using Program 11.2 as well as the modified version just described. What conclusion can you draw?

10. A binary search tree can be used to sort n elements. Write a sort procedure that inserts the n elements `a[1:n]` into an initially empty binary search tree and then performs an inorder traversal putting the numbers into a in sorted order. For simplicity, assume that the numbers in a are distinct. Compare the average run time of the resulting sort procedure with that for insertion sort and heap sort.

11. Write a function to delete the max element from a binary search tree. Your function must have time complexity $O(h)$ where h is the height of the binary search tree. Show that your code has this complexity.

    (a) Use suitable test data to test the correctness of your deletion procedure.

    (b) Create a random list of n elements and a random sequence of insert and delete max operations of length m. Create the latter sequence so that the probability of an insert is approximately 0.5 (therefore, the probability of a delete max is also 0.5). Initialize a max heap and a binary search tree to contain the n elements in the first random list. Now measure the time to perform the m operations, using the max heap as well as the binary search tree. Divide this time by m to get the average time per operation. Do this experiment for $n = 100, 500, 1000, 2000, \cdots, 5000$. Let m be 5000. Tabulate your computing times.

    (c) Based on your experiments, what can you say about the relative merits of the two priority queue schemes?

⋆12. Extend the class `BinarySearchTree` by including the sequential access functions `Begin` and `Next` which, respectively, return a pointer to the first and next element (in ascending order) of a dictionary. Both return zero in case there is no first or next element. The average complexity of both functions (averaged over the retrieval of all elements in the search tree) should be $\Theta(1)$. Show that this is the case. Test the correctness of your codes.

11.2   AVL TREES

11.2.1   Definition

We can guarantee O(log$n$) performance for each search tree operation by ensuring that the search tree height is always O(log$n$). Trees with a worst-case height of O(log$n$) are called **balanced trees**. One of the more popular balanced trees, known as an **AVL tree**, was introduced in 1962 by Adelson-Velskii and Landis.

Definition An empty binary tree is an AVL tree. If T is a nonempty binary tree with T_L and T_R as its left and right subtrees, then T is an AVL tree iff (1) T_L and T_R are AVL trees and (2) $|h_L - h_R| \leq 1$ where h_L and h_R are the heights of T_L and T_R, respectively. ∎

An **AVL search tree** is a binary search tree that is also an AVL tree. Trees (a) and (b) of Figure 11.1 are AVL trees, while tree (c) is not. Tree (a) is not an AVL search tree, as it is not a binary search tree. Tree (b) is an AVL search tree. The trees of Figure 11.3 are AVL search trees.

An **indexed AVL search tree** is an indexed binary search tree that is also an AVL tree. Both the search trees of Figure 11.2 are indexed AVL search trees. In the remainder of this section, we shall not consider indexed AVL search trees explicitly. However, the techniques we develop carry over in a rather straight-forward manner to such trees.

If we are to use AVL search trees to represent a dictionary and perform each dictionary operation in logarithmic time, then we must establish the following properties:

1.   The height of an AVL tree with n elements/nodes is O(log$n$).

2.   For every value of n, $n \geq 0$, there exists an AVL tree. (Otherwise, some insertions cannot leave behind an AVL tree, as no such tree exists for the current number of elements.)

3.   An n-element AVL search tree can be searched in O(*height*) = O(log$n$) time.

4.   A new element can be inserted into an n element AVL search tree so that the result is an $n + 1$ element AVL tree and such an insertion can be done in O(log$n$) time.

5.   An element can be deleted from an n-element AVL search tree so that the result is an $n - 1$ element AVL tree and such a deletion can be done in O(log$n$) time.

Property 2 follows from property 4, so we shall not show property 2 explicitly. Properties 1, 3, 4, and 5 are established in the following subsections.

11.2.2 Height of an AVL Tree

We shall obtain a bound on the height of an AVL tree that has n nodes in it. Let N_h be the minimum number of nodes in an AVL tree of height h. In the worst case the height of one of the subtrees is $h - 1$, and the height of the other is $h - 2$. Both these subtrees are also AVL trees. Hence

$$N_h = N_{h-1} + N_{h-2} + 1, N_0 = 0, \text{ and } N_1 = 1$$

Notice the similarity between this definition for N_h and the definition of the Fibonacci numbers

$$F_n = F_{n-1} + F_{n-2}, F_0 = 0, \text{ and } F_1 = 1.$$

It can be shown (see Exercise 11) that $N_h = F_{h+2} - 1$ for $h \geq 0$. From Fibonacci number theory we know that $F_h \approx \phi^h / \sqrt{5}$ where $\phi = (1 + \sqrt{5})/2$. Hence $N_h \approx \phi^{h+2} / \sqrt{5} - 1$. If there are n nodes in the tree, then its height h is at most $\log_\phi (\sqrt{5}(n + 1)) - 2 \sim 1.44\log_2(n + 2) = O(\log n)$.

11.2.3 Representation of an AVL Tree

AVL trees are normally represented using the linked representation scheme for binary trees. However, to facilitate insertion and deletion, a balance factor bf is associated with each node. The balance factor $bf(x)$ of a node x is defined to be

height of left subtree of x − height of right subtree of x

From the definition of an AVL tree, it follows that the permissible balance factors are −1, 0, and 1. Figure 11.5 shows two AVL search trees and the balance factors for each node.

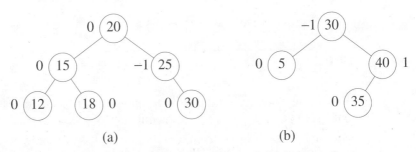

(a)   (b)

The number outside each node is its balance factor

Figure 11.5 AVL search trees

11.2.4 Searching an AVL Search Tree

To search an AVL search tree, we may use the code of Program 11.2 without change. Since the height of an AVL tree with n elements is $O(\log n)$, the search time is $O(n \log n)$.

11.2.5 Inserting into an AVL Search Tree

If we use the strategy of Program 11.3 to insert an element into an AVL search tree, the tree following the insertion may no longer be AVL. For instance, when an element with key 32 is inserted into the AVL tree of Figure 11.5(b), the new search tree is the one shown in Figure 11.6(a). Since this tree contains nodes with balance factors other than -1, 0, and 1, it is not an AVL tree. When an insertion into an AVL tree using the strategy of Program 11.3 results in a search tree that has one or more nodes with balance factors other than -1, 0, and 1, the resulting search tree is **unbalanced**. We can restore balance (i.e., make all balance factors -1, 0, and 1) by shifting some of the subtrees of the unbalanced tree as in Figure 11.6(b).

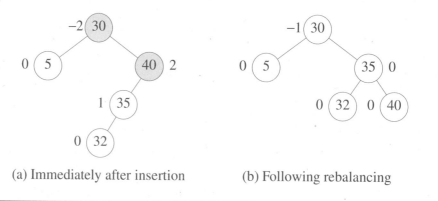

(a) Immediately after insertion   (b) Following rebalancing

Figure 11.6 Sample insertion into an AVL search tree

Before examining the subtree movement needed to restore balance, let us make some observations about the unbalanced tree that results from an insertion.

I1:   In the unbalanced tree the balance factors are limited to -2, -1, 0, 1, and 2.

I2:   A node with balance factor 2 had a balance factor 1 before the insertion. Similarly, a node with balance factor -2 had a balance factor -1 before the insertion.

I3:   The balance factors of only those nodes on the path from the root to the newly inserted node can change as a result of the insertion.

I4:   Let A denote the nearest ancestor of the newly inserted node whose balance factor is either -2 or 2. (In the case of Figure 11.6(a), the A node is the node with key 40.) The balance factor of all nodes on the path from A to the newly inserted node was 0 prior to the insertion.

Node A (see I4) may be identified while we are moving down from the root searching for the place to insert the new element. From I2 it follows that $bf(A)$ was either -1 or 1 prior to the insertion. Let X denote the last node encountered that has such a balance factor. When inserting 32 into the AVL tree of Figure 11.5(b), X is the node with key 40; when inserting 22, 28, or 50 into the AVL tree of Figure 11.5(a), X is the node with key 25; and when inserting 10, 14, 16, or 19 into the AVL tree of Figure 11.5(a), there is no node X.

When node X does not exist, all nodes on the path from the root to the newly inserted node have balance factor 0 prior to the insertion. The tree cannot be unbalanced following the insertion because an insertion changes balance factors by -1, 0, or 1, and only balance factors on the path from the root may change. Therefore, if the tree is unbalanced following the insertion, X exists. If $bf(X) = 0$ after the insertion, then the height of the subtree with root X is the same before and after the insertion. For example, if this height was h before the insertion and if $bf(X)$ was 1, the height of its left subtree X_L was $h-1$ and that of its right subtree X_R was $h-2$ before the insertion (see Figure 11.7(a)). For the balance factor to become 0, the insertion must be made in X_R resulting in an X'_R of height $h-1$ (see Figure 11.7(b)). The height of X'_R must increase to $h-1$ as all balance factors on the path from X to the newly inserted node were 0 prior to the insertion. The height of X remains h and the balance factors of the ancestors of X are the same before and after the insertion, so the tree is balanced.

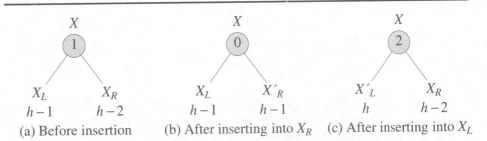

Balance factor of X is inside the node.
Subtree heights are below subtree names.

Figure 11.7 Inserting into an AVL search tree

The only way the tree can become unbalanced is if the insertion causes $bf(X)$ to change from -1 to -2 or from 1 to 2. For the latter case to occur, the insertion must be made in the left subtree X_L of X (see Figure 11.7(c)). Now the height of X'_L must become h (as all balance factors on the path from X to the newly inserted node were 0 prior to the insertion). Therefore, the A node referred to in observation I4 is X.

When the A node has been identified, the imbalance at A can be classified as either an L (the newly inserted node is in the left subtree of A) or R type imbalance. This imbalance classification may be refined by determining which grandchild of A is on the path to the newly inserted node. Notice that such a grandchild exists, as the height of the subtree of A that contains the new node must be at least 2 for the balance factor of A to be -2 or 2. With this refinement of the imbalance classification, the imbalance at A is of one of the types LL (new node is in the left subtree of the left subtree of A), LR (new node is in the right subtree of the left subtree of A), RR, and RL.

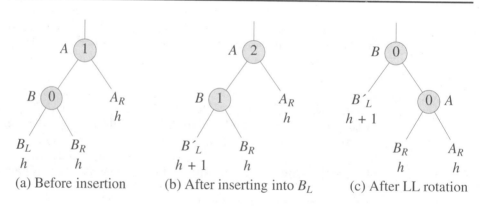

(a) Before insertion   (b) After inserting into B_L (c) After LL rotation

Balance factors are inside nodes.
Subtree heights are below subtree names.

Figure 11.8 An LL rotation

A generic LL type imbalance appears in Figure 11.8. Figure 11.8(a) shows the conditions before the insertion, and Figure 11.8(b) shows the situation following the insertion of an element into the left subtree B_L of B. The subtree movement needed to restore balance at A appears in Figure 11.8(c). B becomes the root of the subtree that A was previously root of, B'_L remains the left subtree of B, A becomes the root of B's right subtree, B_R becomes the left subtree of A, and the right subtree of A is unchanged. The balance factors of nodes in B'_L that are on the path from B to the newly inserted node change as does the balance factor of A. The remaining balance factors are the same as before the rotation. Since the heights of the subtrees of Figures 11.8(a) and (c) are the same, the balance factors of the ancestors (if any) of this subtree are the same as before the insertion. So no nodes with a balance factor other than $-1, 0$, or 1 remain. A single LL rotation has rebalanced the entire tree! You may verify that the rebalanced tree is indeed a binary search tree.

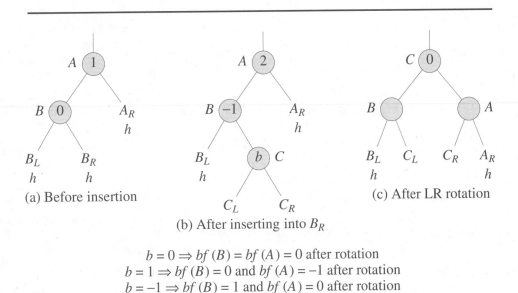

(a) Before insertion

(b) After inserting into B_R

(c) After LR rotation

$$b = 0 \Rightarrow bf(B) = bf(A) = 0 \text{ after rotation}$$
$$b = 1 \Rightarrow bf(B) = 0 \text{ and } bf(A) = -1 \text{ after rotation}$$
$$b = -1 \Rightarrow bf(B) = 1 \text{ and } bf(A) = 0 \text{ after rotation}$$

Figure 11.9 An LR rotation

Figure 11.9 shows a generic LR type imbalance. Since the insertion took place in the right subtree of B, this subtree cannot be empty following the insertion; therefore, node C exists. However, its subtrees C_L and C_R may be empty. The rearrangement of subtrees needed to rebalance appears in Figure 11.9(c). The values of $bf(B)$ and $bf(A)$ following the rearrangement depend on the value, b, of $bf(C)$ just after the insertion but before the rearrangement. The figure gives these values as a function of b. The rearranged subtree is seen to be a binary search tree. Also, since the heights of the subtrees of Figures 11.9(a) and (c) are the same, the balance factors of their ancestors (if any) are the same before and after the insertion. So a single LR rotation at A rebalances the entire tree.

The cases RR and RL are symmetric to the ones we have just seen. The transformations done to remedy LL and RR imbalances are often called **single rotations**, while those done for LR and RL imbalances are called **double rotations**. The transformation for an LR imbalance can be viewed as an RR rotation followed by an LL rotation, while that for an RL imbalance can be viewed as an LL rotation followed by an RR rotation (see Exercise 15).

The steps in the AVL search-tree-insertion algorithm that results from our discussion appear in Figure 11.10. These steps can be refined into C++ code that has a complexity of O(*height*) = O(log*n*). *Notice that a single rotation is sufficient to restore balance if the insertion causes imbalance.*

Step 1: Find the place to insert the new element by following a path from the root as in a search for an element with the same key. During this process, keep track of the most recently seen node with balance factor -1 or 1. Let this node be A. If an element with the same key is found, the insert fails and the remaining steps are not performed.

Step 2: If there is no node A, then make another pass from the root, updating balance factors. Terminate following this pass.

Step 3: If $bf(A) = 1$ and the new node was inserted in the right subtree of A or if $bf(A) = -1$ and the insertion took place in the left subtree, then the new balance factor of A is zero. In this case update balance factors on the path from A to the new node and terminate.

Step 4: Classify the imbalance at A and perform the appropriate rotation. Change balance factors as required by the rotation as well as those of nodes on the path from the new subtree root to the newly inserted node.

Figure 11.10 Steps for AVL search tree insertion

11.2.6 Deletion from an AVL Search Tree

To delete an element from an AVL search tree, we proceed as in Program 11.4. Let q be the parent of the node that was physically deleted. For example, if the element with key 25 is deleted from the tree of Figure 11.5(a), the node containing this element is deleted and the right-child pointer from the root diverted to the only child of the deleted node. The parent of the deleted node is the root, so q is the root. If instead, the element with key 15 is deleted, its spot is used by the element with key 12 and the node previously containing this element deleted. Now q is the node that originally contained 15 (i.e., the left child of the root). Since the balance factors of some (or all) of the nodes on the path from the root to q have changed as a result of the deletion, we retrace this path backwards from q towards the root.

If the deletion took place from the left subtree of q, $bf(q)$ decreases by 1, and if it took place from the right subtree, $bf(q)$ increases by 1. We may make the following observations:

D1: If the new balance factor of q is 0, its height has decreased by 1, and we need to change the balance factor of its parent (if any) and possibly those of its other ancestors.

D2: If the new balance factor of q is either -1 or 1, its height is the same as before the deletion and the balance factors of its ancestors are unchanged.

D3: If the new balance factor of q is either -2 or 2, the tree is unbalanced at q.

Since balance factor changes may propogate up the tree along the path from q to the root (see observation D2), it is possible for the balance factor of a node on this path to become -2 or 2. Let A be the first such node on this path. To restore balance at node A, we classify the type of imbalance. The imbalance is of type L if the deletion took place from A's left subtree. Otherwise, it is of type R. If $bf(A) = 2$ after the deletion, it must have been 1 before. So A has a left subtree with root B. A type R imbalance is subclassified into the types R0, R1, and R$-$1 depending on $bf(B)$. The type R$-$1, for instance, refers to the case when the deletion took place from the right subtree of A and $bf(B) = -1$. In a similar manner type L imbalances are subclassified into the types L0, L1, and L$-$1.

An R0 imbalance at A is rectified by performing the rotation shown in Figure 11.11. Notice that the height of the shown subtree was $h + 2$ before the deletion and is $h + 2$ after. So the balance factors of the remaining nodes on the path to the root are unchanged. As a result, the entire tree has been rebalanced.

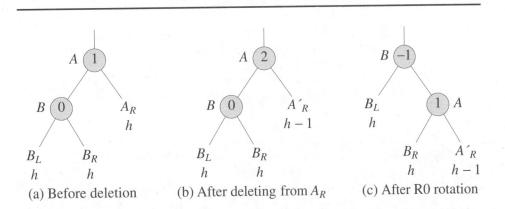

(a) Before deletion   (b) After deleting from A_R (c) After R0 rotation

Figure 11.11 An R0 rotation (single rotation)

Figure 11.12 shows how to handle an R1 imbalance. While the pointer changes are the same as for an R0 imbalance, the new balance factors for A and B are different and the height of the subtree following the rotation is now $h + 1$, which is one less than before the deletion. So if A is not the root, the balance factors of some of its ancestors will change and further rotations may be necessary. Following an R1 rotation, we must continue to examine nodes on the path to the root. *Unlike the case of an insertion, one rotation may not suffice to restore balance following a deletion. The number of rotations needed is $O(\log n)$.*

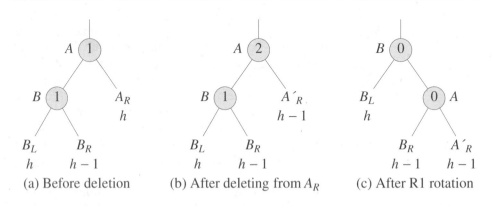

(a) Before deletion   (b) After deleting from A_R (c) After R1 rotation

Figure 11.12 An R1 rotation (single rotation)

The transformation needed when the imbalance is of type R−1 appears in Figure 11.13. The balance factors of A and B following the rotation depend on the balance factor b of the right child of B. This rotation leaves behind a subtree of height $h + 1$, while the subtree height prior to the deletion was $h + 2$. So we need to continue on the path to the root.

LL and R1 rotations are identical; LL and R0 rotations differ only in the final balance factors of A and B; and LR and R−1 rotations are identical.

EXERCISES

13. Prove by induction that the minimum number of nodes in an AVL tree of height h is $N_h = F_{h+2} - 1$, $h \geq 0$.

14. Prove observations I1 through I4 regarding an unbalanced tree resulting from an insertion using the strategy of Program 11.3.

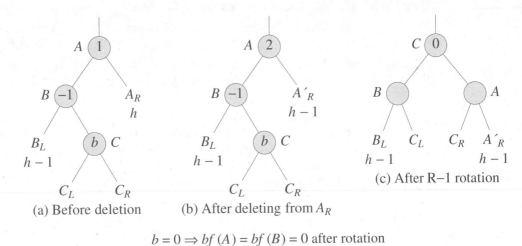

$$b = 0 \Rightarrow bf(A) = bf(B) = 0 \text{ after rotation}$$
$$b = 1 \Rightarrow bf(A) = -1 \text{ and } bf(B) = 0 \text{ after rotation}$$
$$b = -1 \Rightarrow bf(A) = 0 \text{ and } bf(B) = 1 \text{ after rotation}$$

Figure 11.13 An R−1 rotation (double rotation)

15. Draw a figure analogous to Figure 11.7 for the case when $bf(X) = -1$ prior to the insertion.

16. Draw figures analogous to Figures 11.8 and 11.9 for the case of RR and RL imbalances.

17. Start with the LR imbalance shown in Figure 11.9(b) and draw the tree that results when we perform an RR rotation at node B. Observe that an LL rotation on this resulting tree results in the tree of Figure 11.9(b).

18. Draw figures analogous to Figures 11.11, 11.12, and 11.13 for the case of L0, L1, and L−1 imbalances.

★ 19. Develop a C++ class `AVLtree` that includes the binary search tree functions `Search`, `Insert`, `Delete`, and `Ascend`. Fully code all your functions and test their correctness. Your implementations for the first three operations must have complexity O(log$n$), and that for the last operation should be Θ(n). Show that this is the case.

★ 20. Do Exercise 19 for the case when the search tree may contain several elements with the same key. Call the new class `DAVLtree`.

★ 21. Develop a C++ class `IndexedAVLtree` that includes the indexed binary search tree functions `Search`, `Insert`, `Delete`, `Index-Search`, `IndexDelete`, and `Ascend`. Fully code all your functions and test their correctness. Your implementations for the first five operations must have complexity $O(\log n)$ and that for the last operation should be $\Theta(n)$. Show that this is the case.

★ 22. Do Exercise 21 for the case when the search tree may contain several elements with the same key. Call the new class `DIndexedAVLtree`.

23. Explain how you could use an AVL tree to reduce the asymptotic complexity of our solution to the railroad car rearrangement problem of Section 5.5.3 to $O(n \log k)$?

★ 24. Develop a class `IndexedAVLList` that represents a linear list as a binary tree that differs from an AVL tree only in that it may not be a binary search tree. Your implementation should support all the linear list operations defined in Program 3.1. Other than the operation `Search`, all operations should run in logarithmic or less time.

11.3   RED–BLACK TREES

11.3.1   Definition

A **red-black tree** is a binary search tree in which every node is colored either red or black. The remaining properties satisfied by a red-black tree are best stated in terms of the corresponding extended binary tree. Recall, from Section 9.4.1, that we obtain an extended binary tree from a regular binary tree by replacing every null pointer with an external node. The additional properties are

RB1. The root and all external nodes are colored black.

RB2. No root-to-external-node path has two consecutive red nodes.

RB3. All root-to-external-node paths have the same number of black nodes.

An equivalent definition arises from assigning colors to the pointers between a node and its children. The pointer from a parent to a black child is black and to a red child is red. Additionally,

RB1′. Pointers from an internal node to an external node are black.

RB2′. No root-to-external-node path has two consecutive red pointers.

RB3′. All root-to-external-node paths have the same number of black pointers.

Notice that if we know the pointer colors, we can deduce the node colors and vice versa. In the red-black tree of Figure 11.14, the external nodes are solid squares, black pointers are thick lines, and red pointers are thin lines. The colors of the nodes may be deduced from the pointer colors and property RB1. The nodes with 5, 50, 62, and 70 are red, as they have red pointers from their parents. The remaining nodes are black. Notice that every path from the root to an external node has exactly two black pointers and three black nodes (including the root and the external node); no such path has two consecutive red nodes or pointers.

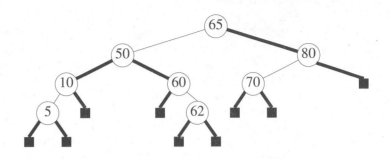

Figure 11.14 A red-black tree

Let the **rank** of a node in a red-black tree be the number of black pointers on any path from the node to any external node in its subtree. So the rank of an external node is zero. The rank of the root of Figure 11.14 is 2, that of its left child is 2, and of its right child is 1.

Lemma 11.1 Let the length of a root-to-external-node path be the number of pointers on the path. If P and Q are two root-to-external-node paths in a red-black tree, then $length(P) \leq 2length(Q)$.

Proof Consider any red-black tree. Suppose that the rank of the root is r. From RB1′ the last pointer on each root-to-external-node path is black. From RB2′ no such path has two consecutive red pointers. So each red pointer is followed by a black pointer. As a result, each root-to-external-node path has between r and $2r$ pointers, so $length(P) \leq 2length(Q)$. To see that the upper bound is possible, consider the red-black tree of Figure 11.14. The path from the root to the left child of 5 has length 4, while that to the right child of 80 has length 2. ∎

Lemma 11.2 Let h be the height of a red-black tree (excluding the external nodes), let n be the number of internal nodes in the tree, and let r be the rank of the root.

(a) $h \leq 2r$

(b) $n \geq 2^r - 1$

(c) $h \leq 2\log_2(n + 1)$

Proof From the proof of Lemma 11.1, we know that no root-to-external-node path has length $> 2r$, so $h \leq 2r$. (The height of the red-black tree of Figure 11.14 with external nodes removed is $2r = 4$.)

Since the rank of the root is r, there are no external nodes at levels 1 through r, so there are $2^r - 1$ internal nodes at these levels. Consequently, the total number of internal nodes is at least this much. (In the red-black tree of Figure 11.14, levels 1 and 2 have $3 = 2^2 - 1$ internal nodes. There are additional internal nodes at levels 3 and 4.)

From (b) it follows that $r \leq \log_2(n + 1)$. This inequality together with (a) yields (c). ∎

Since the height of a red-black tree is at most $2\log_2(n + 1)$, search, insert, and delete algorithms that work in O(h) time have complexity O($\log n$).

Notice that the worst-case height of a red-black tree is more than the worst-case height (approximately $1.44\log_2(n + 2)$) of an AVL tree with the same number of (internal) nodes.

11.3.2   Representation of a Red-Black Tree

Although it is convenient to include external nodes when defining red-black trees, in an implementation, null or zero pointers, rather than physical nodes, represent these nodes. Further, since pointer and node colors are closely related, with each node we need to store only its color or the color of the two pointers to its children. Node colors require just one additional bit per node, while pointer colors require two. Since both schemes require almost the same amount of space, we may choose between them on the basis of actual run times of the resulting red-black tree algorithms.

In our discussion of the insert and delete operations, we shall explicitly state the needed color changes only for the nodes. The corresponding pointer color changes may be inferred.

11.3.3   Searching a Red-Black Tree

We can search a red-black tree with the code we used to search an ordinary binary search tree (Program 11.2). This code has complexity O(h), which is O($\log n$) for a red-black tree. Since we use the same code to search ordinary binary search trees, AVL trees, and red-black trees and since the worst-case height of an AVL tree is least, we expect AVL trees to show the best worst-case performance in applications where search is the dominant operation.

11.3.4   Inserting into a Red-Black Tree

Elements may be inserted using the strategy used for ordinary binary trees (Program 11.3). When the new node is attached to the red-black tree, we need to assign it a color. If the tree was empty before the insertion, then the new node is the root and must be colored black (see property RB1). Suppose the tree was not empty prior to the insertion. If the new node is given the color black, then we will have an extra black node on paths from the root to the external nodes that are children of the new node. On the other hand, if the new node is assigned the color red, then we might have two consecutive red nodes. Making the new node black is guaranteed to cause a violation of property RB3, while making the new node red may or may not violate property RB2. We shall make the new node red.

If making the new node red causes a violation of property RB2, we shall say that the tree has become imbalanced. The nature of the imbalance is classified by examining the new node u, its parent pu, and the grandparent gu of u. Observe that since property RB2 has been violated, we have two consecutive red nodes. One of these red nodes is u, and the other must be its parent; therefore, pu exists. Since pu is red, it cannot be the root (as the root is black by property RB1); u must have a grandparent, gu, which must be black (property RB2). When pu is the left child of gu, u is the left child of pu, and the other child of gu is black (this case includes the case when the other child of gu is an external node), the imbalance is of type LLb. The other imbalance types are LLr (pu is the left child of gu, u is the left child of pu, the other child of gu is red), LRb (pu is the left child of gu, u is the right child of pu, the other child of gu is black), LLb, LRr, RRb, RRr, RLb, and RLr.

Imbalances of the type XYr (X and Y may be L or R) are handled by changing colors, while those of type XYb require a rotation. When we change a color, the RB2 violation may propagate two levels up the tree. In this case we will need to reclassify at the new level, with the new u being the former gu, and apply the transformations again. When a rotation is done, the RB2 violation is taken care of, and no further work is needed.

Figure 11.15 shows the color changes performed for LLr and LRr imbalances; these color changes are identical. Black nodes are shaded dark, while red ones are shaded light. In Figure 11.15(a), for example, gu is black, while pu and u are red; the pointers from gu to its left and right children are red; gu_R is the right subtree of gu; and pu_R is the right subtree of pu. Both LLr and LRr color changes require us to change the color of pu and of the right child of gu from red to black. Additionally, we change the color of gu from black to red provided gu is not the root. Since this color change is not done when gu is the root, the number of black nodes on all root-to-external-node paths increases by one when gu is the root of the red-black tree.

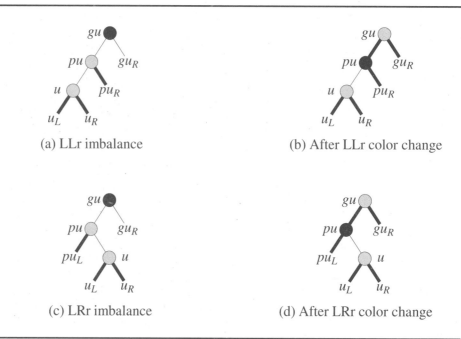

(a) LLr imbalance

(b) After LLr color change

(c) LRr imbalance

(d) After LRr color change

Figure 11.15 LLr and LRr color changes

If changing the color of *gu* to red causes an imbalance, *gu* becomes the new *u* node, its parent becomes the new *pu*, and its grandparent becomes the new *gu* and we continue to rebalance. If *gu* is the root or if the color change does not cause an RB2 violation at *gu*, we are done.

Figure 11.16 shows the rotations performed to handle LLb and LRb imbalances. In Figures 11.16(a) and (b), *u* is the root of pu_L. Notice the similarity between these rotations and the LL (refer to Figure 11.8) and LR (refer to Figure 11.9) rotations used to handle an imbalance following an insertion in an AVL tree. The pointer changes are the same. In the case of an LLb rotation, for example, in addition to pointer changes, we need to change the color of *gu* from black to red and of *pu* from red to black.

In examining the node (or pointer) colors after the rotations of Figure 11.16, we see that the number of black nodes (or pointers) on all root-to-external-node paths is unchanged. Further, the root of the involved subtree (*gu* before the rotation and *pu* after) is black following the rotation; therefore, two consecutive red nodes cannot exist on the path from the tree root to the new *pu*. Consequently, no additional rebalancing work is to be done. *A single rotation (preceded possibly by O(log n) color changes) suffices to restore balance following an insertion!*

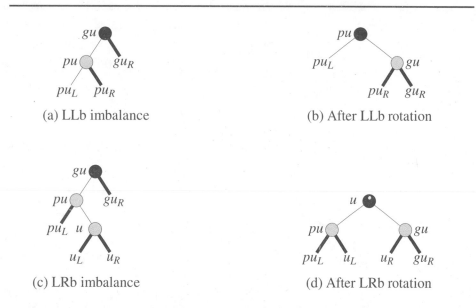

(a) LLb imbalance

(b) After LLb rotation

(c) LRb imbalance

(d) After LRb rotation

Figure 11.16 LLb and LRb rotations for red-black insertion

Example 11.1 Consider the red-black tree of Figure 11.17(a). This figure shows only pointer colors; node colors may be inferred from the pointer colors and the knowledge that the root color is always black. External nodes are shown for convenience. In an actual implementation, the shown black pointers to external nodes are simply null or zero, and external nodes are not represented. Notice that all root-to-external-node paths have two black pointers.

To insert 70 into this red-black tree, we use the algorithm of Program 11.3. The new node is added as the left child of 80. Since the insertion is done into a nonempty tree, the new node is assigned the color red. So the pointer to it from its parent (80) is also red. This insertion does not result in a violation of property RB2, and no remedial action is necessary. Notice that the number of black pointers on all root-to-external-node paths is the same as before the insertion.

Next, insert 60 into the tree of Figure 11.17(b). The algorithm of Program 11.3 attaches a new node as the left child of 70 as in Figure 11.17(c). The new node is red, and the pointer to it is also red. The new node is the u node, its parent (70) is pu, and its grandparent (80) is gu. Since pu and u are red, we have an imbalance. This imbalance is classified as an LLr imbalance (as pu is the left child of gu, u is the left child of pu, and the other child of gu is red). When the LLr color change of Figure 11.15(a) and (b) is performed, we get the tree of Figure 11.17(d). Now u, pu, and gu are each moved two levels up the tree. The node with 80 is the new u node, the root becomes pu, and gu is zero. Since there

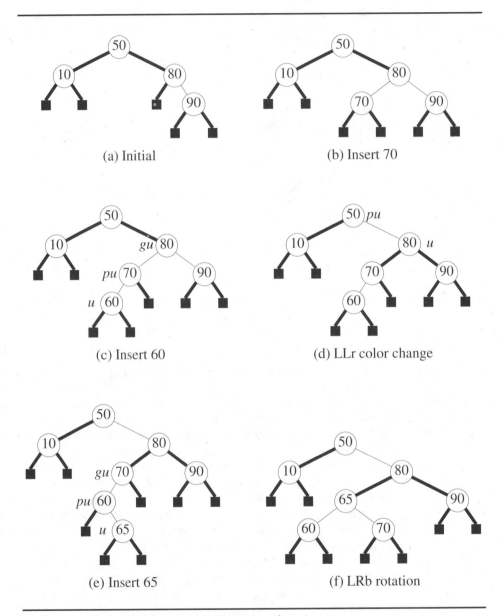

(a) Initial

(b) Insert 70

(c) Insert 60

(d) LLr color change

(e) Insert 65

(f) LRb rotation

Figure 11.17 Insertion into a red-black tree (continues)

is no *gu* node, we cannot have an RB2 imbalance at this location and we are done. All root-to-external-node paths have exactly two black pointers.

Now insert 65 into the tree of Figure 11.17(d). The result appears in Figure 11.17(e). The new node is the *u* node. Its parent and grandparent are, respectively, the *pu* and *gu* nodes. We have an LRb imbalance that requires us to perform the rotation of Figure 11.16(c) and (d). The result is the tree of Figure 11.17(f).

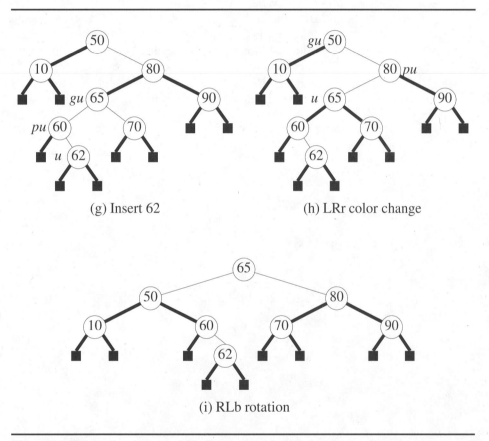

(g) Insert 62

(h) LRr color change

(i) RLb rotation

Figure 11.17 Insertion into a red-black tree (concluded)

Finally, insert 62 to obtain the tree of Figure 11.17(g). We have an LRr imbalance that requires a color change. The resulting tree and the new *u*, *pu*, and *gu* nodes appear in Figure 11.17(h). The color change just performed has caused an RLb imbalance two levels up, we now need to perform an RLb rotation. The rotation results in the tree of Figure 11.17(i). Following a rotation, no further work is needed and we are done. ■

11.3.5   Deletion from a Red-Black Tree

Deletions are performed by first using the deletion algorithm for ordinary binary
search trees (Program 11.4) and then performing remedial color changes and a
single rotation if necessary. Consider the red-black tree of Figure 11.18(a). If
Program 11.4 is used to delete 70, we get the tree of Figure 11.18(b). (If pointer
colors are represented, we will also need to change the color of 90's left pointer
to get this tree.) When 90 is deleted from tree (a), tree (c) results. (If pointer
colors are used, the right-pointer color of 65 will need to be changed to get this
tree.) The deletion of 65 from tree (a) results in tree (d). (Again, if pointer colors
are used, a pointer-color change is needed.) Let y denote the node that takes the
place of the physically deleted node. The y nodes for the deletion examples
appear in Figure 11.18. In the case of Figure 11.18(b), for example, the left child
of 90 was deleted. Its new left child is the external node y.

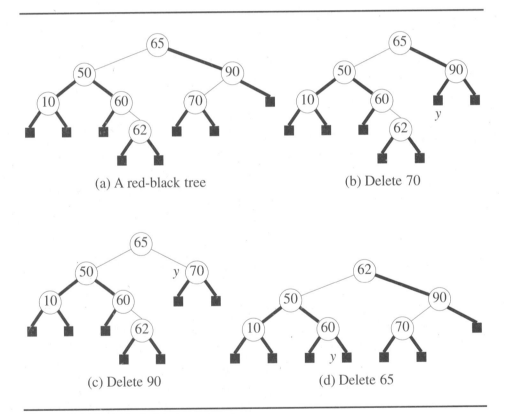

(a) A red-black tree

(b) Delete 70

(c) Delete 90

(d) Delete 65

Figure 11.18 Red-black deletion examples

In the case of tree (b), the deleted node (i.e., the one that contained 70 in tree (a)) was red. Its deletion does not affect the number of black nodes on root-to-external-node paths, and no remedial work is necessary. In tree (c) the deleted node (i.e., the one with 90 in tree (a)) was black, and the number of black nodes (and hence pointers) on paths from the root-to-external-nodes in y is one less than before. Since y is not the new root, an RB3 violation occurs. In tree (d) the deleted node was red, and no RB3 violation occurs. *An RB3 violation occurs only when the deleted node was black and y is not the root of the resulting tree.* No other red-black property violations are possible following a deletion using Program 11.4.

When an RB3 violation occurs, the subtree rooted at y is one black node (or equivalently, one black pointer) deficient; therefore, the number of black nodes (and hence pointers) on paths from the root to external nodes in the sub-tree y is one less than on paths to other external nodes. We shall say that the tree has become **unbalanced**. We classify the nature of the imbalance by identifying the parent py and sibling v of y. When y is the right child of py, the imbalance is of type R. Otherwise, it is of type L. Observe that since y is one black node deficient, v cannot be an external node. If v is a black node, the imbalance is of type Lb or Rb. When v is red, the imbalance is of type Lr or Rr.

First, consider an Rb imbalance. Imbalances of type Lb are handled in a similar way. Rb imbalances may be divided into three subcases on the basis of the number of v's red children. The three subcases are Rb0, Rb1, and Rb2.

When the imbalance type is Rb0, a color change is performed (Figure 11.19). Figure 11.19 shows the two possibilities for the color of py. If py was black prior to the color change, then the color change causes the subtree rooted at py to be one black node deficient. Also, in Figure 11.19(b) the number of black nodes on paths to external nodes in v is one less than before the color change. Therefore, regardless of whether the path goes to an external node in v or y, following the color change, it is one black node deficient. If py is the root of the whole red-black tree, nothing more is to be done. If it is not, then py becomes the new y; the imbalance at y is reclassified, and appropriate remedial action occurs at this new y.

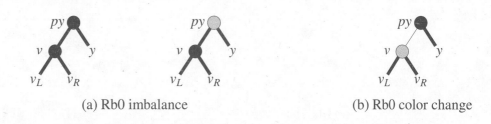

(a) Rb0 imbalance   (b) Rb0 color change

Figure 11.19 Rb0 color change for red-black deletion

When *py* was red before the color change, the number of black nodes on paths to external nodes in *y* increases by one but is unchanged for those in *v*. The entire tree becomes balanced, and we are done.

Rotations are performed when the imbalance type is Rb1 or Rb2. These rotations appear in Figure 11.20. An unshaded node denotes a node that may be either red or black. The color of such a node is not changed as a result of the rotation. Therefore, in Figure 11.20(b) the root of the shown subtree has the same color before and after the rotation—the color of *v* in (b) is the same as that of *py* in (a). You should verify that following the rotation the number of black nodes (and hence black pointers) on paths from the root-to-external-nodes in *y* is increased by one and unchanged on paths from the root to the remaining external nodes. As a result, a rotation rebalances the tree, and no further work is to be done.

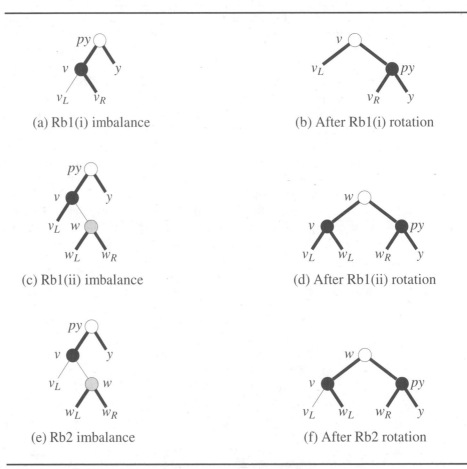

(a) Rb1(i) imbalance   (b) After Rb1(i) rotation

(c) Rb1(ii) imbalance   (d) After Rb1(ii) rotation

(e) Rb2 imbalance   (f) After Rb2 rotation

Figure 11.20 Rb1 and Rb2 rotations for red-black deletion

Next, consider imbalances of type Rr. The case of Lr imbalances is symmetric. Since y is one black node deficient and v is red, both v_L and v_R have at least one black node that is not an external node; therefore, both children of v are internal nodes. Rr imbalances may be subdivided into three cases according to the number of red children (0, 1, or 2) that v's right child has. All three cases of an Rr imbalance are handled by a rotation. The rotations appear in Figures 11.21 and 11.22. Once again, you can verify that the shown rotation restores balance to the entire tree.

(a) Rr0 imbalance   (b) Rr0 rotation

Figure 11.21 Rr0 rotation for red-black deletion

Example 11.2 If we delete 90 from the red-black tree of Figure 11.17(i), we get the tree of Figure 11.23(a). Since the deleted node was not the root and was black, we have an imbalance. The imbalance is of type Rb0, and a color change is performed to get the tree of Figure 11.23(b). Since py was originally a red node, this color change rebalances the tree and we are done.

If we now delete 80 from tree (b), tree (c) results. A red node was deleted, so the tree remains balanced. When 70 is deleted from tree (c), we get tree (d). This time a nonroot black node was deleted, and the tree is unbalanced. The imbalance type is Rr1(ii) (the right child w of v has one red pointer, which is itself the right-child pointer of w). Following an Rr1(ii) rotation, tree (e) is obtained. This tree is balanced. ∎

11.3.6 Implementation Considerations and Complexity

The remedial action taken to rebalance a red-black tree following an insertion or deletion requires us to move back on the path taken from the root to the point of insertion or deletion. This backward movement is easy to do if each node has a parent field in addition to data, left child, right child, and color fields. An alternative to adding a parent field to each node is to save, on a stack, pointers to nodes encountered on the downward path from the root to the point of insertion/deletion. Now we may move back toward the root by performing

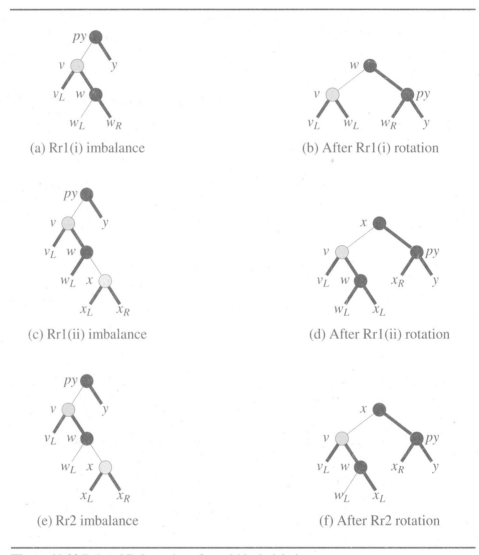

(a) Rr1(i) imbalance

(b) After Rr1(i) rotation

(c) Rr1(ii) imbalance

(d) After Rr1(ii) rotation

(e) Rr2 imbalance

(f) After Rr2 rotation

Figure 11.22 Rr1 and Rr2 rotations for red-black deletion

deletes from the stack of saved pointers. For an n-element red-black tree, the addition of parent fields increases the space requirements by $\Theta(n)$, while the use of a stack increases the space requirements by $\Theta(\log n)$. Although the stack scheme is more efficient on space requirements, the parent-pointer scheme runs slightly faster.

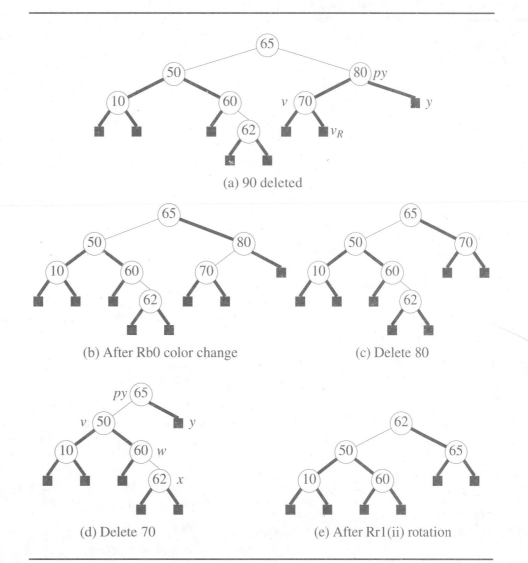

(a) 90 deleted

(b) After Rb0 color change

(c) Delete 80

(d) Delete 70

(e) After Rr1(ii) rotation

Figure 11.23 Deletion from a red-black tree

Since the color changes performed following an insert or delete may propogate back towards the root, $O(\log n)$ of these color changes may be performed. Rotations, on the other hand, guarantee to rebalance the tree. As a result, at most one rotation may be performed following each insert/delete. The time needed for each color change or rotation operation is $\Theta(1)$, the total time needed to insert/delete is $O(\log n)$.

EXERCISES

25. Draw the RRr and RLr color changes that correspond to the LLr and LRr changes of Figure 11.15.

26. Draw the RRb and RLb rotations that correspond to the LLb and LRb changes of Figure 11.16.

27. Draw the Lb0 color change that corresponds to the Rb0 change of Figure 11.19.

28. Draw the Lb1 and Lb2 rotations that correspond to the Rb1 and Rb2 rotations of Figure 11.20.

29. Draw the Lr0, Lr1, and Lr2 rotations that correspond to the Rr0, Rr1, and Rr2 rotations of Figures 11.21 and 11.22.

★ 30. Develop a C++ class `RedBlackTree` that includes the binary search tree functions `Search`, `Insert`, `Delete`, and `Ascend`. Fully code all your functions and test their correctness. Your implementations for the first three operations must have complexity O(log$n$), and that for the last operation should be $\Theta(n)$. Show that this is the case. The implementations of `Insert` and `Delete` should follow the development in the text.

11.4 B-TREES

11.4.1 Indexed Sequential Access Method (ISAM)

AVL and red-black trees guarantee good performance when the dictionary is small enough to reside in internal memory. For larger dictionaries (called **external dictionaries** or **files**) that must reside on a disk, we can get improved performance using search trees of higher degree. Before we jump into the study of these high degree search trees, let us take a look at the popular **indexed sequential access method** (ISAM) for external dictionaries. This method provides good sequential and random access.

In the ISAM method the available disk space is divided into blocks, a block being the smallest unit of disk space that will be input or output. Typically, a block is one track long and can be input or output with a single seek and latency delay. The dictionary elements are packed into the blocks in ascending order and the blocks are used in an order that minimizes the delay in going from one block to the next.

For sequential access the blocks are input in order, and the elements in each block are retrieved in ascending order. If each block contains m elements, the number of disk accesses per element retrieved is $1/m$.

To support random access, an index is maintained. This index contains the largest key in each block. Since the index contains only as many keys as there are blocks and since a block generally houses many elements (i.e., m is usually large), the index is generally small enough to reside in internal memory. To perform a random access of an element with key k, the index is searched for the single block that can contain the corresponding element; this block is retrieved from the disk and searched internally for the desired element. As a result, a single disk access is sufficient to perform a random access.

This technique may be extended to larger dictionaries that span several disks. Now the elements are assigned to disks in ascending order and then to blocks within a disk also in ascending order. Each disk maintains a block index that retains the largest key in each block. Additionally, an overall disk index maintains the largest key in each disk. This index generally resides in memory.

To perform a random access, the disk index is searched to determine the single disk that the desired record might reside on. Next, the block index for this disk is retrieved from the appropriate disk and searched for the block that is to be fetched from the disk. The block is then fetched and searched internally. In the extended scheme a random access requires two disk accesses (one to fetch a block index and another to fetch a block).

Since the ISAM method is essentially a formula-based representation scheme, it runs into difficulty when inserts and deletes are performed. We can partially alleviate this difficulty by leaving space in each block so that a few inserts can be performed without moving elements across block boundaries. Similarly, we can leave empty space in the block after deletes, rather than perform an expensive shift of the elements across block boundaries to use the new free space.

11.4.2 m-way Search Trees

Definition An **m-way search tree** may be empty. If it is not empty, it is a tree that satisfies the following properties:

1. In the corresponding extended search tree (obtained by replacing zero pointers with external nodes), each internal node has up to m children and between 1 and $m - 1$ elements. (External nodes contain no elements and have no children.)

2. Every node with p elements has exactly $p + 1$ children.

3. Consider any node with p elements. Let $k_1, \cdots, k_p$ be the keys of these elements. The elements are ordered so that $k_1 < k_2 < \cdots < k_p$. Let $c_0, c_1, \cdots, c_p$ be the $p + 1$ children of the node. The elements in the subtree with root c_0 have keys smaller than k_1, those in the subtree with root c_p have keys larger than k_p, and those in the subtree with root c_i have keys larger than k_i but smaller than k_{i+1}, $1 \le i < p$. ∎

Although it is useful to include external nodes when defining an *m*-way search tree, external nodes are not physically represented in actual implementations. Rather, a null or zero pointer appears wherever there would otherwise be an external node.

Figure 11.24 shows a seven-way search tree. External nodes are shown as solid squares. All other nodes are internal nodes. The root has two elements (with keys 10 and 80) and three children. The middle child of the root has six elements and seven children; six of these children are external nodes.

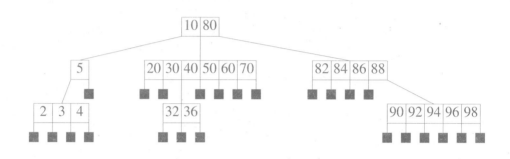

Figure 11.24 A seven-way search tree

Searching an *m*-Way Search Tree

To search the seven-way search tree in Figure 11.24 for an element with key 31, we begin at the root. Since 31 lies between 10 and 80, we follow the middle pointer. (By definition, all elements in the first subtree have key < 10, and all in the third one have key > 80.) The root of the middle subtree is searched. Since $k_2 < 31 < k_3$, we move to the third subtree of this node. Now we determine that $31 < k_1$ and move into the first subtree. This move causes us to fall off the tree; that is, we reach an external node. We conclude that the search tree contains no element with key 31.

Inserting into an *m*-Way Search Tree

If we wish to insert an element with key 31, we search for 31 as above and fall off the tree at the node [32,36]. Since this node can hold up to six elements (each node of a seven-way search tree can have up to six elements), the new element may be inserted as the first one in the node.

To insert an element with key 65, we search for 65 and fall off the tree by moving to the sixth subtree of the node [20,30,40,50,60,70]. This node cannot accomodate additional elements, and a new node is obtained. The new element is put into this node, and the new node becomes the sixth child of [20,30,40,50,60,70].

Deleting from an m-Way Search Tree

To delete the element with key 20 from the search tree of Figure 11.24, we first perform a search. The element is the first element in the middle child of the root. Since $k_1 = 20$ and $c_0 = c_1 = 0$, we may simply delete the element from the node. The new middle child of the root is [30,40,50,60,70]. Similarly, to delete the element with key 84, we first locate the element. It is the second element in the third child of the root. Since $c_1 = c_2 = 0$, the element may be deleted from this node and the new node configuration is [82,86,88].

When deleting the element with key 5, we have to do more work. Since the element to be deleted is the first one in its node and since at least one of its neighboring children (these children are c_0 and c_1) is nonzero, we need to replace the deleted element with an element from a nonempty neighboring subtree. From the left neighboring subtree (c_0), we may move up the element with largest key (i.e., the element with key 4).

To delete the element with key 10 from the root of Figure 11.24, we may replace this element with either the largest element in c_0 or the smallest element in c_1. If we opt to replace it with the largest in c_0, then the element with key 5 moves up and we need to find a replacement for this element in its original node. The element with key 4 is moved up.

Height of an m-Way Search Tree

An m-way search tree of height h (excluding external nodes) may have as few as h elements (one node per level and one element per node) and as many as $m^h - 1$. The upper bound is achieved by an m-way search tree of height h in which each node at levels 1 through $h - 1$ has exactly m children and nodes at level h have no children. Such a tree has $\sum_{i=0}^{h-1} m^i = (m^h - 1)/(m-1)$ nodes. Since each of these nodes has $m - 1$ elements, the number of elements is $m^h - 1$.

As the number of elements in an m-way search tree of height h ranges from a low of h to a high of $m^h - 1$, the height of an m-way search tree with n elements ranges from a low of $\log_m(n + 1)$ to a high of n.

A 200-way search tree of height 5, for example, can hold $32 * 10^{10} - 1$ elements but might hold as few as 5. Equivalently, a 200-way search tree with $32 * 10^{10} - 1$ elements has a height between 5 and $32 * 10^{10} - 1$. When the search tree resides on a disk, the search, insert, and delete times are dominated by the number of disk accesses made (under the assumption that each node is no larger than a disk block). Since the number of disk accesses needed for the search, insert, and delete operations are O(h) where h is the tree height, we need to ensure that the height is close to $\log_m(n + 1)$. This assurance is provided by balanced m-way search trees.

11.4.3   B-Trees of Order m

Definition A **B-tree of order** m is an m-way search tree. If the B-tree is not empty, the corresponding extended tree satisfies the following properties:

1.   The root has at least two children.

2.   All internal nodes other than the root have at least $\lceil m/2 \rceil$ children.

3.   All external nodes are at the same level. ■

The seven-way search tree of Figure 11.24 is not a B-tree of order 7, as it contains external nodes at more than one level (levels 3 and 4). Even if all its external nodes were at the same level, it would fail to be a B-tree of order 7 as it contains nonroot internal nodes with two (node [5]) and three (node [32,36]) children. Nonroot internal nodes in a B-tree of order 7 must have at least $\lceil 7/2 \rceil$ = 4 children. A B-tree of order 7 appears in Figure 11.25. All external nodes are at level 3, the root has three children, and all remaining internal nodes have at least four children. Additionally, it is a seven-way search tree.

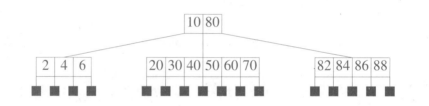

Figure 11.25 A B-tree of order 7

In a B-tree of order 2, no internal node has more than two children. Since an internal node must have at least two children, all internal nodes of a B-tree of order 2 have exactly two children. This observation coupled with the requirement that all external nodes be on the same level implies that B-trees of order 2 are full binary trees. As such, these trees exist only when the number of elements is $2^h - 1$ for some integer h.

In a B-tree of order 3, internal nodes have either two or three children. So a B-tree of order 3 is also known as a 2-3 tree. Since internal nodes in B-trees of order 4 must have two, three, or four children, these B-trees are also referred to as 2-3-4 (or simply 2,4) trees. A 2-3 tree appears in Figure 11.26. Even though this tree has no internal node with four children, it is also an example of a 2-3-4 tree. To build a 2-3-4 tree in which at least one internal node has four children, simply add elements with keys 14 and 16 into the left child of 20.

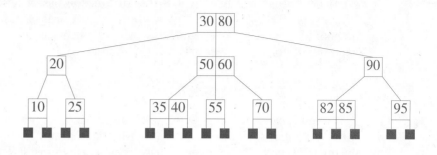

Figure 11.26 A 2-3 tree or B-tree of order 3

11.4.4   Height of a B-Tree

Lemma 11.3 Let T be a B-tree of order m and height h. Let $d = \lceil m/2 \rceil$ and let n be the number of elements in T.

(a) $2d^{h-1} - 1 \leq n \leq m^h - 1$

(b) $\log_m(n + 1) \leq h \leq \log_d(\dfrac{n+1}{2}) + 1$

Proof The upper bound on n follows from the fact that T is an m-way search tree. For the lower bound, note that the external nodes of the corresponding extended B-tree are at level $h + 1$. The minimum number of nodes on levels 1, 2, 3, 4, $\cdots$, $h + 1$ is 1, 2, $2d$, $2d^2$, $\cdots$, $2d^{h-1}$, so the minimum number of external nodes in the B-tree is $2d^{h-1}$. Since the number of external nodes is one more than the number of elements

$$n \geq 2d^{h-1} - 1$$

(b) follows directly from (a). ∎

From Lemma 11.3, it follows that a B-tree of order 200 and height 3 has at least 19,999 elements, and one of the same order and height 5 has at least $2 * 10^8 - 1$ elements. Consequently, if a B-tree of order 200 or more is used, the tree height is quite small even when the number of elements is rather large. In practice, the B-tree order is determined by the disk block size and the size of individual elements. There is no advantage to using a node size smaller than the disk block size, as each disk access reads or writes one block. Using a larger node size involves multiple disk accesses, each accompanied by a seek and latency delay, so there is no advantage to making the node size larger than one block.

Although in actual applications the B-tree order is large, our examples use a small m because a two-level B-tree of order m has at least $2d - 1$ elements. When m is 200, d is 100 and a two-level B-tree of order 200 has at least 199 elements. Manipulating trees with this many elements is quite cumbersome. Our examples involve 2-3 trees and B-trees of order 7.

11.4.5   Searching a B-Tree

A B-tree is searched using the same algorithm as used for an m-way search tree. Since all internal nodes on some root-to-external-node path may be retreived during the search, the number of disk accesses is at most h (h is the height of the B-tree).

11.4.6   Inserting into a B-Tree

To insert an element into a B-tree, we first search for the presence of an element with the same key. If such an element is found, the insert fails because duplicates are not permitted. When the search is unsuccessful, we attempt to insert the new element into the last internal node encountered on the search path. For example, when inserting an element with key 3 into the B-tree of Figure 11.25, we examine the root and its left child. We fall off the tree at the second external node of the left child. Since the left child currently has three elements and can hold up to six, the new element may be inserted into this node. The result is the B-tree of Figure 11.27(a). Two disk accesses are made to read in the root and its left child. An additional access is necessary to write out the modified left child.

Next, let us try to insert an element with key 25 into the B-tree of Figure 11.27(a). This element is to go into the node [20,30,40,50,60,70]. However, this node is full. *When the new element needs to go into a full node, the full node is split.* Let P be the full node. Insert the new element e together with a null pointer into P to get an overfull node with m elements and $m + 1$ children. Denote this overfull node as

$$m, c_0, (e_1,c_1), \cdots, (e_m,c_m)$$

where the e_is are the elements and the c_is are the children pointers. The node is split around element e_d where $d = \lceil m/2 \rceil$. Elements to the left of this one remain in P, and those to the right move into a new node Q. The pair (e_d,Q) is inserted into the parent of P. The format of the new P and Q is

$$P: d-1, c_0, (e_1,c_1), ..., (e_{d-1},c_{d-1})$$
$$Q: m-d, c_d, (e_{d+1},c_{d+1}), ...(e_m,c_m)$$

Notice that the number of children of both P and Q is at least d.

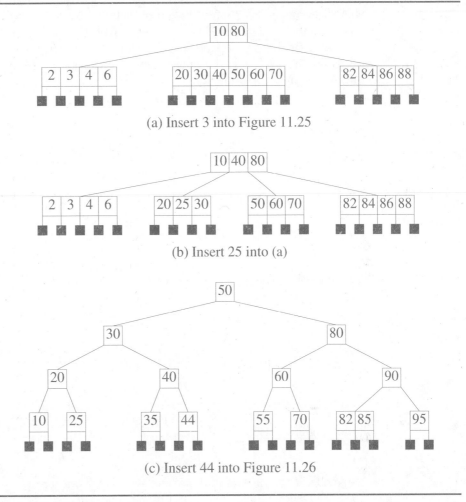

(a) Insert 3 into Figure 11.25

(b) Insert 25 into (a)

(c) Insert 44 into Figure 11.26

Figure 11.27 Inserting into a B-tree

In our example, the overfull node is

$$7, 0 \ (20,0), (25,0), (30,0), (40,0), (50,0), (60,0), (70,0)$$

and $d = 4$. Splitting around e_4 yields the two nodes

$$P: 3, 0, (20,0), (25,0), (30,0)$$
$$Q: 3, 0, (50,0), (60,0), (70,0)$$

When the pair $(40,Q)$ is inserted into the parent of P, we get the B-tree of Figure 11.27(b).

To insert 25 into Figure 11.27(a), we need to get the root and its middle child from the disk. Then we write to disk the two split nodes and the modifed root. The total number of disk accesses is five.

As a final example, consider inserting an element with key 44 into the 2-3 tree of Figure 11.26. This element goes into the node [35,40]. Since the node is full, we get the overfull node

$$3, 0, (35,0), (40,0), (44,0)$$

Splitting around $e_d = e_2$ yields the two nodes

$$P: 1, 0, (35,0)$$
$$Q: 1, 0, (44,0)$$

When we attempt to insert the pair $(40,Q)$ into the parent A of P, we see that this node is full. Following the insertion, we get the overfull node

$$A: 3, P, (40,Q), (50,C), (60,D)$$

where C and D are pointers to the nodes [55] and [70]. The overfull node A is split to create a new node B. The new A and B are

$$A: 1, P, (40,Q)$$
$$B: 1, C, (60,D)$$

Now we need to insert the pair $(50,B)$ into the root. Prior to this insertion, the root has the format

$$R: 2, S, (30,A), (80,T)$$

where S and T are, respectively, pointers to the first and third subtrees of the root. Following the insertion of the pair $(50,B)$, we get the overfull node

$$R: 3, S, (30,A), (50,B), (80,T)$$

This node is split around the element with key 50 to create a new R and a new node U as below:

$$R: 1, S, (30,A)$$
$$U: 1, B, (80,T)$$

The pair $(50,U)$ would normally be inserted into the parent of R. However, since R has no parent, we create a new root with the format

$$1, R, (50,U)$$

The resulting 2-3 tree appears in Figure 11.27(c).

Three disk accesses are made to read in nodes [30,80], [50,60], and [35,40]. For each node that splits, two accesses are made to write the modified node and the newly created node. In our case three nodes are split, so six write accesses are made. Finally, a new root is created and written out. This write takes an additional disk access. The total number of disk accesses is 10.

When an insertion causes s nodes to split, the number of disk accesses is h (to read in the nodes on the search path) + $2s$ (to write out the two split parts of each node that is split) + 1 (to write the new root or the node into which an insertion that does not result in a split is made). Therefore, the number of disk accesses needed for an insertion is $h + 2s + 1$, which is at most $3h + 1$.

11.4.7   Deletion from a B-Tree

Deletion is first divided into two cases: (1) the element to be deleted is in a node whose children are external nodes (i.e., the element is in a leaf), and (2) the element is to be deleted from a nonleaf. Case (2) is transformed into case (1) by replacing the deleted element with either the largest element in its left-neighboring subtree or the smallest element in its right-neighboring subtree. The replacing element is guaranteed to be in a leaf.

Consider deleting the element with key 80 from the B-tree of Figure 11.27(a). Since the element is not in a leaf, we find a suitable replacement. The possibilities are the element with key 70 (i.e., the largest element in the left-neighboring subtree) and 82 (i.e., the smallest element in the right-neighboring subtree). When we use the 70, the problem of deleting this element from the leaf [20,30,40,50,60,70] remains.

If we are to delete the element with key 80 from the 2-3 tree of Figure 11.27(c), we replace it with either the element with key 70 or that with key 82. If we select the 82, the problem of deleting 82 from the leaf [82,85] remains.

Since case (2) may be transformed into case (1) quite easily, we concern ourselves with case (1) only. To delete an element from a leaf that contains more than the minimum number of elements (1 if the leaf is also the root and $\lceil m/2 \rceil - 1$ if it is not) requires us to simply write out the modified node. (In case this node is the root, the B-tree becomes empty.) To delete 50 from the B-tree of Figure 11.27(a), w write out the modified node [20,30,40,60,70], and to delete 85 from the 2-3 tree of Figure 11.27(c), we write out the node [82]. Both cases require h disk accesses to follow the search path down to the leaf and an additional access to write out the modified version of the leaf that contained the deleted element.

When the element is being deleted from a nonroot node that has exactly the minimum number of elements, we try to replace the deleted element with an element from its nearest-left or -right sibling. Notice that every node other than the root has either a nearest-left sibling or a nearest-right sibling or both. For example, suppose we wish to delete 25 from the B-tree of Figure 11.27(b). This deletion leaves behind the node [20,30], which has just two elements. However, since this node is a nonroot node of a B-tree of order 7, it must contain at least three elements. Its nearest-left sibling, [2,3,4,6], has an extra element. The largest element from here is moved to the parent node, and the intervening element (i.e., with key 10) is moved down to create the B-tree of Figure 11.28(a). The number of disk accesses is 2 (to go from the root to the leaf that contains 25) + 1 (to read in the nearest-left sibling of this leaf) + 3 (to write out the changed leaf, its sibling, and its parent) = 6.

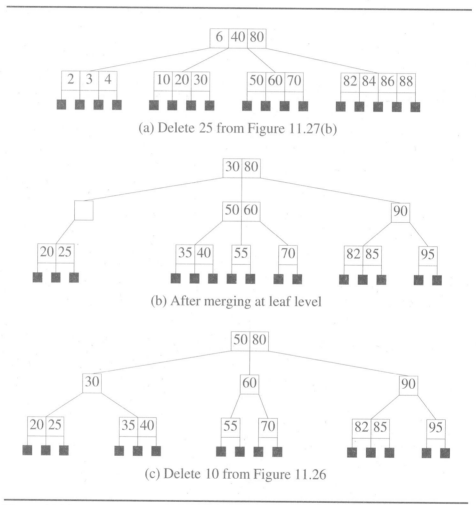

(a) Delete 25 from Figure 11.27(b)

(b) After merging at leaf level

(c) Delete 10 from Figure 11.26

Figure 11.28 Deleting from a B-tree

Suppose that instead of checking the nearest-left sibling of [20,30], we had checked its nearest-right sibling [50,60,70]. Since this node has only three elements, we cannot delete an element. (If the node had four or more, we would have moved its smallest element to the parent and moved the element in the parent that lies between these two siblings into the leaf that is one element short.) Now, we can proceed to check the nearest-left sibling of [20,30]. Performing this check requires an additional disk access, and we are not certain that this nearest sibling will have an extra element. *In the interest of keeping the worst-case disk-access count low, we shall check only one of the nearest siblings of a node that is one element short.*

When the nearest sibling that is checked has no extra elements, we merge the two siblings with the element between them in the parent into a single node. Since the siblings have $d - 2$ and $d - 1$ elements each, the merged node has $2d - 2$ elements. As $2d - 2$ equals $m - 1$ when m is odd and $m - 2$ when m is even, there is enough space in a node to hold this many elements.

In our example the siblings [20,30] and [50,60,70] and the element with key 40 are merged into the single node [20,30,40,50,60,70]. The resulting B-tree is that of Figure 11.27(a). This deletion requires two disk accesses to get to the node [20,25,30], another access to read in its nearest-right sibling, then two more accesses to write out the two nodes that are modified. The total number of disk accesses is five.

Notice that since merging reduces the number of elements in the parent node, the parent may end up being one element short. If the parent becomes one element short, we will need to check the parent's nearest sibling and either get an element from there or merge with it. If we get an element from the nearest-right (-left) sibling, then the left-most (right-most) subtree of this sibling is also taken. If we merge, the grandparent may become one element short and the process will need to be applied at the grandparent. At worst, the shortage will propagate back to the root. When the root is one element short, it is empty. The empty root is discarded, and the tree height decreases by one.

Suppose we wish to delete 10 from the 2-3 tree of Figure 11.26. This deletion leaves behind a leaf with zero elements. Its nearest-right sibling [25] does not have an extra element. Therefore, the two sibling leaves and the in-between element in the parent (10) are merged into a single node. The new tree structure appears in Figure 11.28(b). We now have a node at level 2 that is an element short. Its nearest-right sibling has an extra element. The left-most element (i.e., the one with key 50) moves to the parent, and the element with key 30 moves down. The resulting 2-3 tree appears in Figure 11.28(c). Notice that the left subtree of the former [50,60] has moved also. This deletion took three read accesses to get to the leaf that contained the element that was to be deleted; two read accesses to get the nearest-right siblings of the level 3 and 2 nodes; and four write accesses to write out the four nodes at levels 1, 2, and 3 that were modified. The total number of disk accesses is nine.

As a final example, consider the deletion of 44 from the 2-3 tree of Figure 11.27(c). When the 44 is removed from the leaf it is in, this leaf becomes short one element. Its nearest-left sibling does not have an extra element, and so the two siblings together with the in-between element in the parent are merged to get the tree of Figure 11.29(a). We now have a node at level 3 that is one element short. Its nearest-left sibling is examined and found to have no extra elements, so the two siblings and the in-between element in their parent are merged. The tree of Figure 11.29(b) is obtained. Now we have a level 2 node that is one element short. Its nearest-right sibling has no extra elements, and we perform another merge to get the tree of Figure 11.29(c). Now the root is an element short. Since the root becomes an element short only when it is empty, the root is discarded. The final 2-3 tree is shown in Figure 11.29(d). Notice that when the root is discarded, the tree height reduces by one.

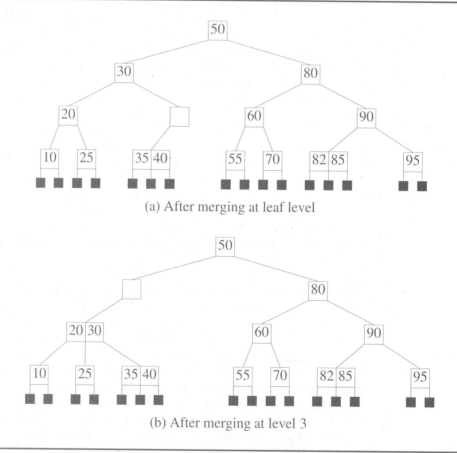

(a) After merging at leaf level

(b) After merging at level 3

Figure 11.29 Deleting 44 from the 2-3 tree of Figure 11.27(c) (continues)

We need four disk accesses to find the leaf that contains the element to be deleted, three nearest-sibling accesses, and three write accesses. The total number is 10.

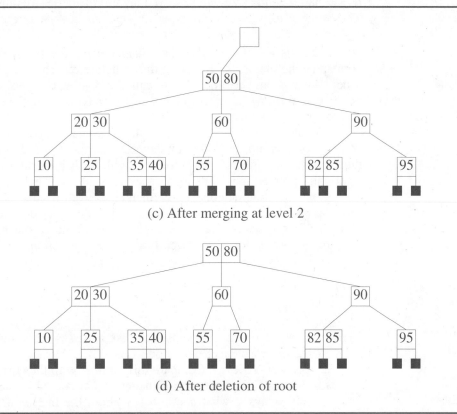

(c) After merging at level 2

(d) After deletion of root

Figure 11.29 Deleting 44 from the 2-3 tree of Figure 11.27(c) (concluded)

The worst case for a deletion from a B-tree of height h is when merges take place at levels h, $h - 1$, $\cdots$, and 3, and at level 2, we get an element from a nearest sibling. The worst-case disk access count is $3h$; (h reads to find the leaf with the element to be deleted) + ($h - 1$ reads to get nearest siblings at levels 2 through h) + ($h - 2$ writes of merged nodes at levels 3 through h) + (3 writes for the modified root and two level 2 nodes).

11.4.8   Node Structure

Our discussion has assumed a node structure of the form

$$s, c_0, (e_1, c_1), (e_2, c_2), \cdots, (e_s, c_s)$$

where s is the number of elements in the node, the e_is are the elements in ascending order of key, and the c_is are children pointers. When the element size is large relative to the size of a key, we may use the node structure

$$s, c_0, (k_1, c_1, p_1), (k_2, c_2, p_2), \cdots, (k_s, c_s, p_s)$$

where the k_is are the element keys and the p_is are the disk locations of the corresponding elements. By using this structure, we can use a B-tree of a higher order. An even higher-order B-tree, called a B´-tree, becomes possible if nonleaf nodes contain no p_i pointers and if in the leaves we replace the null children pointers with p_i pointers.

Another possibilty is to use a balanced binary search tree to represent the contents of each node. Using a balanced binary search tree in this way reduces the permissible order of the B-tree, as with each element we need a left- and right-child pointer as well as a balance factor or color field. However, the CPU time spent inserting/deleting an element into/from a node decreases. Whether this approach results in improved overall performance depends on the application. In some cases a smaller m might increase the B-tree height, resulting in more disk accesses for each search/insert/delete operation.

EXERCISES

31. What is the maximum number of disk accesses made during a search of a B-tree of order $2m$ if each node is two disk blocks and requires two disk accesses to retrieve? Compare this number with the corresponding number for B-tree of order m that uses nodes that are one disk block in size. Based on this analysis, what can you say about the merits of using a node size larger than one block?

32. What is the maximum number of disk accesses needed to delete an element that is in a nonleaf node of a B-tree of order m?

33. Suppose we modify the way an element is deleted from a B-tree as follows: If a node has both a nearest-left and nearest-right sibling, then both are checked before a merge is done. What is the maximum number of disk accesses that can be made when deleting from a B-tree of height h?

★ 34. A 2-3-4 tree may be represented as a binary tree in which each node is colored black or red. A 2-3-4 tree node that has just one element is represented as a black node; a node with two elements is represented as a black node with a red child (the red child may be either the left or right child of the black node); a node with three elements is represented as a black node with two red children.

    (a) Draw a 2-3-4 tree that contains at least one node with two elements and one with three. Now draw it as a binary tree with colored nodes using the method just described.

    (b)   Verify that the binary tree is a red-black tree.

    (c)   Prove that when any 2-3-4 tree is represented as a colored binary tree as described here, the result is a red-black tree.

    (d)   Prove that every red-black tree can be represented as a 2-3-4 tree using the inverse mapping.

    (e)   Verify that the color changes and rotations given in Section 11.4.4 for an insertion into a red-black tree are obtainable from the B-tree insertion method using the mapping in (d).

    (f)   Do part (e) for the case of deletion from a red-black tree.

★ 35.   Develop a class `TwoThree` that implements a 2-3 tree. Include functions to search, insert, and delete. Test the correctness of your code.

★ 36.   Develop a class `TwoFour` that implements a 2-3-4 tree. Include functions to search, insert, and delete. Test the correctness of your code.

11.5 APPLICATIONS

11.5.1 Histogramming

In the histogramming problem we start with a collection of n keys and must output a list of the distinct keys and the number of times (i.e., frequency) each occurs in the collection. Figure 11.30 gives an example with 10 keys. The problem input appears in Figure 11.30(a), and the histogram is presented in Figure 11.30(b) as a table and as a bar chart in Figure 11.30(c). Histogramming is commonly performed to determine the distribution of data. For example, we may histogram the scores on a test, the gray-scale values in an image, the cars registered in Gainesville (the key being the manufacturer), and the highest degree earned by persons living in Los Angeles.

    When the key values are integers in the range zero through r and r is reasonably small, the histogram can be computed in linear time by a rather simple procedure (Program 11.6) that uses the array element $h[i]$ to determine the frequency of the key i. Other integral key types may be mapped into this range to use Program 11.6. For example, if the keys are lowercase letters, we may use the mapping $[a, b, \cdots, z] = [0, 1, \cdots, 25]$.

    Program 11.6 becomes infeasible when the key range is very large as well as when the key type is not integral (for example, when the keys are real numbers). Suppose we are determining the frequency with which different words occur in a text. The number of possible different words is very large compared to the number that might actually appear in the text. In such a situation, we may sort the keys and then use a simple left-to-right scan to determine the number of keys for each distinct key value. The sort can be accomplished in O($n\log n$) time

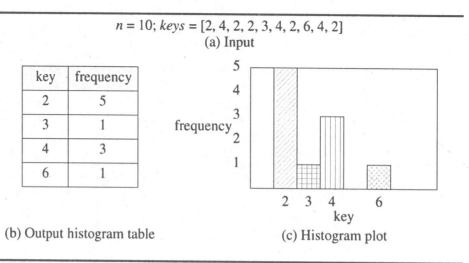

$n = 10; keys = [2, 4, 2, 2, 3, 4, 2, 6, 4, 2]$
(a) Input

key	frequency
2	5
3	1
4	3
6	1

(b) Output histogram table

(c) Histogram plot

Figure 11.30 Histogramming example

(using HeapSort (Program 9.12), for example), and the ensuing left-to-right scan takes $\Theta(n)$ time; the overall complexity is $O(n\log n)$. This solution can be improved upon when the number m of distinct keys is small when compared to n. By using balanced search trees such as AVL and red-black trees, we can solve the histogramming problem in $O(n\log m)$ time. Furthermore, the balanced search tree solution requires only the distinct keys to be stored in memory. Therefore, this solution is appropriate even in situations when n is so large that we do not have enough memory to accomodate all keys (provided, of course, there is enough memory for the distinct keys).

The solution we describe uses a binary search tree and so has expected complexity $O(n\log m)$. By replacing the binary search tree used in this solution with a balanced search tree, the claimed complexity is achieved. In our binary search tree solution, we extend the class BSTree by adding the public member

```
BSTree<E,K>& InsertVisit
            (const E& e, void(*Visit)(E& u));
```

that inserts element e into the search tree provided no element with key equal to e.key exists. In case such an element u exists, function visit is invoked. The code for this member may be obtained from that for Insert (Program 11.3) by replacing the line

```
else throw BadInput(); // duplicate key
```

with the lines

```
void main(void)
{// Histogram of nonnegative integer values.
   int n,  // number of elements
       r;  // values between 0 and r
   cout << "Enter number of elements and range"
        << endl;
   cin >> n >> r;

   // create histogram array h
   int *h;
   try {h = new int[r+1];}
   catch (NoMem)
      {cout << "range is too large" << endl;
       exit(1);}

   // initialize array h to zero
   for (int i = 0; i <= r; i++)
      h[i] = 0;

   // input data and compute histogram
   for (int i = 1; i <= n; i++) {
      int key;  // input value
      cout << "Enter element " << i << endl;
      cin >> key;
      h[key]++;
      }

   // output histogram
   cout << "Distinct elements and frequencies are"
        << endl;
   for (int i = 0; i <= r; i++)
      if (h[i]) cout << i << "   " << h[i] << endl;
}
```

Program 11.6 Simple histogramming program

```
else {Visit(p->data);
      return *this;};
```

Program 11.7 gives the code for the new histogramming program. During an element visit, its frequency count is incremented by one.

```
class eType {
   friend void main(void);
   friend void Add1(eType&);
   friend ostream& operator <<(ostream&, eType);
   public:
      operator int() const {return key;}
   private:
      int key,     // element value
          count;   // frequency
};
ostream& operator<<(ostream& out, eType x)
   {out << x.key << " " << x.count << "    "; return out;}

void Add1(eType& e) {e.count++;}

void main(void)
{// Histogram using a search tree.
   BSTree<eType,int> T;
   int n;   // number of elements
   cout << "Enter number of elements" << endl;
   cin >> n;

   // input elements and enter into tree
   for (int i = 1; i <= n; i++) {
      eType e;   // input element
      cout << "Enter element " << i << endl;
      cin >> e.key;
      e.count = 1;
      // put e in tree unless match already there
      // in latter case increase count by 1
      try {T.InsertVisit(e, Add1);}
      catch (NoMem)
         {cout << "Out of memory" << endl;
          exit(1);}
      }

   // output distinct elements and their counts
   cout << "Distinct elements and frequencies are"
        << endl;
   T.Ascend();
}
```

Program 11.7 Histogramming using a search tree

11.5.2 Best-Fit Bin Packing

The best-fit method to pack n objects into bins of capacity c was described in Section 10.5.1. By using a balanced search tree, we can implement the method to run in $O(n\log n)$ time. The search tree will contain one element for each bin that is currently in use and has nonzero available capacity. Suppose that when object i is to be packed, there are nine bins (a through i) in use that still have some space left. Let the available capacity of these bins be 1, 3, 12, 6, 8, 1, 20, 6, and 5, respectively. Notice that it is possible for two or more bins to have the same available capacity. The nine bins may be stored in a binary search tree with duplicates (i.e., a member of either `DBSTree` or `DAVLtree`), using as key the available capacity of a bin.

Figure 11.31 shows a possible binary search tree for the nine bins. For each bin, the available capacity is shown inside a node, and the bin name, outside. This tree is also an AVL tree. If the object `i` that is to be packed requires `s[i]` = 4 units, we can find the bin that provides the best fit by starting at the root of the tree of Figure 11.31. The root tells us bin h has an available capacity of six. Since object `i` fits into this bin, bin h becomes the candidate for the best bin. Also, since the capacity of all bins in the right subtree is at least six, we need not look at the bins in this subtree in our quest for the best bin. The search proceeds to the left subtree. The capacity of bin b isn't adequate to accomodate our object, so the search for the best bin moves into the right subtree of bin b. The bin, bin i, at the root of this subtree has enough capacity, and it becomes the new candidate for the best bin. From here, the search moves into the left subtree of bin i. Since this subtree is empty, there are no better candidate bins and bin i is selected.

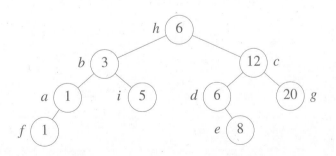

Figure 11.31 AVL with duplicates

As another example of the search for the best bin, suppose `s[i]` = 7. The search again starts at the root. The root bin, bin h, does not have enough capacity for this object, so our quest for a bin moves into the right subtree. Bin c has

enough capacity and becomes the new candidate bin. From here we move into
c's left subtree and examine bin d. It does not have enough capacity to accomodate the object, so we continue with the right subtree of d. Bin e has enough
capacity and becomes the new candidate bin. We then move into its left subtree,
which is empty. The search terminates.

When we find the best bin, we can delete it from the search tree, reduce its
capacity by s[i], and reinsert it (unless its remaining capacity is zero). If we
do not find a bin with enough capacity, we can start a new bin.

To implement this scheme, we can use the class DBSTree to obtain
$O(n\log n)$ expected performance or the class DAVLtree for $O(n\log n)$ performance in all instances. In either case we need to extend the class definition to
include a public member FindGE(k,Kout) that finds the smallest bin capacity Kout that is $\geq$ k. This member takes the form given in Program 11.8. Its
complexity is O(*height*). The code for the class AVLtree is identical.

```
template<class E, class K>
bool DBSTree<E,K>::FindGE(const K& k, K& Kout) const
{// Find smallest element with value >= k.
   BinaryTreeNode<E> *p = root, // search pointer
                     *s = 0;    // pointer to smallest
                                // >= k found so far

   // search the tree
   while (p) {
      // is p a candidate?
      if (k <= p->data) {// yes
         s = p;  // p is a better candidate than s
         // smaller elements in left subtree only
         p = p->LeftChild;}
      else // no, p->data too small, try right subtree
         p = p->RightChild;
   }

   if (!s) return false; // not found
   Kout = s->data;
   return true;
}
```

Program 11.8 Finding the smallest key $\geq$ k

Program 11.9 packs n objects into bins using the best-fit strategy. It uses
the same interface as FirstFit (Program 10.7) uses. As a result, Program
11.9 may be invoked using Program 10.6 so long as the file that contains the
class DBSTree is included into the program using the #include statement.

```
class BinNode {
   friend void BestFitPack(int *, int, int);
   friend ostream& operator<<(ostream&, BinNode);
   public:
      operator int() const {return avail;}
   private:
      int ID,      // bin identifier
          avail;   // available capacity
};

ostream& operator<<(ostream& out, BinNode x)
   {out << "Bin " << x.ID << " " << x.avail;
    return out;}

void BestFitPack(int s[], int n, int c)
{
   int b = 0;                      // number of bins used
   DBSTree<BinNode, int> T;   // tree of bin capacities

   // pack objects one by one
   for (int i = 1; i <= n; i++) {// pack object i
      int k;       // best fit bin number
      BinNode e;   // corresponding node
      if (T.FindGE(s[i], k)) // find best bin
         T.Delete(k, e);     // remove best bin
                             // from tree
      else {// no bin large enough
            // start a new bin
            e = *(new BinNode);
            e.ID = ++b;
            e.avail = c;}

      cout << "Pack object " << i << " in bin "
           << e.ID << endl;

      // update available capacity and put bin
      // in tree unless avail capacity is zero
      e.avail -= s[i];
      if (e.avail) T.Insert(e);
      }
}
```

Program 11.9 Bin packing using best fit

11.5.3 Crossing Distribution

In the crossing-distribution problem, we start with a routing channel with n pins on both the top and bottom of the channel. Figure 11.32 shows an instance with $n = 10$. The routing region is the shaded rectangular region. The pins are numbered 1 through n, left to right, on both the top and bottom of the channel. In addition, we have a permutation C of the numbers $[1, 2, 3, \cdots, n]$. We must use a wire to connect pin i on the top side of the channel to pin C_i on the bottom side. The example in Figure 11.32 is for the case $C = [8, 7, 4, 2, 5, 1, 9, 3, 10, 6]$. The n wires needed to make these connections are numbered 1 through n. Wire i connects top pin i to bottom pin C_i. Wire i is to the left of wire j iff $i < j$.

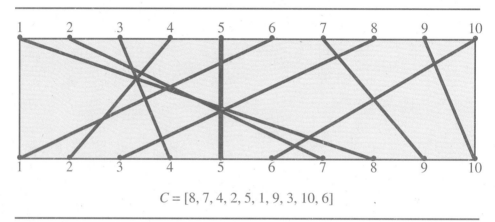

$$C = [8, 7, 4, 2, 5, 1, 9, 3, 10, 6]$$

Figure 11.32 A wiring instance

Figure 11.32 shows that no matter how we route wires 9 and 10 in the given routing region, these wires must cross at some point. Crossings are undesirable as special care must be taken at the crossing point to avoid a short circuit. This special care might, for instance, involve placing an insulator at the point of crossing or routing one wire onto another layer at this point and then bringing it back after the crossover point. Therefore, we seek to minimize the number of crossings. You may verify that the minimum number of crossings is made when the wires are run as straight lines as in Figure 11.32.

Each crossing is given by a pair (i, j) where i and j are the two wires that cross. One way to identify all the crossings is to examine each pair (i, j) of wires and to check whether the straight lines defined by their endpoints intersect. To avoid checking the same pair twice, we may require $i < j$ (note that the crossings $(9, 10)$ and $(10, 9)$ are the same). Let k_i be the number of pairs (i, j), $i < j$, such that wires i and j cross. For the example of Figure 11.32, $k_9 = 1$ and $k_{10} = 0$. In Figure 11.33 we list all crossings and k_i values for the example of Figure

11.32. Row i of this table first gives the value of k_i and then the values of j, $i < j$, such that wires i and j cross. The total number of crossings K may be determined by adding together all k_is. For our example $K = 22$. Since k_i counts the crossings of wire i only with wires to its right (i.e., $i < j$), k_i give the number of right-side crossings of wire i.

i	k_i	Crossings						
1	7	2	3	4	5	6	8	10
2	6	3	4	5	6	8	10	
3	3	4	6	8				
4	1	6						
5	2	6	7					
6	0							
7	2	8	10					
8	0							
9	1	10						
10	0							

Figure 11.33 Crossing table

To balance the routing complexity in the top and lower halves of the channel, we require that each half have approximately the same number of crossings. (One-half should have $\lfloor K/2 \rfloor$ crossings, and the other should have $\lceil K/2 \rceil$ crossings). Figure 11.34 shows a routing of Figure 11.32 in which we have exactly 11 crossings in each half of the channel.

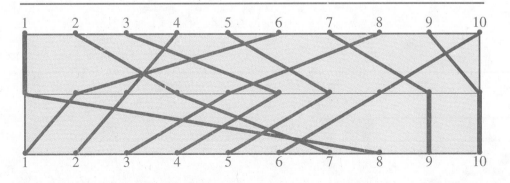

Figure 11.34 Splitting the crossings

The connections in the top half are given by the permutation $A = [1, 4, 6, 3, 7, 2, 9, 5, 10, 8]$. That is, top pin i is connected to center pin A_i. The connections in the bottom half are given by the permutation $B = [8, 1, 2, 7, 3, 4, 5, 6, 9, 10]$. That is, center pin i is connected to bottom pin B_i. Observe that $C_i = B_{A_i}$, $1 \leq i \leq n$. This equality is essential if we are to accomplish the connections given by C.

The crossing numbers k_i and the total number of crossings K can be computed in $\Theta(n^2)$ time by examining each wire pair (i, j). The partitioning of C into A and B can then be computed using a linear list as in Program 11.10.

```
LinearList<int> L(n);
int r = K/2;  // remaining number of crossings
              // needed in top half

// scan wires right to left
int w = n;    // w is current wire
while (r) {   // need more crossings in top half
   if (k[w] < r) {// use all from wire w
                L.Insert(k[w], w);
             r -= k[w];}
   else {// use only r from wire w
         L.Insert(r, w);
         r = 0;}
   w--;}

// determine wire permutation at center
// first w wires have same ordering
for (int i = 1; i <= w; i++)
   X[i] = i;

// ordering of remaining wires is from L
for (int i = w+1; i <= n; i++)
   L.Delete(1, X[i]);

// compute top half permutation
for (int i = 1; i <= n; i++)
   A[X[i]] = i;

   // compute bottom half permutation
for (int i = 1; i <= n; i++)
   B[i] = C[X[i]];
```

Program 11.10 Crossing distribution using a linear list

In the `while` loop, we scan the wires from right to left, determining their relative order at the center of the routing channel. The objective is to have a routing order at the center that requires exactly $r = K/2$ crossings in the top half of the routing channel.

The linear list `L` keeps track of the current ordering, at the center, of the wires so far considered. When wire `w` is considered, we can allocate up to `k[w]` of its crossings with right-side wires to the upper half. The first crossing is with the first wire in `L`, the second with the second wire in `L`, and so on. If c of the `k[w]` right-side crossings of wire `w` are allocated to the upper half, then this wire must cross the first c wires in `L`. In addition, the ordering of wires `w` through `n` is obtained by inserting `w` after the cth wire in `L`. Notice that when wire `w` is considered in the `while` loop of Program 11.10, wires `w+1` through `n` have already been considered and so are in `L`. Further, since `k[w]` cannot exceed the number of wires to the right of wire `w`, `L` has at least `k[w]` wires in it when wire `w` is considered.

When a wire `w` is considered in the `while` loop of Program 11.10, all of its right-side crossings are allocated to the top half unless the remaining number `r` of crossings needed in the top half is less than `k[w]`. In this latter case, `r` of the possible `k[w]` right-side crossings are allocated to the upper half.

When the `while` loop terminates, the wire ordering `X` at the center of the routing channel may be constructed by noting that wires 1 through `w` have no crossings in the upper half and so do not change their relative order in this half. Therefore, `X[1:w]` = [1, 2, $\cdots$, `w`]. The ordering of the remaining wires is given by the list `L`. The first two `for` loops of Program 11.10 construct `X`.

Let us go through the construction of `X` using our example of Figure 11.32. We begin by adding wire 10 to `L` to get `L` = (10). No crossings are generated. Next we add wire 9 to get `L` = (10, 9). The addition of this wire generates one upper half crossing. Then we add wire 8 after the k_8th element to get `L` = (8, 10, 9). The total number of right-side crossings in the upper half remains 1. Next we add wire 7 after the second element of `L`, generating two upper-half crossings. `L` becomes (8, 10, 7, 9) and the additional crossings needed `r` drops to 8. When wire 6 is added, we get `L` = (6, 8, 10, 7, 9); $r = 8$. The addition of wire 5 generates two crossings and results in `L` = (6, 8, 5, 10, 7, 9); $r = 6$. When wire 4 is added after the first element of `L`, one crossing is generated and we get `L` = (6, 4, 8, 5, 10, 7, 9); $r = 5$. Next we add wire 3 to get `L` = (6, 4, 8, 3, 5, 10, 7, 9); $r = 2$. Finally, when wire 2 is considered, we see that although it is capable of generating $k_2 = 6$ crossings, only two of these crossings can be assigned to the top half of the channel. So it is inserted after the second element of the list to get `L` = (6, 4, 2, 8, 3, 5, 10, 7, 9). The remaining wires retain their current relative order.

Now we compute the wire permutation following the routing of the top half by appending `L` to the ordering (1, 2, $\cdots$, w) to obtain `X` = [1, 6, 4, 2, 8, 3, 5, 10, 7, 9].

The permutation A is closely related to X. A[j] tells us which center pin wire j should go to, while X[i] tells us which wire comes to center pin j. The third for loop of Program 11.10 uses this information to compute A. From X and C, B may be computed, as in the fourth for loop.

Since the time needed to insert an element into a linear list of size s is $O(s)$, the while loop of Program 11.10 takes $O(n^2)$ time. The second for loop also takes this much time. The remainder of the code takes $\Theta(n)$ time, so the overall complexity of Program 11.10 is $O(n^2)$. Combining the time requirements of Program 11.10 with the time needed to compute K and the k[i]s, we see that the overall time needed to solve the crossing-distribution problem is $O(n^2)$ when a linear list is used.

We can reduce the complexity of our solution to $O(n\log n)$ by using a balanced search tree rather than a linear list. To obtain a solution with expected complexity $O(n\log n)$, we may use an indexed binary search tree rather than an indexed balanced search tree. The technique is the same in both cases. We will use an indexed binary search tree to illustrate this technique.

First, let us see how to compute the crossing numbers k_i, $1 \le i \le n$. Suppose we examine the wires in the order $n, n-1, \cdots, 1$ and put C_i into an indexed search tree when wire i is examined. For the example of Figure 11.32, we start with an empty tree. We examine wire 10 and insert $C_{10} = 6$ into an empty tree to get the tree of Figure 11.35(a). The number ouside the node is its LeftSize value, and that inside the node is its key (or C value). Note that k_n is always zero, so we set $k_n = 0$. Next we examine wire 9 and insert $C_9 = 10$ into the tree to get the tree of Figure 11.35(b). To make the insertion, we pass over the root that has LeftSize = 1. From this LeftSize value, we know that wire 9's bottom endpoint is to the right of exactly one of the wires seen so far, so $k_9 = 1$. We examine wire 8 and insert $C_8 = 3$ to get the tree of Figure 11.35(c). Since C_8 is the smallest entry in the tree, no wires are crossed and $k_8 = 0$. For wire 7, $C_7 = 9$ is inserted to obtain tree (d). C_7 becomes the third-smallest entry in the tree. We can determine that C_7 is the third-smallest entry by keeping a running sum of the LeftSize values of the nodes whose right subtree we enter. When C_7 is inserted, this sum is 2. So the new element is currently the third smallest. From this information we conclude that its bottom endpoint is to the right of two others in the tree. As a result, $k_7 = 2$. Proceeding in this way, the trees of Figures 11.35(e) through 11.35(i) are generated when we examine wires 6 through 2. Finally, when we examine wire 1, we insert $C_1 = 8$ as the right child of the node with key 7. The sum of the LeftSize values of the nodes whose right subtrees we enter is $6 + 1 = 7$. Wire 1 has a bottom endpoint that is to the right of seven of the wires in the tree, and so $k_1 = 7$.

The time needed to examine wire i and compute k_i is $O(h)$ where h is the current height of the indexed search tree. So all k_is can be computed in expected time $O(n\log n)$ by using an indexed binary search tree or in time $O(n\log n)$ using an indexed balanced search tree.

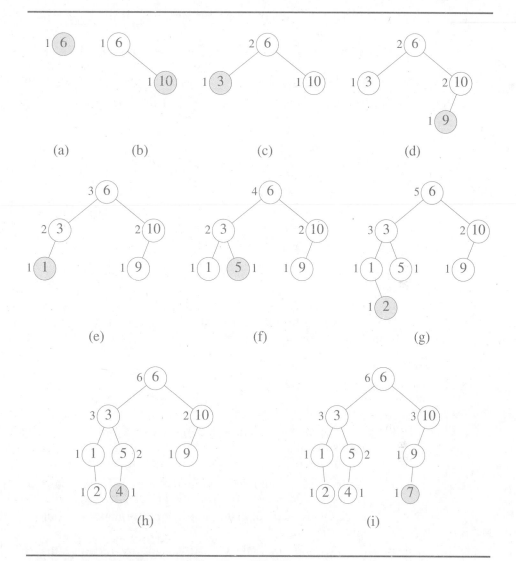

Figure 11.35 Computing the number of crossings

To compute A, we can implement the code of Program 11.10, using a modified indexed search tree. In this modification, elements have no keys. Each element has only a position or rank. Insert(j,e) inserts element e so that it becomes the element with rank j+1. To list the elements in order of rank, we can do an inorder traversal. The time needed by this implementation of Program 11.10 is O($n\log n$).

Another way to obtain the permutation A is to first compute $r = \sum_{i=1}^{n} k_i /2$ and $s =$ smallest i such that $\sum_{l=i}^{n} k_l \le r$. For our example $r = 11$ and $s = 3$. We see that Program 11.10 does all crossings (i.e., with wires whose top point is to the right) for wires n, $n-1$, $\cdots$, s and $r - \sum_{l=s}^{n} k_i$ of those for wire $s-1$ in the top half and the remaining crossings in the bottom half. To get these top-half crossings, we examine the tree following the insertion of C_s. For our example, we examine tree (h) of Figure 11.35. An inorder traversal of tree (h) yields the sequence (1, 2, 3, 4, 5, 6, 9, 10). Replacing these bottom endpoints with the corresponding wire numbers, we get the sequence (6, 4, 8, 3, 5, 10, 7, 9), which gives the wire permutation following the nine crossings represented in Figure 11.35(h). For the additional two crossings, we insert wire $s = 2$ after the second wire in the sequence to get the new wire sequence (6, 4, 2, 8, 3, 5, 10, 7, 9). The remaining wires 1 through $s-1$ are added at the front to obtain (1, 6, 4, 2, 8, 3, 5, 10, 7, 9), which is the X permutation computed in Program 11.10. To obtain X in this way, we need to rerun part of the code used to compute the k_is, perform an inorder traversal, insert wire s, and add a few wires at the front of the sequence. The time needed for all of these steps is O($n\log n$).   A and B may be obtained from X in linear time using the last two `for` loops of Program 11.10.

EXERCISES

37. Write a histogramming program that first inputs the n keys into an array, then sorts this array, and finally makes a left-to-right scan of the array outputting the distinct key values and the number of times each occurs.

38. Write a histogramming program that uses a chained hash table rather than a binary search tree as in Program 11.7, to store the distinct keys and their frequencies. Compare the run-time performance of your new program with that of Program 11.7.

39. (a) Extend the class `DBSTree` by adding the public member `DeleteGE(k,e)`, which deletes the element with smallest key $\ge$ k. The deleted element is returned in e.   `DeleteGE` throws an exception if it fails.

   (b) Use `DeleteGE` (and not `FindGE`) to obtain a new version of `BestFit`.

   (c) Which will run faster? Why?

40. (a)   Use an indexed AVL search tree to obtain an O($n \log n$) solution for the crossing-distribution problem.

  (b)   Test the correctness of your code.

  (c)   Compare the actual run time of this solution to that of the $\Theta(n^2)$ solution described in this section (see Program 11.10). Do this comparison using randomly generated permutations C and $n = 1000$; 10,000; and 50,000.

11.6 REFERENCES AND SELECTED READINGS

AVL trees were invented by G. Adelson-Velskii and E. Landis in 1962. More material on these trees can be found in the book *The Art of Computer Programming: Sorting and Searching* by D. Knuth, Addison-Wesley, Reading, MA, 1973.

Red-black trees were invented by R. Bayer in 1972. However, Bayer called these trees ''symmetric balanced B-trees.'' The red-black terminology is due to Guibas and Sedgewick who studied these trees in greater detail in 1978. The pioneering papers are ''Symmetric Binary B-Trees: Data Structures and Maintenance Algorithms'' by R. Bayer, *Acta Informatica*, 1, 1972, 290–306 and ''A Dichromatic Framework for Balanced Trees'' by L. Guibas and R. Sedgewick, *Proceedings of the 10th IEEE Symposium on Foundations of Computer Science*, 1978, 8–21.

The application of red-black trees to the implementation of priority search trees is described in the paper ''Priority Search Trees'' by E. McCreight, *SIAM Journal on Computing*, 14, 2, 1985, 257–276.

The solution to the crossing-distribution problem is due to S. Cho and S. Sahni (unpublished).

Various search-tree structures that have the same asymptotic complexity are described in the text *Fundamentals of Data Structures in C++* by E. Horowitz, S. Sahni, and D. Mehta, W. H. Freeman, New York, NY, 1994. This text also describes B´-trees and another variant B*-trees.

CHAPTER 12
GRAPHS

BIRD'S-EYE VIEW

Congratulations! You have successfully journeyed through the forest of trees. Awaiting you now is the study of the graph data structure. Surprisingly, graphs are used to model literally thousands of real world problems. Not so surprisingly, we shall see only a very small fraction of these problems in the remainder of this book. This chapter covers the following topics:

- Graph terminology including these terms: *vertex*, *edge*, *adjacent*, *incident*, *degree*, *cycle*, *path*, *connected component*, and *spanning tree*.

- Three types of graphs: undirected, directed, and weighted.

- Common graph representations: adjacency matrix, packed-adjacency lists, and linked-adjacency lists.

- Standard graph search methods: breadth-first and depth-first search.
- Algorithms to find a path in a graph, to find the connected components of an undirected graph, and to find a spanning tree of a connected undirected graph.
- Specifying an abstract data type as an abstract class.

The new C++ features used in this chapter are abstract classes, virtual functions, and virtual base classes.

12.1 DEFINITIONS

Informally, a graph is a collection of vertices or nodes, pairs of which are joined by lines or edges. More formally, a **graph** $G = (V,E)$ is an ordered pair of finite sets V and E. The elements of V are called **vertices** (vertices are also called **nodes** and **points**). The elements of E are called **edges** (edges are also called **arcs** and **lines**). Each edge in E joins two different vertices of V and is denoted by the tuple (i,j), where i and j are the two vertices joined by E.

A graph is generally displayed as a figure in which the vertices are represented by circles and the edges by lines. Examples of graphs appear in Figure 12.1. Some of the edges in this figure are oriented (i.e., they have arrow heads), while others are not. An edge with an orientation is a **directed** edge while an edge with no orientation is an **undirected** edge. The undirected edges (i,j) and (j,i) are the same; the directed edge (i,j) is different from the directed edge (j,i), the former being oriented from i to j and the latter from j to i.[1]

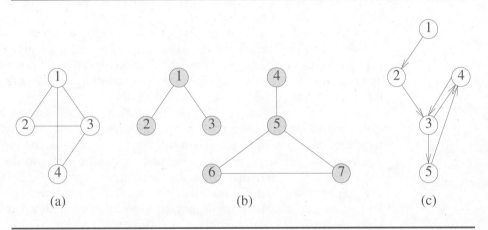

(a)   (b)   (c)

Figure 12.1 Graphs

Vertices i and j are **adjacent** vertices iff (i,j) is an edge in the graph. The edge (i,j) is **incident** on the vertices i and j. Vertices 1 and 2 of Figure 12.1(a) are adjacent, as are vertices 1 and 3; 1 and 4; 2 and 3; and 3 and 4. This graph has no other pairs of adjacent vertices. The edge (1,2) is incident on the vertices 1 and 2 and the edge (2,3) is incident on the vertices 2 and 3.

---

1. Some books use the notation $\{i,j\}$ for an undirected edge and (i,j) for a directed one. Others use (i,j) for an undirected edge and $<i,j>$ for a directed one. This book uses the same notation, (i,j), for both kinds of edges. Whether an edge is directed or not will be clear from the context.

It is sometimes useful to have a slightly refined notion of adjacency and incidence for directed graphs. The directed edge (i,j) is **incident to** vertex j and **incident from** vertex i. Vertex i is **adjacent to** vertex j, and vertex j is **adjacent from** vertex i. In the graph of Figure 12.1(c), vertex 2 is adjacent from 1, while 1 is adjacent to 2. Edge $(1,2)$ is incident from 1 and incident to 2. Vertex 4 is both incident to and from 3. Edge $(3,4)$ is incident from 3 and incident to 4. For an undirected edge, the refinements ''to'' and ''from'' are synonomous.

Using set notation, the graphs of Figure 12.1 may be specified as $G_1 = (V_1, E_1)$; $G_2 = (V_2, E_2)$; and $G_3 = (V_3, E_3)$ where

$$V_1 = \{1,2,3,4\}; \qquad E_1 = \{(1,2), (1,3), (2,3), (1,4), (3,4)\}$$
$$V_2 = \{1,2,3,4,5,6,7\}; \quad E_2 = \{(1,2), (1,3), (4,5), (5,6), (5,7), (6,7)\}$$
$$V_3 = \{1,2,3,4,5\}; \qquad E_3 = \{(1,2), (2,3), (3,4), (4,3), (3,5), (5,4)\}$$

If all the edges in a graph are undirected, then the graph is an **undirected** graph. The graphs of Figures 12.1(a) and (b) are undirected graphs. If all the edges are directed, then the graph is a **directed** graph. The graph of Figure 12.1(c) is a directed graph.

By definition, a graph does not contain multiple copies of the same edge. Therefore, an undirected graph can have at most one edge between any pair of vertices, and a directed graph can have at most one edge from vertex i to vertex j and one from j to i. Also, a graph cannot contain any **self-edges**; that is edges of the form (i,i). A self-edge is also called a **loop**.

Often an undirected graph is simply called a **graph**, and a directed graph is called a **digraph**. In some applications of graphs and digraphs, we shall assign a weight or cost to each edge. When weights have been assigned to edges, we use the terms **weighted graph** and **weighted digraph** to refer to the resulting data object. The term **network** refers to a weighted graph or digraph. Actually, all the graph variants defined here may be regarded as special cases of networks— an undirected (directed) graph may be viewed as an undirected (directed) network in which all edges have the same weight.

12.2 APPLICATIONS

Graphs, digraphs, and networks are used in the analysis of electrical networks; the study of the molecular structure of chemical compounds (particularly hydrocarbons); the representation of airline routes and communication networks; in planning projects, genetic studies, statistical mechanics, social sciences; and in many other situations. In this section we formulate some real-world problems as problems on graphs.

Example 12.1 [*Path Problems*] In a city with many streets, we can say that each intersection is a vertex in a digraph. Each segment of a street that is between two adjacent intersections is represented by either one or two directed edges. Two directed edges, one in either direction, are used if the street segment is two way, and a single directed edge is used if it is a one-way segment. Figure 12.2 shows a hypothetical street map and the corresponding digraph. In this figure there are three streets—1St., 2St,. and 3St.—and two avenues—1Ave. and 2Ave. The intersections are labeled 1 through 6. The vertices of the corresponding digraph (Figure 12.2(b)) have the same labels as given to the intersection in Figure 12.2(a).

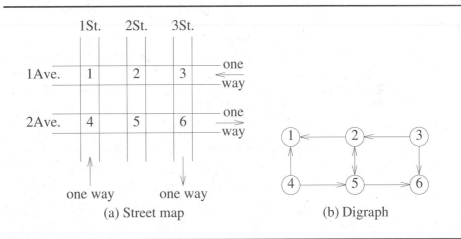

(a) Street map   (b) Digraph

Figure 12.2 Street map and corresponding digraph

A sequence of vertices $P = i_1, i_2, \cdots, i_k$ is an i_1 to i_k **path** in the graph or digraph $G = (V, E)$ iff the edge (i_j, i_{j+1}) is in E for every j, $1 \leq j < k$. There is a path from intersection i to intersection j iff there is a path from vertex i to vertex j in the corresponding digraph. In the digraph of Figure 12.2(b), 5, 2, 1 is a path from 5 to 1. There is no path from 5 to 4 in this digraph.

A **simple path** is a path in which all vertices, except possibly the first and last, are different. The path 5, 2, 1 is a simple path, whereas the path 2, 5, 2, 1 is not.

With each edge in a graph or digraph, we may associate a **length**. The length of a path is the sum of the lengths of the edges on the path. The shortest way to get from intersection i to intersection j is obtained by finding a shortest path from vertex i to vertex j in the corresponding network (i.e., weighted digraph). ■

Example 12.2 [*Spanning Trees*] Let $G = (V, E)$ be an undirected graph. G is **connected** iff there is a path between every pair of vertices in G. The undirected graph of Figure 12.1(a) is connected, while that of Figure 12.1(b) is not. Suppose that G represents a possible communication network with V being the set of cities and E the set of communication links. It is possible to communicate between every pair of cities in V iff G is connected. In the communication network of Figure 12.1(a), cities 2 and 4 can communicate using the communication path 2,3,4, while in the network of Figure 12.1(b), cities 2 and 4 cannot communicate.

Suppose that G is connected. Some of the edges of G may be unneccessary in that G remains connected even if these edges are removed. In the graph of Figure 12.1(a), for example, the graph remains connected even if we remove the edges (2,3) and (1,4).

A graph H is a **subgraph** of another graph G iff its vertex and edge sets are subsets of those of G. A **cycle** is a simple path with the same start and end vertex. For example, 1, 2, 3, 1 is a cycle in the graph of Figure 12.1(a). A connected undirected graph that contains no cycles is a **tree**. A subgraph of G that contains all the vertices of G and is a tree is a **spanning tree** of G. The spanning trees of Figure 12.1(a) appear in Figure 12.3.

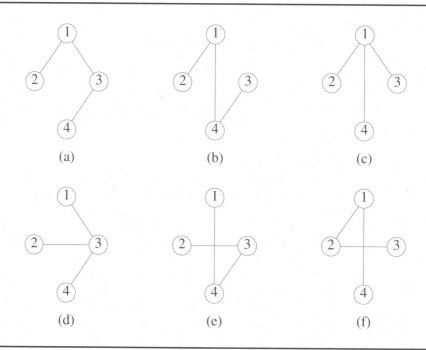

Figure 12.3 Spanning trees of Figure 12.1(a)

A connected graph with n vertices must have at least $n - 1$ edges. Hence when each link of a communication network has the same construction cost, the construction of all links on any one spanning tree minimizes network construction cost and ensures that a communication path exists between every pair of cities. Further, if the links have different (but nonnegative) costs, then the links on a minimum-cost spanning tree (the cost of a spanning tree is the sum of the costs of the edges on it) are to be constructed. Figure 12.4 shows a graph and two of its spanning trees. The spanning tree of Figure 12.4(b) is a minimum-cost spanning tree. ∎

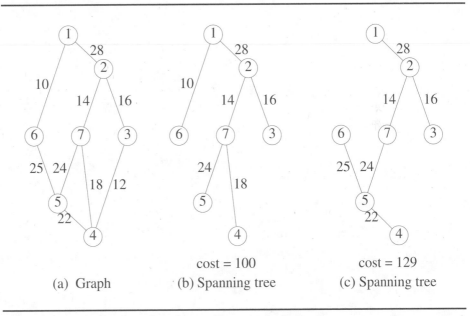

(a) Graph

cost = 100
(b) Spanning tree

cost = 129
(c) Spanning tree

Figure 12.4 Connected graph and two of its spanning trees

Example 12.3 [*Interpreters*] Suppose that you are planning an international convention. All the speakers at this convention know English only. The remaining participants know one of the languages {L1, L2, L3, $\cdots$, Ln}. You have available a set of interpreters who can translate between English and some of the other languages. Your task is to select the fewest number of interpreters needed to translate between English and the remaining languages.

We can formulate the problem as a graph problem in which the graph has two sets of vertices. One set corresponds to interpreters and the other to languages (Figure 12.5). An edge exists between interpreter i and language Lj iff interpreter i can translate between English and this language. Interpreter i **covers** language Li iff an edge connects the interpreter and the language. We want to find the smallest subset of the interpreter vertices that cover the language vertices.

The graph of Figure 12.5 has an interesting property: We can partition the vertex set into two subsets A (the interpreter vertices) and B (the language vertices) so that every edge has one endpoint in A and the other in B. Graphs with this property are **bipartite graphs**. ■

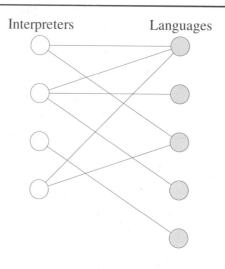

Figure 12.5 Interpreters and languages

12.3   PROPERTIES

Let G be an undirected graph. The **degree** d_i of vertex i is the number of edges incident on vertex i. For the graph of Figure 12.1(a), $d_1 = 3$; $d_2 = 2$; $d_3 = 3$; and $d_4 = 2$.

Property 1 Let $G = (V, E)$ be an undirected graph. Let $|V| = n$; $|E| = e$; and $d_i = $ degree of vertex i.

(a) $\sum_{i=1}^{n} d_i = 2e$

(b) $0 \le e \le n(n-1)/2$

Proof To prove (a), note that each edge in an undirected graph is incident on exactly two vertices. Hence the sum of the degrees of the vertices equals two times the number of edges. For (b), observe that the degree of a vertex lies between 0 and $n - 1$, so the sum of the degrees lies between 0 and $n(n - 1)$. From (a), it now follows that e lies between 0 and $n(n - 1)/2$. ∎

An n-vertex graph with $n(n - 1)/2$ edges is a **complete** graph. Figure 12.6 gives the complete graphs for $n = 1, 2, 3$, and 4. The complete graph on n vertices is denoted K_n.

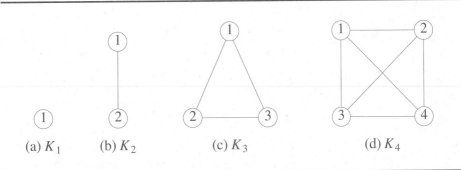

(a) K_1 (b) K_2 (c) K_3 (d) K_4

Figure 12.6 Complete graphs

Let G be a digraph. The **in-degree** d_i^{in} of vertex i is the number of edges incident to i (i.e., the number of edges coming into this vertex). The **out-degree** d_i^{out} of vertex i is the number of edges incident from this vertex (i.e., the number of edges leaving vertex i). For the digraph of Figure 12.1(c), $d_1^{in} = 0$; $d_1^{out} = 1$; $d_2^{in} = 1$; $d_2^{out} = 1$; $d_3^{in} = 2$; and $d_3^{out} = 2$.

Property 2 Let $G = (V, E)$ be a directed graph. Let n and e be as in Property 1.

(a) $0 \leq e \leq n(n-1)$

(b) $\sum_{i=1}^{n} d_i^{in} = \sum_{i=1}^{n} d_i^{out} = e$

Proof Exercise 2 asks you to prove this property. ∎

A **complete** digraph on n vertices contains exactly $n(n - 1)$ directed edges. Figure 12.7 gives the complete digraphs for $n = 1, 2, 3$, and 4.

The terms *in-degree* and *out-degree* may be used in the context of undirected graphs as synonyms for the term *degree*. The definitions provided in this section extend to networks in a rather straightforward way.

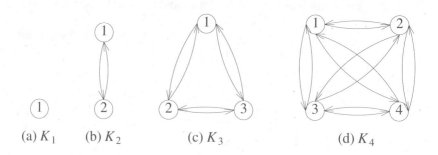

(a) K_1 (b) K_2 (c) K_3 (d) K_4

Figure 12.7 Complete digraphs

EXERCISES

1. For each of the graphs of Figure 12.8, determine the following:
   (a) The in-degree of each vertex.
   (b) The out-degree of each vertex.
   (c) The set of vertices adjacent from vertex 2.
   (d) The set of vertices adjacent to vertex 1.
   (e) The set of edges incident from vertex 3.
   (f) The set of edges incident to vertex 4.
   (g) All directed cycles and their lengths.

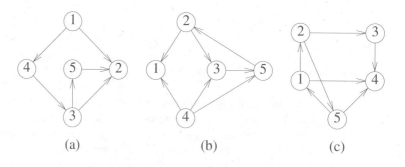

(a)   (b)   (c)

Figure 12.8 Digraphs

2.   Prove Property 2.

3.   Let G be any undirected graph. Show that the number of vertices with odd degrees is even.

4.   Let $G = (V, E)$ be a connected graph with $|V| > 1$. Show that G contains either a vertex of degree 1 or a cycle (or both).

5.   Let $G = (V, E)$ be a connected graph that contains at least one cycle. Let $(i,j) \in E$ be an edge that is on at least one cycle of G. Show that the graph $h = (V, E - \{(i,j)\})$ is also connected.

6.   Prove the following:

   (a)   For every n there exists a connected undirected graph containing exactly $n-1$ edges, $n \geq 1$.

   (b)   Every n-vertex connected undirected graph contains at least $n - 1$ edges. You may use the results of the previous two exercises.

7.   A digraph is **strongly connected** iff it contains a directed path from i to j and from j to i for every pair of distinct vertices i and j.

   (a)   Show that for every n, $n \geq 2$, there exists a strongly connected digraph that contains exactly n edges.

   (b)   Show that every n vertex strongly connected digraph contains at least n edges, $n \geq 2$.

   (c)   Write a procedure to determine whether or not the digraph G is strongly connected.

   (d)   Analyze the time complexity of your procedure for the case when G is represented as an adjacency matrix as well as for the case of a linked-adjacency-list representation.

12.4   THE ADTs *Graph* AND *Digraph*

The abstract data type *Graph* refers exclusively to undirected graphs while the data type *Digraph* refers to directed graphs. The abstract data type specifications of ADTs 12.1 and 12.2 list only a few of the many operations commonly performed on a graph. As we progress through this text, we shall add operations.

The abstract data types *WeightedGraph* and *WeightedDigraph* are similar. Only the specification of the Add operation needs to change to reflect a weight associated with the new edge.

AbstractDataType *Graph* {
  instances
    a set V of vertices and a set E of edges
  operations
    Create(n): create an undirected graph with n vertices and no edges
    Exist(i, j): return `true` if edge (i,j) exists; `false` otherwise
    Edges(): return the number of edges in the graph
    Vertices(): return the number of vertices in the graph
    Add(i, j): add the edge (i,j) to the graph
    Delete(i, j): delete the edge (i,j)
    Degree(i): return the degree of vertex i
    InDegree(i): synonym for degree
    OutDegree(i): synonym for degree
}

ADT 12.1 Abstract data type specification of an undirected graph

AbstractDataType *Digraph* {
  instances
    a set V of vertices and a set E of edges
  operations
    Create(n): create a directed graph with n vertices and no edges
    Exist(i, j): return `true` if edge (i,j) exists; `false` otherwise
    Edges(): return the number of edges in the graph
    Vertices(): return the number of vertices in the graph
    Add(i, j): add the edge (i,j) to the graph
    Delete(i, j): delete the edge (i,j)
    InDegree(i): return the in-degree of vertex i
    OutDegree(i): return the out-degree of vertex i
}

ADT 12.2 Abstract data type specification of a directed graph

EXERCISES

8. Write the ADT specification for a weighted undirected graph *Weighted-Graph*.

9. Write the ADT specification for a weighted digraph *WeightedDigraph*.

12.5   REPRESENTATION OF GRAPHS AND DIGRAPHS

The most frequently used representation schemes for graphs and digraphs are adjacency based: adjacency matrices, packed-adjacency lists, and linked-adjacency lists.

12.5.1   Adjacency Matrix

The **adjacency matrix** of an n-vertex graph $G = (V,E)$ is an $n \times n$ matrix A. Each element of A is either zero or one. We shall assume that $V = \{1, 2, \cdots, n\}$. If G is an undirected graph, then the elements of A are defined as follows:

$$A(i,j) = \begin{cases} 1 & \text{if } (i,j) \in E \text{ or } (j,i) \in E \\ 0 & \text{otherwise} \end{cases} \tag{12.1}$$

If G is a digraph, then the elements of A are defined as follows:

$$A(i,j) = \begin{cases} 1 & \text{if } (i,j) \in E \\ 0 & \text{otherwise} \end{cases} \tag{12.2}$$

The adjacency matrices for the graphs of Figure 12.1 appear in Figure 12.9.

$$
\begin{array}{c}
\begin{array}{cc}
 & \begin{array}{cccc} 1 & 2 & 3 & 4 \end{array} \\
\begin{array}{c} 1 \\ 2 \\ 3 \\ 4 \end{array} &
\left[\begin{array}{cccc}
0 & 1 & 1 & 1 \\
1 & 0 & 1 & 0 \\
1 & 1 & 0 & 1 \\
1 & 0 & 1 & 0
\end{array} \right]
\end{array} \\
\text{(a)}
\end{array}
\qquad
\begin{array}{c}
\begin{array}{cc}
 & \begin{array}{ccccccc} 1 & 2 & 3 & 4 & 5 & 6 & 7 \end{array} \\
\begin{array}{c} 1 \\ 2 \\ 3 \\ 4 \\ 5 \\ 6 \\ 7 \end{array} &
\left[\begin{array}{ccccccc}
0 & 1 & 1 & 0 & 0 & 0 & 0 \\
1 & 0 & 0 & 0 & 0 & 0 & 0 \\
1 & 0 & 0 & 0 & 0 & 0 & 0 \\
0 & 0 & 0 & 0 & 1 & 0 & 0 \\
0 & 0 & 0 & 1 & 0 & 1 & 1 \\
0 & 0 & 0 & 0 & 1 & 0 & 1 \\
0 & 0 & 0 & 0 & 1 & 1 & 0
\end{array} \right]
\end{array} \\
\text{(b)}
\end{array}
\qquad
\begin{array}{c}
\begin{array}{cc}
 & \begin{array}{ccccc} 1 & 2 & 3 & 4 & 5 \end{array} \\
\begin{array}{c} 1 \\ 2 \\ 3 \\ 4 \\ 5 \end{array} &
\left[\begin{array}{ccccc}
0 & 1 & 0 & 0 & 0 \\
0 & 0 & 1 & 0 & 0 \\
0 & 0 & 0 & 1 & 1 \\
0 & 0 & 1 & 0 & 0 \\
0 & 0 & 0 & 1 & 0
\end{array} \right]
\end{array} \\
\text{(c)}
\end{array}
$$

Figure 12.9 Adjacency matrices for the graphs of Figure 12.1

The validity of the following statements is an immediate consequence of (12.1) and (12.2):

1. $A(i,i) = 0, 1 \le i \le n$ for all n-vertex graphs.

2. The adjacency matrix of an undirected graph is symmetric. That is, $A(i,j) = A(j,i), 1 \le i \le n, 1 \le j \le n$.

3. For an n-vertex undirected graph, $\sum_{j=1}^{n} A(i,j) = \sum_{j=1}^{n} A(j,i) = d_i$. (Recall that d_i is the degree of vertex i.)

4. For an n vertex digraph, $\sum_{j=1}^{n} A(i,j) = d_i^{out}$ and $\sum_{j=1}^{n} A(j,i) = d_i^{in}, 1 \le i \le n$.

Mapping the Adjacency Matrix into an Array

The $n \times n$ adjacency matrix A may be mapped into an $(n + 1) \times (n + 1)$ array a of type `int` using the mapping $A(i,j) =$ a$[i][j], 1 \le i \le n, 1 \le j \le n$. If `sizeof(int)` equals 2 bytes, this mapping results in a storage requirement of $2(n + 1)^2$ bytes. Alternatively, we may use an $n \times n$ array—a$[n][n]$—and the mapping $A(i,j) =$ a$[i-1][j-1], 1 \le i \le n, 1 \le j \le n$. Since this alternative requires $2n^2$ bytes, the storage requirement is reduced by $4n + 2$ bytes.

A further reduction by $2n$ bytes results if we use the fact that all diagonal entries are zero and so need not be stored. When the diagonal is eliminated, an upper- and a lower-triangular matrix remain (see Section 4.3.3). These matrices may be compacted into an $(n - 1) \times n$ matrix as in Figure 12.10. The shaded entries represent the lower triangle of the original adjacency matrix.

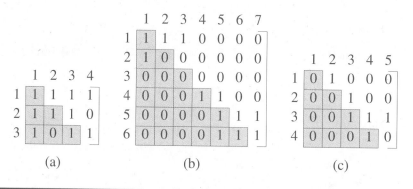

Figure 12.10 Adjacency matrices of Figure 12.9 with diagonals eliminated

A further and more dramatic reduction in storage requirement results if we use the fact that each adjacency matrix entry needs just 1 bit of storage and each array entry has 16 bits. By using an array a of type `unsigned int`, we can pack 16 elements of A into a single element of a. The storage requirements now become $n(n-1)/8$ bytes. This reduction in space requirements comes at a cost in time needed to store and retrieve an adjacency-matrix entry.

For undirected graphs the adjacency matrix is symmetric (see Section 4.3.5), so only the elements above (or below) the diagonal need to be stored explicitly. Hence we need only $(n^2 - n)/2$ bits.

Time Requirements

When adjacency matrices are used, we need $\Theta(n)$ time to determine the set of vertices adjacent to or from any given vertex, and to find the number of edges in the graph. However, we can add or delete an edge in $\Theta(1)$ time.

12.5.2   Packed-Adjacency Lists

In the **packed-adjacency-list** representation of $G = (V, E)$ with $|V| = n$ and $|E| = e$, we use two one-dimensional arrays $h[0:n+1]$ and $l[0:x]$ where $x = e - 1$ if G is a digraph and $x = 2e - 1$ if G is an undirected graph. First we add all vertices adjacent from vertex 1 to l; then we add all vertices adjacent from vertex 2 to l; then we add all vertices adjacent from vertex 3 to l; and so on. (If i and j are adjacent vertices in an undirected graph, then i is adjacent from j and j is adjacent from i). h is set up so that the vertices adjacent from vertex i are in positions $l[h[i]]$, $l[h[i]+1]$, $\cdots$, $l[h[i+1]-1]$ if $h[i] < h[i+1]$. If $h[i] \geq h[i+1]$, then no vertices are adjacent from i. We say that $l[h[i]]$, $l[h[i]+1]$, $\cdots$, $l[h[i+1]-1]$ is the packed-adjacency list for vertex i. The order in which vertices appear in this list is not important. Figure 12.11 gives the packed-adjacency lists corresponding to the graphs of Figure 12.1.

For an undirected graph, the values of h are in the range 0 through $2e$. As this range represents only $2e + 1$ distinct values, each $h[i]$ need to be at most $\lceil \log(2e + 1) \rceil$ bits long. The l entries are each in the range 1 through n. Hence each l needs to be at most $\lceil \log n \rceil$ bits long. The total number of bits needed to store the packed-adjacency lists of an undirected n-vertex e-edge graph is therefore at most $(n + 1)\lceil \log(2e+1) \rceil + 2e \lceil \log n \rceil = O((n + e)\log n)$.

Time Requirements

When e is much less than n^2, the space needed by packed-adjacency lists is less than that needed by an adjacency matrix. If G is an undirected graph, the degree of vertex i is simply $h[i+1] - h[i]$ and the number of edges in G is $h[n+1]/2$. It is easier to determine these quantities when adjacency lists are used than when adjacency matrices are used. The addition of a new edge or the deletion of an old one, however, requires $O(n + e)$ time.

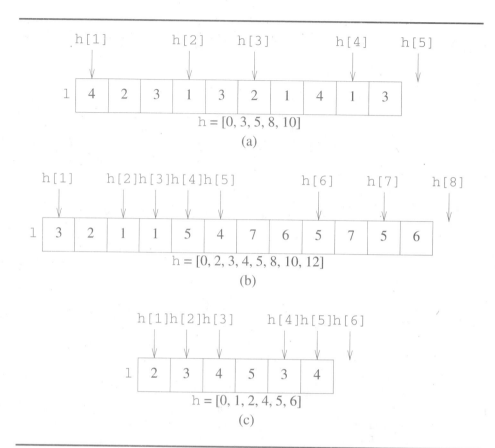

Figure 12.11 Packed-adjacency lists for graphs of Figure 12.1

12.5.3 Linked-Adjacency Lists

In the case of linked-adjacency lists, each adjacency list is maintained as a chain. The class Chain<int> (Program 3.8) may be used for this purpose. In addition, an array h of head nodes of type Chain<int> keeps track of these adjacency lists. h[i].first points to the first node in the adjacency list for vertex i. If x points to a node in the chain h[i], then (i, x->data) is an edge of the graph. Figure 12.12 gives some linked-adjacency-list representations.

If we assume that each pointer and integer is 2 bytes long, the space needed by the linked-adjacency-list representation of an n-vertex graph is $2(n + m + 1)$ where $m = 2e$ for an undirected graph and $m = e$ for a directed graph. The 1 comes from our use of an array h of size $n + 2$ and may be eliminated by using $h[i - 1]$ to point to the chain for vertex i.

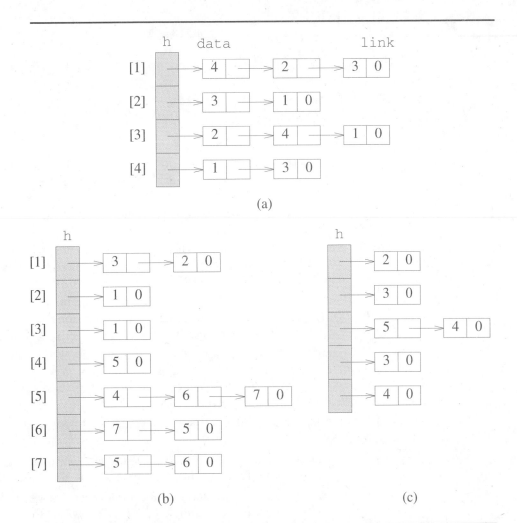

Figure 12.12 Linked-adjacency lists for the graphs of Figure 12.1

Time Requirements

Linked-adjacency lists permit easy addition and deletion of edges. The time needed to determine the number of vertices on an adjacency list is proportional to the number of vertices on that list.

EXERCISES

10. Obtain the following representations for the graphs of Figures 12.5 and 12.8(a):

    (a) Adjacency matrix.

    (b) Packed-adjacency lists.

    (c) Linked-adjacency lists.

11. Let `a` be an $(n-1) \times n$ array that represents the adjacency matrix A of an n-vertex graph. The matrix diagonal is not represented in `a` (see Figure 12.10). Write functions `Store` and `Retrieve` to, respectively, store and retrieve the value of $A(i,j)$. The complexity of each function should be $\Theta(1)$.

12. Do Exercise 11 for the case when the full adjacency matrix (see Figure 12.9) is represented by packing 16 entries of the matrix into a single entry of a one-dimensional array `a` of type `unsigned int`.

13. Do Exercise 11 for the case of an undirected graph for which only the lower triangle is explicitly stored in a one-dimensional array `a`. Assume that each element of `a` is either 0 or 1.

14. Do Exercise 11 for the case of an undirected graph for which only the lower triangle is explicitly stored in a one-dimensional array `a` of type `unsigned int`. Assume that each element of `a` represents 16 elements of the lower triangle of the adjacency matrix.

15. Assume that a directed $n \times n$ adjacency matrix is represented in an $n \times n$ array `a`.

    (a) Write a function to determine the out-degree of a vertex. The complexity of your function should be $\Theta(n)$. Show that this is the case.

    (b) Write a function to determine the in-degree of a vertex. The complexity of your function should be $\Theta(n)$. Show that this is the case.

    (c) Write a function to determine the number of edges in the graph. The complexity of your function should be $\Theta(n^2)$. Show that this is the case.

16. Suppose that an undirected graph is represented using the packed-adjacency list representation (see Figure 12.11).

    (a) Write a function to delete the edge (i,j). What is the time complexity of your code?

    (b) Write a function to add the edge (i,j). What is the time complexity of your code?

17. Do Exercise 16 for the case of a directed graph.
18. Do Exercise 15 for the case when linked-adjacency lists (see Figure 12.12) are used.
19. Do Exercise 16 for the case when linked-adjacency lists are used.
20. Let G be an n-vertex e-edge undirected graph. What is the least value of e for which the adjacency-matrix representation of G uses less space than the packed-adjacency-list representation uses?
21. Do Exercise 20 for the case of a directed graph G.

12.6 REPRESENTATION OF NETWORKS

Networks, whether weighted graphs or digraphs, are generally represented using schemes that are simple extensions of those used for graphs and digraphs. The **cost-adjacency-matrix** representation uses a matrix `C` just like the adjacency-matrix representation does. If $A(i,j)$ is one, then $C(i,j)$ is the cost (or weight) of the corresponding edge. If $A(i,j)$ is zero, then the corresponding edge is not present and $C(i,j)$ equals some prespecified value `NoEdge`. The value of `NoEdge` is chosen so that operations performed by the application on the $C(i,j)$ values are able to distinguish between the presence and absence of an edge. Usually, it suffices to set `NoEdge` to the largest allowable value for the data type of the costs/weights. Figure 12.13 gives possible cost-adjacency matrices for the graphs of Figure 12.1. The symbol ∞ denotes the value of `NoEdge` in use.

	1	2	3	4
1	∞	4	7	8
2	4	∞	2	∞
3	7	2	∞	6
4	8	∞	6	∞

(a)

	1	2	3	4	5	6	7
1	∞	9	5	∞	∞	∞	∞
2	9	∞	∞	∞	∞	∞	∞
3	5	∞	∞	∞	∞	∞	∞
4	∞	∞	∞	∞	3	∞	∞
5	∞	∞	∞	3	∞	6	4
6	∞	∞	∞	∞	6	∞	1
7	∞	∞	∞	∞	4	1	∞

(b)

	1	2	3	4	5
1	∞	8	∞	∞	∞
2	∞	∞	3	∞	∞
3	∞	∞	∞	2	7
4	∞	∞	6	∞	∞
5	∞	∞	∞	5	∞

(c)

Figure 12.13 Possible cost-adjacency matrices for the graphs of Figure 12.1

We can obtain the packed-adjacency-list representation of a network from that of the corresponding unweighted graph or digraph by replacing each entry of *l* with a (vertex, weight) pair. For example, the array *l* for the digraph of Figure 12.1(c) appears in Figure 12.11(c), and a weight assignment to its edges is defined by the cost adjacency matrix of Figure 12.13(c). The array *l* for the corresponding weighted digraph is [(2, 8), (3, 3), (4, 2), (5, 7), (3, 6), (4, 5)]. The array *h* does not change.

We can obtain the adjacency-list representation of a network from that of the corresponding graph by using chains of type `Chain<GraphNode>` where `GraphNode` has two components: `vertex` and `weight`. Figure 12.14 shows the representation for the network that corresponds to the cost-adjacency matrix of Figure 12.13(a). The first component of each node in this figure is `vertex`, and the second is `weight`.

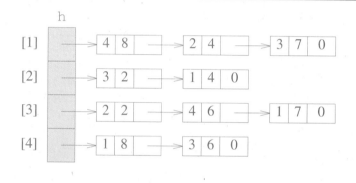

Figure 12.14 Linked-adjacency lists for network of Figure 12.13(a)

EXERCISES

22. Obtain the packed-adjacency-list representations of the networks that correspond to the cost-adjacency matrices of Figures 12.1(a) and (b).

23. Obtain the linked-adjacency-list representations of the networks that correspond to the cost-adjacency matrices of Figures 12.1(a) and (b).

12.7 CLASS DEFINITIONS

12.7.1 The Different Classes

Unweighted digraphs and graphs may be regarded as weighted digraphs and graphs in which each edge has a weight of one. So the abstract data types (*Graph*, *Digraph*, *WeightedGraph*, and *WeightedDigraph*) defined in Section 12.4 are subtypes of a more general abstract data type *Network*.

For each of the four abstract data types of Section 12.4, we considered three possible representations (matrix, packed, and linked) in Sections 12.5 and 12.6. With one C++ class for each abstract data type and representation combination, we will have 12 classes. Only eight of these classes are explicitly considered in this text. We develop the four that correspond to the packed representation in Exercises 33 through 36.

The eight classes we shall develop are `AdjacencyGraph`, `AdjacencyWGraph` (weighted graphs using the matrix representation), `AdjacencyDigraph`, `AdjacencyWDigraph`, `LinkedGraph`, `LinkedWGraph`, `LinkedDigraph`, and `LinkedWDigraph`.

Several pairs of our four abstract data types have an ''IsA'' relationship between them. For example, an undirected graph may be viewed as a directed graph in which edge (i,j) is present whenever edge (j,i) is present; as a weighted undirected graph in which all edge weights are one; or as a weighted digraph in which all edge weights are one and whenever edge (i,j) is present, so also is (j,i). Similarly, a digraph may be viewed as a weighted digraph in which all edge weights are one.

The presence of these relationships makes it easier to develop the eight classes because we can derive one class from another. Although many ''IsA'' relationships exist, we shall employ just a few. It is natural to derive the adjacency-matrix classes from one another and the linked ones from other linked classes. The derivation hierarchy we employ appears as a directed acyclic graph (dag) in Figure 12.15. The class `AdjacencyGraph`, for example, is derived from the class `AdjacencyWGraph`, which, in turn, is derived from the class `AdjacencyWDigraph`. For the linked classes, we have included an additional class `LinkedBase` which represents an array of chains. The use of the class `LinkedBase` avoids replication of functions common to the four linked classes. For the adjacency classes, we did not need to define an additional class as the adjacency classes have a common root class, `AdjacencyWDigraph`, in which functions common to all classes could be defined.

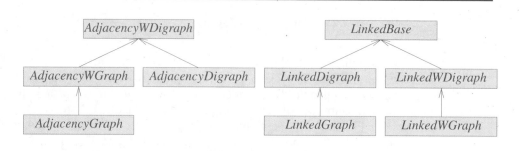

Figure 12.15 Class-derivation hierarchy

12.7.2 Adjacency-Matrix Classes

The root of our adjacency-matrix classes is `AdjacencyWDigraph`, so we begin with this class. Program 12.1 specifies the class. The constructor first allocates space for the two-dimensional array `a` using the function `Make2DArray` of Program 1.13. Then this array is initialized so as to represent the adjacency matrix of an n-vertex graph with zero edges. Its complexity is $\Theta(n^2)$. Our code does not catch any exceptions that might be thrown by `Make2DArray`. The destructor uses the two-dimensional array deallocator of Program 1.14.

```
template<class T>
class AdjacencyWDigraph {
   friend AdjacencyWGraph<T>;
   public:
      AdjacencyWDigraph
              (int Vertices = 10, T noEdge = 0);
      ~AdjacencyWDigraph() {Delete2DArray(a,n+1);}
      bool Exist(int i, int j) const;
      int Edges()  const {return e;}
      int Vertices() const {return n;}
      AdjacencyWDigraph<T>& Add
                    (int i, int j, const T& w);
      AdjacencyWDigraph<T>& Delete(int i, int j);
      int OutDegree(int i) const;
      int InDegree(int i) const;
```

Program 12.1 Cost-adjacency matrix for weighted directed graphs (continues)

```
   private:
      T NoEdge;    // used for absent edge
      int n;       // number of vertices
      int e;       // number of edges
      T **a;       // 2D array
};

template<class T>
AdjacencyWDigraph<T>
   ::AdjacencyWDigraph(int Vertices, T noEdge)
{// Constructor.
   n = Vertices;
   e = 0;
   NoEdge = noEdge;
   Make2DArray(a, n+1, n+1);
   // initalize to graph with no edges
   for (int i = 1; i <= n; i++)
      for (int j = 1; j <= n; j++)
         a[i][j] = NoEdge;
}

template<class T>
bool AdjacencyWDigraph<T>::Exist(int i, int j) const
{// Does edge (i, j) exist?
   if (i < 1 || j < 1 || i > n || j > n
       || a[i][j] == NoEdge) return false;
   return true;
}

template<class T>
AdjacencyWDigraph<T>& AdjacencyWDigraph<T>
                 ::Add(int i, int j, const T& w)
{// Add edge (i,j) to digraph if not present.
   if (i < 1 || j < 1 || i > n ||
       j > n || i == j || a[i][j] != NoEdge)
       throw BadInput();
   a[i][j] = w;
   e++;
   return *this;
}
```

Program 12.1 Cost-adjacency matrix for weighted directed graphs (continues)

```
template<class T>
AdjacencyWDigraph<T>& AdjacencyWDigraph<T>
                ::Delete(int i, int j)
{// Delete edge (i,j).
   if (i < 1 || j < 1 || i > n ||
       j > n || a[i][j] == NoEdge)
      throw BadInput();
   a[i][j] = NoEdge;
   e--;
   return *this;
}

template<class T>
int AdjacencyWDigraph<T>::OutDegree(int i) const
{// Return out degree of vertex i.
   if (i < 1 || i > n) throw BadInput();
   // count out edges from vertex i
   int sum = 0;
   for (int j = 1; j <= n; j++)
      if (a[i][j] != NoEdge) sum++;
   return sum;
}

template<class T>
int AdjacencyWDigraph<T>::InDegree(int i) const
{// Return indegree of vertex i.
   if (i < 1 || i > n) throw BadInput();
   // count in edges at vertex i
   int sum = 0;
   for (int j = 1; j <= n; j++)
      if (a[j][i] != NoEdge) sum++;
   return sum;
}
```

Program 12.1 Cost-adjacency matrix for weighted directed graphs (concluded)

The code for function Exist does not distinguish between the cases when i and/or j may not denote a valid vertex from the case when they do and the edge (i,j) is not present. We could modify the code to throw an OutOfBounds exception in the former case. The same distinction could be made in the add and delete codes. All the codes are rather straightforward, and we shall not elaborate further. The complexity of Exist, Edges, Add, and Delete is $\Theta(1)$, and that of OutDegree and InDegree is $\Theta(n)$.

The remaining three adjacency-matrix classes are specified in Programs 12.2 through 12.4.

```
template<class T>
class AdjacencyWGraph : public AdjacencyWDigraph<T> {
   public:
      AdjacencyWGraph(int Vertices = 10, T noEdge = 0)
         : AdjacencyWDigraph<T>(Vertices, noEdge) {}
      AdjacencyWGraph<T>& Add(int i, int j, const T& w)
         {AdjacencyWDigraph<T>::Add(i,j,w);
          a[j][i] = w;
          return *this;}
      AdjacencyWGraph<T>& Delete(int i, int j)
         {AdjacencyWDigraph<T>::Delete(i,j);
          a[j][i] = NoEdge;
          return *this;}
      int Degree(int i) const {return OutDegree(i);}
};
```

Program 12.2 Cost-adjacency matrix for weighted graphs

```
class AdjacencyDigraph :
              public AdjacencyWDigraph<int> {
   public:
      AdjacencyDigraph(int Vertices = 10)
         : AdjacencyWDigraph<int>(Vertices, 0) {}
      AdjacencyDigraph& Add(int i, int j)
         {AdjacencyWDigraph<int>::Add(i,j,1);
          return *this;}
      AdjacencyDigraph& Delete(int i, int j)
         {AdjacencyWDigraph<int>::Delete(i,j);
          return *this;}
};
```

Program 12.3 Adjacency-matrix representation of a digraph

```
class AdjacencyGraph : public AdjacencyWGraph<int> {
   public:
      AdjacencyGraph(int Vertices = 10)
         : AdjacencyWGraph<int>(Vertices, 0) {}
      AdjacencyGraph& Add(int i, int j)
            {AdjacencyWGraph<int>::Add(i,j,1);
               return *this;}
      AdjacencyGraph& Delete(int i, int j)
            {AdjacencyWGraph<int>::Delete(i,j);
               return *this;}
};
```

Program 12.4 Adjacency-matrix representation of a graph

12.7.3 An Extension to the Class `Chain`

In the linked-list representations, each object is represented as an array of chains where each chain is of type `Chain` (Program 3.8). One of the chain operations we need has not been defined yet. So we include this operation now.

The new public member function (Program 12.5) deletes an element with a prespecified key value. The code searches the chain for an element whose key equals that of `x`. (We assume that `!=` has been overloaded to compare the keys of two elements.) If a matching element is found, it is deleted from the chain and returned in `x`.

12.7.4 The Class `LinkedBase`

As noted in Figure 12.15, the derivation paths for the unweighted- and weighted-graph versions are different. The cause of this difference is that the chain-node type used for weighted graphs and digraphs has a weight field, while that for unweighted graphs and digraphs does not. For unweighted graphs and digraphs, using chain nodes of type `int` is sufficient, while for weighted graphs and digraphs, the chain-node type must include a weight and a vertex field. Despite this difference in the chain-node structure, the codes for several basic functions remains the same. As a result, we introduce a new class `Linked-Base` (Program 12.6), which includes the constructor, destructor, `Edges`, and `OutDegree` functions.

The constructor allocates space for the array of chains. `h[i]` is the chain for vertex `i`, $1 \le i \le n$. The destructor frees the space allocated by the constructor. The complexity of the constructor, destructor, and `Edges` is $\Theta(1)$ and that of `OutDegree(i)` is $\Theta(d_i^{out})$.

```
template<class T>
Chain<T>& Chain<T>::Delete(T& x)
{// Delete element matching x.
   ChainNode<T> *current = first,
                *trail = 0; // one behind current

   // search for match
   while (current && current->data != x) {
      trail = current;
      current = current->link;}
   if (!current) throw BadInput(); // no match

   // match found in node current
   x = current->data; // save matching element

   // remove current from chain
   if (trail) trail->link = current->link;
   else first = current->link; // current is first node

   delete current;  // free node
   return *this;
}
```

Program 12.5 Deleting from a chain by key

12.7.5   Linked Classes

The four linked graph classes we define now are to be declared friends of
LinkedBase. Program 12.7 gives the class LinkedDigraph. We have
added the protected function AddNoCheck, which adds an edge without performing validity checks. We added AddNoCheck because a validity check is
expensive when adjacency lists are used; the check may now be omitted, as we
will know apriori that the edge addition is valid. The complexity of
Exist(i,j) and Add(i,j) is $\Theta(d_i^{out})$; that of AddNoCheck is $\Theta(1)$; that
of Delete(i,j) is $O(d_i^{out} + d_j^{out})$; and that of InDegree is $\Theta(n+e)$.

```
template<class T>
class LinkedBase {
   public:
      LinkedBase(int Vertices = 10)
         {n = Vertices;
          e = 0;
          h = new Chain<T> [n+1];}
      ~LinkedBase() {delete [] h;}
      int Edges() const {return e;}
      int Vertices() const {return n;}
      int OutDegree(int i) const
         {if (i < 1 || i > n) throw OutOfBounds();
          return h[i].Length();}
   private:
      int n;         // number of vertices
      int e;         // number of edges
      Chain<T> *h;  // adjacency list array
};
```

Program 12.6 Base class for linked-adjacency representations

```
class LinkedDigraph : public LinkedBase<int> {
   public:
      LinkedDigraph(int Vertices = 10)
         : LinkedBase<int> (Vertices) {}
      bool Exist(int i, int j) const;
      LinkedDigraph& Add(int i, int j);
      LinkedDigraph& Delete(int i, int j);
      int InDegree(int i) const;
   protected:
      LinkedDigraph& AddNoCheck(int i, int j);
};

bool LinkedDigraph::Exist(int i, int j) const
{// Is edge (i,j) present?
   if (i < 1 || i > n) throw OutOfBounds();
   return (h[i].Search(j)) ? true : false;
}
```

Program 12.7 Linked-adjacency-list representation of a digraph (continues)

```
LinkedDigraph& LinkedDigraph::Add(int i, int j)
{// Add edge (i,j) to the graph.
   if (i < 1 || j < 1 || i > n || j > n || i == j
      || Exist(i, j)) throw BadInput();
   return AddNoCheck(i, j);
}

LinkedDigraph& LinkedDigraph::AddNoCheck(int i, int j)
{// Add edge but do not check for errors.
   h[i].Insert(0,j); // add j to vertex i list
   e++;
   return *this;
}

LinkedDigraph& LinkedDigraph::Delete(int i, int j)
{// Delete edge (i,j).
   if (i < 1 || i > n) throw OutOfBounds();
   h[i].Delete(j);
   e--;
   return *this;
}

int LinkedDigraph::InDegree(int i) const
{// Return indegree of vertex i.
   if (i < 1 || i > n) throw OutOfBounds();
   // count in edges at vertex i
   int sum = 0;
   for (int j = 1; j <= n; j++)
      if (h[j].Search(i)) sum++;
   return sum;
}
```

Program 12.7 Linked-adjacency-list representation of a digraph (concluded)

The class `LinkedGraph` is defined as a derived class of `LinkedDigraph` as in Program 12.8. The complexities of all functions except `InDegree` are the same as for `LinkedDigraph`.

```
class LinkedGraph : public LinkedDigraph {
   public:
      LinkedGraph(int Vertices = 10)
         : LinkedDigraph (Vertices) {}
      LinkedGraph& Add(int i, int j);
      LinkedGraph& Delete(int i, int j);
      int Degree(int i) const {return InDegree(i);}
      int OutDegree(int i) const {return InDegree(i);}
   protected:
      LinkedGraph& AddNoCheck(int i, int j);
};

LinkedGraph& LinkedGraph::Add(int i, int j)
{// Add edge (i,j) to the graph.
   if (i < 1 || j < 1 || i > n || j > n || i ==j
      || Exist(i, j)) throw BadInput();
   return AddNoCheck(i, j);
}

LinkedGraph& LinkedGraph::AddNoCheck(int i, int j)
{// Add edge (i,j), no error checks.
   h[i].Insert(0,j);
   try {h[j].Insert(0,i);}
   // on exception, undo first insert
   // and rethrow same exception
   catch (...) {h[i].Delete(j);
                throw;}
   e++;
   return *this;
}

LinkedGraph& LinkedGraph::Delete(int i, int j)
{// Delete edge (i,j).
   LinkedDigraph::Delete(i,j);
   e++; // compensate
   LinkedDigraph::Delete(j,i);
   return *this;
}
```

Program 12.8 The class LinkedGraph

The class definition for weighted directed graphs appears in Program 12.9. The class `GraphNode` appears in Program 12.10. The code for `InDegree` is the same as for the class `LinkedDigraph` and is not provided in Program 12.9. The complexity of all functions remains the same as for the class `LinkedDigraph`. The class `LinkedWGraph` may now be derived from `LinkedWDigraph` (see Exercise 32).

```cpp
template<class T>
class LinkedWDigraph :
            public LinkedBase<GraphNode<T> > {
   public:
      LinkedWDigraph(int Vertices = 10)
         : LinkedBase<GraphNode<T> > (Vertices) {}
      bool Exist(int i, int j) const;
      LinkedWDigraph<T>& Add(int i, int j, const T& w);
      LinkedWDigraph<T>& Delete(int i, int j);
      int InDegree(int i) const;
   protected:
      LinkedWDigraph<T>&
         AddNoCheck(int i, int j, const T& w);
};

template<class T>
bool LinkedWDigraph<T>::Exist(int i, int j) const
{// Is edge (i,j) present?
   if (i < 1 || i > n) throw OutOfBounds();
   GraphNode<T> x;
   x.vertex = j;
   return h[i].Search(x);
}

template<class T>
LinkedWDigraph<T>& LinkedWDigraph<T>
      ::Add(int i, int j, const T& w)
{// Add edge (i,j).
   if (i < 1 || j < 1 || i > n || j > n || i == j
      || Exist(i, j)) throw BadInput();
   return AddNoCheck(i, j, w);
}
```

Program 12.9 Linked-adjacency lists for weighted digraphs (continues)

```
template<class T>
LinkedWDigraph<T>& LinkedWDigraph<T>
        ::AddNoCheck(int i, int j, const T& w)
{// Add (i,j) with no error checks.
   GraphNode<T> x;
   x.vertex = j; x.weight = w;
   h[i].Insert(0,x);
   e++;
   return *this;
}

template<class T>
LinkedWDigraph<T>& LinkedWDigraph<T>
        ::Delete(int i, int j)
{// Delete edge (i,j).
   if (i < 1 || i > n) throw OutOfBounds();
   GraphNode<T> x;
   x.vertex = j;
   h[i].Delete(x);
   e--;
   return *this;
}

template<class T>
int LinkedWDigraph<T>::InDegree(int i) const
{// Return indegree of vertex i.
   if (i < 1 || i > n) throw OutOfBounds();
   int sum = 0;
   GraphNode<T> x;
   x.vertex = i;
   // check all lists for edge <j,i>
   for (int j = 1; j <= n; j++)
      if (h[j].Search(x)) sum++;
   return sum;
}
```

Program 12.9 Linked-adjacency lists for weighted digraphs (concluded)

```
template <class T>
class GraphNode {
    friend LinkedWDigraph<T>;
    friend LinkedWGraph<T>;
    friend Chain<T>;
    public:
        int operator !=(GraphNode<T> y) const
        {return (vertex != y.vertex);}
        void Output(ostream& out) const
        {out << vertex << " " << weight << " ";}
    private:
        int vertex;   // second vertex of edge
        T weight;     // edge weight
};

template <class T>
ostream& operator<<(ostream& out, GraphNode<T> x)
    {x.Output(out); return out;}
```

Program 12.10 The class `GraphNode`

EXERCISES

24. Write the function `AdjacencyGraph::Input`, which inputs an undirected graph as well as the function `Output`, which outputs the graph. Assume that the input consists of the number of vertices and edges in the graph together with a list of edges. Each edge is given as a pair of vertices. Overload the operator $<<$ so that it may be used to input a graph.

25. Write the function `AdjacencyDigraph::Input`, which inputs a directed graph, as well as the function `Output`, which outputs the graph. Overload the operator $<<$ so that it may be used to input a digraph.

26. Write the function `AdjacencyWGraph::Input`, which inputs an undirected network, as well as the function `Output`, which outputs the graph. Overload the operators $<<$ and $>>$ to provide this capability also.

27. Write the function `AdjacencyWDigraph::Input`, which inputs a directed network, as well as the function `Output`, which outputs the network. Overload the operators $<<$ and $>>$ to provide this capability also.

28. Write the function `LinkedGraph::Input`, which inputs an undirected graph, as well as the function `Output`, which outputs the graph. Overload the operators $<<$ and $>>$ to provide this capability also.

29. Write the function `LinkedDigraph::Input`, which inputs a directed graph, as well as the function `Output`, which outputs the graph. Overload the operators `<<` and `>>` to provide this capability also.

30. Write the function `LinkedWGraph::Input`, which inputs an undirected network, as well as the function `Output`, which outputs the network. Overload the operators `<<` and `>>` to provide this capability also.

31. Write the function `LinkedWDigraph::Input`, which inputs a directed network, as well as the function `Output`, which outputs the network. Overload the operators `<<` and `>>` to provide this capability also.

32. Develop a C++ class `LinkedWGraph` in which weighted undirected graphs are represented using linked-adjacency lists. Derive your class from the class `LinkedWDigraph` (Program 12.9).

33. Develop a C++ class `PackedAdjGraph` in which undirected graphs are represented using packed-adjacency lists. Derive your class from the class `LinearList` (Program 3.1).

34. Develop a C++ class `PackedAdjWGraph` in which weighted undirected graphs are represented using packed-adjacency lists. Derive your class from the class `LinearList` (Program 3.1).

35. Develop a C++ class `PackedAdjDigraph` in which digraphs are represented using packed-adjacency lists. Derive your class from the class `LinearList` (Program 3.1).

36. Develop a C++ class `PackedAdjWDigraph` in which weighted digraphs are represented using packed-adjacency lists. Derive your class from the class `LinearList` (Program 3.1).

12.8 GRAPH ITERATORS

12.8.1 Specification

When writing applications that use any of our graph classes, we need to move along one or more of the rows of the adjacency matrix or along one or more of the chains. These functions are called **iterators**. For the class `Chain`, we defined an additional class, `ChainIterator` (Program 3.18), which provided functions to move from one element of a chain to the next. We may follow the same strategy for our graph classes and define new classes that provide iterator functions for graphs.

For our graph classes, however, we shall embed the iterators within the classes. Exercises 37, 38, and 39 explore the use of new iterator classes. The iterator functions we shall define and their significance follows. These functions use one cursor for each matrix row or linked chain. Consequently, these iterator functions do not support applications that require multiple cursors on the same row or chain.

`Begin(i)`

For an adjacency-list representation, the first vertex on the list for vertex `i` is returned. For an adjacency matrix, the smallest (i.e., first) vertex adjacent from `i` is returned. In both cases a zero is returned if there is no adjacent vertex.

`NextVertex(i)`

Returns the next vertex on the adjacency list for vertex `i` or the next-lowest vertex adjacent from `i`. Again, a zero is returned if there is no next vertex.

`InitializePos()`

Initializes the storage mechanism being used to keep track of the current location in each of the adjacency lists or in each row of the (cost) adjacency matrix.

`DeactivatePos()`

Deactivates the storage mechanism created by `InitializePos()`.

12.8.2 Iterator Functions for Adjacency-Matrix Representations

The iterator functions for adjacency-matrix representations may be implemented by including them as public member functions of the class `AdjacencyWDigraph`. Since the remaining three adjacency classes are derived from this class, they inherit the iterators defined for `AdjacencyWDigraph`.

Since we may be at different locations of different rows of the adjacency matrix, we use an array `pos` to record our location in each row. This variable is defined as a private member of `AdjacencyWDigraph` as below

```
int *pos;  // array of current locations
```

The iterator function codes appear in Program 12.11.

12.8.3 Iterator Functions for Linked-Adjacency Lists

For graphs and networks represented by linked-adjacency lists, we need to add the public members `Initialize` and `DeactivatePos` of Program 12.12 to the class `LinkedBase`. Also, we need to define `pos` as a private member as follows:

```
ChainIterator<T> *pos;
```

We also add the remaining two iterator functions to the classes `Linked-Digraph` and `LinkedWDigraph`. The codes are given in Programs 12.13 and 12.14.

```
void InitializePos() {pos = new int [n+1];}

void DeactivatePos() {delete [] pos;}

template<class T>
int AdjacencyWDigraph<T>::Begin(int i)
{// Return first vertex adjacent to vertex i.
   if (i < 1 || i > n) throw OutOfBounds();

   // look for first adjacent vertex
   for (int j = 1; j <= n; j++)
      if (a[i][j] != NoEdge) {// j is first one
         pos[i] = j; return j;}

   pos[i] = n + 1; // no adjacent vertex
   return 0;
}

template<class T>
int AdjacencyWDigraph<T>::NextVertex(int i)
{// Return next vertex adjacent to vertex i.
   if (i < 1 || i > n) throw OutOfBounds();

   // find next adjacent vertex
   for (int j = pos[i] + 1; j <= n; j++)
      if (a[i][j] != NoEdge) {// j is next vertex
         pos[i] = j;
         return j;}

   pos[i] = n + 1; // no next vertex
   return 0;
}
```

Program 12.11 Iterators for adjacency-matrix representations

```
void InitializePos()
   {pos = new ChainIterator<T> [n+1];}

void DeactivatePos() {delete [] pos;}
```

Program 12.12 Additions to LinkedBase

```
int LinkedDigraph::Begin(int i)
{// Return first vertex adjacent to vertex i.
   if (i < 1 || i > n) throw OutOfBounds();
   int *x = pos[i].Initialize(h[i]);
   return (x) ? *x : 0;
}

int LinkedDigraph::NextVertex(int i)
{// Return next vertex adjacent to vertex i.
   if (i < 1 || i > n) throw OutOfBounds();
   int *x = pos[i].Next();
   return (x) ? *x : 0;
}
```

Program 12.13 Linked-adjacency-list iterators

```
template<class T>
int LinkedWDigraph<T>::Begin(int i)
{// Return first vertex adjacent to vertex i.
   if (i < 1 || i > n) throw OutOfBounds();
   GraphNode<T> *x = pos[i].Initialize(h[i]);
   return (x) ? x->vertex : 0;
}

template<class T>
int LinkedWDigraph<T>::NextVertex(int i)
{// Return next vertex adjacent to vertex i.
   if (i < 1 || i > n) throw OutOfBounds();
   GraphNode<T> *x = pos[i].Next();
   return (x) ? x->vertex : 0;
}
```

Program 12.14 Linked-weighted-digraph iterators

EXERCISES

37. Implement and test an iterator class for `AdjacencyWDigraph`. Your class should provide the same functionality as the iterators in this section provide.

38. Do Exercise 37 for `LinkedDigraph`.

39. Do Exercise 37 for `LinkedWDigraph`.

12.9   LANGUAGE FEATURES

12.9.1   Virtual Functions and Polymorphism

Consider the codes `LinkedGraph::Add` (Program 12.8) and `LinkedDigraph::Add` (Program 12.7). The two codes are identical! Since `LinkedGraph` derives from `LinkedDigraph`, we may be tempted to remove `LinkedGraph::Add` and inherit the `Add` member of `LinkedDigraph`. Suppose we inherit this member. If *G* is of type `LinkedGraph`, then the expression `G.Add(i,j)` invokes the inherited function `LinkedDigraph::Add`, which, in turn, invokes `LinkedDigraph::AddNoCheck`, and the edge is added to chain `i` but not to chain `j`. The behavior of `LinkedDigraph::Add` is **unimorphic**. That is, regardless of whether `LinkedDigraph::Add` is working on objects of type `LinkedDigraph` or on objects of a type derived from `LinkedDigraph`, `LinkedDigraph::Add` behaves in the same way; the same functions are invoked.

Since `LinkedGraph` has a member function `AddNoCheck` of its own, we would like `LinkedDigraph::Add` to invoke `LinkedGraph::AddNoCheck` when it is working on objects of type `LinkedGraph` and to invoke `LinkedDigraph::AddNoCheck` when it is working on objects of type `LinkedDigraph`. That is, we want the behavior of `LinkedDigraph::Add` to be polymorphic; the exact functions invoked should depend on the type of the object the function is working on. We achieve polymorphic behavior by prefixing the declaration of line 10

```
LinkedDigraph& AddNoCheck(int i, int j);
```

of Program 12.7 with the keyword `virtual`, making `LinkedDigraph::AddNoCheck` a **virtual function**. No other changes are made. In particular, we do not add the keyword `virtual` in the function header

```
LinkedDigraph& LinkedDigraph::AddNoCheck(int i, int j)
```

Virtual functions are handled in a special manner. First, consider the case of single inheritance in which each class is either a base class or is derived from exactly one class. Suppose that class A is derived from class B and that A and B together contain at least one virtual function. A virtual function table is constructed for class A. For each virtual function F of A and B, this table contains a pointer to the actual function implementation of F that is to be used when we perform F on an object of type A.

Consider the derivation structure of Figure 12.16, which is an example of single inheritance because each class derives from at most one other class. There are four classes A, B, C, and D. Class A derives from class B, which derives from C, which derives from D. Each box lists the member functions of a class. Class D, for example, contains the virtual functions f and g (in the figure, vf is an abbreviation for virtual f and vg for virtual g) and the non-virtual function h. The functions D::f and D::g simply output the character D, while A::f and A::g output the character A. Although g is not explicitly declared a virtual function in B, it is a virtual function nonetheless as g is virtual in D. *Once a function is declared virtual, it remains virtual in all classes derived from it.*

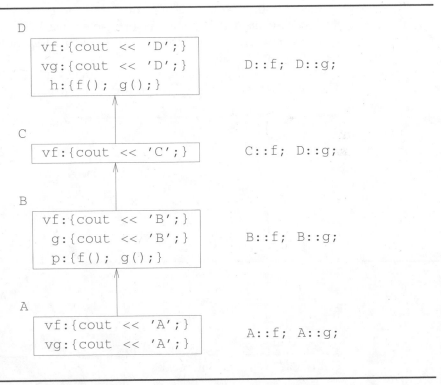

Figure 12.16 Virtual functions

The line to the right of each box of Figure 12.16 gives the virtual function table for the corresponding class. This table contains a pointer to the actual implementation that each class uses for each virtual function. Since D derives from no class, its table contains entries for only the virtual functions defined within D. The table for each remaining class is constructed from that of the class it derives from. For example, we obtain the table for C from that of D by updating the entries for functions redefined in C and adding entries for new virtual functions defined in C. We use the same process to construct the tables for B and A.

Let a, b, c, and d be objects of type A, B, C, and D, respectively. The invocation d.h() uses the virtual function table for the class D to decide which f and g to execute. The output is DD. When c.h() is executed, we use the virtual function table for C to decide which implementation of f and g to execute. The output is CD. The outputs produced by b.h(), b.p(), a.h(), and a.p() are BB, BB, AA, and AA, respectively.

Next consider the case of multiple inheritence in which a class A derives from two or more classes. For example, consider the derivation digraph of Figure 12.17 (a) in which class A derives from B and E. Class A now has two virtual function tables. The first corresponds to the derivation path ABCD and the second to the path AEFG. The first table is used when working on objects of type A along the path ABCD; the second is used when working on objects of type A along the path AEFG. The virtual function table for the first path is constructed from that of B using the same process as used for single inheritance. The table for the second path is constructed from that for E in the same way.

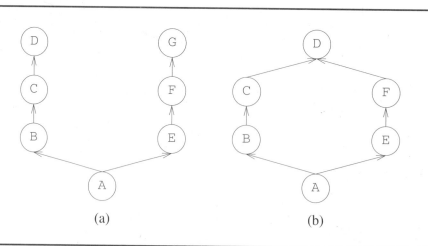

(a)   (b)

Figure 12.17 Derivation hierarchies

Because of the way in which virtual function tables are constructed, we need to designate one of the two virtual function tables of A as the table to use in case some other class, say, X, derives from A. By convention, we use the table for the first mentioned base class. So if class A is declared as

```
class A : public B, public E
```

the table for the path ABCD becomes the table to use for A whenever we are building the table for other classes that derive from A.

12.9.2 Pure Virtual Functions and Abstract Classes

A virtual function that is initialized to zero as in

```
virtual int f(int x, int y) = 0;
```

is a **pure virtual function**. Such a function is given no implementation in the class in which it is declared. A class that contains a pure virtual function is an **abstract class**. If A is an abstract class, then there can be no objects of type A because no method to perform A.f() has been given. There can, however, be pointers to objects of type A.

In Section 12.7 we noted that digraphs, undirected graphs, weighted digraphs, and weighted undirected graphs may all be viewed as networks. Although we defined no class corresponding to a network, we defined two classes for each of the four special network types because at the representation level, we have to distinguish among the four network types. However, it is useful now to define the class Network (Program 12.15) as an abstract class. At present this class contains only pure virtual functions. In subsequent sections we add some nonvirtual functions to Network.

```
class Network {
   public:
      virtual int Begin(int i) = 0;
      virtual int NextVertex(int i) = 0;
      virtual void InitializePos() = 0;
      virtual void DeactivatePos() = 0;
};
```

Program 12.15 The abstract class Network

The additional functions will perform operations on all four special network types regardless of their implementation, a feat made possible by the use of the iterators Begin, NextVertex, InitializePos, and DeactivatePos to move around in a graph. Since these iterators are defined as virtual functions, the actual implementation of each that is invoked will depend on the type of the object being worked on.

12.9.3   Virtual Base Classes

Consider the derivation structure of Figure 12.17 (b). Classes B, C, and D are as in Figure 12.16; class A is class A of Figure 12.16 with the redefinition of g omitted; classes E and F differ from classes B and C, respectively, only in that they output E and F, respectively, rather than B and C. Both C and F derive from D. If a is of type A, then the invocations a.h() and a.p() are ambiguous; in the first case we do not know which of the two virtual function tables of A (i.e., the ones for the paths ABCD and AEFD) is to be used, and in the second we do not know whether a.B::p() or a.E::p() is intended. The invocation a.B::h() invokes D::h() and A's virtual function table for the path ABCD is used. The output is AB. The invocation a.E::h() generates the output AE. Thus the invocation path determines which implementation of the virtual functions of D are used.

In many applications we want to use the same implementation of each virtual function of the common base class D when working on objects of type A regardless of the path used to invoke these functions. We can do so by making D a virtual base class of both C and F. In our example of Figure 12.17, simply making D a virtual base class of C and F is not enough, as the virtual functions f and g of D are redefined on both the ABCD and AEFD paths. As a result, we do not know which definition is to be used. To eliminate this ambiguity, each virtual function of the base class D should be redefined on at most one path from A. For example, suppose that f is redefined to output B in class B, but g is not redefined in A, B, or C, and that g is redefined in E to output E, but f is not redefined in A, E, or F. Class A's virtual function table entries for f and g are the same for both paths ABCD and AEFD. The invocations a.B::h(), a.E::h(), a.E::p() generate the same output BE.

Another consequence of making D a virtual base class of C and F is that objects of type A have only one copy of the data members of D. Regardless of whether D is or is not a virtual base class, objects of types C and F contain the data members of D. In turn, objects of type B contain the data members of C and D, while those of type E contain the data members of E and F. If D is not a virtual base class, objects of type A will contain the data members of B, C, and D via derivation from B and those of E, F, and D via derivation from E. Consequently, there will be two sets of D's data members in each object of type A. When D is a virtual base class, each object of type A will contain only one set of data members from D.

To avoid multiple copies of the data members of a base class, the base class should be declared a virtual base class. To make Network a virtual base class of AdjacencyWDigraph and LinkedBase (for example), we change the class headers to

```
class AdjacencyWDigraph : virtual public Network
class LinkedBase : virtual public Network
```

The headers state that `AdjacencyWDigraph` and `LinkedBase` derive publicly from `Network` and that `Network` is a virtual base class for each. Since the remaining graph classes are derived from `AdjacencyWDigraph` and `LinkedBase`, the members of these remaining classes also obtain access to members of `Network` as a result of these modifications.

In our graph applications, we must define `Network` as a virtual base class of of `AdjacencyWDigraph` and `LinkedBase` because we also define another class `Undirected` that derives from `Network`. The class `Undirected` contains functions that are specialized to undirected graphs and networks. As a result, these functions are to be accessible only from the classes for undirected graphs and networks. Figure 12.18 shows the new derivation structure for our graph classes.

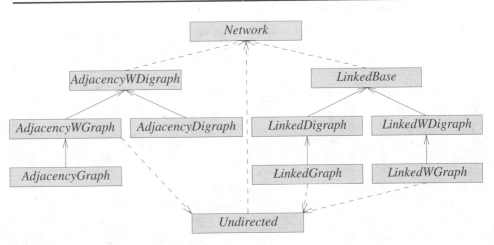

broken arrows designate derivations from a virtual base class

Figure 12.18 Class-derivation hierarchy including `Undirected`

For our linked classes, the pure virtual functions `InitializePos`, `DeactivatePos`, `Begin`, and `NextVertex` of `Network` are defined in `LinkedBase`. Suppose that *G* is of type `LinkedGraph` and `f` is a member of `Network`. Suppose that `LinkedBase` and `Undirected` derive from `Network` in a nonvirtual manner. The invocation `G.f()` is ambiguous, as we do not know which virtual table of `LinkedGraph` is to be used. Further, if we execute `G.g()` where `g` is a member of `Undirected` and `g`, in turn, invokes `f`, which is a member of `Network`, then the path `LinkedGraph -> Undirected -> Network` is used and the pure virtual iterator functions of `Network` are undefined. We can overcome both difficulties by making `Network` a virtual base class of both `LinkedBase` and `Undirected`.

12.9.4   Abstract Classes and Abstract Data Types

We can use abstract classes to specify abstract data types in a formal manner. So far, we have been providing this specification in an informal way. Consider the abstract data type *LinearList* (ADT 2.1), which is an informal specification of the linear-list data structure. It gives the operations that all implementations of a linear list must support. However, we do not have any way to enforce this requirement. *We can enforce compliance with an abstract data type specification by writing it as an abstract class and requiring that all implementations be derived from this abstract class.*

For the linear-list data structure, we may use the abstract class specification of Program 12.16.

```
template<class T>
class AbstractList {
public:
   virtual bool IsEmpty() const = 0;
   virtual int Length() const = 0;
   virtual bool Find(int k, T& x) const = 0;
      //return the k'th element of list in variable x
   virtual int Search(const T& x) const = 0;
      //return position of x
   virtual AbstractList<T>& Delete(int k, T& x) = 0;
      //delete k'th element of list and return in x
   virtual AbstractList<T>&
                   Insert(int k, const T& x) = 0;
      //insert x just after k'th element
   virtual void Output(ostream& out) const = 0;
};
```

Program 12.16 The abstract class `AbstractList`

Notice that all member functions of `AbstractList` are pure virtual functions. Since every implementation of a linear list is required to derive from `AbstractList`, each implementation must provide an implementation of all pure virtual functions. Otherwise, the implementation can have no instances.

To satisfy the requirement that all implementations be derived from the abstract data structure specification, we need to change the class header statements of `LinearList` (Program 3.1) and `Chain` (Program 3.8) to

```
class LinearList : AbstractList<T> {
class Chain : AbstractList<T> {
```

We also need to change the return type of `Insert` and `Delete`. In both classes, the return type for these functions is a reference to `AbstractList`. Therefore, in the class definitons we must replace the statements

```
LinearList<T>& Delete(int k, T& x);
LinearList<T>& Insert(int k, const T& x);
```

and

```
Chain<T>& Delete(int k, T& x);
Chain<T>& Insert(int k, const T& x);
```

with the statements

```
AbstractList<T>& Delete(int k, T& x);
AbstractList<T>& Insert(int k, const T& x);
```

Also, the statements

```
LinearList<T>& LinearList<T>::Delete(int k, T& x)
LinearList<T>& LinearList<T>::
                    Insert(int k, const T& x)
```

are to be replaced by

```
AbstractList<T>& LinearList<T>::Delete(int k, T& x)
AbstractList<T>& LinearList<T>::
                    Insert(int k, const T& x)
```

and the statements

```
Chain<T>& Chain<T>::Delete(int k, T& x)
Chain<T>& Chain<T>::Insert(int k, const T& x)
```

are to be replaced by

```
AbstractList<T>& Chain<T>::Delete(int k, T& x)
AbstractList<T>& Chain<T>::Insert(int k, const T& x)
```

No additional changes are necessary.

Besides providing the ability to enforce compliance with the abstract data type specification, the use of an abstract class as above allows us to code implementation-independent functions as members of the abstract class rather than include the code as a member of each implementation. We shall see examples of the use of this capability in the following sections.

EXERCISES

40. Obtain an abstract class specification `AbstractStack` of a stack (ADT 5.1). Now change the stack implementations `Stack` (Program 5.2) and `LinkedStack` (Program 5.4) so that both derive from `AbstractStack`. Test the correctness of your codes.

41. Obtain an abstract class specification `AbstractQueue` of a queue (ADT 6.1). Now change the queue implementations `Queue` (Program 6.1) and `LinkedQueue` (Program 6.4) so that both derive from `AbstractQueue`. Test the correctness of your codes.

12.10   GRAPH SEARCH METHODS

The number of functions that we can perform on a graph, digraph, or network are too numerous to list here. We have already seen some of these functions (e.g., find a path, find a spanning tree, find our whether the undirected graph is connected), and we shall see some others later in this book. Many functions require us to visit all vertices that can be reached from a given start vertex. (A vertex u is reachable from vertex v iff there is a (directed) path from v to u.) The two standard ways to search for these vertices are **breadth-first search** and **depth-first search**. Although both search methods are popular, the depth-first method is used more frequently to obtain efficient graph algorithms.

12.10.1   Breadth-First Search

Consider the directed graph of Figure 12.19(a). One way to determine all the vertices reachable from vertex 1 is to first determine the set of vertices adjacent from 1. This set is {2,3,4}. Next we determine the set of new vertices (i.e., vertices not yet reached) that are adjacent from vertices in {2,3,4}. This set is {5,6,7}. The set of new vertices adjacent from vertices in {5,6,7} is {8,9}. There are no new vertices adjacent from a vertex in {8,9}; therefore, {1,2,3,4,5,6,7,8,9} is the set of vertices reachable from vertex 1.

This method of starting at a vertex and identifying all vertices reachable from it is called **breadth-first search**. Such a search may be implemented using a queue. A pseudocode version of a possible implementation appears in Figure 12.20.

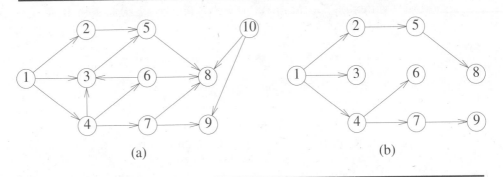

Figure 12.19 Breadth-first search

```
// Breadth first search beginning at vertex v
Label vertex v as reached;
Initialize Q to be a queue with only v in it;
while (Q is not empty) {
    Delete a vertex w from the queue;
    Let u be a vertex (if any) adjacent from w;
    while (u) {
        if (u has not been labeled) {
            Add u to the queue;
            Label u as reached; }
        u = next vertex that is adjacenct from w;
    }
}
```

Figure 12.20 Pseudocode for breadth-first search

If we use the pseudocode of Figure 12.20 on the graph of Figure 12.19(a) with $v = 1$, then vertices 2, 3, and 4 will get added to the queue (assume that they get added in this order) during the first iteration of the outer while loop. In the next iteration of this loop, 2 is removed from the queue, and vertex 5 added to it. Next 3 is deleted from the queue, and no new vertices are added. Then 4 is deleted, and 6 and 7 added; 5 is deleted and 8 added; 6 is deleted, and nothing added; and 7 is deleted, and 9 added. Finally, 8 and 9 are deleted, and the queue becomes empty. The procedure terminates, and vertices 1 through 9 have been marked as reached. Figure 12.19(b) shows the subgraph formed by the edges used to reach the nodes that get visited.

Theorem 12.1 Let N be an arbitrary graph, digraph, or network. Let v be any vertex of N. The pseudocode of Figure 12.20 labels all vertices that are reachable from v (including vertex v).

Proof Exercise 42 asks you to prove this theorem. ∎

12.10.2 The Class `Network`

As indicated by the pseudocode of Figure 12.20, at a suitably high level, the manner in which breadth-first search is performed is independent of whether we are dealing with a graph, digraph, weighted graph, or weighted digraph and is also independent of the particular representation used. However, to implement statements such as

`u = next vertex that is adjacent from w;`

we need to know the implementation in use. We can avoid writing separate code to perform a breadth-first search for each of the implementations by making our breadth-first search (BFS) function a member of the class `Network` (as defined in Program 12.15) and using graph iterators to go from one adjacent vertex to the next.

12.10.3 Implementation of `Network::BFS`

The unified code for breadth-first search (see Program 12.17) closely follows the pseudocode of Figure 12.20. Program 12.17 assumes that `reach[i]` = 0 initially for all vertices and that `label` ≠ 0. All reachable vertices have `reach[i]` set to `label` upon termination.

12.10.4 Complexity Analysis of `Network::BFS`

Each vertex that is reachable from the start vertex v is labeled, added to the queue exactly once, deleted from the queue exactly once, and its row in the adjacency matrix or its linked-adjacency list is traversed exactly once. If s vertices are labeled, then the time for all of these operations is $\Theta(sn)$ when an adjacency matrix is used and $\Theta(\sum_i d_i^{out})$ when a linked-adjacency list is used. In the latter case the sum is done over all i where i is a labeled vertex. For an undirected graph/network, the out-degree of a vertex is considered equal to its degree.

At this point we may wonder what the unified breadth-first search code costs compared to codes customized for each of the representations. Direct implementations for adjacency matrices and linked-adjacency lists appear in Programs 12.18 and 12.19.

```
void Network::BFS(int v, int reach[], int label)
{// Breadth first search.
   LinkedQueue<int> Q;
   InitializePos(); // init graph iterator array
   reach[v] = label;
   Q.Add(v);
   while (!Q.IsEmpty()) {
      int w;
      Q.Delete(w);   // get a labeled vertex
      int u = Begin(w);
      while (u) {// visit adj vertices of w
         if (!reach[u]) {// an unreached vertex
            Q.Add(u);
            reach[u] = label;} // mark reached
         u = NextVertex(w); // next adj vertex of w
         }
      }
   DeactivatePos(); // free iterator array
}
```

Program 12.17 Breadth-first search

```
template<class T>
void AdjacencyWDigraph<T>::BFS
               (int v, int reach[], int label)
{// Breadth first search.
   LinkedQueue<int> Q;
   reach[v] = label;
   Q.Add(v);
   while (!Q.IsEmpty()) {
      int w;
      Q.Delete(w);   // get a labeled vertex
      // label unlabeled vertices adjacent from w
      for (int u = 1; u <= n; u++)
         if (a[w][u] != NoEdge && !reach[u]) {
            Q.Add(u);   // u is not labeled
            reach[u] = label;}
      }
}
```

Program 12.18 Direct implementation of breadth-first search for adjacency-matrix representations

```
void LinkedDigraph::BFS(int v, int reach[], int label)
{// Breadth first search.
   LinkedQueue<int> Q;
   reach[v] = label;
   Q.Add(v);
   while (!Q.IsEmpty()) {
      int w;
      Q.Delete(w);   // get a labeled vertex
      // use pointer p to go down adjacency
      // list for vertex w
      ChainNode<int> *p;
      for (p = h[w].First(); p; p = p->link) {
         int u = p->data;
         if (!reach[u]) {// an unreached vertex
            Q.Add(u);
            reach[u] = label;}
         }
      }
}
```

Program 12.19 Direct BFS implementation for linked graphs and digraphs

On a 50-vertex, undirected, complete graph represented by its adjacency matrix, the execution time of `Network::BFS` was 2.6 times that of `AdjacencyWDigraph::BFS`. For the linked representation, the unified code took 4.5 times the time taken by the customized code.

The differential between the unified and customized codes can be reduced slightly by eliminating some of the unnecessary validity checks that the iterator functions `Begin` and `NextVertex` perform. In the context of `BFS` and possibly other members of `Network` that may be defined later, `Begin` and `NextVertex` are invoked only with a valid vertex parameter. Therefore, we may develop private versions of these functions (say `begin` and `nextVertex`) that do not perform a validity check. When validity checks are not performed, the performance factor 4.5 (for a 50-vertex complete graph) became 3.6.

As indicated above, we can expect to pay a potentially very significant performance penalty when using `Network::BFS` over the customized versions. However, we should keep in mind that several merits are associated with `Network::BFS`. For example, this single code works with all representations, whereas the customized route requires several codes. Consequently, if we introduce new representations, we can use existing members of `Network` with no change provided the iterator functions have been implemented.

12.10.5 Depth-First Search

Depth-first search is an alternative to breadth-first search. Starting at a vertex v, a depth-first search proceeds as follows: First the vertex v is marked as reached and then an unreached vertex u adjacent from v is selected. If such a vertex does not exist, the search terminates. Assume that a u as described exists. A depth-first search from u is now initiated. When this search is completed, we select another unreached vertex adjacent from v. If such a vertex does not exist, then the search terminates. If such a vertex exists, a depth-first search is initiated from this vertex, and so on.

Program 12.20 gives the public Network class member DFS as well as the private member dfs. In the implementation of depth-first search, it is easier to let u run through all vertices adjacent from v, rather than just through the unreached vertices adjacent from v.

```
void Network::DFS(int v, int reach[], int label)
{// Depth first search driver.
   InitializePos(); // init graph iterator array
   dfs(v, reach, label); // do the dfs
   DeactivatePos(); // free graph iterator array
}

void Network::dfs(int v, int reach[], int label)
{// Actual depth-first search code.
   reach[v] = label;
   int u = Begin(v);
   while (u) {// u is adj to v
      if (!reach[u]) dfs(u, reach, label);
      u = NextVertex(v);}
}
```

Program 12.20 Depth-first search

Let us try out DFS on the digraph of Figure 12.19(a). If v = 1, then vertices 2, 3, and 4 are the candidates for the first choice of u. Suppose that the first value assigned to u is 2. The edge used to get to 2 is (1,2). A depth-first search from 2 is now initiated. Vertex 2 is marked as reached. The only candidate for u this time is vertex 5. The edge (2,5) is used to get to 5. A depth-first search from 5 is initiated, and vertex 5 is marked as reached. Using the edge (5,8), vertex 8 is reached and marked. From 8 there are no unreached adjacent vertices, so the algorithm backs up to vertex 5. There are no new candidates for u here, so we back up to 2 and then to 1.

At this point we have two candidates: vertices 3 and 4 for `u`. Assume that 4 is selected. Hence edge (1,4) is used. A depth-first search from 4 is initiated, and vertex 4 is marked as reached. Vertices 3, 6, and 7 are now the candidates for `u`. Assume that vertex 6 is selected. When `u = 6`, vertex 3 is the only candidate for `w`. Edge (6,3) is used to get to 3. A depth-first search from 3 is initiated, and vertex 3 gets labeled as reached. No new vertices are adjacent from 3, and we back up to vertex 6. No new vertices are adjacent from here, so we back up to 4. From 4 we initiate a depth-first search with `u = 7`. Next we reach vertex 9 from which there are no new adjacent vertices. This time we back up all the way to 1. As there are no new vertices adjacent from 1, the algorithm terminates.

For `DFS`, we can prove a theorem analogous to Theorem 12.1; `DFS` labels vertex `v` and all vertices reachable from `v`.

Theorem 12.2 Let N be an arbitrary graph, digraph, or network. Let `v` be any vertex of N. Following the invocation `DFS(v,reach,label)`, `reached[i] = label` for all vertices (including `v`) that are reachable from vertex `v`.

Proof Exercise 43 asks you to prove this theorem. ■

We can also verify that `DFS` and `BFS` have the same time and space complexities. However, the graphs for which `DFS` takes maximum space (i.e., stack space for the recursion) are the graphs on which `BFS` takes minimum space (i.e., queue space). The graphs for which `BFS` takes maximum space are the graphs for which `DFS` takes minimum space. Figure 12.21 gives the best-case and worst-case graphs for `DFS` and `BFS`.

(a) Worst case for *DepthFirstSearch*(1); best case for *BreadthFirstSearch*(1)

(b) Best case for *DepthFirstSearch*(1); worst case for *BreadthFirstSearch*(1)

Figure 12.21 Worst-case and best-case space-complexity graphs

EXERCISES

42. Prove Theorem 12.1.
43. Prove Theorem 12.2.
44. Develop the iterator functions for the class `PackedAdjGraph`.

12.11 APPLICATIONS REVISITED

12.11.1 Finding a Path

We can find a path (see Example 12.1) from one vertex v to another vertex w by starting a search (either breadth first or depth first) at vertex v and terminating the search as soon as we reach vertex w. To actually construct the path, we need to remember the edges used to move from one vertex to the next. For the path problem, the needed set of edges is implicitly stored in the depth-first recursion, so it is easier to develop a path-finding code by using the depth-first strategy. As the recursion unfolds following the labeling of vertex w, the path is constructed backwards from w to v. The code for `FindPath` appears in Program 12.21. This code requires that `Vertices()` be defined as a virtual member of `Network`.

The input parameters to `FindPath` are the start or source vertex (v) for the path and the destination vertex (w). If there is no path from v to w, `FindPath` returns `false`; otherwise, it returns `true`. When a path is found, the path length (i.e., the number of edges on the path) is returned in the parameter `length` and the actual path is returned as a sequence of vertices in the array positions `p[0:length]`. Observe that `p[0] = v` and `p[length] = w`.

`FindPath` first checks for the special case $v = w$. In this case a path of length 0 is returned. If $v \neq w$, `FindPath` invokes the graph iterator function `InitializePos`. Then `FindPath` creates and initializes an array `reach`. The depth-first search for the path is actually performed by the private `Network` member `findPath`, which returns `false` iff no path is found. Function `findPath` is a modified depth-first search. There are essentially two modifications that have been made to a standard depth-first search: (1) `findPath` discontinues the search for reachable vertices as soon as the destination vertex w is reached, and (2) `findPath` records the vertices on the path from the source v to the current vertex u in the array `path`.

`FindPath` and `DFS` have the same complexity.

```
bool Network::FindPath
     (int v, int w, int &length, int path[])
{// Find a path from v to w, return length and path in
 // path[0:length].  Return false if there is no path.
   // first vertex in path is always v
   path[0] = v;
   length = 0;  // current path length
   if (v == w) return true;
   // initialize for recursive path finder
   int  n = Vertices();
   InitializePos();  // iterator
   int *reach = new int [n+1];
   for (int i = 1; i <= n; i++)
      reach[i] = 0;

   // search for path
   bool x = findPath(v, w, length, path, reach);

   DeactivatePos();
   delete [] reach;
   return x;
}

bool Network::findPath(int v, int w, int &length,
                  int path[], int reach[])
{// Actual path finder v != w.
 // Performs a depth-first search for a path to w.
   reach[v] = 1;
   int u = Begin(v);
   while (u) {
      if (!reach[u]) {
         length++;
         path[length] = u; // add u to path
         if (u == w) return true;
         if (findPath(u, w, length, path, reach))
            return true;
         // no path from u to w
         length--; // remove u
         }
      u = NextVertex(v);}
   return false;
}
```

Program 12.21 Find a path in a graph

12.11.2 Connected Graphs and Components

We can determine if an undirected graph *G* is connected (see Example 12.2) by performing either a depth-first or breadth-first search from any vertex and then verifying that all vertices have been labeled as reached. Although this strategy only directly verifies that there is a path from the start vertex of the breadth-first search to every other graph vertex, this verification is sufficient to conclude that a path exists between every pair of vertices. To see the validity of this claim, suppose that *i* is the start vertex of the search and that the search reaches all vertices of the graph. We may construct a path between any two vertices *u* and *v* by using the path from *i* to *u* in the reverse direction and then the path from *i* to *v*. Function Connected (Program 12.22) returns false if the graph is not connected and true if it is. Since the notion of connectedness is defined only for undirected graphs and networks, we define a new class Undirected. The function Connected is a member of Undirected. Figure 12.18 shows the new set of derivations for our graph classes.

```
class Undirected : virtual public Network {
   public:
      bool Connected();
};

bool Undirected::Connected()
{// Return true iff graph is connected.

   int n = Vertices();

   // set all vertices as not reached
   int *reach = new int [n+1];
   for (int i = 1; i <= n; i++)
      reach[i] = 0;

   // mark vertices reachable from vertex 1
   DFS(1, reach, 1);

   // check if all vertices marked
   for (int i = 1; i <= n; i++)
      if (!reach[i]) return false;
   return true;
}
```

Program 12.22 Determine whether an undirected graph is connected

The set C of vertices that are reachable from a vertex i, together with the edges that connect pairs of vertices in C, is a **connected component**. The graph of Figure 12.1(b) has two connected components. One consists of the vertices $\{1, 2, 3\}$ and the edges $\{(1,2), (1,3)\}$, and the other consists of the remaining vertices and edges. In the **component-labeling problem**, we are to label the vertices in a graph so that two vertices are assigned the same label iff they belong to the same component. In the example of Figure 12.1(b), vertices 1 and 2 can be labeled 1, and the remaining vertices labeled 2.

We can label components by making repeated invocations of either depth-first or breadth-first search. We start each invocation at an as yet unlabeled vertex and perform a search, labeling newly reached vertices with a new label. Function LabelComponents (Program 12.23) solves the component-labeling problem. It returns the number of components in the graph. The component labels are returned in the array L. We may use DFS in place of BFS in Program 12.23 and obtain the same results. The complexity of Program 12.23 is $\Theta(n^2)$ when the graph is represented as an adjacency matrix and $\Theta(n+e)$ when we use the linked-adjacency-list representation.

```
int Undirected::LabelComponents(int L[])
{// Label the components of the graph.
 // Return the number of components and set L[1:n]
 // to represent a labeling of vertices by component.

   int n = Vertices();

   // assign all vertices to no component
   for (int i = 1; i <= n; i++)
      L[i] = 0;

   int label = 0;  // ID of last component
   // identify components
   for (int i = 1; i <= n; i++)
      if (!L[i]) {// unreached vertex
         // vertex i is in a new component
         label++;
         BFS(i, L, label);} // mark new component

   return label;
}
```

Program 12.23 Component labeling

12.11.3   Spanning Trees

If a breadth-first search is carried out starting from any vertex in a connected undirected graph or network with n vertices, then from Theorem 12.1 we know that all vertices will get labeled. Exactly n-1 of these vertices are reached in the inner `while` loop of `Network::BFS` (Program 12.17). When a new vertex u is reached in this loop, the edge used to reach u is (w,u). The set of edges used in the inner `while` loop to reach previously unreached vertices is of size n-1. Since this set of edges contains a path from v to every other vertex in the graph, it defines a connected subgraph, which is a spanning tree of G.

Consider the graph of Figure 12.22(a). If a breadth-first search is started at vertex 1, then the edges {(1,2), (1,3), (1,4), (2,5), (4,6), (4,7), (5,8)} are used to reach previously unreached vertices. This set of edges corresponds to the spanning tree of Figure 12.22(b).

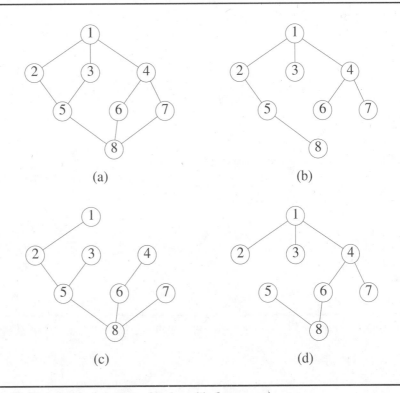

Figure 12.22 A graph and some of its breadth-first spanning trees

A **breadth-first spanning tree** is any spanning tree obtained in the manner just described from a breadth-first search. One may verify that the spanning trees of Figures 12.22 (b), (c), and (d) are all breadth-first spanning trees of the graph of Figure 12.22 (a). (Figures 12.22 (c) and (d) are, respectively, obtained by starting at vertices 8 and 6.)

When a depth-first search is performed in a connected undirected graph or network, exactly $n-1$ edges are used to reach new vertices. The subgraph formed by these edges is also a spanning tree. Spanning trees obtained in this manner from a depth-first search are called **depth-first spanning trees**. Figure 12.23 shows some of the depth-first spanning trees of Figure 12.22(a).

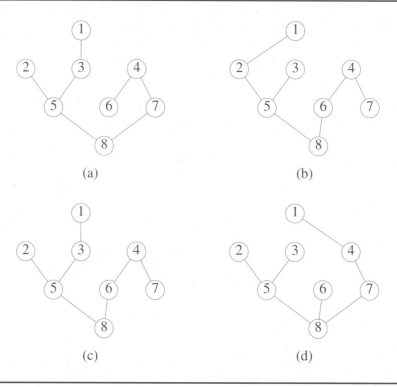

Figure 12.23 Some depth-first spanning trees of Figure 12.22(a)

EXERCISES

45. For the graph of Figure 12.1(a), do the following:

    (a) Obtain a breadth-first spanning tree starting at vertex 1.

    (b) Obtain a breadth-first spanning tree starting at vertex 3.

    (c) Obtain a depth-first spanning tree starting at vertex 1.

    (d) Obtain a depth-first spanning tree starting at vertex 3.

46. Write code for the public member `Undirected::BSpanning-Tree(i,BT)`, which finds a breadth-first spanning tree of a connected undirected graph or network by initiating a breadth-first search at vertex `i`. Your code should throw an exception if it fails because of memory problems; return `false` if it fails because there is no spanning tree (i.e., the graph is not connected); and return `true` if it succeeds. When a spanning tree is found, the edges are to be returned in the array `BT`. Define a suitable type for `BT`.

47. Do Exercise 46 for the case of `Undirected::DSpanning-Tree(i,DT)`, which finds a depth-first spanning tree `DT` beginning at vertex `i`.

48. Write code for the public member `Network::Cycle()`, which determines whether the network has a (directed) cycle. Base your code on either a depth-first or a breadth-first search.

    (a) Prove the correctness of your code.

    (b) Obtain the time and space complexities of your code.

49. Let G be an undirected graph or network. Write C++ code for the function `Undirected::Bipartite(L)`, which returns `false` if G is not a bipartite graph (see Example 12.3) and `true` if it is. In case G is bipartite, the function also returns, in `L`, a labeling of the vertices such that `L[i]` = 1 for vertices in one subset and `L[i]` = 2 for vertices in the other subset. The complexity of your code should be $\Theta(n^2)$ if G has n vertices and is represented as a matrix and $\Theta(n + e)$ if a linked list representation is used. Show that this is the case. (*Hint:* Perform several breadth-first searches, each time beginning at an as yet unreached vertex; assign this unreached vertex to set 1; vertices adjacent from this vertex are assigned to set 2; those adjacent to these set 2 vertices are assigned to set 1; and so on. Also check for conflicting assignments, i.e., the set assignment of a vertex is changed.)

50. Let G be an undirected graph or network. Its **transitive closure** is a 0/1 valued array `TC` such that `TC[i][j]` = 1 iff G has a path with one or more edges from vertex `i` to vertex `j`. Write a function `Undirected::TransitiveClosure(TC)` to compute the transitive

closure matrix of G. The complexity of your function should be $\Theta(n^2)$ time where n is the number of vertices in G. (*Hint:* Use component labeling.)

51. Do Exercise 50 for `Network::TransitiveClosure(TC)`, which is to be used when G is directed. What is the complexity of your algorithm?

CHAPTER 13

THE GREEDY METHOD

BIRD'S-EYE VIEW

Exit the world of data structures. Enter the world of algorithm-design methods.

In the remainder of this book, we study methods for the design of good algorithms. Although the design of a good algorithm for any given problem is more an art than a science, some design methods are effective in solving many problems. You can apply these methods to computer problems and see how the resulting algorithm works. Generally, you must fine-tune the resulting algorithm to achieve acceptable performance. In some cases, however, fine tuning is not possible, and you will have to think of some other way to solve the problem.

Chapters 13 through 17, present five basic algorithm-design methods: the greedy method, divide and conquer, dynamic programming, backtracking, and branch and bound. This list excludes several more advanced methods, such as linear programming, integer programming, neural networks, genetic algorithms, and simulated annealing, which are also widely used. These methods are typically covered in courses dedicated to them.

This chapter begins by introducing the notion of an optimization problem. Next the greedy method, which is a very intuitive method, is described. We use the greeedy method to obtain algorithms for the container-loading, knapsack, topological-ordering, bipartite-cover, shortest paths, and minimum-cost spanning-tree problems.

13.1 OPTIMIZATION PROBLEMS

Many of the examples used in this chapter and in the remaining chapters are **optimization problems**. In an optimization problem we are given a set of **constraints** and an **optimization function**. Solutions that satisfy the constraints are called **feasible solutions**. A feasible solution for which the optimization function has the best possible value is called an **optimal solution**.

Example 13.1 [*Thirsty Baby*] A very thirsty, and intelligent, baby wants to quench her thirst. She has access to a glass of water, a carton of milk, cans of various juices, and bottles and cans of various sodas. In all the baby has access to n different liquids. From past experience with these n liquids, the baby knows that some are more satisfying than others. In fact, the baby has assigned satisfaction values to each liquid. s_i units of satisfaction are obtained by drinking 1 ounce of the ith liquid.

Ordinarily, the baby would just drink enough of the liquid that gives her greatest satisfaction per ounce and thereby quench her thirst in the most satisfying way. Unfortunately, there isn't enough of this most satisfying liquid available. Let a_i be the amount in ounces of liquid i that is available. The baby needs to drink a total of t ounces to quench her thirst. How much of each available liquid should she drink?

We may assume that satisfaction is additive. Let x_i denote the amount of liquid i that the baby should drink. The solution to her problem is obtained by finding real numbers x_i, $1 \leq i \leq n$ that maximize $\sum_{i=1}^{n} s_i x_i$ subject to the constraints

$$\sum_{i=1}^{n} x_i = t \text{ and } 0 \leq x_i \leq a_i, 1 \leq i \leq n.$$

Note that if $\sum_{1}^{n} a_i < t$, then there is no solution to the baby's problem. Even if she drinks all the liquids available, she will be unable to quench her thirst.

This precise mathematical formulation of the problem provides an unambiguous specification of what the program is to do. Having obtained this formulation, we can provide the input/output specification, which takes the form:

Input n, t, s_i, a_i, $1 \leq i \leq n$. n is an integer, and the remaining numbers are positive reals.

Output Real numbers x_i, $1 \leq i \leq n$, such that $\sum_{i=1}^{n} s_i x_i$ is maximum, $\sum_{i=1}^{n} x_i = t$, and $0 \leq x_i \leq a_i$, $1 \leq i \leq n$. Output a suitable message if $\sum_{i=1}^{n} a_i < t$.

The constraints are $\sum_{i=1}^{n} x_i = t$ and $0 \le x_i \le a_i$, and the optimization function is $\sum_{i=1}^{n} s_i x_i$. Every set of x_is that satisfies the constraints is a feasible solution. Every feasible solution that maximizes $\sum_{i=1}^{n} s_i x_i$ is an optimal solution. ∎

Example 13.2 [*Loading Problem*] A large ship is to be loaded with cargo. The cargo is containerized, and all containers are the same size. Different containers may have different weights. Let w_i be the weight of the ith container, $1 \le i \le n$. The cargo capacity of the ship is c. We wish to load the ship with the maximum number of containers.

This problem can be formulated as an optimization problem in the following way: Let x_i be a variable whose value can be either 0 or 1. If we set x_i to 0, then container i is not to be loaded. If x_i is 1, then the container is to be loaded. We wish to assign values to the x_is that satisfy the constraints $\sum_{i=1}^{n} w_i x_i \le c$ and $x_i \in \{0,1\}$, $1 \le i \le n$. The optimization function is $\sum_{i=1}^{n} x_i$.

Every set of x_is that satisfies the constraints is a feasible solution. Every feasible solution that maximizes $\sum_{i=1}^{n} x_i$ is an optimal solution. ∎

Example 13.3 [*Minimum-Cost Communication Network*] We introduced this problem in Example 12.2. The set of cities and possible communication links can be represented as an undirected graph. Each edge has a cost (or weight) assigned to it. This cost is the cost of constructing the link represented by the edge. Every connected subgraph that includes all the vertices represents a feasible solution. Under the assumption that all weights are nonnegative, the set of feasible solutions can be narrowed to the set of spanning trees of the graph. An optimal solution is a spanning tree with minimum cost.

In this problem we need to select a subset of the edges. This subset must satisfy the following constraint: *The set of selected edges forms a spanning tree*. The optimization function is the sum of the weights of the selected edges. ∎

13.2   THE GREEDY METHOD

In the **greedy method** we attempt to construct an optimal solution in stages. At each stage we make a decision that appears to be the best (under some criterion) at the time. A decision made in one stage is not changed in a later stage, so each decision should assure feasibility. The criterion used to make the greedy decision at each stage is called the **greedy criterion**.

Example 13.4 [*Change Making*] A child buys candy valued at less than \$1 and gives a \$1 bill to the cashier. The cashier wishes to return change using the fewest number of coins. Assume that an unlimited supply of quarters, dimes, nickels, and pennies is available. The cashier constructs the change in stages. In each stage a coin is added to the change. This coin is selected using the greedy criterion: *At each stage increase the total amount of change constructed by as much as possible.* To assure feasiblity (i.e., the change given exactly equals the desired amount) of the solution, the selected coin should not cause the total amount of change given so far to exceed the final desired amount.

Suppose that 67 cents in change is due the child. The first two coins selected are quarters. A quarter cannot be selected for the third coin because such a selection results in an infeasible selection of coins (change exceeds 67 cents). The third coin selected is a dime, then a nickel is selected, and finally two pennies are added to the change.

The greedy algorithm has intuitive appeal in that we construct the change using a strategy that our intuition tells us should result in the fewest (or at least close to the fewest) number of coins being given out. We can actually prove that the greedy algorithm just described does indeed generate change with the fewest number of coins (see Exercise 1). ∎

Example 13.5 [*Machine Scheduling*] You are given n tasks and an infinite supply of machines on which these tasks can be performed. Each task has a start time s_i and a finish time f_i, $s_i < f_i$. $[s_i, f_i]$ is the processing interval for task i. Two tasks i and j overlap iff their processing intervals overlap at a point other than the interval start or end. For example, the interval [1, 4] overlaps with [2, 4], but not with [4, 7]. A **feasible** task-to-machine assignment is an assignment in which no machine is assigned two overlapping tasks. Therefore, in a feasible assignment each machine works on at most one task at any time. An **optimal assignment** is a feasible assignment that utilizes the fewest number of machines.

Suppose we have $n = 7$ tasks labeled a through g and that their start and finish times are as shown in Figure 13.1(a). The task-to-machine assignment: Assign task a to machine $M1$, task b to machine $M2$, $\cdots$, task g to machine $M7$ is a feasible assignment that utilizes seven machines. This assignment is not an optimal assignment because other assignments use fewer machines. For example, we can assign tasks a, b, and d to the same machine, reducing the number of utilized machines to five.

A greedy way to obtain an optimal task assignment is to assign the tasks in stages, one task per stage and in nondecreasing order of task start times. Call a machine **old** if at least one task has been assigned to it. If a machine is not old, it is **new**. For machine selection, use the greedy criterion: *If an old machine becomes available by the start time of the task to be assigned, assign the task to this machine; if not, assign it to a new machine.*

task	a	b	c	d	e	f	g
start	0	3	4	9	7	1	6
finish	2	7	7	11	10	5	8

(a) Seven tasks

(b) Schedule

Figure 13.1 Tasks and a three-machine schedule

For our sample data, the greedy algorithm has $n = 7$ stages. The tasks are assigned in the order: a, f, b, c, g, e, d. Stage 1 has no old machines, so a is assigned to a new machine (say $M1$). This machine is now busy from time 0 to time 2 (see Figure 13.1(b)). In stage 2, task f is considered. Since the only old machine is busy when task f is to start, it is assigned to a new machine (say $M2$). When task b is considered in stage 3, we find that the old machine $M1$ is free at time $s_b = 3$, so b is assigned to $M1$. The availability time for $M1$ becomes $f_b = 7$, while that for M_2 is $f_f = 5$. In stage 4, task c is considered. Since neither of the old machines is available at time $s_c = 4$, task c is assigned to a new machine (say $M3$). The availability time of this machine becomes $f_c = 7$. Task g is considered in stage 5 and assigned to machine $M2$, which is the first to become available. Task e is assigned in stage 6 to machine $M1$, and finally in stage 7, task d is assigned to machine $M3$. (Note: task d could also have been assigned to machine $M2$.)

The proof that the described greedy algorithm generates optimal assignments is left as an exercise (Exercise 7). The algorithm may be implemented to have complexity O($n\log n$) by sorting the tasks in nondecreasing order of s_i, using an O($n\log n$) sort (such as heap sort) and then using a min heap of availability times for the old machines. ∎

Example 13.6 [*Shortest Path*] You are given a directed network as in Figure 13.2. The length of a path is defined to be the sum of the costs of the edges on the path. You are to find a shortest path from a start vertex *s* to a destination vertex *d*.

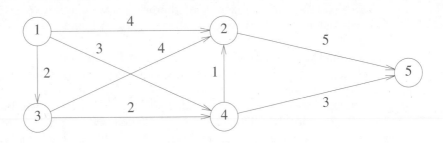

Figure 13.2 Sample digraph

A greedy way to construct such a path is to do so in stages. In each stage, a vertex is added to the path. Suppose that the path built so far ends at vertex *q* and *q* is not the destination vertex *d*. The vertex to add in the next stage is obtained using the greedy criterion: *Select a nearest vertex adjacent from q that is not already on the path.*

This greedy method does not necessarily obtain a shortest path. For example, suppose we wish to construct a shortest path from vertex 1 to vertex 5 in Figure 13.2. Using the greedy method just outlined, we begin at vertex 1 and move to the nearest vertex not already on the path. We move to vertex 3, a distance of only two units. From vertex 3 the nearest vertex we can move to is vertex 4. From vertex 4, we move to vertex 2 and then to the destination vertex 5. The constructed path is 1, 3, 4, 2, 5, and its length is 10. This path is not the shortest 1-to-5 path in the digraph. In fact, several shorter paths exist. For instance, the path 1, 4, 5 has length 6. ■

Now that you have seen three examples of a greedy algorithm, you should be able to go over the applications considered in earlier chapters and identify several of the solutions developed as greedy ones. For example, the Huffman tree algorithm of Section 9.5.3 constructs a binary tree with minimum weighted external path length in $n - 1$ stages. In each stage two binary trees are combined to create a new binary tree. This algorithm uses the greedy criterion: Of the available binary trees, combine two with the least weight.

The LPT-scheduling rule of Section 9.5.2 is a greedy one. It schedules the *n* jobs in *n* stages. First the jobs are ordered by length. Then in each stage a machine is selected for the next job. The machine is selected using the greedy criterion: *Minimize the length of the schedule constructed so far.* This criterion translates into scheduling the job on the machine on which it finishes first. This machine is also the machine that becomes idle first.

Notice that in the case of the machine-scheduling problem of Section 9.5.2, the greedy algorithm does not guarantee optimal solutions. However, it is intuitively appealing and generally produces solutions that are very close in value to the optimal. It uses a rule of thumb that we might expect a human machine scheduler to use in a real scheduling environment. Algorithms that do not guarantee optimal solutions but generally produce solutions that are close to optimal are called **heuristics**. So the LPT method is a heuristic for machine scheduling. Theorem 9.2 states a bound between the finish time of LPT schedules and optimal schedules, so the LPT heuristic has **bounded performance**. A heuristic with bounded performance is an **approximation algorithm**.

Section 10.5.1 stated several bounded performance heuristics (i.e., approximation algorithms) for the bin-packing problem. Each of these heuristics is a greedy heuristic. The LPT method of Section 9.5.2 is also a greedy heuristic. All these heuristics have intuitive appeal and, in practice, yield solutions much closer to optimal than suggested by the bounds given in that section.

The rest of this chapter presents several applications of the greedy method. In some applications the result is an algorithm that always obtains an optimal solution. In others the algorithm is just a heuristic that may or may not be an approximation algorithm.

EXERCISES

1. Show that the greedy algorithm for the change-making problem (Example 13.4) always generates change with the fewest number of coins.

2. Consider the change-making problem of Example 13.4. Suppose that the cashier has only a limited number of quarters, dimes, nickels, and pennies. Formulate a greedy solution to the change-making problem. Does your algorithm always use the fewest number of coins? Prove your result.

3. Extend the algorithm of Example 13.4 to the case when the cashier has $100, $50, $20, $10, $5, and $1 bills in addition to coins and a customer gives u and v cents as payment towards a purchase of x and y cents. Does your algorithm always generate change with the fewest total number of bills and coins? Prove this.

4. Write a C++ program implementing the change-making solution of Example 13.4. Assume that the cashier has bills in the denominations $100, $50, $20, $10, $5, and $1 in addition to coins. Your program should include modules for input (i.e., input amount of purchase and amount given by the customer), output (output the amount of change and a breakdown by denomination), and computation (compute how the change is to be given).

5.   Suppose that some country has coins in the denominations 14, 12, 5, and 1 cents. Will the greedy method of Example 13.4 always generate change with the fewest number of coins? Prove your answer.

6.   (a)   Show that the greedy algorithm of Example 13.5 always finds an optimal task assignment.

   (b)   Program your algorithm so that its complexity is $O(n \log n)$, n is the number of tasks.

★ 7.   Consider the machine-scheduling problem of Example 13.5. Assume that only one machine is available and that we are to select the largest number of tasks that can be scheduled on this machine. For the example, the largest task selection is $\{a, b, e\}$. A greedy algorithm for this task-selection problem would select the tasks in stages. In each stage one task is selected using the following criterion: *From the remaining tasks, select the one that has the least finish time and does not overlap with any of the already selected tasks.*

   (a)   Show that this greedy algorithm obtains optimal selections.

   (b)   Obtain an $O(n \log n)$ implementation of this algorithm. (*Hint:* Use a min heap of finish times.)

13.3   APPLICATIONS

13.3.1   Container Loading

The terminology is from Example 13.2. The ship may be loaded in stages; one container per stage. At each stage we need to decide which container to load. For this decision we may use the greedy criterion: *From the remaining containers, select the one with least weight.* This order of selection will keep the total weight of the selected containers minimum and hence leave maximum capacity for loading more containers. Using the greedy strategy just outlined, we first select the container that has least weight, then the one with the next smallest weight, and so on until either all containers have been loaded or there isn't enough capacity for the next one.

Example 13.7 Suppose that $n = 8$, $[w_1, \cdots, w_8] = [100, 200, 50, 90, 150, 50, 20, 80]$, and $c = 400$. When the greedy algorithm is used, the containers are considered for loading in the order 7, 3, 6, 8, 4, 1, 5, 2. Containers 7, 3, 6, 8, 4, and 1 together weigh 390 units and are loaded. The available capacity is now 10 units, which is inadequate for any of the remaining containers. In the greedy solution we have $[x_1, \cdots, x_8] = [1, 0, 1, 1, 0, 1, 1, 1]$ and $\sum x_i = 6$. ■

Theorem 13.1 The greedy algorithm generates optimal loadings.

Proof We can establish the optimality of the greedy solution in the following way: Let $x = [x_1, \cdots, x_n]$ be the solution produced by the greedy algorithm. Let $y = [y_1, \cdots, y_n]$ be any feasible solution. We shall show that $\sum_{i=1}^{n} x_i \geq \sum_{i=1}^{n} y_i$. Without loss of generality we may assume that the containers have been ordered so that $w_i \leq w_{i+1}$, $1 \leq i \leq n$. We shall transform y, in several steps, into x. Each step of the transformation will produce a new y that is feasible and for which $\sum_{i=1}^{n} y_i$ is no smaller than before the transformation. As a result, $\sum_{i=1}^{n} x_i \geq \sum_{i=1}^{n} y_i$ initially.

From the way the greedy algorithm works, we know that there is a k in the range $[0, n]$ such that $x_i = 1$, $i \leq k$, and $x_i = 0$, $i > k$. Find the least integer j in the range $[1, n]$ such that $x_j \neq y_j$. If no such j exists, then $\sum_{i=1}^{n} x_i = \sum_{i=1}^{n} y_i$. If such a j exists, then $j \leq k$, as otherwise y is not a feasible solution. Since $x_j \neq y_j$ and $x_j = 1$, $y_j = 0$. Set y_j to 1. If the resulting y denotes an infeasible solution, there must be an l in the range $[j+1, n]$ for which $y_l = 1$. Set y_l to 0. As $w_j \leq w_l$, the resulting y is feasible. Also, the new y has at least as many ones as the old y.

By using this transformation several times, we can transform y into x. As each transformation produces a new y that has at least as many ones as the previous y, x has at least as many ones as the original y had. ∎

The C++ code for the greedy container-loading algorithm appears in Program 13.1. Since the greedy method loads containers in increasing order of their weight, Program 13.1 begins by sorting the container weights using an indirect-addressing sort function `IndirectSort` (see Section 3.5 for a definition of indirect addressing). Following the sort, containers are loaded in increasing order of weight. Since the indirect-addressing sort can be carried out in O(nlogn) time (using the heap sort method of Section 9.5.1 or the merge sort method to be developed in Chapter 14) and the remainder of the algorithm takes O(n) time, the overall time complexity of Program 13.1 is O(nlogn).

13.3.2 0/1 Knapsack Problem

In the 0/1 knapsack problem, we wish to pack a knapsack (bag or sack) with a capacity of c. From a list of n items, we must select the items that are to be packed into the knapsack. Each object i has a weight w_i and a profit p_i. In a feasible knapsack packing, the sum of the weights of the packed objects does not exceed the knapsack capacity. An optimal packing is a feasible one with max-

```
template<class T>
void ContainerLoading(int x[],  T w[], T c, int n)
{// Greedy algorithm for container loading.
 // Set x[i] = 1 iff container i, 1<=i<=n is loaded.
 // c is ship capacity, w gives container weights.

    // do indirect addressing sort of weights
    // t is the indirect addressing table
    int *t = new int [n+1];
    IndirectSort(w, t, n);
    // now, w[t[i]] <= w[t[i+1]], 1<=i<n

    // initialize x
    for (int i = 1; i <= n; i++)
       x[i] = 0;

    // select objects in order of weight
    for (int i = 1; i <= n && w[t[i]] <= c; i++) {
       x[t[i]] = 1;
       c -= w[t[i]];}   // remaining capacity

    delete [] t;
}
```

Program 13.1 Loading containers

imum profit. The problem formulation is

$$\text{maximize } \sum_{i=1}^{n} p_i x_i$$

subject to the constraints

$$\sum_{i=1}^{n} w_i x_i \leq c \text{ and } x_i \in \{0,1\}, 1 \leq i \leq n$$

In this formulation we are to find the values of x_i. $x_i = 1$ means that object i is packed into the knapsack, while $x_i = 0$ means that object i is not packed. The 0/1 knapsack problem is really a generalization of the container-loading problem to the case where the profit earned from each container is different. In the context of the knapsack problem, the ship is the *knapsack* and the containers are *objects* that may be packed into the knapsack.

Example 13.8 You are the first-prize winner in a grocery-store contest, and the prize is a free cart load of groceries. There are n different items available in the store, and the contest rules stipulate that you can pick at most one of each. The cart has a capacity of c, and item i takes up w_i amount of cart space. The cost of item i is p_i. Your objective is to fill the cart with groceries that have the maximum value. Of course, you cannot exceed the cart capacity, and you cannot take two of any item. The problem may be modeled using the 0/1 knapsack formulation. The cart corresponds to the knapsack, and the available grocery items correspond to the objects. ∎

Several greedy strategies for the 0/1 knapsack problem are possible. In each of these strategies, the knapsack is packed in several stages. In each stage one object is selected for inclusion into the knapsack using a greedy criterion. One possibility for this greedy criterion is: *From the remaining objects, select the object with maximum profit that fits into the knapsack*. Using this criterion, the object with the largest profit is packed first (provided enough capacity is available), then the one with next largest profit, and so on. This strategy does not guarantee an optimal solution. For instance, consider the case $n = 3$, $w = [100, 10, 10]$, $p = [20, 15, 15]$, and $c = 105$. When we are greedy on profit, we obtain the solution $x = [1, 0, 0]$. The total profit from this solution is 20. The optimal solution is $[0, 1, 1]$. This solution has profit 30.

An alternative is to be greedy on weight. This time the selection criterion is: *From the remaining objects, select the one that has minimum weight and also fits into the knapsack*. Although the use of this criterion yields an optimal solution for the preceding instance, it does not do so in general. Consider the instance $n = 2$, $w = [10, 20]$, $p = [5, 100]$, and $c = 25$. When we are greedy on weight, we obtain the solution $x = [1, 0]$, which is inferior to the solution $[0, 1]$.

Yet another possibility is to be greedy on the profit density p_i/w_i. The selection criterion now is, *From the remaining objects, select the one with maximum p_i/w_i that fits into the knapsack*. This strategy does not guarantee optimal solutions either. For example, try this strategy on the instance $n = 3$, $w = [20, 15, 15]$, $p = [40, 25, 25]$, and $c = 30$.

We should not be too disheartened that none of the considered greedy algorithms can guarantee optimal solutions. The 0/1 knapsack problem is an NP-hard problem (see Section 9.5.2 for a discussion of NP-hard problems), and we probably cannot find a polynomial-time algorithm that solves it. Although packing a knapsack in nondecreasing order of the ratio p_i/w_i does not guarantee an optimal packing, it is an intuitively appealing approach. We expect it to be a good heuristic and produce solutions that are very close to optimal most of the time. In an experiment that involved 600 randomly generated knapsack instances, this greedy heuristic generated optimal solutions for 239. For 583 instances the generated solution had a value within 10 percent of optimal, and all 600 solutions were within 25 percent of optimal. Quite an impressive performance by an algorithm that runs in $O(n \log n)$ time.

We may ask whether the greedy heuristic guarantees solutions that have a value that is within x percent of the optimal value for some x, $x < 100$. The answer is no. To see this, consider the instance $n = 2$, $w = [1, y]$, $p = [10, 9y]$, and $c = y$. The greedy solution is $x = [1,0]$. This solution has value 10. For $y \geq 10/9$, the optimal solution has value $9y$. Therefore, the value of the greedy solution is $(9y - 10)/(9y) * 100$ percent away from the optimal value. For large y, this value approaches 100%.

We can modify the greedy heuristic to provide solutions within x percent of optimal for $x < 100$. First we place a subset of at most k objects into the knapsack. If this subset has weight greater than c, we discard it. Otherwise, the remaining capacity is filled by considering the remaining objects in decreasing order of p_i/w_i. The best solution obtained considering all possible subsets with at most k objects is the solution generated by the heuristic.

Example 13.9 Consider the knapsack instance $n = 4$, $w = [2, 4, 6, 7]$, $p = [6, 10, 12, 13]$, and $c = 11$. When $k = 0$, the knapsack is filled in nonincreasing order of profit density. First we place object 1 into the knapsack, then object 2. The capacity that remains at this time is 5 units. None of the remaining objects fits, and the solution $x = [1, 1, 0, 0]$ is produced. The profit earned from this solution is 16.

Let us now try the greedy heuristic with $k = 1$. The subsets to begin with are $\{1\}$, $\{2\}$, $\{3\}$, and $\{4\}$. The subsets $\{1\}$ and $\{2\}$ yield the same solution as obtained with $k = 0$. When the subset $\{3\}$ is considered, x_3 is set to 1. Five units of capacity remain, and we attempt to use this capacity by considering the remaining objects in nonincreasing order of profit density. Object 1 is considered first. It fits, and x_1 is set to 1. At this time only 3 units of capacity remain, and none of the remaining objects can be added to the knapsack. The solution obtained when we begin with the subset $\{3\}$ in the knapsack is $x = [1, 0, 1, 0]$. The profit earned from this solution is 18. When we begin with the subset $\{4\}$, we produce the solution $x = [1, 0, 0, 1]$ that has a profit value of 19. The best solution obtained considering subsets of size 0 and 1 is $[1, 0, 0, 1]$. This solution is produced by the greedy heuristic when $k = 1$.

If $k = 2$, then in addition to the subsets considered for $k < 2$, we need to consider the subsets $\{1, 2\}$, $\{1, 3\}$, $\{1, 4\}$, $\{2, 3\}$, $\{2, 4\}$, and $\{3, 4\}$. The last of these subsets represents an infeasible starting point and is discarded. For the remaining, the solutions obtained are $[1, 1, 0, 0]$, $[1, 0, 1, 0]$, $[1, 0, 0, 1]$, $[0, 1, 1, 0]$, and $[0, 1, 0, 1]$. The last of these solutions has the profit value 23, which is higher than that obtained from the subsets of size 0 and 1. This solution is therefore the solution produced by the heuristic. ∎

The solution produced by the modified greedy heuristic is k–*optimal*. That is, if we remove up to k objects from the solution and put back up to k, the new solution is no better than the original. Further, the value of a solution obtained in this manner comes within $100/(k+1)$ percent of optimal. When $k = 1$, the solutions are guaranteed to have value within 50 percent of optimal; when $k = 2$, they are guaranteed to have value within 33.33 percent of optimal; and so on. The run time of the heuristic increases with k. The number of subsets to be tried is $O(n^k)$, and $O(n)$ time is spent on each. So the total time taken is $O(n^{k+1})$ when $k > 0$.

The observed performance is far better than suggested by the worst-case bounds. Figure 13.3 summarizes the results of 600 random tests.

		Percent Deviation			
k	0	1%	5%	10%	25%
0	239	390	528	583	600
1	360	527	598	600	
2	483	581	600		

Figure 13.3 Number of solutions within x percent out of 600

13.3.3   Topological Sorting

Often a complex project may be decomposed into a collection of simpler tasks with the property that the completion of all these tasks implies that the project has been completed. For example, the automobile-assembly project may be decomposed into these tasks: place chassis on assembly line, mount axles, mount wheels onto axles, fit seats onto chassis, paint, install brakes, install doors, and so on. A precedence relation exists between certain pairs of tasks. For example, the chassis must be placed on the assembly line before we can mount the axles. The set of tasks together with the precedences may be represented as a digraph— called an **activity on vertex** (AOV) network. The vertices of this digraph represent the tasks, and the directed edge (i,j) denotes the following precedence: task i must complete before task j can start. A six task project appears in Figure 13.4. The edge (1,4) implies that task 1 is to be done before task 4. Similarly, the edge (4,6) implies that task 4 is to be done before task 6. The edges (1,4) and (4,6) together imply that task 1 is to be done before task 6. So the precedence relation is transitive. As a result of this observation, we see that the edge (1,4) is redundant, as the edges (1,3) and (3,4) imply this.

In many situations we must perform the tasks consecutively, for example, the automobile-assembly problem or the many times we buy a consumer product (bicycle, child's swing set, lawn mower, etc.) labeled ''some assembly required.'' We perform the assembly tasks in a sequence dictated by the accompanying instructions. This sequence has the property that for every edge (i,j) in

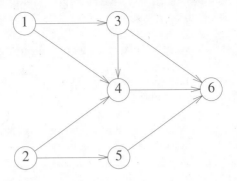

Figure 13.4 A task digraph

the task digraph for the assembly project, task *i* comes before task *j* in the assembly sequence. Sequences that satisfy this property are **topological orders** or **topological sequences**, and the process of constructing a topological order from a task digraph is **topological sorting**.

The task digraph of Figure 13.4 has several topological orders. Three of these orders are 123456, 132456, and 215346. The sequence 142356 is not a topological order, as (for example) task 4 precedes task 3 in this sequence, whereas the task digraph contains the edge (3,4). This sequence violates the precedence dictated by this edge (and others).

We may formulate a greedy algorithm to construct a topological order or sequence. This algorithm constructs the sequence from left to right in stages. In each stage we add a vertex to the sequence. We select the new vertex using the greedy criterion: *From the remaining vertices, select a vertex w that has no incoming edge (v,w) with the property that v hasn't already been placed into the sequence*. Notice that if we add a vertex *w* that violates this criterion (i.e., the digraph has an edge (*v,w*) and vertex *v* is not part of the constructed sequence), then we cannot complete the sequence in a topological order, as vertex *v* will neccessarily come after vertex *w*. A high-level statement of the greedy algorithm appears in Figure 13.5. Each iteration of the `while` loop represents a stage of the greedy algorithm.

Let us try out this algorithm on the digraph of Figure 13.4. We start with an empty sequence V. In the first stage we select the first vertex for V. The digraph has two candidate vertices, 1 and 2, for the first position in the sequence. If we select vertex 2, the sequence becomes V = 2 and stage 1 is complete. In stage 2 we select the second vertex for V. Applying the greedy criterion with V = 2, we see that the candidate vertices are 1 and 5. If we select vertex 5, then V = 25. For the next stage vertex 1 is the only candidate for w. Following stage 3

Let n be the number of vertices in the digraph.
Let V be an empty sequence.
```
while (true) {
```
   Let w be any vertex that has no incoming edge (v,w) such that v is not in V.
   If there is no such w, `break`.
   Add w to the end of V.
   }
`if` (V has fewer than n vertices) the algorithm fails.
`else` V is a topological sequence.

Figure 13.5 Topological sorting

$V = 251$. In stage 4 vertex 3 is the only candidate for w. Thus we add vertex 3 to V to get $V = 2513$. In the next two stages, we add vertices 4 and 6 to get V $= 251346$.

Correctness of the Greedy Algorithm

To establish the correctness of the greedy algorithm, we need to show (1) when the algorithm fails, the digraph has no topological sequence, and (2) when the algorithm doesn't fail, V is, in fact, a topological sequence. (2) is a direct consequence of the greedy criterion used to select the next vertex. For (1) we show in Lemma 13.1 that when the algorithm fails, the digraph has a cycle. When the digraph has a cycle, $q_j q_{j+1} \cdots q_k q_j$, there can be no topological order, as the sequence of precedences defined by the cycle implies that q_j must finish before q_j can start.

Lemma 13.1 If the algorithm of Figure 13.5 fails, the digraph has a cycle.

Proof Note that upon failure $|V| < n$ and there are no candidates for inclusion in V. So there is at least one vertex, q_1, that is not in V. The digraph must contain an edge (q_2, q_1) where q_2 is not in V; otherwise, q_1 is a candidate for inclusion in V. Similarly, there must be an edge (q_3, q_2) such that q_3 is not in V. If $q_3 = q_1$, then $q_1 q_2 q_3$ is a cycle in the digraph. If $q_3 \neq q_1$, there must be a q_4 such that (q_4, q_3) is an edge and q_4 is not in V; otherwise, q_3 is a candidate for inclusion in V. If q_4 is one of q_1, q_2, or q_3, then again the digraph has a cycle. Since the digraph has a finite number n of vertices, continued application of this argument will eventually detect a cycle. ∎

Selection of Data Structures

To refine the algorithm of Figure 13.5 into C++ code, we must decide on a representation for the sequence V, as well as how to detect candidates for inclusion into V. An efficient implementation results if we represent V as a one-dimensional array v; use a stack to keep track of all vertices that are candidates for inclusion into V; and use a one-dimensional array InDegree such that InDegree[j] is the number of vertices j for which (i,j) is an edge of the digraph and i is not a member of V. A vertex j becomes a candidate for inclusion in V when InDegree[j] becomes zero. V is initially the empty sequence, and InDegree[j] is simply the in-degree of vertex j. Each time we add a vertex to V, InDegree[j] decreases by one for all j that are adjacent from the added vertex.

For the digraph of Figure 13.4, InDegree[1:6] = [0, 0, 1, 3, 1, 3] in the beginning. Vertices 1 and 2 are candidates for inclusion in V, as their InDegree value is zero. Therefore, we start with 1 and 2 on the stack. In each stage we remove a vertex from the stack and add that vertex to V. We also reduce the InDegree values of the vertices that are adjacent from the vertex just added to V. If vertex 2 is removed from the stack and added to V in stage 1, we get v[0] = 2 and InDegree[1:6] = [0, 0, 1, 2, 0, 3]. Since InDegree[5] has just become zero, it is added to the stack.

Program 13.2 gives the resulting C++ code. This code is defined as a member function of Network. Consequently, it can be used for both digraphs with and without edge weights. It can also be invoked for undirected graphs (with and without edge weights) in which case incorrect results are obtained as a topological order is defined only for digraphs. To overcome this problem, we can define member functions of AdjacencyGraph, AdjacencyWGraph, LinkedGraph, and LinkedWGraph with the same template. These functions will override the definition in Network and can output an error message. The function Topological returns true if a topological order is found and false if the input digraph does not have a topological order. When a topological order is found, it is returned in v[0:n-1].

Complexity of Network::Topological

The first and third for loops take $\Theta(n)$ time. The total time spent in the second for loop is $\Theta(n^2)$ if we use an (cost) adjacency-matrix representation and $\Theta(n+e)$ if we use a linked-adjacency-list representation. Of the two nested while loops, the outer one may be iterated at most n times. Each iteration adds a vertex w to v and initiates the inner while loop. When adjacency matrices are used, this inner while loop takes $\Theta(n)$ time for each vertex w. When we use linked-adjacency lists, this loop takes d_w^{out} time. Therefore, the time spent on the inner while loop is either $\Theta(n^2)$ or $\Theta(n+e)$. Hence the complexity of Program 13.2 is $\Theta(n^2)$ when we use adjacency matrices and $\Theta(n+e)$ when we use linked-adjacency lists.

```
bool Network::Topological(int v[])
{// Compute topological ordering of digraph vertices.
 // Return true if a topological order is found.
 // In this case return the order in v[0:n-1].
 // Return false if there is no topological order.
   int n = Vertices();

   // Compute in-degrees
   int *InDegree = new int [n+1];
   InitializePos(); // graph iterator array
   for (int i = 1; i <= n; i++) // initialize
      InDegree[i] = 0;
   for (int i = 1; i <= n; i++) {// edges out of i
      int u = Begin(i);
      while (u) {
         InDegree[u]++;
         u = NextVertex(i);}
      }

   // Stack vertices with zero in-degree
   LinkedStack<int> S;
   for (int i = 1; i <= n; i++)
      if (!InDegree[i]) S.Add(i);

   // Generate topological order
   int i = 0;   // cursor for array v
   while (!S.IsEmpty()) {// select from stack
      int w;                  // next vertex
      S.Delete(w);
      v[i++] = w;
      int u = Begin(w);
      while (u) {// update in-degrees
         InDegree[u]--;
         if (!InDegree[u]) S.Add(u);
         u = NextVertex(w);}
      }

   DeactivatePos();
   delete [] InDegree;
   return (i == n);
}
```

Program 13.2 Topological sorting

13.3.4 Bipartite Cover

A bipartite graph (see Example 12.3) is an undirected graph in which the n vertices may be partitioned into two sets A and B so that no edge in the graph connects two vertices that are in the same set (i.e., every edge in the graph has one endpoint in A and the other in B). A subset A' of the set A is said to **cover** the set B (or simply, A' is a cover) iff every vertex in B is connected to at least one vertex of A'. The size of the cover A' is the number of vertices in A'. A' is a minimum cover iff A has no subset of smaller size that covers B.

Example 13.10 Consider the 17-vertex bipartite graph of Figure 13.6. $A = \{1, 2, 3, 16, 17\}$ and $B = \{4, 5, 6, 7, 8, 9, 10, 11, 12, 13, 14, 15\}$. The subset $A' = \{1, 2, 3, 17\}$ covers the set B. Its size is four. The subset $A' = \{1, 16, 17\}$ also covers B and is of size three. A has no subset of size less than three that covers B. Therefore, $A' = \{1, 16, 17\}$ is a minimum cover of B. ∎

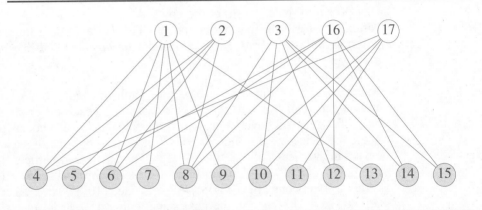

Figure 13.6 Figure for Example 13.10

We shall refer to the problem of finding a minimum cover in a bipartite graph as the **bipartite-cover** problem. In the context of Example 12.3, a minimum cover is useful because it identifies the fewest number of interpreters who can handle the translations at the convention. The bipartite-cover problem is identical to the **set-cover** problem. In this latter problem we are given a collection $S = \{S_1, S_2, \cdots, S_k\}$ of k sets. The members of each set S_i are from the universe U. A subset S' of S covers U iff $\bigcup_{i \in S'} S_i = U$. The number of sets in S' is the size of the cover and S' is a minimum cover iff there is no cover of U of smaller size. We can transform the set-cover problem into the bipartite-cover problem (and vice versa) by using the vertices in A to represent the sets $S_1, \cdots,$ S_k and the vertices in B to represent the elements of the universe U. An edge exists between a vertex in A and one in B iff the corresponding element of U is in the corresponding set of S.

Example 13.11 Let $S = \{S_1, \cdots, S_5\}$, $U = \{4, 5, \cdots, 15\}$, $S_1 = \{4, 6, 7, 8, 9, 13\}$, $S_2 = \{4, 5, 6, 8\}$, $S_3 = \{8, 10, 12, 14, 15\}$, $S_4 = \{5, 6, 8, 12, 14, 15\}$, and $S_5 = \{4, 9, 10, 11\}$. $S' = \{S_1, S_4, S_5\}$ is a cover of size three. No smaller cover exists, so it is a minimum cover. The set-cover instance may be mapped into the bipartite graph of Figure 13.6 using vertices 1, 2, 3, 16, and 17 to represent sets $S_1, S_2, S_3, S_4,$ and S_5, respectively. Vertex j represents universe element j, $4 \le j \le 15$. ■

The set-cover problem is known to be NP-hard. Since the set-cover and bipartite-cover problems are identical, the bipartite-cover problem is also NP-hard. As a result we probably will not be able to develop a fast algorithm to solve it. We can, however, use the greedy method to develop a fast heuristic. One possiblity is to construct the cover A' in stages. In each stage we select a vertex of A for inclusion into the cover. This vertex is selected using the greedy criterion: *Select a vertex of A that covers the largest number of uncovered vertices of B.*

Example 13.12 Consider the bipartite graph of Figure 13.6. Initially $A' = \emptyset$, and no vertex of B is covered. Vertices 1 and 16 each cover six uncovered vertices of B; vertex 3 covers five; and vertices 2 and 17 each cover four. Therefore, in the first stage, we add either vertex 1 or vertex 16 to A'. If we add vertex 16, it covers the vertices $\{5, 6, 8, 12, 14, 15\}$. The uncovered vertices are $\{4, 7, 9, 10, 11, 13\}$. Vertex 1 of A covers four of these uncovered vertices ($\{4, 7, 9, 13\}$), vertex 2 covers one ($\{4\}$), vertex 3 covers one ($\{10\}$), vertex 16 covers zero, and vertex 17 covers four. In the next stage, either 1 or 17 is selected for inclusion into A'. If we choose vertex 1, vertices $\{10, 11\}$ remain uncovered. Vertices 1, 2, and 16 cover none of these uncovered vertices, vertex 3 covers one, and vertex 17 covers two; therefore, we select vertex 17. Now no uncovered vertices remain, and we are done. $A' = \{1, 16, 17\}$. ■

A high-level statement of the greedy covering heuristic appears in Figure 13.7. You should be able to show (1) that the algorithm fails to find a cover iff the initial bipartite graph does not have a cover, and (2) that bipartite graphs exist on which the heuristic will fail to find a minimum cover.

$A´ = \emptyset$
while (more vertices can be covered)
    Add the vertex that covers the largest number of uncovered vertices
    to $A´$.
if (some vertices are uncovered) fail.
else a cover has been found.

Figure 13.7 High-level statement of greedy covering heuristic

Selection of Data Structures and Complexity

To implement the algorithm of Figure 13.7, we need to select a representation for $A´$ and to decide how to keep track of the number of uncovered vertices of B that each vertex of A covers. Since only additions are made to the set $A´$, we can represent $A´$ as a one-dimensional integer array C and use m to keep track of the number of elements in $A´$. We store the members of $A´$ in C[0:m-1].

For a vertex i of A, let New_i be the number of uncovered vertices of B that i covers. In each stage we need to select the vertex with maximum New_i and then update the New_is, as some previously uncovered vertices are now covered. For this update we examine the vertices of B that are newly covered by v. Let j be one such vertex. The New_i value of all vertices of A that cover j is to be reduced by one.

Example 13.13 Consider the graph of Figure 13.6. Initially $(New_1, New_2, New_3, New_{16}, New_{17}) = (6, 4, 5, 6, 4)$. Suppose we select vertex 16 in stage 1, as in Example 13.12. To update the New_is we examine all the newly covered vertices of B. These vertices are 5, 6, 8, 12, 14, and 15. When we examine vertex 5, we reduce the New_i values of vertices 2 and 16 by one because vertex 5 is no longer an uncovered vertex being covered by either 2 or 16. When we examine vertex 6, the counts for vertices 1, 2, and 16 are reduced by one. Similarly, when we examine vertex 8, the counts of 1, 2, 3, and 16 are reduced by one. After we examine all the newly covered vertices, the New_i values are (4, 1, 1, 0, 4). In the next stage we select vertex 1. The newly covered vertices are 4, 7, 9, and 13. When we examine vertex 4, New_1, New_2, and New_{17} are reduced by one; and when we examine vertex 7, only New_1 is reduced by one because vertex 1 is the only vertex that covers 7. ∎

To implement the vertex-selection process, we need to know the New_i values and also which vertices have already been covered. We can use two one-dimensional arrays for this purpose. New is an integer array such that New[i] equals New_i, and Cov is a Boolean array such that Cov[i] equals false if vertex i is not covered and true if it is. We can now refine the high-level statement of Figure 13.7 to obtain the version in Figure 13.8.

```
m = 0;  // current size of cover
New[i] = Degree[i] for all i in A.
Cov[i] = false for all i in B.
while (New[i] > 0 for some i in A) {
   Let v be a vertex with largest New[i].
   C[m++] = v;
   for (all vertices j adjacent from v) {
      if (!Cov[j]) {
         Cov[j] = true;
         Reduce New[k] by one for all vertices adjacent from j.
   }}}
if (some vertices are uncovered) fail.
else a cover has been found.
```

Figure 13.8 Refined version of Figure 13.7

The time spent updating New is $O(e)$ where e is the number of edges in the bipartite graph. It takes $\Theta(n^2)$ time to find the edges of a graph represented by an adjacency matrix and $\Theta(n + e)$ time when we use a linked-adjacency list. The actual update time is either $O(n^2)$ or $O(n + e)$ depending on the graph representation.

The selection of vertex v at the start of each stage takes $\Theta(SizeOfA)$ time where $SizeOfA = |A|$. Since all vertices of A may need to be selected, the number of stages is $O(SizeOfA)$ and the overall complexity of the cover algorithm is either $O(SizeOfA^2 + n^2) = O(n^2)$ or $O(SizeOfA^2 + n + e)$.

Reducing the Complexity

We can reduce the complexity of selecting vertex v at the start of each stage to $\Theta(1)$ time by using a sorted array of New_i values, a max heap, or a max selection tree. With the sorted-array approach, the New_i values need to be sorted at the end of each stage. This sort takes $\Theta(SizeOfB)$ time ($SizeOfB = |B|$) when we use the bin sort (see bin sort in Section 3.8.1) method. As $SizeOfB$ is generally much larger than $SizeOfA$, the sorted-array approach does not yield an overall improvement.

If we use a max heap, then following each stage we need to restructure the heap to account for the change in New values. We can do this restructuring each time a New value is reduced by one. Such a reduction can cause the reduced New value to move at most one level down the heap; therefore, this restructuring costs $\Theta(1)$ per New reduction of one. The total number of reductions is $O(e)$. Hence over all stages of the algorithm only $O(e)$ time is spent maintaining the max heap. Therefore, when we use a max heap, the overall complexity of the cover algorithm is either $O(n^2)$ or $O(n + e)$.

When we use a max selection tree, restructuring the selection tree following the update of each New takes $\Theta(\log SizeOfA)$ time. The best time to do this restructuring is at the end of each stage, rather than after each reduction of a New value by one. The number of restructurings needed is $O(e)$, so the total restructuring time is $O(e \log SizeOfA)$. This time is larger than the restructuring time for a max heap.

However, we can obtain the same time bound as we do when we use a heap by maintaining bins of vertices with the same New value. Since New values may range from zero to $SizeOfB$, $SizeOfB + 1$ bins are needed. Each bin i is a doubly linked list of vertices that have New value i. At the end of a stage, if New[6], for example, has changed from 12 to 4, then we need to move it from bin 12 to bin 4. We can make this move in $\Theta(1)$ time using simulated pointers and an array node of nodes such that node[i] represents vertex i and node[i].left and node[i].right are the doubly linked list pointers. To move vertex 6 from bin 12 to bin 4, we delete node[6] from bin 12 and insert it into bin 4. With this bin scheme the complexity of the covering heuristic is $O(n^2)$ or $O(n + e)$, depending on whether the adjacency matrix or list representation of a graph is used.

Implementation of Doubly Linked Bins

To support the use of doubly linked bins as described above, we define the private members of the class Undirected given in Figure 13.9. Node-Type is a class with private integer members left and right. It is the data type of the doubly linked list nodes. Program 13.3 gives the code for the private members of Undirected.

```
void CreateBins(int b, int n)
   create b empty bins and n nodes

void DestroyBins() {delete [] node;
                    delete [] bin;}

void InsertBins(int b, int v)
   add vertex v to bin b

void MoveBins(int bMax, int ToBin, int v)
   move vertex v from its current bin to bin ToBin

int *bin;
   bin[i] points to first node in doubly linked list for this bin

NodeType *node;
   node[i] represents the node for vertex i
```

Figure 13.9 Private members of Undirected needed to support doubly linked bins

```
void Undirected::CreateBins(int b, int n)
{// Create b empty bins and n nodes.
   node = new NodeType [n+1];
   bin = new int [b+1];
   // set bins empty
   for (int i = 1; i <= b; i++) bin[i] = 0;
}

void Undirected::InsertBins(int b, int v)
{// Insert v into bin b.
   if (!b) return; // do not insert in bin 0
   node[v].left = b; // add at left end
   if (bin[b]) node[bin[b]].left = v;
   node[v].right = bin[b];
   bin[b] = v;
}

void Undirected::MoveBins(int bMax, int ToBin, int v)
{// Move vertex v from its current bin to bin ToBin.
   int l = node[v].left;
   int r = node[v].right;
   // delete from current bin
   if (r) node[r].left = node[v].left;
   if (l > bMax || bin[l] != v) // not left-most one
      node[l].right = r;
   else bin[l] = r; // left-most in bin l
   // add to bin ToBin
   InsertBins(ToBin, v);
}
```

Program 13.3 Definition of bin functions

The function CreateBins dynamically allocates the two arrays: node and bin. node[i] represents vertex i, and bin[i] points to the doubly linked list of vertices with New value i. The for loop sets all doubly linked lists to empty.

Function InsertBins inserts vertex v into bin b provided $b \neq 0$. Since b is the New value of vertex v, $b = 0$ means that vertex v does not cover any vertices of B that are currently uncovered. As a result, there is no advantage to including it in the cover being built, and we can discard the vertex. When $b \neq 0$, vertex v is added to the front of the doubly linked list of vertices with New value b. This addition requires us to insert node[v] to the left of the first node in bin[b]. As the left-most node in a list points to the bin it is in, node[v].left is set to b. If the bin is not empty, then the left pointer of the current first node is set to point to the new first node. Regardless, the right pointer of node[v] may be set equal to bin[b], which is either zero or a pointer to the former first node. Finally, bin[b] is updated to point to the new first node in the list.

MoveBins moves vertex v from its current doubly linked list to that for vertices with New value ToBin. bMax is such that all bins bin[j], $j >$ bMax are empty. The code first determines the nodes to the left and right of node[v] in its current doubly linked list. Next node[v] is extracted from this doubly linked list and then reinserted into bin[ToBin] using the function InsertBins.

Implementation of Undirected::BipartiteCover

This function has an input parameter L that gives the assignment of graph vertices to the sets A and B. L[i] = 1 if vertex i is in A, and L[i] = 2 if the vertex is in B. The function has two output parameters C and m. m is the size of the cover constructed, and C[0:m-1] are the vertices of A that form the cover. The function returns false if the bipartite graph has no cover and true otherwise. The complete code appears in Program 13.4.

Program 13.4 begins by computing the size of the two sets A and B, initializing the necessary doubly linked list structures, creating three arrays, initializing the graph iterators, and creating a stack. Next we initialize the arrays Cov and Change to false and insert the vertices of A into doubly linked lists corresponding to the number of B vertices they cover.

To construct the cover, we examine the doubly linked lists in the order SizeOfB down to one. When we find a nonempty list we add its first vertex v to the cover. This strategy corresponds to selecting vertices with maximum New value. We add the selected vertex to the cover array C and also examine all B vertices adjacent to it. If a vertex j adjacent to v was not already covered, then we set Cov[j] to true to indicate that vertex j is now covered. We also increment the count of covered B vertices. Since j is newly covered, the New value of all A vertices adjacent to it decreases by one. The next while loop decrements these New values and saves the vertices whose New values have been so decremented on a stack. When the Cov values of all vertices adjacent to v have been updated, all New values reflect the number of new vertices that each A vertex can cover. However, the A vertices whose New value has changed as a result of the inclusion of v into the cover are in the wrong doubly linked lists. The next while loop moves these vertices to the proper lists.

```
bool Undirected::BipartiteCover(int L[], int C[],
                                        int& m)
{// Find a cover of the bipartite graph.
 // L is the input vertex labeling, L[i] = 1 iff i is
 // in A.  C is an output array that identifies the
 // cover.  Return false if the graph has no cover.
 // If the graph has a cover, return true;
 // return cover size in m; and cover in C[0:m-1].
   int n = Vertices();

   // create structures
   int SizeOfA = 0;
   for (int i = 1; i <= n; i++) // find size of set A
      if (L[i] == 1) SizeOfA++;
   int SizeOfB = n - SizeOfA;
   CreateBins(SizeOfB, n);
   int *New = new int [n+1];
      // i covers New[i] uncovered vertices of B
   bool *Change = new bool [n+1];
      // Change[i] is true iff New[i] has changed
   bool *Cov = new bool [n+1];
      // Cov[i] is true iff vertex i is covered
   InitializePos();
   LinkedStack<int> S;

   // initialize
   for (int i = 1; i <= n; i++) {
      Cov[i] = Change[i] = false;
      if (L[i] == 1) {// i is in A
         New[i] = Degree(i); // i covers this many
         InsertBins(New[i], i);}}

   // construct cover
   int covered = 0,         // # of covered vertices
       MaxBin = SizeOfB;    // max bin that may be
                            // nonempty
   m = 0;                   // cursor for C
```

Program 13.4 Greedy cover construction (continues)

```
while (MaxBin > 0) {    // search all bins
    // select a vertex
    if (bin[MaxBin]) {       // bin not empty
        int v = bin[MaxBin]; // first vertex
        C[m++] = v;          // add v to cover
        // label newly covered vertices
        int j = Begin(v), k;
        while (j) {
            if (!Cov[j]) {// j not covered yet
                Cov[j] = true;
                covered++;
                // update New
                k = Begin(j);
                while (k) {
                    New[k]--;      // j does not count
                    if (!Change[k]) {
                        S.Add(k);   // stack once only
                        Change[k] = true;}
                    k = NextVertex(j);}
                }
            j = NextVertex(v);}

        // update bins
        while (!S.IsEmpty()) {
            S.Delete(k);
            Change[k] = false;
            MoveBins(SizeOfB, New[k], k);}
        }
    else MaxBin--;
    }

DeactivatePos();
DestroyBins();
delete [] New;
delete [] Change;
delete [] Cov;
return (covered == SizeOfB);
}
```

Program 13.4 Greedy cover construction (concluded)

13.3.5   Single-Source Shortest Paths

In this problem we are given a digraph G with the property that each edge (i,j) has a nonnegative cost (or length) a$[i][j]$. The length of a path is the sum of the costs of the edges on the path. We must find a shortest path from a given source vertex s to each of the vertices (called destinations) in the graph to which there is a path from s. Figure 13.10(a) shows a five-vertex digraph. The number on each edge is its cost. Assume that the source vertex s is 1. The shortest paths from vertex 1 are listed in order of length in Figure 13.10(b). The number preceding each path is its length.

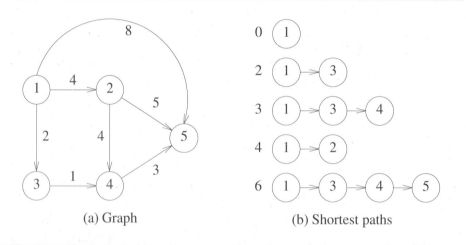

| (a) Graph | (b) Shortest paths |

Figure 13.10 Shortest-paths example

We can solve the shortest-path problem using a greedy algorithm, developed by E. Dijkstra, that generates the shortest paths in stages. In each stage a shortest path to a new destination vertex is generated. The destination vertex for the next shortest path is selected using the greedy criterion: *From the vertices to which a shortest path has not been generated, select one that results in the least path length*. In other words, Dijkstra's method generates the shortest paths in increasing order of length.

We begin with the trivial path from s to itself. This path has no edges and has a length of zero. In each stage of the greedy algorithm, the next shortest path is generated. One strategy that could be used to generate the next shortest path is to look at the shortest path generated so far and extend it by adding the shortest possible edge to it. The resulting new path is a one-edge extension of the shortest path previously generated. This strategy does not work in all cases. An alternative is to look at all of the shortest paths so far generated and, for each of these paths, determine a shortest one-edge extension. Then from all of these possiblities, pick the shortest. This strategy leads to Dijkstra's algorithm.

We can verify that when shortest paths are generated in order of length, the next shortest path to be generated is always a one-edge extension of an already-generated shortest path. In fact, the next shortest path is a shortest one-edge extension of an already-generated shortest path. Such a path must end at a vertex to which a shortest path hasn't as yet been generated. For the example of Figure 13.10, the second path of (b) is a one-edge extension of the first; the third is a one-edge extension of the second; the fourth is a one-edge extension of the first; and the fifth is a one-edge extension of the third.

This observation results in a convenient way to store the shortest paths. We can use an array p such that $p[i]$ gives the vertex that immediately precedes vertex i on the shortest s to i path. For our example $p[1:5] = [0, 1, 1, 3, 4]$. The path from s to any vertex i may be constructed backwards beginning at i and following the sequence, $p[i]$, $p[p[i]]$, $p[p[p[i]]]$, $\cdots$ until we either reach the vertex s or the number 0. In our example if we begin with $i = 5$, we get the vertex sequence $p[i] = 4$, $p[4] = 3$, $p[3] = 1$ $= s$. Therefore, the path is $1, 3, 4, 5$.

To facilitate the generation of shortest paths in increasing order of length, we define $d[i]$ to be the length of the shortest one-edge extension of a path already generated so that the extended path ends at vertex i. When we start, we have only the path from s to s and its length is zero. At this time $d[i]$ equals $a[s][i]$ (a is the cost-adjacency matrix of the digraph) for every vertex i. To generate the next path, we need to select a vertex to which a shortest path hasn't already been generated. Of the vertices that satisfy this requirement, the one for which $d[]$ is minimum is the one at which the next path terminates. When we obtain a new shortest path, the value of $d[]$ may change for some vertices because some of the one-edge extensions of the new shortest paths may yield a smaller value.

Putting these observations together, we get the high-level description of Figure 13.11. Step 1 initializes p to s for all vertices adjacent from s. This initialization records the best information currently available. That is, the shortest path from s to i is a one-edge extension of the shortest path from s to itself. As shorter paths are discovered, $p[i]$ will be updated. When the next shortest path is generated, we need to update d by looking at the one-edge extensions of this path (step 4).

Selection of Data Structures

We need to choose a data structure for the list L of unreached vertices. From this list, we need to extract a vertex with least d (step 3). This extraction can be done in logarithmic time if L is maintained as a min heap (see Section 9.3). Since step 3 is executed $O(n)$ times, the total time spent in step 3 is $O(n \log n)$. However, in step 4 we need to possibly change some d values, as some one-edge extensions of the newly generated shortest path may yield a smaller value

---

Step 1:   Initialize `d[i] = a[s][i], 1≤ i≤ n`.
Set `p[i] = s` for all `i` adjacent from `s`. Set `p[i] = 0` for all other vertices.
Create a list `L` of all vertices for which `p[i] ≠ 0`.

Step 2:   If `L` is empty, terminate. Otherwise, go to step 3.

Step 3:   Delete from `L` the vertex `i` with least value of `d` (ties are broken arbitrarily).

Step 4:   Update `d[j]` to min{`d[j]`, `d[i]+a[i][j]`} for all unreached vertices `j` adjacent from `i`. If `d[j]` changes, set `p[j] = i` and add `j` to `L` in case it isn't already there. Go to step 2.

Figure 13.11 High-level description of shortest-path algorithm

of `d` for some of the unreached vertices. Although key reduction is not a standard min heap operation, it can be done in logarithmic time. Since the total number of key reductions is O(number of edges in the digraph) = $O(n^2)$, the key reduction time is $O(n^2 \log n)$.

The time spent in steps 3 and 4 is $O(n^2)$ if `L` is maintained as an unordered chain. Now each execution of step 3 takes O(`|L|`) = O(n) time, and each key reduction takes $\Theta(1)$ time. (`d[j]` needs to be reduced, and no change is to be made in the chain.)

The refinement of Figure 13.11 into C++ code using an unordered chain appears in Program 13.5. This code uses the classes `Chain` (Program 3.8) and `ChainIterator` (Program 3.18). The `if` conditional inside the last `for` loop can be simplified to

```
if (d[j] > d[i] + a[i][j]))
```

if `NoEdge` is defined to be a sufficiently large number so that no shortest path has length greater than or equal to `NoEdge`. (`NoEdge` should be small enough so that the addition `d[i]+a[i][j]` does not cause an overflow.)

Comments on Complexity
The complexity of Program 13.5 is $O(n^2)$. Any shortest-path algorithm must examine each edge in the graph at least once, since any of the edges could be in a shortest path. Hence the minimum possible time for such an algorithm would be O(e). Since cost-adjacency matrices were used to represent the graph, it takes $O(n^2)$ time just to determine which edges are in the digraph. Therefore, any shortest-path algorithm that uses this representation must take $O(n^2)$. For this representation, then, Program 13.5 is optimal to within a constant factor. Even if a change to adjacency lists is made, only the overall time for the last

```
template<class T>
void AdjacencyWDigraph<T>::ShortestPaths(int s,
                         T d[], int p[])
{// Shortest paths from vertex s, return shortest
 // distances in d and predecessor info in p.
   if (s < 1 || s > n) throw OutOfBounds();
   Chain<int> L; // list of reachable vertices for
                 // which paths have yet to be found
   ChainIterator<int> I;
   // initialize d, p, and L
   for (int i = 1; i <= n; i++){
      d[i] = a[s][i];
      if (d[i] == NoEdge) p[i] = 0;
      else {p[i] = s;
            L.Insert(0,i);}
      }

   // update d and p
   while (!L.IsEmpty()) {// more paths exist
      // find vertex *v in L with least d
      int *v = I.Initialize(L);
      int *w = I.Next();
      while (w) {
         if (d[*w] < d[*v]) v = w;
         w = I.Next();}

      // next shortest path is to vertex *v
      // delete from L and update d
      int i = *v;
      L.Delete(*v);
      for (int j = 1; j <= n; j++) {
         if (a[i][j] != NoEdge && (!p[j] ||
               d[j] > d[i] + a[i][j])) {
            // d[j] decreases
            d[j] = d[i] + a[i][j];
            // add j to L if not already in L
            if (!p[j]) L.Insert(0,j);
            p[j] = i;}
         }
      }
}
```

Program 13.5 Shortest-path program

`for` loop can be brought down to $O(e)$ (because `d` can change only for vertices adjacent from `i`). The total time spent selecting and deleting the minimum-distance vertex from `L` remains $O(n^2)$.

13.3.6 Minimum-Cost Spanning Trees

This problem was considered in Examples 12.2 and Example 13.3. Since every spanning tree of an n-vertex undirected network G has exactly $n - 1$ edges, the problem is to select $n - 1$ edges in such a way that the selected edges form a least-cost spanning tree of G. We can formulate at least three different greedy strategies to select these $n - 1$ edges. These strategies result in three greedy algorithms for the minimum-cost spanning tree problem: Kruskal's algorithm, Prim's algorithm, and Sollin's algorithm.

Kruskal's Algorithm

The Method
Kruskal's algorithm selects the $n - 1$ edges one at a time using the greedy criterion: *From the remaining edges, select a least-cost edge that does not result in a cycle when added to the set of already selected edges*. Note that a collection of edges that contains a cycle cannot be completed into a spanning tree. Kruskal's algorithm has up to e stages where e is the number of edges in the network. The e edges are considered in order of increasing cost, one edge per stage. When an edge is considered, it is rejected if it forms a cycle when added to the set of already selected edges. Otherwise, it is accepted.

Consider the network of Figure 13.12(a). We begin with no edges selected. Figure 13.12(b) shows the current state of affairs. Edge (1,6) is the first edge picked. It is included into the spanning tree that is being built, and the graph of Figure 13.12(c) obtained. Next the edge (3,4) is selected and included into the tree (Figure 13.12(d)). The next edge to be considered is (2,7). Its inclusion into the tree being built does not create a cycle, so we get the graph of Figure 13.12(e). Edge (2,3) is considered next and included into the tree (Figure 13.12(f)). Of the edges not yet considered, (7,4) has the least cost. It is considered next. Its inclusion into the tree results in a cycle, so this edge is rejected. Edge (5,4) is the next edge to be added to the tree being built. The new configuration appears in Figure 13.12(g). The next edge to be considered is the edge (7,5). It is rejected, as its inclusion creates a cycle. Finally, edge (6,5) is considered and included into the tree being built. The inclusion of this edge completes the spanning tree (Figure 13.12(h)). The resulting tree has cost 99.

Figure 13.13 gives a high-level statement of Kruskal's algorithm.

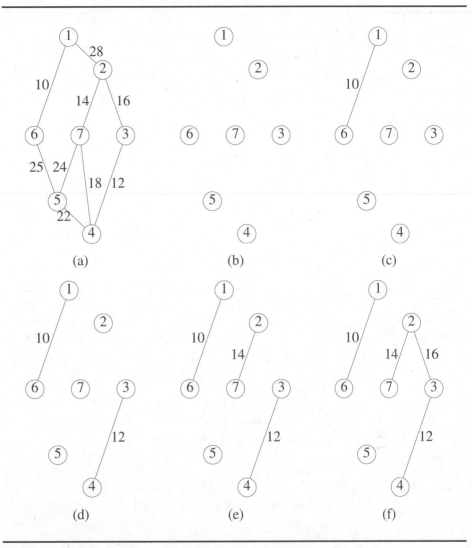

Figure 13.12 Constructing a minimum-cost spanning tree (continues)

Correctness Proof

We may prove that the greedy algorithm of Figure 13.13 always constructs a minimum-cost spanning tree by using the transformation technique used for the loading problem. We need to establish the following: (1) Kruskal's method results in a spanning tree whenever a spanning tree exists, and (2) the spanning tree generated is of minimum cost.

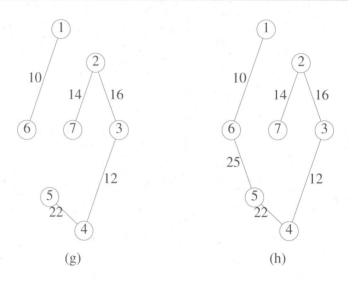

(g)   (h)

Figure 13.12 Constructing a minimum-cost spanning tree (concluded)

// Find a minimum-cost spanning tree in an n-vertex network.
   Let T be the set of selected edges. Initialize $T = \varnothing$.
   Let E be the set of network edges.
   while $(E \neq \varnothing)$ && $(\mid T \mid \neq n-1)$ {
      Let (u,v) be a least cost edge in E.
      $E = E - \{(u,v)\}$. // delete edge from E
      if $((u,v)$ does not create a cycle in T) Add edge (u,v) to T.
      }
   if $(\mid T \mid == n-1)$ T is a minimum-cost spanning tree.
   else The network is not connected and has no spanning tree.

Figure 13.13 High-level statement of Kruskal's algorithm

     Let G be any weighted undirected graph (i.e., G is an undirected network). From Section 12.11.3, we know that an undirected graph G has a spanning tree iff it is connected. Further, the only edges that get rejected (or discarded) in Kruskal's method are those that are currently on a cycle. The deletion of a single edge that is on a cycle of a connected graph results in a graph that is also connected. Hence if G is initially connected, the set of edges in T and E always form a connected graph. Consequently, if G is initially connected, the algorithm cannot terminate with $E = \varnothing$ and $\mid T \mid < n - 1$.

Now let us prove that the constructed spanning tree T is of minimum cost. Since G has a finite number of spanning trees, it has at least one of minimum cost. Let U be such a minimum-cost spanning tree. Both T and U have exactly $n - 1$ edges. If $T = U$, then T is of minimum cost and we have nothing to prove. Therefore, assume that $T \neq U$. Let k, $k > 0$, be the number of edges in T that are not in U. Note that k is also the number of edges in U that are not in T.

We shall show that T and U have the same cost by transforming U into T. This transformation will be done in k steps. At each step the number of edges in T that are not in U will be reduced by exactly 1. Further, the cost of U will not change as a result of the transformation. Consequently, after k steps of transformation U will have the same cost as the initial U and will consist of exactly those edges that are in T. Therefore, T is of minimum cost.

Each step of the transformation involves adding to U one edge from T and removing one edge, f, from U. The edges e and f are selected in the following way:

1. Let e be the least-cost edge in T that is not in U. Such an edge must exist because $k > 0$.

2. When e is added to U, a unique cycle is created. Let f be any edge on this cycle that is not in T. Note that at least one of the edges on this cycle is not in T, because T contains no cycles.

From the way e and f are selected, it follows that $V = U + \{e\} - \{f\}$ is a spanning tree and that T has exactly $k - 1$ edges that are not in V. We need to show that the cost of V is the same as that of U. Clearly, the cost of V is the cost of U plus the cost of edge e minus the cost of edge f. If the cost of e is less than the cost of f, then the spanning tree V has a smaller cost than the tree U, which is impossible. If e has a higher cost than f, then f is considered before e by Kruskal's algorithm. Since f is not in T, Kruskal's algorithm must have discarded f when f was considered for inclusion in T. Hence f together with edges in T having a cost less than or equal to the cost of f must form a cycle. By the choice of e, all these edges are also in U. Hence U must also contain a cycle, but it does not because it is a spanning tree. The assumption that e is of higher cost than f therefore leads to a contradiction. The only possibility that remains is that e and f have the same cost. Hence V has the same cost as U.

Choice of Data Structures and Complexity

To select edges in nondecreasing order of cost, we can set up a min heap and extract edges one by one as needed. When there are e edges in the graph, it takes $\Theta(e)$ time to initialize the heap and $O(\log e)$ time to extract each edge.

The edge set T together with the vertices of G define a graph that has up to n connected components. Let us represent each component by the set of vertices in it. These vertex sets are disjoint. To determine whether the edge (u, v) creates a cycle, we need merely check whether u and v are in the same vertex set (i.e., in the same component). If so, then a cycle is created. If not, then no cycle is created. Hence two Finds on the vertex sets suffice. When an edge is included in T, two components are combined into one and a Union is to be performed on the two sets. The set operations Find and Union can be carried out efficiently using the tree scheme (together with the weighting rule and path compaction) of Section 8.10.2. The number of Finds is at most $2e$, and the number of Unions at most $n-1$ (exactly $n-1$ if the network is connected). Including the initialization time for the trees, this part of the algorithm has a complexity that is just slightly more than $O(n+e)$.

The only operation performed on the set T is that of adding a new edge to it. T may be implemented as an array t of edges with additions being performed at one end. We can add at most $n-1$ edges to T. So the total time for operations on T is $O(n)$.

Summing up the various components of the computing time, we get $O(n + e \log e)$ as the asymptotic complexity of Figure 13.13.

Implementation

Using the data structures just described, Figure 13.13 may be refined into C++ code. We first define the class EdgeNode (Program 13.6), which is the data type for the min heap elements as well as for the spanning-tree array t.

```
template <class T>
class EdgeNode {
   public:
      operator T () const {return weight;}
   private:
      T weight;   // edge weight
      int u, v;   // edge endpoints
};
```

Program 13.6 Data type for Kruskal's algorithm

To make it easier to use the union and find scheme of Section 8.10.2, we define a class UnionFind in which the constructor is the initialization function of Program 8.16, Union is the weighted-union function of Program 8.16, and Find is the path-compacting find function of Program 8.17.

To write a single code that can be used regardless of the network representation, we define a new class UNetwork, which will contain all functions that apply to undirected networks. This class differs from the class Undirected in that the functions of the class Undirected do not require that weights be associated with the edges of the undirected networks on which they operate, while those in UNetwork do. The members of UNetwork will use iterators such as the Begin and NextVertex iterators defined for the class

Network. However, the new iterators will need to return not only the next adjacent vertex but also the weight of the edge to this next vertex. These iterators, together with other functions defined for undirected and directed networks and that require edge weights, may be collected together into a class WNetwork (Program 13.7).

```
template <class T>
class WNetwork : virtual public Network
{
   public:
      virtual void First(int i, int& j, T& c) = 0;
      virtual void Next(int i, int& j, T& c) = 0;
};
```

Program 13.7 The class WNetwork

The actual definitions of First and Next may be added to the classes AdjacencyWDigraph and LinkedWDigraph in the same way that the definitions of Begin and NextVertex were added to these classes. Both classes now need to derive from WNetwork (virtual public). For the members of UNetwork to be accessible from AdjacencyWGraph and LinkedW-Graph, both classes need to derive from UNetwork (virtual public). The code for UNetwork::Kruskal appears in Program 13.8. It requires that Edges() be defined as a virtual member of the class Network and that UNetwork be a friend of EdgeNode. The code returns false if there is no spanning tree and true otherwise. Note that when it returns true, a minimum-cost spanning tree is returned in the array t.

```
template<class T>
bool UNetwork<T>::Kruskal(EdgeNode<T> t[])
{// Find a min cost spanning tree using Kruskal's
 // method.  Return false if not connected.  If
 // connected, return min spanning tree in t[0:n-2].

   int n = Vertices();
   int e = Edges();
   // set up array of network edges
   InitializePos();  // graph iterator
   EdgeNode<T> *E = new EdgeNode<T> [e+1];
   int k = 0;             // cursor for E
```

Program 13.8 C++ code for Kruskal's algorithm (continues)

```
for (int i = 1; i <= n; i++) {
   // get all edges incident to i
   int j;
   T c;
   First(i, j, c);
   while (j) {      // j is adjacent from i
      if (i < j) {// add edge to E
    E[++k].weight = c;
         E[k].u = i;
         E[k].v = j;}
      Next(i, j, c);
      }
   }

// put edges in min heap
MinHeap<EdgeNode<T> > H(1);
H.Initialize(E, e, e);

UnionFind U(n); // union/find structure

// extract edges in cost order and select/reject
k = 0;  // use as cursor for t now
while (e && k < n - 1) {
   // spanning tree not complete &
   // edges remain
   EdgeNode<T> x;
   H.DeleteMin(x); // min cost edge
   e--;
   int a = U.Find(x.u);
   int b = U.Find(x.v);
   if (a != b) {// select edge
      t[k++] = x;
      U.Union(a,b);}
   }

DeactivatePos();
H.Deactivate();
return (k == n - 1);
}
```

Program 13.8 C++ code for Kruskal's algorithm (concluded)

Prim's Algorithm

Prim's algorithm, like Kruskal's, constructs the minimum-cost spanning tree by selecting edges one at a time. The greedy criterion used to determine the next edge to select is *From the remaining edges, select a least-cost edge whose addition to the set of selected edges forms a tree*. Consequently, at each stage the set of selected edges forms a tree. By contrast, the set of selected edges in Kruskal's algorithm forms a forest at each stage.

Prim's algorithm begins with a tree T that contains a single vertex. This vertex can be any of the vertices in the original graph. Then we add a least-cost edge (u, v) to T such that $T \cup \{(u, v)\}$ is also a tree. This edge-addition step is repeated until T contains $n - 1$ edges. Notice that edge (u, v) is always such that exactly one of u and v is in T. A high-level description of Prim's algorithm appears in Figure 13.14. This description also provides for the possibility that the input graph may not be connected. In this case there is no spanning tree. Figure 13.15 shows the progress of Prim's algorithm on the graph of Figure 13.12(a). The refinement of Figure 13.14 into a C++ program and its correctness proof are left as an exercise (Exercise 31).

```
// Assume that the network has at least one vertex.
    Let T be the set of selected edges. Initialize T = ∅.
    Let TV be the set of vertices already in the tree. Set TV = {1}.
    Let E be the set of network edges.
    while (E <> ∅) && (| T | <> n−1) {
        Let (u, v) be a least-cost edge such that u ∈ TV and v ∉ TV.
        if (there is no such edge) break.
        E = E − {(u,v)}. // delete edge from E}
        Add edge (u,v) to T.
    }
    if (| T | == n−1) T is a minimum-cost spanning tree.
    else The network is not connected and has no spanning tree.
```

Figure 13.14 Prim's minimum-spanning-tree algorithm

Prim's algorithm can be implemented to have a time complexity $O(n^2)$ if we associate with each vertex v not in TV a vertex $near(v)$ such that $near(v) \in TV$ and $cost(v, near(v))$ is minimum over all such choices for $near(v)$. The next edge to add to T is such that $cost(v, near(v))$ is minimum and $v \notin TV$.

Sollin's Algorithm

Sollin's algorithm selects several edges at each stage. At the start of a stage, the selected edges together with the n vertices of the graph form a spanning forest. During a stage we select one edge for each tree in this forest. This edge is a minimum-cost edge that has exactly one vertex in the tree. The selected edges

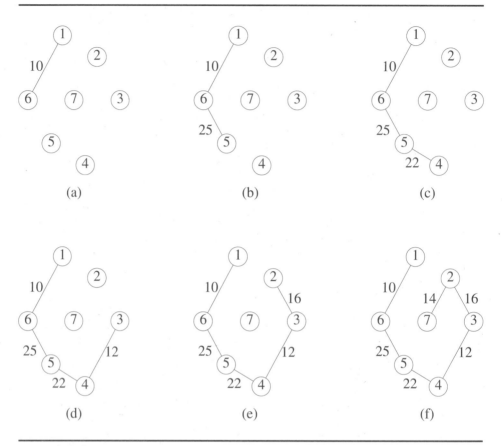

Figure 13.15 Stages in Prim's algorithm

are added to the spanning tree being constructed. Note that two trees in the forest can select the same edge, so we must multiple copies of the same edge. When several edges have the same cost, two trees can select different edges that connect them. In this case also, we must discard one of the selected edges. At the start of the first stage, the set of selected edges is empty. The algorithm terminates when only one tree remains at the end of a stage or when no edges remain to be selected.

Figure 13.16 shows the stages in Sollin's algorithm when it begins with the graph of Figure 13.12(a). The initial configuration of zero selected edges is the same as that shown in Figure 13.12(b). Each tree in this spanning forest is a single vertex. The edges selected by vertices 1, 2, $\cdots$, 7 are, respectively, (1, 6), (2, 7), (3, 4), (4, 3), (5, 4), (6, 1), (7, 2). The distinct edges in this selection are (1, 6), (2, 7), (3, 4), and (5, 4). Adding these edges to the set of selected edges results in the configuration of Figure 13.16(a). In the next stage the tree with vertex set $\{1, 6\}$ selects edge $(6, 5)$, and the remaining two trees select the edge $(2, 3)$. Following the addition of these two edges to the set of selected edges the spanning-tree construction is complete. The constructed spanning tree appears in Figure 13.16(b). The development of Sollin's algorithm into a C++ program and its correctness proof are left as an exercise (Exercise 32).

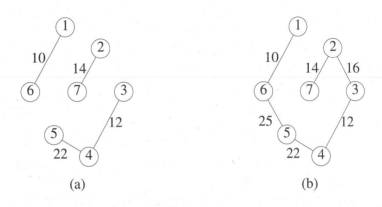

(a)   (b)

Figure 13.16 Stages in Sollin's algorithm

EXERCISES

8. Extend the greedy solution for the loading problem to the case when there are two ships. Does the algorithm always generate optimal solutions?

9. We are given n tasks to perform in sequence. Suppose that task i needs t_i units of time. If the tasks are done in the order $1, 2, \cdots, n$, then task i completes at time $c_i = \sum_{j=1}^{i} t_j$. The average completion time (ACT) is

$$\frac{1}{n} \sum_{i=1}^{n} c_i.$$

   (a) Consider the case of four tasks with task times $(4, 2, 8, 1)$. What is the ACT when the task order is $1, 2, 3, 4$?

   (b) What is the ACT when the task order is $2, 1, 4, 3$?

   (c) A greedy method to construct a task order that tries to minimize the ACT is Construct the order in n stages; in each stage, select from the remaining tasks, one with least task time. For the example of part (a), this strategy results in the task order 4, 2, 1, 3. What is the ACT for this greedy order?

(d)   Write a C++ program that implements the greedy strategy of (c). The complexity of your program should be $O(n\log n)$. Show that this is the case.

(e)   Show that the greedy strategy of (c) results in task orders that have minimum ACT.

10.   If two people perform the n tasks of Exercise 9, we need an assignment of tasks to each and an order in which each person is to perform his/her assigned tasks. The task completion times and ACT are defined as in Exercise 9. A possible greedy method that aims to minimize the ACT is, The two workers select tasks alternately and one at a time; from the remaining tasks, one with least task time is selected; each person does his/her tasks in the order selected. For the example of Exercise 9(a), if person 1 begins the selection process, he/she selects task 4; then person 2 selects task 2, person 1 selects task 1; and finally person 2 selects task 3.

(a)   Write a C++ program to implement this strategy. What is its time complexity?

(b)   Does the outlined greedy strategy always minimize the ACT? Prove your answer.

11.   (a)   Extend the greedy algorithm of Exercise 10 to the case when m persons are available to do the tasks.

(b)   Does your algorithm guarantee optimal solutions? Prove your answer.

(c)   Write C++ code for your algorithm. What is its complexity?

12.   Consider the stack-folding problem of Example 4.4.

(a)   Obtain a greedy algorithm to fold the carton stack into the fewest number of substacks such that no substack is of height more than H.

(b)   Does your algorithm guarantee to fold into the fewest number of substacks always? Prove your answer.

(c)   Write C++ code for your algorithm of (a).

(d)   What is the time complexity of your code of (c).

13.   Write a C++ program for the 0/1 knapsack problem using this heuristic: Pack the knapsack in nondecreasing order of profit density.

14.   Write a C++ program for the 0/1 knapsack problem using the bounded-performance heuristic with $k = 1$.

15.   Prove the error bound on the bounded-performance heuristic for the 0/1 knapsack problem for the case $k = 1$.

16. Write a C++ program for the 0/1 knapsack problem using the bounded-performance heuristic with $k = 2$.

17. Consider the **continuous knapsack problem** in which we require $0 \le x_i \le 1$, rather than $x_i \in \{0, 1\}$. A possible greedy algorithm is, Consider objects in nondecreasing order of profit density; if there is enough remaining capacity to accomodate the object, put it in; if not, put a fraction in to fill the knapsack.

    (a) What is the packing obtained for the instance $n = 3$, $w = [100, 10, 10]$, $p = [20, 15, 15]$, and $c = 105$?

    (b) Prove that this greedy algorithm always generates an optimal solution.

    (c) Write a C++ program that implements this algorithm.

18. The thirsty-baby problem of Example 13.1 is a generalization of the continuous knapsack problem of Exercise 17. Extend the greedy method of Exercise 17 to this problem. Does the algorithm guarantee optimal solutions? Prove your answer.

19. (a) Show that the algorithm of Figure 13.7 fails to find a cover iff the input bipartite graph does not have a cover.

    (b) Give a bipartite graph that has a cover and on which the algorithm of Figure 13.7 fails to find a minimum cover.

20. Trace the working of Figure 13.7 when vertex 1 is selected in stage 1.

21. Devise another greedy heuristic for the bipartite-cover problem. This time use the greedy criterion, If there is a vertex of B that can be covered by only a single vertex of A, select this vertex; otherwise, select a vertex of A that covers the largest number of uncovered vertices.

    (a) Write a high-level statement of the greedy heuristic.

    (b) Refine this greedy heuristic into a C++ function that is a member of the class `Undirected`.

    (c) What is the time complexity of your function?

    (d) Test the correctness of your code.

22. Let G be an undirected graph. A subset S of the vertices of G is a **clique** iff there is an edge between every pair of vertices in S. The size of the clique is the number of vertices in S. A **maximum clique** is a clique of largest size. The problem of finding a maximum clique (i.e., the max clique problem) in a graph is NP-hard.

    (a) Provide a high-level statement of a possible greedy heuristic for the max clique problem.

    (b)   Give an example of a graph on which your heuristic actually produces a maximum clique and also an example on which it does not.

    (c)   Refine the heuristic of (a) into the public member `Undirected ::Clique(int C, int m)` that returns in `m` the size of the largest clique found and in `C` the vertices of this largest clique.

    (d)   What is the time complexity of your code?

23.   Let G be an undirected graph. A subset S of the vertices of G is an **independent set** iff no two vertices of S are connected by an edge. A maximum independent set is an independent set with the maximum number of vertices. Finding the maximum independent set of a graph is NP-hard. Do Exercise 22 for the maximum independent set problem.

24.   A **coloring** of an undirected graph G is an assignment of the labels {1, 2, $\cdots$} to the vertices of G such that no two vertices connected by an edge have the same label. In the graph-coloring problem, we are to color G using the fewest number of distinct colors (labels). The graph-coloring problem is NP-hard. Do Exercise 22 for the graph-coloring problem.

25.   Show that when shortest paths are generated in order of length, the next shortest path to be generated is always a one-edge extension of an already generated shortest path.

26.   Show that the greedy algorithm of Figure 13.11 may not correctly compute the lengths of the shortest paths in a digraph that has one or more edges with negative cost.

27.   Write a function `Path(p,s,i)` that uses the p values computed by the function `ShortestPaths` and outputs a shortest path from vertex `s` to vertex `i`. What is the time complexity of your function?

28.   Write a version of Program 13.5 for the case when the digraph is a member of the class `LinkedWDigraph`. Your function should be defined as a member of this class. What is the time complexity of your function?

29.   Write a version of Program 13.5 for the case when the digraph is a member of the class `LinkedWDigraph` and has only O(n) edges. This time implement `L` as a min heap. What is the time complexity of your function?

30.   Develop a new template class `DNetwork` (directed networks) that is derived from `Network` (Program 12.15). This class will include all functions that apply to directed networks only. For this class, define a function `ShortestPaths` that works on all directed networks regardless of representation. In particular, the function should work for cost-adjacency matrix and linked-list representations. Use the iterator functions defined earlier and introduce new iterator functions as needed. The complexity of your function should remain O(n^2) where n is the number of vertices. Show that this is the case.

⋆ 31.　(a)　Provide a correctness proof for Prim's method (Figure 13.14).

　　　(b)　Refine Figure 13.14 into a C++ program `UNetwork::Prim` with complexity $O(n^2)$.

　　　(c)　Show that the complexity of your program is indeed $O(n^2)$.

⋆ 32.　(a)　Prove that Sollin's algorithm finds a minimum-cost spanning tree for every connected undirected graph.

　　　(b)　What is the maximum number of stages in Sollin's algorithm? Give this as a function of the number of vertices n in the graph.

　　　(c)　Write a C++ program, `UNetwork::Sollin` that finds a minimum-cost spanning tree using Sollin's algorithm.

　　　(d)　What is the complexity of your program?

⋆ 33.　Let T be a tree (not necessarily binary) in which a length is associated with each edge. Let S be a subset of the vertices of T and let T/S denote the forest that results when the vertices of S are deleted from T. We wish to find a minimum-cardinality subset S such that no forest in T/S has a root-to-leaf path of length greater than d.

　　　(a)　Develop a greedy algorithm to find a minimum-cardinality S. (*Hint:* start at the leaves and move toward the root.)

　　　(b)　Prove the correctness of your algorithm.

　　　(c)　What is the complexity of your algorithm? In case it is not linear in the number of vertices in T, redesign your algorithm so that its complexity is linear.

⋆ 34.　Do Exercise 33 for the case when T/S denotes the forest that results from making two copies of each vertex in S. The pointer from the parent goes to one copy, while pointers to the children go from the other copy.

13.4　REFERENCES AND SELECTED READINGS

Greedy approximation algorithms for several problems appear in the paper ''A Survey of Approximately Optimal Solutions to Some Covering and Packing Problems'' by V. Paschos, *ACM Computing Surveys*, 29, 2, 1997, 171–209. An experimental evaluation of greedy algorithms for the minimum-cost spanning-tree problem appears in the paper ''An Empirical Assessment of Algorithms for Constructing a Minimum Spanning Tree'' by B. Moret and H. Shapiro, *DIMACS Series in Discrete Mathematics*, 15, 1994, 99–117.

CHAPTER 14

DIVIDE AND CONQUER

BIRD'S-EYE VIEW

The divide-and-conquer strategy so successfully used by monarchs and colonizers may also be applied to the development of efficient computer algorithms. We begin this chapter by showing how to adapt this ancient strategy to the algorithm-development arena. Then we use the strategy to obtain good algorithms for the minmax problem; matrix multiplication; a problem from recreational mathematics—the defective-chess-board problem; sorting; selection; and a computational geometry problem—find the closest pair of points in two-dimensional space.

This chapter develops the mathematics needed to analyze the complexity of frequently occurring divide-and-conquer algorithms and proves that the divide-and-conquer algorithms for the minmax and sorting problems are optimal by deriving lower bounds on the complexity of these probelms. The derived lower bounds agree with the complexity of the divide-and-conquer algorithms for these problems.

14.1   THE METHOD

The divide-and-conquer methodology is very similar to the modularization approach to software design. Small instances of a problem are solved using some direct approach. To solve a large instance, we (1) divide it into two or more smaller instances, (2) solve each of these smaller problems, and (3) combine the solutions of these smaller problems to obtain the solution to the original instance. The smaller instances are often instances of the original problem and may be solved using the divide-and-conquer strategy recursively.

Example 14.1 [*Detecting a Counterfeit Coin*] You are given a bag with 16 coins and told that one of these coins may be counterfeit. Further, you are told that counterfeit coins are lighter than genuine ones. Your task is to determine whether the bag contains a counterfeit coin. To aid you in this task, you have a machine that compares the weights of two sets of coins and tells you which set is lighter or whether both sets have the same weight.

We can compare the weights of coins 1 and 2. If coin 1 is lighter than coin 2, then coin 1 is counterfeit and we are done with our task. If coin 2 is lighter than coin 1, then coin 2 is counterfeit. If both coins have the same weight, we compare coins 3 and 4. Again, if one coin is lighter, a counterfeit coin has been detected and we are done. If not, we compare coins 5 and 6. Proceeding in this way, we can determine whether the bag contains a counterfeit coin by making at most eight weight comparisons. This process also identifies the counterfeit coin.

Another approach is to use the divide-and-conquer methodology. Suppose that our 16-coin instance is considered a large instance. In step 1, we divide the original instance into two or more smaller instances. Let us divide our 16-coin instance into two 8-coin instances by arbitrarily selecting 8 coins for the first instance (say *A*) and the remaining 8 coins for the second instance *B*. In step 2, we need to determine whether *A* or *B* has a counterfeit coin. For this step we use our machine to compare the weights of the coin sets *A* and *B*. If both sets have the same weight, a counterfeit coin is not present in the 16-coin set. If *A* and *B* have different weights, a counterfeit coin is present and it is in the lighter set. Finally, in step 3 we take the results from step 2 and generate the answer for the original 16-coin instance. For the counterfeit-coin problem, step 3 is easy. The 16-coin instance has a counterfeit coin iff either *A* or *B* has one. So with just one weight comparison we can complete the task of determining the presence of a counterfeit coin.

Now suppose we need to identify the counterfeit coin. We shall define a ''small'' instance to be one with two or three coins. Note that if there is only one coin, we cannot tell whether it is counterfeit. All other instances are ''large'' instances. If we have a small instance, we may identify the counterfeit coin by comparing one of the coins with up to two other coins, performing at most two weight comparisons.

The 16-coin instance is a large instance. So it is divided into two 8-coin instances A and B as above. By comparing the weights of these two instances, we determine whether or not a counterfeit coin is present. If not, the algorithm terminates. Otherwise, we continue with the subinstance known to have the counterfeit coin. Suppose B is the lighter set. It is divided into two sets of four coins each. Call these sets $B1$ and $B2$. The two sets are compared. One set of coins must be lighter. If $B1$ is lighter, the counterfeit coin is in $B1$ and $B1$ is divided into two sets of two coins each. Call these sets $B1a$ and $B1b$. The two sets are compared and we continue with the lighter set. Since the lighter set has only two coins, it is a small instance. Comparing the weights of the two coins in the lighter set, we can determine which is lighter. The lighter one is the counterfeit coin. ■

Example 14.2 [*Gold Nuggets*] Your boss has a bag of gold nuggets. Each month two employees are given one nugget each for exemplary performance. By tradition, the first-ranked employee gets the heaviest nugget in the bag, and the second-ranked employee gets the lightest. This way, unless new nuggets are added to the bag, first-ranked employees get heavier nuggets than second-ranked employees get. Since new nuggets are added periodically, it is necessary to determine the heaviest and lightest nugget each month. You have a machine that can compare the weights of two nuggets and report which is lighter or whether both have the same weight. As this comparison is time-consuming, we wish to determine the heaviest and lightest nuggets, using the fewest number of comparisons.

Suppose the bag has n nuggets. We can use the strategy used in function Max (Program 1.31) to find the heaviest nugget by making $n - 1$ comparisons. After we identify the heaviest nugget, we can find the lightest from the remaining $n - 1$ nuggets using a similar strategy and performing an additional $n - 2$ comparisons. The total number of weight comparisons is $2n - 3$. Two alternative strategies appear in Programs 2.26 and 2.27. The first of these alternative strategies performs $2n - 2$ comparisons, and the second performs at most $2n - 2$ comparisons.

Let us try to formulate a solution that uses the divide-and-conquer method. When n is small, say, $n \leq 2$, one comparison is sufficient to identify the heaviest and lightest nuggets. When n is large (in this case $n > 2$), in step 1 we divide the instance into two or more smaller instances. Suppose we divide the bag of nuggets into two smaller bags A and B, each containing half the nuggets. In step 2 we determine the heaviest and lightest nuggets in A and B. Let these nuggets be H_A (heaviest in A), L_A, H_B, and L_B. Step 3 determines the heaviest overall nugget by comparing H_A and H_B and the lightest by comparing L_A and L_B. We can use the outlined divide-and-conquer scheme recursively to perform step 2.

Suppose $n = 8$. The bag is divided into two bags A and B with four nuggets each. To find the heaviest and lightest nuggets in A, the four nuggets in A are divided into two groups $A1$ and $A2$. Each group contains two nuggets. We can identify the heavier nugget H_{A1} and the lighter one L_{A1} in $A1$ with one comparison. With another comparison, we can identify H_{A2} and L_{A2}. Now by comparing H_{A1} and H_{A2}, we can identify H_A. A comparison between L_{A1} and L_{A2} identifies L_A. So with four comparisons we have found H_A and L_A. We need another four comparisons to determine H_B and L_B. By comparing H_A and H_B (L_A and L_B), we determine the overall heaviest (lightest) nugget. Therefore, the divide-and-conquer approach requires 10 comparisons when $n = 8$. If we use Program 1.31, 13 comparisons are made. When we use Programs 2.26 and 2.27, up to 14 comparisons are made.

Let $c(n)$ be the number of comparisons used by the divide-and-conquer approach. For simplicity, assume that n is a power of two. When $n = 2$, $c(n) = 1$. For larger n, $c(n) = 2c(n/2) + 2$. Using the substitution method (see Example 2.20), this recurrence can be solved to obtain $c(n) = 3n/2 - 2$ when n is a power of two. The divide-and-conquer approach uses almost 25 percent fewer comparisons than the alternative schemes suggested in this example use. ∎

Example 14.3 [*Matrix Multiplication*] The product of two $n \times n$ matrices A and B is a third $n \times n$ matrix C where $C(i,j)$ is given by

$$C(i,j) = \sum_{k=1}^{n} A(i,k)*B(k,j), \ \ 1 \le i \le n, \ \ 1 \le j \le n \tag{14.1}$$

If each $C(i,j)$ is computed using this equation, then the computation of each requires n multiplications and $n-1$ additions. The total operation count for the computation of all terms of C is therefore $n^3 m + n^2(n-1)a$ where m denotes a multiplication and a an addition or subtraction.

To formulate a divide-and-conquer algorithm to multiply the two matrices, we need to define a ''small'' instance, specify how small instances are multiplied, determine how a large instance may be subdivided into smaller instances, state how these smaller instances are to be multiplied, and finally describe how the solutions of these smaller instances may be combined to obtain the solution for the larger instance. To keep the discussion simple, let's assume that n is a power of two (i.e., n is one of the numbers 1, 2, 4, 8, 16, $\cdots$).

To begin with, let us assume that $n = 1$ is a small instance and that $n > 1$ is a large instance. We shall modify this assumption later if we need to. Since a small matrix is a 1×1 matrix, we can multiply two such matrices by multiplying together the single element in each.

Consider a large instance, that is, one with $n > 1$. We can divide such a matrix A into four $n/2 \times n/2$ matrices A_1, A_2, A_3, and A_4 as shown in Figure 14.1(a). When n is greater than one and a power of two, $n/2$ is also a power of two. So the smaller matrices satisfy our assumption on the matrix size also. The matrices B_i and C_i, $1 \le i \le 4$ are defined in a similar way. The matrix product we are to perform may be represented as in Figure 14.1(b). We may use Equation

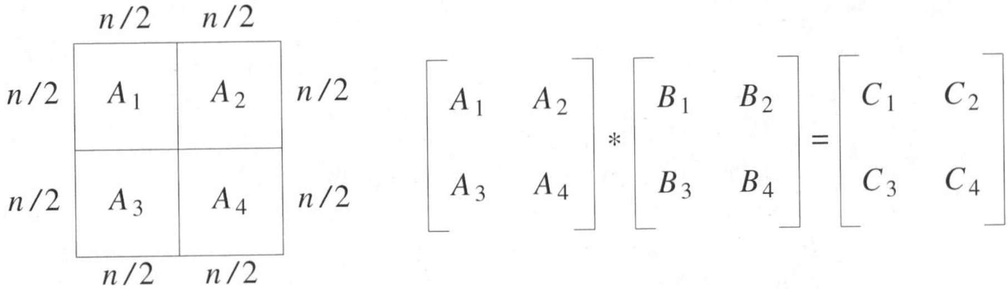

(a) Dividing A into four

(b) $A * B = C$

Figure 14.1 Dividing a matrix into smaller ones

14.1 to verify that the following equations are valid:

$$C_1 = A_1 B_1 + A_2 B_3 \qquad (14.2)$$

$$C_2 = A_1 B_2 + A_2 B_4 \qquad (14.3)$$

$$C_3 = A_3 B_1 + A_4 B_3 \qquad (14.4)$$

$$C_2 = A_3 B_2 + A_4 B_4 \qquad (14.5)$$

These equations allow us to compute the product of A and B by performing eight multiplications and four additions of $n/2 \times n/2$ matrices. We can use these equations to complete our divide-and-conquer algorithm. In step 2 of the algorithm, the eight multiplications involving the smaller matrices are done using the divide-and-conquer algorithm recursively. In step 3 the eight products are combined using a direct matrix addition algorithm (see Program 2.19). The complexity of the resulting algorithm is $\Theta(n^3)$, the same as the complexity of Program 2.24, which uses Equation 14.1 directly. The divide-and-conquer algorithm will actually run slower than Program 2.24 because of the overheads introduced by the instance-dividing and -recombining steps.

To get a faster algorithm, we need to be more clever about the instance-dividing and -recombining steps. A scheme, known as Strassen's method, involves the computation of seven smaller matrix products (versus eight in the preceding scheme). The results of these seven smaller products are matrices D, E, $\cdots$, J, which are defined as

$$D = A_1 (B_2 - B_4)$$

$$E = A_4 (B_3 - B_1)$$

$$F = (A_3 + A_4) B_1$$

$$G = (A_1 + A_2)B_4$$
$$H = (A_3 - A_1)(B_1 + B_2)$$
$$I = (A_2 - A_4)(B_3 + B_4)$$
$$J = (A_1 + A_4)(B_1 + B_4)$$

The matrices D through H may be computed by performing seven matrix multiplications, six matrix additions, and four matrix subtractions. The components of the answer may be computed using another six matrix additions and two matrix subtractions as below:

$$C_1 = E + I + J - G$$
$$C_2 = D + G$$
$$C_3 = E + F$$
$$C_4 = D + H + J - F$$

Let us try this scheme on a multiplication instance with $n = 2$. Sample A and B matrices together with their product C are given below:

$$\begin{bmatrix} 1 & 2 \\ 3 & 4 \end{bmatrix} * \begin{bmatrix} 5 & 6 \\ 7 & 8 \end{bmatrix} = \begin{bmatrix} 19 & 22 \\ 43 & 50 \end{bmatrix}$$

Since $n > 1$, the matrix multiplication instance is divided into four smaller matrices as in Figure 14.1(a), each smaller matrix is a 1×1 matrix and has a single element. The 1×1 multiplication instances are small instances, and they are solved directly. Using the equations for D through J, we obtain:

$$D = 1(6-8) = -2$$
$$E = 4(7-5) = 8$$
$$F = (3 + 4)5 = 35$$
$$G = (1 + 2)8 = 24$$
$$H = (3-1)(5 + 6) = 22$$
$$I = (2-4)(7 + 8) = -30$$
$$J = (1 + 4)(5 + 8) = 65$$

From these values the components of the answer are computed as follows:

$$C_1 = 8 - 30 + 65 - 24 = 19$$
$$C_2 = -2 + 24 = 22$$
$$C_3 = 8 + 35 = 43$$
$$C_4 = -2 + 22 + 65 - 35 = 50$$

For our 2×2 instance, the divide-and-conquer algorithm has done seven multiplications and 18 add/subtracts. We could have computed C by performing eight multiplications and seven add/subtracts using Equation 14.1 directly. For the divide-and-conquer scheme to be faster, the time cost of a multiply must be more than the time cost of 11 add/subtracts.

If Strassen's instance-dividing scheme is used only when $n \geq 8$ and smaller instances are solved using Equation 14.1, then the case $n = 8$ requires seven multiplications of 4×4 matrices and 18 add/subtracts of matrices of this size. The multiplications take $64m + 48a$ operations each, and each matrix addition or subtraction takes $16a$ operations. The total operation count is $7(64m + 48a) + 18(16a) = 448m + 624$. The direct method has an operation count of $512m + 448a$. A minimum requirement for Strassen's method to be faster is that the cost of $512 - 448$ multiplications be more than that of $624 - 448$ add/subtracts. Or one multiply should cost more than approximately 2.75 add/subtracts.

If we consider a "small" instance to be one with $n < 16$, the Strassen's decomposition scheme is used only for matrices with $n \geq 16$; smaller matrices are multiplied using Equation 14.1. The operation count for the divide-and-conquer algorithm becomes $7(512m + 448a) + 18(64a) = 3584m + 4288a$ when $n = 16$. The direct method has an operation count of $4096m + 3840a$. If the cost of a multiplication is the same as that of an add/subtract, then Strassen's method needs time for 7872 operations plus overhead time to do the problem division. The direct method needs time for 7936 operations plus time for the `for` loops and other overhead items in the program. Even though the operation count is less for Strassen's method, it is not expected to run faster because of its larger overhead.

For larger values of n, the difference between the operation counts of Strassen's method and the direct method becomes larger and larger. So for suitably large n, Strassen's method will be faster. Let $t(n)$ denote the time required by Strassen's divide-and-conquer method. Since large instances are recursively divided into smaller ones until each instance becomes of size k or less (k is at least eight and may be larger depending on the implementation and computer characteristics), the recurrence for t is

$$t(n) = \begin{cases} d & n \leq k \\ 7t(n/2) + cn^2 & n > k \end{cases} \tag{14.6}$$

where cn^2 represents the time to perform 18 add/subtracts of $n/2 \times n/2$ matrices as well as the time to divide the instance of size n into the smaller instances. Using the substitution method, this recurrence may be solved to obtain $t(n) = \Theta(n^{\log_2 7})$. Since $\log_2 7 \sim 2.81$, the divide-and-conquer matrix multiplication algorithm represents an asymptotic improvement over the direct scheme that has complexity $\Theta(n^3)$. ∎

Implementation Note

The divide-and-conquer methodology naturally leads to recursive algorithms. In many instances, these recursive algorithms are best implemented as recursive programs. In fact, in many cases all attempts to obtain nonrecursive programs result in the use of a stack to simulate the recursion stack. However, in some instances, it is possible to implement the divide-and-conquer algorithm as a non-recursive program without the use of such a stack and in such a way that the resulting program is faster, by a constant factor, than the natural recursive implementation. The divide-and-conquer algorithms for the gold nuggets problem (Example 14.2) and the merge sort method (Section 14.3) can both be implemented without the use of recursion so as to obtain fast programs that do not directly simulate the recursion.

Example 14.4 [*Gold Nuggets*] The work done by the algorithm of Example 14.2 to find the lightest and heaviest of eight nuggets is described by the binary tree of Figure 14.2. The leaves of this tree denote the eight coins (a, b, $\cdots$, h). Each shaded node represents an instance containing all the leaves in its subtree. Therefore, root A represents the problem of finding the lightest and heaviest of all eight nuggets, while node B represents the problem of finding the lightest and heaviest of the nuggets a, b, c, and d. The algorithm begins at the root. The eight-nugget instance represented by the root is divided into two four-nugget instances represented by the nodes B and C. At B the four-nugget instance is divided into the two-nugget instances D and E. We solve the two-nugget instance at node D by comparing the nuggets a and b to determine which is heavier. After we solve the problems at D and E, we solve the problem at B by comparing the lighter coins from D and E, as well as the heavier coins at D and E. We repeat this process at F, G, and C and then at A.

We can classify the work of the recursive divide-and-conquer algorithm as follows:

1. Divide a large instance into many smaller ones, each of size 1 or 2, during a downward root-to-leaf pass of the binary tree of Figure 14.2.

2. Compare the nuggets in each smaller size 2 instance to determine which nugget is heavier and which is lighter. This comparison is done at nodes D, E, F, and G. For size 1 instances the single nugget is both the smaller and lighter nugget.

3. Compare the lighter nuggets to determine which is lightest. Compare the heavier nuggets to determine which is heaviest. These comparisons are done at nodes A through C.

This classification of the work leads to the nonrecursive code of Program 14.1 to find the location of the minimum and maximum of the n weights `w[0:n-1]`. This program returns `false` if $n < 1$ and returns `true` otherwise.

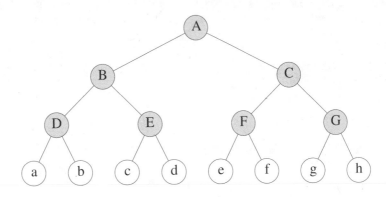

Figure 14.2 Finding the lightest and heaviest of eight nuggets

When $n \geq 1$, Program 14.1 sets Min and Max so that w[Min] is the least weight and w[Max] is the largest weight. The cases $n < 1$ and $n = 1$ are handled first. If $n > 1$ and odd, the first weight w[0] becomes the candidate for minimum and maximum. This step leaves us with an even number of weights w[1:n-1] to account for in the for loop. When n is even, the first two weights are compared outside the for loop and Min and Max are set to the location of the smaller and larger weight, respectively. Again, we are left with an even number of weights w[2:n-1] to account for in the for loop.

In the for loop the outer if finds the larger and smaller of the pair (w[i], w[i+1]) being compared. This work corresponds to the category 2 work in our classification of the work of our divide-and-conquer algorithm. The embedded ifs find the smallest of the smaller weights and the largest of the larger weights. This work is the category 3 work.

The for loop compares the smaller of each pair to the current minimum weight w[Min] and compares the larger to the current maximum weight w[Max]. Min and Max are updated if necessary.

For the complexity analysis, we see that when n is even, one comparison is made outside the for loop and $3(n/2-1)$ inside. The total number of comparisons is $3n/2-2$. When n is odd, no comparisons are made outside the for loop. However, $3(n-1)/2$ comparisons are made inside. Therefore, regardless of whether n is odd or even, a total of $\lceil 3n/2 \rceil - 2$ comparisons are made, $n > 0$. ∎

```
template<class T>
bool MinMax(T w[], int n, T& Min, T& Max)
{// Locate min and max of w[0:n-1].
 // Return false if fewer than one element.
   // special cases, n <= 1
   if (n < 1) return false;
   if (n == 1) {Min = Max = 0;
                return true;}

   // initialize Min and Max
   int s;  // start point for loop
   if (n % 2) {// n is odd
      Min = Max = 0;
      s = 1;}
   else {// n is even, compare first pair
         if (w[0] > w[1]) {
             Min = 1;
             Max = 0;}
         else {Min = 0;
               Max = 1;}
         s = 2;}

   // compare remaining pairs
   for (int i = s; i < n; i += 2) {
      // find larger of w[i] and w[i+1]
      // then compare larger with w[Max]
      // and smaller with w[Min]
      if (w[i] > w[i+1]) {
          if (w[i] > w[Max]) Max = i;
          if (w[i+1] < w[Min]) Min = i + 1;}
      else {
          if (w[i+1] > w[Max]) Max = i + 1;
          if (w[i] < w[Min]) Min = i;}
      }

   return true;
}
```

Program 14.1 Nonrecursive program to find the min and max

EXERCISES

1. Extend the divide-and-conquer method of Example 14.1 to the case of $n > 1$ coins. How many weight comparisons are done?

2. Consider the counterfeit-coin problem of Example 14.1. Suppose that the information "counterfeit coins are lighter than genuine ones" is changed to "counterfeit coins and genuine coins do not have the same weight." Also assume that the coin bag contains n coins.

   (a) Formulate a divide-and-conquer algorithm that either outputs the message "there is no counterfeit coin" or identifies the counterfeit coin. Your algorithm should recursively divide large problem instances into two smaller ones. How many weight comparisons are needed to identify the counterfeit coin (in case such a coin exists)?

   (b) Repeat part (a) with the requirement that large instances are divided into three smaller ones.

3. (a) Write C++ programs that implement both schemes of Example 14.2 to find the maximum and minimum of n elements. Use recursion to implement the divide-and-conquer scheme.

   (b) Programs 2.26 and 2.27 are two other codes to find the maximum and minimum of n elements. What is the minimum and maximum number of comparisons made by each?

   (c) Compare the run times of the codes of (a) and (b) as well as the code of Program 14.1 for $n = 100; 1000;$ and 10,000. For the code of Program 2.27 use both the average- and worst-case times. The two codes of (a) and that of Program 2.26 should have the same average- and worst-case times.

   (d) Note that unless the comparison cost is very high, the divide-and-conqer algorithm will not outperform the others on worst-case data. Why? Will it ever outperform Program 2.27 on the average-time measure? Why?

4. Show that the divide-and-conquer matrix-multiplication algorithm that results from the direct application of Equations 14.2 through 14.5 has complexity $\Theta(n^3)$. From this analysis conclude that the resulting program will be slower than Program 2.24.

5. Use the substitution method to show that the solution to recurrence 14.6 is $\Theta(n^{\log_2 7})$.

★ 6. Program Strassen's matrix-multiplication algorithm and experiment with different values of k (see Equation 14.6) to determine which value results in best performance. Now compare the run times of your program with those for Program 2.24. It is sufficient to do this comparison for the case when n

is a power of two.

7. When n is not a power of two, we may add rows and columns to the matrices to obtain larger matrices whose size is a power of two. Suppose that the smallest number of rows and columns are added so that the resulting matrix size m is a power of two.

    (a)   How large can the ratio m/n be?

    (b)   What matrix entries should you use for the new rows and columns so that when the new matrices A' and B' are multiplied, the product of the original matrices A and B appears in the top-left corner of C'?

    (c)   The run time of Strassen's method to multiply A' and B' is $\Theta(m^{2.81})$. What is the run time as a function of n?

14.2 APPLICATIONS

14.2.1 Defective Chessboard

A **defective chessboard** is a $2^k \times 2^k$ board of squares with exactly one defective square. Figure 14.3 shows some of the possible defective chessboards for $k \le 2$. The defective square is shaded. Note that when $k = 0$, there is only one possible defective chessboard (Figure 14.3(a)). In fact, for any k there are exactly 2^{2k} different defective chessboards.

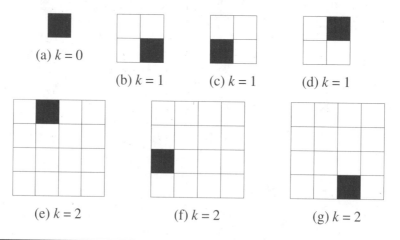

(a) $k = 0$

(b) $k = 1$ (c) $k = 1$ (d) $k = 1$

(e) $k = 2$ (f) $k = 2$ (g) $k = 2$

Figure 14.3 Defective chessboards

In the defective-chessboard problem, we are required to tile a defective chessboard using triominoes (Figure 14.4). In this tiling two triominoes may not overlap, triominoes should not cover the defective square, and triominoes must cover all other squares. With these constraints the number of triominoes to be used becomes $(2^{2k} - 1)/3$. We can verify that $(2^{2k} - 1)/3$ is a whole number. A defective chessboard with $k = 0$ is easily tiled, as it has no nondefective squares. The number of triominoes used in the tiling is zero. When $k = 1$, there are exactly three nondefective squares and these squares are covered using a triomino in one of the orientations of Figure 14.4.

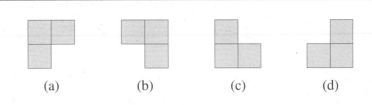

(a)   (b)   (c)   (d)

Figure 14.4 Triominoes with different orientations

The divide-and-conquer method leads to an elegant solution to the defective-chessboard problem. The method suggests reducing the problem of tiling a $2^k \times 2^k$ defective chessboard to that of tiling smaller defective chessboards. A natural partitioning of a $2^k \times 2^k$ chessboard would be into four $2^{k-1} \times 2^{k-1}$ chessboards as in Figure 14.5(a). Notice that when such a partitioning is done, only one of the four smaller boards has a defect (as the original $2^k \times 2^k$ board had exactly one defective square). Tiling one of the four smaller boards corresponds to tiling a defective $2^{k-1} \times 2^{k-1}$ chessboard. To convert the remaining three boards to defective boards, we place a triomino at the corner formed by these three. Figure 14.5(b) shows this placement for the case when the defect in the original $2^k \times 2^k$ chessboard falls into the upper left $2^{k-1} \times 2^{k-1}$ board. We can use this partitioning technique recursively to tile the entire $2^k \times 2^k$ defective chessboard. The recursion terminates when the chessboard size has been reduced to 1×1. The chessboard's only square now has a defect, and no triominoes are to be placed.

We can code this divide-and-conquer algorithm as the recursive C++ function `TileBoard` (Program 14.2). This function assumes that a global two-dimensional integer array `Board` represents the chessboard, `Board[0][0]` represents the top-left corner square of the chessboard. This function also assumes a global integer variable `tile` that is initially zero. The input parameters to this function are

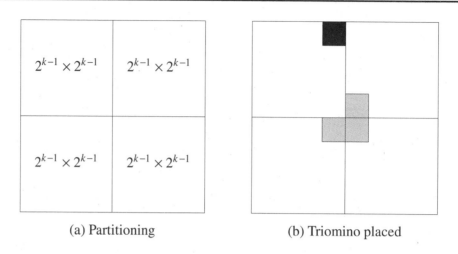

(a) Partitioning	(b) Triomino placed

Figure 14.5 Partitioning a $2^k \times 2^k$ board

tr $\cdots$ the row of the top-left square in the chessboard

tc $\cdots$ the column of the top-left square in the chessboard

dr $\cdots$ the row that contains the defective square

dc $\cdots$ the column with the defective square

size $\cdots$ the number of rows or columns in the chessboard

The function is invoked as `TileBoard(0,0,dr,dc,size)` where size $= 2^k$. The number of tiles needed to tile the defective chessboard is $(\text{size}^2 - 1)/3$. Function `TileBoard` represents these tiles by the integers 1 through $(\text{size}^2 - 1)/3$ and labels each nondefective square of the chessboard with the number of the tile that covers it.

Let $t(k)$ denote the time taken by `TileBoard` to tile a $2^k \times 2^k$ defective chessboard. When $k = 0$, size equals 1 and a constant d amount of time is spent. When $k > 0$, four recursive calls are made. These calls take $4t(k-1)$ time. In addition to this time, time is spent testing the if conditionals and tiling three nondefective squares. Let this time be denoted by the constant c. We obtain the following recurrence for t:

$$t(k) = \begin{cases} d & k = 0 \\ 4t(k-1) + c & k > 0 \end{cases} \qquad (14.7)$$

```
void TileBoard(int tr, int tc, int dr, int dc, int size)
{// Tile a defective chessboard.
   if (size == 1) return;
   int t = tile++,  // tile number to use
       s = size/2;  // quadrant size

   // tile top-left quadrant
   if (dr < tr + s && dc < tc + s)
      // defect is in this quadrant
      TileBoard(tr, tc, dr, dc, s);
   else {// no defect in this quadrant
         // place tile t in bottom-right corner
         Board[tr + s - 1][tc + s - 1] = t;
         // tile the rest
         TileBoard(tr, tc, tr+s-1, tc+s-1, s);}

   // tile top-right quadrant
   if (dr < tr + s && dc >= tc + s)
      // defect is in this quadrant
      TileBoard(tr, tc+s, dr, dc, s);
   else {// no defect in this quadrant
         // place tile t in bottom-left corner
         Board[tr + s - 1][tc + s] = t;
         // tile the rest
         TileBoard(tr, tc+s, tr+s-1, tc+s, s);}

   // tile bottom-left quadrant
   if (dr >= tr + s && dc < tc + s)
      // defect is in this quadrant
      TileBoard(tr+s, tc, dr, dc, s);
   else {// place tile t in top-right corner
         Board[tr + s][tc + s - 1] = t;
         TileBoard(tr+s, tc, tr+s, tc+s-1, s);}

   // tile bottom-right quadrant
   if (dr >= tr + s && dc >= tc + s)
      // defect is in this quadrant
      TileBoard(tr+s, tc+s, dr, dc, s);
   else {// place tile t in top-left corner
         Board[tr + s][tc + s] = t;
         TileBoard(tr+s, tc+s, tr+s, tc+s, s);}
}
```

Program 14.2 Tiling a defective chessboard

We may solve this recurrence using the substitution method (see Example 2.20) to obtain $t(k) = \Theta(4^k) = \Theta$(number of tiles needed). Since we must spend at least $\Theta(1)$ time placing each tile, we cannot obtain an asymptotically faster algorithm than divide and conquer.

14.2.2   Merge Sort

We can apply the divide-and-conquer method to the sorting problem. In this problem we must sort n elements into nondecreasing order. The divide-and-conquer method suggests sorting algorithms with the following general structure: if n is one, terminate; otherwise, partition the collection of elements into two or more subcollections; sort each; combine the sorted subcollections into a single sorted collection.

Suppose we limit ourselves to partitioning the n elements into two subcollections. Now we need to decide how to perform this partitioning. One possibility is to put the first $n - 1$ elements into the first subcollection (say, A) and the last element into the second subcollection (say, B). A is sorted using this partitioning scheme recursively. Since B has only one element, it is already sorted. Following the sort of A, we need to combine A and B, using the function `insert` of Program 2.10. Comparing the resulting sort algorithm with `InsertionSort` (Program 2.15), we see that we have really discovered the recursive version of insertion sort. The complexity of this sort algorithm is $O(n^2)$.

Another possibility for the two-way partitioning of n elements is to put the element with largest key in B and the remaining elements in A. Then A is sorted recursively. To combine the sorted A and B, we need merely append B to the sorted A. If we find the element with largest key using the function `Max` of Program 1.31, the resulting sort algorithm is a recursive formulation of `SelectionSort` (Program 2.7). If we use a bubbling process (Program 2.8) to locate and move the element with largest key to the right-most position, the resulting algorithm is a recursive version of `BubbleSort` (Program 2.9). In either case the sort algorithm has complexity $\Theta(n^2)$. This complexity can be made $O(n^2)$ by terminating the recursive partitioning of A as soon as A is known to be in sorted order (see Examples 2.16 and 2.17).

The partitioning schemes used to arrive at the three preceding sort algorithms partitioned the n elements into two very unbalanced collections A and B. A has $n - 1$ elements, while B has only 1 element. Let us see what happens when this partitioning is done in a more balanced way, that is, when A gets a fraction n/k of the elements and B gets the rest. Now both A and B are to be sorted by recursive application of the divide-and-conquer scheme. To combine the sorted A and B, we use a process called *merge*, which combines two sorted sequences into one.

Example 14.5 Consider the 8 elements with keys [10, 4, 6, 3, 8, 2, 5, 7]. If we pick $k = 2$, then [10, 4, 6, 3] and [8, 2, 5, 7] are to be sorted independently. The result is [3, 4, 6, 10] and [2, 5, 7, 8]. To merge these two sorted sequences, we begin at the front of each. The smaller element (2) is moved to the result sequence. Next 3 and 5 are compared, and 3 is moved to the result sequence. Then 4 and 5 are compared, and 4 is placed in the result sequence. Next 6 and 5 are compared, and so on.

If we pick $k = 4$, then the sequences [10, 4] and [6, 3, 8, 2, 5, 7] are to be sorted. The result of sorting these sequences independently is [4, 10] and [2, 3, 5, 6, 7, 8]. When these sorted sequences are merged, we obtain the desired eight-element sorted sequence. ∎

Figure 14.6 is a high-level statement of the divide-and-conquer sort algorithm that results when the number of smaller instances created is 2 and the partitioning is such that A gets n/k elements.

```
template<class T>
void sort(T E, int n)
{// Sort the n elements in E.  k is global.
  if (n >= k) {
    i = n/k;
    j = n-i;
    Let A consist of the first i elements in E.
    Let B consist of the remaining j elements in E.
    sort(A,i);
    sort(B,j);
    merge(A,B,E,i,j); // merge from A and B into E
    }
  else  sort E using insertion sort.
}
```

Figure 14.6 Pseudocode for divide-and-conquer sort

From our brief description of merge, it is evident that n elements can be merged in $O(n)$ time. Let $t(n)$ be the worst-case time of the divide-and-conquer sort algorithm (Figure 14.6). We obtain the following recurrence for t

$$t(n) = \begin{cases} d & n < k \\ t(n/k) + t(n - n/k) + cn & n \geq k \end{cases}$$

where c and d are constants. $t(n)$ is minimum when $n/k \approx n - n/k$. Therefore, the minimum occurs when $k = 2$, that is, when the two smaller instances are of approximately the same size. *Divide-and-conquer algorithms usually have optimal performance when the smaller instances created are of approximately the same size.*

Setting $k = 2$ in the recurrence for $t(n)$, we get the following recurrence:

$$t(n) = \begin{cases} d & n \leq 1 \\ t(\lfloor n/2 \rfloor) + t(\lceil n/2 \rceil) + cn & n > 1 \end{cases}$$

The presence of the floor and ceiling operators makes this recurrence difficult to solve. We can overcome this difficulty by solving the recurrence only for values of n that are a power of two. In this case the recurrence takes the simpler form

$$t(n) = \begin{cases} d & n \leq 1 \\ 2t(n/2) + cn & n > 1 \end{cases}$$

We can solve this recurrence using the substitution method, and the result is $t(n) = \Theta(n \log n)$. Although the recurrence that was solved is valid only when n is a power of 2, the asymptotic bound obtained is valid for all n because $t(n)$ is a nondecreasing function of n. Since $t(n) = \Theta(n \log n)$, this time represents the best- and worst-case complexity of merge sort. Further, since the best- and worst-case complexities are the same, the average complexity of merge sort is also given by $\Theta(n \log n)$.

Refinement of Figure 14.6 into C++ Code

Figure 14.6 with $k = 2$ is the sorting method known as **merge sort** (or more precisely **two-way merge sort**). Let us now proceed to refine Figure 14.6 with $k = 2$ (i.e., merge sort) into a C++ function to sort n elements. The easiest way to do this refinement is to represent the elements as a linked chain (i.e., as a member of the class Chain (Program 3.8)). In this case we divide E into two roughly equal lists by moving down to the $(n/2)$th node and breaking the chain. The merge procedure should be capable of merging two sorted chains together. We shall not complete the refinement using chains, as we wish to compare the performance of the resulting C++ code with that of heap and insert sort. Neither of these latter sorting methods was coded using a linked representation for the collection of elements.

To be compatible with our earlier sort functions, the merge sort function must begin with the element collection E in an array a and return the sorted sequence in the same array. With this requirement the refinement of Figure 14.6 takes the following course. When E is divided in two, we can avoid copying the two halves into A and B and simply keep track of the left and right ends of each half. We can then perform the merge with the sequences to be merged in a initially. We can merge the sequences into a new array b and then copy them back into a. The refined version of Figure 14.6 appears in Figure 14.7.

```
template<class T>
MergeSort( T a[], int left, int right)
{// Sort the elements in a[left:right].
   if (left < right) {// at least 2 elements
      int i = (left + right)/2; // midpoint
      MergeSort(a,left,i);
      MergeSort(a,i+1,right);
      Merge(a,b,left,i,right); // merge from a into b
      Copy(b,a,left,right); // put result back into a
      }
}
```

Figure 14.7 Divide-and-conquer sort refinement

We can improve the performance of Figure 14.7 in many ways. For example, we can eliminate the recursion easily. If we examine this program carefully, we see that the recursion simply divides the element list repeatedly until we are left with segments of size 1. The merging that takes place after this division into segments of size 1 is best described for the case when n is a power of 2. The segments of size 1 are merged to get sorted segments of size 2. These segments of size 2 are then merged to get sorted segments of size 4. The merge process is repeated until a single sorted sequence of size n remains. Figure 14.8 shows the merging (and copying) that takes place when $n = 8$. The square brackets denote the start and end of sorted segments.

initial segments [8] [4] [5] [6] [2] [1] [7] [3]

merge to b   [4 8]   [5 6]   [1 2]   [3 7]

copy to a   [4 8]   [5 6]   [1 2]   [3 7]

merge to b   [4 5 6 8]   [1 2 3 7]

copy to a   [4 5 6 8]   [1 2 3 7]

merge to b   [1 2 3 4 5 6 7 8]

copy to a   [1 2 3 4 5 6 7 8]

Figure 14.8 Merge sort example

An iterative version of merge sort begins by merging pairs of adjacent segments of size 1, then it merges pairs of adjacent segments of size 2, and so on. We can eliminate virtually all the copying from b to a by merging alternately from a to b and from b to a. The iterative merge sort algorithm appears in Program 14.3.

```
template<class T>
void MergeSort(T a[], int n)
{// Sort a[0:n-1] using merge sort.
   T *b = new T [n];
   int s = 1;  // segment size
   while (s < n) {
      MergePass(a, b, s, n); // merge from a to b
      s += s;
      MergePass(b, a, s, n); // merge from b to a
      s += s;
      }
}
```

Program 14.3 Iterative merge sort

To complete our sorting code, we need to specify the function MergePass. In our C++ development, the function MergePass (Program 14.4) simply determines the left and right ends of the segments to be merged. The actual merging of a pair of segments is done by function Merge (Program 14.5.), which requires defining the operator <= on elements of type T. If a user-defined type is used, the operator <= must be overloaded. Writing Merge in this way permits us to sort on any field of the element. The overloading of <= simply compares the desired fields.

Natural Merge Sort
Natural merge sort is a variant of the basic merge sort (Program 14.3) algorithm just described. It starts by merging the existing sorted segments within the input sequence. For example, the element list [4, 8, 3, 7, 1, 5, 6, 2] contains the sorted segments [4, 8], [3, 7], [1, 5, 6], and [2]. These segments can be identified by making a left-to-right scan of the element list, looking for positions i such that element i is larger than element $i + 1$. In the case of the preceding list, we identify four sorted segments. Segments 1 and 2 are merged to get [3, 4, 7, 8], and segments 3 and 4 are merged to get [1, 2, 5, 6]. Finally, these two segments are merged to get the single sorted segment [1, 2, 3, 4, 5, 6, 7, 8]. Thus only two merge passes are made over the data. Program 14.3 would begin with segments of size 1 and make three merge passes. As an extreme example, suppose the input element list is already sorted and has n elements. Natural merge sort would

```
template<class T>
void MergePass(T x[], T y[], int s, int n)
{// Merge adjacent segments of size s.
   int i = 0;
   while (i <= n - 2 * s) {
      // merge two adjacent segments of size s
      Merge(x, y, i, i+s-1, i+2*s-1);
      i = i + 2 * s;
      }

   // fewer than 2s elements remain
   if (i + s < n) Merge(x, y, i, i+s-1, n-1);
   else for (int j = i; j <= n-1; j++)
           // copy last segment to y
           y[j] = x[j];
}
```

Program 14.4 Merge pass

```
template<class T>
void Merge(T c[], T d[], int l, int m, int r)
{// Merge c[l:m]] and c[m:r] to d[l:r].
   int i = l,     // cursor for first segment
       j = m+1,   // cursor for second
       k = l;     // cursor for result

   // merge until i or j exits its segment
   while ((i <= m) && (j <= r))
      if (c[i] <= c[j]) d[k++] = c[i++];
      else d[k++] = c[j++];

   // take care of left overs
   if (i > m) for (int q = j; q <= r; q++)
                 d[k++] = c[q];
   else for (int q = i; q <= m; q++)
           d[k++] = c[q];
}
```

Program 14.5 Merge

identify exactly one sorted segment and make no merge passes, while Program 14.3 would make $\lceil \log_2 n \rceil$ merge passes. So natural merge sort would complete in $\Theta(n)$ time, while Program 14.3 would take $\Theta(n \log n)$ time.

14.2.3 Quick Sort

We can also use the divide-and-conquer approach to arrive at another totally different sort method called **quick sort**. In this method the n elements to be sorted are partitioned into three segments (or groups)—a left segment *left*, a middle segment *middle*, and a right segment *right*. The middle segment contains exactly one element; no element in *left* has a key larger than the key of the element in *middle*; and no element in *right* has a key that is smaller than that of the middle element. As a result, the elements in *left* and *middle* can be sorted independently, and no merge is required following the sorting of *left* and *right* The element in *middle* is called the **pivot** or **partitioning element**. The sort method is described more precisely by the code of Figure 14.9.

```
// Sort a[0:n-1] using quick sort.
```
Select an element from `a[0:n-1]` for *middle*. This element is the pivot.
Partition the remaining elements into the segments *left* and *right* so that
   no element in *left* has a key larger than that of the pivot and
   no element in *right* has a key smaller than that of the pivot.
Sort *left* using quick sort recursively.
Sort *right* using quick sort recursively.
The answer is *left* followed by *middle* followed by *right*.

Figure 14.9 High-level statement of quick sort

Consider the element list [4, 8, 3, 7, 1, 5, 6, 2]. Suppose we pick the element with key 6 as the pivot. Then 6 is in *middle*; 4, 3, 1, 5, and 2 are in *left*, and 8 and 7 are in *right*. When *left* has been sorted, the keys are in the order 1, 2, 3, 4, 5. When *right* has been sorted, its keys are in the order 7, 8. Putting the elements in *right* after the element in *middle* and those in *left* before the one in *middle*, we get the sorted sequence [1, 2, 3, 4, 5, 6, 7, 8].

The partitioning of the element list into *left*, *middle*, and *right* can be done in place (Program 14.6). In this refinement the pivot is always the element at position 1. Other choices that result in improved performance are possible. One such choice is discussed later in this section.

Program 14.6 remains correct when we change the $<$ and $>$ in the conditionals of the `do-while` statements are to $<=$ and $>=$, respectively. Experimental evidence suggests that the average performance of quick sort is better

```
template<class T>
void QuickSort(T *a, int n)
{// Sort a[0:n-1] using quick sort.
 // Requires a[n] must have largest key.
   quickSort(a, 0, n-1);
}

template<class T>
void quickSort(T a[], int l, int r)
{// Sort a[l:r], a[r+1] has large value.
   if (l >= r) return;
   int i = l,        // left-to-right cursor
       j = r + 1;    // right-to-left cursor
   T pivot = a[l];

   // swap elements >= pivot on left side
   // with elements <= pivot on right side
   while (true) {
      do {// find >= element on left side
         i = i + 1;
         } while (a[i] < pivot);
      do {// find <= element on right side
         j = j - 1;
         } while (a[j] > pivot);
      if (i >= j) break;  // swap pair not found
      Swap(a[i], a[j]);
      }

   // place pivot
   a[l] = a[j];
   a[j] = pivot;

   quickSort(a, l, j-1); // sort left segment
   quickSort(a, j+1, r); // sort right segment
}
```

Program 14.6 Quick sort

when it is coded as in Program 14.6. All attempts to eliminate the recursion from this procedure result in the introduction of a stack. The last recursive call can, however, be eliminated without the introduction of a stack. We leave the elimination of this recursive call as an exercise (Exercise 13).

Program 14.6 requires $O(n)$ recursion stack space. The space requirements can be reduced to $O(\log n)$ by simulating the recursion using a stack. In this simulation the smaller of the two segments *left* and *right* is sorted first. The boundaries of the other segment are put on the stack.

The worst-case computing time for quick sort is $\Theta(n^2)$, and it is achieved, for instance, when *left* is always empty. However, if we are lucky and *left* and *right* are always of about the same size, then the complexity is $\Theta(n\log n)$. Therefore, the best-case complexity of quick sort is $\Theta(n\log n)$ (Exercise 16). Surprisingly, the average complexity of quick sort is also $\Theta(n\log n)$.

Theorem 14.1 The average complexity of `QuickSort` is $\Theta(n\log n)$.

Proof Let $t(n)$ denote the average time needed to sort an n-element array. When $n \leq 1$, $t(n) \leq d$ for some constant d. Suppose that $n > 1$. Let s be the size of the left segment following the partitioning of the elements. Because the pivot element is in the middle segment, the size of the right segment is $n - s - 1$. The average time to sort the left and right segments is $t(s)$ and $t(n - s - 1)$, respectively. The time needed to partition the elements is bounded by cn where c is a constant. Since s can have any of the n values 0 through $n - 1$ with equal probability, we obtain the following recurrence:

$$t(n) \leq cn + \frac{1}{n}\sum_{s=0}^{n-1}[t(s) + t(n - s - 1)]$$

We can simplify this recurrence as follows:

$$t(n) = cn + \frac{2}{n}\sum_{s=0}^{n-1}t(s) \leq cn + \frac{4d}{n} + \frac{2}{n}\sum_{s=2}^{n-1}t(s) \tag{14.8}$$

Now using induction on n we show that $t(n) \leq kn\log_e n$ for $n > 1$ and $k = 2(c + d)$. Here $e \sim 2.718$ is the base of natural logarithms. The induction base covers the case $n = 2$. From Equation 14.8 we obtain $t(2) \leq 2c + 2d \leq kn\log_e 2$. For the induction hypothesis we assume $t(n) \leq kn\log_e n$ for $2 \leq n < m$ where m is an arbitrary integer that is greater than 2. In the induction step we need to prove $t(m) \leq km\log_e m$. From Equation 14.8 and the induction hypothesis, we obtain

$$t(m) \leq cm + \frac{4d}{m} + \frac{2}{m}\sum_{s=2}^{m-1}t(s) \leq cm + \frac{4d}{m} + \frac{2k}{m}\sum_{s=2}^{m-1}s\log_e s \tag{14.9}$$

To proceed further we use the following facts:

- $s\log_e s$ is an increasing function of s.

- $\displaystyle\int_2^m s\log_e s\ ds < \frac{m^2\log_e m}{2} - \frac{m^2}{4}$

Using these facts and Equation 14.9, we obtain

$$t(m) < cm + \frac{4d}{m} + \frac{2k}{m}\int_2^m s\log_e s\ ds$$

$$< cm + \frac{4d}{m} + \frac{2k}{m}\left[\frac{m^2\log_e m}{2} - \frac{m^2}{4}\right]$$

$$= cm + \frac{4d}{m} + km\log_e m - \frac{km}{2}$$

$$< km\log_e m \quad\blacksquare$$

The table of Figure 14.10 compares the average and worst-case complexities of the sort methods developed in this book.

Method	Worst	Average
Bubble sort	n^2	n^2
Count sort	n^2	n^2
Insertion sort	n^2	n^2
Selection sort	n^2	n^2
Heap sort	$n\log n$	$n\log n$
Merge sort	$n\log n$	$n\log n$
Quick sort	n^2	$n\log n$

Figure 14.10 Comparison of sort methods

Median-of-three quick sort is a variant of Program 14.6 that has better average performance. In this variant we do not necessarily use `a[1]` as the pivot. Note that Program 14.6 selects the pivot by setting `pivot` to `a[1]`. In a median-of-three quick sort, the pivot is chosen to be the median of the three elements {`a[1]`, `a[(1+r)/2]`, `a[r]`}. For example, if these elements have keys {5, 9, 7}, then `a[r]` is used as the value of `pivot`. To implement the median-of-three rule, it is easiest to swap the element in the median position with that at a[1] and then proceed as in Program 14.6. If a[r] is the median element, then we swap a[1] and a[r] just before pivot is set to a[1] in Program 14.6 and proceed as in the remainder of the code.

The observed average times for QuickSort appear in Figure 14.11. This figure includes the times for merge, heap, and insertion sort. For each n a minimum of 100 randomly generated integer instances were run. These random instances were constructed by making repeated calls to the function random in stdlib.h. If the time taken to sort these instances was less than 10 clock ticks (see Section 2.6), then additional random instances were sorted until the total time taken was at least this much. The times reported in Figure 14.11 include the time taken to set up the random data. For each n the time taken to set up the data and the time for the remaining overheads included in the reported numbers is the same for all sort methods. As a result, the data of Figure 14.11 is useful for comparative purposes. The data of this figure, for $n \leq 100$, is plotted in Figure 14.12.

n	insert	heap	merge	quick
10	0.000068	0.000126	0.000108	0.000081
20	0.000151	0.000234	0.000222	0.000148
30	0.000267	0.000360	0.000323	0.000224
40	0.000416	0.000502	0.000434	0.000304
50	0.000594	0.000646	0.000541	0.000385
60	0.000809	0.000791	0.000646	0.000468
70	0.001057	0.000946	0.000855	0.000552
80	0.001340	0.001103	0.000971	0.000638
90	0.001626	0.001260	0.001090	0.000726
100	0.001984	0.001423	0.001216	0.000814
200	0.006593	0.003140	0.002498	0.001733
300	0.015934	0.004950	0.004194	0.002693
400	0.026923	0.006593	0.005495	0.003688
500	0.041758	0.008791	0.007143	0.004696
600	0.060440	0.010989	0.008242	0.005495
700	0.080220	0.012637	0.009890	0.006593
800	0.106044	0.015385	0.012088	0.008242
900	0.132418	0.017033	0.012637	0.008791
1000	0.164835	0.019231	0.014835	0.009890

Times are in seconds

Figure 14.11 Average times for sort methods

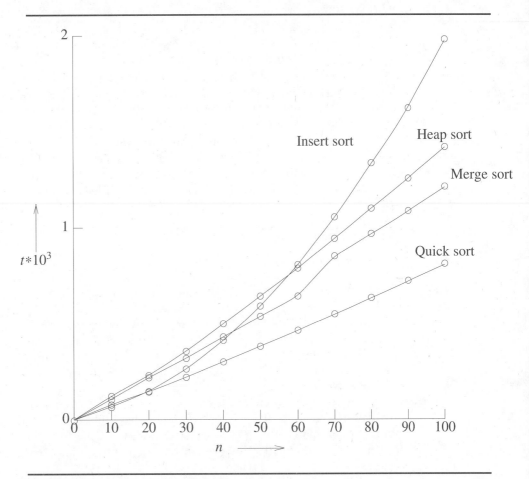

Figure 14.12 Plot of average times

As Figure 14.12 shows, quick sort outperforms the other sort methods for suitably large n. We see that the breakeven point between insertion and quick sort is a little below 20. The exact breakeven point can be found experimentally by obtaining run-time data for n = 15, 16, 17, 18, and 19. Let the exact breakeven point be nBreak. For average performance, insertion sort is the best sort method (of those tested) to use when n ≤ nBreak, and quick sort is the best when n > nBreak. We can improve on the performance of quick sort for n > nBreak by combining insertion and quick sort into a single sort function by replacing the following statement in Program 14.6

```
if (l >= r) return;
```

with the code

```
if (r - 1 < nBreak) {InsertionSort(a,l,r);
                     return;}
```

Here `InsertionSort(a,l,r)` is a function that sorts `a[l:r]`, using the insertion sort method. The performance measurement of the modified quick sort code is left as an exercise (Exercise 20). Further improvement in performance may be possible by replacing `nBreak` with a smaller value (see Exercise 20).

For worst-case behavior most implementations will show merge sort to be best for $n > c$ where c is some constant. For $n \leq c$ insertion sort has the best worst-case behavior. The performance of merge sort can be improved by combining insertion sort and merge sort (see Exercise 21).

14.2.4 Selection

In this problem we are given an array `a[0:n-1]` of n elements and are to determine the kth smallest element. This element is the element in position `a[k-1]` following a sort of the array. Consider the case n = 8; each element has the two fields `key` and `ID` where `key` is an integer and `ID` is a character. Let the eight elements be [(12, *a*), (4, *b*), (5, *c*), (4, *d*), (5, *e*), (10, *f*), (2, *g*), (20, *h*)]. Then suppose that following a sort we have the array [(2, *g*), (4, *d*), (4, *b*), (5, *c*), (5, *e*), (10, *f*), (12, *a*), (20,*h*)]. If k = 1, we return the element with `ID` *g*; if k = 8, we return the element with `ID` *h*; if k = 6, we return the element with `ID` *f*; and if k = 2, we return the element with `ID` *d*. Actually, in this last case we have some flexibility, as the sort could have placed either of the elements with `ID`s *d* and *b* into `a[1]`, because both have the same `key`. Therefore, either may be returned. However, if one element is returned when k = 2, the other should be returned when k = 3.

One application of the selection problem is finding the median element. In this case $k = \lceil n/2 \rceil$. Medians are useful statistical quantities that are reported often in the media, for example, median salary, median age, and median height. Other values of k are also useful. For example, we can divide a population into quartiles by finding the `n/4`, `n/2`, and `3n/4` elements.

We can solve the selection problem in O(nlogn) time by first sorting the n elements (for example, using heap sort or merge sort) and then picking off the element in position `a[k-1]`. We can obtain better average performance by using quick sort (see Figure 14.11), even though this method has an inferior asymptotic complexity of $O(n^2)$.

We can adapt the code of Program 14.6 to the selection problem so as to obtain an even faster solution. If the partitioning element `a[l]` is to be placed in `a[j]` following the execution of the two `while` loops, then `a[l]` is known to be the `j-l+1`th element of `a[l:j]`. If we are looking for the kth element in `a[l:r]` and `j-l+1` equals `k`, then the answer is `a[l]`; if `j-l+1 < k`, then the element we are looking for is the `k-j+l-1`th element of *right*; otherwise, it is the `k`th element of *left*. Therefore, we need to make either zero or one recursive call. The code for the new selection program appears in Program 14.7. A `for` or `while` loop can replace the recursive calls made by `Select` (see Exercise 25).

The worst-case complexity of Program 14.7 is $\Theta(n^2)$. This worst case is achieved, for example, when *left* is always empty and the `k`th element is in *right*. However, if *left* and *right* are always of the same size or differ in size by at most one, then we get the following recurrence for the time needed by Program 14.7:

$$t(n) \le \begin{cases} d & n \le 1 \\ t(\lfloor n/2 \rfloor) + cn & n > 1 \end{cases} \tag{14.10}$$

If we assume that n is a power of two, the floor operator may be dropped and the recurrence solved, using the substitution method, to obtain $t(n) = \Theta(n)$. By selecting the partitioning element more carefully, the worst-case time also becomes $\Theta(n)$. The more careful way to select the partitioning element is to use the **median-of-medians** rule in which the n elements of a are divided into n/r groups for some integer constant r. Each of these groups, except possibly the last one, contains exactly r elements. Next we find the median of each group by sorting the r elements in each group and then selecting the one in the middle position. The median of these n/r medians is computed, using the selection algorithm recursively, and used as the partitioning element.

Example 14.6 [*Median of Medians*] Consider the case $r = 5$, $n = 27$, and $a = [2, 6, 8, 1, 4, 10, 20, 6, 22, 11, 9, 8, 4, 3, 7, 8, 16, 11, 10, 8, 2, 14, 15, 1, 12, 5, 4]$. These 27 elements may be divided into the six groups [2, 6, 8, 1, 4], [10, 20, 6, 22, 11], [9, 8, 4, 3, 7], [8, 16, 11, 10, 8], [2, 14, 15, 1, 12], and [5, 4]. The medians of these six groups are 4, 11, 7, 10, 12, and 4, respectively. The median of the elements [4, 11, 7, 10, 12, 4] is 7. This median is used as the partitioning element. With this choice of the pivot, we get *left* = [2, 6, 1, 4, 6, 4, 3, 2, 1, 5, 4], *middle* = [7], and *right* = [8, 10, 20, 22, 11, 9, 8, 8, 16, 11, 10, 8, 14, 15, 12]. If we are to find the kth element for $k < 12$, only *left* needs to be examined; if $k = 12$, the element is the pivot, and if $k > 12$, the 15 elements of *right* need to be examined. In this last case we need to find the $k - 12$'th element of *right*. ∎

Theorem 14.2 When the partitioning element is chosen using the median-of-medians rule, the following statements are true:

(a) If $r = 9$, then $\max\{ |\,left\,|, |\,right\,| \} \le 7n/8$ for $n \ge 90$.

```
template<class T>
T Select(T a[], int n, int k)
{// Return k'th smallest element in a[0:n-1].
 // Assume a[n] is a dummy largest element.
   if (k < 1 || k > n) throw OutOfBounds();
   return select(a, 0, n-1, k);
}

template<class T>
T select(T a[], int l, int r, int k)
{// Return k'th smallest in a[l:r].
   if (l >= r) return a[l];
   int i = l,         // left to right cursor
       j = r + 1;  // right to left cursor
   T pivot = a[l];

   // swap elements >= pivot on left side
   // with elements <= pivot on right side
   while (true) {
      do {// find >= element on left side
         i = i + 1;
         } while (a[i] < pivot);
      do {// find <= element on right side
         j = j - 1;
         } while (a[j] > pivot);
      if (i >= j) break;  // swap pair not found
      Swap(a[i], a[j]);
      }

   if (j - l + 1 == k) return pivot;

   // place pivot
   a[l] = a[j];
   a[j] = pivot;

   // recursive call on one segment
   if (j - l + 1 < k)
      return select(a, j+1, r, k-j+l-1);
   else return select(a, l, j-1, k);
}
```

Program 14.7 Find the kth element

(b)   If $r = 5$ and all elements of a are distinct, then $\max\{\,|\,\textit{left}\,|,\ |\,\textit{right}\,|\,\} \leq 3n/4$ for $n \geq 24$.

Proof Exercise 23 asks you to prove this theorem. ▪

From Theorem 14.2 and Program 14.7, it follows that if the median-of-medians rule with $r = 9$ is used, the time $t(n)$ needed to select the kth element is given by the following recurrence:

$$t(n) = \begin{cases} cn\log n & n < 90 \\ t(\lceil n/9 \rceil) + t(\lfloor 7n/8 \rfloor) + cn & n \geq 90 \end{cases} \qquad (14.11)$$

This recurrence assumes that an $n\log n$ method is used when $n < 90$ and that larger instances are solved using divide and conquer with the median-of-medians rule. Using induction, you can show (Exercise 24) that $t(n) \leq 72cn$ for $n \geq 1$. When the elements are distinct, we may use $r = 5$ to get linear time performance.

14.2.5   Closest Pair of Points

In this problem you are given n points (x_i, y_i), $1 \leq i \leq n$ and are to find two that are closest. The distance between two points i and j is given by the following formula:

$$\sqrt{(x_i - x_j)^2 + (y_i - y_j)^2)}$$

Example 14.7 Suppose that n equal-size holes are to be drilled into a sheet of metal. If any two holes are too close, metal failure may occur during the drilling process. By determining the minimum distance between any two holes, we can assess the probabilty of such a failure. This minimum distance corresponds to the distance between a closest pair of points. ▪

We can solve the closest-pair-of-points problem in $\Theta(n^2)$ time by examining all $n(n-1)/2$ pairs of points, computing the distance between the points in each pair, and determining the pair for which this distance is minimum. We shall call this method the *direct approach*. The divide-and-conquer method suggests the high-level algorithm of Figure 14.13.

This algorithm uses the direct approach to small instances and solves large instances by dividing them into two smaller instances. One instance (say, A) will be of size $\lceil n/2 \rceil$, and the other (say, B) of size $\lfloor n/2 \rfloor$. The closest pair of points in the original instance falls into one of the three categories: (1) both points are in A (i.e., it is a closest pair of A); (2) both points are in B; and (3) one point is in A, and the other in B. Suppose we determine the closest pair in each

---

```
if  (n is small) {Find the closest pair using the direct approach.
                  return;}
```
// *n* is large
Divide the point set into two roughly equal parts *A* and *B*.
Determine the closest pairs of points in *A* and *B*.
Determine the closest point pair such that one point is in *A* and the other in *B*.
From the three closest pairs computed, select the one with least distance.

Figure 14.13 Finding a closest pair of points

---

of these categories. The pair with the least distance is the overall closest pair. The closest pair in category 1 can be determined by using the closest-pair algorithm recursively on the smaller point set *A*. The closest pair in *B* can be similarly determined.

To determine the closest pair in category 3, we need a different method. The method depends on how the points are divided into *A* and *B*. A reasonable way to do this division is to cut the plane by a vertical line that goes through the median x_i value. All points to the left of this line are in *A*; all to the right are in *B*; and those on the line are distributed between *A* and *B* so as to meet the size requirements on *A* and *B*.

Example 14.8 Consider the 14 points *a* through *n* of Figure 14.14(a). These points are plotted in Figure 14.14(b). The median $x_i = 1$, and the vertical line $x = 1$ is shown as a broken line in Figure 14.14(b). The points to the left of this line (i.e., points *b*, *c*, *h*, and *n*) are in *A*, and those to the right of the line (i.e., points *a*, *e*, *f*, *j*, *k*, and *l*) are in *B*. Of the points *d*, *g*, and *m* that are on the line, two are added to *A* and one to *B* so that *A* and *B* have seven points each. Suppose that *d* and *m* are assigned to *A*, and *g* is assigned to *B*. ∎

Let δ be the smaller of the distances between the points in the closest pairs of *A* and *B*. For a pair in category 3 to be closer than δ, each point of the pair must be less than distance δ from the dividing line. Therefore, we can eliminate from consideration all points that are a distance ≥ δ from this line. The broken line of Figure 14.15 is the dividing line. The shaded box has width 2δ and is centered at the dividing line. Points on or outside the boundary of this box are eliminated. Only the points inside the shaded region need be retained when determining whether there is a category 3 pair with distance less than δ.

Let R_A and R_B, respectively, denote the points of *A* and *B* that remain. If there is a point pair (*p*, *q*) such that $p \in A$, $q \in B$, and *p* and *q* are less than δ apart, then $p \in R_A$ and $q \in R_B$. We can find this point pair by considering the points in R_A one at a time. Suppose that we are considering point *p* of R_A and that *p*'s *y*-coordinate is $p.y$. We need to look only at points *q* in R_B with *y*-

label	a	b	c	d	e	f	g
x_i	2	0.5	0.25	1	3	2	1
y_i	2	0.5	1	2	1	0.7	1
label	h	i	j	k	l	m	n
x_i	0.6	0.9	2	4	1.1	1	0.7
y_i	0.8	0.5	1	2	0.5	1.5	2

(a) The 14 points

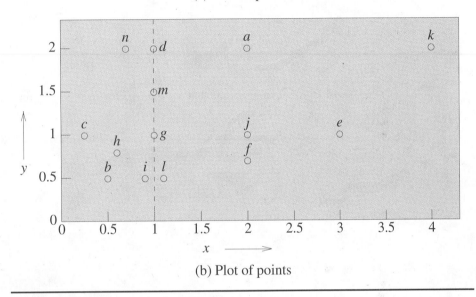

(b) Plot of points

Figure 14.14 Fourteen-point instance

coordinate $q.y$ such that $p.y - \delta < q.y < p.y + \delta$ and see whether any is less than distance δ from p. The region of R_B that contains these points q appears in Figure 14.16(a). Only the points of R_B within the shaded $\delta \times 2\delta$ box need be paired with p to see whether p is part of a category 3 pair with distance less than δ. This $\delta \times 2\delta$ region is p's **comparing region**.

Example 14.9 Consider the 14 points of Example 14.8. The closest point pair in A (see Example 14.8) is (b, h) with a distance of approximately 0.316. The closest point pair in B is (f, j) with a distance of 0.3. Therefore, $\delta = 0.3$. When determining whether there is a category 3 pair with distance less than δ, all points other than d, g, i, l, and m are eliminated from consideration, as each is $\geq \delta$ distant from the dividing line that has x-coordinate 1. We have $R_A = \{d, i, m\}$ and $R_B = \{g, l\}$. Since there are no points in the comparing regions of d and g, only

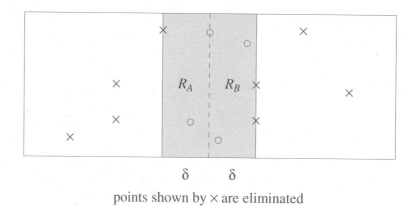

points shown by × are eliminated

Figure 14.15 Eliminating points that are too far from the dividing line

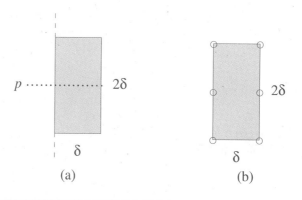

Figure 14.16 Comparing region for p

point i needs to be considered further. The comparing region of i contains only point l. We compute the distance between i and l and find that it is less than δ. (i, l) is therefore the closest pair. ∎

Since all points on the boundary of or inside the $\delta \times 2\delta$ comparing region are at least δ apart, the number of such points cannot exceed six. Figure 14.16(b) shows the only way to place six points while satisfying the minimum distance δ requirement. So each point of R_A is paired with at most six points of R_B when determining a closer category 3 pair.

Choice of Data Structures

To implement the divide-and-conquer algorithm of Figure 14.13, we need to decide what exactly is a "small" instance and also decide how to represent the points. Since the closest pair of a set of less than two points is not defined, we must ensure that our division process does not create sets of size less than two. The creation of sets with fewer than two points can be avoided if our divide-and-conquer algorithm considers sets with fewer than four points as small.

Three quantities: label, x-coordinate, and y-coordinate are associated with each point. Assuming integer labels, each point can be represented using the class Point1 (Program 14.8). The operator <= has been overloaded to facilitate sorting of the point set by x-coordinate, using the merge sort program of Program 14.3.

```
class  Point1 {
   public:
      int operator<=(Point1 a) const
      {return (x <= a.x);}
   private:
      int ID;        // point identifier
      float x, y;   // point coordinates
};

class  Point2 {
   public:
      int operator<=(Point2 a) const
      {return (y <= a.y);}
   private:
      int p;         // index to same point in array X
      float x, y;   // point coordinates
};
```

Program 14.8 Point classes

The input n points may be represented in an array X. Suppose that the points in X have been sorted by their x-coordinate. If at any stage of the division process the points under consideration are X$[l:r]$, then we may obtain A and B by first computing $m = (l + r)/2$. The points X$[l:m]$ are in A, and the remaining points are in B.

After we compute the closest pairs in A and B, we need to compute R_A and R_B and then determine whether there is a closer pair with one point in R_A and the other in R_B. The test of Figure 14.16 may be implemented in a simple way if the points are sorted by their y-coordinate. A list of the points sorted by y-coordinate are maintained in another array using the class Point2 (Program 14.8). Notice that for this class, the operator <= has been overloaded so as to facilitate sorting by *y*-coordinate. The field p is used to index back to the same point in the X array.

With the necessary data structures determined, let us examine the resulting code. First we define a template function dist (Program 14.9) that computes the distance between two points a and b. For our application T may be Point1 or Point2, and dist must be a friend of both Point1 and Point2.

```
template<class T>
inline float dist(const T& u, const T& v)
{// Distance between points u and v.
    float dx = u.x - v.x;
    float dy = u.y - v.y;
    return sqrt(dx * dx + dy * dy);
}
```

Program 14.9 Computing the distance between two points

The function closest (Program 14.10) returns false if the number of points is fewer than two and true if we succeed. Upon success, the closest pair of points is returned in the parameters a and b. The distance between these two points is returned in the parameter d. The code begins by verifying that we have at least two points. Then the points in X are sorted by *x*-coordinate, using MergeSort (Program 14.3). Next the points are copied into an array Y and sorted by *y*-coordinate. Following this sort, $Y[i].y \le Y[i + 1].y$, and for each *i*, $Y[i].p$ gives point *i*'s location in the array X. After the preprocessing, we invoke function close (Program 14.11). This function does the actual computation of the closest pair.

Function close (Program 14.11) determines the closest pair from among the points X[1:r]. These points are assumed to be sorted by their *x*-coordinate. Y[1:r] is the same points sorted by their *y*-coordinate. Z[1:r] is available as space for temporary results. Upon completion the closest pair is returned in a and b. The distance between these two points is returned in d, and the array Y is restored to its input status. The function does not modify the array X.

We begin by taking care of small instances; that is, instances with fewer than four points. Since no instance of size less than two is created by the division process, we need to handle the cases of two and three points. These cases are handled by trying out all possibilities. When the number of points exceeds three, the instance is divided into two smaller instances *A* and *B* by computing m = (l+r)/2. The points X[1:m] are in *A*, and the points X[m+1:r] are in *B*. The corresponding sorted by y lists are created in Z[1:m] and

```
bool closest(Point1 X[], int n, Point1& a,
                               Point1& b, float& d)
{// Find closest pair from n >= 2 points.
 // Return false if fewer than two points.
 // Otherwise, return closest points in a and b.
   if (n < 2) return false;

   // sort on x-coordinate
   MergeSort(X,n);

   // create a point array sorted on y-coordinate
   Point2 *Y = new Point2 [n];
   for (int i = 0; i < n; i++) {
      // copy point i from X to Y and index it
      Y[i].p = i;
      Y[i].x = X[i].x;
      Y[i].y = X[i].y;
      }
   MergeSort(Y,n);   // sort on y-coordinate

   // create temporary array needed by close
   Point2 *Z = new Point2 [n];

   // find closest pair
   close(X,Y,Z,0,n-1,a,b,d);

   // delete arrays and return
   delete [] Y;
   delete [] Z;
   return true;
}
```

Program 14.10 Preprocess and invoke close

Z[m+1:r] from the sorted by y list Y[l:r] by scanning the list Y from left to right and determining which points are in A and which in B. The roles of Y and Z are interchanged, and two recursive calls are made to obtain the closest pairs in A and B. Upon return from these recursive calls, Z is guaranteed to be unaltered, but Y is not. However, only Y[l:r] may have changed. Y[l:r] is reconstructed from Z[l:r] by merging (Program 14.5) the sublists corresponding to A and B.

```
void close(Point1 X[], Point2 Y[], Point2 Z[],
      int l, int r, Point1& a, Point1& b, float& d)
{// X[l:r] is sorted by x-coordinate.
 // Y[l:r] is sorted by y-coordinate.
   if (r-1 == 1) {// two points
      a = X[l];
      b = X[r];
      d = dist(X[l], X[r]);
      return;}

   if (r-1 == 2) {// three points
      // compute distance between all pairs
      float d1 = dist(X[l], X[l+1]);
      float d2 = dist(X[l+1], X[r]);
      float d3 = dist(X[l], X[r]);
      // find closest pair
      if (d1 <= d2 && d1 <= d3) {
         a = X[l];
         b = X[l+1];
         d = d1;
         return;}
      if (d2 <= d3) {a = X[l+1];
                     b = X[r];
                     d = d2;}
      else {a = X[l];
            b = X[r];
            d = d3;}
      return;}
```

Program 14.11 Computation of closest pair of points (continues)

To implement the test of Figure 14.16, we first scan the array segment Y[l:r] that contains the points under consideration sorted by y and accumulate points that are $< \delta$ from the dividing line (see Figure 14.15) in sorted order of y in another array Z[1:k-1]. The pairing of each point p of R_A with all points in its comparing region of R_B is divided into two parts: (1) pairing with points in the comparing region of R_B that have y-coordinate $\geq$ p.y and (2) pairing with points that have y-coordinate $\leq$ p.y. These two parts may be implemented by pairing each point Z[i], $1 \leq$ i $<$ k (regardless of whether it is in R_A or R_B) with a point Z[j], i$<$j, for which Z[j].y-Z[i].y $< \delta$. For each Z[i], the points that get examined lie inside the $2\delta \times \delta$ region shown in Figure 14.17. Since the points in each $\delta \times \delta$ subregion are at least δ apart, the

```
// more than 3 points, divide into two
int m = (l+r)/2;      // X[l:m] in A, rest in B

// create sorted by y lists in Z[l:m] & Z[m+1:r]
int f = 1,      // cursor for Z[l:m]
    g = m+1;   // cursor for Z[m+1:r]
for (int i = 1; i <= r; i++)
   if (Y[i].p > m) Z[g++] = Y[i];
   else Z[f++] = Y[i];

// solve the two parts
close(X,Z,Y,l,m,a,b,d);
float dr;
Point1 ar, br;
close(X,Z,Y,m+1,r,ar,br,dr);

// make (a,b) closer pair of the two
if (dr < d) {a = ar;
          b = br;
              d = dr;}

Merge(Z,Y,l,m,r);// reconstruct Y

// put points within d of mid point in Z
int k = 1;  // cursor for Z
for (int i = 1; i <= r; i++)
   if (fabs(Y[m].x - Y[i].x) < d) Z[k++] = Y[i];

// search for closer category 3 pair
// by checking all pairs from Z[1:k-1]
for (int i = 1; i < k; i++){
   for (int j = i+1; j < k && Z[j].y - Z[i].y < d;
              j++){
      float dp = dist(Z[i], Z[j]);
      if (dp < d) {// closer pair
                d = dp;
                a = X[Z[i].p];
                b = X[Z[j].p];}
      }
   }
}
```

Program 14.11 Computation of closest pair of points (concluded)

number in each subregion cannot exceed four. So the number of points Z[j] that each Z[i] is paired with is at most seven.

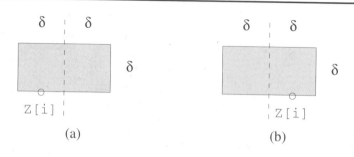

(a)   (b)

Figure 14.17 Region of points paired with Z[i]

Complexity Analysis

Let $t(n)$ denote the time taken by function close on a set of n points. When $n < 4$, $t(n)$ equals some constant d. When $n \geq 4$, it takes $\Theta(n)$ time to divide the instance into two parts, reconstruct Y after the two recursive calls, eliminate points that are too far from the dividing line, and search for a better category 3 pair. The recursive calls take $t(\lceil n/2 \rceil)$ and $t(\lfloor n/2 \rfloor)$ time, respectively. Therefore, we obtain the recurrence

$$t(n) = \begin{cases} d & n < 4 \\ t(\lfloor n/2 \rfloor) + t(\lceil n/2 \rceil) + cn & n \geq 4 \end{cases}$$

which is the same as the recurrence for merge sort. Its solution is $t(n) = \Theta(n\log n)$. The additional work done by function closest consists of sorting X, creating Y and Z, and sorting Y. The total time for this additional work is also $\Theta(n\log n)$. So the overall time complexity of the divide-and-conquer closest-pair code is $\Theta(n\log n)$.

EXERCISES

8. Write a complete program for the defective-chessboard problem. Include modules to welcome the user to the program; input the chessboard size and location of the defect; and output the tiled chessboard. The output is to be provided on a color monitor using colored tiles. No two tiles that share a common boundary should be colored the same. Since the chessboard is a planar figure, it is possible to color the tiles in this way using at most four

colors. However, for this exercise, it is sufficient to devise a greedy coloring heuristic that attempts to use as few colors as possible.

9. Solve recurrence 14.7 using the substitution method.

10. Write a merge sort code that works on chains of elements. The output should be a sorted chain. Make your function a member of the class `Chain` (Program 3.8).

11. Write the function `NaturalMergeSort` that implements a natural merge sort. The input and output configurations are the same as for Program 14.3.

12. Write a natural merge sort code that sorts a chain of elements. Your function should be a member of the class `Chain` (Program 3.8).

13. Replace the last recursive call to `quickSort` in (Program 14.6) with a `while` loop. Compare the average run time of the resulting sort function with that of Program 14.6.

14. Rewrite Program 14.6 using a stack to simulate the recursion. The new code should stack the boundaries of only the smaller of the segments *left* and *right*.

    (a) Show that the stack space needed is O(log n).

    (b) Compare the average run time of Program 14.6 with that of the new code.

15. Show that the worst-case time complexity of `QuickSort` is $\Theta(n^2)$.

16. Suppose that the partitioning into *left*, *middle*, and *right* is always such that *left* and *right* have the same size when n is odd and *left* has one element more than *right* when n is even. Show that under this assumption, the time complexity of Program 14.6 is $\Theta(n\log n)$.

17. Show that $\int s\log_e s \; ds = \dfrac{s^2\log_e s}{2} - \dfrac{s^2}{4}$. Use this result to show that $\displaystyle\int_{2}^{m} s\log_e s \; ds < \dfrac{m^2\log_e m}{2} - \dfrac{m^2}{4}$.

18. Compare the worst-case and average times of Program 14.6 when the median-of-three rule is used to the times when it is not used. Do this comparison experimentally using suitable test data and $n = 10, 20, \cdots, 100, 200, 300, 400, 500, 1000$.

19. Do Exercise 18 using a random number generator rather than the median-of-three rule to select the pivot element.

20. At the end of the quick sort section, we suggested combining two sort methods: quick sort and insertion sort. The combined algorithm is essentially a quick sort that reverts to an insertion sort when the size of a segment is less than or equal to `ChangeOver = nBreak`. Can we obtain a

faster algorithm by using a different value for `ChangeOver`? Why? Experiment with different values of `ChangeOver` and see what happens. Determine the best value of `ChangeOver` for the case of average performance.

21. In this exercise we shall develop a sort procedure with best worst-case performance.

    (a) Compare the worst-case run times of insertion, bubble, selection, heap, merge, and quick sort. The worst-case input data for insertion, bubble, selection, and quick sort are easy to generate. For merge sort, write a program to generate the worst-case data. This program will essentially unmerge a sorted sequence of n elements. For heap sort, estimate the worst-case time using random permutations.

    (b) Use the results of part (a) to obtain a composite sort function that has the best worst-case performance. More likely than not, your composite procedure will include only merge and insertion sort

    (c) Run an experiment to determine the worst-case run time of your composite function. Compare the performance with that of the original sort procedures.

    (d) Plot the worst-case times of the seven sort functions on a single graph sheet.

22. Use the substitution method to solve Equation 14.8 for the case when n is a power of two.

★ 23. Prove Theorem 14.2.

★ 24. Use induction to show that Equation 14.11 implies $t(n) \leq 72cn$ for $n \geq 1$.

25. Program 14.7 needs O(n) space for the recursion stack. This space can be entirely eliminated by replacing the recursive calls with a `while` or `for` loop. Rewrite Program 14.7 in this way. Compare the run time of the two versions of the selection code.

26. Recode Program 14.7 using a random number generator to select the partitioning element. Experimentally compare the average performance of the two codes.

27. Recode Program 14.7 using the median-of-medians rule with $r = 9$.

28. In an attempt to speed Program 14.11, we might eliminate the square root operator from the computation of the distance between two points and instead work with the square of the distance. Finding the closest pair is the same as finding a pair with minimum squared distance. What changes need to be made to Program 14.11? Experiment with the two versions and measure the performance improvement you can achieve.

29. Rewrite Program 14.11 making `Point1` a template class in which the type of the field `ID` is user determined.

30. Devise a faster algorithm to find the closest pair of points when all points are known to lie on a straight line. For example, suppose the points are on a horizontal line. If the points are sorted by x-coordinate, then the nearest pair contains two adjacent points. Although this strategy results in an $O(n\log n)$ algorithm if we use `MergeSort` (Program 14.3), the algorithm has considerably less overhead than Program 14.10 and so runs faster.

31. Consider the closest-pair-of-points problem. Suppose that instead of sorting the points by x-coordinate initially, we use function `Select` (Program 14.7) to find the median x_i and divide the points into A and B.

    (b) Write a high-level description of the resulting algorithm for the closest-pair problem.

    (c) What is the complexity of your algorithm?

    (d) Comment on whether or not you expect the new algorithm to be faster than Program 14.11.

14.3 SOLVING RECURRENCE EQUATIONS

The complexity of many divide-and-conquer algorithms is given by a recurrence of the form

$$t(n) = \begin{cases} t(1) & n = 1 \\ a * t(n/b) + g(n) & n > 1 \end{cases} \tag{14.12}$$

where a and b are known constants. We shall assume that $t(1)$ is known and that n is a power of b (i.e., $n = b^k$). Using the substitution method, we can show that

$$t(n) = n^{\log_b a}[t(1) + f(n)] \tag{14.13}$$

where $f(n) = \sum_{j=1}^{k} h(b^j)$ and $h(n) = g(n)/n^{\log_b a}$.

Figure 14.18 tabulates the asymptotic value of $f(n)$ for various values of $h(n)$. This table allows us to easily obtain the asymptotic value of $t(n)$ for many of the recurrences we encounter when analyzing divide-and-conquer algorithms.

Let us consider some examples using this table. The recurrence for binary search when n is a power of 2 is

$$t(n) = \begin{cases} t(1) & n = 1 \\ t(n/2) + c & n > 1 \end{cases}$$

$h(n)$	$f(n)$
$O(n^r), r < 0$	$O(1)$
$\Theta((\log n)^i), i \geq 0$	$\Theta(((\log n)^{i+1})/(i+1))$
$\Omega(n^r), r > 0$	$\Theta(h(n))$

Figure 14.18 $f(n)$ values for various $h(n)$ values

Comparing this recurrence with (14.11), we see that $a = 1$, $b = 2$, and $g(n) = c$. Therefore, $\log_b(a) = 0$, and $h(n) = g(n)/n^{\log_b a} = c = c(\log n)^0 = \Theta((\log n)^0)$. From Figure 14.18, we obtain $f(n) = \Theta(\log n)$. Therefore, $t(n) = n^{\log_b a}(c + \Theta(\log n)) = \Theta(\log n)$.

For the merge sort recurrence, we obtain $a = 2$, $b = 2$, and $g(n) = cn$. So $\log_b a = 1$, and $h(n) = g(n)/n = c = \Theta((\log n)^0)$. Hence $f(n) = \Theta(\log n)$ and $t(n) = n(t(1) + \Theta(\log n)) = \Theta(n \log n)$.

As another example, consider the recurrence

$$t(n) = 7t(n/2) + 18n^2, n \geq 2 \text{ and } n \text{ a power of } 2$$

that corresponds to the recurrence for Strassen's matrix-multiplication method (recurrence 14.6) with $k = 1$ and $c = 18$. We obtain $a = 7$, $b = 2$, and $g(n) = 18n^2$. Therefore, $\log_b a = \log_2 7 \approx 2.81$ and $h(n) = 18n^2/n^{\log_2 7} = 18n^{2-\log_2 7} = O(n^r)$ where $r = 2 - \log_2 7 < 0$. Therefore, $f(n) = O(1)$. The expression for t(n) is

$$t(n) = n^{\log_2 7}(t(1) + O(1)) = \Theta(n^{\log_2 7})$$

as $t(1)$ is assumed to be a constant.

As a final example, consider the following recurrence

$$t(n) = 9t(n/3) + 4n^6, n \geq 3 \text{ and a power of } 3$$

Comparing this recurrence with (14.11), we obtain $a = 9$, $b = 3$, and $g(n) = 4n^6$. Therefore, $\log_b a = 2$ and $h(n) = 4n^6/n^2 = 4n^4 = \Omega(n^4)$. From Figure 14.12, we see that $f(n) = \Theta(h(n)) = \Theta(n^4)$. Therefore,

$$t(n) = n^2(t(1) + \Theta(n^4)) = \Theta(n^6)$$

as $t(1)$ may be assumed constant.

EXERCISES

32. Use the substitution method to show that Equation 14.13 is the solution to the recurrence 14.12.

33. Use the table of Figure 14.18 to solve the following recurrences. In each case assume $t(1) = 1$.

(a) $t(n) = 10t(n/3) + 11n$, $n \geq 3$ and a power of 3

(b) $t(n) = 10t(n/3) + 11n^5$, $n \geq 3$ and a power of 3

(c) $t(n) = 27t(n/3) + 11n^3$, $n \geq 3$ and a power of 3

(d) $t(n) = 64t(n/4) + 10n^3\log^2 n$, $n \geq 4$ and a power of 4

(e) $t(n) = 9t(n/2) + n^2 2^n$, $n \geq 2$ and a power of 2

(f) $t(n) = 3t(n/8) + n^2 2^n \log n$, $n \geq 8$ and a power of 8

(g) $t(n) = 128t(n/2) + 6n$, $n \geq 2$ and a power of 2

(h) $t(n) = 128t(n/2) + 6n^8$, $n \geq 2$ and a power of 2

(i) $t(n) = 128t(n/2) + 2^n/n$, $n \geq 2$ and a power of 2

(j) $t(n) = 128t(n/2) + \log^3 n$, $n \geq 2$ and a power of 2

14.4   LOWER BOUNDS ON COMPLEXITY

$f(n)$ is an **upper bound** on the complexity of a problem iff at least one algorithm solves this problem in $O(f(n))$ time. One way to establish an upper bound of $f(n)$ on the complexity of a problem is to develop an algorithm whose complexity is $O(f(n))$. Each algorithm developed in this book established an upper bound on the complexity of the problem it solved. For example, until the discovery of Strassen's matrix-multiplication algorithm (Example 14.3), the upper bound on the complexity of matrix multiplication was n^3, as the algorithm of Program 2.24 was already known and this algorithm runs in $\Theta(n^3)$ time. The discovery of Strassen's algorithm reduced the upper bound on the complexity of matrix multiplication to $n^{2.81}$.

$f(n)$ is a **lower bound** on the complexity of a problem iff every algorithm for this problem has complexity $\Omega(f(n))$. To establish a lower bound of $g(n)$ on the complexity of a problem, we must show that *every* algorithm for this problem has complexity $\Omega(g(n))$. Making such a statement is usually quite difficult as we are making a claim about all possible ways to solve a problem, rather than about a single way to solve it.

For many problems we can establish a trivial lower bound based on the number of inputs and/or outputs. For example, every algorithm that sorts n elements must have complexity $\Omega(n)$, as every sorting algorithm must examine each element at least once or run the risk that the unexamined elements are in the wrong place. Similarly, every algorithm to multiply two $n \times n$ matrices must have complexity $\Omega(n^2)$, as the result contains n^2 elements and it takes $\Omega(1)$ time to produce each of these elements, and so on. Nontrivial lower bounds are known for a very limited number of problems.

In this section we establish nontrivial lower bounds on two of the divide-and-conquer problems studied in this chapter—finding the minimum and maximum of n elements and sorting. For both of these problems we limit ourselves to **comparison algorithms**. These algorithms perform their task by making comparisons between pairs of elements and possibly moving elements around; they do not perform other operations on elements. The minmax algorithms of Chapter 2, as well as those proposed in this chapter, satisfy this property, as do all the sort methods studied in this book except for bin sort and radix sort (Sections 3.8.1 and 3.8.2).

14.4.1 Lower Bound for the Minmax Problem

Program 14.1 gave a divide-and-conquer function to find the minimum and maximum of n elements. This function makes $\lceil 3n/2 \rceil - 2$ comparisons between pairs of elements. We shall show that every comparison algorithm for the minmax problem must make at least $\lceil 3/n \rceil - 2$ comparisons between the elements. For purposes of the proof, we assume that the n elements are distinct. This assumption does not affect the generality of the proof, as distinct element inputs form a subset of the input space. In addition, every minmax algorithm must work correctly on these inputs as well as on those that have duplicates.

The proof uses the **state space method**. In this method we describe the start, intermediate, and finish states of every algorithm for the problem as well as how a comparison algorithm can go from one state to another. Then we determine the minimum number of transitions needed to go from the start state to the finish state. This minimum number of transitions is a lower bound on the complexity of the problem. The start, intermediate, and finish states of an algorithm are abstract entities, and there is no requirement that an algorithm keep track of its state explicitly.

For the minmax problem, the algorithm state can be described by a tuple (a,b,c,d) where a is the number of elements that the minmax algorithm still considers candidates for the maximum and minimum elements; b is the number of elements that are no longer candidates for the minimum, but are still candidates for the maximum; c is the number of elements that are no longer candidates for the maximum, but are still candidates for the minimum; and d is the number of elements that the minmax algorithm has determined to be neither the minimum nor the maximum. Let A, B, C, and D denote the elements in each of the preceding categories.

When the minmax algorithm starts, all n elements are candidates for the min and max. So the start state is $(n,0,0,0)$. When the algorithm finishes, there are no elements in A, one in B, one in C, and $n-2$ in D. Therefore, the finish state is $(0,1,1,n-2)$. Transitions from one state to another are made on the basis of comparisons between pairs of elements. When two elements from A are compared, the smaller element can be placed in C and the larger in B. (Recall that all elements are distinct, so we cannot get an equal compare.) The following state transition is possible:

$$(a,b,c,d) \rightarrow (a-2,b+1,c+1,d)$$

Other possible transitions follow.

- When comparisons between elements of B are made, the possible transition is

$$(a,b,c,d) \rightarrow (a,b-1,c,d+1)$$

- When comparisons between elements of C are made, the possible transition is

$$(a,b,c,d) \rightarrow (a,b,c-1,d+1)$$

- When an element of A is compared with an element of B, the possible transitions are
$(a,b,c,d) \rightarrow (a-1,b,c,d+1)$ (the A element is greater than the B element)
$(a,b,c,d) \rightarrow (a-1,b,c+1,d)$ (the A element is smaller than the B element)

- When an element of A is compared with an element of C, the possible transitions are
$(a,b,c,d) \rightarrow (a-1,b,c,d+1)$ (the A element is smaller than the C element)
$(a,b,c,d) \rightarrow (a-1,b+1,c,d)$ (the A element is greater than the C element)

Although other comparisons are possible, none of these comparisons can guarantee a state change. Examining the possible state changes, we see that when n is even, the quickest way to go from the start state $(n,0,0,0)$ to the finish state $(0,1,1,n-2)$ is to do $n/2$ comparisons between elements in A, $n/2-1$ between those in B, and $n/2-1$ between those in C. The total number of comparisons is $3n/2-2$. When n is odd, the fastest way to go from the start state to the finish state is to make $\lfloor n/2 \rfloor$ comparisons between elements in A, $\lfloor n/2 \rfloor - 1$ comparisons between elements in B, $\lfloor n/2 \rfloor - 1$ comparisons between elements in C, and up to two more comparisons involving the remaining element of A. The total count is $\lceil 3n/2 \rceil - 2$.

Since no comparison algorithm for the minmax problem can go from the start state to the finish state making fewer than $\lceil 3n/2 \rceil - 2$ comparisons between pairs of elements, this number is a lower bound on the number of comparisons every minmax comparison algorithm must make. Hence Program 14.1 is an optimal comparison algorithm for the minmax problem.

14.4.2 Lower Bound for Sorting

A lower bound of $n \log n$ on the worst-case complexity of every comparison algorithm that sorts n elements can be established using the state space method. This time the algorithm state is given by the number of permutations of the n elements that are still candidates for the output permutation. When the sort algorithm starts, all $n!$ permutations of the n elements are candidates for the sorted output and when the algorithm terminates, only one candidate permutation remains. (As for the minmax problem, we assume the n elements to be sorted are distinct.)

When two elements a_i and a_j are compared, the current set of candidate permutations is divided into two groups—one group retains permutations that are consistent with the outcome $a_i < a_j$, and the other set retains those that are consistent with the outcome $a_i > a_j$. Since we have assumed that the elements are distinct, the outcome $a_i = a_j$ is not possible. For example, suppose that $n = 3$ and that the first comparison is between a_1 and a_3. Prior to this comparison, as far as the algorithm is concerned, all six permutations of the elements are candidates for the sorted permutation. If $a_1 < a_3$, then the best the algorithm can do is eliminate the permutations (a_3, a_1, a_2), (a_3, a_2, a_1), and (a_2, a_3, a_1). The remaining three permutations must be retained as candidates for the output.

If the current candidate set has m permutations, then a comparison produces two groups, one of which must have at least $\lceil m/2 \rceil$ permutations. A worst-case execution of the sort algorithm begins with a candidate set of size $n!$, reduces this to one of size at least $n!/2$, then reduces the candidate set further to one of size at least $n!/4$, and so on until the size of the candidate set becomes one. The number of reduction steps (and hence comparisons needed) is at least $\lceil \log n! \rceil$.

Since $n! \geq \lceil n/2 \rceil^{\lceil n/2 \rceil - 1}$, $\log n! \geq (n/2 - 1)\log(n/2) = \Omega(n \log n)$. Hence every sort algorithm that is a comparison algorithm must make $\Omega(n \log n)$ comparisons in the worst case.

We can arrive at this same lower bound using a **decision-tree** proof. In such a proof we model the progress of an algorithm using a tree. At each internal node of this tree, the algorithm makes a comparison and moves to one of the children based on the outcome of this comparison. External nodes are nodes at which the algorithm terminates. Figure 14.19 shows the decision tree for `InsertionSort` (Program 2.15) while sorting the three-element sequence `a[0:2]`. Each internal node has a label of the type `i:j`. This label denotes a comparison between `a[i]` and `a[j]`. If `a[i]` < `a[j]`, the algorithm moves to the left child. A right child move occurs when `a[i]` > `a[j]`. Since the elements are distinct, the case `a[i]` = `a[j]` is not possible. The external nodes are labeled with the sorted permutation that is generated. The left-most path in the decision tree of Figure 14.19 is followed when `a[1]` < `a[0]`, `a[2]` < `a[0]`, and `a[2]` < `a[1]`; the permutation at the left-most external node is `(a[2],a[1],a[0])`.

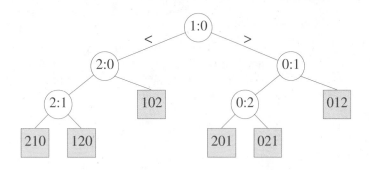

Figure 14.19 Decision tree for `InsertionSort` when n = 3

Notice that each leaf of a decision tree for a comparison sort algorithm defines a unique output permutation. Since every correct sorting algorithm must be able to produce all $n!$ permutations of n inputs, the decision tree for every correct comparison sort algorithm must have at least $n!$ external nodes. Because a tree whose height is h has at most 2^h external nodes, the decision tree for a correct comparison sort algorithm must have a height that is at least $\lceil \log_2 n! \rceil = \Omega(n \log n)$. Therefore, every comparison sort algorithm must perform $\Omega(n \log n)$ comparisons in the worst case. Further, since the average height of every binary tree that has $n!$ external nodes is also $\Omega(n \log n)$, the average complexity of every comparison sort algorithm is also $\Omega(n \log n)$.

The preceding lower-bound proof shows that heap sort and merge sort are optimal worst-case sort methods (as far as asymptotic complexity is concerned) and heap sort, merge sort, and quick sort are optimal average-case methods.

EXERCISES

34. Use the state space method to show that every comparison algorithm that finds the maximum of n elements makes at least $n - 1$ comparisons between pairs of elements.

35. Show that $n! \geq \lceil n/2 \rceil^{\lceil n/2 \rceil - 1}$.

36. Draw the decision tree for `InsertionSort` when $n = 4$.

37. Draw the decision tree for `MergeSort` (Program 14.3) when $n = 4$.

38. Let $a_1, \cdots, a_n$ be a sequence of n elements. Elements a_i and a_j, $i < j$, are **inverted** iff $a_i > a_j$. The number of pairs (i, j) such that a_i and a_j are inverted is the **inversion number** of the element sequence.

(a) What is the inversion number of the sequence 6, 2, 3, 1?

(b) What is the maximum inversion number possible for a sequence of n elements?

(c) Suppose that a sort method compares only pairs of adjacent elements and then possibly swaps them (this is essentially what bubble, selection, and insertion sort do). Show that sort methods of this type must perform $\Omega(n^2)$ comparisons.

CHAPTER 15

DYNAMIC PROGRAMMING

BIRD'S-EYE VIEW

Dynamic programming is arguably the most difficult of the five design methods we are studying. It has its foundations in the principle of optimality. We can use this method to obtain elegant and efficient solutions to many problems that cannot be so solved using either the greedy or divide-and-conquer methods. After describing the method, we consider its application to the solution of the knapsack, image-compression, matrix-multiplication-chains, shortest-paths, noncrossing subset of nets, and component-folding problems.

15.1 THE METHOD

In dynamic programming, as in the greedy method, we view the solution to a problem as the result of a sequence of decisions. In the greedy method we make irrevocable decisions one at a time using a greedy criterion. However, in dynamic programming, we examine the decision sequence to see whether an optimal decision sequence contains optimal decision subsequences.

Example 15.1 [*Shortest Path*] Consider the digraph of Figure 12.2. We wish to find a shortest path from the source vertex $s = 1$ to the destination vertex $d = 5$. We need to make decisions on the intermediate vertices. The choices for the first decision are 2, 3, and 4. That is, from vertex 1 we may move to any one of these vertices. Suppose we decide to move to vertex 3. Now we need to decide on how to get from 3 to 5. If we go from 3 to 5 in a suboptimal way, then the 1-to-5 path constructed cannot be optimal, even under the restriction that from vertex 1 we must go to vertex 3. For example, if we use the suboptimal path 3, 2, 5 with length 9, the constructed 1-to-5 path 1, 3, 2, 5 has length 11. Replacing the suboptimal path 3, 2, 5 with an optimal one 3, 4, 5 results in the path 1, 3, 4, 5 of length 9.

So for this shortest-path problem, suppose that our first decision gets us to some vertex v. Although we do not know how to make this first decision, we do know that the remaining decisions must be optimal for the problem of going from v to d. ∎

Example 15.2 [*0/1 Knapsack Problem*] Consider the 0/1 knapsack problem of Section 13.4. We need to make decisions on the values of $x_1, \cdots, x_n$. Suppose we are deciding the values of the x_is in the order 1, 2, $\cdots, n$. If we set $x_1 = 0$, then the available knapsack capacity for the remaining objects (i.e., objects 2, 3, $\cdots, n$) is c. If we set $x_1 = 1$, the available knapsack capacity is $c - w_1$. Let $r \in \{c, c - w_1\}$ denote the remaining knapsack capacity.

Following the first decision, we are left with the problem of filling a knapsack with capacity r. The available objects (i.e., 2 through n) and the available capacity r define the *problem state* following the first decision. Regardless of whether x_1 is 0 or 1, $[x_2, \cdots, x_n]$ must be an optimal solution for the problem state following the first decision. If not, there is a solution $[y_2, \cdots, y_n]$ that provides greater profit for the problem state following the first decision. So $[x_1, y_2, ..., y_n]$ is a better solution for the initial problem.

Suppose that $n = 3$, $w = [100, 14, 10]$, $p = [20, 18, 15]$, and $c = 116$. If we set $x_1 = 1$, then following this decision, the available knapsack capacity is 16. $[x_2, x_3] = [0, 1]$ is a feasible solution to the two-object problem that remains. It returns a profit of 15. However, it is not an optimal solution to the remaining two-object problem, as $[x_2, x_3] = [1, 0]$ is feasible and returns a greater profit of 18. So $x = [1, 0, 1]$ can be improved to [1, 1, 0]. If we set $x_1 = 0$, the available capacity for the two-object instance that remains is 116. If the subsequence $[x_2, x_3]$ is not an optimal solution for this remaining instance, then $[x_1, x_2, x_3]$ cannot be optimal for the initial instance. ■

Example 15.3 [*Airfares*] A certain airline has the following airfare structure: From Atlanta to New York or Chicago, or from Los Angeles to Atlanta, the fare is \$100; from Chicago to New York, it is \$20; and for passengers connecting through Atlanta, the Atlanta to Chicago segment is only \$20. A routing from Los Angeles to New York involves decisions on the intermediate airports. If problem states are encoded as (origin, destination) pairs, then following a decision to go from Los Angeles to Atlanta, the problem state is, we are at Atlanta and need to get to New York. The cheapest way to go from Atlanta to New York is a direct flight with cost \$100. Using this direct flight results in a total Los Angeles-to-New York cost of \$200. However, the cheapest routing is Los Angeles—Atlanta—Chicago—New York with a cost of \$140, which involves using a suboptimal decision subsequence for the go from Atlanta to New York problem (Atlanta—Chicago—New York).

If instead we encode the problem state as a triple (*tag*, *origin*, *destination*) where *tag* is zero for connecting flights and one for all others, then once we reach Atlanta, the state becomes (0, Atlanta, New York) for which the optimal routing is through Chicago. ■

When optimal decision sequences contain optimal decision subsequences, we can establish recurrence equations, called **dynamic-programming recurrence equations**, that enable us to solve the problem in an efficient way.

Example 15.4 [*0/1 Knapsack*] In Example 15.2, we saw that for the 0/1 knapsack problem, optimal decision sequences were composed of optimal subsequences. Let $f(i,y)$ denote the value of an optimal solution to the knapsack instance with remaining capacity y and remaining objects $i, i+1, \cdots, n$. From Example 15.2, it follows that

$$f(n,y) = \begin{cases} p_n & \text{if } y \geq w_n \\ 0 & 0 \leq y < w_n \end{cases} \tag{15.1}$$

and

$$f(i,y) = \begin{cases} \max\{f(i+1,y), f(i+1,y-w_i) + p_i\} & \text{if } y \geq w_i \\ f(i+1,y) & 0 \leq y < w_i \end{cases} \tag{15.2}$$

By making use of the observation that optimal decision sequences are made up of optimal subsequences, we have obtained a recurrence for f. $f(1,c)$ is the value of the optimal solution to the knapsack problem we started with. Recurrence 15.2 may be used to determine $f(1,c)$ either recursively or iteratively. In the iterative approach, we start with $f(n,*)$, as given by Equation 15.1 and then obtain $f(i,*)$ in the order $i = n-1, n-2, \cdots, 2$ using recurrence 15.2. Finally, $f(1,c)$ is computed using 15.2.

For the instance of Example 15.2, we see that $f(3,y) = 0$ if $0 \leq y < 10$, and 15 if $y \geq 10$. Using recurrence (15.2), we obtain $f(2,y) = 0$ if $0 \leq y < 10$, 15 if $10 \leq y < 14$; 18 if $14 \leq y < 24$; and 33 if $y \geq 24$. The optimal solution has value $f(1,116) = \max\{f(2,116), f(2, 116 - w_1) + p_1\} = \max\{f(2,116), f(2,16) + 20\}$ $= \max\{33, 38\} = 38$.

To obtain the values of the x_is, we proceed as follows: If $f(1,c) = f(2,c)$, then we may set $x_1 = 0$ because we can utilize the c units of capacity getting a return of $f(1,c)$ from objects 2, $\cdots$, n. In case $f(1,c) \neq f(2,c)$, then we must set $x_1 = 1$. Next we need to find an optimal solution that uses the remaining capacity $c - w_1$. This solution has value $f(2,c-w_1)$. Proceeding in this way, we may determine the value of all the x_is.

For our sample instance, we see that $f(2,116) = 33 \neq f(1,116)$. Therefore, $x_1 = 1$ and we need to find x_2 and x_3 so as to obtain a return of $38 - p_1 = 18$ and use a capacity of at most $116 - w_1 = 16$. Note that $f(2,16) = 18$. Since $f(3,16) = 14 \neq f(2,16)$, $x_2 = 1$; the remaining capacity is $16 - w_2 = 2$. Since $f(3,2) = 0$, we set $x_3 = 0$. ∎

When dynamic programming is used, we first set up a recurrence for the value of the optimal solution by making use of the **principle of optimality**, which states that no matter what the first decision, the remaining decisions must be optimal with respect to the state that results from this first decision. Since the principle of optimality may not hold for some formulations of some problems, it is necessary to verify that it does hold for the problem being solved. *Dynamic programming cannot be applied when this principle does not hold.* After we solve the recurrence equation for the value of the optimal solution, we perform a **traceback** step in which the solution itself is constructed.

It is very tempting to write a simple recursive program to solve the dynamic-programming recurrence. *However, as we shall see in subsequent sections, unless care is taken to avoid recomputing previously computed values, the recursive program will have prohibitive complexity.* When the recursive program is designed to avoid this recomputation, the complexity is drastically reduced. The dynamic-programming recurrence may also be solved by iterative code that naturally avoids recomputation of already computed values. Although this iterative code has the same time complexity as the "careful" recursive code, the former has the advantage of not requiring additional space for the recursion stack. As a result, the iterative code generally runs faster than the careful recursive code.

15.2 APPLICATIONS

15.2.1 0/1 Knapsack Problem

Recursive Solution

The dynamic-programming recurrence equations for the 0/1 knapsack problem were developed in Example 15.4. A natural way to solve a recurrence such as 15.2 for the value $f(1,c)$ of an optimal knapsack packing is by a recursive program such as Program 15.1. This code assumes that p, w, and n are global and that p is of type int. The invocation F(1,c) returns the value of $f(1,c)$.

```
int F(int i, int y)
{// Return f(i,y).
   if (i == n) return (y < w[n]) ? 0 : p[n];
   if (y < w[i]) return F(i+1,y);
   return max(F(i+1,y), F(i+1,y-w[i]) + p[i]);
}
```

Program 15.1 Recursive function for knapsack problem

Let $t(n)$ be the time this code takes to solve an instance with n objects. We see that $t(1) = a$ and $t(n) \le 2t(n-1) + b$ for $n > 1$. Here a and b are constants. This recurrence solves to $t(n) = O(2^n)$.

Example 15.5 Consider the case $n = 5$, $p = [6, 3, 5, 4, 6]$, $w = [2, 2, 6, 5, 4]$, and $c = 10$. To determine $f(1,10)$, function F is invoked as F(1,10). The recursive calls made are shown by the tree of Figure 15.1. Each node has been labeled by the value of y. Nodes on level j have $i = j$. So the root denotes the invocation F(1,10). Its left and right children, respectively, denote the invocations F(2,10) and F(2,8). In all, 28 invocations are made. Notice that several invocations redo the work of previous invocations. For example, $f(3,8)$ is computed twice, as are $f(4,8)$, $f(4,6)$, $f(4,2)$, $f(5,8)$, $f(5,6)$, $f(5,3)$, $f(5,2)$, and $f(5,1)$. If we save the results of previous invocations, we can reduce the number of invocations to 19 because we eliminate the shaded nodes of Figure 15.1. ∎

As observed in Example 15.5, Program 15.1 is doing more work than necessary. To avoid computing the same $f(i,y)$ value more than once, we may keep a list L of $f(i,y)$s that have already been computed. The elements of this list are triples of the form $(i,y,f(i,y))$. Before making an invocation F(i,y), we see whether the list L contains a triple of the form $(i,y,*)$ where $*$ denotes a wildcard. If so, $f(i,y)$ is retrieved from the list. If not, the invocation is made

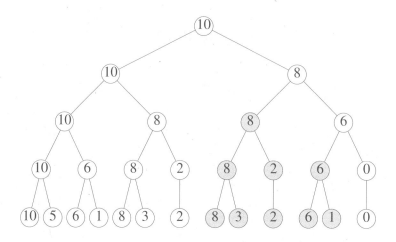

Figure 15.1 Tree of recursive calls

and then the triple $(i,y,f(i,y))$ added to L. L may be stored as a hash table (see Section 7.4) or as a binary search tree (see Chapter 11).

Iterative Solution with Integer Weights

We can devise a fairly simple iterative algorithm (Program 15.2) to solve for $f(1,c)$ when the weights are integer. This algorithm is based on the strategy outlined in Example 15.4, and it computes each $f(i,y)$ exactly once. Program 15.2 uses a two-dimensional array `f[][]` to store the values of the function f. The code for the traceback needed to determine the x_i values that result in the optimal filling appears in Program 15.2.

The complexity of function `Knapsack` is $\Theta(nc)$ and that of `Traceback` is $\Theta(n)$.

Tuple Method *(Optional)*

There are two drawbacks to the code of Program 15.2. First, it requires that the weights be integer. Second, it is slower than Program 15.1 when the knapsack capacity is large. In particular, if $c > 2^n$, its complexity is $\Omega(n2^n)$. We can overcome both of these shortcomings by using a tuple approach in which for each i, $f(i,y)$ is stored as an ordered list $P(i)$ of pairs $(y,f(i,y))$ that correspond to the y values at which the function f changes. The pairs in each $P(i)$ are in increasing order of y. Also, since $f(i,y)$ is a nondecreasing function of y, the pairs are also in increasing order of $f(i,y)$.

```
template<class T>
void Knapsack(T p[], int w[], int c, int n, T** f)
{// Compute f[i][y] for all i and y.

    // initialize f[n][]
    for (int y = 0; y < w[n]; y++)
       f[n][y] = 0;
    for (int y = w[n]; y <= c; y++)
       f[n][y] = p[n];

    // compute remaining f's
    for (int i = n - 1; i > 1; i--) {
       for (int y = 0; y < w[i]; y++)
          f[i][y] = f[i+1][y];
       for (int y = w[i]; y <= c; y++)
          f[i][y] = max(f[i+1][y],
                        f[i+1][y-w[i]] + p[i]);
    }
    f[1][c] = f[2][c];
    if (c >= w[1])
       f[1][c] = max(f[1][c], f[2][c-w[1]] + p[1]);
}

template<class T>
void Traceback(T **f, int w[], int c, int n, int x[])
{// Compute x for optimal filling.
    for (int i = 1; i < n; i++)
       if (f[i][c] == f[i+1][c]) x[i] = 0;
       else {x[i] = 1;
             c -= w[i];}
    x[n] = (f[n][c]) ? 1 : 0;
}
```

Program 15.2 Iterative computation of f and x

Example 15.6 For the knapsack instance of Example 15.5, the f function is given in Figure 15.2. When $i = 5$, the function f is completely specified by the pairs $P(5) = [(0,0), (4,6)]$. The pairs $P(i)$ for $i = 4$, 3, and 2 are $[(0,0), (4,6), (9,10)]$, $[(0,0), (4,6), (9,10), (10,11)]$, and $[(0,0), (2,3), (4,6), (6,9), (9,10), (10,11)]$.

To compute $f(1,10)$, we use recurrence 15.2 which yields $f(1,10) = \max\{f(2,10), f(2,8) + p_1\}$. From $P(2)$, we get $f(2,10) = 11$, and $f(2,8) = 9$ ($f(2,8) = 9$ comes from the pair (6,9)). Therefore, $f(1,10) = \max\{11, 15\} = 15$.

To determine the x_i values, we begin with x_1. Since $f(1,10) = f(2,6) + p_1$, $x_5 = 1$. Since $f(2,6) = f(3,6-w_2) + p_2 = f(3,4) + p_2$, $x_2 = 1$. $x_3 = x_4 = 0$ because $f(3,4) = f(4,4) = f(5,4)$. Finally, since $f(5,4) \neq 0$, $x_5 = 1$. ∎

						y					
i	0	1	2	3	4	5	6	7	8	9	10
5	0	0	0	0	6	6	6	6	6	6	6
4	0	0	0	0	6	6	6	6	6	10	10
3	0	0	0	0	6	6	6	6	6	10	11
2	0	0	3	3	6	6	9	9	9	10	11

Figure 15.2 f function for Example 15.6

If we examine the pairs in each $P(i)$, we see that each pair $(y, f(i,y))$ corresponds to a different combination of 0/1 assignments to the variables x_i, $\cdots, x_n$. Let (a,b) and (c,d) be pairs that correspond to two different 0/1 assignments to x_i, $\cdots, x_n$. If $a \geq c$ and $b < d$, then (a,b) is dominated by (b,c). Dominated assignments do not contribute pairs to $P(i)$. If two or more assignments result in the same pair, only one is in $P(i)$.

Under the assumption that $w_n \leq c$, $P(n) = [(0,0), (w_n,p_n)]$. These two pairs correspond to x_n equal to zero and one, respectively. For each i, $P(i)$ may be obtained from $P(i+1)$. First, compute the ordered set of pairs Q such that (s,t) is a pair of Q iff $w_i \leq s \leq c$ and $(s-w_i, t-p_i)$ is a pair of $P(i+1)$. Now Q has the pairs with $x_i = 1$ and $P(i+1)$ has those with $x_i = 0$. Next, merge Q and $P(i+1)$ eliminating dominated as well as duplicate pairs to get $P(i)$.

Example 15.7 Consider the data of Example 15.6. $P(5) = [(0,0), (4,6)]$, so $Q = [(5,4), (9,10)]$. When merging $P(5)$ and Q to create $P(4)$, the pair $(5,4)$ is eliminated because it is dominated by the pair $(4,6)$. As a result, $P(4) = [(0,0), (4,6), (9,10)]$. To compute $P(3)$, we first obtain $Q = [(6,5), (10,11)]$ from $P(4)$. Next, merging with $P(4)$ yields $P(3) = [(0,0), (4,6), (9,10), (10,11)]$. Finally, to get $P(2)$, $Q = [(2,3), (6,9)]$ is computed from $P(3)$. Merging $P(3)$ and Q yields $P(2) = [(0,0), (2,3), (4,6), (6,9), (9,10), (10,11)]$. ∎

Since the pairs in each $P(i)$ represent different 0/1 assignments to x_i, $\cdots$, x_n, no $P(i)$ has more than 2^{n-i+1} pairs. When computing $P(i)$, Q may be computed in $\Theta(|P(i+1)|)$ time. The time needed to merge $P(i+1)$ and Q is also $\Theta(|P(i+1)|)$. So all the $P(i)$s may be computed in $\Theta(\sum_{i=2}^{n} |P(i+1)|) = O(2^n)$ time. When the weights are integer, $|P(i)| \leq c + 1$. In this case the complexity becomes $O(\min\{nc, 2^n\})$.

15.2.2 Image Compression

As defined in Section 6.4.3, a digitized image is an $m \times m$ matrix of pixels. In this section, we assume that each pixel has a gray value between 0 and 255. So it takes at most 8 bits to store a pixel. If each pixel is stored using the maximum of 8 bits, the total space needed is $8m^2$ bits. We can reduce the storage needs by using a **variable bit scheme** in which different pixels are stored using a different number of bits.

Pixel values 0 and 1 need only 1 bit each; values 2 and 3 need 2 bits each; values 4, 5, 6, and 7 need only 3 bits each; and so forth. When this variable bit scheme is used, we go through the following steps:

1. [*Linearize image*] The $m \times m$ image matrix is converted into a $1 \times m^2$ matrix using (say) the snakelike row-major ordering in Figure 15.3(a).

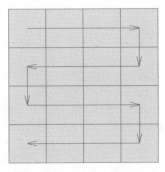

(a) Snakelike row-major order   (b) Grayscale values

Figure 15.3 A digitized image

2. [*Create segments*] The pixels are divided into segments such that the pixels in each segment require the same number of bits. Each segment is a contiguous chunk of pixels, and segments are limited to 256 pixels. If there are more than 256 contiguous pixels with the same bit requirement, they are represented by two or more segments.

3. [*Create files*] Three files *SegmentLength*, *BitsPerPixel*, and *Pixels* are created. The first of these files contains the length (minus one) of the segments created in step 2. Each entry in this file is 8 bits long. The file *BitsPerPixel* gives the number of bits (minus one) used to store each pixel in the segment. Each entry in this file is 3 bits long. The file *Pixels* is a binary string of pixels stored in the variable-bit format.

4.   [*Compress files*] Each of the three files created in 3 is compressed to reduce its space requirements.

The performance of this compression scheme (in terms of achieved compression ratio) depends very much on the presence of long segments that require a small number of bits.

Example 15.8 Consider the 4×4 image of Figure 15.3(b). The gray values in snakelike row-major order are 10, 9, 12, 40, 50, 35, 15, 12, 8, 10, 9, 15, 11, 130, 160, and 240. The number of bits needed to store each of these pixels is 4, 4, 4, 6, 6, 6, 4, 4, 4, 4, 4, 4, 4, 8, 8, and 8, respectively. When the pixels are divided into segments of equal bit requirements, we get the four segments [10, 9, 12], [40, 50, 35], [15, 12, 8, 10, 9, 15, 11], and [130, 160, 240].

The file *SegmentLength* is 2, 2, 6, 2 and *BitsPerSegment* is 3, 5, 3, 7. The file *Pixels* contains the 16 gray values in snakelike row-major order. The first three are stored using 4 bits each, the next three using 6 bits each, the next seven using 4 bits each, and the last three using 8 bits each. The first 30 bits of this file represents the first six pixels. These 30 bits are

$$1010\ 1001\ 1100\ 111000\ 110010\ 100011$$

The space needed to store the three files is 32 bits for *SegmentLength*, 12 bits for *BitsPerSegment*, and 82 bits for *Pixels*. The total is 126 bits. If the image was stored using a fixed 8 bits per pixel, the storage requirements would be $8 \times 16 = 128$ bits. For the sample image, we achieve a modest saving of 2 bits. ∎

Suppose that following step 2, we have n segments. The length of a segment and the bits per pixel for that segment are referred to as the **segment header**. Each segment header needs 11 bits of space. Let l_i and b_i, respectively, denote the length and bits per pixel for segment i. The space needed to store the pixels of segment i is $l_i * b_i$. The total space required for the three files created in step 2 is $11n + \sum_{i=1}^{n} l_i b_i$. The space requirements can be reduced by combining some pairs of adjacent segments into one. If segments i and $i+1$ are combined, then the combined segment has length $l_i + l_{i+1}$. Each pixel now has to be stored using $\max\{b_i, b_{i+1}\}$ bits. Although this technique increases the space needed by the file *Pixels*, it reduces the number of headers by one.

Example 15.9 If we combine segments one and two of Example 15.8, the *SegmentLength* file becomes 5, 6, 2 and *BitsPerSegment* becomes 5, 3, 7. The first 36 bits of *Pixels* now represent the new first segment. These bits are

$$001010\ 001001\ 001100\ 111000\ 110010\ 100011$$

The remainder of *Pixels* is unchanged. The space needed by the files *SegmentLength* and *BitsPerPixel* has decreased by 11 bits as the number of headers is one less than before. The space needed by *Pixels* has increased by 6 bits for a net savings of 5 bits. The total space requirements are now 121 bits. ■

In this section we wish to develop an algorithm to take the n segments created in step 2 and combine adjacent segments so as to produce a new set of segments that has minimum space requirements. After we combine the segments, we can use other techniques such as the LZW method (Section 7.5) and Huffman coding (Section 9.5.3) to further compress the three files.

Let s_q be the space requirements for an optimal combining of the first q segments. Define $s_0 = 0$. For an instance with $i > 0$ segments, suppose that, in an optimal combining C, segment i is combined with segments $i-1, i-2, \cdots,$ and $i-r+1$, but not with segment $i-r$. The space s_i needed by the combining C is

space needed by segments 1 through $i - r + lsum(i-r+1,i) * bmax(i-r+1,i) + 11$

where $lsum(a,b) = \sum_{j=a}^{b} l_j$ and $bmax(a,b) = \max\{b_a, \cdots, b_b\}$. If segments 1 through $i - r$ are not combined optimally in C, then we change their combining to one with a smaller space requirement and hence reduce the space requirement of C. So in an optimal combining C, segments 1 through $i - r$ must also be combined optimally. That is, the principle of optimality holds. With this observation, the space requirements for C become

$$s_i = s_{i-r} + lsum(i-r+1,i) * bmax(i-r+1,i) + 11$$

The only possibilities for r are the numbers 1 through i for which *lsum* does not exceed 256 (recall that segment lengths are limited to 256). Although we do not know which is the case, we do know that since C has a minimum space requirement, r must yield the minimum space requirement over all choices. So we get the recurrence

$$s_i = \min_{\substack{1 \le k \le i \\ lsum(i-k+1,i) \le 256}} \{s_{i-k} + lsum(i-k+1,i) * bmax(i-k+1,i)\} + 11 \qquad (15.3)$$

Let kay_i denote the value of k that yields the minimum. s_n is the space requirement of an optimal combining of the n segments, and an optimal combining may be constructed using the *kay* values.

Example 15.10 Suppose that five segments are created following step 2. Let their lengths be [6, 3, 10, 2, 3] and let their bit per pixel requirements be [1, 2, 3, 2, 1]. To compute s_n using Equation 15.3, we need the values of $s_{n-1}, \cdots, s_0$.

s_0 is zero. For s_1, we get

$$s_1 = s_0 + l_1*b_1 + 11 = 17$$

and $kay_1 = 1$. s_2 is given by

$$
\begin{aligned}
s_2 &= \min\{s_1 + l_2b_2, \, s_0 + (l_1+l_2)*\max\{b_1,b_2\}\} + 11 \\
&= \min\{17 + 6, \, 0 + 9*2\} + 11 \\
&= 29
\end{aligned}
$$

and $kay_2 = 2$. Continuing in this way, we obtain $s_1 \cdots s_5 = [17, 29, 67, 73, 82]$ and $kay_1 \cdots kay_5 = [1, 2, 2, 3, 4]$.

Since $s_5 = 82$, the optimal space combining uses 82 bits of space. We can determine this combining by beginning at kay_5. Since $kay_5 = 4$, s_5 was obtained from Equation 15.3 by setting $k = 4$. The optimal combining consists of the optimal combining for segments 1 through $(5-4) = 1$ followed by the segment that results from combining segments 2, 3, 4, and 5. We are left with just two segments, the original segment 1 and the combination of segments 2 through 5. ∎

Recursive Solution

Recurrence 15.3 may be solved recursively for s_i and kay_i. The recursive code appears in Program 15.3.   `l`, `b`, and `kay` are one-dimensional global integer arrays.   `L` is the segment length restriction (256), and `header` is the space needed for a segment header (11). The invocation `S(n)` returns the value of s_n and also sets the `kay` values. The invocation `Traceback(kay,n)` outputs the optimal combining.

As for the complexity $t(n)$ of Program 15.3, we see that $t(0) = c$ for some constant c and $t(n) \le \sum_{j=\max\{0,n-256\}}^{n-1} t(j) + n$ when $n > 0$. The solution to this recurrence is $t(n) = O(2^n)$. The complexity of `Traceback` is $\Theta(n)$.

Recursive Solution without Recomputations

The complexity of function `S` can be reduced to $\Theta(n)$ by avoiding the recomputation of previously computed s_is. Notice that there are only n different s_is.

Example 15.11 Consider the five-segment instance of Example 15.10. When computing s_5, recursive calls are made to compute $s_4, \cdots, s_0$. When computing s_4, recursive calls are made to compute $s_3, \cdots, s_0$. Therefore, s_4 is computed once, and s_3 twice. Each computation of s_3 computes s_2 once, so s_2 is computed a total of four times. s_1 is computed 16 times! ∎

We can avoid the recomputation of the s_i's by saving previously computed s_is in an array `s`. The new code for function `S` appears in Program 15.4.   `s` is a global integer array that has been initialized to zero.

```
int S(int i)
{// Return S(i) and compute kay[i].
   if (i == 0) return 0;
   // compute min term of Eq. 15.3 for k = 1
   int lsum = l[i], bmax = b[i];
   int s = S(i-1) + lsum * bmax;
   kay[i] = 1;

   // compute min term for remaining k and find min
   for (int k = 2; k <= i && lsum+l[i-k+1] <= L;
                        k++) {
      lsum += l[i-k+1];
      if (bmax < b[i-k+1]) bmax = b[i-k+1];
      int t = S(i-k);
      if (s > t + lsum * bmax) {
         s = t + lsum * bmax;
         kay[i] = k;}
   }

   return s + header;
}


void Traceback(int kay[], int n)
{// Decompose into segments.
   if (n == 0) return;
   Traceback(kay, n-kay[n]);
   cout << "New segment begins at "
        << (n - kay[n] + 1) << endl;
}
```

Program 15.3 Recursive computation of s, kay, and an optimal combining

To determine the time complexity of Program 15.4, we shall use an **amorti-zation scheme** in which we charge different components of the total time to different entities and then add up the charges for these entities. When computing an s_i, the cost of an invocation S(j) is charged to s_j if s_j has not been computed and to s_i if it has. (This s_j in turn offloads the cost of computing new s_qs to the individual s_qs.) The cost of the remainder of Program 15.4 is charged to s_i. This remainder is $\Theta(1)$ because L is a constant (256) and each l_i is at least one. The total amount charged to each s_i is constant, and the number of s_is is n. Therefore, the total work done is $\Theta(n)$.

```
int S(int i)
{// Compute S(i) and kay[i].
 // Avoid recomputations.
   if (i == 0) return 0;
   if (s[i] > 0) return s[i]; // already computed
   // compute s[i]
   // first compute min term of Eq. 15.3 for k = 1
   int lsum = l[i], bmax = b[i];
   s[i] = S(i-1) + lsum * bmax;
   kay[i] = 1;

   // compute min term for remaining k and update
   for (int k = 2; k <= i && lsum+l[i-k+1] <= L; k++){
      lsum += l[i-k+1];
      if (bmax < b[i-k+1]) bmax = b[i-k+1];
      int t = S(i-k);
      if (s[i] > t + lsum * bmax) {
         s[i] = t + lsum * bmax;
         kay[i] = k;}
   }

   s[i] += header;
   return s[i];
}
```

Program 15.4 Recursive computation avoiding recomputations

Iterative Solution

A $\Theta(n)$ iterative solution is obtained if we use Equation 15.3 to compute $s_1, \cdots,$ s_n in this order. This way, when an s_i is to be computed, the needed s_js have already been computed. The resulting code appears in Program 15.5. The function Traceback (Program 15.3) can be used, without change, to determine the optimal combining.

15.2.3 Matrix Multiplication Chains

An $m \times n$ matrix A and an $n \times p$ matrix B can be multiplied in $\Theta(mnp)$ time (see Exercise 16, Chapter 2). We shall use mnp as a measure of the time needed to multiply the two matrices. Suppose we are to multiply three matrices A, B, and C. There are two ways in which we can accomplish this task. In the first, we multiply A and B to get the product matrix D and then multply D and C to get the

```
void Vbits(int l[], int b[], int n, int s[],
                                    int kay[])
{// Compute s[i] and kay[i] for all i.
   int L = 256, header = 11;
   s[0] = 0;
   // compute s[i] using Eq. 15.3
   for (int i = 1; i <= n; i++) {
      // compute min term for k = 1
      int lsum = l[i],
          bmax = b[i];
      s[i] = s[i - 1] + lsum * bmax;
      kay[i] = 1;

      // compute for remaining k and update
      for (int k = 2; k <= i && lsum+l[i-k+1] <= L;
                                    k++) {
         lsum += l[i-k+1];
         if (bmax < b[i-k+1]) bmax = b[i-k+1];
         if (s[i] > s[i-k] + lsum * bmax) {
               s[i] = s[i-k] + lsum * bmax;
               kay[i] = k;}
      }

      s[i] += header;
   }
}
```

Program 15.5 Iterative computation of s and kay

desired result. This multiplication order can be written as $(A * B) * C$. The second way is $A * (B * C)$. Although both multiplication orders obtain the same result, one may take a lot more computing time than the other.

Example 15.12 Suppose that A is a 100×1 matrix, B is a 1×100 matrix, and C is a 100×1 matrix. Then the time needed to compute $A * B$ is 10,000. Since the result is a 100×100 matrix, the time needed to perform the multiplication with C is 1,000,000. The overall time needed to compute $(A * B) * C$ is therefore 1,010,000. $B * C$ can be computed in 10,000 units of time. Since the result is a 1 $\times$ 1 matrix, the time needed for the multiplication with A is 100. The total time needed to compute $A * (B * C)$ is therefore 10,100! Furthermore, when computing $(A * B) * C$, we need 10,000 units of space to store $A * B$, however, when $A * (B * C)$ is computed, only one unit of space is needed for $B * C$.

As an example of a real problem that can benefit from computing the matrix product $A * B * C$ in the proper order, consider the registration of two three-dimensional images. In the registration problem, we are to determine the amount by which one image needs to be rotated, translated, and shrunk (or expanded) so that it approximates the second. One way to perform this registration involves doing about 100 iterations of computation. Each iteration computes the following 12×1 vector T:

$$T = \sum A(x,y,z) * B(x,y,z) * C(x,y,z)$$

Here, A, B, and C are, respectively, 12×3, 3×3, and 3×1 matrices. (x,y,z) gives the coordinates of a voxel, and the sum is done over all voxels. Let t be the number of computations needed to compute $A(x,y,z) * B(x,y,z) * C(x,y,z)$ for a single voxel. Assume that the image is of size $256 \times 256 \times 256$ voxels. In this case the total number of computations needed for the 100 iterations is approximately $100 * 256^3 * t \sim 1.7 * 10^9 t$. When the three matrices are multiplied from left to right, $t = 12 * 3 * 3 + 12 * 3 * 1 = 144$. When we multiply from right to left, $t = 3 * 3 * 1 + 12 * 3 * 1 = 45$. The left-to-right computation requires approximately $2.4 * 10^{11}$ operations, while the right-to-left computation requires about $7.5 * 10^{10}$ operations. On a computer that can do 100 million operations per second, the first scheme would take 40 minutes and the second would take 12.5 minutes. ∎

When we are to compute the matrix product $A * B * C$, only two multiplication orders are possible (left to right and right to left). We can determine the number of operations each order requires and go with the cheaper one. In a more general situation, we are to compute the matrix product $M_1 \times M_2 \times \cdots \times M_q$ where M_i is an $r_i \times r_{i+1}$ matrix, $1 \leq i \leq q$. Consider the case $q = 4$. The matrix product $A * B * C * D$ may be computed in any of the five following ways:

$$A * ((B * C) * D) \qquad A * (B * (C * D))$$
$$(A * B) * (C * D) \qquad ((A * B) * C) * D \qquad (A * (B * C)) * D$$

The number of different ways in which the product of q matrices may be computed increases exponentially with q. As a result, for large q it is not practical to evaluate each multiplication scheme and select the cheapest.

We can use dynamic programming to determine an optimal sequence of pairwise matrix multiplications to use. The resulting algorithm runs in $\Theta(q^3)$ time. Let M_{ij} denote the result of the product chain $M_i \times \cdots \times M_j$, $i \leq j$, and let $c(i,j)$ be the cost of the optimal way to compute M_{ij}. Let $kay(i,j)$ be such that the optimal computation of M_{ij} computes $M_{ik} \times M_{k+1,j}$. An optimal computation of M_{ij} therefore comprises the product $M_{ik} \times M_{kj}$ preceded by optimal computations of M_{ik} and M_{kj}. The principle of optimality holds, and we obtain the dynamic-programming recurrence that follows.

$$c(i,i) = 0, \ 1 \le i \le q$$

$$c(i,i+1) = r_i r_{i+1} r_{i+2} \text{ and } kay(i,i+1) = i, \ 1 \le i < q$$

$$c(i,i+s) = \min_{i \le k < i+s} \{c(i,k) + c(k+1,i+s) + r_i r_{k+1} r_{i+s+1}\},$$
$$1 \le i \le q-s, \ 1 < s < q$$

$$kay(i,i+s) = \text{value of } k \text{ that obtains the above minimum}$$

The above recurrence for c may be solved recursively or iteratively. $c(1,q)$ is the cost of the optimal way to compute the matrix product chain and $kay(1,q)$ defines the last product to be done. The remaining products can be determined using the kay values.

Recursive Solution

As in the case of the 0/1 knapsack and image-compression problems, any recursive solution must be implemented so as to avoid computing the same $c(i,j)$ and $kay(i,j)$ values more than once otherwise, the complexity of the algorithm is too high.

Example 15.13 Consider the case $q = 5$ and $r = (10, 5, 1, 10, 2, 10)$. The dynamic-programming recurrence yields

$$c(1,5) = \min\{c(1,1) + c(2,5) + 500, c(1,2) + c(3,5) + 100, \qquad (15.4)$$
$$c(1,3) + c(4,5) + 1000, c(1,4) + c(5,5) + 200\}$$

Four of the needed cs have $s = 0$ or 1. Their values are immediately computable from the dynamic-programming equations. We get $c(1,1) = c(5,5) = 0$; $c(1,2) = 50$; $c(4,5) = 200$. For $c(2,5)$, we get

$$c(2,5) = \min\{c(2,2) + c(3,5) + 50, \ c(2,3) + c(4,5) + 500, \qquad (15.5)$$
$$c(2,4) + c(5,5) + 100\}$$

$c(2,2) = c(5,5) = 0$, $c(2,3) = 50$, and $c(4,5) = 200$. For $c(3,5)$ and $c(2,4)$ we need to use the recurrences

$$c(3,5) = \min\{c(3,3) + c(4,5) + 100, \ c(3,4) + c(5,5) + 20\}$$
$$= \min\{0 + 200 + 100, \ 20 + 0 + 20\}$$
$$= 40$$

and

$$c(2,4) = \min\{c(2,2) + c(3,4) + 10, \ c(2,3) + c(4,4) + 100\}$$
$$= \min\{0 + 20 + 10, \ 50 + 0 + 20\}$$
$$= 30$$

These computations also yield $kay(3,5) = 4$ and $kay(2,4) = 2$. Now we know all the values needed to compute $c(2,5)$. Substituting these values in Equation 15.5, we get

$$c(2,5) = \min\{0 + 40 + 50,\ 50 + 200 + 500,\ 30 + 0 + 100\} = 90$$

and so $kay(2,5) = 2$. To use Equation 15.4 to compute $c(1,5)$, we still need values for $c(3,5)$, $c(1,3)$, and $c(1,4)$. Proceeding as above, we obtain the values 40, 150, and 90. The corresponding kay values are 4, 2, and 2. Substituting into Equation 15.4, we get

$$c(1,5) = \min\{0 + 90 + 500,\ 50 + 40 + 100, 150 + 200 + 1000, \\ 90 + 0 + 200\} = 190$$

and $kay(1,5) = 2$.

The optimal multiplication sequence has cost 190. The sequence can be determined by examining $kay(1,5)$, which equals 2. So the last multiplication to perform is $M_{12} \times M_{35}$. Since both M_{12} and M_{35} are to be computed optimally, the kay values may be used to figure out how. $kay(1,2) = 1$, so M_{12} is computed as $M_{11} \times M_{22}$. Also, since $kay(3,5) = 4$, M_{35} is optimally computed as $M_{34} \times M_{55}$. M_{34} in turn is computed as $M_{33} \times M_{44}$, so the optimal multiplication sequence is

Multiply M_{11} and M_{22} to get M_{12}
Multiply M_{33} and M_{44} to get M_{34}
Multiply M_{34} and M_{55} to get M_{35}
Multiply M_{12} and M_{35} to get M_{15}

∎

The recursive code to determine $c(i,j)$ and $kay(i,j)$ appears in Program 15.6. Function C assumes that r is a global one-dimensional array and that kay is a global two-dimensional array. It returns the value of $c(i,j)$ and also sets kay[a][b] = $kay(a,b)$ for all a and b for which $c(a,b)$ is computed during the computation of $c(i,j)$. Function Traceback uses the kay values computed by C to determine the optimal multiplication sequence.

Let $t(q)$ be the complexity of function C when $j - i + 1 = q$ (i.e., when M_{ij} is composed of q matrices). We see that when q is one or two, $t(q) = d$ where d is a constant. When $q > 2$, $t(q) = 2\sum_{k=1}^{q-1} t(k) + eq$ where e is a constant. For $q > 2$, $t(q) > 2t(q-1) + e$. So $t(q) = \Omega(2^q)$. The complexity of function Traceback is $\Theta(q)$.

```
int C(int i, int j)
{// Return c(i,j) and compute kay(i,j) = kay[i][j].
   if (i == j) return 0;   // one matrix
   if (i == j - 1) {       // two matrices
      kay[i][i+1] = i;
      return r[i]*r[i+1]*r[i+2];}

   // more than two matrices
   // set u to min term for k = i
   int u = C(i,i) + C(i+1,j) + r[i]*r[i+1]*r[j+1];
   kay[i][j] = i;

   // compute remaining min terms and update u
   for (int k = i+1; k < j; k++) {
      int t = C(i,k) + C(k+1,j) + r[i]*r[k+1]*r[j+1];
      if (t < u) {// smaller min term
         u = t;
         kay[i][j] = k;}
   }

   return u;
}

void Traceback(int i, int j, int **kay)
{// Output best way to compute Mij.
   if (i == j) return;
   Traceback(i, kay[i][j], kay);
   Traceback(kay[i][j]+1, j, kay);
   cout << "Multiply M " << i << ", " << kay[i][j];
   cout << " and M " << (kay[i][j]+1) << ", " << j
        << endl;
}
```

Program 15.6 Recursive computation of $c(i,j)$ and $kay(i,j)$

Recursive Solution without Recomputations

By avoiding the recomputation of c (and hence kay) values previously computed, the complexity can be reduced to $\Theta(q^3)$. To avoid the recomputation, we need to save the values of the $c(i,j)$s in a global array $c[\ ][\ ]$, which is initialized to zero. The new recursive code for function C appears in Program 15.7.

```
int C(int i, int j)
{// Return c(i,j) and compute kay(i,j) = kay[i][j].
 // Avoid recomputations.

   // check if already computed
   if (c[i][j] > 0) return c[i][j];

   // c[i][j] not computed before, compute now
   if (i == j) return 0;   // one matrix
   if (i == j - 1) {// two matrices
                   kay[i][i+1] = i;
                   c[i][j] = r[i]*r[i+1]*r[i+2];
                   return c[i][j];}

   // more than two matrices
   // set u to min term for k = i
   int u = C(i,i) + C(i+1,j) + r[i]*r[i+1]*r[j+1];
   kay[i][j] = i;

   // compute remaining min terms and update u
   for (int k = i+1; k < j; k++) {
      int t = C(i,k) + C(k+1,j) + r[i]*r[k+1]*r[j+1];
      if (t < u) {// smaller min term
                 u = t;
                 kay[i][j] = k;}
   }

   c[i][j] = u;
   return u;
}
```

Program 15.7 Computing $c(i,j)$ without recomputations

To analyze the complexity of the modified function C (Program 15.7), we shall again use the cost amortization method. Observe that the invocation C(1,q) causes each $c(i,j)$, $1 \le i \le j \le q$ to be computed exactly once. For $s = j - i > 1$, the computation of each requires s amount of work in addition to the work done computing the needed $c(a,b)$s that haven't as yet been computed. This additional work is charged to the $c(a,b)$s that are being computed for the first time. These $c(a,b)$s, in turn, offload some of this charge to the first time cs that need to be computed during the computation of $c(a,b)$. As a result, each $c(i,j)$ is charged s amount of work. For each s, $q - s + 1$ $c(i,j)$s are computed.

The total cost is therefore $\sum_{s=1}^{q-1} s(q-s+1) = \Theta(q^3)$.

Iterative Solution

The dynamic programming recurrence for c may be solved iteratively, computing each c and *kay* exactly once, by computing the $c(i,i+s)$s in the order $s = 2, 3, \cdots, q-1$.

Example 15.14 Consider the five-matrix instance of Example 15.13. We begin by initializing $c(i,i)$ to zero, $1 \le i \le 5$. Next we compute $c(i,i+1)$ for $i = 1, \cdots,$ 4. $c(1,2) = r_1 r_2 r_3 = 50$, $c(2,3) = 50$, $c(3,4) = 20$, and $c(4,5) = 200$. The corresponding *kay* values are 1, 2, 3, and 4.

When $s = 2$, we get

$$c(1,3) = \min\{c(1,1) + c(2,3) + r_1 r_2 r_4, c(1,2) + c(3,3) + r_1 r_3 r_4\}$$
$$= \min\{0 + 50 + 500, 50 + 0 + 100\} = 150$$

and $kay(1,3) = 2$. $c(2,4)$ and $c(3,5)$ are computed in a similar way. Their values are 30 and 40. The corresponding *kay* values are 2 and 3.

When $s = 3$, we compute $c(1,4)$ and $c(2,5)$. All the values needed to compute $c(2,5)$ (see Equation 15.5) are known. Substituting these values, we get $c(2,5) = 90$ and $kay(2,5) = 2$. $c(1,4)$ is computed from a similar equation. Finally, when $s = 4$, only $c(1,5)$ is to be computed. The equation is 15.4. All quantities on the right side are known. ∎

The iterative code to compute the c and kay values is function MatrixChain (Program 15.8). Its complexity is $\Theta(q^3)$. We can use the traceback function of Program 15.6 to determine the optimal multiplication sequence following the computation of kay.

15.2.4 All Pairs Shortest Paths

Let G be a directed graph in which each edge has a cost (or length) assigned to it. The cost (length) of any directed path in this graph is the sum of the costs (lengths) of the edges on this path. For any pair of vertices (i,j), there may be several paths from vertex i to vertex j. These paths may differ in their costs. A path from i to j that has the minimum cost from among all i to j paths is called a **shortest *i*-to-*j*** path.

```
void MatrixChain(int r[], int q, int **c, int **kay)
{// Compute costs and kay for all Mij's.

   // initialize c[i][i], c[i][i+1], and kay[i][i+1]
   for (int i = 1; i < q; i++) {
     c[i][i] = 0;
     c[i][i+1] = r[i]*r[i+1]*r[i+2];
     kay[i][i+1] = i;
     }
   c[q][q] = 0;

   // compute remaining c's and kay's
   for (int s = 2; s < q; s++)
      for (int i = 1; i <= q - s; i++) {
         // min term for k = i
         c[i][i+s] = c[i][i] + c[i+1][i+s]
                     + r[i]*r[i+1]*r[i+s+1];
         kay[i][i+s] = i;

         // remaining min terms
         for (int k = i+1; k < i + s; k++) {
            int t = c[i][k] + c[k+1][i+s]
                    + r[i]*r[k+1]*r[i+s+1];
            if (t < c[i][i+s]) {// smaller min term
               c[i][i+s] = t;
               kay[i][i+s] = k;}
            }
         }
}
```

Program 15.8 Iterative computation of c and kay

Example 15.15 Consider the digraph of Figure 15.4. Some of the paths from vertex 1 to vertex 3 are

1.   1, 2, 5, 3
2.   1, 4, 3
3.   1, 2, 5, 8, 6, 3
4.   1, 4, 6, 3

The lengths of these paths are, respectively, 10, 28, 9, 27. By inspecting the graph, we see that path 3 is the shortest 1-to-3 path in this graph. ■

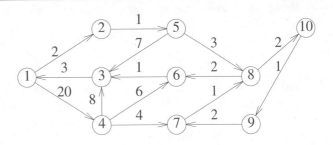

Figure 15.4 A digraph

In the **all-pairs shortest-paths problem**, we are to find a shortest path between every pair of vertices in a directed graph G. That is, for every pair of vertices (i,j), we are to find a shortest path from i to j as well as one from j to i. In all, $n(n-1)$ shortest paths are to be found for an n-vertex digraph. We shall assume that G contains no negative-length cycles. Under this assumption, for every pair of vertices (i,j), there is always a shortest path that contains no cycles. When the digraph has a cycle whose length is less than zero, some shortest paths have length $-\infty$, as they involve going around the negative-length cycle indefinitely.

Let the n vertices of G be numbered 1 through n. Let $c(i,j,k)$ denote the length of a shortest path from i to j that has no intermediate vertex larger than k. Hence $c(i,j,0)$ is the length of the edge $<i, j>$ in case this edge is in G. It is 0 if $i = j$ and ∞ otherwise. $c(i,j,n)$ is the length of a shortest path from i to j.

Example 15.16 For the digraph of Figure 15.4, $c(1,3,k) = \infty$ for $k = 0, 1, 2, 3$; $c(1,3,4) = 28$; $c(1,3,k) = 10$ for $k = 5, 6, 7$; $c(1,3,k) = 9$ for $k = 8, 9, 10$. Hence the shortest 1-to-3 path has length 9. ∎

How can we determine $c(i,j,k)$ for any k, $k > 0$? There are two possibilities for a shortest i-to-j path that has no intermediate vertex larger than k. This path may or may not have k as an intermediate vertex. If it does not, then its length is $c(i,j,k-1)$. If it does, then its length is $c(i,k,k-1) + c(k,j,k-1)$. $c(i,j,k)$ is the smaller of these two quantities. So we obtain the recurrence

$$c(i,j,k) = \min\{c(i,j,k-1), c(i,k,k-1) + c(k,j,k-1)\}, k > 0$$

The above recurrence formulates the solution for one k in terms of the solutions for $k - 1$. Obtaining solutions for $k - 1$ should be easier than obtaining those for k directly. If the above recurrence is solved recursively, the complexity of the resulting procedure is excessive. Let $t(k)$ be the time needed to solve the recurrence recursively for any i, j, k combination. From the recurrence, we see that $t(k) = 2t(k-1) + c$. Using the substitution method, we obtain $t(n) = \Theta(2^n)$. So the time needed to obtain all the $c(i, j, n)$ values is $\Theta(n^2 2^n)$.

The values $c(i, j, n)$ may be obtained far more efficiently by noticing that some $c(i, j, k-1)$ values get used several times. By avoiding the recomputation of $c(i, j, k)$s that were computed earlier, all c values may be determined in $\Theta(n^3)$ time. This strategy may be implemented recursively as we did for the matrix chain problem (see Program 15.7) or iteratively. We shall develop only the iterative code. Our first attempt at developing this iterative code results in the pseudocode of Figure 15.5.

```
// Find the lengths of the shortest paths.
   // initialize c(i,j,0)
   for (int i = 1; i <= n; i++)
      for (int j = 1; j <= n; j++)
         c(i,j,0) = a(i,j); // a is the cost-adjacency matrix

   // compute c(i,j,k) for 0 < k <= n
   for (int k = 1; k <= n; k++)
      for (int i = 1; i <= n; i++)
         for (int j = 1; j <= n; j++)
            if (c(i,k,k-1) + c(k,j,k-1) < c(i,j,k-1))
               c(i,j,k) = c(i,k,k-1) + c(k,j,k-1);
            else c(i,j,k) = c(i,j,k-1);
```

Figure 15.5 Initial shortest-paths algorithm

Observe that $c(i,k,k) = c(i,k,k-1)$ and that $c(k,i,k) = c(k,i,k-1)$ for all i. As a result, if $c(i,j)$ replaces $c(i,j,*)$ throughout Figure 15.5, the final value of $c(i,j)$ will be the same as $c(i,j,n)$. With this observation, Figure 15.5 may be refined into the C++ code of Program 15.9. This refinement uses the class `AdjacencyWDigraph` defined in Program 12.1. Function `AllPairs` returns, in `c`, the lengths of the shortest paths. In case there is no path from `i` to `j`, `c[i][j]` is set to `NoEdge`. This function also computes `kay[i][j]` such that `kay[i][j]` is the largest k that is on a shortest `i`-to-`j` path. The `kay` values may be used to construct a shortest path from one vertex to another (see function `OutputPath` of Program 15.10).

The time complexity of Program 15.9 is readily seen to be $\Theta(n^3)$. Program 15.9 takes O(n) time to output a shortest path.

Example 15.17 A sample cost array `a` appears in Figure 15.6(a). Figure 15.6(b) gives the `c` array computed by Program 15.9, and Figure 15.6(c) gives the `kay` values. From these `kay` values, we see that the shortest path from 1 to 5 is the

```
template<class T>
void AdjacencyWDigraph<T>::AllPairs(T **c, int **kay)
{// All pairs shortest paths.
 // Compute c[i][j] and kay[i][j] for all i and j.
   // initialize c[i][j] = c(i,j,0)
   for (int i = 1; i <= n; i++)
      for (int j = 1; j <= n; j++) {
         c[i][j] = a[i][j];
         kay[i][j] = 0;
         }
   for (int i = 1; i <= n; i++)
      c[i][i] = 0;

   // compute c[i][j] = c(i,j,k)
   for (int k = 1; k <= n; k++)
      for (int i = 1; i <= n; i++)
         for (int j = 1; j <= n; j++) {
            T t1 = c[i][k];
            T t2 = c[k][j];
            T t3 = c[i][j];
            if (t1 != NoEdge && t2 != NoEdge &&
               (t3 == NoEdge || t1 + t2 < t3)) {
                  c[i][j] = t1 + t2;
                  kay[i][j] = k;}
            }
}
```

Program 15.9 Computation of c and kay

shortest path from 1 to $kay[1][5] = 4$ followed by the shortest path from 4 to 5. The shortest path from 4 to 5 has no intermediate vertex on it, as $kay[4][5] = 0$. The shortest path from 1 to 4 goes through $kay[1][4] = 3$. Repeating this process, we determine that the shortest 1-to-5 path is 1, 2, 3, 4, 5. ■

15.2.5   Noncrossing Subset of Nets

In the crossing-distribution problem of Section 11.5.3, we are given a routing channel with n pins on either side and a permutation C. Pin i on the top side of the channel is to be connected to pin C_i on the bottom side, $1 \leq i \leq n$. The pair (i, C_i) is called a **net**. In all, we have n nets that are to be connected or routed.

```
void outputPath(int **kay, int i, int j)
{// Actual code to output i to j path.
   if (i == j) return;
   if (kay[i][j] == 0) cout << j << ' ';
   else {outputPath(kay, i, kay[i][j]);
         outputPath(kay, kay[i][j], j);}
}

template<class T>
void OutputPath(T **c, int **kay, T NoEdge,
                       int i, int j)
{// Output shortest path from i to j.
   if (c[i][j] == NoEdge) {
      cout << "There is no path from " << i << " to "
           << j << endl;
      return;}
   cout << "The path is" << endl;
   cout << i << ' ';
   outputPath(kay,i,j);
   cout << endl;
}
```

Program 15.10 Output a shortest path

0	1	4	4	8		0	1	2	3	4		0	0	2	3	4
3	0	1	5	9		3	0	1	2	3		0	0	0	3	4
2	2	0	1	8		2	2	0	1	2		0	0	0	0	4
8	8	9	0	1		5	5	3	0	1		5	5	5	0	0
8	8	2	9	0		4	4	2	3	0		3	3	0	3	0
		(a)						(b)						(c)		

Figure 15.6 Shortest-paths example

Suppose that we have two or more routing layers of which one is a *preferred layer*. For example, in the preferred layer it may be possible to use much thinner wires, or the resistance in the preferred layer may be considerably less than in other layers. Our task is to route as many nets as possible in the preferred layer. The remaining nets will be routed, at least partially, in the other layers. Since two nets can be routed in the same layer iff they do not cross, our task is equivalent to finding a maximum noncrossing subset (MNS) of the nets. Such a subset has the property that no two nets of the subset cross. Since net (i, C_i) is completely specified by i, we may refer to this net as net i.

Example 15.18 Consider the example of Figure 10.17 that has been redrawn as Figure 15.7. The nets (1,8) and (2,7) (or equivalently, the nets 1 and 2) cross and so cannot be routed in the same layer. The nets (1,8), (7,9), and (9,10) do not cross and so can be routed in the same layer. These three nets do not constitute a MNS as there is a larger subset of noncrossing nets. The set of four nets {(4,2), (5,5), (7,9), (9,10)} is an MNS of the routing instance given in Figure 10.17. ■

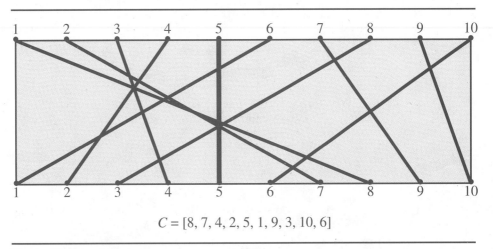

$$C = [8, 7, 4, 2, 5, 1, 9, 3, 10, 6]$$

Figure 15.7 A wiring instance

Let $MNS(i,j)$ denote an MNS under the constraint that all pairs (u, C_u) in the MNS have $u \leq i$ and $C_u \leq j$. Let $size(i,j)$ be the size (i.e., number of nets) of $MNS(i,j)$. Note that $MNS(n,n)$ is an MNS for the input instance and that $size(n,n)$ is its size.

Example 15.19 For the example of Figure 10.17, $MNS(10,10)$ is the answer we seek. As pointed out in Example 15.18, $size(10,10) = 4$. Nets (1,8), (2,7), (7,9), (8,3), (9,10), and (10,6) cannot be members of $MNS(7,6)$ because either their top pin number is greater than 7 or their bottom pin number is greater than 6. So we are left with four nets that are eligible for membership in $MNS(7,6)$. These nets appear in Figure 15.8. The subset {(3,4), (5,5)} is a noncrossing subset of size two. There is no noncrossing subset of size three. So $size(7,6) = 2$. ■

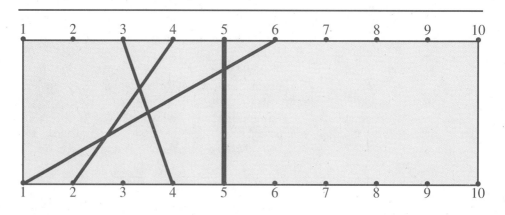

Figure 15.8 Nets of Figure 15.7 that may be in $MNS(7,6)$

When $i = 1$, the net $(1, C_1)$ is the only candidate for membership in $MNS(1,j)$. This net can be a member only when $j \geq C_1$. So we obtain

$$size(i,j) = \begin{cases} 0 & \text{if } j < C_1 \\ 1 & j \geq C_1 \end{cases} \tag{15.6}$$

Next, consider the case $i > 1$. If $j < C_i$, then the net (i, C_i) cannot be part of $MNS(i,j)$. In this case all nets (u, C_u) in $MNS(i,j)$ have $u < i$ and $C_u < j$. Therefore,

$$size(i,j) = size(i-1,j), \quad j < C_i \tag{15.7}$$

If $j \geq C_i$, then the net (i, C_i) may or may not be in $MNS(i,j)$. If it is, then no nets (u, C_u) such that $u < i$ and $C_u > C_i$ can be members of $MNS(i,j)$, as nets of this form cross (i, C_i). All other nets in $MNS(i,j)$ must have $u < i$ and $C_u < C_i$. The number of such nets in $MNS(i,j)$ must be M_{i-1,C_i-1}; otherwise, $MNS(i,j)$ doesn't have the maximum number of nets possible. If (i, C_i) is not in $MNS(i,j)$, then all nets in $MNS(i,j)$ have $u < i$; therefore $size(i,j) = size(i-1,j)$. Although we do not know whether the net (i, C_i) is in $MNS(i,j)$, of the two possibilities, the one that gives the larger MNS must hold. Therefore,

$$size(i,j) = \max\{size(i-1,j), size(i-1,C_i-1) + 1\}, \quad j \geq C_i \tag{15.8}$$

Although Equations 15.6 through 15.8 may be solved recursively, our earlier examples have shown that the recursive solution of dynamic-programming recurrences is inefficient even when we avoid recomputation of previously computed values. So we consider only an iterative solution. For this iterative solution, we use Equation 15.6 to first compute $size(1,j)$. Next we compute $size(i,j)$ for $i = 2, 3, \cdots, n$ in this order of i using Equations 15.7 and 15.8. Finally, we use a traceback to determine the nets in $MNS(n,n)$.

Example 15.20 Figure 15.9 shows the $size(i,j)$ values obtained for the example of Figure 15.7. Since $size(10,10) = 4$, we know that the MNS for this instance has four nets. To find these four nets, we begin at $size(10,10)$. $size(10,10)$ was computed using Equation 15.8. Since $size(10,10) = size(9,10)$, it follows from the reasoning used to obtain Equation 15.8 that there is an MNS of size 4 that does not include net 10. We must now find $MNS(9,10)$. Since $size(9,10) \neq size(8,10)$, $MNS(9,10)$ must include net 9. The remainder of the nets in $MNS(9,10)$ also constitute $MNS(8,C_9-1) = MNS(8,9)$. Since $size(8,9) = size(7,9)$, net 8 may be excluded from the MNS. So we proceed to determine $MNS(7,9)$ which must include net 7 as $size(7,9) \neq size(6,9)$. The remainder of the MNS is $MNS(6,C_7-1) = MNS(6,8)$. Net 6 is excluded as $size(6,8) = size(5,8)$. Net 5 is added to the MNS, and we proceed to determine $MNS(4,C_5-1) = MNS(4,4)$. Net 4 is excluded, and then net 3 is added to the MNS. No other nets are added. The traceback yields the size 4 MNS {3, 5, 7, 9}.

Notice that the traceback does not require $size(10,j)$ for values of j other than 10. We need not compute the values that are not required. ∎

i						j					
	1	2	3	4	5	6	7	8	9	10
1	0	0	0	0	0	0	0	1	1	1
2	0	0	0	0	0	0	1	1	1	1
3	0	0	0	1	1	1	1	1	1	1
4	0	1	1	1	1	1	1	1	1	1
5	0	1	1	1	2	2	2	2	2	2
6	1	1	1	1	2	2	2	2	2	2
7	1	1	1	1	2	2	2	2	3	3
8	1	1	2	2	2	2	2	2	3	3
9	1	1	2	2	2	2	2	2	3	4
10	1	1	2	2	2	3	3	3	3	4

Figure 15.9 $size(i,j)$s for the instance of Figure 15.7

The iterative codes to compute the $size\,(i,j)$s and then the MNS appears in Program 15.11. Function `MNS` computes the $size\,(i,j)$ values in a two-dimensional array `MN`. The mapping is $size\,(i,j)$ = `size[i][j]`. `size[i][j]` = $size\,(i,j)$ is computed for $1 \le i < n, 0 \le j \le n$ as well as for $i = j = n$. The time taken by this computation is $\Theta(n^2)$. Function `Traceback` returns, in `Net[0:m-1]`, the nets that form an MNS. This function takes $\Theta(n)$ time, so the total time taken by the dynamic-programming algorithm for the MNS problem is $\Theta(n^2)$.

15.2.6   Component Folding

Engineers follow several different design styles when they design electronic circuits. Two of these styles are **bit-slice designs** and **standard-cell designs**. In the former the electronic circuit is first designed as a stack of components, as shown in Figure 15.10(a). Each component C_i has a width w_i and a height h_i. The width of the component is an integer number of **slices**. The design of Figure 15.10(a) is a four-slice design. The wires that connect components follow the slice. That is, wires may connect from slice j of component C_i to slice j of component C_{i+1}. If one of these components isn't j slices wide, then there are no slice j wires between them. When the bit-slice design of Figure 15.10(a) is to be realized as part of a larger system, it is allocated some amount of space on a very (large scale integrated) VLSI chip. This allocation is done either by placing a restriction on the width of the space or on its height. The problem now is to fold the stack into the allocated space so as to minimize the unspecified dimension (i.e., if the height is restricted to H, the width W of the area into which the stack is folded is to be minimized). Minimizing this dimension is equivalent to minimizing the area because the other dimension is fixed.

A component stack is folded in a snakelike manner. At each fold point the components get rotated by 180 degrees. In the example of Figure 15.10(b), a 12-component stack has been folded into four vertical stacks. The fold points are C_6, C_9, and C_{10}. The width of a folded stack is the number of slices required by the widest component in the slice. In the example of Figure 15.10(b), the stack widths are 4, 3, 2, and 4. The height of a folded stack is obtained by summing the heights of the components in each stack and taking the maximum of these sums. In Figure 15.10(b) the sum of component heights is maximum for stack 1. The height of this stack determines the height of the rectangle needed to enclose all stacks.

In realistic cases of the component folding problem, we need to account for the additional space needed to carry the wires from one stack to the next. For example, in Figure 15.10(b) the wires between C_5 and C_6 get bent because C_6 is a fold point. These wires need vertical space below C_5 and C_6 so they can cross from stack 1 to stack 2. Let r_i denote the height allowance required in case C_i is

```
void MNS(int C[], int n, int **size)
{// Compute size[i][j] for all i and j.

   // initialize size[1][*]
   for (int j = 0; j < C[1]; j++)
      size[1][j] = 0;
   for (int j = C[1]; j <= n; j++)
      size[1][j] = 1;

   // compute size[i][*], 1 < i < n
   for (int i = 2; i < n; i++) {
      for (int j = 0; j < C[i]; j++)
         size[i][j] = size[i-1][j];
      for (int j = C[i]; j <= n; j++)
         size[i][j] = max(size[i-1][j],
                          size[i-1][C[i]-1]+1);
   }

   size[n][n] = max(size[n-1][n],
                size[n-1][C[n]-1]+1);
}

void Traceback(int C[], int **size, int n, int Net[],
                        int& m)
{// Return MNS in Net[0:m-1].
   int j = n;   // max bottom pin number allowed
   m = 0;        // cursor for Net
   for (int i = n; i > 1; i--)
      // is net i in MNS?
      if (size[i][j] != size[i-1][j]){// yes
         Net[m++] = i;
         j = C[i] - 1;}

   // is net 1 in MNS?
   if (j >= C[1])
      Net[m++] = 1;   // yes
}
```

Program 15.11 Finding a maximum noncrossing subset of nets

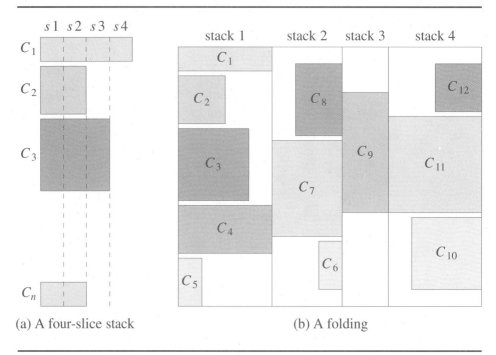

(a) A four-slice stack   (b) A folding

Figure 15.10 A component stack and a folded layout

a fold point. Now the height needed to accomodate stack 1 is $\sum_{i=1}^{5} h_i + r_6$. The height needed by stack 2 is $\sum_{i=6}^{8} h_i + r_6 + r_9$.

In standard cell designs, an electronic circuit is first designed as a linearly ordered list of components that have the same height. Suppose that the components are $C_1, \cdots, C_n$ in this linear order. Next the components are folded into equal-width rows as in Figure 15.11. In this figure 12 standard cells are folded into four equal-width rows. The fold points are C_4, C_6, and C_{11}. Between pairs of adjacent standard cell rows, we use a routing channel to make the electrical connections between cells in different rows. The fold points detrmine the required channel heights for the routing. Let l_i denote the channel height needed when C_i is a fold point. In the example of Figure 15.11, the height of routing channel 1 is l_4, that of channel 2 is l_6, and that of channel 3 is l_{11}.

The folding of bit-slice stacks, as well as of standard cells, leads to several problems that may be solved using dynamic programming.

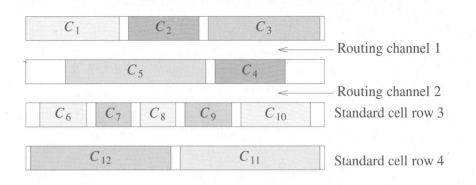

Routing channel 1

Routing channel 2

Standard cell row 3

Standard cell row 4

Figure 15.11 Standard cell folding

Folding of Equal-Width Bit-Slice Components

Define $r_1 = r_{n+1} = 0$. The height requirement of a stack composed of the components C_i through C_j is $\sum_{k=i}^{j} l_k + r_i + r_{j+1}$. Suppose that all components of a bit-slice design have the same width w. First consider the case when the height H of the rectangle into which the folding is to be done is given, and we are to minimize its width. Let W_i be the width of a minimum-width folding of the components C_i through C_n into a rectangle of height H. In case such a folding is not possible (for example, when $r_i + h_i > H$), let $W_i = \infty$. Notice that W_1 is the width of the best folding possible for all n components.

When folding the components C_i through C_n, we need to decide on the fold points. Suppose these decisions are made for the stacks in left-to-right order. If the first decision is to fold at C_{k+1}, then C_i through C_k are in the first stack. For the overall folding to have minimum width, the remaining components C_{k+1} through C_n must be folded in an optimal manner. Hence the principle of optimality holds, and dynamic programming may be used to solve the problem. When the first fold point $k+1$ is known, we get the equality

$$W_i = w + W_{k+1} \tag{15.9}$$

Since we do not know the first fold point, we need to try out all feasible fold points and select the one for which Equation 15.9 gives the minimum W_i. Let $hsum(i,k) = \sum_{j=i}^{k} h_j$. For $k+1$ to be a feasible fold point, $hsum(i,k) + r_i + r_{k+1}$ must not exceed H. Using this obsrvation, we obtain the following dynamic-programming recurrence:

$$W_i = w + \min\{W_{k+1} \mid hsum(i,k) + r_i + r_{k+1} \le H, \ i \le k \le n\} \qquad (15.10)$$

Here $W_{n+1} = 0$ and in case there is no feasible fold point $k + 1$, then W_i is ∞. Recurrence 15.10 may be solved iteratively for W_1 by computing the W_is in the order $W_n, W_{n-1}, \cdots, W_1$. The computation of W_i involves the examination of at most $n - i + 1$ W_{k+1}s and can be done in $O(n - k)$ time. So the time needed to compute all W_is is $O(n^2)$. By saving the values of k that yield each minimum in 15.10, we can use an $O(n)$ traceback to compute the optimal fold points.

Let us consider another folding problem involving equal-width components. This time the width W of the rectangle into which the folding is to be done is known, and we are to minimize its height. Since each folded stack has width w, the maximum number of stacks in the folded layout is $s = W/w$. Let $H_{i,j}$ be the height of a minimum-height folding of $C_i, \cdots, C_n$ into a rectangle of width jw. $H_{1,s}$ is the minimum height into which all n components can be folded. When $j = 1$, no folding is permitted, and so

$$H_{i,1} = hsum(i,n) + r_i, \ 1 \le i \le n$$

Also, when $i = n$, there is only one component and no folding is possible. Therefore,

$$H_{n,j} = h_n + r_n, \ 1 \le j \le s$$

For other $H_{i,j}$, folding is possible. If the first fold is at $k + 1$, then the first stack has a height of $hsum(i,k) + r_i + r_{k+1}$. The remaining components must be folded using a width of at most $(j-1) * w$. To ensure optimality of the overall folding, the remaining components should be folded with minimum height. So

$$H_{i,j} = \max\{hsum(i,k) + r_i + r_{k+1}, H_{k+1,j-1}\} \qquad (15.11)$$

Since we do not know the first fold point, we try out all possible fold points and pick the one for which the right side of Equation 15.11 is minimum. The resulting recurrence is

$$H_{i,j} = \min_{i \le k < n} [\max\{hsum(i,k) + r_i + r_{k+1}, H_{k+1,j-1}\}] \qquad (15.12)$$

This recurrence may be solved iteratively for $H_{i,j}$, $1 \le i \le n$, $1 \le j \le s$ by computing the $H_{i,j}$s first for $j = 2$, then $j = 3$, and so on. The time needed to compute the $H_{i,j}$s for each j is $O(n^2)$, so it takes $O(sn^2)$ time to compute all $H_{i,j}$s. By saving the k values that yield the minimums in recurrence 15.12, we can determine the optimal fold points by a tracback procedure of complexity $O(n)$.

Folding of Variable-Width Bit-Slice Components

First consider the case when the height H of the rectangle into which the folding is to be done is given and its width is to be minimized. Let W_i be as in Equation 15.10. Using an argument similar to that used to derive Equation 15.10, we obtain

$$W_i = \min\{wmin\,(i,k) + W_{k+1} \mid hsum\,(i,k)+r_i+r_{k+1} \leq H, \; i \leq k \leq n\} \qquad (15.13)$$

Here $W_{n+1} = 0$, and $wmin\,(i,k) = \min_{i \leq j \leq k}\{w_j\}$. This recurrence may be solved in a manner similar to Equation 15.10. The time needed is $O(n^2)$.

When the width, W, of the folded layout is given, the minimum-height folding may be obtained using a binary search over the $O(n^2)$ posssible values, $h\,(i,j) + r_i + r_{j+1}$, for this height. For each height checked, we use Equation 15.13 to determine whether there is a folding with width $\leq W$. The total time needed to find the minimum height for which the folding can be done into a rectangle of width at most W is $O(n^2 \log n)$.

Standard Cell Folding

We shall use w_i to denote the width of cell C_i. Each cell has height h. When the width W of the standard cell rows is fixed, the layout area is minimized by minimizing the height of the folding. Consider any minimum-height folding of the components C_i through C_n. Suppose that the first fold point is C_{s+1}. The folding of the components C_{s+1} through C_n must use minimum height; otherwise, we can use a lesser height folding of these components and thereby get an even lesser height folding of C_i through C_n. So the principle of optimality holds, and the dynamic-programming method may be used.

Let $H_{i,s}$ be the minimum height when components C_i through C_n are folded into a rectangle of width W with the first fold being at C_{s+1}. Let $wsum\,(i,s) = \sum_{j=i}^{s} w_j$. We may assume that no component has width greater than W; otherwise, there is no feasible folding. For $H_{n,n}$, we see that there is just one component, and no routing is needed. Therefore, $H_{n,n} = h$. For $H_{i,s}$, $1 \leq i < s \leq n$, we see that if $wsum\,(i,s) > W$, the folding is infeasible. If $wsum\,(i,s) \leq W$, components C_i and C_{i+1} are in the same standard cell row and the height of the routing channel just below is l_{s+1} (define $l_{n+1} = 0$). As a result

$$H_{i,s} = H_{i+1,k} \qquad (15.14)$$

When $i = s < n$, the first standard cell row contains only C_i. The height of this row is h, and the height of the routing channel just below is l_{i+1}. The cells C_{i+1} through C_n are folded optimally. Therefore,

$$H_{i,i} = \min_{i < k \leq n}\{H_{i+1,k}\} + l_{i+1} + h \qquad (15.15)$$

To find the minimum height-folding, we first use Equations 15.14 and 15.15 to determine $H_{i,s}$, $1 \le i \le s \le n$. The height of the minimum-height folding is given by $\min\{H_{1,s}\}$. We can use a traceback procedure to determine the fold points that result in the minimum-height folding.

EXERCISES

1. Modify Program 15.1 so that it also computes the values of the x_is that result in an optimal packing.

2. Modify Program 15.1 to use a lookup table to determine if an $f(i,y)$ has been computed before. If so, obtain the value from the table. If not, make a recursive call to compute this value.

3. Define the 0/1/2 knapsack problem to be

$$\text{maximize } \sum_{i=1}^{n} p_i x_i$$

subject to the constraints

$$\sum_{i=1}^{n} w_i x_i \le c \text{ and } x_i \in \{0,1,2\}, \ 1 \le i \le n$$

Let f be as defined for the 0/1 knapsack problem.

(a) Obtain equations similar to 15.1 and 15.2 for the 0/1/2 knapsack problem.

(b) Assume that the ws are integer. Write a program similar to Program 15.2 to compute f as a two-dimensional array and then to determine an optimal assignment of values for x.

(c) What is the complexity of your program?

4. The two-dimensional 0/1 knapsack problem is defined as

$$\text{maximize } \sum_{i=1}^{n} p_i x_i$$

subject to the constraints

$$\sum_{i=1}^{n} v_i x_i \le c, \ \sum_{i=1}^{n} w_i x_i \le d, \text{ and } x_i \in \{0,1\}, \ 1 \le i \le n$$

Let $f(i,y,z)$ denote the value of an optimal solution to the two-dimensional knapsack problem with objects i through n, $c = y$, and $d = z$.

(a) Obtain equations similar to 15.1 and 15.2 for $f(n,y,z)$ and $f(i,y,z)$.

(b) Assume that the vs and ws are integer. Write a program similar to Program 15.2 to compute f as a three-dimensional array and then to determine an optimal assignment of values for x.

(c) What is the complexity of your program?

★ 5. Write C++ code implementing the tuple method. Include a traceback function to determine the x_i values that define an optimal packing.

6. When the restriction on segment length is eliminated (i.e., $L = \infty$ in Program 15.3), the time complexity of Program 15.3 is given by the recurrence

$$t(0) = c \text{ for some constant } c \text{ and } t(n) = \sum_{j=0}^{n-1} t(j) + n \text{ when } n > 0.$$

(a) Use the fact that $t(n-1) = \sum_{j=0}^{n-2} t(j) + n - 1$ to conclude that $t(n) = 2t(n-1) + 1$ for $n > 0$.

(b) Now show that $t(n) = \Theta(2^n)$.

7. Write an iterative version of function `Traceback` (Program 15.3). What can you say about the relative merits of the two versions?

8. Write code for steps 1 and 2 of the variable-bit image-compression scheme.

9. Show that $\sum_{s=1}^{q-1} s(q - s + 1) = \Theta(q^3)$.

10. Only the upper triangle of the arrays `c` and `kay` are used when solving the matrix-multiplication recurrence. Rewrite the code of Program 15.6 defining `c` and `kay` to be members of the class `UpperMatrix` (see Section 4.3.4).

11. Write a version of Program 15.9 that will work on members of the class `LinkedWDigraph`. The asymptotic complexity of your code should be the same as that of Program 15.9.

12. Let G be a directed acyclic graph with n vertices. Assume that the vertices in G have been labeled 1 through n such that if $<i,j>$ is an edge of G, then $i < j$. Let $l(i,j)$ be the length of the edge $<i,j>$.

(a) Use dynamic programming to obtain a procedure that determines the length of a longest path in G. Your procedure should work in $O(n + e)$ time where e is the number of edges in G.

(b) Write a procedure that uses the results of your procedure for part (a) and constructs a path of longest length. The complexity of your procedure should be $O(p)$ where p is the number of vertices on the path constructed.

13. Modify Program 15.9 so that it starts with an adjacency matrix of a directed graph and computes its reflexive transitive closure matrix RTC. RTC[i][j] = 1 if there is a directed path from vertex i to vertex j that uses zero or more edges. RTC[i][j] = 0 otherwise. The complexity of your code should be $\Theta(n^3)$ where n is the number of vertices in the graph.

14. Write an $O(n^2)$ iterative C++ program to find optimal fold points for bit-slice stacks with equal-width components. Use Equation 15.10.

15. Do Exercise 14 using recurrence 15.12. This time the complexity of your code should be $O(sn^2)$.

16. Find a minimum-width folding of a stack of variable-width components. Use Equation 15.13. The complexity of your algorithm should be $O(n^2)$.

17. Use the development of Section 15.2.6 to arrive at an $O(n^2 \log n)$ algorithm to find a minimum height folding into a rectangle of width W. The bit-slice components have different widths.

18. Use Equations 15.14 and 15.15 to determine a minimum height folding of n standard cells. Your algorithm should run in $O(n^2)$ time. Can you think of a way to use these equations to obtain a $\Theta(n)$ time algorithm for this problem?

★ 19. In Section 13.3.3 we saw that a project may be decomposed into several tasks and that these tasks may be performed in topological order. Let the tasks be numbered 1 through n so that task 1 is done first, then task 2 is done, and so on. Suppose that we have two ways to perform each task. Let $C_{i,1}$ be the cost of doing task i the first way and $C_{i,2}$ the cost of doing it the second way. Let $T_{i,1}$ be the time it takes to do task i the first way, and let $T_{i,2}$ be the time when the task is done the second way. Assume that the Ts are integers. Obtain a dynamic-programming algorithm to determine the least-cost way to complete the entire project in no more than t time. Assume that the cost of the project is the sum of the task costs and the total time is the sum of the task times. (*Hint:* Let $cost(i,j)$ be the least cost with which tasks i through n can be completed in time j.) What is the complexity of your algorithm?

★ 20. A machine has n components. For each component, there are three suppliers. The weight of component i from supplier j is $W_{i,j}$, and its cost is $C_{i,j}$, $1 \le j \le 3$. The cost of the machine is the sum of the component costs, and its weight is the sum of the component weights. Write a dynamic-programming algorithm to determine from which supplier to buy each component so as to have the lightest machine with cost no more than c. Assume that the costs are integer. (*Hint:* Let $w(i,j)$ be the least-weight machine composed of components i through n that costs no more than j.) What is the complexity of your algorithm?

★ 21. Do Exercise 20 but this time define $w(i,j)$ to be the least-weight machine composed of components 1 through i that costs no more than j.

★ 22. String s is a subsequence of string a if s can be obtained from a by deleting some of the characters in a. The string "onion" is a subsequence of "recognition." s is a common subsequence of a and b iff it is a subsequence of both a and b. The length of s is its number of characters. Obtain a dynamic-programming algorithm to find a longest common subsequence of the strings a and b. (*Hint:* Let $a = a_1 a_2 \cdots a_n$ and $b = b_1 b_2 \cdots b_m$. Define $l(i,j)$ to be the length of a longest common subsequence of the strings $a_i \cdots a_n$ and $b_j \cdots b_m$.) What is the complexity of your algorithm?

★ 23. Do Exercise 22 but this time define $l(i,j)$ to be the length of a longest common subsequence of the strings $a_1 \cdots a_i$ and $b_1 \cdots b_j$.

★ 24. In the **string-editing problem**, you are given two strings $a = a_1 a_2 \cdots a_n$ and $b = b_1 b_2 \cdots b_m$ and three cost functions C, D, and I. $C(i,j)$ is the cost of changing a_i to b_j, $D(i)$ is the cost of deleting a_i from a, and $I(i)$ is the cost of inserting b_i into a. String a may be changed to string b by performing a sequence of change, delete, and insert operations. Such a sequence is called an **edit sequence**. For example, we could delete all the a_is and then insert the b_is, or when $n \geq m$, we could change a_i to b_i, $1 \leq i \leq n$, and then delete the remaining a_is. The cost of a sequence of operations is the sum of the individual operation costs. Write a dynamic-programming algorithm to determine a least-cost edit sequence. (*Hint:* Define $c(i,j)$ to be the cost of a least-cost edit sequence that transforms $a_1 \cdots a_i$ into $b_1 \cdots b_j$.) What is the complexity of your algorithm?

15.3 REFERENCES AND SELECTED READINGS

More information on image compression methods is provide in the book *Image and Video Compression Standards* by V. Bhaskaran and K. Konstantinides, Kluwer Academic Publishers, Boston, 1995. The variable bit scheme of Section 15.2.2 is from "State of the Art Lossless Image Compression" by S. Sahni, B. Vemuri, F. Chen, C. Kapoor, C. Leonard, and J. Fitzsimmons, Technical Report, University of Florida, 1997.

An O($n \log n$) algorithm for the matrix-multiplication-chains problem may be found in the papers "Computation of Matrix Chain Products" parts I & II, by T. Hu and M. Shing, *SIAM Journal on Computing*, 11, 1982, 362–372 and 13, 1984, 228–251.

The dynamic-programming algorithm for the noncrossing subset of nets problem is based on the work reported in the paper "Finding a Maximum Planar Subset of a Set of Nets in a Channel" by K. Supowit, *IEEE Transactions on Computer-Aided Design of Integrated Circuits and Systems*, 6, 1, 1987, 93–94.

Our discussion of bit-slice and standard-cell folding is based on the papers ''Optimal Folding of Bit Sliced Stacks'' by D. Paik and S. Sahni, *IEEE Transactions on Computer-Aided Design of Integrated Circuits and Systems*, 12, 11, 1993, 1679–1685; ''Folding a Stack of Equal Width Components'' by V. Thanvantri and S. Sahni, *IEEE Transactions on CAD of ICAS*, 14, 6, 1995, 775–780; and ''Optimal Folding of Standard and Custom Cells'' by V. Thanvantri and S. Sahni, *ACM Transactions on Design Automation and Electronic Systems*, 1996. The second paper uses **parametric search** to obtain faster algorithms than the dynamic programming algorithms described in this book. The last paper show how Equations 15.14 and 15.15 may be solved in $\Theta(n)$ time. These three papers also consider other variants of the folding problem.

CHAPTER 16

BACKTRACKING

BIRD'S-EYE VIEW

A sure-fire way to find the answer to a problem is to make a list of all candidate answers, examine each, and following the examination of all or some of the candidates, declare the identified answer. In theory, this approach should work whenever the candidate list is finite and when it is possible to identify the answer following the examination of all or some of the candidates. In practice, the approach isn't very useful because the number of candidates is often much too large (say, exponential, or even factorial in the instance size). As a result, even the fastest computers are able to complete the examination of the candidates in reasonable time only when the instance size is quite small.

Backtracking and branch and bound are two ways to make a systematic examination of the candidate list. Such a systematic examination of the candidate list often results in significant run-time savings in both the worst and expected cases. In fact, these methods often enable us to eliminate the explicit examination of a large subset of the candidates while still guaranteeing that the answer will be found if the algorithm is run to termination. As a result, these methods are often able to obtain solutions to large instances.

This chapter focuses on the backtracking method. This method is used to obtain algorithms for the container-loading, knapsack, max-clique, traveling-salesperson, and board-permutation problems.

16.1 THE METHOD

Backtracking is a systematic way to search for the solution to a problem. The solution provided in Section 5.5.6 for the rat in a maze problem utilized this technique. In backtracking we begin by defining a **solution space** for the problem. This space must include at least one (optimal) solution to the problem. In the case of the rat in a maze problem, we may define the solution space to consist of all paths from the entrance to the exit. For the case of the 0/1 knapsack problem (see Sections 13.4 and 15.2) with n objects, a reasonable choice for the solution space is the set of 2^n 0/1 vectors of size n. This set represents all possible ways to assign the values 0 and 1 to x. When $n = 3$, the solution space is $\{(0,0,0),$ $(0,1,0), (0,0,1), (1,0,0), (0,1,1), (1,0,1), (1,1,0), (1,1,1)\}$.

The next step is to organize the solution space so that it can be searched easily. The typical organization is either a graph or a tree. Figure 16.1 shows a graph organization for a 3×3 maze. All paths from the vertex labeled (1,1) to the vertex labeled (3,3) define an element of the solution space for a 3×3 maze. Depending on the placement of obstacles, some of these paths may be infeasible.

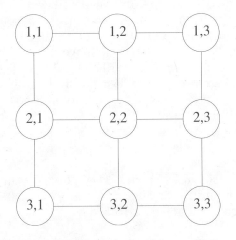

Figure 16.1 Solution space for a 3×3 maze

A tree organization for the three-object 0/1 knapsack solution space appears in Figure 16.2. The label on an edge from a level i node to a level $i + 1$ node gives the value of x_i. All paths from the root to a leaf define an element of the solution space. The path from the root to leaf H defines the solution $x =$ [1,1,1]. Depending on the values w and c, some or all of the root-to-leaf paths may define infeasible solutions.

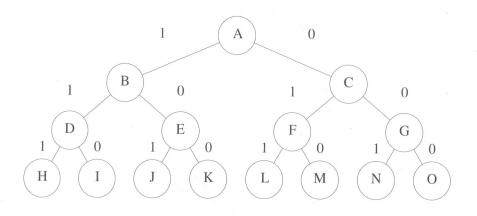

Figure 16.2 Solution space for a three-object knapsack

Once we have defined an organization for the solution space, this space is searched in a depth-first manner beginning at a start node—the entrance node (1,1) in the rat in a maze problem or the root node in the case of the 0/1 knapsack problem. This start node is both a **live** node and the **E-node** (expansion node). From this E-node, we try to move to a new node. If we can move to a new node from the current E-node, then we do so. The new node becomes a live node and also becomes the new E-node. The old E-node remains a live node. If we cannot move to a new node, the current E-node dies (i.e., it is no longer a live node) and we move back (i.e., backtrack) to the most recently seen live node that remains. This live node becomes the new E-node. The search terminates when we have found the answer or when we run out of live nodes to back up to.

Example 16.1 [*Rat in a Maze*] Consider the 3×3 rat in a maze instance given by the matrix of Figure 16.3(a). We shall search this maze using the solution space graph of Figure 16.1.

```
0  0  0        1  1  0        1  1  1
0  1  1        0  1  1        0  1  1
0  0  0        0  0  0        0  0  0
   (a)            (b)            (c)
```

Figure 16.3 Mazes

Every path from the entrance of the maze to the exit corresponds to a path from vertex (1,1) to vertex (3,3) in the graph of Figure 16.1. However, some of the (1,1) to (3,3) paths in this graph do not correspond to entrance to exit paths in the example.

The search begins at position (1,1), which is the only live node at this time. It is also the E-node. To avoid going through this position again, we set *maze* (1,1) to 1. From this position, we can move to either (1,2) or (2,1). For the particular instance we are dealing with, both moves are feasible as the maze has a zero at each position. Suppose we choose to move to (1,2). *maze* (1,2) is set to 1 to avoid going through here again. The status of *maze* is as in Figure 16.3(b). At this time we have two live nodes (1,1), and (1,2). (1,2) becomes the E-node. From the current E-node, there are three moves possible in the graph of Figure 16.1. Two of these moves are infeasible as the maze has a 1 in these positions. The only feasible move is to (1,3). We move to this position and set *maze* (1,3) to 1 to avoid going through here again. The maze of Figure 16.3(c) is obtained. The graph of Figure 16.1 indicates two possible moves from (1,3). Neither of these moves is feasible, so the E-node (1,3) dies and we back up to the most recently seen live node, which is (1,2). No feasible moves from here remain, and this node also dies. The only remaining live node is (1,1). This node becomes the E-node again and we have an untried move that gets us to position (2,1). The live nodes now are (1,1), and (2,1). Continuing in this way, we reach position (3,3). At this time the list of live nodes is (1,1), (2,1), (3,1), (3,2), (3,3). This list also gives the path to the exit.

Program 5.13 is a backtracking algorithm to find a path in a maze. ∎

Example 16.2 [*0/1 Knapsack*] Consider the knapsack instance $n = 3$, $w = [20, 15, 15]$, $p = [40, 25, 25]$, and $c = 30$. We search the tree of Figure 16.2 beginning at the root. The root is the only live node at this time. It is also the E-node. From here we can move to either B or C. Suppose we move to B. The live nodes now are A and B. B is the current E-node. At node B the remaining capacity r is 10, and the profit earned cp is 40. From B we can move to either D or E. The move to D is infeasible, as the capacity needed to move there is $w_2 = 15$. The move to E is feasible, as no capacity is used in this move. E becomes the new E-node. The live nodes at this time are A, B, and E. At node E, $r = 10$ and $cp = 40$. From E, we have two possible moves (i.e., to nodes J and K). The move to node J is infeasible, while that to K is not. Node K becomes the new E-node. Since K is a leaf, we have a feasible solution. This solution has profit value $cp = 40$. The values of x are determined by the path from the root to K. This path (A, B, E, K) is also the live-node sequence at this time. Since we cannot expand K further, this node dies and we back up to E. Since we cannot expand E further, it dies too.

Next we back up to B, which also dies and A becomes the E-node again. It can be expanded further, and node C is reached. Now $r = 30$ and $cp = 0$. From C we can move to either F or G. Suppose we move to F. F becomes the new E-node, and the live nodes are A, C, and F. At F, $r = 15$ and $cp = 25$. From F we can move to either L or M. Suppose we move to L. Now $r = 0$ and $cp = 50$. Since L is a leaf and it represents a better feasible solution than the best found so far (i.e., the one at node K), we remember this feasible solution as the best solution. Node L dies, and we back up to node F. Continuing in this way, we search the entire tree. The best solution found during the search is the optimal one. ■

Example 16.3 [*Traveling Salesperson*] In this problem we are given an *n* vertex network (either directed or undirected) and are to find a cycle of minimum cost that includes all *n* vertices. Any cycle that includes all *n* vertices of a network is called a **tour**. In the **traveling-salesperson problem**, we are to find a least-cost tour.

A four-vertex undirected network appears in Figure 16.4. Some of the tours in this network are 1,2,4,3,1; 1,3,2,4,1; and 1,4,3,2,1. The tours 2,4,3,1,2; 4,3,1,2,4; and 3,1,2,4,3 are the same as the tour 1,2,4,3,1, while the tour 1,3,4,2,1 is the reverse of the tour 1,2,4,3,1. The cost of the tour 1,2,4,3,1 is 66; that of 1,3,2,4,1 is 25; and that of 1,4,3,2,1 is 59. 1,2,4,3,1 is the least-cost tour in the network.

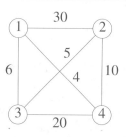

Figure 16.4 A four-vertex network

As the name suggests, the traveling-salesperson problem may be used to model the territory covered by a salesperson. The vertices represent the cities (including the home base) in the salesperson's territory. The edge costs give the travel time (or cost) required to go between two cities. A tour represents the path taken by the salesperson when visiting all cities in his/her territory and then returning home.

We can use the traveling-salesperson problem to model other problems. Suppose we are to drill a number of holes on a sheet of metal or on a printed circuit board. The location of the holes is known. The holes are drilled by a robot drill that begins at its base position, travels to each hole location, drills, and then returns to its base. The total time is that to drill all holes plus the drill travel time. The time to drill all holes is independent of the order in which they are drilled. However, the drill travel time is a function of the length of the tour used by the drill. Therefore, we wish to find a tour of minimum length.

As another example, consider a manufacturing environment in which a particular machine is to be used to manufacture n different items. The items are manufactured repeatedly using a manufacturing cycle. In one cycle all n items are manufactured in sequence, and then we are ready to begin the next cycle. In the next cycle the same manufacturing sequence is used. For example, if the machine is used to paint red, white, and blue cars in this sequence, then following the painting of the blue cars, we begin the sequence again with the red cars followed by the blue ones, then the white ones, again the red ones, and so on. The cost of one cycle includes the actual cost of manufacturing the items plus the cost of changing over from one item to the next. Although the actual cost of manufacturing the items is independent of the sequence in which the items are manufactured, the changeover cost depends on the sequence. To minimize the changeover cost, we may define a directed graph in which the vertices represent the items, and the edge $<i,j>$ has a cost equal to that of changing from the manufacture of item i to that of item j. A minimum-cost tour defines a least-cost manufacturing cycle.

Since a tour is a cycle that includes all vertices, we may pick any vertex as the start (and hence the end). Let us arbitrarily select vertex 1 as the start and end vertex. Each tour is then described by the vertex sequence $1, v_2, \cdots, v_n, 1$ when $v_2, \cdots, v_n$ is a permutation of $(2, 3, \cdots, n)$. The possible tours may be described by a tree in which each root-to-leaf path defines a tour. Figure 16.5 shows such a tree for the case of a four-vertex network. The edge labels on the path from the root to a leaf define a tour (when 1 is appended). For example, the path to node L represents the tour 1,2,3,4,1, while the path to node O represents the tour 1,3,4,2,1. Every tour in the network is represented by exactly one root-to-leaf path in the tree. As a result, the number of leaves in the tree is $(n-1)\,!$.

A backtracking algorithm will find a minimum-cost tour by searching the solution space tree in a depth-first manner, beginning at the root. A possible search using the network of Figure 16.4 would move from node A to B to C to F to L. At L the tour 1,2,3,4,1 is recorded as the best tour seen so far. Its cost is 59. From L we backtrack to the live node F. As F has no unexamined children, it is killed and we backtrack to node C. C becomes the E-node, and we move forward to G and then to M. We have now constructed the tour 1,2,4,3,1 whose cost is 66. Since this tour isn't superior to the best tour we have, we discard it and backtrack to G, then C, and then B. From B the search moves forward to D and then to H and N. The tour 1,3,2,4,1 defined at N has cost 25 and is better than the previous best tour. We save 1,3,2,4,1 as the best tour seen so far. From N the search backtracks to H and then to D. At D we can again move forward. We reach node O. Continuing in this way, we search the entire tree; 1,3,2,4,1 is the least-cost tour. ∎

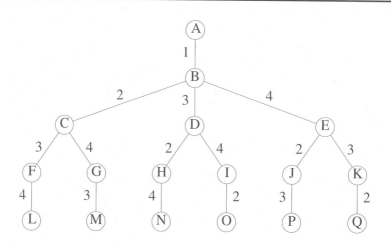

Figure 16.5 Solution space tree for a four-vertex network

When the problem we are to solve asks for a subset of n elements that optimizes some function, the solution space tree is called a **subset tree**. So the solution space tree for an n-object 0/1 knapsack instance is a subset tree. Such a tree has 2^n leaf nodes and $2^{n+1} - 1$ total nodes. As a result, every algorithm that moves through all nodes in the tree must spend $\Omega(2^n)$ time. When the problem asks for an n-element permutation that optimizes some function, the solution space tree is a **permutation tree**. Such a tree has $n!$ leaves and so every algorithm that moves through all nodes of the tree must spend $\Omega(n!)$ time. Note that the tree of Figure 16.5 is for the case when we are looking for the best permutation of the vertices $\{2, 3, 4\}$. Vertex 1 is the first and last vertex of the tour.

We can speed the search for an optimal solution by determining whether or not a newly reached node can possibly lead to a solution better than the best found so far. If it cannot, then there is no point moving into any of its subtrees and the node may be immediately killed. Strategies that are used to kill live nodes are called **bounding functions**. In Example 16.2 we used the following bounding function: Kill nodes that represent infeasible solutions. For the traveling salesperson problem, we could use this bounding function: If the cost of the partial tour built so far isn't less than that of the best tour found to this point, kill the current node. If we use this bounding function on the example of Figure 16.4, then by the time we reach node I, we have found the tour 1,3,2,4,1 with cost 25. At node I the partial tour is 1,3,4 whose cost is 26. By completing this partial tour into a full tour, we cannot get a tour with cost less than 25. There is no point in searching the subtree with root I.

Summary

The steps involved in the backtracking method are

1. Define a solution space that includes the answer to the problem instance.

2. Organize this space in a manner suitable for search.

3. Search the space in a depth-first manner using bounding functions to avoid moving into subspaces that cannot possibly lead to the answer.

An interesting feature of backtracking implementations is that the solution space is generated while the search is conducted. At any time during the search, only the path from the start node to the current E-node is saved. As a result, the space needs of a backtracking algorithm are typically O(length of longest path from the start node). This feature is important because the size of the solution space organization is usually exponential or factorial in length of the longest path. So the solution space organization needs excessive memory if stored in its entirety.

EXERCISES

1. Consider the 0/1 knapsack instance: $n = 4$, $w = [20, 25, 15, 35]$, $p = [40, 49, 25, 60]$, and $c = 62$.

   (a) Draw the solution space tree for 0/1 knapsack instances with $n = 4$.

   (b) Trace the working of a backtracking algorithm on this tree (use the ps, ws, and c values given in this exercise). Clearly label the nodes in the order in which the backtrack algorithm first reaches them. Identify the nodes that do not get reached.

2. (a) Draw the solution space tree for traveling-salesperson instances with $n = 5$.

   (b) Trace the working of a backtracking algorithm on this tree (use the instance of Figure 16.6). Clearly label the nodes in the order in which the backtrack algorithm first reaches them. Identify the nodes that do not get reached.

3. Mary and Joe practice tennis together every Saturday. They begin with a basket of 120 balls each and continue until both baskets are empty. Then they need to pick up 240 balls from around the tennis court. Mary and Joe pick up the balls by retrieving his/her empty basket; filling it with balls; and returning the now full basket to its original position. Mary picks up the balls on her side of the net, while Joe picks up the remaining balls. Describe how the traveling-salesperson problem can help Mary and Joe determine the order in which they should pick up balls so that they walk the minimum distance.

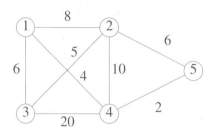

Figure 16.6 Instance for Exercise 2.

16.2 APPLICATIONS

16.2.1 Container Loading

The Problem
In Section 13.3 we considered the problem of a loading a ship with the maximum number of containers. Now we shall consider a variant of this problem in which we have two ships and n containers. The capacity of the first ship is c_1, and that of the second c_2. w_i is the weight of container i and $\sum_{i=1}^{n} w_i \leq c_1 + c_2$. We wish to determine whether there is a way to load all n containers. In case there is, then such a loading is to be determined.

Example 16.4 When $n = 3$, $c_1 = c_2 = 50$, and $w = [10, 40, 40]$, we can load containers 1 and 2 onto the first ship and container 3 onto the second ship. If the weights are $[20, 40, 40]$, then we cannot load the containers onto the ships. ∎

When $\sum_{i=1}^{n} w_i = c_1 + c_2$, the two-ship loading problem is equivalent to the **sum-of-subset** problem in which we are given n numbers and asked to find a subset (if it exists) that sums to c_1. When $c_1 = c_2$ and $\sum_{i=1}^{n} w_i = 2c_1$, the two-ship loading problem is equivalent to the **partition problem**. In this latter problem, we are given n numbers a_i, $1 \leq i \leq n$ and asked to find a subset (if it exists) that sums to $(\sum_{i=1}^{n} a_i)/2$. Both the partition and sum-of-subset problems are NP-hard problems and remain NP-hard even if the instances are limited to integer numbers. So we do not expect to solve the two-ship-loading problem in polynomial time.

You may verify that the following strategy to load the two ships succeeds whenever there is a way to load all n containers: (1) load the first ship as close to its capacity as possible and (2) put the remaining containers into the second ship. To load the first ship as close to capacity as possible, we need to select a subset of containers with total weight as close to c_1 as possible. This selection can be made by solving the 0/1 knapsack problem

$$\text{maximize } \sum_{i=1}^{n} w_i x_i$$

subject to the constraints:

$$\sum_{i=1}^{n} w_i x_i \le c_1 \text{ and } x_i \in \{0,1\}, \, 1 \le i \le n$$

When the weights are integer, we can use the dynamic-programming solution of Section 15.2 to determine the best loading of the first ship. The time needed is $O(\min\{c_1, 2^n\})$ with the tuple method. We can use the backtracking method to develop an $O(2^n)$ algorithm that can outperform the dynamic-programming algorithm on some (though not all) instances.

First Backtracking Solution

Since we are to find a subset of the weights with sum as close to c_1 as possible, we use a subset space that may be organized into a binary tree as in Figure 16.2. The solution space will be searched in a depth-first manner for the best solution. We use a bounding function to prevent the expansion of nodes that cannot possibly lead to the answer. If Z is a node on level $j + 1$ of the tree, then the path from the root to Z defines values for x_i, $1 \le i \le j$. Using these values, define cw (current weight) to be $\sum_{i=1}^{j} w_i x_i$. If $cw > c_1$, then the subtree with root Z cannot contain a feasible solution. We can use this test as our bounding function. Define a node to be **infeasible** iff its cw value exceeds c_1.

Example 16.5 Suppose that $n = 4$, $w = [8, 6, 2, 3]$, and $c_1 = 12$. The solution space tree is the tree of Figure 16.2 with one more level of nodes. The search begins at the root A, and $cw = 0$. If we move to the left child B, then $cw = 8$, which is $\le c_1 = 12$. The subtree with root B contains a feasible node, and we move to node B. From node B we do not move to node D because $cw + w_2 > c_1$; therefore, no leaves in this subtree represent feasible solutions. Instead, we move directly to node E. This move doesn't change cw. The next move is to node J as the cw value here is 10. The left child of J has a cw value of 13, which exceeds c_1, so the search does not move there. Instead, we make a move to the right child of J, which is a leaf. At this point we have found a subset with weight

$cw = 10$. The x_i values are obtained from the path from A to the right child of J. These x_i values are $[1, 0, 1, 0]$.

The backtrack algorithm now backs up to J and then to E. From E we can again move down the tree to node K where $cw = 8$. Its left subtree has cw value 11, and we move there. Since we have reached a leaf, we see whether the cw value exceeds the best found so far. It does, so this leaf represents a better solution than $[1, 0, 1, 0]$. The path to this leaf has x values $[1, 0, 0, 1]$.

From this leaf we back up to node K. Now we can move to K's right child, which is a leaf with $cw = 8$. This leaf doesn't represent a better solution than the best found so far, so we back up to K, E, B, and A. The root is the first node reached from which we can move down again. The algorithm moves to C and searches this subtree. ■

Program 16.1 is the backtracking algorithm that results when we use the preceding bounding function. Function `MaxLoading` returns the maximum subset sum that is $\leq$ c. It does not find the subset that has this weight. We shall later refine the code so as to find this subset. `MaxLoading` employs a recursive function `maxLoading` that is a member of the class `Loading`, which has been defined so as to reduce the number of parameters in `maxLoading`. The invocation `maxLoading(1)` actually does the search of the solution space. `maxLoading(i)` explores the subtree rooted at a level `i` node that is specified implicitly. The subsolution defined by the path from the root to this node has a weight of `cw`, and the weight of the best solution found so far is `bestw`. These variables, along with the other variables associated with a member of the class `Loading`, are initialized by `MaxLoading`.

If `i > n`, we have reached a leaf node. The solution defined by this leaf has weight `cw`, which is guaranteed to be $\leq$ c, as the search does not move to infeasible nodes. If `cw > bestw`, the value of the best solution found so far is updated. When `i` $\leq$ n, we are at a node Z that has two children. The left child represents the case `x[i] = 1`. We can move here only if `cw+w[i]` $\leq$ c. When we move to the left child, `cw` increases by `w[i]` and we reach a level `i+1` node. The subtree of which this node is the root is searched recursively. Upon completion of this search, we return to node Z. To get its `cw` value, we need to decrease the current `cw` by `w[i]`. The right subtree of Z has not been searched. Since this subtree represents the case `x[i] = 0`, the search may move there without a feasibility check because the right child of a feasible node is always feasible.

Notice that the solution space tree is not constructed explicitly by `max-Loading`. Function `maxLoading` spends $\Theta(1)$ time at each node that it reaches. The number of nodes reached is $O(2^n)$, so its complexity is $O(2^n)$. The function also uses $\Theta(n)$ space for the recursion stack.

```
template<class T>
class Loading {
   friend MaxLoading(T [], T, int);
   private:
      void maxLoading(int i);
      int n;      // number of containers
      T *w,       // container weight array
        c,        // capacity of first ship
        cw,       // weight of current loading
        bestw;    // weight of best loading so far
};

template<class T>
void Loading<T>::maxLoading(int i)
{// Search from level i node.
   if (i > n) {// at a leaf
      if (cw > bestw) bestw = cw;
      return;}
   // check subtrees
   if (cw + w[i] <= c) {// try x[i] = 1
      cw += w[i];
      maxLoading(i+1);
      cw -= w[i];}
   maxLoading(i+1);// try x[i] = 0
}

template<class T>
T MaxLoading(T w[], T c, int n)
{// Return weight of best loading.
   Loading<T> X;
   // initialize X
   X.w = w;
   X.c = c;
   X.n = n;
   X.bestw = 0;
   X.cw = 0;

   // compute weight of best loading
   X.maxLoading(1);
   return X.bestw;
}
```

Program 16.1 First backtracking code for the loading problem

Second Backtracking Solution

We can improve the expected performance of function `maxLoading` by not moving into right subtrees that cannot possibly contain better solutions than the best found so far. Let `bestw` be the weight of the best solution found so far. Let Z be a node at level `i` of the solution space tree and let `cw` be as above. No leaf in the subtree with root Z has weight more than `cw+r` where $r = \sum\limits_{j=i+1}^{n} w[j]$ is the weight of the remaining containers. Therefore, when `cw+r` $\leq$ `bestw`, there is no need to search the right subtree of Z.

Example 16.6 Let n, w, and c_1 be as in Example 16.5. With the new bounding function, the search proceeds as with the old one until we reach the first leaf (which is the right child of J). `bestw` is set to 10; we back up to E and then move down to the left child of K where `bestw` is updated to 11. We do not move to the right child of K, because at this right child `cw = 8`, `r = 0`, and `cw+r` $\leq$ `bestw`. Instead, we back up to node A. Again, we do not move to the right child C, because at C `cw = 0`, `r = 11`, and `cw+r` $\leq$ `bestw`.

The strengthened bounding function has avoided the search of the right subtree of A as well as the right subtree of K. ∎

When we use the strengthened bounding function, we get the code of Program 16.2. This code assumes that a private member `r` of type `T` has been added to the class definition of `Loading` (Program 16.1). Notice that the new code does not check whether a reached leaf has more weight than the previous best. Such a check is unneccessary because the strengthened bounding function disallows moves to nodes that cannot yield a better solution. As a result, each leaf that is reached represents a better solution than all previously reached leaves. Although the complexity of the new code remains $O(2^n)$, it is expected to examine fewer nodes than Program 16.1 examines.

Finding the Best Subset

To determine the subset of containers that has weight closest to `c`, it is necessary to add code to remember the best subset found so far. To remember this subset, we add the parameter `bestx` to `MaxLoading`. `bestx` is an integer array of zeroes and ones so that container `i` is in the best subset iff `bestx[i]` = 1. The new code appears in Program 16.3.

This code assumes that two private data members `x` and `bestx` are added to `Loading`. Both of these data members are one-dimensional arrays of type `int`. The array `x` is used to record the path from the search tree root to the current node (i.e., it saves the x_i values on this path), and `bestx` records the best solution found so far. Whenever a leaf with a better value is reached, `bestx` is updated to represent the path from the root to this leaf. The 1s on this

```
template<class T>
void Loading<T>::maxLoading(int i)
{// Search from level i node.
   if (i > n) {// at a leaf
      bestw = cw;
      return;}
   // check subtrees
   r -= w[i];
   if (cw + w[i] <= c) {// try x[i] = 1
      cw += w[i];
      maxLoading(i+1);
      cw -= w[i];}
   if (cw + r > bestw) // try x[i] = 0
      maxLoading(i+1);
   r += w[i];
}

template<class T>
T MaxLoading(T w[], T c, int n)
{// Return weight of best loading.
   Loading<T> X;
   // initialize X
   X.w = w;
   X.c = c;
   X.n = n;
   X.bestw = 0;
   X.cw = 0;
   // initial r is sum of all weights
   X.r = 0;
   for (int i = 1; i <= n; i++)
      X.r += w[i];

   // compute weight of best loading
   X.maxLoading(1);
   return X.bestw;
}
```

Program 16.2 Refinement of Program 16.1

```
template<class T>
void Loading<T>::maxLoading(int i)
{// Search from level i node.
   if (i > n) {// at a leaf
      for (int j = 1; j <= n; j++)
         bestx[j] = x[j];
      bestw = cw; return;}
   // check subtrees
   r -= w[i];
   if (cw + w[i] <= c) {// try x[i] = 1
      x[i] = 1;
      cw += w[i];
      maxLoading(i+1);
      cw -= w[i];}
   if (cw + r > bestw) {// try x[i] = 0
      x[i] = 0;
      maxLoading(i+1);}
   r += w[i];
}

template<class T>
T MaxLoading(T w[], T c, int n, int bestx[])
{// Return best loading and its value.
   Loading<T> X;
   // initialize X
   X.x = new int [n+1];
   X.w = w;
   X.c = c;
   X.n = n;
   X.bestx = bestx;
   X.bestw = 0;
   X.cw = 0;
   // initial r is sum of all weights
   X.r = 0;
   for (int i = 1; i <= n; i++)
      X.r += w[i];
   X.maxLoading(1);
   delete [] X.x;
   return X.bestw;
}
```

Program 16.3 Code to report best loading

path identify the containers to be loaded. Space for the array x is allocated by `MaxLoading`.

Since `bestx` may be updated $O(2^n)$ times, the complexity of `maxLoading` is $O(n2^n)$. This complexity can be reduced to $O(2^n)$ using one of the following strategies:

1. First run the code of Program 16.2 to determine the weight of the best loading. Let this weight be `W`. Then run a modified version of the code of Program 16.3. The modified version begins with `bestw = W` enters right subtrees so long as `cw+r` ≥ `bestw` and terminates the first time a leaf is reached (i.e., the first time `i > n`).

2. Modify the code of Program 16.3 so that the path from the root to the best leaf encountered so far is saved incrementally. Specifically, if we are at a level `i` node, then the path to the best leaf is given by `x[j]`, $1 \le j < i$ and `bestx[j]`, $j \le i \le n$. This way, each time the algorithm backs up by one level, one `x[i]` is stored in `bestx`. Since the number of times the algorithm backs up is $O(2^n)$, the additional cost is $O(2^n)$.

An Improved Iterative Version

The code of Program 16.3 can be improved to reduce its space requirements. We can eliminate the recursion-stack space, which is $\Theta(n)$, as the array x retains all the information needed to move around in the tree. As illustrated in Example 16.5, from any node in the solution space tree, our algorithm makes a series of left-child moves until no more can be made. Then if a leaf has been reached, the best solution is updated. Otherwise, it tries to move to a right child. When either a leaf is reached or a right-child move is not worthwhile, the algorithm moves back up the tree to a node from which a possibly fruitful right child move can be made. This node has the property that it is the nearest node on the path from the root that has `x[i]` = 1. If a move to the right child is fruitful, it is made and we again attempt to make a series of left-child moves. If the move to the right child is not fruitful, we back up to the next node with `x[i]` = 1. This motion of the algorithm through the tree can be coded as an iterative algorithm as in Program 16.4. Unlike the recursive code, this code moves to a right child before checking whether it should. If the move should not have been made, it backs up. The time complexity of the iterative code is the same as that of Program 16.3.

```
template<class T>
T MaxLoading(T w[], T c, int n, int bestx[])
{// Return best loading and its value.
 // Iterative backtracking version.
   // initialize for root
   int i = 1;  // level of current node
   // x[1:i-1] is path to current node
   int *x = new int [n+1];
   T bestw = 0,  // weight of best loading so far
     cw = 0,      // weight of current loading
      r = 0;      // sum of remaining container weights
   for (int j = 1; j <= n; j++)
      r += w[j];

   // search the tree
   while (true) {
      // move down and left as far as possible
      while (i <= n && cw + w[i] <= c) {
         // move to left child
         r -= w[i]; cw += w[i];
         x[i] = 1; i++;}
      if (i > n) {// leaf reached
         for (int j = 1; j <= n; j++)
            bestx[j] = x[j];
         bestw = cw;}
      else {// move to right child
            r -= w[i]; x[i] = 0; i++;}
      // back up if necessary
      while (cw + r <= bestw) {
         // this subtree does not have a better
         // leaf, backup
         i--;
         while (i > 0 && !x[i]) {
            // backup from a right child
            r += w[i]; i--;}
         if (i == 0) {delete [] x; return bestw;}
         // move to right subtree
         x[i] = 0; cw -= w[i]; i++;
         }
      }
}
```

Program 16.4 Iterative loading code

16.2.2 0/1 Knapsack Problem

The 0/1 knapsack problem is an NP-hard problem for which were considered greedy heuristics in Section 13.4 and developed dynamic-programming algorithms in Section 15.2. In this section we develop a backtracking algorithm for this problem. Since we are to select a subset of objects for inclusion into the knapsack such that the profit obtained is maximum, the solution space is organized as a subset tree (Figure 16.2). The backtracking algorithm is very similar to that for the loading problem of Section 16.2. As in the development of Section 16.2, let us initially develop a recursive algorithm that finds the maximum profit obtainable. Later, this algorithm can be refined to code that finds the subset of objects to be included in the knapsack so as to earn this much profit.

As in the case of Program 16.2, left branches are taken whenever the left child represents a feasible node; right branches are taken when there is a possiblity that the right subtree contains a better solution than the best found so far. A simple way to decide whether or not to move into the right subtree is to define r to the sum of profits of the objects yet to be considered and add r to the profit (cp) earned at the current node. If $r + cp$ is less than or equal to the profit ($bestp$) of the best solution found so far, the right subtree need not be searched. A more effective way is to order the remaining objects by profit density (p_i/w_i), fill the remaining capacity by putting in objects in decreasing order of density, and use a fraction of the first such object that doesn't fit.

Example 16.7 Consider the instance $n = 4$, $c = 7$, $p = [9, 10, 7, 4]$, and $w = [3, 5, 2, 1]$. The profit densities of these objects are $[3, 2, 3.5, 4]$. When the knapsack is packed in decreasing order of density, object 4 is packed first, then object 3 is packed, and then object 1. Following the packing of these three objects, the available capacity is 1. This capacity is adequate for 0.2 of object 2. Putting in 0.2 of this object yields a profit of 2. The solution constructed is $x = [1, 0.2, 1, 1]$, and the corresponding profit is 22. Although this solution is infeasible (x_2 is 0.2 while it should be either zero or one), its value 22 can be shown to be no less than the best feasible solution. Therefore, we know that the 0/1 knapsack instance has no solution with value more than 22.

The solution space tree is that of Figure 16.2 with one additional level of nodes. When we are at node B of the solution space tree, $x_1 = 1$ and the profit earned so far is $cp = 9$. The capacity used at this node is $cw = 3$. The best additional profit we can earn is by filling the remaining capacity $cleft = c - cw = 4$ in order of denisty. That is, first put in object 4, then object 3, and then 0.2 of object 2. Therefore, the value of the best solution in the subtree A is at most 22.

When we are at node C, $cp = cw = 0$ and $cleft = c = 7$. Loading the remaining capacity by density, objects 4 and 3 are packed and then 0.8 of object 2 is packed. This packing yields a profit of 19. No node in subtree C can yield greater profit.

At node E, $cp = 9$, $cw = 3$, *cleft* = 4. Only objects 3 and 4 remain to be considered. When these objects are considered in order of density, object 4 is packed first and then object 3. So no node in subtree E has value more than cp + 4 + 7 = 20. If we have already found a solution with value 20 or more, there is no point in searching subtree E. ∎

A good way to implement this bounding function is to first sort the objects by density. Assume this sort has been done. The class `Knap` (Program 16.5) has been defined so as to reduce the number of parameters to the bounding function `Bound` (Program 16.6) and to the recursive function `Knapsack` (Program 16.7), which computes the value of the best knapsack packing. This reduction in parameters in turn reduces the recursion-stack space needed and also reduces the time for each invocation of `Knapsack`. Notice the similarity between function `Knapsack` and function `maxLoading` (Program 16.2). Also note that the bounding function is computed only for right-child moves. For left-child moves, the bounding function value at the left child is the same as at its parent.

```
template<class Tw, class Tp>
class Knap {
   friend Tp Knapsack(Tp *, Tw *, Tw, int);
   private:
      Tp Bound(int i);
      void Knapsack(int i);
      Tw c;        // knapsack capacity
      int n;       // number of objects
      Tw *w;       // array of object weights
      Tp *p;       // array of object profits
      Tw cw;       // weight of current packing
      Tp cp;       // profit of current packing
      Tp bestp;    // max profit so far
};
```

Program 16.5 The class `Knap`

Before we can invoke function `Knapsack` of Program 16.7, we need to sort the objects by density and also ensure that the sum of weights exceeds the knapsack capacity. For purposes of the sort, we define the class `Object` (Program 16.8). Notice that the `<=` operator has been defined so that the merge sort program (Program 14.3) will sort into decreasing order of density.

Program 16.9 verifies that the sum of weights exceeds the knapsack capacity, sorts the objects, and performs other initializations necessary before `Knap::Knapsack` can be invoked. The complexity of `Knap::Knapsack`

```
template<class Tw, class Tp>
Tp Knap<Tw, Tp>::Bound(int i)
{// Return upper bound on value of
 // best leaf in subtree.
   Tw cleft = c - cw;  // remaining capacity
   Tp b = cp;           // profit bound
   // fill remaining capacity
   // in order of profit density
   while (i <= n && w[i] <= cleft) {
      cleft -= w[i];
      b += p[i];
      i++;
      }

   // take fraction of next object
   if (i <= n) b += p[i]/w[i] * cleft;
   return b;
}
```

Program 16.6 Knapsack bounding function

```
template<class Tw, class Tp>
void Knap<Tw, Tp>::Knapsack(int i)
{// Search from level i node.
   if (i > n) {// at a leaf
      bestp = cp;
      return;}
   // check subtrees
   if (cw + w[i] <= c) {// try x[i] = 1
      cw += w[i];
      cp += p[i];
      Knapsack(i+1);
      cw -= w[i];
      cp -= p[i];}
   if (Bound(i+1) > bestp) // try x[i] = 0
      Knapsack(i+1);
}
```

Program 16.7 Recursive function for 0/1 knapsack problem

```
class Object {
   friend int Knapsack(int *, int *, int, int);
   public:
      int operator<=(Object a) const
      {return (d >= a.d);}
   private:
      int ID;  // object identifier
      float d; // profit density
};
```

Program 16.8 The class `Object`

is $O(n2^n)$, as the bounding function has complexity $O(n)$, and it is computed at $O(2^n)$ right children.

16.2.3   Max Clique

A subset U of the vertices of an undirected graph G defines a **complete subgraph** iff for every u and v in U, (u,v) is an edge of G. The **size** of a subgraph is the number of vertices in it. A complete subgraph is a **clique** of G iff it is not contained in a larger complete subgraph of G. A **max clique** is a clique of maximum size.

Example 16.8 In the graph of Figure 16.7(a), the subset $\{1,2\}$ defines a complete subgraph of size 2. This subgraph is not a clique, as it is contained in a larger complete subgraph (i.e., the one defined by $\{1,2,5\}$). $\{1,2,5\}$ defines a max clique of the graph. The vertex sets $\{1,4,5\}$ and $\{2,3,5\}$ define other max cliques. ■

A subset U of vertices of G defines an empty subgraph iff for every u and v in U, (u,v) is *not* an edge of G. The subset is an **independent set** of G iff it is not contained in a larger subset of vertices that also defines an empty subgraph of G. A **max independent set** is an independent set of maximum size. For any graph G, its **complement** G is a graph that has the same vertex set. Further, (u,v) is an edge of G iff it is not an edge of G.

Example 16.9 The graph of Figure 16.7(b} is the complement of the graph of Figure 16.7(a), and vice versa. $\{2,4\}$ defines an empty subgraph of Figure 16.7(a). It is also a max independent set of this graph. Although $\{1,2\}$ defines an empty subgraph of Figure 16.7(b), it is not an independent set because it is contained in $\{1,2,5\}$, which also defines an empty subgraph. $\{1,2,5\}$ is one of the max independent sets of Figure 16.7(b). ■

```
template<class Tw, class Tp>
Tp Knapsack(Tp p[], Tw w[], Tw c, int n)
{// Return value of best knapsack filling.
   // initialize for Knap::Knapsack
   Tw W = 0;  // will be sum of weights
   Tp P = 0;  // will be sum of profits
   // define an object array to be sorted by
   // profit density
   Object *Q = new Object [n];
   for (int i = 1; i <= n; i++) {
      // array of profit densities
      Q[i-1].ID = i;
      Q[i-1].d = 1.0*p[i]/w[i];
      P += p[i];
      W += w[i];
      }
   if (W <= c) return P;  // all objects fit
   MergeSort(Q,n);  // sort by density

   // create member of Knap
   Knap<Tw, Tp> K;
   K.p = new Tp [n+1];
   K.w = new Tw [n+1];
   for (int i = 1; i <= n; i++) {
      // Ps and Ws in density order
      K.p[i] = p[Q[i-1].ID];
      K.w[i] = w[Q[i-1].ID];
      }
   K.cp = 0;
   K.cw = 0;
   K.c = c;
   K.n = n;
   K.bestp = 0;

   // find best profit
   K.Knapsack(1);

   delete [] Q;
   delete [] K.w;
   delete [] K.p;
   return K.bestp;
}
```

Program 16.9 Preprocessor for Program 16.7

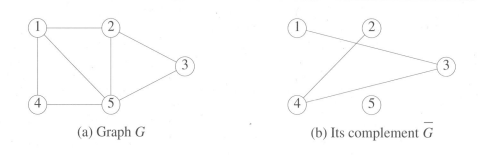

(a) Graph G (b) Its complement $\bar{G}$

Figure 16.7 A graph and its complement

Notice that if U defines a complete subgraph of G, then it also defines an empty subgraph of $\bar{G}$, and vice versa. So there is a correspondence between the cliques of G and the independent sets of $\bar{G}$. In particular, a max clique of G defines a max independent set of $\bar{G}$.

The **max-clique** problem is to find a max clique of the graph G. Similarly, the **max-independent-set** problem is to find a max-independent set of G. Both problems are NP-hard. We can solve one using an algorithm for the other. For example, if we have an algorithm that solves the max-clique problem, we can solve the max-independent-set problem by first computing the complement of the given graph and then finding a max clique in the complement graph.

Example 16.10 Suppose we have a collection of n animals. We may define a **compatibility graph** G that has n vertices. (u,v) is an edge of G iff animals u and v are compatible. A max clique of G defines a largest subset of mutually compatible animals.

In Section 15.6 we considered the problem of finding a maximum size non-crossing subset of nets. We can also formulate this problem as a max-independent-set problem. Define a graph in which each vertex represents a net. There is an edge between two vertices iff the corresponding nets cross. So a maximum independent set of the graph corresponds to a maximum size subset of noncrossing nets. When the nets have one endpoint at the top of the routing channel and the other at the bottom, a maximum size subset of noncrossing nets can be found in polynomial time (actually in $\Theta(n^2)$ time) using dynamic programming. When the endpoints of a net may lie anywhere in the plane, no polynomial-time algorithm to find a maximum size subset of noncrossing nets is known. ∎

The max-clique and max-independent-set problems may be solved by $O(n2^n)$-time backtracking algorithms. In both a subset solution space tree (Figure 16.2) may be used. Consider the max-clique problem. The recursive backtracking algorithm is very similar to Program 16.3. When attempting to move to the left child of a level i node Z of the space tree, we need to verify that there is an edge from vertex i to every other vertex, j, for which $x_j = 1$ on the path from the root to Z. When attempting to move to the right child of Z, we need to verify that enough vertices remain so that there is a possibility of finding a larger clique in the right subtree.

The backtracking algorithm may be implemented as a member of the class `AdjacencyGraph` (Program 12.4) by first adding the private `static` members `x` (integer array, used to store path to current node), `bestx` (integer array, used to save best solution found so far), `bestn` (number of vertices in `bestx`), and `cn` (number of vertices in `x`) to this class. These members have been made `static` members because we envision finding the max clique one graph at a time. So all instances of `AdjacencyGraph` can share these variables.

The function `maxClique` (Program 16.10) is a private member of `AdjacencyGraph`, while `MaxClique` is a public member. Function `maxClique` does the actual search of the solution space tree, while `MaxClique` initializes the necessary variables. The invocation `MaxClique(v)` returns the size of the max clique. It also sets the integer array `v` so that `v[i] = 0` iff vertex `i` is not a member of the found max clique.

16.2.4 Traveling Salesperson

The solution space for the traveling-salesperson problem (Example 16.3) is a permutation tree. Such a tree may be searched using function `Perm` (Program 1.10), which generates all permutations of a list of elements. If we begin with $x = [1, 2, \cdots, n]$, then we can generate the solution space for the n-vertex traveling-salesperson problem by generating all permutations of x_2 through x_n. Since `Perm` generates all permutations with the same prefix together, it is easy to modify `Perm` so that it does not generate permutations that have an invalid prefix (i.e., the prefix does not define a path) or a prefix that cannot be completed into better tours than the best found so far. Notice that in a permutation space tree, the permutations defined by the leaves in any subtree have the same prefix (see Figure 16.5). Therefore, eliminating certain prefixes from consideration is equivalent to not entering certain subtrees during the search.

The backtracking algorithm for the traveling-salesperson problem is best implemented as a member of the class `AdjacencyWDigraph` (Program 12.1). As in our other examples, we shall have two member functions `tSP` and `TSP`. The former is a protected or private member, and the latter a public member. The function `G.TSP(v)` returns the cost of a least-cost tour; the tour itself is returned in the integer array `v`. If the network has no tour, the value `NoEdge` is returned. `TSP` is essentially a preprocessor for `tSP`, which does a

```
void AdjacencyGraph::maxClique(int i)
{// Backtracking code to compute largest clique.
   if (i > n) {// at leaf
      // found a larger clique, update
      for (int j = 1; j <= n; j++)
         bestx[j] = x[j];
      bestn = cn;
      return;}
   // see if vertex i connected to others
   // in current clique
   int OK = 1;
   for (int j = 1; j < i; j++)
      if (x[j] && a[i][j] == NoEdge) {
         // i not connected to j
         OK = 0;
         break;}
   if (OK) {// try x[i] = 1
      x[i] = 1;   // add i to clique
      cn++;
      maxClique(i+1);
      x[i] = 0;
      cn--;}
   if (cn + n - i > bestn) {// try x[i] = 0
      x[i] = 0;
      maxClique(i+1);}
}

int AdjacencyGraph::MaxClique(int v[])
{// Return size of largest clique.
 // Return clique vertices in v[1:n].
   // initialize for maxClique
   x = new int [n+1];
   cn = 0;
   bestn = 0;
   bestx = v;

   // find max clique
   maxClique(1);

   delete [] x;
   return bestn;
}
```

Program 16.10 Max clique

recursive backtrack search in the permutation space tree. TSP assumes that x (integer array to hold path to current node), bestx (integer array to hold best tour found so far), cc (variable of type T to hold cost of partial tour at current node), and bestc (variable of type T to hold cost of best solution found so far) have been defined as static data members of AdjacencyWDigraph. The preprocessor TSP appears in Program 16.11. tSP(2) searches a tree that contains all permutations of x[2:n].

```
template<class T>
T AdjacencyWDigraph<T>::TSP(int v[])
{// Traveling salesperson by backtracking.
 // Return cost of best tour, return tour in v[1:n].
   // initialize for tSP
   x = new int [n+1];
   // x is identity permutation
   for (int i = 1; i <= n; i++)
      x[i] = i;
   bestc = NoEdge;
   bestx = v;  // use array v to store best tour
   cc = 0;

   // search permutations of x[2:n]
   tSP(2);

   delete [] x;
   return bestc;
}
```

Program 16.11 Preprocessor for traveling-salesperson backtracking

Function tSP appears in Program 16.12. Its structure is the same as that of function Perm (Program 1.10). When i equals n, we are at the parent of a leaf of the permutation tree and need to first verify that there is an edge from vertex x[n-1] to x[n], as well as one from x[n] back to the start vertex 1. If both edges exist, we have found a new tour. In this case we need to see whether this tour is the best found so far. If it is, we record the tour and its cost in bestx and bestc, respectively.

When i < n, we examine the children of the current level i-1 node and move to one of these children only if there is (1) an edge from x[i-1] to x[i] (if so, x[1:i] defines a path in the network) and (2) the cost of the path x[1:i] is less than the cost of the best tour found so far (if not, the path cannot be completed into a better tour). The variable cc keeps track of the cost of the path so far constructed.

```
template<class T>
void AdjacencyWDigraph<T>::tSP(int i)
{// Backtracking code for traveling salesperson.
   if (i == n) {// at parent of a leaf
      // complete tour by adding last two edges
      if (a[x[n-1]][x[n]] != NoEdge &&
          a[x[n]][1] != NoEdge &&
          (cc + a[x[n-1]][x[n]] + a[x[n]][1] < bestc ||
          bestc == NoEdge)) {// better tour found
          for (int j = 1; j <= n; j++)
             bestx[j] = x[j];
          bestc = cc + a[x[n-1]][x[n]] + a[x[n]][1];}
      }
   else {// try out subtrees
      for (int j = i; j <= n; j++)
         // is move to subtree labeled x[j] possible?
         if (a[x[i-1]][x[j]] != NoEdge &&
             (cc + a[x[i-1]][x[i]] < bestc ||
              bestc == NoEdge)) {// yes
            // search this subtree
            Swap(x[i], x[j]);
            cc += a[x[i-1]][x[i]];
            tSP(i+1);
            cc -= a[x[i-1]][x[i]];
            Swap(x[i], x[j]);}
      }
}
```

Program 16.12 Recursive backtracking for traveling salesperson

Excluding the cost of updating `bestx` whenever a better tour is found, `tSP` takes $O((n-1)!)$ time. The updating time is $O(n*(n-1)!)$, as $O((n-1)!)$ updates take place and each costs $\Theta(n)$ time. So the overall complexity is $O(n!)$. We can reduce the number of search tree nodes visited by `tSP` by using stronger conditions for the cost of a path (see Exercise 16).

16.2.5 Board Permutation

The board-permutation problem arises in the design of large electronic systems. The classical form of this problem has n circuit boards that are to be placed into slots in a cage (Figure 16.8). Each permutation of the n boards defines a

placement of the boards into the cage. Let $B = \{b_1, \cdots, b_n\}$ denote the n boards. A set $L = \{N_1, \cdots, N_m\}$ of m nets is defined on the boards. Each N_i is a subset of B. These subsets need not be disjoint. Each net is realized by running a wire through the boards that constitute the net.

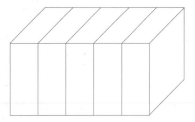

Figure 16.8 Cage with slots

Example 16.11 Let $n = 8$ and $m = 5$. Let the boards and nets be as given below.

$$B = \{b_1, b_2, b_3, b_4, b_5, b_6, b_7, b_8\}$$
$$L = \{N_1, N_2, N_3, N_4, N_5\}$$
$$N_1 = \{b_4, b_5, b_6\}$$
$$N_2 = \{b_2, b_3\}$$
$$N_3 = \{b_1, b_3\}$$
$$N_4 = \{b_3, b_6\}$$
$$N_5 = \{b_7, b_8\}$$

Figure 16.9 shows a possible permutation for the boards. The edges denote the wires that have to be run between the boards. ∎

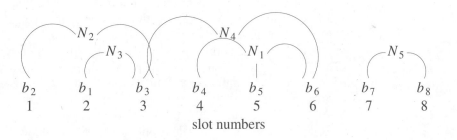

Figure 16.9 Board wiring

Let x denote a board permutation. Board x_i is placed into slot i of the cage when the placement is done using permutation x_i. *density* (x) is the maximum number of wires that cross the gap between any pair of adjacent slots in the cage. For the permutation of Figure 16.9, the *density* is 2. Two wires cross the gaps between slots 2 and 3, slots 4 and 5, and slots 5 and 6. The gap between slots 6 and 7 has no wires, and the remaining gaps have one wire each.

Card cages are designed with a uniform gap size (i.e., the space between adjacent slots is the same). This gap size therefore determines the size of the cage. The gap size itself must be adequate to accommodate the number of wires that must pass through it. Hence the gap size (and in turn the cage size) is determined by *density* (x).

The objective of the board-permutation problem is to find a permutation of the boards that has least *density*. Since this problem is an NP-hard problem, it is unlikely it can be solved by a polynomial-time algorithm and a search method such as backtracking is an attractive way to solve it. The backtracking algorithm will search a permutation space for the best board permutation.

We may represent the input as an $n \times m$ integer array `B` such that `B[i][j]` is 1 iff net N_j includes board b_i. Let `total[j]` be the number of boards that include net N_j. For any partial board permutation `x[1:i]`, let `now[j]` be the number of boards in `x[1:i]` that include net N_j. Net N_j crosses the gap between slots `i` and `i+1` iff `now[j] > 0` and `now[j]` $\neq$ `total[j]`. The wire density between slots `i` and `i+1` may be computed by using this test to determine which wires cross the gap between the two slots. The maximum of the wire densities between slots `k` and `k+1` for $1 \le k \le i$ gives the density of the partial permutation.

Our implementation of the backtracking algorithm for the board-permutation problem uses the class `Board` (Program 16.13). Program 16.14 gives the private method `BestOrder` and Program 16.15 gives the preprocessor function `ArrangeBoards`. `ArrangeBoards` returns the density of the best board arrangement. The best arrangement is returned in the array `bestx`.

`ArrangeBoards` creates `X` which is a member of the class `Board` and initializes the variables associated with it. In particular, `total` is initialized so that `total[j]` equals the number of boards with net `j`, and `now[1:n]` is set to zero corresponding to a null partial permutation. The invocation `X.BestOrder(1,0)` searches the permutation tree of `x[1:n]` for a best completion of the null permutation whose density is zero. In general, `X.BestOrder(i, cd)` finds the best completion of the partial permutation `x[1:i-1]`. This partial permutation has density `cd`.

Function `BestOrder` (Program 16.14) has the same structure as Program 16.12, which also searches a permutation space. This time, when `i` equals `n`, all boards have been placed and `cd` is the density of the complete permutation. Since the algorithm completes only those permutations that are better than the

```
class Board {
   friend ArrangeBoards(int**, int, int, int []);
   private:
      void BestOrder(int i, int cd);
      int *x,         // path to current node
          *bestx,     // best arrangement found so far
          *total,     // total[j] = number of boards
                      // with net j
          *now,       // now[j] = number of boards in
                      // partial arrangement with net j
          bestd,      // density of bestx
          n,          // number of boards
          m,          // number of nets
          **B;        // 2D board array
};
```

Program 16.13 Class definition of Board

best found so far, we need not verify that cd is less than bestd. When i <
n, the permutation is not complete. x[1:i-1] defines the partial permutation
at the current tree node, and cd is its density. Each child of this node expands
this partial permutation by adding one board at the end. For each such expansion, the new density ld is computed, and only those nodes for which ld <
bestd are searched. Other nodes and their subtrees are not searched.

At each node of the permutation tree, function BestOrder spends $\Theta(m)$
time computing the density at each child. So the total time spent computing
these densities is O(mn!). In addition, O(n!) time is spent generating permutations and O(mn) time is spent updating the best. Note that each update reduces
bestd by at least one, and on termination bestd ≥ 0. So the number of
updates is O(m). The overall complexity of BestOrder is O(mn!).

```
void Board::BestOrder(int i, int cd)
{// Backtracking search of permutation tree.
   if (i == n) {// all boards placed
      for (int j = 1; j <= n; j++)
         bestx[j] = x[j];
      bestd = cd;}
   else // try out subtrees
      for (int j = i; j <= n; j++) {
         // try child with board x[j] as next one

         // update now & compute density at last slot
         int ld = 0;
         for (int k = 1; k <= m; k++) {
            now[k] += B[x[j]][k];
            if (now[k] > 0 && total[k] != now[k])
               ld++;
         }

         // update ld to be overall density of
         // partial arrangement
         if (cd > ld) ld = cd;

         // search subtree only if it may
         // contain a better arrangement
         if (ld < bestd) {// move to child
            Swap(x[i], x[j]);
            BestOrder(i+1, ld);
            Swap(x[i], x[j]);}

         // reset now
         for (int k = 1; k <= m; k++)
            now[k] -= B[x[j]][k];
      }
}
```

Program 16.14 Search the permutation tree

```
int ArrangeBoards(int **B, int n, int m, int bestx[])
{// Return best density.
 // Return best arrangement in bestx.
   Board X;
   // initialize X
   X.x = new int [n+1];
   X.total = new int [m+1];
   X.now = new int [m+1];
   X.B = B;
   X.n = n;
   X.m = m;
   X.bestx = bestx;
   X.bestd = m + 1;

   // initialize total and now
   for (int i = 1; i <= m; i++) {
      X.total[i] = 0;
      X.now[i] = 0;
      }

   // initialize x to identity permutation
   // and compute total
   for (int i = 1; i <= n; i++) {
      X.x[i] = i;
      for (int j = 1; j <= m; j++)
         X.total[j] += B[i][j];
      }

   // find best arrangement
   X.BestOrder(1,0);

   delete [] X.x;
   delete [] X.total;
   delete [] X.now;
   return X.bestd;
}
```

Program 16.15 Preprocessor for `BestOrder` (Program 16.14)

EXERCISES

4. Prove that the two-ship-loading strategy in which the first is loaded as close to its capacity as possible finds a feasible loading whenever there is a way to load all containers.

5. Experiment with the codes of Programs 16.3 and 16.4 to determine their relative run-time performance.

6. Write a new version of Program 16.3 that uses strategy 1 to achieve a time complexity of $O(2^n)$.

7. Modify Program 16.3 using strategy 2 to reduce its time to $O(2^n)$.

8. Write a recursive backtracking algorithm for the sum of subset problem. Notice that in this case we can terminate as soon as a subset with sum c_1 is found. There is no need to remember the best solution found so far. Your code should not use an array such as x used in Program 16.3. Rather, the solution should be reconstructed as the recursion unfolds after finding a subset with sum c_1.

9. Refine Programs 16.7 and 16.9 so that they compute a 0/1 array x that corresponds to the best packing of the knapsack.

10. Obtain an iterative backtracking algorithm for the 0/1 knapsack problem. Your algorithm should be similar to Program 16.4. Notice that `Knap::Bound` can be modified to return the last object i that was packed into the knapsack and so avoid remaking the left moves made by `Bound` and move directly to the left-most node moved to by `Bound`.

11. Write an iterative version of Program 16.10 that corresponds to Program 16.4. What can you say about the relative merits of the two versions?

12. Write a version of Program 16.10 that begins by sorting the vertices into decreasing order of degree. Do you expect this version to work any better than Program 16.10.

13. Write a backtracking algorithm for the max-independent-set problem.

14. Rewrite the max-clique code (Program 16.10) as members of the class `UNetwork`. The same code should work on members of the classes `AdjacencyGraph`, `AdjacencyWGraph`, `LinkedGraph`, and `LinkedWGraph` (see Section 12.7).

15. Let G be a directed graph with n vertices. Let Max_i be the cost of the most expensive edge that leaves vertex i.

    (a) Show that every traveling-salesperson tour has a cost less than
    $$\sum_{i=1}^{n} Max_i + 1.$$

(b) Use this bound as the initial value of `bestc`. Rewrite `TSP` and `tSP`, simplifying the code where possible.

16. Let G be a directed graph with n vertices. Let $MinOut_i$ be the cost of the least expensive edge that leaves vertex i.

   (a) Show that all traveling-salesperson tours with the prefix x_1 through x_i cost at least $\sum_{j=2}^{i} A(x_{j-1}, x_j) + \sum_{j=i}^{n} MinOut_{x_j}$ where $A(u,v)$ is the cost of the edge $<u,v>$.

   (b) Use the result of (a) to obtain a stronger condition than

   ```
   if (a[x[i-1]][x[j]] != NoEdge &&
       (cc + a[x[i-1]][x[i]] < bestc ||
        bestc == NoEdge))
   ```

   which is used in Program 16.12 to determine when to move to a child node. The first sum is easily computed from `cc`, and the second is easily computed by maintaining in a new variable `r` the sum of the `MinOut[i]` values of the vertices not included in the path so far constructed.

   (c) Test the new version of `tSP` to see how many nodes of the permutation tree it visits compared to the number visited by Program 16.12.

17. Consider any board arrangement. The length of a net is the distance between the first and last boards that include this net. For the board arrangement of Figure 16.9, the first board that includes N_4 is in slot 3 and the last in slot 6. The net length is therefore 3. The length of net N_2 is 2 because its first board is in slot 1 and its last in slot 3. The length of the longest net in the arrangement of Figure 16.9 is 3. Write a backtracking code to find the board arrangement that has the smallest maximum length. Test the correctness of your code.

18. [*Vertex Cover*] Let G be an undirected graph. A subset U of its vertices is a **vertex cover** iff for every edge (u,v) of G, either u or v or both are in U. The number of vertices in U is the **size** of the cover. $\{1,2,5\}$ is a vertex cover of size three in the graph of Figure 16.7(a). Write a backtracking algorithm to find a vertex cover of least size. What is its complexity?

19. [*Simple Max Cut*] Let G be an undirected graph and let U be any subset of its vertices. Let V be the remaining vertices of G. The number of edges with one endpoint in U and the other in V is the size of the **cut** defined by U. Write a backtracking algorithm to find the size of the maximum cut as well as the corresponding U. What is its complexity?

20. [*Machine Design*] A certain machine consists of n components. Each component is available from three vendors. Let w_{ij} be the weight of component i available from vendor j and let c_{ij} be its cost. Write a

backtracking algorithm to determine the least-weight machine that can be constructed at a cost no more than c. What is its complexity?

21.   [**Network Design**] A petroleum delivery network has been represented as a directed weighted acyclic graph G. G has a vertex s called the **source** vertex. This vertex is the source from which the petroleum flows to the remaining vertices. The in-degree of s is zero. Each edge weight gives the distance between the two vertices it connects. The pressure loss as petroleum flows through the network is a function of the distance travelled. To ensure proper operation of the network, it is necessary to maintain a certain minimum pressure P_{min} throughout the network. To maintain this minimum pressure, pressure boosters may be placed at some or all of the vertices of G. A pressure booster restores the pressure to the maximum allowable level, P_{max}. Let d be the distance petroleum can flow before its pressure drops from P_{max} to P_{min}. In the **booster-placement problem**, we need to place the minimum number of boosters so that petroleum flows a distance no more than d before encountering a booster. Write a backtracking algorithm for the booster-placement problem. What is its complexity?

22.   [*n* **Queens**] In the n-queens problem, we wish to find a placement of n queens on an $n \times n$ chessboard such that no two queens attack. Two queens are said to **attack** iff they are in the same row, column, diagonal, or antidiagonal of the chessboard. Hence we may assume that in any feasible solution, queen i is placed in row i of the chess board. So we are interested only in determining the column placement of each queen. Let c_i denote the column that queen i is placed in. If no two queens attack, then $[c_1, \cdots, c_n]$ is a permutation of $[1, 2, \cdots, n]$. The solution space for the n queens problem can therefore be limited to all permutations of $[1, 2, \cdots, n]$.

   (a)   Organize the n queens solution space as a tree.

   (b)   Write a backtracking procedure to search this tree for a feasible placement of the n queens.

★ 23.   Write a function to search a subset space tree, which is a binary tree, by backtracking. The parameters to your function should include functions to determine whether a node is feasible, compute a bound at this node, determine if this bound is better than another value, and so on. Test your code by using it on the loading and 0/1 knapsack problems.

★ 24.   Do Exercise 23 for permutation space trees.

★ 25.   Write a function to search a solution space by backtracking. The parameters to your function should include functions to generate the next child of a node, determine whether this next child is feasible, compute a bound at this node, determine if this bound is better than another value, and so on. Test your code by using it on the loading and 0/1 knapsack problems.

CHAPTER 17

BRANCH AND BOUND

BIRD'S-EYE VIEW

All good things must come to an end. We are at the last chapter of this book. Fortunately, most of the concepts used in this chapter have been developed in earlier ones. Like backtracking, branch and bound searches a solution space that is often organized as a tree. The common tree organizations are the subset and permutation trees introduced in Chapter 16. However, unlike backtracking, which searches these tree organizations in a depth-first manner, branch and bound usually searches these trees in either a breadth-first or least-cost manner. The applications considered in this chapter are the same as those of Chapter 16. Consequently, it should be easy for you to see the similarities and differences between the backtracking and branch-and-bound methods.

Since the space requirements of branch-and-bound algorithms are often considerably more than those of their backtracking counterparts, backtracking is often more successful at finding the answer in memory-limited situations.

17.1 THE METHOD

Branch and bound is another way to systematically search a solution space. It differs from backtracking primarily in the way an E-node is expanded. Each live node becomes an E-node exactly once. When a node becomes an E-node, all new nodes that can be reached using a single move are generated. Generated nodes that cannot possibly lead to a (optimal) feasible solution are discarded. The remaining nodes are added to the list of live nodes and then one node from this list is selected to become the next E-node. The selected node is extracted from the list of live nodes and expanded. This expansion process is continued until either the answer is found or the list of live nodes becomes empty.

There are two common ways to select the next E-node (though other possibities exist):

- **First-in First-out (FIFO)**
  This scheme extracts nodes from the list of live nodes in the same order as they are put into it. The live node list behaves as a queue.

- **Least Cost or Max Profit**
  This scheme associates a cost or profit with each node. If we are searching for a solution with least cost, then the list of live nodes can be set up as a min heap. The next E-node is the live node with least cost. If we want a solution with maximum profit, the live node list can be set up as a max heap. The next E-node is the live node with maximum profit.

Example 17.1 [*Rat in a Maze*] Consider the rat in a maze instance of Figure 16.3(a) and the solution space organization of Figure 16.1. In a FIFO branch and bound, we begin with (1,1) as the E-node and an empty live node list. The maze position (1,1) is set to 1 to prevent a return to this position. (1,1) is expanded, and its neighbor nodes (1,2) and (2,1) are added to the queue (i.e., the list of live nodes). Positions (1,2) and (2,1) are set to 1 in the maze to prevent moving to these positions again. The maze now is as in Figure 17.1(a), and the E-node (1,1) discarded.

1	1	0		1	1	1		1	1	1
1	1	1		1	1	1		1	1	1
0	0	0		0	0	0		1	0	0
	(a)				(b)				(c)

Figure 17.1 FIFO branch and bound in a maze

Node (1,2) is removed from the queue and expanded. Its three neighbors (see the solution space of Figure 16.1) are examined. Only (1,3) represents a feasible move (the remaining two nodes represent moves to blocked positions), and it is added to the queue. This maze position is set to 1 and the status of *maze* is as in Figure 17.1(b). Node (1,2) is discarded. The next E-node is extracted from the queue. It is (2,1). When this E-node is expanded, node (3,1) is added to the queue, *maze* (3,1) is set to 1, and node (2,1) discarded. *maze* is as in Figure 17.1(c), and the queue has the nodes (1,3) and (3,1) on it. (1,3) becomes the next E-node. Since this E-node does not get us to any new nodes, it is discarded and (3,1) becomes the new E-node. At this time the queue is empty. Node (3,1) gets us to node (3,2), which is now added to the queue, and (3,1) discarded. (3,2) is the next E-node. Expanding this node, we reach the exit (3,3), and the search terminates.

A FIFO search of a maze has the desirable property that the path found (if any) is a shortest path from the entrance to the maze. Observe that the path found by backtracking may not be a shortest path. Interestingly, we have already seen the code for a FIFO branch-and-bound search of a maze. The wire-routing code of Program 6.11 when run with the start position (1,1) and finish position (n,n) performs a FIFO branch-and-bound search of the maze and determines the shortest start-to-finish path. ∎

Example 17.2 [*0/1 Knapsack*] We shall carry out both a FIFO and a maximum profit branch-and-bound search on the knapsack instance $n = 3$, $w = [20, 15, 15]$, $p = [40, 25, 25]$, and $c = 30$. The FIFO version uses a queue to keep track of live nodes, as these nodes are to be extracted in FIFO order. The max-profit version uses a max heap, as E-nodes are selected from among the live nodes in decreasing order of profit earned at the live node or in decreasing order of an estimate of the maximum profit earned at any leaf in the live node's subtree. The instance we are using is the same as that used in Example 16.2, and the solution space tree is that of Figure 16.2.

The FIFO branch-and-bound search begins with the root A as the E-node. At this time the live node queue is empty. When node A is expanded, nodes B and C are generated. As both are feasible, they are added to the live-node queue, and node A is discarded. The next E-node is node B. It is expanded to get nodes D and E. D is infeasible and discarded, while E is added to the queue. Next C becomes the E-node. When expanded, it leads to nodes F and G. Both are feasible and added to the queue. The next E-node E gets us to J and K. J is infeasible and discarded. K is a feasible leaf and represents a possible solution to the instance. Its profit value is 40.

The next E-node is node F. Its children L and M are generated. L represents a feasible packing with profit value 50, while M represents a feasible packing with value 15. G is the last node to become the E-node. Its children N and O are both feasible. The search now terminates because the live-node queue is empty. The best solution found has value 50.

Notice that a FIFO branch and bound working on a solution space tree is very much like a breadth-first search of the tree with the root as the start vertex. The major difference is that subtrees of infeasible nodes are not searched.

The max profit branch-and-bound algorithm begins with node A of the solution space tree as the initial E-node. The max heap of live nodes is initially empty. Expanding the initial E-node yields the nodes B and C. Both are feasible and are inserted into the heap. The profit earned at node B is 40 (as $x_1 = 1$ here), while that earned at C is 0. A is discarded, and B becomes the next E-node, as its profit value is larger than that of C. When B is expanded, the nodes D and E are generated. D is infeasible and discarded. E is added to the heap. E becomes the next E-node, as its profit value is 40, while that of C is 0. When E is expanded, the nodes J and K are generated. J is infeasible and discarded. K represents a feasible solution. This solution is recorded as the best found so far, and K discarded. Only one live node, node C, remains. This live node becomes the new E-node. Nodes F and G are generated and inserted into the max heap. F has a profit of 25 and becomes the next E-node. Nodes L and M are generated. Both are discarded, as they are leaf nodes. The solution corresponding to L is recorded as the best found so far. Finally, G becomes the E-node, and the nodes N and O generated. Both are leaves and are discarded. Neither represents a solution that is better than the best found so far, so no solution update takes place. The heap is empty, and there is no next E-node. The search terminates with J representing the optimal solution.

As in the case of backtracking, *the search for an optimal solution can be speeded by using a bounding function*. This function places an upper bound on the maximum profit that can possibly be obtained by expanding a particular node. If a node's bound isn't larger than the profit of the best solution found so far, it may be discarded without expansion. Further, in the case of a max profit branch and bound, nodes may be extracted from the max heap in nonincreasing order of the profit bound, rather than by the actual profit for the node. This strategy to extract nodes gives preference to live nodes that are likely to lead to good leaves, rather than to nodes that have already earned large profit. ∎

Example 17.3 [*Traveling Salesperson*] Consider the four-city traveling-salesperson instance of Figure 16.4. The corresponding solution space organization is the permutation tree of Figure 16.5. A FIFO branch-and-bound would begin with node B as the initial E-node and an empty queue of live nodes. When B is expanded, the nodes C, D, and E are generated. As there is an edge from vertex 1 to each of the vertices 2, 3, and 4, all three of these nodes are feasible and all three are added to the queue. The E-node B dies, and the next E-node is the first live node on the queue. Node C is the next E-node. When this node is expanded, nodes F and G are generated. Both are added to the queue because the graph of Figure 16.4 has an edge from vertex 2 to both vertex 3 and vertex 4. Next D becomes the E-node, and then E becomes the E-node. Now the live node queue contains the nodes F through K.

The next E-node is F. It is expanded to obtain node L, which is a leaf. A tour has been found. Its cost is 59. The next E-node G gets us to leaf M, which defines a tour whose cost is 66. When node H becomes the E-node, the leaf N that represents a tour of cost 25 is reached. The next E-node is I. It represents the partial tour 1,3,4 whose cost, 26, is more than that of the best tour found so far. So I is not expanded. Finally, J and K become E-nodes and get expanded. Following this expansion, the queue is empty, and the algorithm terminates with node N identifying the best tour.

Instead of searching the solution space tree in a FIFO manner, we could search in a least-cost manner, using a min heap to store the live nodes. This search also begins with node B as the E-node and an empty live node list. When B is expanded, the nodes C, D, and E are generated and added to the min heap. Of the nodes in the min heap, E has least cost (the partial tour 1,4 has cost 4) and becomes the new E-node. E is expanded, and the nodes J and K are added to the min heap. These nodes have a cost of 14 and 24, respectively. The least-cost node in the min heap is now D. It becomes the E-node, and H and I are generated. The min heap now contains the nodes C, H, I, J, and K. Of these nodes, H has least cost. H is the next E-node. It is expanded, and the tour 1,3,2,4,1 of cost 25 is completed. Node J is the next E-node. When it is expanded, we reach node P, which represents a tour of cost 25. Nodes K and I are the next two E-nodes. As the cost of I exceeds that of the best solution found so far, the search terminates; none of the remaining live nodes can get us to a better solution.

As in the case of the knapsack example (Example 17.2), we can use a bounding function to reduce the number of nodes generated and expanded. Such a function will determine a lower bound on the minimum-cost tour that can possibly be obtained by expanding a particular node. If a node's bound isn't smaller than the cost of the best tour found so far, it may be discarded without expansion. Further, in the case of a least-cost branch and bound, nodes may be extracted from the min heap in nondecreasing order of the cost bound. ∎

As mentioned in the preceding examples, we can use bounding functions to reduce the number of nodes of the solution space tree that are generated. When developing a bounding function, we should keep in mind that our primary objective is to solve the instance using the least amount of time and using no more memory than is available to us. *Solving the problem by generating the least number of nodes is not the primary objective.* As a result, we need a bounding function that pays for its computation time by a corresponding reduction in the number of nodes generated.

Backtracking generally has a memory advantage over branch and bound. The memory needed by backtracking is O(length of longest path in the solution space organization), while that needed by branch and bound is O(size of solution space organization). For a subset space, backtracking requires $\Theta(n)$ memory, while the branch-and-bound methods considered require $O(2^n)$ memory. For a permutation space, backtracking requires $\Theta(n)$ memory, while branch and bound needs $O(n\ !)$. Although a max-profit or least-cost branch and bound has intuitive appeal over backtracking and might be expected to examine fewer nodes on many inputs, the space needs might exceed what is available sooner than the time needs of backtracking exceed the length of time we are willing to wait for the answer.

EXERCISES

1. In a **last-in first-out (LIFO)** branch-and-bound search, the list of live nodes behaves as a stack. Describe the progress of such a method on the knapsack instance of Example 17.2. How does LIFO branch and bound differ from backtracking?

2. Consider the 0/1 knapsack instance with $n = 4$, $p = [4, 3, 2, 1]$, $w = [1, 2, 3, 4]$, and $c = 6$.

    (a) Draw the solution space tree for a four-object knapsack instance.

    (b) Trace through the working of a FIFO branch-and-bound search, as was done in Example 17.2.

    (c) Use function `Bound` (Program 16.6) to determine the maximum profit obtainable at any leaf in a subtree. Use this bound together with the value of the best solution determined so far to decide whether or not to add a node to the live node list. Which nodes of the solution space tree are generated by a FIFO branch and bound that uses this mechanism?

    (d) Trace through the working of a max-profit branch-and-bound search, as was done in Example 17.2.

    (e) Which nodes of the solution space tree are generated during a max-profit branch and bound when the bounding function of (c) is used?

17.2   APPLICATIONS

17.2.1   Container Loading

FIFO Branch and Bound

The container-loading problem of Section 16.2.1 essentially requires us to find a maximum loading of the first ship. This problem is a subset-selection problem and the solution space organization is a subset tree. The FIFO branch-and-bound analog of Program 16.1 is Program 17.1. Like Program 16.1, Program 17.1 finds only the weight of a maximum loading.

```
template<class T>
void AddLiveNode(LinkedQueue<T> &Q, T wt,
                     T& bestw, int i, int n)
{// Add node weight wt to queue Q if not leaf.
   if (i == n) {// feasible leaf
       if (wt > bestw) bestw = wt;}
   else Q.Add(wt); // not a leaf
}


template<class T>
T MaxLoading(T w[], T c, int n)
{// Return value of best loading.
 // Use FIFO branch and bound.
   // initialize for level 1 start
   LinkedQueue<T> Q;   // live-node queue
   Q.Add(-1);          // end-of-level marker
   int i = 1;          // level of E-node
   T Ew = 0,           // weight of E-node
     bestw = 0;        // best weight so far

   // search subset space tree
   while (true) {
      // check left child of E-node
      if (Ew + w[i] <= c) // x[i] = 1
         AddLiveNode(Q, Ew + w[i], bestw, i, n);

      // right child is always feasible
      AddLiveNode(Q, Ew, bestw, i, n); // x[i] = 0

      Q.Delete(Ew);       // get next E-node
      if (Ew == -1) {     // end of level
         if (Q.IsEmpty()) return bestw;
         Q.Add(-1);       // end-of-level marker
         Q.Delete(Ew);    // get next E-node
         i++;}            // level number of Ew
   }
}
```

Program 17.1 FIFO branch-and-bound search for container loading

Function `MaxLoading` does the branch-and-bound search of the solution space tree. The linked queue `Q` keeps track of live nodes. Only the weight associated with each live node is stored in the queue. The queue also stores the weight −1 to mark the end of a level of live nodes. Function `AddLiveNode` is used to add nodes (i.e., their weights to the live node queue). This function begins by checking whether `i` (the level of the current E-node) equals `n`. If so, we are at a leaf. Leaves are not added to the queue, as these nodes cannot be expanded. Leaves that are reached define feasible solutions, and each is checked for being better than the best found so far. When `i < n`, the node is added to the queue.

`MaxLoading` begins by initializing `i = 1` (current E-node is the root) and `bestw = 0` (value of best loading found so far). At this time, there are no live nodes in the queue. A −1 is added to the queue to indicate that we are at the end of level 1. The weight associated with the current E-node is given by `Ew`. In the `while` loop, we first see whether the left child of the E-node is feasible. If so, `AddLiveNode` is invoked. Then the right child is added. (This child is guaranteed to be feasible.) Notice that `AddLiveNode` may fail as we may not have enough memory to add a node to the queue. `AddLiveNode` does not catch the `NoMem` exception that `Q.Add` may throw. The catching of this exception is left to the user.

When both children of the E-node have been generated, the E-node dies and we extract the next E-node from the queue. The queue cannot be empty at this time because it must contain at least the end-of-level marker −1. If we have reached the end of a level, then we see whether any live nodes from the next level are present. These nodes are present iff the queue is not empty. When live nodes from the next level are present, we add an end-of-level marker to the queue and begin to process the live nodes at the next level.

The time and space requirements of `MaxLoading` are $O(2^n)$.

An Improvement

We may attempt the refinement used in Program 16.2. In this refinement, a right child was pursued only if the weight associated with it plus the weight (r) of the remaining containers exceeds `bestw`. In Program 17.1 `bestw` doesn't get updated until `i` equals `n`. Prior to this time, the right-child test always succeeds as `bestw = 0` and `r > 0`. When `i` equals `n`, no more nodes are added to the queue. So the right-child test is of no use at this time.

To make the right-child test effective, we need to update `bestw` earlier. We know that the weight of the best loading is the maximum of the weights associated with the feasible nodes in the subset tree. Since these associated weights increase only when a move is made to a left child, we may update `bestw` at all such moves. This observation results in the code of Program 17.2. When a live node is added to the queue, `wt` cannot exceed `bestw` and so `bestw` is not updated. A single statement, inserted directly into `MaxLoading`, now replaces the function `AddLiveNode`.

```
template<class T>
T MaxLoading(T w[], T c, int n)
{// Return value of best loading.
 // Use FIFO branch and bound.
   // initialize for level 1 start
   LinkedQueue<T> Q;    // live-node queue
   Q.Add(-1);           // end-of-level marker
   int i = 1;           // level of E-node
   T Ew = 0,            // weight of E-node
     bestw = 0,         // best weight so far
     r = 0;             // remaining weight at E-node
   for (int j = 2; j <= n; j++)
     r += w[i];

   // search subset space tree
   while (true) {
       // check left child of E-node
       T wt = Ew + w[i];   // weight of left child
       if (wt <= c) {      // feasible left child
          if (wt > bestw) bestw = wt;
          // add to queue unless leaf
          if (i < n) Q.Add(wt);}

       // check right child
       if (Ew + r > bestw && i < n)
          Q.Add(Ew);       // may have a better leaf

       Q.Delete(Ew);       // get next E-node
       if (Ew == -1) {     // end of level
          if (Q.IsEmpty()) return bestw;
          Q.Add(-1);       // end-of-level marker
          Q.Delete(Ew);    // get next E-node
          i++;             // level of E-node
          r -= w[i];}      // remaining weight at E-node
       }
}
```

Program 17.2 Improved version of Program 17.1

Finding the Best Subset

To be able to find the best subset, we need to store paths from the live nodes to the tree root. Then when we have determined which leaf gives the best loading, we can traverse the path to the root setting the x values. The data type of the elements in the queue of live nodes is QNode (Program 17.3). Here LChild equals true iff the node is the left child of its parent.

```
template<class T>
class  QNode {
   private:
      QNode *parent;  // pointer to parent node
      bool LChild;    // true iff left child of parent
      T weight;       // weight of partial solution
                      // defined by path to this node
};
```

Program 17.3 The class QNode

The new branch-and-bound code appears in Program 17.4. The time overhead of invoking function AddLiveNode that has a large number of parameters may be eliminated by making this function an inline function. The use of an inline function increases the space requirements slightly as the resulting code is longer. Alternatively, we may define AddLiveNode and MaxLoading as members of a class through which they can share variables such as Q, i, n, bestw, E, bestE, and bestx, which can be defined as class members.

The code of Program 17.4 doesn't delete nodes of type QNode. One way to delete these nodes is to save pointers to all nodes created by AddLiveNode and then delete these nodes at the end.

Max-Profit Branch and Bound

In a max-profit branch-and-bound search of the subset tree, the list of live nodes is a max-priority queue. Each live node x in the queue has an upper weight (or max profit) associated with it. This upper weight is the weight associated with the node x plus the weight of the remaining containers. Live nodes become E-nodes in decreasing order of their upper weight. Notice that if x is a node with upper weight x.uweight, then no node in its subtree has weight more than x.uweight. From this observation and the observation that the weight associated with a leaf node equals its upper weight, we conclude that when a leaf becomes the E-node in a max-cost branch and bound, no remaining live node can lead to a leaf with more weight. Therefore, we may terminate the search for the best loading.

```
template<class T>
void AddLiveNode(LinkedQueue<QNode<T>*> &Q, T wt,
     int i, int n, T bestw, QNode<T> *E,
     QNode<T> *&bestE, int bestx[], bool ch)
{// Add a level i weight wt live node to the
 // queue Q if not leaf.  New node is a child
 // of E.  ch is true iff new node is the left
 // child.  If feasible leaf set bestx[n] to ch.
   if (i == n) {// feasible leaf
      if (wt == bestw) {
         // best so far
         bestE = E;
         bestx[n] = ch;}
      return;}

   // not a leaf, add to queue
   QNode<T> *b;
   b = new QNode<T>;
   b->weight = wt;
   b->parent = E;
   b->LChild = ch;
   Q.Add(b);
}

template<class T>
T MaxLoading(T w[], T c, int n, int bestx[])
{// Return value of best loading.  Return best
 // loading in bestx.  Use FIFO branch and bound.
   // initialize for level 1 start
   LinkedQueue<QNode<T>*> Q;   // live-node queue
   Q.Add(0);               // 0 is end-of-level pointer
   int i = 1;              // level of E-node
   T Ew = 0,               // weight of E-node
     bestw = 0,            // best weight so far
     r = 0;                // remaining weight at E-node
   for (int j = 2; j <= n; j++)
      r += w[i];
   QNode<T> *E = 0,     // current E-node
            *bestE;     // best E-node so far
```

Program 17.4 Branch-and-bound code that also computes the best subset (continues)

```
      // search subset space tree
   while (true) {
      // check left child of E-node
      T wt = Ew + w[i];
      if (wt <= c) {// feasible left child
         if (wt > bestw) bestw = wt;
         AddLiveNode(Q, wt, i, n, bestw, E,
                              bestE, bestx, true);}

      // check right child
      if (Ew + r > bestw) AddLiveNode(Q, Ew, i, n,
                        bestw, E, bestE, bestx, false);

      Q.Delete(E);      // next E-node
      if (!E) {         // end of level
         if (Q.IsEmpty()) break;
         Q.Add(Q);      // end-of-level pointer
         Q.Delete(E);   // next E-node
         i++;           // level of E-node
         r -= w[i];}    // remaining weight at E-node

      Ew = E->weight;   // weight of new E-node
      }

   // construct x[] by following path from
   // bestE to root, x[n] set by AddLiveNode
   for (int j = n - 1; j > 0; j--) {
      bestx[j] = bestE->LChild;   // bool to int
      bestE = bestE->parent;
      }

   return bestw;
}
```

Program 17.4 Branch-and-bound code that also computes the best subset (concluded)

This strategy may be implemented in one of two ways. In the first each live node resides in the max-priority queue alone. In this case each node must contain the path from the root of the subset tree to the node. This information is needed to determine the x values once we have identified the leaf that yields the best loading. In the second strategy, in addition to placing each live node into the max-priority queue, the node is entered into a separate tree structure that represents the portion of the subset tree generated. When the best leaf is identified, the corresponding x values are determined by following the path from the leaf to the root. We shall use this second implementation method. Exercise 8 explores the first method.

The max-priority queue may be represented as a max heap of type Heap-Node (Program 17.5). uweight is the upper weight of the live node, level is the level of the subset tree at which the live node resides, and ptr points to the live node in the subset tree. Nodes in the subset tree are of type bbnode, which is also defined in Program 17.5. Nodes are extracted from the max heap using their uweight value.

```
class bbnode {
   private:
      bbnode *parent;  // pointer to parent node
      bool LChild;     // true iff left child of parent
};

template<class T>
class HeapNode {
   public:
      operator T () const {return uweight;}
   private:
      bbnode *ptr;   // pointer to live node
      T uweight;     // upper weight of live node
      int level;     // level of live node
};
```

Program 17.5 bbnode and HeapNode classes

The function AddLiveNode (Program 17.6) adds a new live node to the subset tree, using a node of type bbnode, and also inserts it into the max heap, using a node of type HeapNode. AddLiveNode needs to be declared a friend of both bbnode and HeapNode.

The function MaxLoading (Program 17.6) begins by defining a max heap whose capacity is 1000. Consequently, we can solve instances that have at most 1000 live nodes in the priority queue at any time. For larger instances we will need to define a larger max heap. Next the array r of remaining weights is initialized. The sum of the weights of the remaining containers for a level i+1 node (i.e., a node at which decisions have already been made for x[1:i]) is given by $r[i] = \sum_{j=i+1}^{n} w[j]$. The variable E points to the current E-node in the subset tree, and Ew is the weight associated with this node; its level is given

```
template<class T>
void AddLiveNode(MaxHeap<HeapNode<T> > &H, bbnode *E,
                 T wt, bool ch, int lev)
{// Add a level lev live node with upper weight
 // wt to max heap H.  New node is a child of E.
 // ch is true iff new node is the left child.
   bbnode *b = new bbnode;
   b->parent = E;
   b->LChild = ch;
   HeapNode<T> N;
   N.uweight = wt;
   N.level = lev;
   N.ptr = b;
   H.Insert(N);
}

template<class T>
T MaxLoading(T w[], T c, int n, int bestx[])
{// Return value of best loading.  Return best
 // loading in bestx.
 // Use max-profit branch and bound.
   // define a max heap for up to
   // 1000 live nodes
   MaxHeap<HeapNode<T> > H(1000);
   // define array of remaining weights
   // r[j] sum of weights w[j+1:n]
   T *r = new T [n+1];
   r[n] = 0;
   for (int j = n-1; j > 0; j--)
      r[j] = r[j+1] + w[j+1];

   // initialize for level 1 start
   int i = 1;            // level of E-node
   bbnode *E = 0;        // current E-node
   T Ew = 0;             // weight of E-node
```

Program 17.6 Max-profit branch and bound (continues)

```
    // search subset space tree
    while (i != n+1) {// while not at leaf
        // check children of E-node
        if (Ew + w[i] <= c) {// feasible left child
            AddLiveNode(H, E, Ew+w[i]+r[i], true, i+1);}
        // right child
        AddLiveNode(H, E, Ew+r[i], false, i+1);

        // get next E-node
        HeapNode<T> N;
        H.DeleteMax(N); // cannot be empty
        i = N.level;
        E = N.ptr;
        Ew = N.uweight - r[i-1];
        }

    // construct bestx[] by following path
    // from E-node E to the root
    for (int j = n; j > 0; j--) {
        bestx[j] = E->LChild;  // bool to int
        E = E->parent;
        }

    return Ew;
}
```

Program 17.6 Max-profit branch and bound (concluded)

by `i`. Initially, the root is the E-node. As a result, we begin with `i = 1` and `Ew = 0`. Since we do not store the root explicitly, we set `E` to zero initially.

The `while` loop generates the left and right children of the current E-node. If the left child is feasible (i.e., its weight does not exceed the capacity), it is added to the subset tree and to the max heap as a level `i+1` node. The right child of a feasible node is guaranteed to be feasible and so is always added to the set subtree and max heap. Following this addition, the next E-node is extracted from the max heap. In case there is no next E-node, there is no feasible solution. If the next E-node is a leaf (i.e., it is a level `n+1` node), it represents the optimal loading. This loading is determined by following the path from this leaf to the root.

Comments on Implementation

1. The use of a max heap to represent the max-priority queue of live nodes requires us to predict the maximum size of this queue (1000 in the implementation of Program 17.6). We can avoid the need for this prediction by using a pointer-based representation of a priority queue, rather than an array-based one. One such representation is the leftist tree of Section 9.4.

2. Define `bestw` to be the maximum weight associated with any of the feasible nodes generated so far. The priority queue of live nodes may contain several nodes whose `uweight` value does not exceed `bestw`. These nodes cannot possibly lead to the best leaf. Their presence in the priority queue is taking valuable queue space and also contributing to the time needed to insert/delete. We should eliminate them. One elimination strategy is to test `uweight > bestw` before inserting a node into the priority queue. However, since `bestw` increases as the algorithm progresses, nodes that passed this test at the time of insertion may fail it later on. A more aggressive strategy is to also apply the test whenever `bestw` increases and delete from the priority queue all nodes with `uweight < bestw`. This strategy requires us to delete nodes with least `uweight`. Hence we need a priority queue that supports the operations insert, delete max, and delete min. Such a priority queue is called a **double-ended** priority queue. Data structures for double-ended priority queues appear in the references provided in Chapter 9.

17.2.2   0/1 Knapsack Problem

A max-profit branch-and-bound algorithm for the 0/1 knapsack problem may be developed using the function `Bound` of Program 16.6 to compute for each live node `N` an upper profit `up` such that no node in the subtree with root `N` has profit value more than `uprofit`. The max heap of live nodes uses `uprofit` as the key field. Each entry of the max heap is of type `HeapNode` where `HeapNode` has the private data members `uprofit`, `profit`, `weight`, `level`, and `ptr`. The fields `level` and `ptr` have the same significance as they had in the loading problem (Program 17.5). For any node `N`, `N.profit` is the profit associated with it, `N.uprofit` is its upper profit, and `N.weight` is the weight associated with it. The data type `bbnode` is as in Program 17.5. Nodes are extracted from the max heap using their `uprofit` value.

The code of Program 17.7 uses a class `Knap` that is very similar to the class `Knap` (Program 16.5) defined for the backtracking solution to this problem. The only differences in the data members of the two versions of `Knap` are that in Program 17.7 (1) `bestp` is no longer a member and (2) `bestx` is a new member that is a pointer to `int`. The significance of this new data member is that `bestx[j]` = 1 iff object i is in the knapsack in the optimal packing. The function `AddLiveNode` adds a new live node to both the subset tree, using a node of type `bbnode`, and to the max heap, using a node of type `HeapNode`. This function is very similar to the corresponding function used for the loading problem (Program 17.6). Therefore, the code is omitted.

```
template<class Tw, class Tp>
Tp Knap<Tw, Tp>::MaxProfitKnapsack()
{// Return profit of best knapsack filling.
 // Set bestx[i] = 1 iff object i is in knapsack in
 // best filling.  Use max-profit branch and bound.
   // define a max heap for up to
   // 1000 live nodes
   H = new MaxHeap<HeapNode<Tp, Tw> > (1000);

   // allocate space for bestx
   bestx = new int [n+1];

   // initialize for level 1 start
   int i = 1;
   E = 0;
   cw = cp = 0;
   Tp bestp = 0;        // best profit so far
   Tp up = Bound(1);    // maximum possible profit
                        // in subtree with root E

   // search subset space tree
   while (i != n+1) {// not at leaf
      // check left child
      Tw wt = cw + w[i];
      if (wt <= c) {// feasible left child
         if (cp+p[i] > bestp) bestp = cp+p[i];
         AddLiveNode(up, cp+p[i], cw+w[i], true, i+1);}
         up = Bound(i+1);

      // check right child
      if (up >= bestp) // right child has prospects
          AddLiveNode(up, cp, cw, false, i+1);
```

Program 17.7 Max-profit branch and bound for the 0/1 knapsack problem (continues)

```
            // get next E-node
            HeapNode<Tp, Tw> N;
            H->DeleteMax(N); // cannot be empty
            E = N.ptr;
            cw = N.weight;
            cp = N.profit;
            up = N.uprofit;
            i = N.level;
            }

      // construct bestx[] by following path
      // from E-node E to the root
      for (int j = n; j > 0; j--) {
         bestx[j] = E->LChild;
         E = E->parent;
         }
      return cp;
}
```

Program 17.7 Max profit branch-and-bound for the 0/1 knapsack problem (concluded)

Function `MaxProfitKnapsack` performs the max-profit branch-and-bound search on the subset tree. The function assumes that the objects are in order of profit density. This ordering may be arrived at using a preprocessor that is very similar to that used for the backtracking algorithm given in Program 16.9. `MaxProfitKnapsack` begins by initializing the max heap of live nodes and creating an array `bestx` in which the best knapsack packing can be stored. Since the object indexes may have changed as a result of the reordering by profit density, it is necessary to map the solution generated by `MaxProfitKnapsack` back to the original object indexes. This mapping can be done using the ID fields of Q (see Program 16.9).

In `MaxProfitKnapsack`, E is the current E-node, `cw` is the weight associated with this node, and `cp` the profit. `up` is an upper bound on the profit of any node in the subtree with root E. The `while` loop is iterated until a leaf becomes the E-node. Since no node remaining in the max heap has an upper profit that is more than the profit at this leaf, this leaf defines an optimal packing. This packing is determined by following the path from the leaf to the root.

The structure of the `while` loop of `MaxProfitKnapsack` is very similar to that of the `while` loop of Program 17.6. First we check the feasiblity of the left child of the E-node. If this child is feasible, it is added to the subset tree as well as to the live-node list (i.e., the max heap). The right child is added only if its `Bound` value indicates it might lead us to the best packing.

17.2.3 Max Clique

The solution space tree for the clique problem (Section 16.2.3) is also a subset tree. Let us use the same max profit branch-and-bound implementation strategy as used for the loading and knapsack problems. The nodes in the portion of the solution space tree constructed are of type `bbnode`, while the max-priority queue elements are of type `CliqueNode`. Each `CliqueNode` has the fields `cn` (number of vertices in the clique represented by this node), `un` (maximum possible clique size for any leaf in this node's subtree), `level` (level of the node in the solution space tree), `ch` (ch is one iff the node is the left child of its parent), and `ptr` (pointer to node in the solution space tree). For `un` we simply use the value `cn+n-level+1`. As a result, we can eliminate either the `cn` or the `level` field because from `un` and either `cn` or `level`, the other can be computed. When an element is to be extracted from the max-priority queue, we select an element with maximum `un`. In our implementation of Program 17.8, `CliqueNode` includes all three of the fields `cn`, `un`, and `level`. The inclusion of these fields makes it easier to experiment with alternative definitions of `un`. The function `AddCliqueNode` adds a live node to the subset tree being constructed and also adds it to the max heap. The code is very similar to the code for the corresponding function for the loading and knapsack problems and is omitted.

The function `BBMaxClique` performs a max-profit branch-and-bound search of the subset solution space tree. The root of this tree is the initial E-node. This node is not explicitly represented in the constructed tree. For this E-node, `cn` (size of clique represented by E-node) is zero, as no vertices have been selected for inclusion into the clique. The level of the E-node is designated by variable `i`. This initial value of `i` is one, as the initial E-node is the root of the subset tree. The size of the best clique constructed so far is saved in `bestn`.

In the `while` loop, E-nodes are expanded until a leaf (i.e., a level `n+1` node) becomes the E-node. For a leaf node, `un = cn`. Since all remaining nodes have a `un` value ≤ that of the current E-node, they cannot lead to a larger clique than the clique represented by this E-node. Therefore, the max clique has been found. The clique itself is constructed by following the path from the E-node leaf to the root of the constructed subset tree.

To expand a nonleaf E-node, we first consider its left child. At the left child a new vertex `i` is included into the clique being constructed. This inclusion is possible only if an edge exists between vertex `i` and each of the vertices already included at the E-node. To determine the feasiblity of the left child, we follow the path from the E-node to the root, determining which vertices are included and also verifying that each included vertex is connected to vertex `i` by an edge. If the left child is feasible, we add it to the max-priority queue as well as to the subset tree being constructed. Next we add the right child

```
int AdjacencyGraph::BBMaxClique(int bestx[])
{// Max profit branch-and-bound code to find
 // a max clique.
   // define a max heap for up to
   // 1000 live nodes
   MaxHeap<CliqueNode> H(1000);
   // initialize for level 1 start
   bbnode *E = 0;  // current E-node is root
   int i = 1,      // level of E-node
      cn = 0,      // size of clique at E
      bestn = 0;   // size of largest clique so far
   // search subset space tree
   while (i != n+1) {// while not at leaf
      // see if vertex i is connected to others
      // in current clique
      bool OK = true;
      bbnode *B = E;
      for (int j = i - 1; j > 0; B = B->parent, j--)
         if (B->LChild && a[i][j] == NoEdge) {
            OK = false;
            break;}
      if (OK) {// left child feasible
         if (cn + 1 > bestn) bestn = cn + 1;
         AddCliqueNode(H, cn+1, cn+n-i+1, i+1, E,
      if (cn + n - i >= bestn)
         // right child has prospects
         AddCliqueNode(H, cn, cn+n-i, i+1, E, false);
      // get next E-node
      CliqueNode N;
      H.DeleteMax(N); // cannot be empty
      E = N.ptr;
      cn = N.cn;
      i = N.level;
      }
   // construct bestx[] by following path
   // from E to root
   for (int j = n; j > 0; j--) {
      bestx[j] = E->LChild;
      E = E->parent;}
   return bestn;
}
```

Program 17.8 Branch-and-bound max-clique code

provided that its subtree could contain a leaf that represents a max clique.

Since every graph has a max clique, we do not need to test for an empty heap when deleting from the max heap. The `while` loop is exited only when we reach a feasible leaf.

17.2.4 Traveling Salesperson

The traveling-salesperson problem was introduced in Section 16.2.4. The solution space for this problem is a permutation tree. As in the case of max-profit and least-cost branch-and-bound searches of subset trees, there are two possibilities for the implementation. In one we use only a priority queue in which each element contains the path to the root. In the other we maintain the portion of the solution space tree that is generated and a priority queue of live nodes. In the latter case the priority-queue elements do not contain the path to the root. The implementation in this section uses the former approach, though the latter could also have been used.

Since we are looking for a least-cost traveling-salesperson route, we shall employ a least-cost branch and bound. The implementation uses a min-priority queue of live nodes. The nodes in this queue are of type `MinHeapNode`. Each node of this type has the fields `x` (a permutation of the numbers 1 through n with `x[0]` being 1), `s` (an integer such that the path from the root of the permutation tree to this node defines the tour prefix `x[0:s]` and the vertices yet to be visited by the tour are `x[s+1:n-1]`), `cc` (cost of tour prefix represented by the path from the solution space tree root to this node), `lcost` (least possible cost of any leaf in this node's subtree), and `rcost` (sum of costs of least cost out bound edges from vertices `x[s:n-1]`). When data of type `MinHeapNode<T>` is converted to th data type `T`, the result is the `lcost` value. The branch-and-bound code appears in Program 17.9.

Program 17.9 begins by creating a min heap with capacity 1000. This min heap represents the min-priority queue of live nodes. Live nodes are extracted from the min heap on the basis of their `lcost` value. Next we compute the cost `MinOut` of the cheapest outbound edge from each vertex in the digraph. If some vertex has no outbound edge, the digraph has no tour and we terminate. If each vertex has an outbound edge, a least-cost branch and bound is initiated. We begin with the child of the root (node B in Figure 16.5) as the first E-node. At this node the tour prefix constructed is just the single vertex 1. Therefore, $s = 0$, `x[0]` $= 1$, and `x[1:n-1]` are the remaining vertices (2, 3, $\cdots$, n). The tour prefix 1 has cost zero, so `cc` $= 0$. Also, $rcost = \sum_{i=1}^{n} MinOut[i]$. In the program, `bestc` gives the cost of the best tour found so far. Initially, no tour has been found, so `bestc` is set to `NoEdge`.

```
template<class T>
T AdjacencyWDigraph<T>::BBTSP(int v[])
{// Min-cost branch-and-bound
 // traveling-salesperson code.
   MinHeap<MinHeapNode<T> > H(1000); // for live nodes
   T *MinOut = new T [n+1];
   // compute MinOut[i] = cost of min-cost edge
   // leaving vertex i
   T MinSum = 0;   // sum of min-cost out edges
   for (int i = 1; i <= n; i++) {
      T Min = NoEdge;
      for (int j = 1; j <= n; j++)
         if (a[i][j] != NoEdge &&
                (a[i][j] < Min || Min == NoEdge))
            Min = a[i][j];
      if (Min == NoEdge) return NoEdge; // no route
      MinOut[i] = Min;
      MinSum += Min;}
   // initial E-node is tree root
   MinHeapNode<T> E;
   E.x = new int [n];
   for (int i = 0; i < n; i++)
      E.x[i] = i + 1;
   E.s = 0;                // partial tour is x[1:0]
   E.cc = 0;               // its cost is zero
   E.rcost = MinSum;   // will go up by this or more
   T bestc = NoEdge;   // no tour found so far
   // search permutation tree
   while (E.s < n - 1) {// not at leaf
      if (E.s == n - 2) {// parent of leaf
         // complete tour by adding 2 edges
         // see if new tour is better
         if (a[E.x[n-2]][E.x[n-1]] != NoEdge &&
             a[E.x[n-1]][1] != NoEdge && (E.cc +
             a[E.x[n-2]][E.x[n-1]] + a[E.x[n-1]][1]
             < bestc || bestc == NoEdge)) {
            // better tour found
            bestc = E.cc + a[E.x[n-2]][E.x[n-1]]
                        + a[E.x[n-1]][1];
            E.cc = bestc; E.lcost = bestc;
            E.s++; H.Insert(E);}
         else delete [] E.x;}  // done with E-node
```

Program 17.9 Least-cost branch and bound for traveling salesperson (continues)

```
        else {// generate children
            for (int i = E.s + 1; i < n; i++)
                if (a[E.x[E.s]][E.x[i]] != NoEdge) {
                    // feasible child, bound path cost
                    T cc = E.cc + a[E.x[E.s]][E.x[i]];
                    T rcost = E.rcost - MinOut[E.x[E.s]];
                    T b = cc + rcost;   // lower bound
                    if (b < bestc || bestc == NoEdge) {
                        // subtree may have better leaf
                        // save root in max heap
                        MinHeapNode<T> N;
                        N.x = new int [n];
                        for (int j = 0; j < n; j++)
                            N.x[j] = E.x[j];
                        N.x[E.s+1] = E.x[i];
                        N.x[i] = E.x[E.s+1];
                        N.cc = cc;
                        N.s = E.s + 1;
                        N.lcost = b;
                        N.rcost = rcost;
                        H.Insert(N);}
                }   // end of feasible child
            delete [] E.x;}   // done with this node

        try {H.DeleteMin(E);}         // get next E-node
        catch (OutOfBounds) {break;} // no nodes left
        }

    if (bestc == NoEdge) return NoEdge; // no route
    // copy best route into v[1:n]
    for (int i = 0; i < n; i++)
        v[i+1] = E.x[i];

    while (true) {// free all nodes in min heap
        delete [] E.x;
        try {H.DeleteMin(E);}
        catch (OutOfBounds) {break;}
        }

    return bestc;
}
```

Program 17.9 Least-cost branch and bound for traveling salesperson (concluded)

The `while` loop expands E-nodes until we reach one that is a leaf. A leaf is detected by noticing that when `s = n-1`, the tour prefix is `x[0:n-1]`; this prefix includes all `n` vertices of the digraph. Hence a live node with `s = n-1` represents a leaf. By the nature of the algorithm, a leaf has `lcost` and `cc` equal to the cost of the tour it represents. Since all remaining live nodes have an `lcost` value at least as much as that of the first leaf extracted from the min heap, none of these remaining nodes can lead to a better leaf. Therefore, the search for an optimal tour may terminate as soon as a leaf becomes the E-node.

The body of the `while` loop is split into two cases. The first is for E-nodes with `s = n-2`. At this time the E-node is the parent of a single leaf. If this leaf defines a feasible tour and if the tour cost is less than that of the best tour found so far, the leaf is inserted into the min heap. Otherwise, the leaf is discarded, and we move on to the next E-node.

All other E-nodes fall into the second case handled in the body of the `while`. Now we generate each child of the E-node. Since the E-node represents the feasible path `x[0:s]`, the feasible children are those for which `<x[s],x[i]>` is an edge of the digraph and `x[i]` is one of `x[s+1:n-1]`. For each feasible child we compute the cost `cc` of the prefix (`x[0:s]`, `x[i]`) by adding the cost of the edge `<x[s],x[i]>` to `E.cc`. Since every tour that has this prefix must also contain an edge that leaves each of the remaining vertices, no leaf can have a cost less than `cc` plus the sum of the costs of the cheapest edge that leaves each of the remaining vertices. We use this bound as the value of `lcost` of the child generated. We add this new child to the live-node list (i.e., the min heap) if its `lcost` is less than the cost `bestc` of the best tour found so far.

If the digraph contains no tour, Program 17.9 returns the value `NoEdge`. Otherwise, it returns the cost of the optimal tour. The vertex sequence corresponding to this tour is returned in the array `v`.

17.2.5 Board Permutation

The solution space for the board-permutation problem (Section 16.2.5) is a permutation tree. We can perform a least-cost branch-and-bound search of this tree to find a least-density board arrangement. We use a min-priority queue, each element of which represents a live node and is of type `BoardNode`. Each object of type `BoardNode` has the fields `x` (a board permutation); `s` (boards `x[1:s]` are fixed in positions 1 through `s`, respectively); `cd` (density of the board arrangement `x[1:s]`, including wires going to the right of `x[s]`); and `now` (`now[j]` is the number of boards in `x[1:s]` that contain net `j`). Also, when an object of type `BoardNode` is converted to type `int`, the result is the `cd` value of the object. The branch-and-bound code appears in Program 17.10.

```
int BBArrangeBoards(int **B, int n, int m,
                                   int* &bestx)
{// Least-cost branch and bound, m nets, n boards.
   MinHeap<BoardNode> H(1000);   // for live nodes
   // Initialize first E-node, total, and bestd.
   BoardNode E;
   E.x = new int [n+1];
   E.s = 0;    // partial permutation is E.x[1:s]
   E.cd = 0;   // density of E.x[1:s]
   E.now = new int [m+1];
   int *total = new int [m+1];
   // now[i] = number of boards in x[1:s] with net i
   // total[i] = number of boards with net i
   for (int i = 1; i <= m; i++) {
      total[i] = 0;
      E.now[i] = 0;
      }
   for (int i = 1; i <= n; i++) {
      E.x[i] = i; // permutation is 12345...n
      for (int j = 1; j <= m; j++)
         total[j] += B[i][j]; // boards with net j
      }
   int bestd = m + 1;   // best density found so far
   bestx = 0;           // null pointer

   do {// expand E-node
      if (E.s == n - 1) {// one child only
         int ld = 0; // local density at last board
         for (int j = 1; j <= m; j++)
            ld += B[E.x[n]][j];
         if (ld < bestd) {// better permutation
            delete [] bestx;
            bestx = E.x;
            bestd = max(ld, E.cd);
            }
         else delete [] E.x;
         delete [] E.now;}
```

Program 17.10 Least-cost branch and bound for the board-permutation problem (continues)

```
         else {// generate children of E-node
         for (int i = E.s + 1; i <= n; i++) {
            BoardNode N;
            N.now = new int [m+1];
            for (int j = 1; j <= m; j++)
               // account for nets in new board
               N.now[j] = E.now[j] + B[E.x[i]][j];
            int ld = 0; // local density at new board
            for (int j = 1; j <= m; j++)
               if (N.now[j] > 0 && total[j] != N.now[j])
                  ld++;
            N.cd = max(ld, E.cd);
            if (N.cd < bestd) {// may lead to better leaf
               N.x = new int [n+1];
               N.s = E.s + 1;
               for (int j = 1; j <= n; j++)
                  N.x[j] = E.x[j];
               N.x[N.s] = E.x[i];
               N.x[i] = E.x[N.s];
               H.Insert(N);}
            else delete [] N.now;}

            delete [] E.x;} // done with E-node

         try {H.DeleteMin(E);} // next E-node
         catch (OutOfBounds) {return bestd;}  // no E-node
         } while (E.cd < bestd);

      // free all nodes in min heap
      do {delete [] E.x;
          delete [] E.now;
          try {H.DeleteMin(E);}
          catch (...) {break;}
          } while (true);

      return bestd;
}
```

Program 17.10 Least-cost branch and bound for the board-permutation problem (concluded)

The code of Program 17.10 initializes the E-node to be the tree root. No board has been placed at this node. Therefore, $s = 0$, $cd = 0$, $now[i] = 0$ for $1 \leq i \leq n$, and x is any permutation of the numbers 1 through n. The array total is initialized such that $total[i]$ is the number of boards that contain net i. The best board permutation found so far is saved in the array bestx and its density is saved in bestd. A do-while loop examines the E-nodes one at a time. At the end of each iteration of this loop, the next E-node is selected by extracting, from the min heap of live nodes, a node with least cd. If this node's cd value is $\geq$ bestd, then none of the remaining live nodes can lead to board permutations with density less than bestd and the algorithm terminates.

The do-while loop considers two cases for the E-node. The first arises when $s = n-1$. At this time $n-1$ boards have been placed, and the E-node is the parent of a leaf of the solution space tree. The permutation corresponding to this leaf is x. Its density is computed, and bestd and bestx updated if necessary.

In the second case the E-node has two or more children. Each child N is generated, and the density N.cd of the partial permutation $(x[1:s+1])$ corresponding to the child is computed. The child N is saved in the min-priority queue only if N.cd < bestd. Notice that when N.cd $\geq$ bestd, all leaves in its subtree have density $\geq$ bestd and do not represent board permutations better than bestx.

EXERCISES

3. Add code to Program 17.4 to save pointers to all nodes created by AddLiveNode on a linked queue. MaxLoading should use this information to delete all created nodes before terminating.

4. The method to delete all nodes created by AddLiveNode described in this section waits until the end to delete the nodes. However, nodes that have no live children and no generated leaf can be deleted right away. Similarly, level n nodes that do not have a child with weight bestw can also be deleted. Discuss how you might implement a scheme that deletes uneeded nodes as soon as is possible. Describe the time/space trade-offs involved in implementing your scheme. Do you recommend it?

5. In the context of Program 17.6, define bestw to be the maximum of the weights associated with the feasible nodes generated so far. Modify Program 17.6 so that a new live node is added to the subset tree and max heap iff its uweight is greater than or equal to bestw. You will also need to add code to initialize and update bestw.

6. Write a max-profit branch-and-bound code for the loading problem, using only a max-priority queue. That is, do not maintain the portion of the solution space tree generated (as is done in Program 17.6). Each priority queue node will now contain the path to the tree root.

7. Modify Program 17.6 so that all nodes of type `bbnode` and `HeapNode` are deleted at the end.

8. Write a max-profit branch-and-bound code for the 0/1 knapsack problem using only a max-priority queue. That is, do not maintain the portion of the solution space tree generated. Each priority-queue node will now contain the path to the tree root.

9. Modify Program 17.7 so that all nodes of type `bbnode` and `HeapNode` are deleted at the end.

10. (a) In Program 17.8 right children with `un` value $\geq$ `bestn` are added to the max heap. Will the program still work correctly if only right children with `un` > `bestn` are added? Why?

    (b) Does the program add left children with `un` $\geq$ `bestn` to the max heap?

    (c) Modify the program so that only nodes with `un` > `bestn` are added to the max heap and to the solution space subtree being constructed.

11. Consider the subset space tree for the max-clique problem. For any level `i` node `X` of the subset tree, let `MinDegree(X)` be the minimum of the degrees of the vertices included at `X`.

    (a) Show that no leaf in the subtree with root `X` can represent a clique of size more than `X.un` = min{`X.cn+n-i+1`, `MinDegree(X)+1`}.

    (b) Rewrite `BBMaxClique` using this definition of `X.un`.

    (c) Compare the run times as well as the number of solution space tree nodes generated by the two versions of `BBMaxClique`.

12. Write a max-profit branch-and-bound code for the max-clique problem, using only a max-priority queue. That is, do not maintain the portion of the solution space tree generated. Each priority-queue node will now contain the path to the tree root.

13. Modify Program 17.8 so that all nodes of type `bbnode` and `CliqueNode` are deleted at the end.

14. Modify Program 17.9 so that nodes with `s` = `n-2` are not entered into the priority queue. Rather, the best permutation found so far is saved in an array `bestp`. The algorithm terminates when the next E-node has `lcost` $\geq$ `bestc`.

15. Write a version of Program 17.9 in which we use parent pointers to explicitly retain the portion of the solution space tree examined by the algorithm (as in Program 17.7) and the priority-queue entries contain the fields `lcost`, `cc`, `rcost`, and `ptr` (pointer to corresponding node in solution space tree) only.

16. Write a FIFO branch-and-bound code for the board-permutation problem. Your code must output both the best board arrangement and its density. Use suitable test data to test the correctness of your code.

17. Write a FIFO branch-and-bound algorithm to find a board arrangement that minimizes the length of the longest net (see Exercise 17 of Chapter 16).

18. Do Exercise 17 using a least-cost branch and bound.

19. Write a least-cost branch-and-bound algorithm for the vertex-cover problem of Exercise 18 of Chapter 16.

20. Write a max-cost branch-and-bound algorithm for the simple max-cut problem of Exercise 19 of Chapter 16.

21. Write a least-cost branch-and-bound algorithm for the machine-design problem of Exercise 20 of Chapter 16.

22. Write a least-cost branch-and-bound algorithm for the network-design problem of Exercise 21 of Chapter 16.

23. Write a FIFO branch-and-bound algorithm for the n-queens-placement problem of Exercise 22 of Chapter 16.

★24. Do Exercise 23 of Chapter 16 for FIFO branch and bound.

★25. Do Exercise 24 of Chapter 16 for FIFO branch and bound.

★26. Do Exercise 25 of Chapter 16 for FIFO branch and bound.

★27. Do Exercise 23 of Chapter 16 for least-cost branch and bound.

★28. Do Exercise 24 of Chapter 16 for least-cost branch and bound.

★29. Do Exercise 25 of Chapter 16 for least-cost branch and bound.

★30. Do Exercise 25 of Chapter 16 for arbitrary branch and bound. For this exercise, you will need to pass functions to add live nodes and select the next E-node as parameters.

INDEX